C000212359

A Dictionary of Herefordshire Biography

A Dictionary of Herefordshire Biography

Philip Weaver

Logaston Press

LOGASTON PRESS
Little Logaston Woonton Almeley
Herefordshire HR3 6QH
www.logastonpress.co.uk

First published by Logaston Press 2105

ISBN 978 1 906663 97 1

Typeset by Logaston Press
and printed and bound in Poland by www.lfbookservices.co.uk

Contents

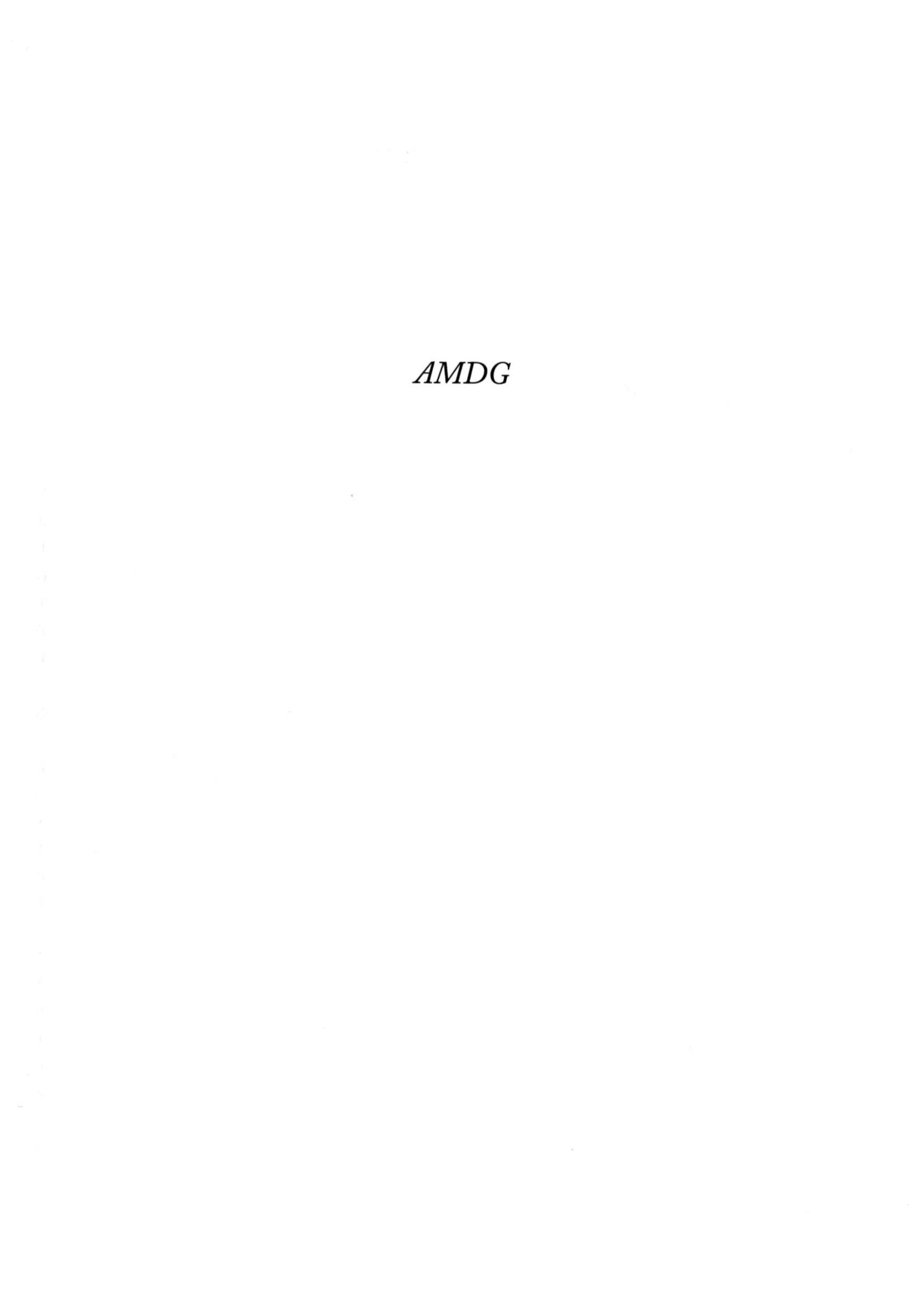

AMDG

Introduction

We possess no other life, no other living sap, than the treasures stored up from the past and digested, assimilated and created afresh by us.

Simone Weil, *The Need For Roots*

'Not a mile visually unrewarding,' Pevsner wrote of the rolling border county of Herefordshire, lying between the Malverns and the Black Mountains, between the rocky chasm of the Wye as it dives into the Forest of Dean and the crags of Bringewood. Its churches and black and white houses, its old towns and castles are unique. There is the great Norman Cathedral of Hereford with its chained library and Mappa Mundi, the Regency confection of Smirke's Eastnor Castle; the icing sugar Gothick of Shobdon Church and the 12th-century strangeness of the Herefordshire School of Sculptors in a dozen Norman churches. All these bear witness to the many people who were born here or somehow drawn here.

The land is full of the traces left by nameless men and women who lived in and moved across Herefordshire for a million years, leaving a 300,000-year-old hand axe at Mathon; an accumulation of Ice Age rubbish in King Arthur's Cave; a Bronze Age urn also from Mathon and now restored in the City Museum. The Romans came this way as well, and settled as though they meant to stay, but in the end their towns at Kenchester, Weston under Penyard and Leintwardine, where there were streets of shops and houses, some grand like the one that yielded the mosaic now in Hereford Museum, were left to crumble beneath the fields. Tribal dignitaries of the Dobunni tribe, their families and slaves, passed across this land too, but of their lives we now know almost nothing.

The builders of old houses and churches were once celebrated, like the 12th-century carpenters who made the great columns for the Bishop's Palace and the 13th-century masons who built the beautiful church at Madley. In the middle ages the traces left include more written evidence, like the contract naming the builder of the Cathedral chapter house. But mostly the written records only tell us the history of kings and bishops, nobility and gentry, those who ruled, judged and administered here; the great families like the Bohuns and Briouzes, Coningsbys and Crofts, Mortimers and Scudamores. When humble folk are remembered, it is often because of their part in tragedy, like Christina Cray, a swineherd sentenced to death when a stray pig joined her herd; little Emma Foulger, accidentally shot by her brother; a philanthropic bookseller driven mad by the law. Later the records expand, and finally thousands of past Herefordians ask to be noticed.

The stories that can be told are not only of Herefordshire people born and bred, but of many interesting men and women who came here, like Rafael Sabatini the Hollywood film script writer; Admiral Nelson, miles from the sea; the Wordsworths on holiday. There are also a dragon, some ghosts, a pigeon, apples, cows and sheep, and a cannon.

Finding out about one's family is good fun, and it's even more fun to find out about everyone else's. Some families are well-known like the Mortimers with their *Chronicle*, and the Harleys, who are still here to ask. Monarchs and celebrities are well-known nationally but the difficulty is finding out what they did when they came here: Nelson enjoyed the Wye and stayed over with his friend near Ross; Dickens bought a donkey as a surprise for his agent's children.

Finding out can be hard work – in the excellent Hereford Record Office; on the many on-line genealogy sites; keeping an eye open for snippets in books and pamphlets that have nothing to do with one's present quarry; filling in gaps with chance remarks in conversations; and most enjoyably, getting out on field work, amongst the memorials of Holme Lacy Church say, or in Hellens Manor House etc. There are so many helpful people to thank. The biggest surprise for me has been the way people connect up with each other. The commonest word in this book is 'qv' (or '*quod vide*' - for which see), which sends you on to someone else, then on again, for ever ...

Those people I have let in to this book are only a fraction of the fascinating stories longing to be told. If you know of an interesting person, born before 1900, let me know, and their story can be added to those here.

Philip Weaver
Ledbury

A note from the publishers

We have opted to present the dictionary entries in strict alphabetical order for ease of reference. This means that in a very few cases (we make it four), entries for the same family are interspersed with others who happen to have the same surname but are unrelated. (The entries themselves make this clear.) Another consequence of alphabetical order is that members of the same family are presented not chronologically but alphabetically, in the hope that this will help the reader to track down a particular Roger Mortimer, say, or Edward Harley. The author has provided illuminating summaries of the history of the families (each presented in a text box at the appropriate point) to help you find your way around their entries. In the case of the Skidmores and Scudamores, different spellings of earlier and later members of the same family mean that they are separated by alphabetic tyranny, and this is also true of Cornewalls and Cornwalls; but the cross-references provided will help to make the connections.

Abel, John (1579-1675), master carpenter, was born at Sarnesfield. He and Joanna his wife were probably Catholics. Tradition says he lived at nearby Woodmanton in a house still extant. He is credited with many old timber buildings of the area, like the great Market Hall at Hereford, since demolished. John Scudamore d.1671, qv) employed him in the restoration of Dore Abbey (1634), where he rebuilt the roof on great carved brackets, created the screen below, and built the bell tower and frame. His carving of goggle-eyed, large-breasted caryatids often with beards is distinctive, as are his gnomic Latin and English texts. They can be seen on the Dore Abbey screen, around the Market House at Leominster and on a screen at Monnington Court. He built market houses at Kington, Brecon and Leominster. That at Leominster (1634) stood at the junction of Broad and High Streets. It formed the entrance to the Buttercross, and was used as public offices and magistrates' court with an open poultry and butter market underneath. It was bought by John Arkwright (qv, d.1858) who in 1858 re-erected it in its present location near the Priory Church as The Grange. Although much changed it gives a strong flavour of Abel. Some of the inscriptions have been traced to familiar sources of the time like St Jerome and Cato the Elder*; one, 'Where justice rules there virtue flows', has been adopted as the motto on Leominster's Arms. Abel built Lady Margaret Hawkins (qv) Grammar School in Kington (1625-9) for which his contract survives, and restored St Bartholomew Church, Vowchurch, building a timber frame inside the walls to hold his roof. In the 1640s the 60-year-old Abel was at his most inventive. Thomas Blount (qv) says he was in Hereford at the time of the Scottish siege during the Civil War constructing devices like the gunpowder mill for governor Barnabas Scudamore (qv) and a corn mill for which he won King Charles' thanks. John Webb (qv) refers to a siege engine called 'the Sow' which Abel built to deploy against the garrison at Canon Frome in October 1645. He worked on Tyberton Court for William Brydges (qv, d.1688) and plans of 1652 for a house survive, giving his fee as £30. Extreme old age brought poverty and he was supported with a small pension. Abel died aged 96 and was buried alongside his two wives on 31 January 1675 in Sarnesfield churchyard. Blount gives his original epitaph as:

This craggy Stone a covering is for an Architector's Bed
That lofty Buildings raised high, yet now lyes low His Head
His line and Rule, so Death concludes, are locked up in Store
Build they that list or they that wist for He can Build no More.
His House of Clay could Hold no Longer,
May Heavens joy frame Him a Stronger.
Vive ut vivas in vitam aeternam.

Abel's son, also John, was living in Sarnesfield in 1699 when he was churchwarden.

* Abel's text reads: 'Vive Deo gratvs; crimine mvndatvs; toti mvndo tvmvlatvs; semper transire paratvs'. And: 'Where jvstice rule there virtu flow - Vive ut post vivas sat cito si sat bene – Like columns doo vpprop the fabric of a building so noble gentri doo svpport the honor of a kingdom'. On the south side he has 'in memoria Eterna erit jvstvs – 1633'.

Abercrombie, Lascelles (1881-1938), poet, was born on 9 January 1881 in Cheshire into a wealthy stockbroker's family. He was a pupil at Malvern College. He was fond of literature and the classics and determined to make his living from writing, and having read chemistry at Manchester University he turned to journalism and poetry. In 1908 he married Catherine, daughter of Owen Gwatkin, a surgeon, and after a year in Liverpool the couple moved to Much Marcle in Herefordshire. His sister Ursula and

her husband Alex Whaley were leasing Hellens, the old manor house at Much Marcle, from its owner Charles Walwyn Radcliffe Cooke (qv) and they let the Abercrombies have a year's lease at Monks Walk Cottage on the estate. They spent 1911 here in some poverty with Lascelles writing reviews and poetry. His first success was self published from Monks Walk: *Mary and the Bramble,* praised by Edward Thomas and Yeats. Next year Ursula found them 'The Gallows' at Ryton just over the border in Gloucestershire on her friend Lord Beauchamp's estate. Here, in the Dymock area, Abercrombie formed the nucleus for the group of friends now known as the Dymock Poets. He drew to the area the recently married Wilfrid Gibson, who moved to 'The Old Nail Shop' at Greenway Cross a few miles south of Ledbury. Abercrombie and Gibson had John Drinkwater and Rupert Brooke to stay which in turn attracted Robert Frost and his family to the area for nearly a year. Following Frost, in August 1914, came Edward (qv) and Helen Thomas with their children; W.H. Davies, Eleanor Farjeon, Arthur Ransome also visited. It was at 'The Gallows' that the Abercrombies with Rupert Brooke, John Drinkwater and Wilfrid Gibson produced *New Numbers* as an organ for their own poetry. The group dispersed in the course of the First World War. Abercrombie worked in munitions in Liverpool, later becoming an eminent university lecturer. He was thought of in his time as one of the best of the new Georgian Poets, writing in a style that brought the drama and rhythms of ordinary speech to poetry. He died on 27 October 1938 as a result of diabetes.

Abrahall, John (1389-1443), MP for Hereford, was from a family settled in Archenfield, Foy and Eaton Tregoz. His grandfather was Sir William and father Richard Abrahall; his aunt, Katherine, was the first wife of Sir Richard de la Bere (qv, d.1382). John married Margaret, widow of Sir William Hampton of Hampton Mapnors, later called Hampton Court, and had the use of the manor during her lifetime. His third wife Peryn was the daughter of Sir Thomas Whitney (qv, fl.1415). He was escheator in the Marches, a JP and a commissioner on government business. He bought the manor of Gillow in Hentland from the Pembridge (qv) family. Other Abrahalls lived at Eaton Tregoz and Ingestone Court. He was involved in a lawless feud between John Talbot (qv, d.1453) and the Skidmores (qv John (II) Skidmore) and with a band of Archenfield men committed murders and looting, kidnapping and rustling from Ross to Ludlow without restraint. His private army numbered a thousand at one time. When the widow of one victim brought the matter to the King's Bench, the Abrahalls' threats had it dismissed. His election as an MP in the 1420s and '30s seems to have been rigged. But he died intestate and greatly in debt with his heir William (1437-87) a minor. There was an inquiry in Hereford which led to riots there. When valuable silver plate of his was located in the keeping of John Fuyster, a Hereford merchant, Fuyster refused to give it up, claiming Abrahall had given it him in exchange for a house in Hereford. In the 15th and 16th centuries Abrahalls lived at Caradoc Court, which they brought from the de la Mares (qv Richard de la Mare) by marriage and in 1594 a John Abrahall sold it to Rowland Scudamore (qv, d.1631). A John Abrahall married Ann, daughter of Watkyn Vaughan (qv) of Hergest. In the 17th century they were vicars of Foy, with several wall monuments in the church. Anthony Wood, the 17th-century Oxford biographer, recorded that a John Abrahall, son of the parson of Foy, hanged himself in his rooms at Balliol College, Oxford in 1676. Their arms feature an 'urchin' or hedgehog, often seen in the Ross area in association with the Kyrle family (qv) with whom they intermarried. A John Abrahall married Dorothy, daughter of Francis Kyrle (qv). Their motto was 'J'ay guardé le foy'.

Adam (*c.*1186-1216), the first recorded abbot of the Cistercian abbey of Dore, was a powerful, ambitious intellectual connected with Bishop William de Vere's (qv) brilliant court at Hereford Cathedral. He rebuilt the transept crossing and east end at Dore, founded in 1147 by Robert fitz Harold (qv) in an Early English style at variance with Cistercian principles of simplicity. His polygonal chapter house, its plan recovered by Roland Paul (qv), was the model for others. This and the great nave with its ceremonial west end and all the monastic buildings disappeared after the Dissolution. Adam wrote a treatise on music (there was an organ at Dore Abbey) and other manuscripts by him exist. He was accused by detractors like Gerald of Wales (qv) of rapacity in securing lands and money through spiritual pressure, but it is probably true to say that the laity clamoured to be associated with the abbey. He wrote a verse epigram attacking Gerald, who was defended by the poet Simon de Fresne (qv). His successor abbots were Adam II (*c.*1216-36), Stephen of Worcester (1236-57) and Henry. M.R. James (qv) found a letter from the Precentor of Hereford asking Abbot Henry to take care of his mentally frail predecessor Stephen who was being detained at Dore.

Adam of Aylton (early 14th century) was chaplain to Bishop Orleton (qv).

Adam of Usk (*c.*1365-1430), *Adda o Frynbuga* in Welsh, chronicler, was a servant of Edmund (III) Mortimer (qv), who commissioned him to write a history of his family. Edmund sent Adam to Oxford where he became a doctor of canon law. He accompanied Bolingbroke (qv Henry IV) on his march from Bristol to Chester in pursuit of Richard II (qv) and advised him on the legality of the king's deposition. He seems to have been unruly and Henry IV banished him at one time. When Adam was in Rome in 1404, at Bishop Trefnant's (qv) death, the Pope appointed him Bishop of Hereford but King Henry disallowed it, appointing Mascall (qv) instead. Adam wrote a Latin chronicle dealing with English history from 1377 to 1421 which illuminates the condition of mediaeval Britain at that time. He witnessed the Peasants' Revolt; he writes about his patrons the Mortimers and Glyn Dŵr's (qv) revolt in detail and calls Lady Abergavenny (qv under William (V) de Beauchamp) an evil Jezebel.

Adam, Robert (1728-92), architect, was born in Kirkaldy, Fife on 3 July 1728 and educated in Edinburgh where the family moved, mixing with figures from the Scottish Enlightenment like David Hume and Adam Smith. His father and brothers were all architects and Robert was apprenticed at his older brother John's office. He travelled in Italy absorbing contemporary and ancient fashions and was especially influenced by the ruins of Diocletian's palace on the Croatian coast. In Britain his designs became fashionable. Sir George Amyand (qv George Cornewall d.1819) commissioned him to design a new mansion at Moccas (1775-81), the

builder being Anthony Keck (qv). Adam's style is seen in the Round Room and the Oval Stair. Sir Uvedale Price (qv) employed him at Foxley Hall, Yazor and he drew up plans for the court at Brampton Bryan (1777), romantically presented as a Roman camp. There is a room at Gaines near Whitbourne in his style. His manner had become less fashionable by the time of his death but elements of his style remained popular mannerisms through the Victorian period and can be seen in many town terraces. He never married and is buried in Westminster Abbey.

Ælfgar (*c*.1010-*c*.63), magnate, was the son of Earl Leofric (qv) of Mercia and Godgifu, known as Lady Godiva (qv). He married Ælfgifu and their son Edwin became Earl of Mercia after him. Their other children were Morcar (qv), Burgheard and Edith. He was granted the earldom of East Anglia when Tostig Godwinson was exiled in 1051. When he was exiled for treason he raised a fleet in Viking Ireland and sailed to Wales to ally himself with Gruffydd ap Llywelyn (qv) and wreak revenge. They marched on Leominster and then Hereford where they were opposed, on 24 October 1055, somewhere near the Whitecross, by the Norman Earl Ralph (qv). He had mounted his Herefordshire men on horseback in the Norman fashion, but they were used to fighting on foot and fled letting the wild forces of Ælfgar and Gruffydd sack Hereford, destroy Ralph's castle and burn Æthelstan's (qv) new cathedral, looting the rich shrine of Ethelbert (qv). After this crime Ælfgar was reinstated and in 1057 succeeded on his father's death to his earldom of Mercia. In 1058 however he was exiled again, this time an action perhaps driven by Harold Godwinson, later to be King Harold II (qv) who had become Earl of Wessex as well as Herefordshire after Ralph's death. Ælfgar again allied himself with Gruffydd to whom he married his daughter Edith (qv, d.after 1066). He was reinstated in his earldom of Mercia but died soon after.

Æthelbald (d.757), King of Mercia and England south of the Humber 716-57, was of the royal house of Mercia and secured the throne as

prophesied by his kinsman St Guthlac (qv) after early vicissitudes. A strong king, he took control of semi-independent kingdoms like the Hwicce and the Magonsaete (of the Herefordshire area) and his writ ran in East Anglia, London and even Kent. He was probably responsible for the founding of St Guthlac's monastery on the banks of the Wye in Hereford and presented it with relics of the saint. He appointed Cuthbert (qv) Bishop of Hereford and then Archbishop of Canterbury. In 743 the *Anglo-Saxon Chronicle* records a joint attack on the Welsh west of Hereford by Æthelbald and forces of Wessex. He was murdered at Seckington, Warwickshire in 757 by his bodyguard and buried in the royal Mercian cenotaph at Repton after which a visionary claimed to have seen him in Hell. In the churchyard at Repton there is a stone that may show a carving of Æthelbald on horseback with a large moustache (see above). After his death there was civil war from which Offa (qv) emerged successful.

Æthelflad (870-918), 'Lady of the Mercians', was the daughter of King Alfred and married Ethelred, ealdorman of Mercia. She was pious and an effective war leader after her husband's death. She was a great builder of *burhs* and fortified Hereford as a base for her attack on the

King of Brycheiniog's palace at Llangorse. A part of the bank and palisade of her fortifications has been found behind Cantilupe Street. She may have brought St Guthlac's (qv) relics to Hereford from Crowland. She was buried at St Oswald's Priory in Gloucester. After her death Mercia was absorbed into greater Wessex under her brother Edward the Elder (qv).

Æthelstan (895-939), King of England 924-39, was the eldest son of Edward the Elder (qv) and Queen Ecgwyn his first wife, and grandson of King Alfred. He is the first Saxon king to be regarded as king of all England and was significant in a European context. He successfully continued his father's policy of retaking the Danelaw and extended his influence into Cornwall, Wales, Northumbria and even Scotland. He ordered that all *burhs* should have mints and one was set up in Hereford, recently strengthened by his aunt Æthelflad (qv). A coin of Æthelstan's from the mint at Hereford can be seen in Hereford Museum; Hunlaf was the moneyer. Mercian coins omitted his head on the obverse, still suspicious of this intruder from Wessex. It was at Hereford in 927, after his defeat of the Vikings at York, that Æthelstan summoned the five Welsh kings to meet him, including Hywel Dda, Owain of Gwent and Idwal, King of Gwynedd. They agreed to pay him tribute and that the Wye should be their border. A charter was issued for the Dunsaete recording how the border was to be administered. These were an Anglian group settled in Archenfield (a name that derives from the Welsh kingdom of Ergyng and ultimately perhaps from the Roman town of *Ariconium*). In 937 Æthelstan and his half-brother Edmund won a great victory over the combined forces of Olaf Guthfrithson lord of the Danes of Dublin, Constantine King of Scotland and Owen of Strathclyde at the Battle of Brunanburh. This was the most important Anglo-Saxon battle before Hastings and enabled Æthelstan to add his inscription *Rex totius Britanniae* to his coinage, and to be called *the Glorious*. He died on 27 October 939 in Gloucester and was buried in his favourite abbey at Malmesbury where his effigy remains. He had no children and was succeeded by 18-year-old Edmund.

Æthelstan (*c*.990-1056), Bishop of Hereford 1015-56, agreed the western boundary of his diocese with the Welsh and received their submission to his spiritual authority; and established his eastern boundary with Worcester. He rebuilt Hereford Cathedral in stone probably on the site of St John's Cloister to the south-east of the present cathedral, where Silas Taylor (qv) saw its foundations. As he was blind in his later years a neighbouring Welsh bishop, Tremerig, was his suffragan. At the consecration Æthelstan presented the cathedral with an ancient book of 8th-century gospels. In 1055 Earl Ælfgar (qv) with Prince Gruffydd ap Llewelyn (qv) and a Welsh force raided across the border, burning Hereford along with its new cathedral. Three canons, Ordgar, Godo, and Eilmar with his four sons made a vain stand at the cathedral gates but were all killed. Many were burnt to death inside the cathedral. The shrine and bones of St Ethelbert were looted and dispersed, but the frail Gospel Book was saved. In it is minuted the decision of a court presided over by Bishop Æthelstan concerning a land dispute at Aylton (qv Thurkil). It is now kept in the cathedral archives and is used at the consecration of new bishops and deans. After this disaster Æthelstan retired to his palace at Bosbury where he died on 10 February 1056. He was buried in the ruins of his cathedral, probably under the northern range of the vicars choral houses. The area stood desolate for over a century. Æthelstan was a pious, much loved bishop but attempts to have him canonised came to nothing in the new Norman regime.

Alfred of Marlborough (d.*c*.1086), also called Alured, was a pre-Conquest Norman tenant of the king in several shires including Herefordshire where he held much land including the manor of Ewyas Harold. His daughter Agnes married Turstin (qv). She failed to secure inheritance of her father's estates which were split up amongst the Conqueror's Marcher lords and is mentioned in Domesday as a feudal tenant of the Mortimers (qv) at Wigmore.

Alington, Cyril Argentine (1872-1955), Dean of Durham Cathedral, was born on 22 October 1872 in Ipswich and educated at Marlborough School and Trinity College, Oxford. He married the Hon Hester Lyttleton in 1904. He was successively headmaster of Shrewsbury and Eton and finally Dean of Durham. In 1951 he retired to Treago Castle, St Weonards, to live with one of his four daughters, Lavinia, who had married Sir Roger Aubrey Baskerville Mynors (qv), and here he died on 16 May 1955. He is buried and memorialised in Durham Cathedral.

Alkmund (d.*c*.800) was a royal saint from Northumbria martyred in Mercia and buried first in Derby where there are remains of his shrine, then in Shrewsbury Abbey. Aymestrey's church is dedicated to him with St John the Baptist (qv). His feast day is 19 March.

Allen, Bennet (1736-1819), clergyman and journalist, was baptised on 26 August 1736 at Yazor, Herefordshire, the second son of the vicar James Allen (*c*.1700-76) and his wife Elizabeth Bennet. He was educated at Wadham College, Oxford and ordained in 1761. In 1766 he left for a Maryland parish with an introduction from its proprietor Lord Baltimore. He antagonised everyone there but for ten years managed to hold on to his rich living, surviving duels and public punishments. He returned to London when the War of Independence started and the lurid stories told about him were used in the American novelist Winston Churchill's novel *Richard Carvel* (1899). Back in London he took up journalism. Libelling a man he had known in America in one article, he was challenged to a duel and killed his opponent. He got his penalty reduced to a six-month term of imprisonment and was presented with a public collection on his release. He died aged 83 at Ilford, Essex at the house of Bamber Gascoyne, an admirer.

Allen, John (1789-1829), bookseller and antiquary, was baptised on 4 August 1789 at Hereford, the son of John Allen (*c*.1754-1828), bookseller and printer from London and Mary Thomas (*c*.1753-1827). Allen was described as 'principal bookseller in the County' and provided Hereford with a subscription library – membership 4 shillings a quarter. John Allen jr. was a precocious antiquarian and wrote an unfinished history of the county. In 1820 he translated from Latin the charter given to Hereford by William III (qv) in 1697 and had it printed. He was present at the public dinner honouring Joseph Hume (qv) in Hereford in 1821. He collected a bibliography of books, pamphlets and printed ephemera relating to Herefordshire which he printed on his father's press as *Bibliotheca Herefordensis* (1821), the earliest county bibliography published in England. He wrote antiquarian articles for the *Hereford Independent* which he published as *Collectanea Herefordensis* in 1825. Allen was involved in founding Hereford Library and presented many books. Amongst them, however, unknown to him, was a pamphlet whose author had been prosecuted for libel. By placing it in the library Allen was said to be repeating the libel and was prosecuted in his turn at the April 1822 Hereford Assizes. There was great public sympathy for him and his solicitors waived their fee but he was found guilty and the £400 fine meant the family firm had to be sold. His father and mother died shortly after and Allen sought anonymity in London. In 1827 he was admitted to Bethlem Lunatic Asylum and subsequently transferred to the Hereford Asylum where he died on 16 August 1829 aged 40.

Allen, Thomas (*c*.1540-1632), mathematician, antiquary and astrologer, was born on 21 December in 1540 or '42 in Uttoxeter, Staffordshire. He was educated at Trinity College, Oxford but settled at Gloucester Hall where there was no chapel and, as a Roman Catholic, he could avoid the oath of allegiance to the Church of England. He studied mathematics and astrology and lectured on geography to students, influencing such as Robert Hues and Richard Hakluyt (qqv). He was involved in the founding of Thomas Bodley's library and made a collection of scientific manuscripts which he left to his friend Sir Kenelm Digby who later presented them to the Bodleian. A sociable man, he was welcome at John Scudamore's (qv, d.1623) great house at Holme Lacy. Like many mathematicians of his time he was suspected of necromancy. When John Aubrey (qv) later stayed at Holme Lacy it was still told of Allen that he:

happened to forgett his Watch in the Chamber-windowe. [Watches were then rarities.] The Maydes came in to make the Bed, and hearing a thing in a case cry Tick Tick Tick presently concluded that that was his Devill and tooke it by the string with the tongues, and threw it out of the windowe into the Mote (to drown the Devill). It so happened that the string hung on a sprig of an elder that grew out of the Mote; and this confirmed them that t'was the Devill. So the good old Gentleman gott his watch again.

In Allen's case there were grounds for suspicion as he gave astrological consultations, laid ghosts and owned Dr Dee's (qv) scrying glass: an obsidian mirror for observing spirits (now in the British Museum). He performed an exorcism for the Reeds (qv) of Bronsil Castle. An old college servant told Aubrey (qv) that Allen would find spirits coming up his stairs like bees. Allen died at Gloucester Hall on 30 September 1632 and was buried in Trinity College Chapel.

Andrew of St Victor (12th century), first abbot of Wigmore Abbey, was a celebrated Victorine monk of the Augustinian order. The abbey had been founded by Hugh (II) de Mortimer (qv), based first at Shobdon then, after several moves, at Wigmore. Andrew studied and taught at Paris, at the Augustinian Abbey of St Victor, where he wrote a commentary on Ezekiel. The Victorines formed a distinct group in the nascent University of Paris at this time, having a more mystical approach than the Aristotelians. Andrew returned to resume his abbacy of Wigmore. A 12th-century capital in nearby Rock Church pictured the Ark of the Church, and this has been linked with the treatise of his colleague Hugh of St Victor (d.1141) called *Didascalion* in which a similar image of the ark is described (qv also Brian of Lingen). The sculptures at Rock are associated with the Herefordshire School of Sculpture (qv) and suggest a link between them and Victorine thought. Herefordshire in the 12th century was a centre of European learning.

Andrews, Joyce (1546-1660) lived in Felton to the reputed age of 114. She was commemorated at the time of her death in an attractive portrait that now hangs in Hereford Museum and

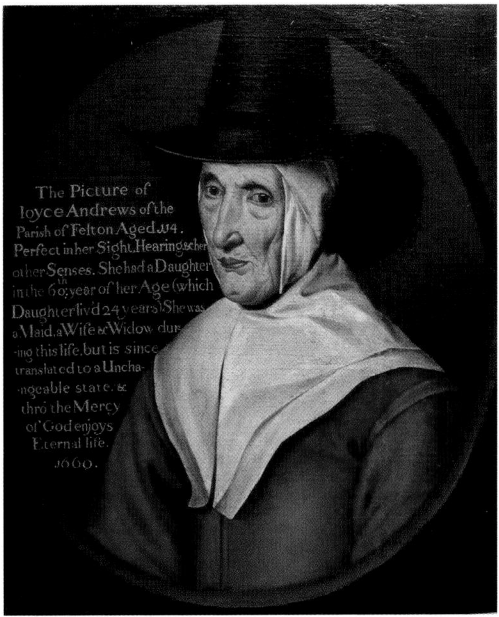

shows her in a high black felt hat now thought of as traditionally Welsh. Joyce was presumably a relative of John Prise (qv) of nearby Wistaston Court, as John Duncumb (qv) says the painting was hung with the family portraits in the great hall there. She was said to have had a daughter when she was 60; her daughter died aged 24.

Anne (1665-1714), Queen of Great Britain 1702-14, was born on 6 February 1665 the youngest daughter of James Duke of York and Anne Hyde. Her father, James II, abdicated on the invasion of William of Orange who had married her older sister Mary. Anne succeeded William III in 1702. She visited the Foleys (qv) at Stoke Edith House and left behind her straw hat, which can now be seen in Hereford Museum. She died, childless, on 1 August 1714, the last member of the House of Stuart, and was succeeded by George of Hanover.

Anthony, Charles (1802-83), 'the Father of Modern Hereford', editor and proprietor of the *Hereford Times*, was born in Manchester on 22 September 1802. After his parents' death he was brought up by his grandfather in Hereford and educated at Cheltenham College. He married Elizabeth Warrington. He bought the *Hereford Times* in 1832 with help from local Liberals and refounded it as a broadsheet of four pages of six columns, an organ for Liberal ideas. The cover price of the new newspaper was 7d of which 4d was tax at a time when an agricultural worker's wage might be 7/6 a week. Anthony successfully campaigned for the abolition of this 'tax on knowledge'. The paper was originally published in two separate editions, the *North County Edition* and the *City & South Edition*. In 1838 he opened new offices in Widemarsh Street. He was editor for many years and wrote articles for the paper throughout his life. He was remembered as a hands-on, indeed physical editor, not averse to ejecting obstreperous visitors personally from the front desk. In 1858 the *Hereford Times* moved to Maylord Street. He was six times Mayor of Hereford between 1836 and 1885, an alderman, a JP and a reforming Liberal at the centre of the changes experienced in Hereford in the 19th century: the coming of the railways; the building of Barrs Court Railway Station and the Eign railway bridge; the building of the first iron bridge over the Wye at Hunderton; the installation of a new drainage system; the new cattle market. He campaigned for them all and was a supporter of female suffrage. Conditions in Hereford in the early 19th century were shocking and as a citizen, a campaigning editor and town councillor Anthony worked against this civic neglect (qv Timothy Curley) and was instrumental in securing the Improvement Act of 1854 through which councils might raise revenue to spend on civic projects. He presided over the opening of the more sanitary butter, poultry and meat markets and helped bring about the enlargement of the Shire Hall. He was very much involved with education in Herefordshire and was noted for his books on the British Empire. He died on 5 February 1883 and was buried at St Bartholomew's, Holmer where his monument can be seen. His funeral was attended by 5,000 citizens and the business of Hereford stopped for the day.

Apperley: the family was originally from Deerhurst, Gloucs, appearing in the Much Marcle, Woolhope, Fownhope area after Elizabeth de Apperley married Sir Thomas de Brugge (qv) in 1380. They were connected with other county families like the Scudamores, Kyrles and Danseys (qqv).

Apperley, Thomas (1674-1735) was perhaps born in Little Hereford where his Dansey relatives lived, although his parents, Anthony Apperley and Anne Cornewall (qv), lived in Fownhope. He went to a school in Little Hereford run by a Mr Lewis, and attended St John's College, Cambridge, where he became a fellow. He graduated MD in 1704. He married Elizabeth (1673-1743) daughter of James Westfaling (qv under Herbert Westfaling, d.1705) of Rudhall and practised physick at Grafton. He wrote medical books, one a treatise on smallpox in which he praised the efficacy of the saffron grown in Herefordshire as antidote to poisons. He thought the soil in the county particularly good for it and praised the saffron grown in the garden of the college of vicars choral. He and his father were buried in Hereford Cathedral. Another branch of the family is found at Ashperton through the 17th and 18th centuries.

d'Aqua, David (13th century), prebendary of Hereford Cathedral, bought land that would generate an income in order to distribute simnel cake amongst the clergy in his memory. Commemorative simnel cake continued to be eaten at the cathedral till the 16th century when the fund was given to the Cathedral School.

Aquablanca, John de (d.1320), Dean of Hereford 1262-1320, was the nephew of Bishop Peter de Aquablanca (qv). The influx of the Savoyards into Herefordshire in the train of Queen Eleanor, wife of Henry III (qv), caused unrest and John's collation as dean was delayed. Francis Havergal (qv) thought it wasn't until 1278 that he was able to take up office but even so his tenure was a long one, covering Bishop Thomas Cantilupe's (qv) episcopal reign and up to his canonisation in 1320. He rebuilt much in the cathedral in the latest Decorated style, viz the eastern transepts, the chancel, the south nave aisle and he reroofed the nave aisles. The great central tower with its ballflower decoration that is a speciality of Herefordshire was rebuilt on inadequate foundations and was to cause trouble later. He also built a south-west tower which was to bring down half the nave in the 18th century. Of his time also is the beautiful stained glass in the western window of the south wall of the lady chapel. Miracles occurred at the Cantilupe grave and Dean John moved his bones into the spacious new north transept. At his death the dean left bequests of money for the fabric of county churches such as Ledbury, Clehonger and Withington.

Aquablanca, Peter de (d.1268), Bishop of Hereford 1240-68, was a great contrast to his quiet predecessor Ralph de Maidstone (qv). He had come over in the train of Henry III's Queen Eleanor of Provence as her uncle William of Savoy's steward, spoke no English, was very fat and filled offices with his relatives. He was said to be the most hated prelate in England, Matthew Paris saying 'his memory exhaled a sulphurous stench'. There was a backlash of violence in Herefordshire and in 1252 his chaplain Bernard Prior of Campagne, a proctor in the county during his absences, was murdered while saying Mass in the bishop's chapel of St Mary Magdalene. The bishop's own life was threatened and his barns were burnt. Peter was often at Court or on diplomatic missions for King Henry who used him for difficult negotiations and the raising of money. In his absence services were neglected and the cathedral grew disused. In 1260 he granted an indulgence to all who contributed to the rebuilding of Dore Abbey. When the Welsh Prince Llewelyn ab Iorwerth (qv) began raiding the Marches, Bishop Peter complained to Henry that Herefordshire was in confusion. However when the king arrived to organise defences Bishop Peter had fled to Gloucester and had to be ordered to return to his see. But his fear was well grounded as in 1262 he was besieged in Hereford Castle and captured in his cathedral by Roger de Clifford (qv) and supporters of Simon de Montfort (qv) who locked him up in Walter de Baskerville's (qv) castle of Eardisley and plundered his palace. His release was negotiated but the barons were pardoned and Bishop Peter fled to Savoy to beautify his beloved church of Aiguebelle, leaving his lands in the barons' hands. Bishop Peter is said to be the prelate captured by Robin Hood (qv under Hood) in Barnesdale and held for a ransom. But it is interesting to note that the services he ordained for Savoy were after the *Use of Hereford*. In 1268 Peter returned to his see, made his will and died at his favourite palace of Sugwas on 27 November 1268. His heart was buried where it had always been, at Aiguebelle, Savoy, but his body was interred in Hereford cathedral in the magnificent north transept built as a setting for his tomb, and his unwilling canons were forced by the Pope to pay for it. Tomb and transept are amongst the most splendid architecture in the cathedral, in mid 13th century French fashion, with straight sided arches and Purbeck marble shafts such as Henry was using at Westminster Abbey. The style was copied in other churches in Herefordshire and is seen eg. in the north door at Ledbury. His nephew John de Aquablanca's (qv) tomb lies near by. Peter de Aquablanca, that extraordinary prelate, was seen again more recently when his tomb was opened during repair work in 1925.

Arkwright, John (1785-1858), Richard's (qv) eldest son, married Sarah, daughter of Sir Hungerford Hoskyns (qv) of Harewood Park. The great Hampton Court estate, with woods, waterfalls and bisected by the River Lugg and the Humber Brook, was a wonderful playground for his 12 children. He brought in enthusiastic amateur architect Charles Hanbury Tracy to remodel the house but the expense proved too much for even the Arkwright fortune and he was dropped. Joseph Paxton (qv), head gardener of Chatsworth and future designer of the Crystal Palace, designed and built the conservatory on the south front of the house (*c.*1845). He funded the renovation and moving of The Grange, Leominster to its present position.

Arkwright, John Hungerford (1833-1905), eldest son of John (qv) and Sarah, was Lord Lieutenant of Herefordshire and JP. He married Dot, Charlotte Lucy Davenport, a keen plantswoman who named a primrose, *Evelyn Arkwright*, after her daughter and won an award of merit for *Evelyn's Beacon*. Building projects at Hampton Court, under Clerk of Works Edward Hinch (qv), drained their finances and Dot began to sell seeds of her primroses to supplement their income. Arkwright founded the Hereford Herd Book Society in 1878 and was its first president.

Arkwright, John Stanhope (1872-1954), footballer and politician, son of John Hungerford Arkwright (qv) and Charlotte, was born in London on 10 July 1872 and educated at Eton and Christ's Church, Oxford. He was a noted footballer and played right wing for Hereford Town Football Club in the Birmingham League. In 1910 he found the two bells with their quarter jacks (the carved elmwood figures that struck the bells with axes at each quarter) from the old Town Hall, demolished 50 years before, on a market stall and presented them to Hereford. They had stood on each side of the clock on the Town Hall's lantern and are now in the Old House near where they originally stood. In 1905 he married Stephanie (1883-1947) daughter of Stephen Robinson of Lynhales, a breeder of Hereford cattle. He was elected Conservative MP for Hereford unopposed in the 1906 General Election and held the seat until his retirement in 1912. In that year he sold Hampton Court and moved to Kinsham Court, a smaller house which he bought from his late brother-in-law. He had always written verse and here in 1934 he composed *Oh Valiant Hearts* for which he was knighted. The words came to him in Leominster and a verse is carved on the war memorial there. It was chosen to be sung as a hymn before George V at Westminster Abbey and on the same day in Hereford Cathedral. After the war it became known as *The Remembrance Hymn* and has been sung at every Remembrance Day service since. It was collected in his book of patriotic verse *The Supreme Sacrifice.* Vaughan Williams (qv) set it to a traditional tune but the version written by Charles Harris (qv), rector of Colwall, is the remembered one. Sir John was a Freeman and Chief Steward of the City of Hereford. He was, like his mother, a keen gardener and is known for the propagation of daffodils, and for developing *Lychnis arkwrightii*. He died at Lower Court, Kinsham on 19 September 1954 and was buried in St Mary's, Byton.

Arkwright, Richard (1755-1843), landowner, was the son of Sir Richard Arkwright (1732-92), inventor of cotton spinning machinery. He inherited a fortune which he increased by his own industrial efforts and through banking, becoming the 'richest commoner in England' at his death. He and his wife Mary had 11 children. He bought land during the Napoleonic Wars when it was cheap including, in 1817, the Hampton Court Estate at Dinmore. He spent lavishly putting house and estate in order and increasing its size. His architect was Sir Jeffry Wyatville (qv), who was working for his neighbour Sir Uvedale Price (qv).

Armitage, Arthur (1812-92), born at Burton Court at Linton near Ross, the twelfth child of Whaley (1767-1855) and Eleonora Armitage, became, like his father, a barrister. He married Isabel Jane Perceval (1830-1921) and lived at Dadnor, Bridstow where he farmed 400 acres. He was the bailiff of the Herefordshire estates of Guy's Hospital, JP and Deputy Lieutenant of Herefordshire. He was President of the Woolhope Club in 1879. Isabel was a fine watercolourist and her paintings are in the Woolhope Club archive.

Armitage, Eleonora (1865-1961), botanist, was the fifth child of Arthur (qv) and Isabel. She was a younger colleague of botanists Augustin Ley and William Purchas (qqv) who lived nearby and made bryological discoveries new to the county from her Bridstow home where she lived, unmarried, until almost the end of her long life. She wrote papers on liverworts and was a founding member of the Moss Exchange Club, and its president in 1939 when it became the British Bryological Society.

Armstrong, Herbert Rowse (1870-1922), murderer, was born in 1870 at Newton Abbot, Devon. He read law at Cambridge, sponsored by wealthier relatives, and became a solicitor. In 1906 he joined a law practice in Hay, buying a house nearby in Cusop Dingle. He prospered and married Katherine Friend, a Devon girl he had known from his youth, and they had three children. Armstrong was a major in France during the Great War. On his return he was appointed clerk to the justices at Hay Magistrates Court. He was a small, slight man and his wife a forceful, dominating woman. It seemed that Armstrong met another woman in London and, frustrated by life at home, started giving his wife small amounts of arsenic from preparations he used in the garden. Mrs Armstrong was treated by their family doctor who, as she was

becoming delusional, committed her to Barnwood Asylum in Gloucestershire. She recovered sufficiently to be discharged home but worsened again and died without suspicions being aroused. Armstrong then attempted to murder a rival solicitor with arsenic-laced scones and chocolates. The solicitor was related to the chemist from whom Armstrong bought his arsenic and discreet investigations were started. Police watched Armstrong from the Hay clock tower as he went to buy the poison at the chemist and gathered evidence that led to his trial. The case was heard at Hereford Magistrates Court, Armstrong being brought to Hereford every day from Gloucester Gaol. Despite engaging good defence counsel he was found guilty, hanged at Gloucester Gaol on 31 May 1922 and buried in the prison yard, the only solicitor to be hanged for murder in Britain. For many years his waxwork was displayed in Madame Tussaud's, looking all the more sinister for his dapper, calm appearance.

Arthur (fl.500 AD), King, is associated with several places in Herefordshire. Remarkable and ancient landscape features are often linked to legendary heroes and one associated with the mythical king is Arthur's Stone on Merbach Hill near Dorstone, where Kilvert (qv) loved to walk. The 6,000-year-old standing stones formed the central chamber and passageway of a much larger mound. Legend says it is the burial site of a king defeated by Arthur. One derivation of *Arthur's Stone* and indeed Dorstone is *Thor's Stone*. Arthur's last battle with his nephew Mordred (qv) is believed by some to have been fought at Wormelow (the worm referring to Arthur's dragon standard). Arthur's son Amyr is also believed to have been buried under Wormelow Tump, now destroyed by road works. Under The Doward near Ganarew where the Wye runs through a deep canyon is King Arthur's Cave, where Arthur and his knights rest until Britain calls them again. The geologist and archaeologist Revd W.S. Symonds (qv) excavated the cave floor and found the bones of rhinoceros, lion and hyena.

d'Athée, Gerard (d.*c*.1215), was a captain of mercenaries appointed by King John (qv) in 1208 as Sheriff of Herefordshire and a counterweight to the Briouze influence in the Marches (qv for example William (III) de Briouze). He was expected to provide effective leadership in a troubled region when the Briouze family were in exile in France. However, as he is condemned by name in King Henry III's (qv) reissue of Magna Carta, he must have fallen from favour, a victim of Briouze resurgence.

Atkins, Ivor Algernon (1869-1953), organist, was born on 29 November 1869 in Llandaff. He was sub-organist to his friend George Sinclair (qv) at Hereford Cathedral (1890-93) having followed him from Truro Cathedral. Later he was choirmaster and organist at Worcester Cathedral for over 50 years. He is known for his edition of Allegri's *Miserere* with its famous top C. He was a friend of Elgar (qv) with whom he prepared an edition of Bach's *St Matthew Passion*. Elgar dedicated *Pomp and Circumstance* to Atkins. He was knighted in 1921.

Atkins, Richard (1559-81), Protestant martyr, was born in Ross into a Roman Catholic family. At 19, an illiterate nailsmith, he converted to Protestantism and began behaving oddly. He stitched a gallows on his shirt and spoke wildly against Queen Elizabeth but was tolerated as a madman. In 1581 he set off to confront the Pope in Rome. Here, raving and feverish, he was taken to the English College and nursed back to health. He was declared sane at a madhouse but tolerated as mad by the Inquisition. Eventually he made himself such a nuisance with his public criticism of the Pope and an attack on the officiating priest in St Peter's that he was detained and, on 2 August 1581, burnt as a heretic. Foxe's *Book of Martyrs* and the authorities in Rome give opposing views of his end, but a martyr's death seems to have been his desire.

Atkinson, William (*c*.1773-1839), architect, was born in Durham and began life as a carpenter. His father was the bishop's carpenter and put his son in contact with James Wyatt (qv), who took him on as a pupil and gained him entry to the Royal Academy Schools in London. Finding patrons, Atkinson built country houses and succeeded Wyatt as architect to the Board of Ordnance. A commission in Herefordshire was Garnons at Mansell Gamage for John Geers Cotterell (qv) who had waited in vain for Wyatt to start work. Atkinson designed the house (1815-30) next to Cotterell's old Jacobean manor, with which it was intended to harmonise. The old house was later pulled down and further work to the new was added by Reginald Blomfield (qv) and others. He was consulted by Charles Hanbury Tracy about alterations at Hampton Court for John Arkwright (qv, d.1858). Atkinson was a keen geologist and botanist and had a collection of rare trees at his house at Paddington where he died on 22 May 1839.

Atlay, James (1817-94), Bishop of Hereford 1869-94, was born on 3 July 1817 at Wakerley in Northamptonshire. He was educated at Grantham and Oakham schools and St John's College, Cambridge where he remained as a tutor for some years. He was ordained in 1843 and appointed vicar of Leeds in 1859 when he married Frances Turner. In 1869 Disraeli made him Bishop of Hereford. Atlay was a conservative high churchman. He was much seen about

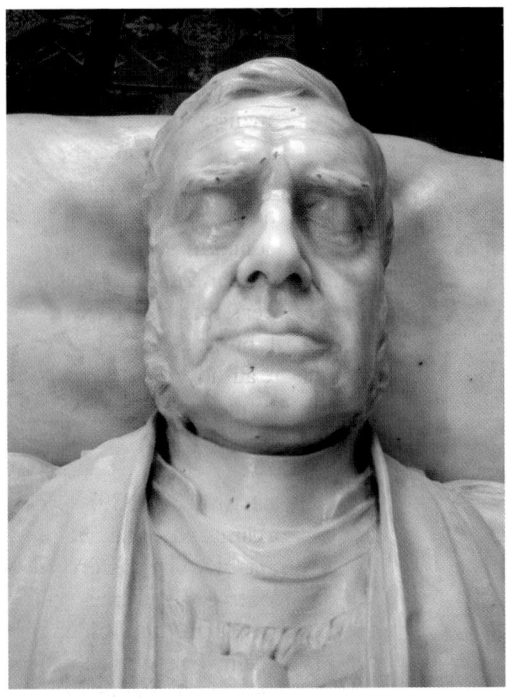

the diocese and popular with the clergy. His archbishop described him as 'the most beautiful combination of enthusiasm, manliness, and modesty'. Kilvert (qv) however called him 'overbearing and imperious' and related how Atlay mistook a curate for his candidate for confirmation and despite protestation forcibly confirmed him. His 25-year reign was one of the longest for a Bishop of Hereford. He died on 24 December 1894 and was buried outside the cathedral in the lady arbour. There is a portrait of him in the bishop's palace and his marble effigy in the north transept by James Forsyth (1897) (see above) is a masterpiece. There were several children: Revd George Atlay, a missionary, was murdered at Lake Nyasa in August 1895; his brass is in Hereford Cathedral. Another, Charles Atlay, was killed in March 1900 at Ladysmith during the Boer War.

Attey, John (*c*.1580-1640), musician and composer, was born at Ross. He was music master to the Earl and Countess of Bridgewater's daughters at Ashridge, Little Gaddesdon, Herts; they described him as 'Gentleman and Practitioner in Music'. He is best known for his *Book of Ayres* for four parts and lute, in the manner of John Dowland. A popular song of his is *Sweet was the song the Virgin sung*. He died at Ross in 1640.

> **Aubrey**: A family from Brecknockshire who became wealthy through trading in London; one was a salter. They bought the manor of Clehonger in the early 17th century and have remained evident in the area until recent times. Some seem to have been dogged by bad luck: Sir Samuel especially, but also the hapless biographer John, who lost all except his charm and good friends.

Aubrey, Harcourt (d.1779), a wealthy landowner of Clehonger, refounded Mary Price's (qv) almshouses in Berrington Street, Hereford which were thereafter called Aubrey's Almshouses. His wife Elizabeth was a granddaughter of a Mr Elfe who had managed the charity after Mrs Price's death. They had a son Richard (d.1803). His and the family's monument can be seen in the nave of All Saints Church, Clehonger.

Aubrey, Herbert (d.1671), of Clehonger, son of Samuel (qv), married Elizabeth née Bedell (d.1676). Both are buried in All Saints, Clehonger, commemorated on a wall tablet with others of the Aubrey family who continued to live at Belmont until 1788 when it burnt down and was rebuilt by James Wyatt (qv). They had a son Herbert (qv, d.1691).

Aubrey, Herbert (*c*.1635-91), son of Herbert Aubrey (d.1671), lived at the Blackfriars, Hereford, and was MP for Hereford in 1681 and 1682. He married Joyce, daughter of John Brydges (qv, d.1652) of Priors Court, and they had three sons and two daughters. He was one of the relatives with whom John Aubrey (qv) stayed.

Aubrey, John (1626-97), antiquarian and biographer, was the eldest of the three surviving sons of Richard Aubrey (qv, d.1652) and Deborah. He was born on 12 March 1626 at Easton Piers near Kington St Michael in Wiltshire, with family roots in Herefordshire. His education at Trinity College, Oxford was interrupted by the Civil Wars and he was called home to his lasting sadness. He inherited Burlton Court and other Herefordshire property on the death of his father and often stayed with relatives in the county. He found Hereford folk had 'a brisk spirit, clear voices, speak quick ... longaevous [long-lived], not covetous and stingy but hospitable, quick witted'. He enjoyed their tales of the Herefordshire fairies and, realizing such stories were dying out, devoted his life to collecting them. He took notes from everyone he met, never with much order, 'tumultuarily as if tumbled out of a sack', leaving gaps with 'quaere' in the margin, meaning to follow it up but never getting round to it. He sold Burlton Court to his friend Dr Thomas Willis (qv Browne Willis), who had 'haire ... like a red pig', and his other property at Stretford near Leominster to another friend, Bishop Herbert Croft (qv). His biographical information, or gossip, which he called '*Schediasmata*, pieces written extempore on the spur of the moment', were unpublished until Andrew Clarke's *Brief Lives* of 1898. He wrote many other historical papers most still unpublished. In *Monumenta Britannica* he makes innovative attempts at dating through comparisons, looking at handwriting, clothing, architecture etc. In the section *Chronologia Architectonica* he records his study of Hereford Cathedral, where he particularly enjoyed the chancel vaulting. Aubrey was drawn into expensive law suits and increasing debt. He did not have an orderly mind and his money disappeared, as did his property and finally even his beloved library. Finally he was reduced to living off the charity and in the houses of friends and relations like those at Clehonger and Brampton Abbots. His 'chiefest friend' (one of his fourteen *amici*) was Sir John Hoskyns (qv, d.1705) of Harewood Park where he often stayed; another was Sir John Scudamore (qv, d.1671) of Holme Lacy. He was sociable and optimistic, seeing his rootless life as one of freedom: 'I had never quiet til divested of all', and he relaxed into 'a happy delitescency'. It was not ideal for his antiquarian and 'chorographic' researches though and he brought none of his varied and considerable researches into publishable form. His filing system, which he carried on horseback from house to house, was a 'dust basket' stuffed with papers. The tetchy Anthony Wood, with whom he freely shared his researches, ungratefully called him 'magotie-headed and sometimes little better than crazed'. Wood predicted he would meet his death rushing downstairs to catch a departing celebrity. But unlike Wood, Aubrey was a kind, likeable man, and it is for the gossip he relates in *Brief Lives* that we remember him. He says rightly 'how these curiosities would be quite forgotten, did not such idle fellows as I am put them down'. He died (of a stroke) as he had lived, travelling between friends' houses, and was buried in St Mary Magdalen, Oxford on 7 June 1697.

Aubrey, Richard (1603-52), son of John (qv under William Aubrey) and Rachel, was born at Burlton Court, Burghill. He married Deborah (1610-86), the daughter and heir of Isaac and Israel Lyte, who brought him property at Easton Piers in Wiltshire where they moved. His son

John (qv) recalled that he was educated to hawking but not much else. Burlton Court is now a farmhouse.

Aubrey, Samuel (1580-1645), knight, was a cousin of Dr William (qv) and son of Morgan Aubrey of Aston Ingham. Morgan was a London salter with origins in Brecknockshire who bought the manor of Clehonger. Samuel was knighted by King Charles in 1620 and was High Sheriff of the county. He lived in old Belmont Abbey on the banks of the Wye. In 1643 the Parliamentary army commandeered the house before besieging Hereford, evicting the family and imprisoning Sir Samuel in Bristol. On his release he found his way home, where he died. He is buried in Hereford Cathedral.

Aubrey, William (*c*.1529-95), Queen Elizabeth's Master of Requests and her 'little doctor', was from Brecknockshire. He was a kinsman of John Dee (qv) and a relation of the Vaughans. There were many related Aubreys in the Marches. He married Wilgiford Williams of Oxford and was buried in Old St Pauls, where there was a monument to him. His son John bought Burlton Court at Burghill and married Rachel Danvers from Wiltshire. They were buried at St Mary's Burghill, where there is a large brass to Aubrey, Rachel and their two children.

Audley: The family were from Staffs, with their seat at Heleigh (or Heighley) Castle. There were various creations of the barony of Audley. Margery, the daughter of Roger (VI) Mortimer and Philippa, married John Lord Audley, and Marcle was her dower; thus the Audleys became lords of the manors of Marcle and Monnington.

Audley, Edmund (1439-1524), Bishop of Hereford 1492-1502, was the second son of James Tuchet, 5th Baron Audley, and his second wife, Eleanor Holland. He took the surname Audley when his older brother became Baron Audley to indicate his association with him and the Yorkist cause, then in the ascendant. This paid off as his rise was rapid and he accumulated livings and prebends around the country, including the prebend of Colwall in 1464 aged only 25. He was archdeacon of the East Riding of Yorkshire, of Essex and a canon of St George's Chapel, Windsor, a sign of the king's approval. He was made Bishop of Rochester in 1480 and on 22 June 1492 was translated to Hereford. He was bishop for ten years before moving to Salisbury. On Henry VII's death he was a testator of his will. He was a learned humanist but not it seems humane, as he fiercely persecuted dissent and the owning of religious books in English, burning a Lollard in Salisbury for every year of his 20-year reign as bishop there. Audley had a magnificent two-storey chantry chapel built on the south side of the lady chapel in Hereford Cathedral 1516-24 where prayers could be said for his soul, not long before such practices were abolished. Its painted saints are still visible and the upper storey is rich in panelling and pendentives. He built another chapel in Salisbury Cathedral where, dying at Ramsbury on 23 August 1524, he was buried.

Audley, Hugh (d.1347), Earl of Gloucester, was proprietor of the manor of Marcle by 1301, called Marcle Audley, with its manor house, Hellens where his franklin Walter de Helyon (qv) lived, and castle south of the church. Sir Hugh married Margaret, widow of Piers Gaveston and daughter of Gilbert de Clare, Earl of Gloucester in April 1317, becoming earl himself in 1337. His son Sir Hugh married Isolde (as her second husband), the daughter of Edmund (I) Mortimer (qv), and it may be their effigies that rest in the Kyrle chapel of Much Marcle Church.

Audley, James (1316-69), KG, was the eldest son of Sir James Audley, an Oxfordshire knight and nephew and heir of Sir Hugh to whom he paid a pair of silver spurs for Hellens. He fought under the Black Prince (qv Edward of Woodstock) at Crécy (1346) and showed great valour at Poitiers (1356) for which he was granted a pension by Prince Edward. He was a founding knight of the Order of the Garter. Prince

Edward is said to have stayed at Hellens and his feathers are carved on the mantel in the old Hall. Sir James was a governor in King Edward's French territories and was buried at Poitiers.

Audley, Katherine (b.*c.*1272), 'recluse of Ledbury' or anchoress, was the daughter of Sir John Giffard, Baron of Brimpsfield, Gloucs. She married Sir Nicholas de Audley in 1287. They had a son Richard (b.1298) and daughter Ella, who married Sir James de Perrers. After the death of her husband and father the wealthy widow began to dispose of her properties and became a recluse. According to a prophecy, Katherine would found her cell where bells rang without human aid. She travelled from Wenlock (then within the diocese of Hereford) accompanied by her maid Mabel and various miracles: near Stanford Bishop their horses were stolen and recovered through prayer; at Stretton Grandison a spring appeared, forming St Katherine's Well. At Ledbury the church bells rang spontaneously and she knew this was where she should settle. The Hazle nearby was an Audley property and her cell was probably founded here. A document refers to her as at Ledbury in 1313 and in 1322 Edward II (qv) awarded her a pension of £30 pa. She is spoken of at Ledbury as Saint Katherine and confused with St Katherine of Alexandria, patron of St Katherine's Hospital. The baptistery or north chapel at Ledbury (built *c.*1330) may have been intended as a shrine for 'the blessed Katherine'. Wordsworth and Coleridge (qqv) have celebrated her in poems.

Augustine (d.604), saint and first Archbishop of Canterbury, was a Benedictine monk sent on a mission from Rome to Britain by St Gregory in 603 to negotiate conformity with bishops of the Celtic church and convert the pagan English. Bede places the synod in the territory of the Hwicce under an oak and local tradition places this at Stanford Bishop. The independent British bishops decided that if he stood to greet them they would negotiate with him but if he remained seated on his throne, pride would disqualify him. He did not rise to greet them and agreement between the churches was postponed for a century. A possibly Anglo-Saxon chair known as St Augustine's Throne can be seen in St James's Church, Stanford Bishop. St Augustine had better luck in Kent, baptising many before his death soon after. His feast day in England is 26 May.

Aurelianus, Ambrosius (5th century) was a military leader of an old Roman family who maintained some degree of command in a Britain being overrun by the Saxons. Described by Gildas and Bede as *dux* and in Welsh legend called *Emrys Wledig*, he halted the Saxon advance at Mons Badonicus. Legend says that Croft Ambrey bears his name.

Averill, John (fl.1851), was the minister of Ledbury's Congregational chapel, which he found too small and damp. He organised its rebuilding and it was rededicated, as can be read on the parapet, in 1852. Here Elizabeth Barrett (qv) came with her father to worship.

B

Bach, John (d.1777), schoolmaster and surveyor of Hereford, designed gardens at Stoke Edith (1766) for Thomas Foley (qv, d.1777) and at Newport, Almeley (1767), introducing a fashionable informality. Coloured maps survive of these projects, as do his surveys of Much Birch, Monnington and the Widemarsh area of Hereford. The Bach family were found in the Leominster area in the 17th century, and a John Bach was a 'writing master' and bailiff of Leominster.

Backhouse, Robert Ormston (1854-1940), **Sarah Elizabeth** (1857-1921) and **William Ormston** (1885-1962) were Quaker horticulturists. Robert, a son of William Backhouse of Darlington, married Sarah Elizabeth Dodgson in 1884 and they moved to Sutton Court at Sutton St Nicholas. Sarah and Robert continued the work with which the Backhouse family had long been involved on the hybridisation of narcissi, interested in developing a pink-cupped flower. Sarah was awarded the Barr Cup in 1916 for her hybridizing work but it was not until after her death that Robert finally produced the first pink-cupped, white-perianthed variety, named *Mrs R. O. Backhouse* in her honour. Robert Backhouse died at Sutton Court on 10 April 1940. Their son William was educated at Trinity Hall, Cambridge, and worked for a period of five years at the Cambridge Plant Breeding Station and the John Innes Institute before becoming a geneticist for the Argentine government. He returned to Sutton Court in 1945 to continue the family work on narcissi, dying there in 1962.

Badham, John (fl 1660-88) was organist at Hereford Cathedral 1660-88 at a salary of £12 per annum. He was clearly in straitened circumstances, perhaps because of the vicissitudes of the Civil Wars, as extra payments were made him by Dean and Chapter. His job included teaching the choristers to play the organ and other instruments and to keep the song books in good order; and he was let off the parochial duties which were required of his predecessor before the Civil Wars – one Hugh Davies (organist 1630-44). There would have been no organ at the end of the Interregnum and a small organ was borrowed for him. Badham wrote several anthems, including *Praise the Lord*; *Oh Lord Thou has Searched me out* and *How doth the City sit Sorrowfull*, for which he received extra payments from the Chapter. He had a son, Charles (fl.1698-1716), who also wrote anthems and who was appointed minor canon at St Paul's, London. John was succeeded in post by Henry Hall (qv), who had been Badham's assistant organist.

Baggallay, Richard (1816-88), MP for Hereford, was born in Stockwell, London on 13 May 1816, the son of a Lord Chief Justice, and educated at Gonville and Caius College, Cambridge. He was called to the bar in 1843 and was QC in 1861. In 1847 he married Marianne (13 June 1824-20 June 1895), daughter of Henry Charles Lacy, MP for Bodmin. They had five sons and four daughters. He was elected MP for Hereford in 1865 as a reforming conservative

and was Solicitor General in Disraeli's administration. When the government fell in 1868 he lost his seat and ministerial position, but was knighted. He was later MP for Hove, Sussex and was again appointed Solicitor General and finally Attorney General. He died in Hove on 13 November 1888. Baggallay Street in Hereford is named after him.

Bagnall, Gibbons (1719-1800), clergyman and poet, was born in Windsor the son of a prosperous wine merchant and educated at Balliol College, Oxford and King's College, Cambridge. In 1757 he married Sarah Reeve of Windsor. Appointed vicar of Holme Lacy, he was headmaster of Hereford Cathedral School from 1749 to 1778. As prebendary of Piona Parva (Pyon) and Barsham at Hereford, he was the canon in residence on Easter Monday 1786 when the west end of the cathedral fell. He was also rector of Upton Bishop and, from 1783, vicar of Sellack. He wrote poetry, publishing *Education: an Essay* (1765) and a verse translation of Fénelon's *Adventures of Telemachus*. He died on 31 December 1800.

Baker, Beatrice May (1876-1973), headmistress, was born at 2 High Street, Hereford on 4 May 1876, the third daughter of Edward Joseph Baker, a prosperous tailor, and Catherine Pugh. All three daughters and their brother went to Hereford Cathedral School. Beatrice took a BA degree at Royal Holloway College, taught in Cardiff and became headmistress and proprietor of Badminton House, Bristol, which she transformed into a successful private school. She was at the forefront of international peace initiatives by the League of Nations, visited Geneva annually with pupils and took in refugees including Indira Nehru, during the time her father was in prison. She died in Somerset on 28 September 1973.

Baker, Henry Williams (1821-77), hymn writer and clergyman, was born in London on 27 May 1821, the eldest son of Vice-Admiral Sir Henry Loraine Baker. He was educated at Trinity College, Cambridge, and ordained in 1846. He was curate at Great Horkesley, Essex and was then presented to the vicarage of Monkland, near Leominster in 1851 where he remained until his death. There was no vicarage at Monkland so Baker built one to his own design and cost, calling it Horkesley House. It had a private chapel with its own organ. Baker chose his domestic staff for their choral abilities and in this way maintained the best choir in the county. With the support of Bishop Hampden (qv), he built a school for 60 children, one of the most successful of village schools. In 1859 he succeeded his father as 3rd Baronet. Sir Henry was the force behind *Hymns Ancient and Modern* (1861), as well as a source of funds. This became the Church of England's most loved and used anthology of hymns and a constant best-seller. Although seen by some as too Tractarian, Baker tried to ensure a balanced approach. He wrote many hymns himself, including *The King of Love My Shepherd Is* and the popular harvest-thanksgiving hymn *Praise Oh Praise our God and King*. All Saints, Monkland was originally the chapel of a small Benedictine abbey and had become dilapidated. Sir Henry commissioned George Street (qv) to rebuild it (1866) after a Tractarian model. Street reused original fabric where possible, keeping the Norman tufa windows and the tower arch. The much admired organ in the church was designed by Baker and Sir Frederick Gore Ouseley (qv). John Wilkes (qv) played there and supplied the tune that came to be called *Monkland* as a setting for Milton's *Let Us With a Gladsome Mind*, which Baker included in *Hymns A&M*, giving the village wide celebrity. Sir Henry remained unmarried, developing strong ideas about the celibacy of the clergy after a Laetitia Bonner refused him, marrying instead Revd W. Edwards, vicar of Orleton. The stained glass in the east window at St George, Orleton commemorates Laetitia. Baker's housekeeper was his sister Jessy Baker (1825-1907). He died on 12 February 1877 in his vicarage, and was buried in the churchyard. Thirty years later Jessy was buried next to him. A stained glass window and a brass (from colleagues at *Hymns A&M*) commemorate Baker in his church. In 1893 Street's design for a lych-gate was built as a further memorial.

Baldwin, Samuel (fl.1606-45) was a stonemason from an established family of masons in Gloucester. He made the table tombs at Ross for John and Mary Rudhall (qv John Rudhall d.1636), and at Marcle for John and Sybil Kyrle (qv John Kyrle, d.1650); and the wonderful Smalman (qv Francis Smalman) wall-monument at Kinnersley of 1639. He is credited with Bishop Herbert Westfaling's (qv) now tombless effigy in the north transept of Hereford Cathedral and a wall monument to Sir Walter Pye (qv) at Much Dewchurch. He is buried in St Nicholas's, Gloucester. His son Stephen continued the business.

Ballard, Ernest (1870-1952) horticulturist, fruit grower and chemist, youngest son of Stephen Ballard (qv), was born on 2 May 1870 at The Winnings, Colwall. He studied chemistry to help with the family vinegar business. In 1899 he married his first cousin Ella de Quincey (1870-1920) and they lived at Old Court, Colwall near the Winnings, where they had four children. Here he developed his nursery and concentrated on developing the modern Michaelmas Daisy, producing the double *Beauty of Colwall.* Ernest worked on Hepaticas, discovering the hybrid media Ballardii, and varieties of Aubretias, Iberis, Hellebores, Fritillaria, Nerines and Cyclamen. In 1949 he was awarded the RHS gold medal. He died at Staplow on 30 March 1952. His son Philip Ernest's wife Helen, living at Old Country Farm, Mathon, continued his work on Hellebores to acclaim. Ernest's head nurseryman Percy Picton bought Old Court Nursery at Ernest's death. The Picton family still run the nursery, which now has the national collection of asters.

Ballard, Philip (1800-87), Stephen's brother (qv), worked with him on the Hereford and Gloucester canal. He was a Hereford town councillor living at The Knoll, Church Road, Tupsley. On 19 October 1887 the wealthy old man was burgled by James Jones and Alfred Scandrett (both 1864-88), who beat him with an axe causing his later death. Scandrett, who had wielded the axe, tried to kill Jones in the dock. Philip's niece, Stephen's daughter, Ada had been staying with her uncle and appeared as a witness in Hereford Court, writing to the burglars later in prison. They were hanged in March 1888 in Hereford Gaol and buried in the yard. The hangman was James Berry (qv).

Ballard, Robert (1802-78), Stephen's brother (qv), was a Ledbury brickmaker who made the bricks for his brother's engineering projects, including the five million required for the Ledbury Viaduct, all made on site. This splendid structure still stands by Ledbury railway station. In 1870 his son Robert (1839-1912) moved to Australia, where, like his uncle Stephen, he built railways. There is a town in North Queensland called Ballard after him.

Ballard, Stephen (1804-91), civil engineer, was born at Malvern Link on 5 April 1804 the fifth of the seven children of Philip Ballard (1771-1842), an attorney from Ross, and Charlotte Baylis from Ledbury. Philip, Charlotte and a daughter of that name are remembered on a wall plaque in Ledbury Church. Stephen was educated in Worcester but left early for a horticultural apprenticeship in Middlesex, later returning to work with the Worcester builder Henry Lucy. He became clerk of a Ledbury consortium led by Robert Biddulph (qv) that intended to finish building the Hereford and Gloucester canal, long stranded outside Ledbury (qv Josiah Clowes). He quickly took the project over and, aged 26, picking up experience from other jobs and learning as he went, built five locks to bring it into Ledbury town, then, over the next 18 years, through cuttings and over bridges on into Hereford. His diaries describe walking to the site from Malvern for a 4am start, and working through till 9pm before walking back. This was too much for his apprentice Samuel Willcox, whom he left sleeping at the workings; in future he would erect temporary shelters at the canal head. When the canal reached Withington in February 1844 there was a grand celebration before Ballard left for his next job. The canal opened in 1845 and the price of coal in Hereford dropped steeply. It was the last of the canals, completed in the railway age, and the railway companies immediately offered to buy it. Ironically the company made most of

its profits by carrying railway equipment. John Masefield (qv) remembered the painted boats on the canal at Ledbury. Ballard was an original thinker and an inventor: he created a machine for breaking up ice on the canal, as well as a horse-drawn steam engine that burnt weeds before the age of herbicides and a device for cleaning and reusing old bricks. He wrote books, one on the benefit of light railways in rural areas. He was an early member of the Institute of Civil Engineers in the heroic days of Brunel, Brassey and Telford. He won the Telford gold medal and went into partnership with Brassey. His skills were much sought after: he was asked to survey the Panama Canal, and to build railways on the Continent, in India and Canada. He married Maria Bird, whom he had met while draining the Fens near Peterborough. They settled at The Winnings, Colwall which he built along with other houses in the area. Here they had several sons and daughters, and he farmed and grew fruit, winning awards for his jams and vinegar. He became involved with the Malvern to Hereford railway line, which was being tunneled under his land. This required drilling through the very hard granites of the Malverns and the softer rocks at Ledbury, where fossils were found. The line ran over the Leadon Valley on the Ledbury Viaduct, a striking feat of engineering, 19 metres tall with 31 slender arches, and another elegant structure, the Skew Bridge. He built three stations, one at Tarrington for Lady Emily Foley (qv). He built Jubilee Drive through the Malverns against local opposition and, by Act of Parliament, founded the Malvern Hills Conservators to prevent building on the Hills. Ballard was loved by his workforce although the navvies and their wild drinking scared him. He describes the trails of men with their families crossing the Malverns looking for work, stopping in his large porch at The Winnings for soup which he kept ready for them. He was a kind, charitable man, teetotal and opposed to capital punishment. A keen observer of nature, his notes and sketches are preserved in Hereford Record Office. He died on 14 November 1891 and is buried with other members of his family on his estate in the spoil dug out of his railway tunnel below.

Ballard, Thomas (1798-1855), artist, older brother of Stephen (qv), painted the copy of *The Last Supper* that hangs behind the altar in St Michael's, Ledbury. A contemporary copy of Leonardo's fresco in Milan by Leonardo's assistant Giampietrino was bought in 1821 by the Royal Academy, where Ballard saw and copied it in 1826. (The Royal Academy's copy is now in Magdalen College chapel, Oxford.) He lived in Ledbury's Homend. A son, Thomas (1836-1908), was also an artist. Another, John Edy Ballard (b.1841), was a Ledbury grocer.

de Balun: A Norman family from Ballon, Le Mans. Hamelin de Balun and his sons came to England with the Conqueror and were granted much land in east Wales, founding Abergavenny Castle. Hamelin's daughter Emmeline married Reginald de Breteuil (qv Roger de Breteuil), who took the name de Balun. After the fall of the Lacy family in 1096 the de Baluns were granted the large manor of Marcle, centred on Mortimer's Castle, of which a mound remains near Much Marcle Church. With the Bohuns, Briouzes and Mortimers (qqv) the de Baluns guarded the Marches. The manor passed from them to the Audleys (qv) in the 13th century.

Balun, John de (d.1235), baron, was the son of Reginald (d.1203). When de Balun joined the barons' rebellion against King John (qv) he forfeited his lands, although they were later recovered from Henry III (qv). He witnessed Henry III's reissue of Magna Carta and was a benefactor of Aconbury Priory. He married Joanna, daughter of the unfortunate William (III) de Briouze (qv), whose downfall was probably responsible for de Balun losing his lands. John and Joanna had at least three sons, the eldest of whom, John, succeeded him.

Balun, Walter de (d.*c.*1284), a descendant of John (qv), married Isolde (d.*c.*1336), daughter of Edmund (I) de Mortimer (qv). After Walter's death she married Hugh Audley (qv), the start of the Audley presence in what was called Marcle Audley.

Banks, Richard (1792-1871) arrived in Kington in 1814 and bought a half-share in James Davies' successful legal practice. Banks married Davies' niece, the heiress Esther Davies (qv Esther Crummer).

Banks, Richard William (1819-91), eldest of six children of Richard (qv) and Esther, married Emily Rosa Hartland (1835-1924)

in 1858. They moved into Ridgebourne on the Hergest estate, near Kington and had a daughter and a son, William. He was a banker and lawyer, a keen naturalist, an archaeologist and distinguished geologist. Roderick Murchison (qv) drew attention to his work at the meeting of the British Association at Glasgow in 1855 and read a paper by him to the Geological Society later in that year. *Pteraspis banksii* and *Himantopterus banksii* were so named in recognition of the collections he had made of the *Pterygoti* in the Kington locality. Murchison acknowledged his assistance in the 3rd edition of his *Siluria* in 1859. He planted Yeld Wood at Hergest with exotic trees including the huge Douglas Firs.

Banks, Thomas (1735-1805), sculptor, was born in London but spent his childhood in Ross-on-Wye and went to school there. The eldest of the three sons of William Banks, he was surveyor to the 4th Duke of Beaufort at Badminton and learnt the principles of architecture and drawing with him. He won a travelling scholarship at the Royal Academy and, as a sculptor in London, met and worked with important practitioners of the mid 18th century including Peter Scheemakers, John Flaxman and Joseph Nollekens. After a period in Russia working for Catherine the Great, he returned to take London by storm with a series of large scale heroic and moving works of group sculpture. His best known work is *Shakespeare attended by Painting and Poetry*, now in the garden of New Place, Stratford-upon-Avon. He died in London on 2 February 1805.

Banks, William Hartland (1876-1930), only son of Richard William (qv) and Emily, married Dorothy Alford (1876-1937) in 1894 and they had three daughters. He was a banker, traveller and photographer, as well as a passionate

plantsman and gardener. His garden design was influenced by the writings of William Robinson. In 1912 he bought the Hergest Estate and created Hergest Croft Gardens with 50 acres of rare trees and shrubs, and especially fine rhododendrons. The Banks family still own Hergest Croft.

Bannister, Arthur Thomas (b.1861), vicar of Ewyas Harold, wrote a history of his parish published by Jakeman & Carver (qv) in 1902 that includes a detailed account of William fitz Osbern's (qv) castle, as far as he could make it out, and of the town, which was one of the biggest in Herefordshire in the 12th century. He later published *Herefordshire and its place in English History* and *The Place Names of Herefordshire* (1916). He was an editor for the Cantilupe Society, and published *The Register of Adam de Orleton* (qv). He was a canon residentiary of Hereford Cathedral (1909-36) and precentor (1916-36). He followed Canon Capes (qv) as keeper of the archives (1914-35) and worked with F.C. Morgan (qv) in ordering the cathedral library. In 1927 he published a scholarly catalogue of manuscripts with an introduction by M.R. James (qv). He was an authority on the history of the cathedral and was Master of the Fabric. He ran a crammers establishment for university entrance at Ewyas Harold rectory. Brian Hatton (qv), a pupil in 1905, was impressed with the other students' talk of motors and women and made caricatures of Bannister and his pupils. Bannister was a member of the Woolhope Club, whose *Transactions* record his antiquarian papers.

Barber, William George Storr (1876-1934), monumental mason, was born 28 January 1876 at Castle Camps, Cambridge the son of Revd G.R. Barber. He was apprenticed to Alfred Ursell, mason of Ross. In 1903 he married Florence, daughter of John Jay, a mason of Leominster, and moved to 88 Bargates, Leominster. He had a workshop in Etnam Street where he made church monuments and war memorials. They later moved to Aylestone House, Hereford. He designed and sculpted the marble reredos for Mitcheldean Church (1913), made war memorials for Aberdeen and for March in Cambridgeshire and designed a memorial for the Royal Marines, with whom he had served, at Plymouth Hoe. In Leominster he carved the statue of St Ethelbert in a niche on the front of St Ethelbert's Church in Bargates (1908). He designed and built Leominster's War Memorial by the Priory Church, which is inscribed with a verse from John Stanhope Arkwright's (qv) *Remembrance Hymn*. Other work in the county includes a cross in Weobley Church (1920), a hooded figure in Pudleston Church (1921) and war memorials at Almeley and Dilwyn. He was chairman of the YMCA and of the Hereford WEA, and was much involved with the Hereford Drama Festival. His lungs were weakened by the effects of stone dust and he moved to stay with a son in Kent where he died on 19 October 1934.

Barker, Edward Henry Lingen (1838-1917), Hereford architect, built the Victoria Eye Hospital in Hereford (1889), now converted to private housing, and designed Board Schools in several counties, such as that at Garway (1886-7) and Woolhope (1878), where he added the vicarage in 1879. He built cottages in Gwynne Street, Hereford (1864) and in Shobdon, and built The Croft (1890) at Vowchurch. The archway into St Peter's graveyard in Commercial Street and the gates on Shobdon Court drive are both of 1881. He altered the ground floor of the Old House in High Town, Hereford (1882-3) and restored John Abel's (qv) gravestone (1886). He lived at 144 Ledbury Road, Hereford, which he built for himself in 1881. He was diocesan architect for Pembrokeshire and built much in Wales, and also worked in Ireland.

Barksdale, Clement (1609-87), clergyman and author, was the son of John Barksdale and was born on St Clement's Day, 23 November 1609 at Winchcombe, Gloucs. Educated at Merton College and Gloucester Hall, Oxford, and ordained, at 28 he was appointed headmaster of Hereford Cathedral School, becoming a vicar choral and rector of St Nicholas, Hereford. The next five years were a time of sieges and alarms at Hereford, until 1646 when he was evicted by the Presbyterians (qv William Lowe). He found succour with the Chandos family of Sudely Castle near Winchcombe, and became their chaplain and a rector nearby. He married and both his sons, Charlton and Charles, became vicars. A moderate Anglican, he attempted to unite opposing factions and preached tolerance. He produced many books and is remembered for his translation of Grotius, his great love. He died in January 1687 and is buried at Naunton, his last cure.

Barneby: The Barneby family acquired the Brockhampton estate on Bringsty Common from the Habingtons in the 16th century. In the previous century it had been with the Domultons (qv), who built the charming black and white house so admired today. In the early 18th century the manor was conveyed by marriage to the Lutleys, who incorporated the Barneby name into their own to maintain continuity. They built a mansion on the hill above the old manor house and renovated the old house. The large estate with its farms was finally vested in the National Trust, where it remains.

Barneby, Edmund, see **Edmund Higginson**

Barneby, Penelope (b.1679), the heiress of Brockhampton, married Philip Lutley of Loughton Hall and Bromcroft Castle, Shropshire in 1707.

Barneby, Richard (d.1597) acquired the Brockhampton estate on Bringsty Common when he married the heiress Mary Habington (d.1574) from Ombersley. The Habingtons had the estate from the Domultons (qv John Domulton). Barneby commissioned the Dutch monumental sculptor Gerard Holleman to make an enjoyably flamboyant tomb for him and Mary in St Michael Bockleton a few miles east of Brockhampton, just in Worcs.

Barneby, William (1846-95) inherited the Salt Marsh estate, near Bromyard, after his uncle Edmund's death (qv Edmund Higginson), with the enormous new Saltmarshe Castle. In the 20th century the estate, now unsustainably large, was let and finally sold. The estate agent's catalogue in 1953 described how 'the terrace gardens and surrounding woods and parklands combine to complete the natural setting of the site on which the castle stands'. But the castle was demolished in 1955; two castellated lodges alone remain, and William Nesfield's (qv) terraces are now a caravan park.

Barneby, William Henry (fl.1870s), the younger brother of John Habington Barneby Lutley (qv), commissioned Thomas Henry Wyatt (qv) to build Bredenbury Court (1873) (now St Richard's School) near Bromyard. In 1877 he paid for the rebuilding of St Andrew's Church, Bredenbury on a new site, with a new pulpit and organ.

Barneby Lutley, Bartholomew Richard (1713-83) was the youngest son of Penelope Barneby (qv) and Philip Lutley. On coming of age he added his mother's family name Barneby. In 1756 he married his cousin Betty Freeman (qv under John Freeman, d.1764) of Gaines at nearby Whitbourne. In the 1760s he started to lay out the estate grounds and commissioned Thomas Farnolls Pritchard (qv) to build Brockhampton House (*c*.1764).

Barneby Lutley, John (1757-1817), Bartholomew's (qv) son, was Sheriff of Herefordshire. In 1792 he married Elizabeth (d.1833), the daughter of Robert Bulkeley. Their children were John, William and Elizabeth (1793-1852), who married Robert Biddulph Phillips (qv, d.1864). He died on 11 February 1817.

Barneby Lutley, John Habington (d.1906) was the son of John Barneby (qv John Barneby Lutley). He married Emily Chetwynd-Talbot (1844-86) in 1864 and remodelled the interiors at Brockhampton. The estate descended to Col John Talbot Lutley who, dying childless, bequeathed it to the National Trust in 1946.

Barnsley, William (d.1734), lawyer, retired from the Inner Temple to Eardisley. He bought the manor from his cousin, another William Barnsley, who had acquired it from the Baskervilles (qv Benhail Baskerville) in the late 1600s. William lived at Castle House while he built himself Eardisley Park House. He married Jane L'Estrange, 30 years his junior, a descendant of the Duppa family (qv under Brian Duppa) and served as Deputy Sheriff of Herefordshire. HE made a will leaving everything to Jane, but she predeceased him. He had a stroke in the dovecote at Eardisley Park and died intestate. His estranged son, also William Barnsley, was convinced by his father's man of business and solicitor Mansell Powell (qv) that his father had intended to leave his estate to Powell. In support of his position, Powell produced a will bequeathing the estate to himself and a Samuel Barnsley, who claimed to be a cousin. The probate court approved this will but many years later the deserted wife of one John Cartwright (qv), a scrivener who knew Barnsley's hand, arrived from London to expose her husband, whom she suspected of forging the will. Her allegations were taken up by Elizabeth (1710-73), wife of the genuine heir, over 30 years after Barnsley senior's death. The will was re-examined, witnesses were recalled and probate was withdrawn. It transpired that Powell had paid Cartwright to write out the will and the 'cousin' to stand as heir. Powell and Barnsley were sentenced to prison but Cartwright was hanged. William was declared a lunatic and to be incapable of managing his affairs, and by this time most of the estate had gone in chancery costs, but his wife Elizabeth was able to live at Eardisley Park. The affair is said to have inspired Dickens' (qv) *Bleak House*, with its brilliant attack on the Court of Chancery. There are Barnsley epitaphs in Eardisley Church: old Barnsley's reads:

> *Bubble's broken, but death's the gate of life ...*

while that to Elizabeth and William the younger reads:

> *After tedious and lengthy law-suits lasting 34 years, at length they overcame. Conquerors!'*

de la Barre, John (d.1483), son of Sir Thomas (qv, d.1420) and Alice, inherited much land in Herefordshire and elsewhere. He married Joan (d.1484) and they are the subjects of a splendid brass in All Saints, Clehonger which depicts the details of their fashionable clothing, armour and heraldry. Joan half-turns to her husband with a smile and raised hands while her little dogs bark up at her. Their daughter married a member of the Bodenham family (qv) and conveyed the Rotherwas mansion and estate to her husband.

de la Barre, Richard (*c.*1130-*c.*1202), ecclesiastic, held a prebend in Hereford and served Henry II (qv) on diplomatic missions to the Pope during the Becket (qv) affair. He was a justice under Henry and his son King John (qv).

de la Barre, Richard (d.1386), canon of Hereford Cathedral, is the subject of a brass (now in the ambulatory) which shows him in his cope in the head of a cross.

de la Barre, Thomas (*c.*1349-1419), of Barre's Court, Holmer and Rotherwas, was the son of Thomas de la Barre (d.1388) of Rotherwas, and Hawise, sister and co-heir of Sir Richard Pembridge (qv, d.1375). He inherited lands through the Pembridges and from his wife Elizabeth (d.1420), daughter of Sir William Croyser and widow of Sir Ralph Camoys and of Sir Edward Kendale. On his father's death he came into the Rotherwas estate, and he possessed other lands at Tarrington, Holmer, Allensmore, Little Marcle and Lyde. He lived at Barre's Court (now the site of Hereford railway station) and Ayot St Lawrence, Herts. Knighted by 1373, he was Sheriff of Hereford in 1385, 1388-9 and 1395-6, a JP for the Shire and MP for Hereford in 1386, 1402 and 1416, and for Herts., thanks to his uncle Pembridge. He became an influential member of the households of Edward III (qv) and Richard II (qv), who in 1384 appointed him surveyor of the King's Haye, the royal forest south of Hereford, and paid him large annuities. He fought for Richard on his Irish campaign in 1394-5. However, he transferred easily to the usurping Henry IV's (qv) service and continued to serve with Henry V (qv); both Henrys confirmed his privileges. He continued to amass estates in Herefordshire and Herts. He was involved in the future Henry V's arrangements for combatting Glyn Dŵr's (qv) rebellion. He stood surety for his neighbours Leonard Hakluyt of Eaton Hall and Thomas (I) Walwyn of Stoke Edith (qqv); all three men were royal servants involved in prosecuting Lollards. In 1416 Hereford Cathedral chapter appointed him steward of four of their local manors. In 1419 as JP his son Thomas (qv, d.1420) was brought before him charged with armed robbery and other crimes. This must have been difficult for the ageing father, and he died later that year, closely followed by his widow.

de la Barre, Thomas, (d.1420), son of Thomas (qv, d.1419) and Elizabeth, married Lord John Talbot's (qv, d.1453) sister Alice. There was great anarchy in Herefordshire at this time and Thomas became involved in Lord John's bloody feuds. Having committed serious crimes including armed robbery and abductions, he was brought before his father as JP in 1419 and had to be referred to higher courts at Westminster. He died the following year, leaving his young son, John (qv), heir to the great estates. His widow Alice and Lord John Talbot, her brother, were appointed custodians of all the lands. His daughter Margaret married Richard de la Hay (qv under Thomas de la Hay, d.1440) and his daughter Elizabeth married Sir Edmund Cornewall (fl.1450).

Barrett, Edward Barrett Moulton (1785-1857), was born in Jamaica, the son of a plantation owner, and educated in England. In 1805 he married Mary Graham-Clarke (d.1828) and they lived at Coxhoe Hall, Co. Durham. In 1809 he bought the 472-acre estate of Hope End, near Ledbury from Sir Henry Tempest (qv) and moved there with his three oldest children Elizabeth (the poet), Edward and Henrietta. He was a wealthy man as a result of the proceeds of his Jamaican slave-run sugar plantation, and was appointed High Sheriff of Herefordshire for 1814. He commissioned John Claudius Loudon (qv) to design a 'Hindoo' style house with minarets and lay out the surrounding park. After his wife's death he and Elizabeth often worshipped at Ledbury Congregational Chapel. With the abolition of slavery and poor management of the estate Edward's wealth dwindled and Hope End was sold to Thomas Heywood (qv). The Barretts moved several times, finally arriving in Wimpole Street, London where Edward died in 1857. He was buried in Ledbury Church with his wife and one of their daughters. Their wall plaque on the east wall of the north aisle in St Michael's Church shows a soul climbing heavenly stairs towards an open door.

Barrett Browning, Elizabeth (1806-61), poet, eldest child of Edward Moulton Barrett (qv) was born at Coxhoe Hall, Co. Durham on 6 March 1806 but grew up from the age of three at Hope End near Ledbury. Known as *Ba* to her many brothers and sisters, she was a precocious child and well educated by her doting father for whom she was 'the laureate of Hope End'; she was closest to her brother Edward or *Bro*. She wrote her early poems here: *The Romance of the Swan's Nest*, *The Lost Bower* etc. In her long poem *Aurora Leigh* (1857), set at Hope End and the neighbourhood, she recalls the view from her room:

... the lawn,
Which, after sweeping broadly round the house,
Went trickling through the shrubberies in a stream
Of tender turf, and wore and lost itself
Among the acacias, over which you saw
The irregular line of elms by the deep lane
Which stopt the grounds and dammed the overflow
Of arbutus and laurel.

She was a scholar of Greek and her early poetry dealt with themes from Greek philosophy and history. She befriended Hugh Stuart Boyd, a blind classicist, who had admired her poem *An*

Essay on Mind, published privately by her father, and visited him over the hills at Malvern to read the classics to him. Sir Uvedale Price (qv) valued her learning, asking her, aged 20, to proofread his essay on Greek and Latin pronunciation, and she prized Price's friendship highly. A lung complaint (possibly tuberculosis) left her frail, and a slip from her pony in the Malverns damaged her spine and circumscribed her life. The family arrived in Wimpole Street in 1838 with Elizabeth reduced to a reclusive invalid. Encouraged by her friend Mary Russell Mitford, she continued writing poetry and attracted celebrity and the attentions of the handsome young poet, Robert Browning, with whom she finally eloped. Her father and brothers never forgave her, refusing even to open her letters. Elizabeth and Robert made their life in Florence, where her mature verse was written. They had a child known as Pen. She died on 29 June 1861 and was buried in Florence. Robert died almost 30 years later in 1889. Ledbury remembers her in the Barrett-Browning Institute.

Barrow, Jonathan (fl.1718), builder, originally from Monmouth, lived at Bridstow. He erected the sundial on the Wilton bridge at Ross in 1718. It has a cube dial with four faces. The inscription reads:

Esteem thy precious time
Which pass so swift away,
Prepare then for eternity
And do not make delay.

It marked the boundary between two parishes.

Barston, John (fl.1701), educated at Oxford, was appointed Presbyterian minister of Aylton during the Commonwealth. He was ejected in 1662 but was licensed as a nonconformist preacher and in 1701 was the minister of Ledbury's Congregational Chapel.

Baskerville: a Herefordshire family named from Bosqueville in Normandy who claimed descent from the Emperor Charlemagne. A Nicholas de Basqueville fought beside his cousin Duke William at Hastings in 1066. They owed feudal allegiance, during times of baronial unrest, to such as the Bohuns, the Cliffords and the Lacys (qqv), and the Crown. They were based at Eardisley for 600 years; the castle mound within a moat can be seen to the west of the church of St Mary Magdalene where their helms once hung. After 1200 they controlled Bredwardine Castle, which guarded an important crossing of the Wye south of the church. Again, earthworks are all that remain, but a carved figure in the church is called 'the Sheela of the Baskervilles'. The wolf's head of their arms gripping a broken spear in its mouth with five drops of blood could have inspired Conan Doyle (qv).

Baskerville, Benhail (d.1685), one of the children of Thomas (qv under Humphrey Baskerville) and Frances, was recorded as living in the ruins of Eardisley Castle in poverty in the 1670s and was buried in St Andrew's Church, Bredwardine. Eardisley Park was later sold to the London solicitor William Barnsley (qv).

Baskerville, Hannibal (1597-1668), antiquarian, was the only son of Sir Thomas (d.1597, qv) and Mary. He was educated by Henry Peacham and at Brasenose College. He secured his inheritance and his mother's dower estates from his Scudamore stepfather, Sir James (qv, d.1619). As his second wife he married his cousin Mary Morgan (1602-44), the daughter of his uncle Nicholas Baskerville and widow of John Morgan. They are said to have had 18 children.

Baskerville, Humphrey (d.1647), knight, was born at Eardisley Castle and married Elizabeth, daughter of Sir Thomas Coningsby (qv, d.1625). In 1645 Barnabas Scudamore (qv), the Governor of Hereford, returning from an attack on Abergavenny, attacked and burnt Eardisley Castle and Church. Sir Humphrey died on 3 April 1647. His son Thomas (d.1682) married Frances Pember and they had many children including Benhail (qv); Thomas's daughter Philippa married a Coningsby cousin.

Baskerville, James (*c*.1436-94) of Eardisley, the son of John (qv, d.1455), married Catherine (also known as Sybil), daughter, of Sir Walter Devereux (qv, d.1459). Their daughter Joan (b.1476) married James Scudamore (qv, d.1553) and their daughter Elizabeth married Watkyn Vaughan (qv, d.1504). Sir James Baskerville fought for Henry VII (qv) at Stoke and was made knight banneret on the battlefield for his valour.

Baskerville, James (d.1546) married Elizabeth, daughter of John Breynton of Sugwas. Their three sons were James, John and Thomas. He was an esquire at Court in 1516 and was knighted at Anne Boleyn's coronation. He was a JP from 1511, Mayor of Hereford in 1523 and twice Sheriff of Hereford. Sir James was MP for Herefordshire in 1536.

Baskerville, James (by 1506-72) of Eardisley, son of Sir James (qv, d.1546), married Elizabeth, daughter of Sir Walter Devereux (qv, d.1558), 3rd Lord Ferrers, who promoted his career. He was MP for Herefordshire at Thomas Cromwell's suggestion with John Scudamore (qv, d.1571). He was a JP in the county, and after his father, had commission of oyer and terminer in the Midlands (i.e. to determine treasons). He supervised the delivery of prisoners to Hereford Castle. His daughter Sybil married his ward Robert Whitney (qv, d.1567). He was knighted in 1547, and Sheriff of Hereford in 1548/9 and 1550/1. He was buried in Eardisley Church and his brother John succeeded him.

Baskerville, John (1408-55), knight, was born at Eardisley on 12 February 1408, the son of Richard Baskerville the rector (qv under 14th-century Richard Baskerville). When he was still a boy he followed Henry V (qv) to Agincourt. He married Isabel, daughter of John Touchet, Lord Audley, and their children included James, John, Henry, Humphrey and Sybil, who married Richard Rowdon (d.1455) and had a son, John.

Baskerville, Ralph de (d.1127) married Sybil, daughter of Adam de Port (qv). Her mother, Bertha, was a daughter of William (II) de Briouze (qv) and granddaughter of Miles, 1st Earl of Hereford (qv Miles of Gloucester).

Baskerville, Ralph de (1134-94), married a daughter of Lord Clifford (qv). The sources say he had a duel with his father-in-law over disputed Baskerville territory in which Lord Clifford was killed. The two knights depicted fighting on the font in Eardisley Church have been thought to represent this duel, but modern research believes otherwise. Legend tells how the White Cross was erected at the site of the duel, just to the north of Hereford. Ralph himself was murdered in Northants *c.*1194 and was succeeded by his son Roger.

Baskerville, Richard died in 1177, in which year the estate and castle of Eardisley was taken back into the king's hands.

Baskerville, Richard (14th century), Lord of Eardisley, was High Sheriff of Hereford and knight of the shire, representing Hereford in Edward II (qv) and III's (qv) Parliaments. His son, grandson and great-grandsons were all Richards, one a rector of Eardisley in 1373.

Baskerville, Robert de (d.1109) held five estates strung along the northern side of the Wye Valley between Wales and Hereford. He married Agnes, granddaughter of Gruffydd ap Llywelyn (qv), and lived in Eardisley Castle. They had a son, Ralph (qv, d.1127).

Baskerville, Thomas (d.1597), soldier and sea captain, the younger son of Henry and Anne Baskerville of Hereford, lived at Wolvershill and Brinsop. He was a kinsman of Robert Devereux, 2nd Earl of Essex (qv, d.1601), a JP and escheator for the Crown. A distinguished soldier, he fought under Robert Dudley in the Low Countries, where he was knighted. He was MP for Carmarthen and arranged help for poor soldiers from Elizabeth's campaigns on the Continent. He accompanied Sir Francis Drake and Sir John Hawkins (qv Margaret Hawkins) on their last expedition to the Indies. When Drake died, Sir Thomas buried him at sea, took command and brought the expedition home. He married Mary Throckmorton of Gloucestershire and his letters to '*sweet Mal*' survive. He was given command of English forces in the Low Countries where Mary gave birth to their son Hannibal (qv). Shortly after, on 4 June 1597, Sir Thomas died of a fever in Picardy and was buried in Old St Paul's with an inscription recording his noble deeds. Mary then married Sir James Scudamore (qv, d.1619), with whom she had another nine children, but less happy relations. She died and was buried at Sunningwell, Berkshire, on 17 October 1632.

Baskerville, Thomas (1630-1700), topographer, fourth of Hannibal's (qv) 18 children, was born at Bayworth House, Sunningwell, the estate his grandfather had bought. This was where, in 1649, he witnessed the great Leveller gathering before their encounter with Cromwell at Burford. From then on he spent the rest of his life travelling. He went at least once to see his family's property in Herefordshire; in 1674 he made lively and pungent notes of the people and markets he saw, which Thomas Hearne (qv, d.1735)) thought hopelessly whimsical. He was a noted eccentric and called himself (Hearne said) the King of Jerusalem. He prepared his papers for the press, but died before he saw them published, and they eventually came into the possession of Richard Rawlinson (qv). The son of his old age, Matthew Thomas (d.1721), dissipated the Berkshire estate with drunkenness.

Baskerville, Walter (13th century), a grandson of Roger de Baskerville (qv under Ralph de Baskerville, d.1194), was granted back the manor of Eardisley by Humphrey (IV) de Bohun in 1251, and was granted a licence by the Bishop of Hereford to hold services in the castle chapel in 1272. The Baskervilles were to represent the county in Parliament for the next 400 years. The region was liable to attack by the Welsh and the Baskervilles were a key part of its defences: in 1262 Llywelyn ap Gruffydd (qv) ravaged the area on his way to attack Hereford. Bishop Peter de Aquablanca (qv) was arrested by the barons and placed in custody at Eardisley Castle until King Henry III (qv) had him released.

Baskerville, Walter (*c.*1459-1508), knight, married Ann Jenkyn and was escheator of Herefordshire and the Marches. He died on 13 October 1508 and is buried in St Andrew's, Bredwardine.

Bateman: James Bateman's rise to wealth and power was astonishing. On buying the Shobdon estate he was brought closer to the Harleys, the other political power of the age, and Bateman's credit was of great use to the government, especially abroad. He purchased honours and offices. His Herefordshire estates were worth £14,000 at his death. His son and heir, Viscount Bateman, and his son John allowed younger brother Dicky Bateman (qv) a free hand at Shobdon, and supported by connoisseur Horace Walpole (qv), he made free use of it. The loss of old Shobdon Church is not to our taste, but preserving choice pieces of medieval sculpture was ahead of its time.

Bateman, James (*c.*1660-1718) KG, financier, was the son of Joas Bateman (d.1704), a wealthy London merchant of Dutch origin. He married Esther (d.1709), daughter and co-heiress of John Searle of Finchley, and they had four sons and three daughters. He was Lord Mayor of London, an MP, one of the first governors of the Bank of England, and then chairman of the South Sea Company before the bubble burst. He was a brilliant financier and one of the richest men in Britain, and bought the Order of the Garter and the Shobdon estate in Herefordshire. He died on 10 November 1718.

Bateman, John (1721-1802), 2nd Viscount Bateman, was the son of Sir William (qv) and nephew and heir of Richard (qv). He married Elizabeth Sambrooke. He was elected MP for Leominster (1768-84), though as his viscountcy was Irish it did not entitle him to sit in parliament. He was Lord Lieutenant for Herefordshire from 1747 to his death and in 1756 he was appointed to the Privy Council. He was chief steward for Leominster and John Price (qv) dedicated his history of Leominster to him. T.A. Knight (qv) named a species of pear *Shobdon Court* in his honour. He died on 2 March 1802.

Bateman, Richard (1705-73), connoisseur, was the third son of Sir James Bateman (qv). He travelled widely, collecting voraciously and on his return *c.*1730 bought The Grove, Windsor as his main residence and to hold his collections. It was decorated under the influence of Sir Horace Walpole (qv) in a Chinese and, later, a Gothick style. Older brother John allowed him a free hand on the Shobdon estate and he replaced the Norman church of St John's (qv Merlimond) with its 12th-century Herefordshire School (qv) carvings with a confection of white and gold, recently restored. The distinctive carvings from the old church appealed to Bateman's antiquarian taste, and he re-erected the Norman doors and chancel arch on the hill as a frame for the sculptures. He also pulled down old Shobdon Court and replaced it with one in Walpole's Strawberry Hill Gothick style (*c.*1765). His architect may have been Henry Flitcroft (qv), but the taste is Walpole's. It was demolished in 1933, and a rebuilt wing is all that remains. The Shobdon Arches have outlasted Shobdon Court and can be seen, much weathered, on the rise near the church. There is a plaster cast of one tympanum in the V&A, and the work can be seen in G.R. Lewis's (qv) lithographs of 1852. 'Dicky' Bateman died on 1 March 1773.

Bateman, William (1695-1744), Baron Culmore and Viscount Bateman, was the eldest son of Sir James (qv) and Esther. In 1720 he married Lady Anne Spencer (1702-69), the granddaughter of the Duke of Marlborough. A

grand gilt chest made as a wedding present by James Moore the cabinet maker is now in the V&A. He was Whig MP for Leominster 1721-2. He was created Baron Culmore and Viscount Bateman in 1725 and was invested KB in 1732. He was a great traveller and collector. When in Herefordshire he lived at Shobdon Court; there is an inn called the Bateman Arms in the village. In 1732 he was elected Fellow of the Royal Society. Lord Bateman died in Paris in December 1744 leaving his son John (qv) as his heir.

Bayley, Robert Slater (1801-59) was a Congregational minister in Hereford from 1857-9 and lived in Eign Gate with his wife Mary and their children. Born in Birmingham, he had also ministered to congregations in Lincolnshire, London and Sheffield, where he helped found the People's College and published his monthly periodical, the *People's College Journal*. He supported Chartism and wrote a pamphlet in its defence. He died in All Saints parish, Hereford on 15 November 1859.

Baylis, James, see under **Reynolds, Thomas**

Bayly, John (1596-1633), clergyman, was born in Herefordshire, the son of Lewis Bayly (qv) and was educated at Exeter College, Oxford, where he spent much of his life. He graduated DD in 1630 and was a chaplain to Charles I (qv). He published two of his sermons: *The Angell Guardian* and *The Light Enlightening*. He was married and had children.

Bayly, Lewis (*c*.1575-1631), Bishop of Bangor, was born at Carmarthen, the son of a clergyman. He married Judith Appleton (d.1608), a knight's daughter of Herefordshire, where they had three sons and a daughter. He was an effective and learned preacher and attracted the attention of James I (qv), who appointed him chaplain to Prince Henry and gave him several livings, and later made him Bishop of Bangor. He provided offices and benefices for his sons John (qv), Theodore and Thomas (qv), claiming that nepotism was natural in a father. He wrote the popular *Practice of Piety*, a very influential work in that it was one of the two books John Bunyan's wife brought to him as her dowry and was responsible for his conversion. He was granted a BD from Oxford 1611. He married a wealthy second wife and they had a son Nicholas, his main heir. A quarrelsome man, he was at odds with his dean. King James imprisoned him for refusing to read *The Book of Sports* from the pulpit.

Bayly, Thomas (*c*.1600-*c*.57), Royalist divine, Lewis Bayly's (qv) youngest son with Judith, was educated at Magdalene College, Cambridge. He was ordained and made a priest by his father in his Province of Bangor, later becoming subdean of Wells. He was awarded DD in the besieged

Oxford of 1644. A Royalist officer in the Civil Wars, and present at the siege of Raglan Castle, he continued to attack the Puritan establishment during the Commonwealth and was imprisoned in Newgate, where he wrote *Herba parietis*, his reflections in prison. He also reflected on the similarity of Anglicanism and Catholicism in *Certamen religiosum* (1649). Travelling abroad after his release and conscious of the religious anarchy at home, he converted to Catholicism.

Beale, John (1608-83), scientist, philosopher, gardener, writer, clergyman, was born in April 1608 at Yarkhill, the son of Thomas Beale (1575-1620), a lawyer, gentleman farmer and cider apple grower. His mother Joanna (1576-1660) was Sir Walter Pye's (qv) sister. He was educated at Worcester Cathedral School and Eton, where he knew Sir Henry Wotten, and King's College, Cambridge. He found he had a 'photographic memory', and learnt by heart all he came across in the classics, philosophy and in his scientific reading where he became increasingly interested in horticulture and agriculture. Instead of buying a book it is said that he would pass his eye over it in the bookshop and have its contents in his mind. He was ordained and at Cambridge lectured on scientific subjects *extempore*, but his emphasis on experiment was too radical and he was not popular. He gained an entry at Court in the 1620s through his Pye uncles but became disenchanted with the policies of King Charles and Archbishop Laud (qqv). He travelled on the Continent with his nephew collecting rare manuscripts. On his return he was given a rectory in Somerset but was ejected during the Commonwealth. Back in Hereford, he married Jane Mackworth; their eldest son John (d.1684) became a physician and went to Jamaica in 1675. The young family fled Hereford during the siege of 1645 but his wife had Parliamentarian connections who helped them. At one point Beale was Master of St Katherine's Hospital in Ledbury but he was ejected in favour of John Tombes (qv). In the 1650s he received the living of Stretton Grandison thanks to the patronage of Sir Richard and Elizabeth Hopton (qv). During the Commonwealth he was a member of the governing committee in Herefordshire, establishing an Association of Ministers in the county. He bought the manor of Cobhall at Allensmore in 1652 and experimented with growing cider apples on the poor soil, using the Redstreak (qv) and Genet Moyle apples, writing up his findings in *A Treatise on Fruit Trees* (1653). He corresponded with Samuel Hartlib who thought highly of him and published his letters as *Herefordshire Orchards, a Pattern for All England* (1657). He also wrote *Observations on some parts of Bacon's Natural History as it concerns fruit trees, fruits and flowers* (1658). Protector Cromwell noticed him but Beale refused his patronage. Through Hartlib he met John Evelyn (qv), Henry Oldenburg and Robert Boyle. He was the most important Baconian or experimental philosopher of his period, working on horticulture, agriculture, forestry, botany, diet, astronomy, optics, technology, trade, education, and writing on theological matters. He thought that experiments should be disseminated to improve and expand industry and that scientific agriculture would be the base for national progress. Beale's vision of enlightenment and industrial revolution was prophetic. At the Restoration he was appointed chaplain to Charles II and had standing and competency. He was a founding member of the Royal Society where in 1662 President Oldenburg read his paper *Aphorisms concerning cider* about his experiments at Cobhall. He helped Evelyn write *Pomona* (1664) which incorporated much of his *Aphorisms* and, through the Royal Society, arranged to have grafts of Redstreak and Genet Moyle distributed across the country. In 1677 Beale wrote *Nurseries, Orchards, Profitable Gardens and Vineyards Encouraged*, continuing his mission to expand useful knowledge. He died in Yeovil, Somerset where he was buried on 16 April 1683. The Beale family continued to be found in Herefordshire; around 1800 Mary Anne Beale (d.1859) married William Symonds (qv, d.1840).

Beaton, Donald (1802-63), gardener from Ross-shire, was born on 8 March 1802 into a Gaelic-speaking family. He developed his horticultural skills at Beaufort Castle where he learned English. He developed a special interest in the hybridisation of garden plants in Perth and London, and then became head gardener and estate manager at Haffield, Donnington for William Gordon (qv). Here he experimented with his colour theories in bedding plants. In 1837 he married Lydia Penn at Eastnor and after her death in 1850 remarried to Jane Parfett. He wrote garden journalism, publicising his ideas of bedding, and retired to Surrey where he died on 31 October 1863. Darwin called him clever but cocksure.

Beauchamp: The senior branch were earls of Warwick, whilst baronies were created for lesser branches. The title Baron Bergavenny was created for Sir William, a younger son, in 1392, and Baron Powick is another example. Like many noble families the Beauchamps have a complex web of inter relationships with an impenetrable cousinage. The family's focus was not in Herefordshire but they have left us the mysterious Bronsil Castle under the Malverns and provided the county with a bishop.

Beauchamp, Richard de (1396-1422), 2nd Baron Bergavenny and 1st Earl of Worcester, was son and heir of William (V) de Beauchamp (qv) and Joan. He married Isabel le Despenser (qv under Edward Despenser). Their daughter Elizabeth was Baroness Bergavenny.

Beauchamp, Richard de (*c*.1425-81), Bishop of Hereford 1448-50, was born in Wiltshire the son of Sir Walter Beauchamp. Sir Richard Beauchamp (qv, d.1503) was his nephew. Beauchamp was a childhood friend of Henry VI and at Court from an early age. He was educated at Exeter College, Oxford and made Bishop of Hereford in his early 20s. It was a mediaeval custom at Hereford for a bishop on his enthronement to walk barefoot and bareheaded from St Guthlac's (qv) Priory, where the County Hospital now is, through the Bishop's or Byster's Gate to the cathedral, and Beauchamp actually did this. He was a conscientious diocesan bishop, travelling widely in his diocese and making a visitation in 1450. After only two years he was translated to Salisbury, where the bishop had just been murdered. He was much loved by Henry VI, who made him his treasurer and liked to have him near. Despite this intimacy Richard found no difficulty, like his kinsman and namesake Richard de Beauchamp (qv, d.1503), in transferring allegiance to Edward IV (qv) when, as the Earl of March, he seized the throne in 1461. He was a capable architect and superintended the building of Edward's great chapel of St George at Windsor, where he was appointed its first chancellor. He died in his palace at Salisbury on 18 October 1481 and is buried in Salisbury Cathedral.

Beauchamp, Richard de (*c*.1430-1503), 2nd Baron Powick, was the son of John (d.1475), 1st Baron Beauchamp of Powick, Lord Treasurer. The family were descended from the Beauchamp Earls of Warwick and received some benefit after the 13th Earl's death. He had estates in Worcestershire and a fortified house at Bronsil (first mentioned in 1240 in relation to Ledbury Hospital). Sir Richard married Elizabeth, daughter of Humphrey Stafford of Grafton, in 1447. They had a boy who died young and three girls: Elizabeth (d.1503) who married Robert, 2nd Baron Willoughby de Broke; Anne who married Richard Lygon of Madresfield and Margaret who married Oliver Reed (qv Reed family) of Lugwardine. Beauchamp's wife had an adulterous relationship with a neighbour, Thomas Burdet, and was accused of plotting Beauchamp's death by sorcery with others; these men were further accused of 'imagining the death of the king' (Edward IV), convicted of treason and hanged at Tyburn. Beauchamp acquired 300 acres of the bishop's hunting chase at Eastnor when his uncle Richard (qv, d.1481) was Bishop of Hereford and was given permission by Henry VI (qv) to impark. At Bronsil he built a most up to date castle and in 1450 and 1457 was licensed to crenellate in these troubled times: the Lancastrian defeat at St Albans was in 1455. The castle was rectangular in structure with polygonal corner turrets, standing within a double moat, and adorned with lakes and extensive pleasure gardens. The Buck brothers (qv) sketched the ruins in 1731 with towers and walls standing. Beauchamp had been Henry VI's treasurer and was remembered for his wisdom and courage. In the 1450s, in response to Henry's mental incapacity, he seems to have shifted allegiance to the Duke of York. It is recorded that he harassed Queen Margaret's army and in 1471 fought at the Battle of Tewkesbury on the Yorkist side. There are two versions of Lord Beauchamp's death: the more sober locates it at home on 19 January 1503, but the legend is that he died fighting in Italy and his unquiet spirit, bewailing its scattered bones, returned to haunt his beloved Bronsil. He was survived by his daughters and co-heirs Elizabeth, Anne and Margaret. Margaret and her husband Oliver Reed lived at the castle, with its charming pleasure gardens, extensive hunting park and unquiet paternal ghost.

Beauchamp, William (V) de (1344-1411) 1st Baron Bergavenny, was the fourth son of Thomas de Beauchamp, 11th Earl of Warwick (1314-60) and Katherine (d.1369), daughter of Roger (V) Mortimer (qv), 1st Earl of March. He married Joan (1375-1435) daughter of Richard Fitzalan, Earl of Arundel and Elizabeth, daughter of William de Bohun (qv). Their daughter, Joan (1396-1430), married James Butler, 4th Earl of Ormond, one of whose descendants was Anne Boleyn. William's older sister Maud (b.1335) married Roger de Clifford, 5th Baron Clifford of Westmorland. William was Roger (VII) Mortimer's executor when he died in Ireland in 1398, along with colleagues Kynard de la Bere (qv) and Thomas Oldcastle (qv). He died on 8 May 1411 and was buried in Blackfriars Priory in Hereford where he endowed a chantry. He left a will in English, perhaps a sign of Lollardy. Lady Joan was called an 'evil Jezebel' by the chronicler Adam of Usk (qv) and indeed, when acting as overseer of Thomas (II) Walwyn's (qv) will, she tried to seize one of his manors with armed men. She died on 14 November 1435 and was buried beside William in the Blackfriars.

Beauclerk, James (1709-87), Bishop of Hereford 1745-87, was born at Windsor the son of Charles Beauclerk, 1st Duke of St Albans and the illegitimate son of Charles II and Nell Gwynne (qv). His mother Diana de Vere was descended from a 12th-century Bishop of Hereford. Tall, distinguished and said to resemble his royal grandfather, he was appointed Bishop of Hereford at the young age of 36. He was often at odds with the Dean and Chapter and neither side did much to shore up the deteriorating fabric of the cathedral. Funds were spent on cosmetic work such as the repaving of the choir in 1774, and unhelpful repairs: Thomas Symonds (qv, d.1791), surveyor of the fabric, underpinned the north-west tower with its evident cracks and started filling in the chapels below. The real problem, the lateral force of the central tower, was not understood and on Easter Sunday 17 April 1786, a year before the bishop's death, the whole west end collapsed bringing with it the western half of the nave. Beauclerk had made attempts to move to a richer diocese but was genuinely interested in his see; he spent much time there, held a visitation in 1765 (for which extensive minutes can be seen) and ordained his clergy in person. He died unmarried on 20 October 1787, his main beneficiary being his secretary Richard Jones.

He is commemorated by a plaque with his arms on the north wall of the north-east transept.

Beaumont, James (d.1750) was a preacher from Radnorshire. In 1741 he was preaching at Dilwyn and later at Leominster, and was officially recognized by the Methodists. He was violently beaten by conservative locals and was reported dead, but his ministry at Leominster attracted followers. They became known as the Unitas Fratrum church and rented a room for their meetings. They adopted Moravian practices and were held to be antinomian. Beaumont retired to Haverfordwest where he died on 22 June 1750.

Beaumont, Robert (1104-68), 2nd Earl of Leicester, called *Le Bossu* or hunchback, was created King Stephen's (qv) lieutenant in Herefordshire. His estates were concentrated in Leicestershire and his twin brother Waleran's in Normandy. He was more interested in his lands in Normandy, and Stephen allowed him to retire there in 1140. He was a literate and learned man and became Henry II's (qv) chief justiciar. He founded and was buried in Leicester Abbey.

Beccicus (*c.*3rd century AD) was a Dobunni Celt who dedicated an altar found at Michaelchurch with the inscription 'Deo trivii Beccicus donavit aram' – Beccicus gave this altar to the god of the crossroads, i.e. a public meeting place. The altar was discovered in 1820 by Revd John Webb (qv), who had it restored and placed in St Michael's Church at Michaelchurch.

Becket, Thomas (1118-70), Archbishop of Canterbury 1162-70, a Cheapside merchant's son, was advanced by Henry II (qv) to be his chancellor and then archbishop. Henry was famously wrong in believing that Becket would be his pliable tool and instead Becket obstinately defended the privileges of the Church. On 29 December 1170, having returned from exile, Becket was assassinated in Canterbury Cathedral by four knights who believed they were acting at Henry's behest (qv Richard de Britto). Henry did public penance and Becket was canonised only three years later by Pope

Alexander III in an immense wave of popular devotion. In Leominster the Archbishop of Canterbury, John Pecham (qv), dedicated the Forbury Chapel to him and in the 19th century a chapel in Leominster's Bargates was dedicated to him. There is a 14th-century stained glass figure of him and St Thomas de Cantilupe of Hereford (qv) in Credenhill Church (see above). Hereford Cathedral has a Limoges-enamelled casket of *c.*1200 that contained a relic of St Thomas. It shows the murder and entombment of the saint and must have been commissioned by Bishop William de Vere (qv) who had known Becket. The casket was disposed of at the Reformation but hidden by the recusant Bodenham family (qv Roger Bodenham). By the 18th century it had come into the possession of Thomas Russell, a canon of Hereford who returned it to the cathedral where its importance was recognised by F.T. Havergal (qv).

Bedo, John (fl.1535), forger, is recorded in Hereford archives as being punished for 'falsifying the King's letters'. In a letter to the Mayor of Hereford he is described as of 'crafty and untrue disposition'; with one William Blast, he forged the old Corporation seal for gain. His punishment is depicted on a 14th-century misericord in Hereford Cathedral that shows a man tied on a horse backwards. In Bedo's case he was to be led by his accomplices through Hereford Market in this position to spend the day in the pillory and the night in the city gaol.

Benbow, John (1800-74), farmer and Mormon, was born on 1 April 1800, son of Thomas and Anne Benbow, tenant farmer of Grendon Court, Grendon Warren near Bromyard. In 1826 he married a local girl, Jane Holmes. Dissatisfied with the Methodists, he and others broke away to form the United Brethren and with his money built a chapel at Gadfield Elm near Staunton (near Newent). His brother William, while working in Hanley, had been baptised by Wilford Woodruff, an elder from the Church of the Latter Day Saints of America, or Mormons, and brought him to the Benbows' Hill Farm at Castle Frome. In his memoir *Leaves From my Journal*, Woodruff described Benbow as a wealthy farmer with 300 acres, in a chapter on his time in Herefordshire. In 1840 Jane and John were baptised in the farm pond, which is now a site of pilgrimage for American Mormons. The other Mormon elders Brigham Young and Willard Richards joined Woodruff in proselytizing the Ledbury area and, helped by the agricultural depression, converted about 1,800 people, many baptised in the Hill Farm pond. Benbow was appointed an elder of the Mormon congregation and presented the Gadfield Elm chapel to the Mormons as a permanent base. It remains today, refurbished, the oldest Mormon chapel in the world. It was at a council meeting on the Herefordshire Beacon that it was decided to publish the *Book of Mormon* in Britain. Most of the converts chose to emigrate to America. The poor were funded by Benbow and others like Edward Ockey, who sold his farm, Moorend for the purpose. Another was William Carter (qv) who married Benbow's sisters Ellen and Elizabeth after the polygamous Mormon fashion.

Bennett, Robert (*c*.1530-1617), Bishop of Hereford 1603-17, was born at Baldock, Hertfordshire and educated at Trinity College, Cambridge, an erudite man and a keen racquets

player. He came to the notice of Lord Burghley through his vehement anti-Catholicism and was made Dean of Windsor in 1596. He was outspoken and argumentative and made enemies. Queen Elizabeth (qv) appointed him to the see of Hereford and James I (qv) had him consecrated – James thought he had a pleasing countenance. Bennett found the county 'stuffed with recusants' and his own clergy sympathetic to them, but he could not persuade his patron to give him a commission to tackle the problem. On hearing from the vicar of Allensmore that Alice Wellington (qv), a Catholic recusant he had excommunicated, had been buried in the parish churchyard by night, he sent a party to arrest those responsible, but they were set upon by angry parishioners. One tragic result of his zeal was the cruel execution in 1610 of the elderly Jesuit priest Father Roger Cadwallador (qv), who had long been in retirement. Bennett was an evangelical preacher and tried to treat with nonconformists in his see. There were complaints about the nonconformity of the rector of Brampton Bryan, Thomas Pierson (qv), but he was protected by his patron Robert Harley (qv, d.1656). He dealt effectively with lax clerical standards through education and dismissals. His health was undermined by worry and the poor climate, and he died on 25 October 1617. He was buried in Hereford Cathedral in a tomb of his own design, but all that remains of this is the alabaster effigy. Wood says it was placed behind his wife's seat on the north side of the choir, so it is still in its original place, but now sharing a ledge with Bishop Giles de Braose (qv Giles de Briouze) of 400 years before. Bennett presented a manuscript of Nicholas Hereford's (qv Nicholas de Hereford) 'Cider Bible' to the cathedral.

Benson, George (1614-92), Dean of Hereford, was educated at Oriel and Queen's Colleges, Oxford. At the Restoration he was made Doctor of Divinity and appointed canon residentiary of Hereford and Master of the Fabric during the great repairs. He later became archdeacon of Hereford and in 1672 dean. He was also Master of St Katherine's Hospital, Ledbury and rector of Cradley. He agreed to his friend Bishop Herbert Croft's (qv) visitation. Benson died on 24 August 1692 and was buried in his cathedral on the right of the high altar. During the Cottinghams' restoration (qv Lewis Nockalls Cottingham and his son Nockalls) his grave was discarded but retrieved by George Gilbert Scott (qv), and Lord Saye and Sele (qv Frederick Fiennes) paid to have it positioned in the south-east transept, restoring its charming affinity with his neighbour, in death as in life, Bishop Croft (qv), hands figured clasped across the stones.

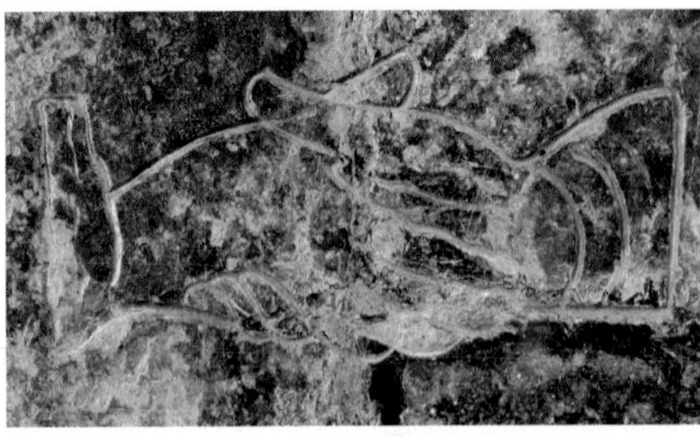

Benson, Martin (1689-1752), Bishop of Gloucester, was born on 23 April 1689 in Cradley rectory, the son of Revd John Benson (1652-1713) and his wife Catherine Martin (d.1725). He accompanied Thomas Fermor (qv under William Fermor), Baron Leominster, on his Grand Tour and after various appointments was made Bishop of Gloucester in 1735.

Bentham, George (1800-84), botanist, was born on 22 September 1800, the third of the five children of Samuel and Maria Bentham of Plymouth. His mother was a knowledgeable botanist and her brother was Jeremy Bentham (1748-1832), who was interested in classification. George travelled widely across Napoleonic Europe with his parents, learning the languages and botanising. He returned to train for the law in London where he lived as his Uncle Jeremy's assistant. Staying at Kentchurch in 1833, he met and married Sarah Brydges (d.1881), younger daughter of Sir Harford Jones-Brydges (qv). In 1842 they moved to Pontrilas Court to be near his sister-in-law, called Sarah Laura, who had married John Lucy Scudamore (qv) of Kentchurch Court. Bentham devoted his time to botanical research at Kew Gardens. He was a friend and supporter of Darwin. His name is

joined with Hooker as co-author of *The Handbook of the British Flora*, although the work is mostly Bentham's, edited by Hooker after his death. He also wrote an autobiography. On his retirement he was regarded as one of the great scientists of his age. He collected such a vast amount of botanical material that transferring it to Kew required four railway wagons. Amongst other gifts to Kew was a table in which Jeremy Bentham's pet mouse lived. He was an early member of the Woolhope Club and a long serving President of the Linnaean Society. He died in London on 10 September 1884 and is buried with his wife in Brompton Cemetery.

Bentley, Samuel (1823-1908), rector of Bosbury 1879-97, was born in Islington, Middlesex. He graduated from St Catherine's College, Cambridge and was ordained in 1849. In 1853 he was curate at Ashton Keynes in Wiltshire, where he married Frances Baden from Stoke Newington in Middlesex. As rector of Bosbury he wrote *A Short Account of the Church, Episcopal Manor and other Objects of Interest in Bosbury, Herefordshire* in 1881. He was rural dean in the Frome deanery.

de la Bere, Kynard (d.1402), heir of Sir Richard (d.1382, qv) and his first wife, bought Kinnersley Castle from his stepmother Sybil (qv under Richard de la Bere, d.1382). He married Katherine, widow of Sir John Pecche of Arden, Warks and they had a son Richard and a daughter Agnes. He was MP for Herefordshire in the 1380s and '90s and stood surety for his neighbour John Croft in 1381. He was Richard II's (qv) esquire and accompanied him on his Scottish expedition, and had been knighted by 1387. As JPs in the county he and Leonard Hakluyt (qv) were instructed to round up the Lollard supporters of Walter Brut (qv). He opposed rebels in the county and Welsh incursions. He fought in Sir Edmund (IV) Mortimer's (qv) Radnorshire campaign against Owain Glyn Dŵr (qv) and was killed in the disastrous defeat at Pilleth on 22 June 1402. His will shows Lollard tendencies. His son Richard seems to have made an armed raid on Eardisley in 1414 during a general breakdown of order in west Herefordshire and John ap Harry (qv) was called out to subdue him.

de la Bere, Richard (1320-82), the second son of John and Agnes, married, as his second wife, Sybil, daughter and heiress of William de Kynardsley (qv) who brought him lands at Kinnersley. They were also proprietors of nearby Letton with lands in other counties. Richard was a friend of the Black Prince (qv Edward of Woodstock), receiving gifts and grants of land at 'Le Nokes' and Bredwardine. At an engagement with Philip VI of France near Crécy on 25 August 1346 he saved the prince's life, for which service he was knighted, granted livery of a coat of arms and became constable of the prince's castle of Emlyn and his chamberlain. He was Sheriff of Herefordshire in 1354 and 1356 and was a knight of the shire in Edward III's Parliament. He and his wife died in 1382 and were buried in the Blackfriars, Hereford's Dominican friary, which had been granted dispensation to bury the laity.

de la Bere, Richard (d.1514) is the subject, with his two wives Anne and Elizabeth and their 21 children, of a brass in Hereford Cathedral. The de la Beres disappear from the county in the 16th century; Kinnersley Castle was bought by Roger Vaughan (qv, fl.1550).

de la Bere, Robert (fl.1340), with his wife Margaret, is the subject of monumental sculpture in the Church of St Cosmas and St Damian (qv), Stretford. The figures of his son Sir John

and John's wife Agnes lie nearby, identified by the heraldry; Agnes was the daughter of Payne de Turberville. They lived at Stretford and at Weobley Castle on the Gower.

> **Berington**: An old Herefordshire family associated with the place of that name, variously written as Beritune, Barrington etc., originally from Barentin in Normandy at the time of the Conquest. Their arms are three running, collared greyhounds. Their seat at Berrington passed to the Cornewalls (qv) by the 14th century, but they were also found at Cowarne Court, Much Cowarne, where they succeeded the Syfervast family, and Winsley House, Dinmore. Recusancy was noted at both places. John Berington's daughter Mary (1626-1704), for instance, became an Augustinian nun at Bruges under the name Sister Xaveria. Robert Berington was Mayor of Hereford in 1442 and his son, Thomas, for three terms in 1462, 1465 and 1470. They were Royalists in the Civil Wars and were present at the siege of Goodrich Castle in 1645. There is a monument to John Berington (d.1617) and Joyce his wife in St Lawrence, Bishopstone, where in 1723 Anne Berrington founded almshouses which are extant. In the 18th century Beringtons moved into Little Malvern Court, just over the border in Worcs, and they are still there.

Berington, George (fl.1595) of Winsley House, Dinmore was persuaded by Father Cadwallador (qv) to train as a Roman Catholic priest at Valladolid in 1595. The Beringtons hid Cadwallador after the 'Whitsun Riot' disturbances at Allensmore in 1605. A John Berington's daughter Sybil (d.1605) married John Skippe (qv, d.1619) and is buried in Ledbury Church.

Berington, Joseph (1743-1827), Roman Catholic priest, was born on 16 January 1743 at Winsley House, near Dinmore, the son of John Berington and his wife, Winifred Hornyold. Her brother Bishop John Hornyold taught Joseph before sending him to the English College at Douai to train for the priesthood. His sister Elizabeth was the mother of William Lambe (qv), and his cousin Charles Berington also became a Catholic bishop. Joseph was ordained in 1770 and became a professor of philosophy at Douai. He was too liberal for the college, though, and returned to take charge of the Wolverhampton Mission. His liberal views and disagreement with the Pope attracted censure, but he found protectors. He was friendly with such members of the Midlands Enlightenment as Priestley, Boulton and James Watt (qv) and published tracts arguing for religious tolerance, believing that salvation resided in all Christian believers. His major work *A Literary History of the Middle Ages* (with an introduction by William Hazlitt) further expanded his views. He died and is buried in his parish of Buckland, Berks.

Berkeley, James (1275-1327), Bishop of Exeter, was the fourth son of Thomas, Baron Berkeley. He studied at Oxford, was ordained and became a doctor of theology. He acquired a large number of prebends and canonries including Hereford, where he lived for many years in a canon's house by the cathedral, revered for his saintly life. In 1326 he was appointed Bishop of Exeter, but died almost immediately after. 1327 was the date of Edward II's (qv) murder at Berkeley Castle, James's family home. The Berkeleys were known to support Roger (V) Mortimer (qv) the king's nemesis, and Queen Isabella (qv). At Exeter a cult grew up around Berkeley's tomb and there was talk of canonisation, but the political situation changed with Mortimer's execution.

Bernard, Mountague (1820-82), international lawyer, was born at Tibberton Court, Gloucestershire on 28 January 1820, the son of a Jamaica plantation owner. He was educated at Trinity College Oxford and called to the bar at Lincoln's Inn. After a career in international law, where he attempted to harmonise international legal systems, he retired to live with relatives at Overross, Ross-on-Wye where he died on 2 September 1882.

Berry, James (1852-1913), itinerant hangman from Bradford, was employed at county gaols as required. He was frequently brought to Hereford for executions, famously turning off James Jones and Alfred Scandrett, the murderers of Philip Ballard (qv) in 1887. He was an indiscreet man famous for his celebratory post-execution drinking sessions, in the course of which the rope was auctioned off. In eight years he hanged 131 convicted murderers.

Best, John (1569-1637), residentiary canon of Hereford Cathedral (1612-35), was prebend of Moreton Parva (1607-37) and master of the fabric in 1614-15. He was canon librarian of the cathedral library at the turn of the 16th century and was active in the cleaning of archive material and preparing presses and cupboards for the books after Queen Elizabeth's (qv) officials had found the library in a ruinous condition. Later he assisted Dr Thornton (qv) in the great reorganisation when the new chained library was resited in the lady chapel. When the bookbinder John Cooper (qv) returned refurbished volumes in the 1620s, it was Dr Best who received them.

Béthune, Robert de (d.1148), Bishop of Hereford 1131-48, came from a knightly Flemish family that had settled in Buckinghamshire. He trained to be a schoolmaster, then studied under Guillaume de Champeaux at his school of Notre Dame. He made his vows as an Augustinian canon at Llanthony in the Black Mountains shortly after the priory's foundation, and planted a cell of the priory at Weobley. He was prior of Llanthony by 1127 and in 1130 Henry I (qv) made him bishop of the vacant see of Hereford. Béthune was an austere, pious and active bishop of his diocese, increasingly thought of as a saint. He was reported to have miraculously healed a beggar at the gates of his palace in Ledbury's market place. A three-day market at Ledbury was granted him by King Stephen (qv) at high mass in Hereford Cathedral at Whitsun 1138, to be held at the feast of its patrons Sts Peter and Paul (29 June), and also a three-day market at Ross. Under Béthune the cathedral was consecrated (1142). He formed a chapter of canons under Ralph (qv) the first dean, with a treasurer, chancellor and precentor. These were lawless times of civil war between Stephen (qv) and Matilda. For the peace of his see he pragmatically supported the ruler of the moment, Stephen at first, then Matilda when her forces captured the king and the powerful local magnate Miles of Gloucester (qv), Earl of Hereford, put pressure on him to do so; then Stephen again. Geoffrey Talbot (qv, d.1140) seized Hereford Castle for Matilda, but Stephen drove him out. In pursuing Talbot to Shrewsbury the suspicious Stephen took Robert in his train to keep an eye on him. When conditions at Llanthony became insecure during the Anarchy he provided refuge for the monks at Hereford and, with Earl Miles, helped them found a second home at Gloucester, granting them income from Here-

fordshire lands and churches. The ruins of both Llanthonys can still be seen. He looked after the canons of Shobdon when Hugh (I) de Mortimer (qv) had confiscated their land, mediating with Mortimer on their behalf and persuading him to allow them to settle at Wigmore in 1148. Bishop Robert was one of the three bishops Stephen allowed to go to the Council of Rheims, where he died on 16 April 1148. In a deathbed confession he admitted his affection for the storks and peacocks he kept at Hereford and for his too-much-loved black dog with the white feet. His body was returned to Hereford Cathedral for burial encased in the carcass of an ox. On its way miracles were performed; an unofficial cult flourished at his tomb and his Dean and Chapter tried unsuccessfully to have him canonised. William of Wycombe (qv), his chaplain, wrote his life. A later,14th-century effigy can be seen in the south choir aisle of the cathedral.

Beuno (*c*.545-640), saint, from a princely family of Gwent, was educated at Caerwent and ordained a priest, learned in scripture. He was granted lands at Llanveynoe (which means the enclosure of Beuno) at Longtown in the British Kingdom of Ewyas, Herefordshire. Here *c*.600 AD he founded a monastery of which nothing now remains except the short-armed cross in the churchyard, which is believed to be connected with the house. The church is now dedicated to St Peter (qv). He performed many miracles: one involved his niece St Winifred, who had refused the advances of her suitor Caradoc. He, enraged, had her decapitated. Her uncle Beuno however replaced her head miraculously, and at the site a healing well was found – Holywell – which became the most important venue for pilgrimages in Wales. Beuno retired to Clynnog on the Lleyn where in 640 he died and was buried. Miracles occurred at his tomb and children with rickets and epilepsy used to be left there overnight for healing. His feast day is 21 April.

Bevan, Edward (1770-1860), apiarist, was born on 8 July 1770 in London but moved to Hereford as a child after the death of his parents to live with his mother's father, a Hereford apothecary. He went to Hereford Cathedral School and was apprenticed to a Hereford surgeon. He qualified as a physician and practised at Stoke and in Cheshire, later retiring to Woodland Cottage, Bridstow where he began to experiment with bee-keeping, helped by his wife, his niece Marianne Thomas and a neighbouring vicar (qv Richard Walond). He published his results as *The Honey-Bee* (1827). He also gave a paper on the subject to the Hereford Literary, Philosophical and Antiquarian Institution and exhibited at the Great Exhibition of 1851. He was a founder member of the Royal Entomological Society in 1833. He lived in Carmarthenshire for a few years but in 1849 moved to St Owen Street, Hereford where, on 31 January 1860, he died. He is considered the father of modern bee-keeping.

Bezant, Aaron Walter (1824-after 1881), clockmaker, jeweller and dealer in sewing machines and pianos, had a shop at 5 & 6 Widemarsh Street, Hereford. Bezant is a Suffolk name and Aaron was born there on 12 December 1824. His wife Matilda (b.1823) and her younger sister Kate, who were from Norfolk, worked in the business with six other employees and Robert Davies, Bezant's apprentice. They had two sons, Luke and Matthew. The church clock at Weobley is an example of his work.

Biddulph: A family from Biddulph in Staffs, claiming Saxon origins, the name meaning wolf-killer. Coming to Ledbury they acquired New House, thought by Pevsner to be the finest black and white building in the county. It sits in its own deer park. Biddulphs became discreetly celebrated and enormously wealthy bankers in partnership with their neighbours the Cocks (qv) family. They were high ranking army officers and one, Sir Thomas, a close servant to Queen Victoria. The last Ledbury Biddulph died recently but the family survive elsewhere.

Biddulph, Anthony (b.1584), was the son of Simon Biddulph and Joyce Floyer. He married Elizabeth, daughter of Robert Palmer and they lived at Hazle Court near Ledbury.

Biddulph, Anthony (*c.*1666-1718), was the son of Robert Biddulph and Mary Cullen. He married Constance, daughter of Francis Hall (qv Elizabeth Hall). In 1688 he bought New House, the great black and white mansion at Ledbury's Top Cross, reputedly the finest in Herefordshire, which stands in its own deer park. They had two sons, Robert and Michael. He was High Sheriff of Herefordshire in 1694. The effigies of Anthony and Constance recline with splendid hauteur at the west end of Ledbury Church over the family vault.

Biddulph, Francis (1734-1800), banker, was baptised at Ledbury on 3 March 1734. He set up as a goldsmith in St Paul's churchyard and in 1757 invited his friends James and Thomas Sommers Cocks (qqv) to help him found a bank. Largely with Cocks' finances the partners established the house of Cocks, Biddulph & Co. and in 1759 the firm moved to 43 Charing Cross. The bank was well known for its aristocratic patrons and discretion and was the banker of Hereford Cathedral. The bank was eventually absorbed by Barclays. Biddulph never married and died intestate in Brighton on 25 October 1800.

Biddulph, John (1768-1845) was born at New House on 17 March 1768, the youngest of Michael Biddulph's (qv, d.1800) four sons. He married Augusta Roberts and they had two sons and a daughter, Mary Ann (d.1892), who married Robert Martin (1808-97) of Overbury, Tewkesbury, a partner of the famous Grasshopper Bank of Lombard Street, where their son John Biddulph Martin (1841-97) was partner in turn. He was interested in geology and subscribed to Murchison's (qv) Silurian system, and was also a prominent archer of the Hereford Bowmeeting. He bought Hazle Court, Ledbury and gave a part, Haffield, to his nephew William Gordon (qv), who brought in Smirke (qv), then at Eastnor, to design Haffield House. He was a leading member of the board of the Ledbury Canal Company (qv Stephen Ballard). He died on 25 November 1845.

Biddulph, John Michael Gordon (1869-1949), 2nd Baron Biddulph, was the eldest son of Sir Robert (qv, d.1918), born in London on 19 November 1869 with Ledbury Park his seat in Herefordshire. He was educated at Eton and Christ Church, Oxford and was a director of Martins Bank. In 1896 he married Marjorie daughter of Lt-Col William Mure. Their daughter Adelaide married Henry Yorke (qv under Philip Yorke), the novelist who wrote under the nom de plume Henry Green. He was Deputy Lieutenant and a JP for Herefordshire and died on 17 December 1949.

Biddulph, Michael (1724-1800), son of Robert (qv, d.1772) and Anne, married Penelope (1733-1818), daughter of John Dandridge of Malvern. Their daughter Penelope married Adam Gordon and their son was William Gordon (qv).

Biddulph, Michael (1834-1923), 1st Baron Biddulph, banker, was born on 17 February 1834 the son of Robert (qv, d.1864) and educated at Harrow. In 1864 he married Adelaide (d.1872), daughter of General Jonathan Peel. After her death he married, in 1877, Elizabeth daughter of Charles Yorke, 4th Earl of Hardwicke and widow of Henry Adeane. Biddulph was a partner of the family bank Cocks, Biddulph & Co. He

was Liberal MP for Hereford county (1865-86) and of Ross-on-Wye after constituency changes. He was Deputy Lieutenant of the county and in 1903 was created Baron Biddulph of Ledbury. He died on 6 April 1923 in Ledbury and was buried in Donnington Church. The dedication of St Peter's Church, Ledbury was changed to St Michael in his memory.

Biddulph, Robert (1682-1772), son of Anthony (qv, d.1718) was born in October 1682 at New House, later called Ledbury Park. He married Anne Joliffe (1690-1760) of Cofton Hall, Worcs. Of their seven children, Francis (qv) inherited New House.

Biddulph, Robert (1801-64) was born on 3 March 1801 the son of John (qv, d.1845). He was a Whig MP for Hereford between 1832 and 1837, JP and Deputy Lieutenant for Herefordshire. He married Elizabeth, daughter of George Palmer of Nazeing Park, Essex in 1830 and their sons were Michael (qv, d.1923) and Robert (qv, d.1918). He died on 28 February 1864 and his wife died in January 1899.

Biddulph, Robert (1835-1918), army officer, younger brother of Michael Biddulph (qv, d.1923) was born in London on 26 August 1835. He was educated at the Royal Military Academy, Woolwich and joined the Royal Artillery in 1853. He fought in the Crimea at the Alma, Balaclava and the siege of Sevastopol. He was in India during the Mutiny, present during the capture of Lucknow and fought in the Oudh. He served in Sir James Hope Grant's campaign in China in 1860 and, returning to India, was promoted lieutenant colonel in 1863. In 1864 he married Sophia (d.1905), daughter of Revd Anthony Lewis Lambert, a Hampshire rector, and they had four sons and six daughters. He was Governor of Gibraltar and in 1900 returned home to the War Office. He funded Ledbury Cottage Hospital in 1891, replacing an earlier hospital on the other side of the street. He was created KCMG in 1880, GCMG in 1886 and GCB in 1899. He died in London on 18 November 1918 and was buried in St Michael's Church, Ledbury, where there is a memorial to him.

Biddulph, Robert Myddelton (1761-1814), born at Colwall on 22 March 1761, was the son and heir of Michael Biddulph. Inheriting the Biddulph fortune, he made another trading in Bengal. He returned home, and in 1801 married the wealthy heiress Charlotte, daughter of Richard Myddelton MP of Chirk Castle, and assumed his wife's name by royal licence. He was elected MP for the county 1796-1802 through the management of Duke of Norfolk (qv Charles Howard) as a way of excluding the sitting Whig MP George Cornewall (qv, d.1819), under the banner 'the Friend of Peace and Liberty'. When Cornewall was later re-elected, Biddulph was returned for Denbigh (1806-12). He died on 30 August 1814 and is buried in Ledbury Church..

Biddulph, Robert Myddelton (1805-72), eldest son and heir of Robert (qv, d.1814) and Charlotte, married Frances, daughter of William Mostyn-Owen. Their son Richard (1837-1913) lived at Chirk Castle. He rose to the rank of colonel in the army.

Biddulph, Thomas Myddelton (1809-78), courtier and army officer, born on 29 July 1809, was the second son of Robert (qv, d.1814) and Charlotte. He was educated at Eton and served in the 1st Life Guards, becoming a general in 1877. In 1851 Baron Stockmar appointed him master of Queen Victoria's household. He married Mary, one of the queen's maids of honour, and daughter of Frederick Seymour and Lady Mary Gordon. He was created KCB and appointed Keeper of the Queen's Privy Purse, supervising her finances and trusted to negotiate royal grants, always an anxiety for Victoria. In 1877 he became a member of the Privy Council. From 1866 until his death he was receiver-general of the Duchy of Cornwall and, from 1873, of the Duchy of Lancaster. Sir Thomas was always in close attendance on the queen and he died near Balmoral on 28 September 1878.

Binyon, Brightwen (1846-1905), architect, was born on 30 May 1846 at Victoria Park, Manchester, and named Brightwen after his mother's family. His maternal aunt Eliza and her husband moved in artistic circles in London and were related to Laurence Binyon (qv) and Edmund Gosse. Binyon was a pupil of Alfred Waterhouse and started his own architectural practice in Ipswich. He married Rachel Cudworth. He was elected ARIBA and designed public buildings including the Ipswich Corn Exchange and Swindon Town Hall, and rebuilt his Brightwen relations' house The Grove, Stanmore. He won the competition to design the Barrett-Browning Institute in Ledbury as a memorial to Elizabeth Barrett (qv). It was built on the site of a tannery by local builder George Hill at a cost of £2,330 and opened by Sir Henry Rider Haggard (qv) in 1896. In 1938 Ledbury Public Library moved into the building and was opened by poet laureate John Masefield (qv). Binyon died on 21 September 1905.

Binyon, Robert Laurence (1869-1943), poet, was born into a Quaker family on 10 August 1869 at Lancaster. They moved to Hoe Court, Colwall where he spent his childhood. From his poem 'For the Fallen' are the lines often read at Remembrance Day services:

Age shall not weary them, nor the years condemn.
At the going down of the sun and in the morning,
We will remember them.

Birch, John (1615-91), Parliamentarian officer and governor of Hereford, was born on 7 September 1615, the eldest son of Samuel Birch (d.1669), a Presbyterian Elder of Ardwick Manor near Manchester. With his brother Samuel he went to Bristol, where he set up as a merchant. Here he married Alice, daughter of Thomas Deane and the widow of a business friend, and they had five children. When Prince Rupert (qv) laid siege to Bristol in the Civil War Birch raised a force of volunteers but Bristol fell and he fled to London. Here he raised a regiment of which he was colonel. He served under William Waller (qv) and his early successes impressed Cromwell. In 1645 he received a commission to distress Hereford, which had resisted a siege by the Scottish Army. He appeared before Hereford on 18 December 1645, a freezing, snowy day, having lost some of his men to severe cold. Feinting a retreat, he hid in the old ruins of St Guthlac's Priory beyond Byster's Gate, sending a few men dressed as workmen into Hereford where they seized the gate and admitted Birch's force. A gleeful pamphlet describing this stratagem can be seen in the cathedral library. Parliament granted his force £60,000 and appointed him joint Governor of Hereford with Wroth Rogers (qv). He set up his HQ in what is now Castle Cliffe House on Castle Green and began allocating the houses of the vicars choral to needy persons. The following June he besieged Goodrich Castle, the last Royalist stronghold in Herefordshire, where Sir Henry Lingen (qv) and his garrison were holding out. Birch had the heavy mortar Roaring Meg (qv) cast in the Forest of Dean and pounded the castle into submission. He then joined Thomas Fairfax

at Raglan Castle with Meg. Birch bought up sequestered estates and confiscated church property. He stood for Parliament when Humphrey Coningsby (qv, d.1692) was purged in 1646 but was beaten by Sir Edward Harley (qv, d.1700), although he was later elected MP for Leominster. His irregularly paid troops were rowdy in the streets and jeered at the papistical Anglican services in the cathedral. He tried to have them posted to Ireland but they mutinied and imprisoned him and his brother Major Samuel Birch (d.1693); after which he retired with his family to The Homme in Dilwyn. He was purged from the Long Parliament of 1648 by Colonel Pride and, increasingly disillusioned with the radicalised Parliamentary rump, treated with Charles II at Worcester in 1651, although he left before the battle. Cromwell regarded Birch as delinquent, and had him arrested at his favourite house, Whitbourne, near Bromyard, the old bishops' palace which he had bought cheap. He was locked up and imprisoned in Hereford Castle; he later claimed to have been arrested 21 times in all. By the late 1650s he publicly declared for a Restoration. He was again elected for Leominster and held offices in Richard Cromwell's Parliament. He was also elected to the restored Long Parliament. At the Restoration he vainly tried to persuade Richard Baxter to accept the bishopric of Hereford. He was forced to disgorge much church property although he managed to make money from the transactions. In 1661 he bought nearby Garnstone from Roger Vaughan (d.1672, qv under Thomas Tomkyns) and rebuilt the house, as recorded by Thomas Dingley (qv). Birch continued to represent Weobley in Restoration parliaments where he warned against Popish plots and absolute monarchy, until ejected in 1683. He was protected from the effects of his occasional rashness by his friend Edward Harley. He retired to enlarge and improve his Garnstone estate and restored Weobley Church. James II was planning to make Birch Deputy Lieutenant of Hereford at his abdication. When news of William of Orange's invasion reached Birch he joined with Harley and presented William with money collected from the Herefordshire gentry. With renewed popularity he was elected MP for Weobley again and, aged 74, made frequent speeches to King William's Parliament. He died at Garnstone House on 10 May 1691 and is buried in Weobley Church where there is a standing statue of him (see above). Bishop Ironside (qv) thought the monument intrusive and removed its railings but the martial statue still gestures in the chancel. Birch's secretary John Roe wrote a *Military Memoir* of him, which was edited by John Webb (qv) in 1864. A legend portrays Birch's niece Alice and her lover Charles Clifford trapped in Goodrich Castle while her uncle was besieging it, and both are said to have drowned trying to escape. Their ghosts haunt the place.

Birch, Sarah, John's (qv) youngest daughter, was allowed to inherited Garnstone on condition she married her cousin, John Birch. This she did. Her husband John Birch in 1701 became MP of Weobley until his death in 1735. Garnstone descended through the female line to the Peploes (qv Samuel Peploe).

Birch, Thomas, John's (qv) brother, was rector of Hampton Bishop near Hereford 1654-83. He was a fellow of Manchester collegiate church and a correspondent of Richard Baxter.

Bird, Charles John (1777-1854), William Bird's (qv) fourth son, was born on 11 July 1777 at Drybridge House. He went to the Cathedral School and aged nine, while on a picnic, heard the cathedral's west front collapse and saw the great cloud of dust. He was educated at Magdalene College, Cambridge and ordained. He received the living of Dinedor from the Duke of Norfolk (qv Charles Howard) and Mordiford from the Foleys (qv Edward Foley, d.1803) and lived at Mordiford rectory where he had a collection of fossils and antiquities. His 21 volumes of historical notes on Herefordshire were acquired by W.H. Cooke (qv) who made use of them in completing Duncumb's (qv) history of the county. As a JP he was severe with the Welsh drovers who brought their beasts to market on the Sabbath. He was a founding member of the Herefordshire Philosophical Society in 1836. He died on 6 December 1854 and is buried in Mordiford churchyard.

Bird, Thomas (1772-1836), attorney, William's (qv) third son, was born at Drybridge House, Hereford on 2 March 1772 and educated at Hereford Cathedral School. He was clerk of the peace with an office in the new Shire Hall. He was a prominent Freemason and Master of Palladian Lodge in Hereford. Bird owned a timber and shipbuilding yard on the Wye below Castle Green which, after his death, the bishop pulled down to improve his view. Bird was a notable collector of antiquities, buying the papers of James Hill (qv), which found their way, via Walter Pilley (qv), into the Hereford Record Office. His son Thomas Hugh Bird (d.1868) was vicar of Yarkhill. His children continued to live at Drybridge House, which is now a day care centre.

Bird, William (d.1795), attorney, was the son of Benjamin Bird, who had built Drybridge House in St Martin's Street, Hereford in 1742. William was Mayor of Hereford in 1773 and a JP. He married Hannah; their daughter Anne married Behning Wentworth (qv), and their sons Charles (qv) and Thomas (qv) played a prominent part in Herefordshire life.

Birmingham, William, Dean of Hereford 1362-75, was from a Staffordshire family, tenants of the Dudleys, who were prominent in the early commercial development of Birmingham. William was appointed Dean of Hereford by Pope Urban V in November 1362 following Dean Thomas Trillek (qv). His contract with Thomas of Cambridge (qv) for the cathedral chapter house is extant.

Birt, James (1741-1804), residentiary canon of Hereford, prebend of Gorwall and Overbury. His father, Philip Birt (1719-63), was also prebendary of Hereford. He was vicar of Woolhope, Fownhope and Fawley, and Master of St Katherine's Hospital, Ledbury from 1785, living in the Master's House. He attempted to regularise the lax conditions at the hospital and raised rents to provide revenue for repairs and subsidy for the inmates. He started the process that led to the pulling down of Butcher Row and the building of the southern half of the almshouses. John Lidiard's map of Ledbury (1788) calls the Master's House 'Canon Birt's House'.

Bisse, Philip (1666-1721), Bishop of Hereford 1713-21, and Thomas his brother (qv) were born at Oldbury on the Hill, Gloucestershire, sons of the rector Revd John Bisse. Philip was educated at Winchester and New College, Oxford. In 1710 he was consecrated Bishop of St David's and in 1713 Bishop of Hereford, assisted by the patronage of his cousin Robert Harley (qv, d.1724) to beat the favourite, Adam Ottley (qv). In 1704 he married Bridget (1661-1718), daughter of Thomas Osborne, 1st Duke of Leeds and widow of Charles fitz Charles, Earl of Plymouth, the king's illegitimate son by Catherine Pegg. Bisse had been Bridget's chaplain. He supported Harley at Westminster and was a conscientious diocesan bishop. He modernised the cathedral and his palace after centuries of decay with largely cosmetic works and pulled down the chapter house. He walled off the choir from the lady chapel to the east and the noisy nave to the west with screens painted with classical architectural features, creating a Georgian room in the middle of the ancient fabric. He had a free hand in the cathedral as his dean, John Tyler (qv) was also Bishop of Llandaff. He was Queen Anne's chaplain and a Fellow of the Royal Society. Dr Bisse died at Westminster on 6 September 1721 and was buried in Hereford Cathedral where an expensive marble tomb was erected, of which only a panel remains.

Bisse, Thomas (1675-1731), cleric, was educated at Corpus Christi College, Oxford. He was rector of Cradley and one of the portionists of the Ledbury living. In 1716 his brother the bishop (Philip Bisse, qv) appointed him chancellor of the cathedral, prebendary of Colwall and rector of Weston-under-Penyard, replacing Joseph Harvey (qv), a non-juror. His parishes were managed by curates. The cathedral choirs of Hereford, Gloucester and Worcester had occasionally sung together and Bisse with his experience of musical festivals in London, arranged for a grand festival to be held on a regular annual basis at each cathedral city in rotation, starting in about 1716. This was the genesis of the Three Choirs Festival, Britain's oldest musical festival. He was a stirring preacher and some of the sermons he gave at these festivals were printed: *On the Beauty of Holiness in the Common Prayer* (1716) is still in print. He died on 22 April 1731.

Blake, Thomas (1825-1901), a Baptist of humble beginnings, became a wealthy landowner in Ross-on-Wye and bought the fine early-17th-century mansion Alton Court, home of the Markyes (qv) which he renovated *c.*1885. He had radical political views and was a benefactor of the local poor: in 1886 he built a pumping station in a field beside the house to provide Ross with its water supply. He left land

to the town on the steep bank between Wye Street and the Wye which in 1907 became the Blake Memorial Gardens.

Blashill, Thomas (1831-1905), FRIBA, was an architect whose father was the Cotterells' (qv) agent at Garnons. Chief architect for London County Council, he was interested in the monastic settlements of Herefordshire and the Marches and wrote studies of them. A founding member of the Woolhope Club, he was president in 1882 and at its half centenary in 1901, and he led visits to several monastic sites. He discovered that Dore Abbey chapter house was 12-sided, a rarity in austere Cistercian houses, and he ascertained the length of the nave. With Roland Paul (qv) he campaigned for funds for the restoration of the remains of the abbey. He rebuilt St John the Baptist, Yarkhill in 1863 with his partner Charles Ainslie (1820-63) and built the school. He restored Putley Church (1876) where he found Roman remains, and worked at the school and Putley Court. He restored several other Herefordshire churches such as St Peter, Dormington (1877) and St Andrew, Hampton Bishop (1879); and he built schools at Westhide (1863), and for Lady Foley (qv) at Tarrington (1875).

Blomfield, Arthur (1829-99), architect, built the Dean Leigh (qv) library at Hereford Cathedral in 1895 onto the western arm of the cloisters. The new library building of 1996 is an extension to this building. He rebuilt the chancel of Bodenham Church in 1891 and supplied furnishings such as the reredos. Thomas Hardy trained as an architect in Blomfield's office. He was Vice President of RIBA, an associate RA and knighted in 1889.

Blomfield, Reginald (1856-1942), was Sir Arthur Blomfield's (qv) nephew and trained in his office. He modernised Garnons for John Richard Geers Cotterell (qv) in 1908-9 and built the war memorial at Eye in 1919, the year he was knighted. He was a fellow of the RA and President of RIBA 1912-14.

Bloomfield, Robert (1766-1823), poet, was born on 3 December 1766 at Honington, Suffolk. His father, a tailor, died of smallpox while Robert was young, leaving his wife and children in poverty. Robert learnt to read and write from his mother, a schoolteacher, and began writing poetry. Poverty drove him to work on a relative's farm, but he was not strong enough for the work and joined his older brothers in London where he learnt to make shoes and worked on his own education. He had his first work published in 1800: *The Farmer's Boy*, a long poem on farming life influenced by Thomson's *Seasons*, with woodcuts by Bewick. It was praised by Robert Southey and John Clare drew from it. He was compared with George Crabbe and Wordsworth (qv) in his depiction of the common round and called the cobbler-poet. Bloomfield married and started a family of his own but, generous to his brothers and mother beyond his means, was never free from money worries. He continued cobbling and made Aeolian harps, and the Duke of Grafton granted him an allowance. Bloomfield loved the Wye and Herefordshire was for him 'a land of delight'. He lodged at the Swan in Ross in summer 1807 with a party of friends, and they sailed up the river enjoying the steep banks, the Courtfield, Welsh Bicknor, 'Hereford with all her towers', as the castle was still standing, and Clifford's castle. He kept a poetic journal of the trip, *The Banks of the Wye: a Poem* (1811). The book was a commercial success but the publisher defaulted and Bloomfield earned little from it. He retired dejected to Bedfordshire in debt and poor health and on 19 August 1823 died and was buried in Campton churchyard. His epitaph rightly refers back to his verse: 'Let His Wild Native Wood Notes Tell the Rest'.

Blore, Edward (1787-1879), architect, was born in Derby on 13 September 1787. He was an artistic child with a gift for architectural sketches which, when his father became mad, he sold to support the family. He picked up his antiquarian knowledge from Gothick romances. His father died in 1819 and he married Sarah Ann Hodges and they lived in London, bringing up five daughters and three sons. He received important commissions including the rebuilding of Lambeth Palace (1829-31), work at Hampton Court Palace and the design of Goodrich Court (1828) for Samuel Meyrick (qv). At Goodrich he created a German Schloss with turrets and battlements to vie with the

castle opposite and to be both country house and a museum for Meyrick's collection of mediaeval armour. Blore designed rooms in different mediaeval styles: the banqueting hall was admired as especially authentic, although Wordsworth (qv) hated it. The style of Goodrich Court, sadly demolished, can be evoked from Blore's Monmouth Gatehouse (1837) on the Monmouth Road, and Ye Olde Hostelrie in the village. He worked in a classical style at Buckingham Palace and there is an early classical monument by him in St Mary's Church at Stoke Edith to Edward Foley of 1810. Blore was a likeable man with many highly placed contacts; his practice was efficiently run and increasingly successful and he became rich. He died in London on 4 September 1879 and was buried in Highgate cemetery.

Blount: The family was connected with other gentry families of the Marches. In the mid 15th century John, younger son of Sir Humphrey Blount of Kinlet, married an Eye heiress of Eye Manor (qv under Osbert de Eye). The Blounts were related to the Cornewalls (qv) at nearby Berrington and lived at Eye Manor until it passed to Ferdinando Gorges (qv). In the 1570s Catherine, daughter of Edward Blount, married Sir James Croft (qv, d.1590) as his second wife.

Blount, Myles (1584-1663) was the son of Roger Blount and Mary Berington of a Roman Catholic family long established at Grendon Bishop and Orleton. He married Anne Bustard (d.1669) of Adderbury, Oxfordshire and they had three sons and six daughters, one of whom, Anne, married Wallop Brabazon (qv). Myles died at Adderbury on 27 November 1663. A brass commemorates him in Orleton Church.

Blount, Thomas (1618-79), antiquarian and lexicographer, was the eldest of the nine children of Myles (qv) and Anne, born at Bordesley at Tardebigge, Worcs. As Blount's Catholicism barred him from university he read law at the Inner Temple and was called to the bar in 1648. He wrote a series of reference books such as *Glossographia* (1656) a dictionary of difficult words and a book of legal instances, both of which were plagiarised. In around 1650 he married Anne Church of Essex and moved to Orleton Manor, one of the finest half-timbered houses in the county. Charles II stayed here and in the early 18th century Alexander Pope (qv) wrote poetry in the chamber above the porch. In the 1670s Blount started work on his *History of Herefordshire*, compiled in parish order, which was read in its manuscript form by his neighbour William Brome (qv). It was never published and of the two manuscript volumes he left at his death the first was lost when Sir Robert Cornwall (qv) borrowed it, although it partially survives in transcriptions made by others. The second manuscript volume (L-Z) is in the Hereford Record Office. Blount died on 26 December 1679 and is buried in the chancel of St George's Church, Orleton where there is a brass to him. Blount's daughter Elizabeth (1662-1724) lived on at Orleton. Teresa and Martha Blount, friends of Pope (qv), seem to have been descendants of the family. Blounts continued in the county: in 1821 Emma daughter of William Blount of Orleton married Henry Matthews (qv, d.1828).

le Blund, Aaron (fl.later 13th century), son of Elias Blund of London, was a prominent Jewish financier in Hereford after the decline of Hamo's (qv) dynasty.

Bodenham: The family, from Bodenham, acquired the Rotherwas estate in 1483 from the de la Barre family by marriage. There was a timber-framed house with chapel of *c*.1300, lying between Dinedor Hill and the south bank of the Wye. Sir Roger rebuilt Rotherwas House in 1611 as one of the grand houses of the county. They became staunch Catholics and were Royalists through the Civil Wars. Through sequestrations and fines Rotherwas House became ruinous and was not rebuilt until their fortunes were restored in 1732. Then Sir Charles employed James Gibbs to build a large Palladian mansion. In the 20th century the unwieldy house again deteriorated until the estate was auctioned off and the house demolished in 1926. The chapel remains in the care of English Heritage.

Bodenham, Cecily (d.1543) was the daughter of Roger Bodenham (qv) and Joan Bromwich of Rotherwas. She was known to Henry VIII and Anne Boleyn. She became a nun at Kington St Michael Priory, Wiltshire which, in 1511, was robbed by a local curate who abducted Cecily. In 1534 she bought the position of Abbess of Wilton Abbey from Thomas Cromwell and, five years later, readily complied with the abbey's dissolution. In return she was given a large pension and retired to a pleasant Wiltshire farm with ten of the sisters. There is a portrait of her in Minneapolis Institute of Arts.

Bodenham, Charles (fl.1728-32) had James Gibbs build Rotherwas House at Dinedor in 1732, retaining fittings from its predecessor of 1611. Panelling surviving from the earlier house was later bought by and erected at Amherst College Massachusetts, USA.

Bodenham, Charles de la Barre (d.1880) inherited the estate in 1865 and employed Peter Paul Pugin (qv Pugin) to renovate the chapel. He died without an heir in 1874 and the Dinedor estate of 2,500 acres passed through his Polish widow to be used by refugees and for war work.

Bodenham, Roger (1545-1623), baronet, built Rotherwas House. He married a Catholic wife and having, it is said, been cured of leprosy in the waters of St Winifred's Well at Holywell, north Wales (qv Beuno), he was converted himself. The Becket (qv) reliquary were preserved through penal times and it is now often on show in the cathedral.

Bodley, George Frederick (1827-1907), architect and designer, was born in Hull on 14 March 1827. The family moved to Brighton where George met C.E. Kempe (qv). He was encouraged to take up architecture by Sir George Gilbert Scott (qv), whose brother had married Bodley's sister, and Bodley became his first pupil. Combining middle pointed gothic and continental gothic forms with architectural guidelines from John Ruskin's writings, Bodley developed a style suitable for modern use that came to typify high Victorian architecture. He had a long partnership with Thomas Garner. Bodley's first church, built when he was 27, was Christ Church at Llangrove (1854-6), Herefordshire, built for Catherine Marriott (qv). In 1860 he rebuilt St James's at Canon Frome with a beautiful rose window in the north chapel, its glass by Clayton and Bell (qv). In 1864 he restored St James's, Wigmore, rebuilt the chancel of St George's in nearby Burrington, and supplied plans for a

new school at Brampton Abbotts. While he was working with Garner on the renovation of St Mary's, Almeley in 1868 he met his future wife Minna (1851-1933), the daughter of Thomas Reavely (qv) of nearby Kinnersley Castle. They married in St James's, Kinnersley, where Bodley has left wall paintings in the nave and chancel. He designed a new organ case in the church as a wedding present for Minna as he was a good organist, and designed wallpaper for Kinnersley Castle. They had one son, George. He rebuilt Letton Court and rectory in red brick for the Blissett family, but the building burnt down in 1924. His next commissions were the repair of St Michael's, Lyonshall and St Michael's, Kingsland where more of his wall decoration can be seen. In 1889 the churchwardens of Eardisley Church commissioned a chalice and paten from him. A late work is the attractive Paraclete Chapel at Hom Green, Walford, built to commemorate Lionel Trafford (qv). It was finished in 1906; having been left unused for some time, it is now the venue for occasional recitals. Bodley died on 21 October 1907 and was buried in St James's, Kinnersley, where his grave can be seen.

Bodvoc (fl.15-10BC) ruled the Dobunni, a Celtic tribe whose territory in Roman times covered Gloucestershire and part of Herefordshire. He struck coins at Bagendon, the Dobunni cantonal capital, refounded by the Romans as *Corinium Dobunnorum*, now Cirencester. They possibly occupied the hillfort at Credenhill, though Herefordshire lay at the junction of three tribal territories and the local people may even have had their own identity. The Romans built a town below the hill, called *Castra Magna* or *Magnis* (near Kenchester). An inscription on a milestone found there (qv Numerian) indicates that the area was administered as Dobunni territory. Coins of Bodvoc have been found at *Ariconium*, an industrial centre near Weston-under-Penyard. Dobunnic coins date from between *c*.35BC and the arrival of the Romans, rulers who followed Bodvoc being named on their coins as Anted (10BC-AD10), Comux (10-15), Eisu (15-30), and Catti (15-43), all probably abbreviations. Five hundred years later a Bodvoc was buried at Margam near Swansea 50 miles to the west, showing the continuity of Celtic culture through much upheaval.

Bohun, earls of Hereford. The Bohun badge, a swan, was a rebus based on the pronunciation *bow-an*. The first was Humphrey, Lord of St George de Bohon in the Norman Cotentin and known as *cum barba* because of his beard, unusual among Normans. Dugdale (qv) says he was related by marriage to the Conqueror and fought with him at Hastings. Humphrey (I) (d.*c*.1123), his second son, founded the English family of Bohun, in Wiltshire initially. His grandson Humphrey (II) (d.1165) married Margaret (d.1187), daughter of Miles of Gloucester (qv), Earl of Hereford, and she brought the earldom of Hereford to the Bohuns and also the hereditary office of high constable. Their son Humphrey (III) de Bohun (*c*.1134-81) married Margaret of Huntingdon (1145-1201), daughter of Henry of Scotland, whose first marriage was to the Duke of Brittany, King William's ally. With Humphrey (IV) the earldom of Essex was added to their titles. There were nine Humphreys alone, the saintly Matilda (qv Humphrey VI), twins, William and Edward (b.1312, qqv), and a royal duke, Henry (IV). The ninth and last Humphrey (qv), the 7th Earl, had no male heirs and the great Bohun estates spread across the country were divided between his daughters. King Richard II granted the title, now advanced to a dukedom, to his cousin Henry Bolingbroke and on Henry's usurpation of the throne the title merged into that of the Crown, where it remains.

Bohun, Edward de (1312-34), twin brother of William (qv), married Margaret, daughter of William 2nd Baron de Ros but had no children. He was Constable of England and a friend of the young Edward III (qv). He drowned rescuing a soldier during Edward's Scottish campaign.

Bohun, Henry de (*c.*1176-1220), 1st Earl of Hereford, was the son of Humphrey (III) de Bohun and Margaret of Huntingdon (d.1201), daughter of Henry of Scotland and the Earl of Northumberland. He was brought up by his grandmother, Margaret of Hereford (qv), who passed her father's title Earl of Hereford to him, as a new creation, along with the hereditary office of Constable of England. He was one of the barons appointed to enforce the Magna Carta. He married Maud (d.1236) daughter of Geoffrey fitz Peter, 1st Earl of Essex and their son was Humphrey (IV) (qv). Like most of the barons of England he was frequently at odds with King John (qv), who at one time took control of the Bohun lands. He made peace with the new king, Henry III (qv) and died on pilgrimage to the Holy Land on 1 June 1220.

Bohun, Humphrey (IV) de (after 1199-1275), 2nd Earl of Hereford and 1st Earl of Essex, son of Henry (qv), married Maud (d.1241), daughter of Raoul de Lusignan. He added the earldom of Essex to his titles in succession to his father-in-law. His daughter Maud married Anselm Marshal (qv under William the Marshal), and she was buried at the abbey of Llanthony Secunda, Gloucester. Humphrey next married Maud de Avenbury (d. 8 October 1273), sister of Giles, Dean of Hereford. He stood godfather to Henry III's (qv) son Prince Edward (qv Edward of Woodstock), and was appointed keeper of the southern Marches to protect Herefordshire against the incursions of Llywelyn ap Gruffydd (qv). He died on 24 September 1275 and was buried by Maud at Llanthony.

Bohun, Humphrey (V) de (*c.*1221-65), 'the Good', married Eleanor daughter of William (V) de Briouze (qv); one of their sons was Humphrey (VI) (qv). Their daughter Alice (*c.*1233-55) married Roger de Tosni, lord of Flamstead. He fought in the Crusades, returning in 1252. He was wounded at the Battle of Evesham and died on 27 October 1265 in captivity at Beeston Castle, near Chester, predeceasing his father. Prince Edward (qv Edward I) gave some of his castles to Roger (III) Mortimer (qv).

Bohun, Humphrey (VI) de (*c.*1249-98), 3rd Earl of Hereford and 2nd of Essex, was a minor at the death of his grandfather, Humphrey (IV) (qv) and was made the ward of Gilbert de Clare, Earl of Gloucester. He married the pious Matilda, daughter of Enguerrand de Fiennes, in 1275 and they had a son, Humphrey (VII) (qv). His Herefordshire estates became increasingly important in Edward I's (qv) Welsh wars. He feuded with his powerful Marcher neighbours and also fought to recover territory from Llywelyn ap Gruffydd. He went on pilgrimage to Santiago de Compostela. As hereditary High Constable he accompanied Edward I on his Scottish wars. He died on 31 December 1298 and was buried at his castle of Pleshey in Essex. When Matilda died in 1318 she was buried in Dore Abbey where there was a miracle-working fragment of the True Cross. Her tomb became the focus of miracles and made Dore Abbey a centre for pilgrimage.

Bohun, Humphrey (VII) de (1276-1322), 4th Earl of Hereford and 3rd of Essex, was born at Pleshey Castle, the Bohuns' Essex seat. Rich and elegant, he married Princess Elizabeth of Rhuddlan (qv). At the Battle of Bannockburn in 1314 he challenged Robert the Bruce to single combat but was captured and exchanged later for the Bruce's queen and daughter, who had fallen into English hands. His nephew Henry de Bohun came across the Bruce during this battle, riding a pony without armour and charged him on his great war horse but at the last minute Bruce turned aside and killed Henry with a blow from his axe. Bohun and the Mortimers put down the rebellion of Llywelyn Bren in Glamorgan in 1316. As Edward II's (qv) brother-in-law, Humphrey was initially close to him, but with other barons he was alienated by Edward's reliance on his favourite Gaveston. When Gaveston returned, breaking the terms of his exile, de Bohun and other barons captured him and sentenced him to death. He opposed the Despensers' greed and malign influence over Edward and they were exiled. However the Despensers returned and with the king drove the barons to defeat on 16 March 1322 at the Battle of Boroughbridge, where Humphrey was killed. His daughter, Margaret, married Hugh Courtenay, 10th Earl of Devon and their son William Courtenay (qv) became Bishop of Hereford.

Bohun, Humphrey (IX) de (1342-73), 7th Earl of Hereford, 6th Earl of Essex and 2nd Earl of Northampton, was the son of William (qv) and Elizabeth. He travelled to Italy in 1366 to arrange Lionel, Duke of Clarence's marriage to a Visconti princess. He saw service in Edward III's (qv) French wars. He married Joan, daughter of Richard Fitzalan 10th Earl of Arundel (qv under Edmund Fitzalan), in 1359 but they had no male heirs and their titles became extinct. His daughter Mary married Henry Bolingbroke, (qv Henry IV), who was created Duke of Hereford. Mary died when their son, the future Henry V (qv), was young and the princes were brought up by their grandmother, the Countess Joan. The other daughter, Eleanor, (*c*.1366-99) married Thomas of Woodstock, Duke of Gloucester, youngest son of Edward III. Their daughter was Anne of Gloucester (qv William Bourchier).

Bohun, Joanna de, see **Kilpeck, Joanna de**

Bohun, John de (1306-35), 5th Earl of Hereford, eldest surviving son of the 12 children of Humphrey (VII) (qv), had to wait until the fall of the Despensers in 1326 before he was permitted to assume his titles: the earldoms of Hereford and Essex and Constable of England. He married Alice Fitzalan (qv), daughter of the Earl of Arundel, and then later Margaret Bassett. He must have had some incapacity as William and Edward (qv under William), his twin brothers, customarily deputed for him.

Bohun, William de, (1312-60), 6th Earl of Hereford and 1st of Northampton, was, with his twin Edward (qv), a son of Humphrey (VII) and Elizabeth. Both took part in Edward III's (qv) arrest of Roger (V) Mortimer (qv) at Nottingham Castle in 1330. William married Elizabeth Badlesmere, widow of Roger (V) Mortimer's son Edmund (II) (qv), intending to heal the enmity. He and his twin Edward were prominent in Edward III's Scottish wars. He was rewarded with the Earldom of Northampton and created one of the first Knights of the Garter. His friendship with Edward III helped the Bohun family and led to the rehabilitation of his stepson Roger (VI) de Mortimer, grandson of the traitor Roger (V). His daughter Elizabeth married Richard Fitzalan, Earl of Arundel and Surrey, in 1359. He died on 16 September 1360 and was buried in Walden Abbey, Essex. His brother Humphrey (VIII) succeeded to his titles but died in 1361.

Bonner, Edmund (1495-1569) was nominated Bishop of Hereford in 1538 but before he could be consecrated was elected Bishop of London. He had been educated in Broadgates Hall (later Pembroke College) Oxford, supporting himself by working in the kitchens. After ordination he ingratiated himself with Henry VIII (qv) by appealing to the Pope to reverse the king's excommunication. He was unhappy with Edward VI's (qv) Protestant reforms and persecuted Protestants cruelly in Mary's (qv) reign. Foxe vilified him; John Aubrey (qv) said he pursued a young boy for unguarded words he had repeated and had him burnt to death. Under Elizabeth (qv) he was arrested and died in the Marshalsea in 1569.

Booker, Luke (1762-1835), clergyman and writer, was the son of a Nottingham schoolmaster born on 20 October 1762. He was ordained and held curacies. His brother-in-law, Richard Blakemore, installed him as rector of the beautiful, isolated church of St James, Tedstone Delamere before George Gilbert Scott's (qv) restoration 50 years later. He was also vicar of Dudley. He raised much money for charities by his sermons, wrote poetry, sensational pamphlets, a melodrama and historical guides. He was much married, a JP in the county and died on 1 October 1835.

Booth, Charles (d.1535), Bishop of Hereford 1516-35, was the son of Roger of Mollington in Cheshire and educated at Pembroke College, Cambridge, where he was appointed Doctor of

Law. He was amongst Prince Arthur's group of advisers and a prebendary of Hereford in 1490. In 1516 he became Bishop of Hereford and in 1519 celebrated with a grand convocation where the cathedral's institutions were confirmed, in English (the use of English rather than Latin for such a purpose being a rarity at that time). He got on well with Dean Frowcester (qv). As a friend of Prince Arthur's widow Catherine of Aragon he followed her to Court when she married Henry VIII (qv). He seems to have been against the marriage but conformed after threats from the king. His is the magnificent outer porch of the cathedral, with a chapel in the upper room dedicated to St Mary, which recently housed the chained library; the two turrets hold narrow stairs. The door that stands beside the porch was intended by Bishop Booth to lead into the oratory of the Good Shepherd, but this was never built. He repaired Monthalt House in Old Fish Street, the Bishop of Hereford's lodging in London, and its chapel. He died on 5 May 1535 at his manor of Whitbourne and was buried in the cathedral beside his porch. Booth had good relations with the city council and left them money in his will for a good dinner in his memory. He also left some precious books to the cathedral library where they remain safely chained.

Booth, James Charles (1703-78), lawyer, came from a Catholic family descended from Bishop Booth (qv) with estates in Herefordshire. Booth was educated at Magdalen College, Oxford and the Middle Temple and became the most famous conveyancer of his age, consulted by kings. He married Mary, daughter of politician John Sharp and built Whitfield Court (1755-60) near Wormbridge in the old Forest of Treville. He died on 15 January 1778 and was buried in East Barnet, Hertfordshire.

Bosa (fl.833), a Chancellor of King Witlaf of Mercia, is supposed to have given his name to Bosbury. He witnessed a royal charter to Crowland Abbey dated 833.

Boughton, Charles William, later Rouse-Boughton, and finally Boughton-Rouse (1747-1821), 9th Baronet Boughton, was the second son of Shuckburgh (qv) and Mary. He was born in Worcester but the family home was now Poston Court, Vowchurch. He went to Bengal at 17 as a Writer (a junior civil servant) and held various judicial offices with the East India Company. In England he was MP for Evesham (1780) and in 1782 married Catherine, daughter of William Pearce of Downton Hall. They had a son and two daughters. He changed his name to Boughton-Rouse in 1769 and in 1791 was appointed 1st Baronet Boughton-Rouse, of Rouse Lench by Pitt for his services to the government. (The Rouse Lench connection came from his mother's family.) In 1794, on the death of his brother Edward, he became 9th Baronet Boughton of Lawford Parva. He lived at Downton Hall, Shropshire, devoting himself to agriculture, and was noted for a new breed of pig.

Boughton, Edward (*c.*1742-94), 8th Baronet Boughton, of Lawford Parva, was the eldest son of Shuckburgh (qv) and Mary. He lived on his Vowchurch lands at Poston Court. He sold off his estates outside Herefordshire in order to improve those in the county, employing Sir William Chambers (qv) to build him a hunting lodge at Poston. He died on 26 February 1794.

Boughton, Shuckburgh (*c.*1703-63) was the son of Sir William Boughton and his second wife Catherine Shuckburgh. His brother Edward married a Shuckburgh cousin. This Edward's son Sir Theodosius was murdered by his brother-in-law, causing Shuckburgh to inherit the Boughton estates in several counties including those in the Vowchurch area, which he added to by purchases from Lord Arthur Somerset (qv). He married Mary, eldest daughter of Algernon Greville, Lord Brooke (qv Arthur Somerset). After Shuckburgh's death Mary was one of Queen Charlotte's Women of the Bedchamber.

Boughton, Stephen (1572-1637), of Buckinghamshire, was educated at Magdalen College Oxford. He was chaplain and subdean of the Chapel Royal, Windsor and in 1605 perpetual vicar of St Bartholomew's, Much Marcle with Yatton, and rector of Dinedor. The patron of the Much Marcle living was Walter Pye (qv). He was involved in arrangements for James I's funeral. He married Elizabeth (d.1623), daughter of Sir John Kyrle (qv, d.1650). She is buried in the church where a memorial plaque shows her at prayer.

Boulers, Reginald (*c*.1400-59), Bishop of Hereford 1451-3, was educated and ordained at Oxford and became Doctor of Theology. A Benedictine monk at the Abbey of St Peter's, Gloucester, he rose to be Abbot in 1437. He declined the bishopric of Llandaff and Henry VI (qv) employed him on diplomatic missions and the administration of territories in France. His abbey property was attacked in Gloucester in 1450, and Jack Cade's rebels named him one of Henry's evil councillors. He fled to the Duke of York's protection at Ludlow where news reached him of his nomination to the bishopric of Hereford, and he was consecrated in February 1451. In 1453 he was translated to the see of Coventry and Lichfield. He acted as mediator between the Duke of York and King Henry. He died in 1459 at his Warwickshire manor and was buried in the lady chapel at Lichfield Cathedral.

Boulter, John a baker and **Carwardine, Lancelot** a farmer at Fairtree, Ledbury were given the running of Ledbury Workhouse in the 19th century. They paid a rent of £330 pa and took the benefits. For this they agreed to: *furnish the poor ... with good wholesome and sufficient meat, drink, wearing apparell, washing, lodging and all other necessaries. Particularly as to eatables and drinkables they will provide for such poor objects as are grown up to full age in the following manner – on Mondays, for breakfast, dinner and supper, one pound of bread and four ounces of cheese, on Tuesdays, Thursdays and Saturdays the like quantities, on Wednesdays one pound of bread, two ounces of cheese and one pound of meat before it is boiled and the like of Fridays and Sundays, also a proper quantity of wholesome pudding and meat broth every day except Wednesday when there shall be meat broth for breakfast. They are to allow poor objects going out to work four ounces of bread and two ounces of cheese extraordinary each working day. They are to brew good beer not weaker than three bushels of malt good Ledbury measure to one hundred and fifteen gallons of water, and are to allow each poor object a sufficient quantity with meals according to the custom of the workhouse. In case of lameness or sickness they are to provide an apothecary and surgeon and all medicines and applications. When meat is allowed they are to provide not only good but a sufficient quantity of garden stuff and vegetables. They are not to force upon the poor objects in any one year more than four quarters of bull beef – i.e. two hinder quarters and two forequarters.*

Bourchier, William (*c*.1374–1420, Count of Eu in Normandy, soldier, came of an Essex family, neighbours of Thomas of Woodstock, Duke of Gloucester (qv under Humphrey (IX) de Bohun). Through Woodstock, Bourchier accompanied Richard II (qv) to Ireland where he was knighted by him. Gloucester was arrested and murdered by the arbitrary king in 1397 and King Richard himself was soon deposed and dead. But Bourchier weathered the troubles and was taken up by the new king, Henry IV (qv). Henry was worried about Welsh incursions and used Bourchier to organize the defences of the Marches castles. One of the greatest landowners in the Marches at this time was Anne of Gloucester (qv in Humphrey (IX) de Bohun), widow of his late patron, and it was in one of her castles, Huntington, that they met and fell in love clandestinely. As Anne was close to the throne this was not welcome news to the new dynasty but Bourchier won the match through loyalty and valour. He fought at Agincourt and was granted a rich French prisoner, the Comté Eu, whose title he took as part ransom. While he was fighting in France Anne exchanged letters with the Abbot of Llanthony which survive in the Public Record Office. Anne's Bohun inheritance was eventually recovered by the Bourchier family, who became great names of the 15th and 16th centuries. Their granddaughter Cecily was to marry John Devereux, 2nd Baron Ferrers (qv, d.1501).

Bourn, Daniel (fl.1744-54), wool and cotton dealer of Leominster, invented a cotton carding engine which he patented in 1748 and installed in his Leominster factory, its rotating cylinders driven by the River Lugg. Water mills were widely used in Leominster for fulling cloth and grinding grain. Cotton production was in decline in the area, however, and in 1754 the Leominster cotton workers, seeing mechanization as a threat to their jobs, burnt down Bourn's factory. His losses amassed to over £1,600 and, disheartened, he gave up his endeavours, but Richard Arkwright senior (qv) was impressed by the process and adopted it as the basis of his water frame spinning machine.

Bourne, Robert (1832-1915) of Cowarne Court, Much Cowarne, was the son of Revd Robert Burr Bourne and his wife Eliza Jane of Crayford, Kent. He married Anna Eliza Baker (b.*c*.1836) and their son was Col Gilbert Charles Bourne (d.1933), who married Constance Croft (qv Croft family). Their daughter Anne Beatrice married Sir Elliott Wood (qv). His father, Revd Bourne, bought the Cowarne Park Estate and had a Jacobean-style mansion built (by John Cotton 1852-3), surrounded by a large park, well wooded with pleasure gardens and lakes. By the 1960s the house had been demolished and features of the park lost. The estate farm, Home Farm, and a lodge by Cotton are all that remain. Revd Bourne had St Mary's Church, Much Cowarne restored by Charles Heather (qv), following a fire caused by a lightning strike in 1840. In 1857 Robert Bourne jr was Captain in Her Majesty's 54th Regiment, rising to the rank of lieutenant colonel. He was JP for Worcestershire and Deputy Lieutenant of Herefordshire.

Bowers, James (fl.1860-1904) was a Hereford builder employed at a time of major changes at the centre of 19th-century Hereford. In 1860 the Town Council contracted with him for the new hop and wool markets on the north side of High Town where the Redstreak (qv) public house had stood. In 1873 he built Kempson's (qv) Library and Museum in Broad Street for about £6,000; and Cheers' (qv) new Town Hall on St Owen Street, finished in 1904 30% over the estimate at £24,000.

Box, Sidney (fl.1914-23), campaigner for agricultural workers' welfare, was a member of the National Union of Agricultural Workers. He proposed strike action in 1914 for a minimum wage for farm workers of 20 shillings for a 60-hour week, 1 shilling a week extra at threshing time, 4d an hour overtime and time and a half at harvest. Government figures showed agricultural wages in Herefordshire were 3 shillings a week below the national average and in response some farmers and landowners raised the labourer's wage by this amount. With the First World War came government price and wage guaran-

tees. Box stood as Labour MP for Hereford in 1923 but came last. There is a Sidney Box Drive in Hereford.

Boycott, Arthur Edwin (1877-1938), naturalist and pathologist, was the son of William Boycott, a Hereford solicitor. He was born at The Grange, Broomy Hill, Hereford on 6 April 1877. He went to Hereford Cathedral School and won a scholarship to Oriel College, Oxford, where he read natural sciences and became a Doctor of Medicine. He married Constance, the daughter of Will Agg, in 1904 and they had two sons. He engaged in research into the physiology of the blood in London Hospitals, and at Porton Down during the war. In Herefordshire he studied snails and made important discoveries which were reported in the Woolhope Club transactions. Professor Boycott served on the Royal Society's council and with the Royal Society of Medicine. Suffering from tuberculosis, he lived with his son at Ewen Farm, near Cirencester, and died on 12 May 1938.

Brabazon, Wallop (*c.*1581-after 1642), of Eaton Grange near Leominster, was the second son of Sir Edward Brabazon and Mary Smith. In 1630 he was High Sheriff of Herefordshire. He was a commissioner of array for the Royalist forces in the Civil War and one of the Nine Worthies of Herefordshire (see index). He married Anne Blount (qv under Myles Blount); their son Henry married Anne Lyster and lived in Hereford. Wallop, their youngest, (d.1702) was his grandfather's heir and is buried with his wife Katherine and his father in the family vault of Leominster Priory, where there is an inscription. After Wallop junior's death there was litigation about the ownership of Eaton Grange. John Price's (qv) history of Leominster says the Brabazons owned an ancient fortification overlooking Hay Lane called Comfort Castle, the site of the townspeople's games in ancient times.

Brampton, Bryan de (fl.1295) is recorded as having a tower at Brampton Bryan in 1295, having held Brampton Bryan Castle for the Mortimers (qv) since the 11th century. In 1179 the Bramptons were involved with Hugh (II) de Mortimer (qv) in the founding of Wigmore Abbey. The castle gatehouse was under construction in the early 14th century as ballflower decoration shows. There were five Bryan de Bramptons in the 13th century; the last was without male heir and his daughter Margaret de Brampton married Robert Harley (qv, d.1349) in 1309. There is a contemporary effigy in St Barnabas Church, Brampton Bryan of Lady Margaret holding her heart.

Brent-Dyer, Elinor Mary (1894-1969), children's writer, was born on 6 April 1894 in South Shields and, having trained as a teacher, began writing stories. She and her mother moved to Hereford in 1933. Elinor worked first as a governess in Peterchurch then, in 1938, opened the Margaret Roper School in Bodenham Road, Hereford, where she was headmistress until it closed in 1948. She began to have success with the Chalet School stories. They were set in the Austrian Tyrol where she had been on holiday but clearly dealt with her own experiences as headmistress in Hereford. After the Anschluss the fictional Chalet School was moved to a country house (based on Michaelchurch Court) in a village near 'Armiford' in Herefordshire, and Hereford and the Golden Valley are described. She wrote 101 books altogether and there were 59 books in the Chalet School series: the longest set of school stories written to date. After 1964 she moved in with friends in Redhill, Surrey where she died on 20 September 1969. The Friends of the Chalet School have placed a plaque on the Bodenham Road school building.

Breteuil, Roger de or **fitz William** (fl.1071-87), Earl of Hereford, magnate and rebel, was the second son of William fitz Osbern (qv) and Adelize de Tosny. He inherited his father's extensive English territories but, rebelling in 1075, raised a force in Herefordshire against the Conqueror. He was captured before he could cross the Severn, however, and spent the rest of his life in prison, his possessions granted to others. His holdings such as Clifford Castle went to his uncle Ralph de Tosny (qv). His sons Reynold and Roger served the Conqueror's youngest son Henry I but were never to recover their patrimony.

Breton, John de (d.1275), or John Brito, Bishop of Hereford 1269-75, was the son of John and Margaret of Dore. He was keeper of the wardrobe and steward to King Edward I, and was a royal justice on eyre. He was Sheriff of Hereford from 1254 to 1257 and is thought to have written a practical book of laws, the *Britton*, from which he is named. He graduated as a Doctor and became a canon of Hereford Cathedral before being elected as bishop in 1269. He was associated with his notorious predecessor Bishop Peter de Aquablanca (qv) and subject with Peter to the barons' anger. When bishop he tried to expel the Savoyard relations of his predecessor, but met with violent resistance. He made his own relative, Thomas, a canon of Hereford, however, and he appointed Thomas de Cantilupe (qv), de Montfort's man and his successor bishop. He died in debt to the king and Edward seized his property. His body was buried in Hereford Cathedral but his heart went to Dore Abbey where his parents were buried. An effigy at the abbey shows him in episcopal raiment holding his heart (qv Roland Paul).

Brewster, John (d.1684) was born in Gloucester, where his father John owned property, including the Sword Inn, with more in Hereford. His father had been Sheriff of Gloucester in 1612 and 1617 and Mayor in 1632. John junior was a London apothecary who returned to live at Burton Court, Eardisland. He married Margaret and they had a son, William (qv). After her death he married Blanche Louth, with whom he had eight children, the oldest being Benjamin. He and Margaret are buried in the chancel of St Mary's, Eardisland. Blanche, John's widow, married Thomas de la Hay (qv) of Urishay Castle, Peterchurch in 1686. A daughter, Elizabeth, married James Gwynn. Her portrait (1690) is in the Hereford Museum and Art Gallery collection. The Gwynns lived on at Burton Court and had a son William, who was an attorney at Neath.

Brewster, William (1665-1715), physician and antiquarian, the only son of John (qv) and Margaret, was baptised at St Mary's, Eardisland on 9 November 1665. He was educated at Hereford Cathedral School, then at St John's College, Oxford where he associated with non-jurors including Brome, Hicks and Hearne (qqv). He graduated D.Med in 1697, studied anatomy in London and practised as a physician in Hereford where he married Susan daughter of Francis Brydges (qv). He and John Maylord (qv) bought the Blewhouse in Widemarsh Street from Lady Throckmorton for £1,610 in 1697, another house in Bewell Street for £444 and some others adjoining. He pulled the Blewhouse down and built the Mansion House which his friend William Brome (qv) said was the most elegant house in Hereford. It had large, pleasant gardens (now Tesco's car park) and a bowling green, now part of the pub of that name. Brewster died here on 7 June 1715 and was buried in the east cloister at Hereford Cathedral. In his will he left his important library to All Saints Church, Hereford where it was chained for parishioners' use, after the fashion of the cathedral library, with which it has now been combined. Books were also given to the Bodleian via Hearne and to St John's. Susan continued to live at the Mansion House, leaving it to her Brydges cousin after her death. Later it was bought by Hereford Corporation as extra office space until the new Town Hall was built in St Owen Street. Burton Court remained with the Brewsters until bought by John Clowes (qv) in 1865.

Brian of Lingen (fl.late 12th century), priest, is believed to be the author of a book of advice for nuns and anchoresses called, in its various manuscripts, *Ancrene Riwle* or *Ancrene Wisse*. Brian, an Augustinian canon of Wigmore Abbey, wrote in a local Herefordshire dialect at the end of the 12th century. He addressed his 'dear sisters', a group of Augustinian canonesses, at Limebrook and Deerfold, not far from Wigmore Abbey and the castle, where one of the manuscripts was found. He shows himself to be a cultivated and humane man, an experienced spiritual director who gave sympathetic advice to the religious of these small houses. The *Ancrene Wisse* is connected with a group of writings in a similar dialect called the *Katherine Group* which showed the influence of Victorine thought and it cannot be a coincidence that the Abbot of Wigmore Abbey was Andrew of St Victor (qv). English prose surviving from this time is rare and this example of the English of Herefordshire is unique.

Bridget (d.523) is the patron saint of Bridstow church and village. Popular in the early Middle Ages, St Bride is variously emblematised by a milking cow, a flame and corn especially twisted into a cross. She is a bringer of comfort and her feast day is 1 February.

Brihtric (10th century) was a moneyer at Hereford Mint during King Æthelstan's (qv) reign. The mint was on the fortified enclosure which Edward the Elder built on Castle Green. A coin bearing his name can be seen in Hereford Museum.

de Briouze (or Braose): A powerful family of knights from Briouze in Normandy who fought at Hastings. They were Lords of Bramber and Bramber Castle, Sussex was their base, but by the 12th century they were in Herefordshire, stiffening the defences of the Marches. They were violently acquisitive with respect to both the Welsh and their neighbours, and William (II) was known as 'the terror of the Marches'. By the 13th century they owned 16 castles throughout the Norman British Isles, but they fell foul of the dangerous King John (qv), whose treachery was more than a match for even the Briouze might. When William (V) was caught in bed with Prince Llywelyn's wife Joan (King John's daughter) he was publicly hanged. There was a bishop in the 13th century (qv Giles/Gilbert de Briouze) but their bright light burned out with William (V) who left only daughters, and the great Briouze estates in the county passed to the Mortimers, the Bohuns, the Cantilupes *et al.*

Briouze, Giles or **Gilbert de** (1170-1215), Bishop of Hereford 1200-15, the son of William (III) (qv), owed his bishopric to the favour King John (qv) was showing to his father at that time. Giles was bishop in times of conflict between King John and the barons and during the Interdict of Pope Innocent of 1208-14. An active, indeed warlike prelate, he did much building in the cathedral and maintained an office for diocesan business. He fled the wrath of John with relatives, going into exile in France after his father's rampage in Herefordshire, and spent much of his episcopate helping French bishops. He returned with other exiled bishops after the Pope had lifted the Interdict against England. In 1214 Giles made an alliance with Llywelyn ab Iorwerth (qv) which his brother Reginald (qv) sealed by marrying Llywelyn's daughter Gwladus. Giles died on 17 November 1215 in Worcester during negotiations for the release of his imprisoned nephews, the sons of William (IV) de Briouze (qv). He was buried in Hereford Cathedral and his later effigy lies in the north choir aisle holding a tower to symbolise his building work. He was succeeded as bishop by his Dean, Hugh de Mapenore (qv).

Briouze, Loretta de (d.*c*.1266), Countess of Leicester, daughter of William (III) (qv), married Robert de Breteuil, Earl of Leicester, who died on Crusade. She went with her family into exile and on return, like her sister Annora, entered an anchorage at Hackington, near Canterbury.

Briouze, Reginald de (d.1228), third son of William (III) (qv), married Graecia, daughter of William Brewer. After her death he allied himself with Llywelyn ab Iorwerth (qv) in rebellion against King John (qv), and married his daughter, Gwladus (qv). He and his brother, Bishop Giles (qv), seized their lands back from King John but had to pay a large fine.

Briouze, William (I) de (11th century), Lord of Bramber, was given lands in West Sussex after the Conquest, centred on Bramber Castle. His son Philip (d.1130s), 2nd Lord of Bramber, married Aenor of Totnes and won lands in Herefordshire and Wales.

Briouze, William (II) de (died after 1193), 3rd Lord of Bramber, son of Philip de Briouze (qv under William I) married Bertha of Hereford, one of the daughters of Miles of Gloucester (qv), Earl of Hereford and Brecknock, through whom he acquired further lands in the Marches. Their daughter Sybil (*c*.1157-1228) married first William de Ferrières, then Adam de Port (qv). William supported King Stephen (qv) during the Anarchy but was loyal to Henry II (qv) and assisted him in his invasion of Ireland. Henry appointed William Sheriff of Hereford. A powerful, violent man, he was 'the terror of the Marches'.

Briouze, William (III) de (d.1211), magnate, son of William (II) (qv) and one of the great landowners of the Marches, was Sheriff of Hereford under Richard I. He married Matilda de St Valéry (d.1210) and they had some 16 children. He helped King John (qv) secure his kingdom and was a bulwark against the Welsh. He was allowed to increase his territories in the Marches, picking up the barony of Kington which Adam de Port (qv) had forfeited. He was pardoned the debts he and his father had amassed, including £50 to the Jews of Hereford (qv Hamo). John began to distrust the might of the Briouzes, however, and turned against him, which led to the unrest of the Barons' Wars of the early 13th century. Briouze and Matilda may have known that John had murdered his nephew Arthur and so John sought to silence them. Matilda and her sons met King John in Hereford and handed over the de Briouze castles of Hay, Brecon and Radnor, but Briouze was furious and went on the rampage trying to recapture the castles. He burnt Brecon and its priory to the ground, sacked Leominster and took Weobley Castle, burning the town and massacring everyone he caught. The *Dore Abbey Chronicles* report that Briouze fled to Ireland in 1208. John captured his wife and son William (IV) and starved them to death in Corfe Castle. Briouze fled to France and died near Paris on 4 September 1211; he was buried in the abbey of St Victoire at Paris. Just before his own death John authorized one of Briouze's daughters, Margaret, to found the Grandmontine Priory at Craswall for the souls of her father, mother and brother, perhaps showing remorse. In 1216 she founded a priory for Augustinian nuns at Aconbury, whose church is now a diocesan storehouse. Margaret married Walter de Lacy (qv, d.1241). Of his other daughters Matilda married Gruffydd ap Rhys (II) (d.1201), the son of Lord Rhys (qv) of Deheubarth, Joanna married her father's client John de Balun (qv), Loretta (qv) married Robert de Breteuil and Annora married Hugh (III) de Mortimer (qv). Having been captured with her mother and brother, she was fortunate to be released by the Pope's order, and she entered an anchorage at Hackington.

Briouze, William (IV) de (d.1210), the eldest son of William (III) (qv), married Matilda the daughter of Richard de Clare, Earl of Hertford and they had four sons. He was murdered by King John with his mother in 1210. (See under William (III) de Briouze.) John also imprisoned his sons in Corfe Castle but they were released by Henry III (qv) in 1218.

Briouze, William (V) de (*c*.1200-30), son of Reginald (qv) and Graecia, married Eva daughter of William Marshal (qv), 2nd Earl of Pembroke. In 1228 Llywelyn the Great (qv) captured him, ransoming him for £2,000, and Briouze arranged a marriage between his daughter Isabella and Llywelyn's only son, Prince Dafydd. On a visit to Llywelyn at Easter 1230, however, Briouze was found in bed with Llywelyn's wife Joan, King John's daughter, and publicly hanged by Llywelyn on 2 May 1230. Eva married off her remaining daughters: Maud (*c*.1224-1301) to her cousin Roger (III) de Mortimer (qv); Eleanor (*c*.1226-51) to Humphrey (V) de Bohun (qv); and Eva (*c*.1227-55) to William (III) de Cantilupe (qv). With this the Briouze connection with Herefordshire ends, although *c*.1280 a Giles de Briouze (d.*c*.1305) married Maud de Whitney (qv); and Alice de Briouze married Ralph St Owen (qv St Owen, Ralph) in the 14th century.

Brito, John, see under **John le Breton**

Britto, Richard de (fl.1170), or Breton, one of the four knights that murdered Thomas Becket (qv) on 29 December 1170, lived in

Dorstone Castle. He was a follower of William fitz Empress, a brother of Henry II, whose marriage Becket had not allowed and who is said to have died of a broken heart in consequence. Britto's sword is said to have broken while hacking at the archbishop's head. The four knights were excommunicated by the Pope and required to go on lengthy pilgrimages.

Britto, Richard de (d.1275) rebuilt St Faith's Church at Dorstone in memory of his ancestor, Richard de Britto (qv, fl.1170), providing a chantry chapel for expiatory prayer. An inscription dedicates the chapel to the Virgin Mary 'as promised' in 1256. He built the Pandy Inn to house the workmen and is himself buried in St Faith's. A pewter chalice was found in his grave indicating that he was a priest but it has since been stolen. Bishop John de Breton (qv) of Hereford was a relative.

Britton, John (1771-1857), antiquary and topographer, was born on 7 July 1771 of humble origins in Wiltshire. He went to London and, as the impoverished apprentice of a wine merchant, began to educate himself. He published over 100 illustrated guides to Britain starting with *Beauties of Wiltshire* (1801). The 27 volumes of *The Beauties of England and Wales* took him 20 years to complete. He visited Herefordshire in 1798

on a walking tour, calling on Uvedale Price (qv), whom he greatly admired, at Foxley. He stayed in Hereford studying, measuring and drawing Hereford Cathedral, meeting John Thelwall (qv) in a bookshop. He published his work on Hereford Cathedral in his *Architectural Antiquities of Great Britain* and in his most successful multiple publication the *Cathedral Antiquities of England.* The illustrations in his *Engravings of the Cathedrals* (1814-35 in 14 volumes) were meticulously measured, drawn and described using the best engravers of his time. He supplied topographical plates for the work of the Pugins (qv), father and son. He was, like Pugin, a tireless worker and often on the brink of bankruptcy. He stands with Pugin and Ruskin as the originator of the Victorian gothic revival style. He was devoted to his wife and on her death married her niece. At the end of his life he wrote his autobiography. He died in London on 2 January 1857.

Brockhampton: The family (12th-13th centuries) was associated with the estate of that name east of Bromyard. A ruined 12th-century chapel from their time is said to be haunted. The name means a settlement by a brook and their house stood by a ford across the Paradise Brook, a tributary of the Teme. In 1283 the estate was sold to Robert de Furches (qv) and later to the Domultons (qv), descendants of the Brockhamptons and the builders of the timber-framed house, Lower Brockhampton.

Brodbelt, Ann (1751-1827), letter writer, was born on 1 January 1751 in Spanish Town, Jamaica, one of the two children of Thomas Penoyre (qv) of The Moor, Clifford. On 1 January 1770 Ann married the physician Francis Rigby Brodbelt (1746-95), son of Daniel and Anna Maria Brodbelt of Spanish Town, where they set up home. Dr Brodbelt provided medical care to wealthy plantation-owning families and was doctor to the prison. They had three children: a son, Francis (1771-1827), and two daughters, Ann (1774-1828), and Jane (1779-1856), all educated in England because Dr Brodbelt believed strongly in female education. Francis inherited The Moor when the Penoyre line died out at Clifford. Ann is remembered for the letters she wrote to the girls over the next ten years, published by her descendant, Geraldine Mozley, under the title *Letters to Jane from Jamaica* (1938). They vividly describe the English attempt at genteel life in Jamaica under the constant threat of disease and revolt. In 1795 Dr Brodbelt died and Ann returned to England to live with her daughters and then in Bath. On her death on 6 September 1827 she was buried in the Penoyre family grave at Clifford Church.

Brome, William (1664-1745), antiquarian, son of John Brome, was born at Eau Withington, north-east of Hereford and educated at Christ Church, Oxford. He married Jane, daughter of Griffiths Raignold, Registrar of Hereford and they had a large family. Brome's sister married Joseph Harvey (qv), the headmaster of Hereford Cathedral School. Brome was a non-juror, refusing to foreswear his oath to James II after his exclusion; his ability to travel was restricted and most professions were closed to him. He was a friend of the Jacobite diarist and antiquarian Thomas Hearne (qv, d.1735). Many non-jurors engaged in antiquarian research to find evidence that the House of Orange had usurped the throne, and Anglo-Saxon studies advanced greatly in this period. Brome knew Thomas Blount (qv) and had read his manuscript notes for a history of Herefordshire. George Hickes (qv), Anglo-Saxon scholar and non-juring bishop hid with Brome at Eau Withington for more than a year in 1697, a period he is said to have remembered as the best part of his life. He was also a friend of Hereford physician William Brewster (qv), Edward Harley (qv, d.1741) and Susanna Hopton (qv), whom he memorably described. He was buried in the chancel of St Peter's Church, Withington. Brome's daughter Elizabeth (1703-97) married William Jauncey (b.1690) of All Saints Parish, Hereford and they were buried at Stretton Grandison. Bromes lived at Eau Withington throughout the 18th century: a James Brome (d.1770) married Mercy Beata Geers (qv under Thomas Geers d.1750) in 1745.

Bromyard, John (fl.1326-82), Dominican friar at the Blackfriars Priory in Widemarsh, Hereford (established 1322), was licensed to hear confessions in Herefordshire in 1326. He wrote a series of guides to help preachers with their sermons and was himself an influential preacher. In 1382 he became chancellor of Cambridge University.

Brookes, Henry (1816-84), shoemaker and fossil collector, was baptised in Eastnor on 29 December 1816, the son of John Brookes, a carpenter employed on the building of Eastnor Castle, and his wife Anne. He was apprenticed to a Ledbury tanner and became a cobbler. In 1842 he married Ann, daughter of Benjamin Bennett of the Packhorse Inn in Ledbury's Homend, where they brought up their large family. He was an amateur geologist and inspected the fossiliferous Aymestrey and Downton beds at Dog Hill, Ledbury in the 1850s when they were exposed by work on the Worcester to Hereford railway line. In these Silurian and Devonian strata Brookes and George Piper (qv) found fossils that supported Murchison's (qv) controversial claims for a new system in the Lower Paleozoic which he had christened *Silurian*. Brookes displayed his large fossil collection on the walls of his house and was visited by such students of geology as the members of the Woolhope Club. He was captain of Ledbury belltower. He died in Ledbury on 16 April 1884.

Broughton, Edward (*c*.1570-*c*.1650), from an old Kington family, married Isabel, daughter of Rafe Beeston and lived in the Manor House at Canon Pyon. John Aubrey (qv) talked to him in 1646 when he was nearly 80 and thought him the handsomest man he ever saw, 'very wise ... of an admirable Elocution'. He was Col Massey's (qv) commissary in the Civil Wars and one of the committee that administered the Herefordshire region for Parliament. Aubrey's grandfather Lyte lived near him and remembered Broughton's great gift for praying and, his grandmother added, his wife was as good as he was. Aubrey notes his experiments with fertilisation of the land: 'He was the first that used the Improvement of Land by Soape-Ashes when he lived at Bristowe, where they then threw it away ... This I had from himself.'

Broughton, Elizabeth 'Bess' (*c*.1620-*c*.70), courtesan, the daughter of Edward (qv) and Isabel, was 'a most exquisite beautie, as finely shaped as Nature could frame; had a delicate Witt'. Aubrey heard she 'lost her Maydenhead to a poor young fellow' at Canon Pyon, now 'a pittifull poor old weaver, Clarke of the Parish'. Her father tried locking her up but she climbed down a rope and went to London where 'her price was very deare'. She was the Earl of Dorset's mistress for a time. Aubrey had heard that at last she 'gott the Pox, of which she died'. He relates some indecent songs that were sung about her in London and quotes a passage about her in Ben Jonson's *Execrations against Vulcan*.

Brown, Jonathan, Dean of Hereford 1637-43, was educated at Gloucester Hall, Oxford and ordained. He married Ann Barne Lovelace (a half sister of Richard Lovelace the poet). His daughter Ann married Herbert Croft (qv, d.1691) who succeeded him as dean. Brown, rector of London parishes, was appointed a canon and Dean of Hereford. He graduated as Doctor of Divinity. Bishop Lindsell (qv) tried to hold a visitation but Brown resisted him. Dean and chapter came under the Presbyterian scrutiny of Sir Robert Harley (qv, d.1656), who reported to Parliament on the superstitious practices in Hereford – a 'babel of confusion', it seemed to him. Cathedral statutes were revised under Bishop Wren (qv), but civil war loomed and Dean Brown died in the disturbances and was buried at Hartingfordbury Church, Herts, where he had been vicar in quieter times.

Brown, Lancelot 'Capability' (1716-83), landscape designer, was born in Northumberland where he learnt his trade. He married Bridget Wayett in 1744 and they had a daughter Bridget and three sons. By the age of 25 he had

become Viscount Cobham's head gardener at Stowe and he was later employed by George III. He was known for his quick assessment of the capabilities of the estate. Marking out the broad outlines of his vision, he would leave specialist supervisors in charge of the works: a lake-maker, builder, nurseryman etc. He worked on Croome Park estate throughout his career and designed the house there. His last project was the park at Berrington (1775) which Thomas Harley (qv, d.1804) had recently bought. Brown brought in his partner and son-in-law Henry Holland (qv) to design Berrington Hall. Brown chose the location for the house and laid out the site with sweeping views to the Black Mountains, having his lake-makers dig the 14-acre 'Pool' below by hand. He planted the semi-natural landscape, for which he was famous, with groups of trees and shrubs, only now in their full maturity. The view from the dining-room windows across the park forms a 'picturesque' Claudian image, pastoral yet restrained. He also placed a walled garden with rare fruit trees by the house. He worked at Moccas Park for Sir George Amyand (qv Cornewall), improving and enhancing the deer park with its ancient oaks and chestnuts. Brown died while still working on 6 February 1783 and was buried on his estate at Fenstanton, (now Hunts). During his last years he had begun to be seen as old-fashioned by doyens of the picturesque such as T.A. Knight and Uvedale Price (qqv).

Brown, Thomas (1798-1880), Roman Catholic Bishop of Newport and Menevia, was born in Bath and educated at Acton Burnell, near Shrewsbury where a Benedictine community from Douai was in exile. He joined them as Brother Joseph and in 1814 they moved to Downside Abbey, near Bath, where St Thomas of Hereford's (qv Cantilupe) skull is held. Brown was ordained priest and engaged in polemic at a time when Roman Catholicism was being legalized. He was the first bishop of a large diocese which included Herefordshire and Wales. In 1854 he was involved in the founding of Belmont Abbey, given by Francis Wegg-Prosser (qv), which became his cathedral when his diocese was curtailed. His home was Manor House, Lower Bullingham where he died on 12 April 1880. He was buried at Belmont Priory where there is a monument to him made by E.W. Pugin (qv) in 1880.

Browne: A Much Dewchurch family who bought the Harewood estate from the Thornhills (qv) in 1547. The estate had been given to the Knights Templar of Garway by King John (qv) in 1215 and the Brownes built a preceptory which passed to the Knights Hospitaller. They spent a fortune building a large house with several towers, which left them impoverished; it was sold to Bennet Hoskyns (qv) in 1654.

Broy, William de (fl.1293) was a Norman knight who held Aylton manor from the king. His feudal rent was a mounted man for 40 days a year, but was commuted by cash-hungry King Edward I (qv) to 24 shillings p.a. William himself had 38 tenants. In the late 13th century he gave 6 acres of land at Aylton to Little Malvern Priory on which to found a monastery. Aylton Priory survived until the dissolution of the minor houses in 1536 and a structure survives today as Priors Court. Two priors from this small house have left a trace in the historical record: Adam and William (qqv).

Brugge, Elizabeth (*c*.1510-68), daughter of Rowland Brugge of The Ley, Weobley, married, secondly, Sir Ralph Vane (d.1552) a distinguished soldier. They lived at Penshurst until Vane, a supporter of Edward Seymour, Duke of Somerset, was executed after Seymour's fall. Elizabeth was a patron of Robert Crowley (qv) and other Protestants, for which she suffered under Queen Mary (qv), going into hiding. She died and was buried at Holborn.

Brugge, Walter (fl.1380-1400), a well-educated priest, was Roger (VII) Mortimer's (qv) receiver-general. Mortimer was away in Ireland for much of his short life and was dependent on Brugge for his financial affairs. He rewarded Brugge with a prebendary at St David's and the archdeaconry of Meath in Ireland.

Brut, Walter or **Bryt** (fl.1393), astronomer and Lollard, from the Welsh gentry, was educated at Merton College, Oxford, a centre of astronomical studies. He taught astronomy there and was the author of the treatise *Theorica planetarum* on the movement of the planets and other astronomical works. He was the 'Gualterius Bryte' who was tried for heresy before Bishop Mascall (qv) in Hereford in 1393. Brut's eloquent defence and recantation in Latin are extant but the outcome is unclear; he presumably won his case. Langland (qv) mentions him favourably in *Piers Plowman*: 'he said him the sothe'. Bishop Trefnant (qv) was frustrated by the ease with which Herefordshire Lollards recanted but then continued to preach heresy.

Brute, Aaron (18th century) stonemason and building contractor, lived at Blaenavon near Abergavenny, Monmouthshire. He dug a level iron ore mine near Forgeside and an iron bridge and horse-drawn railway to serve it, with a row of terraced housing erected for his workers. The Brute family of monumental masons (fl.1721-1850) are noted in Herefordshire for their rustic rococo wall plaques in many of the churches in the west of the county. A typical one at Walterstone signed by Aaron is to Nicholas Price (d.1775). Clodock and

Rowlestone have several with charming sentimental verses, viz.:

These lovely babes so young and fair
Cut off by early doom
Just came to show how sweet these flowers
In paradise do bloom.

Bryant, Andrew (fl.1822-35), cartographer, surveyed 13 counties including, in 1835, Herefordshire in a 1½ inch: 1 mile format. He was driven out of business in 1835 by the government's new Ordnance Survey.

Brydges (also Brugge and Bridges): a family descended from Sir Simon de Brugge (b.1272), who married Mary Solers (qv) of Bridge Sollers; their son was Sir John de Brugge. A branch of the family settled in Gloucestershire where they married into the Chandos barony. In Bishop Swinfield's (qv) *Household Rolls* a Thomas de Brugge is recorded as his 'pugilus' or champion. In the 14th century they began to represent the county in Parliament; their seat was at The Ley, Weobley where *c.*1380 Sir Thomas Brugge married Elizabeth, daughter of Nicholas de Apperley (qv) of Deerhurst. Their offspring were frequently Sheriffs of Hereford. Sir John de Brugge (*c.*1368-1436) of Ross was Garter King of Arms. The main Brydges seat was Wilton Castle from the 1550s and they were buried at Peterstow. They were also found at Tyberton Court and Dewsall Court, Old Colwall and Bosbury.

Brydges, Charles (d.1619), second son of Sir John (qv, d.1557), married Jane Carne, another relation of the Greys. He bought Wilton Castle from his mother's uncle William Grey (qv), 13th Lord Wilton, for 25,000 crowns.

Brydges, Giles (*c.*1573-1637), 1st Baronet of Wilton Castle, eldest son of Charles (qv), was educated at St Albans Hall, Oxford. He married Mary, daughter of Sir James Scudamore (qv, d.1619). Through Chandos patronage he was MP for Tewkesbury in 1621-2, and through that of his father-in-law MP for Herefordshire 1625-9 and High Sheriff of Herefordshire in 1628. He was created 1st Baronet Brydges in 1627.

Brydges, Henry (1708-71), 2nd Duke of Chandos and Viscount Wilton of Wilton Castle, was born on 17 January 1708, the second son and heir of James (qv, d.1744). George II called him 'a hot-headed, passionate, half-witted coxcomb'. He represented Hereford in Parliament from 1727 to 1734. In 1728 he married Lady Mary (1710-38), daughter of Charles Bruce, the 4th Earl of Elgin and she bore him his heir, James Brydges, who would be the 3rd Duke. After Lady Mary's death and that of his father Henry witnessed a wife sale at an inn in Newbury. The woman, Anne Wells, was a chambermaid at the inn and, touched by her patient acquiescence as she stood with a halter around her neck in the inn yard, the Duke bought her, marrying her on Christmas Day 1744. This unconventional marriage lasted until Anne's death in 1759. In 1767, he married for the third time to Elizabeth (1731-1813) daughter of Sir John Major. He died on 28 November 1771. The Brydges now have little connection with the county. See William Egerton for Edward Brydges (1712-80) and his son Sir Egerton Brydges (1762-1837).

Brydges, James (1555-1603) rebuilt The Ley at Weobley as a splendid timber-framed house.

Brydges, James (1642-1714), 3rd Baronet of Wilton and 8th Baron Chandos of Sudeley, was born in September 1642 at Dewsall Court. He was educated at St John's College, Oxford. He married Elizabeth Barnard (1643-1719) from a family of bankers and they had 14 children. He was Sheriff of Herefordshire 1667-8. He inherited the barony of Chandos from the Gloucestershire branch of the family when William Brydges, 7th Baron Chandos (qv John Chandos) died. He was Ambassador of the Turkey Company to Constantinople. His daughter Mary married his neighbour Sir Hungerford Hoskyns (qv, d.1767) and his eldest son James (qv, d.1744) became the 1st Duke of Chandos. Sir James died on 16 October 1714 and was buried at Aconbury.

Brydges, James (1674-1744), 1st Duke of Chandos, Privy Councillor, was born at Dewsall Court on 6 January 1674, the son and heir of Sir James (qv, d.1714). He was educated at Westminster School and New College, Oxford, learning to enjoy books and music but leaving without a degree. He travelled in Germany, making contacts in the Electoral Court at Hanover that were to prove useful in the coming reign. In 1695 he married Mary (1668-1712), daughter of Sir Thomas Lake of Cannons, Middlesex and they had two sons. Cannons, one of the most splendid houses in England of its time, now became the seat of the Brydges family. He rebuilt it in a majestic style satirised by Alexander Pope (qv) as 'Timon's Villa', using the best architects of the day. It is now demolished. Another property, Aconbury House in Herefordshire, was sold to Guy's Hospital in 1730. He was MP for Hereford from 1698 to 1714 and had a residence in Castle Street, Hereford. He was created Viscount Wilton and Earl Carnarvon and, in 1719, Duke of Chandos. In 1720 he presented Hereford Cathedral with £50 for Bishop Philip Bisse's (qv) renovations and sent his picture agent in Genoa 'forty dozen of Herefordshire Redstreak Cider' (qv Redstreak). He was a Fellow of the Royal Society and a commissioner to the Admiralty. Marlborough made him paymaster of the queen's forces from which he made a great amount of money. After the death of Mary he married Cassandra Willoughby (1670-1735), daughter of his aunt Emma Barnard. The new King George I created him Duke of Carnarvon. On the death of the much loved Duchess Cassandra in 1735 he married, thirdly, Lydia Catharina (1693-1750) the wealthy widow of Sir Thomas Davall and daughter of John Vanhatten, a London merchant. His eldest son died and the next, Henry Marquess of Carnarvon, became his heir. The duke died at Cannons on 9 August 1744 and was buried in St Lawrence's, Little Stanmore, with his first two wives. His wives kept a

record of family life in which the duke is shown as generous, sympathetic and kindly if formal: on beating an opponent in a duel for instance he apologised and invited him to dinner. Contemporaries thought him princely. He was a great patron of music and Handel wrote *Acis and Galatea* and the Chandos Anthems while staying at Cannons.

Brydges, John (1492-1557), 1st Lord Chandos of Sudeley, was born at Coberley, Gloucs. The eldest son of Sir Giles Brydges, knight of the body to Henry VIII, he himself served the king both as groom of the chamber and with diplomatic and military service, for which he was knighted. He owned the manor of Lugwardine which he sold to Richard Warnecombe (qv). He married Elizabeth (d.1559), daughter of Edmund Grey 9th Baron Grey of Wilton (qv). They had seven sons, including Edmund Brydges (d.1573), 2nd Baron Chandos, Charles (qv), and three daughters. Lady Jane Grey (qv), a distant relation of his wife, asked for his support to hold the throne but Brydges, a Catholic, did not respond and in fact was responsible for the collapse of Wyatt's rebellion by threatening to fire on him if he crossed London Bridge to enter London. He accompanied Queen Mary (qv) into London and was later rewarded by her consort Philip with the barony of Sudeley.

Brydges, John (1623-52), 2nd Baronet, a son of Sir Giles (qv), married Mary, daughter and heiress of John Pearle (qv) of Dewsall. As her dower she brought the Jacobean manor house Dewsall Court, which can still be seen. She had previously been married to Sir William Hinson of Pengethley. Their son John Brydges (d.1669) of Priors Court married a daughter of Herbert Aubrey (qv, d.1691). Sir John acquired from the Pearles (qv) the conventual buildings of Aconbury Priory, which he rebuilt as his residence. He served in Ireland during the Civil War to keep clear of the conflict in England. He refused to let a garrison into Wilton Castle, which Silas Taylor (qv) called 'a very faire, sweet dwelling house'. Although it was not defensible, Governor Barnabas Scudamore (qv) and Sir Henry Lingen (qv) burnt it down one Sunday while the family were at church. Brydges died of smallpox on 21 February 1652 and is buried at Peterstow.

Brydges, John (1671-1742) of Bosbury was the second son of William and Ursula Brydges of Colwall. He was a lawyer at New Inn, London where he died on 4 August 1742. He was buried in Holy Trinity Church, Bosbury, and his nephew, John Brydges (1711-44), placed a wall plaque by Thomas White (qv) to commemorate him. This also records another John Brydges, who died on 14 January 1744, son of Thomas and Margaret Brydges of Bosbury. Another member of the Old Colwall branch, Elizabeth (d.*c*.1710), married Bridstock Harford (qv under Richard Harford). This branch subsequently adopted Brydges as a surname. Dr William Brewster (qv) married Susan the daughter of Francis Brydges of Castle Street, Hereford, and persuaded Brydges to give his friend William Brome (qv), a restricted non-juror, permission to travel to Oxford in 1710. The Brydges inherited Brewster's house in Widemarsh Street, the Mansion House.

Brydges, William (1601-88), a son of Sir Giles, bought the estate of Tyberton from Kynard de la Bere (qv) in 1650 and had John Abel (qv) rebuild Tyberton Court and repair the dilapidated chapel, adding a steeple and bells. The oldest of his four sons, Marshall Brydges (1634-1709), inherited the estate and became High Sheriff of Herefordshire. Marshall's eldest son Francis William was a barrister at the Middle Temple. He settled Tyberton on his son William, who began to build a grander house and church, using John Wood of Bath (qv) who had worked for his cousin the Duke of Chandos (qv). Tyberton Court was sadly demolished but the church rebuilt at this time (1728-31) remains, with its rich carving on the eastern apse. It is instructive to note that St Mary's, despite all the rebuilding, keeps its Norman south door. The family was proud of its modernity *and* its antiquity.

Buca (fl.early 8th century) was the servant of King Æthelbald of Mercia, who gave him three hides of land at Acton Beauchamp for a religious community. Lay control of religious foundations was common at this time but beginning to be deprecated. A fragment of an early 9th-century cross shaft has been used as a lintel in this isolated church.

Buchanan, Robert (1852-1920) was born in Glasgow. He married Jeanie Rae Turnbull (d.1937) and they had three daughters. After time in the army and ranching in America Robert bought a flour mill in Liverpool and his two sons, Alan and Robert, were born. In 1912 he bought the Bosbury House estate for his eldest son Alan, but Alan was killed in 1915 at the Battle of Hooge and his other son Robert was unwilling to manage the farms. So, in memory of Alan, his father offered most of the estate to the Board of Agriculture to be held on trust as smallholdings for discharged servicemen, retaining Bosbury House and some farmland. Robert and Jeanie Rae are buried in Bosbury churchyard. Hereford Council took over the management of the Trust in 1972.

Buck, Marian (1857-1947), educationalist, was born Marian Walker at Birstall near Leicester in 1851, the daughter of a boot and shoe manufacturer. She moved with her father to Stanley Hill, Bosbury while a child but married Dr William Edgar Buck (d.1886) in Leicester; they had no children. In 1877 they founded the Leicester School of Cookery which became the North Midland Training School of Cookery in 1890. She published several cookery books and, after Dr Buck's death, moved to Camp End House at British Camp in Herefordshire, founding a residential school at Evendine Court, Colwall with Anna Brander and Mary Worthington, which provided domestic training for girls. She retired to Bosbury and, in 1907, designed and had built The Noverings as her home. She acquired land and properties in Bosbury and bought the Old Vicarage from Willoughby Baskerville Mynors (qv); she presented the vicarage to the parish as the village hall. She also presented the war memorial to Bosbury. A window in the church is dedicated to her.

Buck, Samuel (1696-1779) and **Nathaniel** (*c*.1700-between 1760 and 1774) were topographical draughtsmen from Yorkshire who, saddened by the neglect of antiquities, set out to record and engrave the ancient monuments of England and Wales. They began in 1726 from their base in Soho, London, initially with William Stukeley (qv), systematically covering the country. Samuel married Catherine Faussett in 1727 and Nathaniel a Rebecca. By the 1730s the brothers had reached Herefordshire, where they sketched Bronsil, Brampton Bryan, Wigmore and Goodrich Castles and buildings in the City of Hereford, engraving them back in London. Their work was published in *Views of Ruins of Castles & Abbeys in England 1726-1739* which could be bought in individual sheets. Their travels and recording work continued for a long time after this. After Nathaniel's death Samuel, despite their labours, lived in poverty and was supported by subscription from admirers. He died aged 83 on 17 August 1779 and was buried in St Clement Danes.

Buckler, John Chessell (1793-1894), architect, was the eldest son of John Buckler, land agent for Oxford University and an artist who produced etchings of historic buildings and interested his son in the practice of architecture. Buckler junior was employed by John Habington Barney Lutley (qv) in 1871 to restore the 15th-century manor house Lower Brockhampton near Bromyard, creating the house we see today. He was drastic by modern standards and removed the upper floor in the Hall. It had been used as a farmhouse ever since the Barneby family built Brockhampton House on higher ground (qv Bartholomew Barneby Lutley). He wrote and illustrated books on the history of British architecture.

du Buisson, Edmund (d.1914), rector of Breinton, had the dilapidated church rebuilt (1868-70) by Kempson (qv), who also built the rectory (1866-7), now Breinton Grange, for his curates. Revd du Buisson built a school for 40 children. He lived at Breinton Court with his wife Charlotte and their five children. One of his daughters, Edith, was a watercolourist and another, Lucy, played the harmonium in church and married a curate but died young. His son John Clement du Buisson (1871-1938), educated at Hereford Cathedral School and Magdalen College, Oxford, was Dean of St Asaph's. His grandson Henry Victor was Bishop of Lebombo Land in northeastern South Africa and is buried in Breinton churchyard; the east window of St Michael's is dedicated to Revd du Buisson.

Bull, Henry Graves (1818-85), physician and naturalist, was born in Northants a farmer's son and studied medicine at the Northampton Infirmary and at Edinburgh and Paris Universities. He came to Hereford in 1841, living at Harley House by the cathedral where a plaque now commemorates him. Here he was joined by his widowed mother and a sister. Dr Bull began his medical practice at Hereford Dispensary, where he treated patients for the next 40 years. He married Elizabeth Read (1831-1915) in 1854 and had four sons, who

all went to the Hereford Cathedral School, and four daughters. He was appointed physician to the Infirmary (the neglected building can be seen in Union Street) where he was amongst the first to use ether in operations. This was an unpaid post which he filled for the rest of his life. He was also Medical Officer at Hereford Prison. His interest in the health of the poor led to research into the incidence of infectious diseases, especially in St Owen's Parish of Hereford, the most disease-ridden. He attributed this to the open drains, the contaminated wells and the filthy state of the Castle Pool and was called as an expert witness by the 1853 Board of Health inquiry. He helped set up the Hereford Friendly Society and was involved in the founding of the free Permanent Library in Broad Street, acting as librarian. He was a member of the Herefordshire Literary, Philosophical and Antiquarian Institution but as a botanist found the society too antiquarian and, in 1851, helped start the Woolhope Naturalists' Field Club. A special interest was fungi and he led the club's celebrated annual Fungus Forays, out of which grew the British Mycological Society. He chaired the committee and gave the project constant guidance. Reference to Dr Bull – a bull and some toadstools – is found amongst the terracotta carvings on the façade of Kempson's library building in Broad Street. Another interest was mistletoe, on which he contributed a paper. He was an authority on species of fruit and a member of the club's Pomona Committee. With Dr Hogg (qv) of the RHS he was appointed general editor of the *Herefordshire Pomona, or The Apple Trees of Herefordshire* (1878) which listed known species of apple and pear. The two folio volumes were beautifully illustrated in Bull's drawing room by his eldest daughter Edith (1860-1921), helped by a professional artist, Alice Blanche Ellis (qv). They painted watercolours of the fruit described which were then reproduced by a chromo-lithographic process in Belgium and published by the Hereford firm Jakeman & Carver (qv). Bull cooperated with Hogg on their synopsis of the Pomona: *The Apple and the Pear as Vintage Fruits* (1880), where he cites various writers on the virtues of Herefordshire's Redstreak (qv) cider apple. He was President of the Woolhope Club and long the editor of its *Transactions*, and was working on his *Notes on the Birds of Herefordshire* in 1885 when he died. His daughter Maude (d.1951) made great contributions to the cataloguing of the cathedral library.

Bull, John (*c*.1563-1628), organist and composer, was born either at Old Radnor in the diocese of Hereford or in Hereford City where he certainly lived as a child. He was a chorister in Hereford Cathedral and in 1582 was appointed organist and, soon after, master of the choristers. In 1583 Elizabeth's statute for reorganising music in cathedrals came into effect and Bull oversaw its implementation in Hereford. He had an often turbulent relationship with Dean and Chapter but kept rooms in Hereford for many years. Bull had studied with William Byrd at Oxford and Cambridge. In 1586 he was appointed organist of the Chapel Royal and over the years he played before Queen Elizabeth, King James and Prince Henry. From 1596 to 1607 he was professor of music at

Gresham College, where he gave twice weekly lectures, and made musical instruments. He married an Elizabeth Walter in 1617 and they had a child. In 1617, fleeing from legal action in England, he was appointed organist at Antwerp Cathedral, and court musician for Archduke Albrecht in Brussels. He died in 1628, a brilliant keyboard performer and a master of counterpoint, an innovative and learned composer for the keyboard, viol and voice. He is commemorated in Hereford Cathedral with a plaque.

Bulmer, Charles Henry (1833-1918), rector of Credenhill, married Mary Grace Parnell Cockrem. He came from a family of Hereford wine merchants and cider makers and made prize-winning cider and perry. He was a Woolhope Club member and as President when the Pomona Committee was formed, he invited Dr Hogg (qv) of the RHS to assist them.

Bulmer, Edward Frederick (1865-1941) and **Henry Percival** (1867-1919), cider-makers, sons of Revd Charles Bulmer (qv), were born at the rectory, Credenhill: Fred on 26 May 1865 and Percy on 28 January 1867. Percy (below left) went to the Hereford Cathedral School (1880-86), but was often ill at home. He experimented with fruit from the orchard to improve the cider his father made. Cider was crude at this time but Percy saw a market for a superior drink and, advised by his father, in the autumn of 1887 began to produce a small amount of cider in a more scientific manner. Fred (below right) went to Hereford Cathedral and Shrewsbury Schools and read classics at King's College, Cambridge. He helped Percy in the vacations and, on leaving university, joined him in the project. The cider they made won prizes from the first: in Paris in 1888 and at the Royal Agricultural Show in 1889. Encouraged by their success they and their father raised funds, bought adjoining land and invested in modern industrial equipment. Percy handled the science, investigating the latest production methods on the Continent, while Fred did the marketing. He pioneered modern advertising on posters and in the press and presented the celebrated Woodpecker brand. Production went up 500%. Percy married Susan Ball (1871-1968) and they had four sons. Fred married Sophie Ritter (1874-1968) and they had three sons and three daughters. The brothers remained partners until Percy became ill and retired in 1918. When Fred retired in 1938 Bulmers had become the biggest cider producer in Britain, producing four million gallons a year. In 1970 it became a public limited company. H.P. Bulmer & Co. had a programme of social care, introducing a family benefits scheme and superannuation, and the firm built housing for its workers and funded the rebuilding of Hereford Cathedral's Henry Willis (qv) organ in the

1930s, as their woodpecker logo on the organ attests. Percy Bulmer died on 2 December 1919 from cancer aged 52 at his home, Longmeadow in Hereford, and Fred on 2 September 1941 aged 76 at Adam's Hill, Breinton. There is a plaque to them all in Credenhill Church.

Bunn, Frances (1871-1921) was an enamellist from West Bromwich who trained at Birmingham Municipal School of Art, where she was a star pupil, winning the Board of Education's Silver Medal in 1903. She painted in enamels on copper, often portraits. A good example of her work can be seen in Hereford Cathedral commemorating G.R. Sinclair (qv), the director of music, at his organ. Some of her works are held in the Birmingham and the Victoria and Albert museums.

Burgh, Hubert de (*c.*1160-1243), 1st Earl of Kent, was High Sheriff of Herefordshire in 1215. He was loyal to John in the Barons' Wars and is mentioned in Magna Carta as advisor to the king. During King Henry III's minority he was Regent of England. His three wives were Beatrice de Warrenne with whom he had two sons, Isabel, the divorced wife of King John, and Princess Margaret of Scotland. He was governor of Hereford Castle until 1223, when he was required to surrender it to Bishop Hugh Foliot (qv). He is buried at Holborn Blackfriars.

Burghill: the family were based at Withington through the centuries.

Burghill, Arnold of Thinghall Parva married, as his second wife, Grizell, co-heiress of John Prise of Ocle Pychard. They had a daughter, Catherine, who married Alexander Stanhope (qv).

Burghill, John (*c.*1330-1414), bishop, was the son of Thomas and Sybilla, an armigerous family of Thinghill, Withington. He had two brothers, William and Thomas and at least one sister. He entered the Dominican House of Blackfriars at Hereford, the preaching order whose priory ruins can be seen off Widemarsh Street, where he was a protégé of Prior Rushook (qv). He was made a priest by Bishop John Trillek (qv) in 1354. Rushook was a confessor of Richard II (qv) and introduced Burghill into the royal household, where he also became a confessor and a friend of the young king. Rushook arranged for Burghill to succeed him as Bishop of Llandaff, being consecrated by the Pope in Rome in 1396. In 1398 Richard had Burghill translated to the richer see of Coventry and Lichfield, attending his enthronement personally. Burghill was close to the king during Rushook's disgrace and accompanied him on his Irish expedition. He witnessed Bolingbroke's usurpation as Henry IV (qv) and Richard II's death, probably by starvation. He was the only bishop to attend Richard's funeral in 1400, aged about 70. He retired to his diocese and died at Lichfield in 1414.

Burghill, Richard (d.1492) is the subject of a brass in Hereford Cathedral on which he is described as master and instructor. This is presumably an early reference to the Cathedral School.

Burhill, Robert (*sic*) (1572-1641), clergyman, descended from the Burghill family, was born at Dymock, Gloucs. He was a fellow at Oxford noted for his Greek and Hebrew learning, and was elected to a Hereford canonry and the rectory of Peterstow in 1604. He wrote and assisted in the writing of others' books. He was DD in 1632, and died at his Norfolk rectory of Northwold where he is buried.

Burley, Simon (*c.*1336-88), knight and courtier, was the son of a Herefordshire gentry family, perhaps in the Lyonshall area where he later held lands. He served under Edward the Black Prince (qv Edward of Woodstock) in France and Spain, was captured and exchanged. He married Marguerite de Beausse. He was tutor to Richard II (qv) and became his close friend. He helped arrange the king's marriage and was rewarded with the Order of the Garter and lands along the Marches from the Mortimer (qv) estates, and was granted the right to hold a market at Lyonshall. In 1384 he became Warden of the Cinque Ports. He was involved in the Lords Appellant revolt (qv Henry IV) and, as a royal favourite, was arraigned and executed at Tower Hill on 5 May 1388, despite the king's pleading. Richard later erected a monument to him at St Mary Graces, a Cistercian abbey in Smithfield, London.

Burne-Jones, Edward Coley (1833-98), artist, stayed whilst young with his friends the Caswells in Hereford and attended services at the cathedral. He remembered the beauty of the cathedral in contrast with the noise of his industrial Birmingham home as paradise, his wife Georgiana recorded. She thought he owed his conversion to Anglo-Catholicism to the experience. He met his friend Revd John Goss in Hereford, and Goss introduced him to the ideas of the Oxford Movement and to Newman's sermons which had an influence on him. Mr Caswell encouraged Burne-Jones' attempts to draw and introduced him to his relation Charles Spozzi, a Hereford art collector with whom Burne-Jones stayed, enjoying the Cox (qv) drawings on his walls. There is much work by Burne-Jones in the county, mostly stained glass made by Morris & Co. from reused cartoons, in Coddington, Dormington, St Peter's Hereford, Ledbury, Leysters and Moreton on Lugg.

The Morris & Co. tapestries (1902) at Brockhampton by Ross are also from cartoons drawn in 1879 by Burne-Jones, originally for stained glass for Salisbury Cathedral.

Burnel, Matilda (fl. before 1318) was a venerable matron who was buried before the high altar of Dore Abbey. A manuscript in Hereford Cathedral library records a miracle that was associated with Matilda's remains in 1318 and drew pilgrims.

Butler, John (1717-1802), Bishop of Hereford 1788-1802, was born in Hamburg on 27 December 1717. He was educated at University College, Oxford and ordained. He became chaplain at Court and preached before the House of Commons. He pleased the Whig administration with his popular pamphlets and, assiduous at Court, was rewarded with the archdeaconry of Surrey (1769-82). In 1777 he secured the bishopric of Oxford and in 1788 was translated to the see of Hereford. He chose James Wyatt (qv), whom he had met at Oxford, as architect to replace the fallen west front of Hereford Cathedral, a choice universally regretted. Another friend from Oxford, Revd Napleton (qv) became his chaplain. He was more in evidence at Hereford than his predecessor, Bishop Beauclerk (qv), holding three visitations and maintaining clerical discipline. He married twice but had no children. He published *Select Sermons* (1801) and died on 10 December 1802. There is a copper wall-plaque to him in the eastern ambulatory of the cathedral.

Byfield, George (*c.*1756-1813), architect, was a pupil of Sir Robert Taylor before opening his own office in London. In 1793 he exhibited designs for alterations to Kinnersley Castle for Thomas Clutton. In 1799 he worked at Madresfield Court for the Earl of Beauchamp and, in the same year, he built the chapel at Brockhampton by Bromyard for John Barneby Lutley (qv) in Regency Gothick, unusual for him. Inside is a neo-classical monument by Byfield to his patron's father Bartholomew Barneby Lutley (qv). The charming little building with its small tower has recently been renovated and is in occasional use. He built the Lower Lodge, which stands off the Worcester to Bromyard road on the edge of the Brockhampton Estate, in another of his styles, with a sturdy portico modelled on St Paul's Covent Garden. He regularly exhibited at the Royal Academy, his work often showing the influence of Robert Adam (qv). He died in London on 8 August 1813.

Byron, George Gordon (1788-1824), 6th Baron Byron, poet of the Romantic Revival movement, was born on 22 January 1788. Lord Byron shocked Regency society with his morals and amongst his lovers was Jane Elizabeth Harley (qv), Countess of Oxford, Lord Harley's estranged wife, whose 'autumnal charms' suited Byron. He stayed at Eywood (near Titley) and, in 1812-3, Kinsham Court. Here, sitting under the great cedar, he wrote the first two cantos of *Childe Harold* and dedicated the poem to Lady Oxford. He was a friend of Charles Skinner Matthews (qv), a son of Dr John Matthews of Belmont where he also stayed. He died on 19 April 1824 of a fever contracted at Missolonghi where he was fighting for Greek independence.

C

Cadwallador, Roger (1567-1610), Roman Catholic priest, was born at Stretton Sugwas the eldest son of a prosperous yeoman, John Cadwallador. The family was pious and learned, bilingual in Welsh and English. In 1590 Roger went to Rheims to train as a priest, and he was ordained at Valladolid. He returned to Herefordshire in 1593 and travelled the county on foot, saying mass in Catholic houses like Whitfield and Stretton Courts. In 1595 he encouraged the Beringtons of Winsley House at Hope under Dinmore to send their son George (qv) to Valladolid for training as a Jesuit priest. His activity was noticed by Bishop Bennett (qv); Cadwallador was sheltered by the Beringtons but was arrested at Easter 1610 and tried for treason. As there was plague in Hereford at that time he was forced to walk, loaded with chains, to Leominster, where, on 27 August 1610, he was hanged, drawn and quartered. His head was placed on the Cross House in Broad Street and his four quarters were set up on Lugg Bridge, South Street, Bargates, and Etnam Street. Near the Bargates site in 1897 Peter Paul Pugin (qv) built the RC Church of St Ethelbert's. On the south side of this church a chapel is dedicated to him and stained glass windows commemorate his execution. One of the half-length figures on John Abel's (qv) Market House seems to grimace in anguish and may represent Cadwallador. Abel, a Catholic, probably witnessed the martyrdom. Cadwallador was one of the English martyrs beatified by Pope John Paul on 22 November 1987.

Calwe, William (d.1409) was a chantry priest of St Peter's (now St Michael's) Church, Ledbury. A brass in the chancel shows him kneeling in prayer with the verse:

Sey Pat Nost for Sere William Calwe
Who loved well God and alle halwe

This is an early date for a rhyming couplet in English; it asks us to say an 'Our Father' for Calwe, who loved God and all saints so well. In Thomas Dingley's (qv) 1684 drawing of the complete brass Calwe kneels before St Peter, then patron of the church. The executors of John and Joanna Hope, including an Alice Pauncefoot (qv), founded the chantry (active from 1384) to pray for the Hopes' souls. Calwe is believed to have lived in a house by the churchyard. In a grant of land dated 1376 he is mentioned as chaplain of St Katherine's Hospital, Ledbury.

Cam: The family practised medicine in Hereford for more than a century. In 1729 John Cam, a surgeon, bought Wargrave House on St Owen Street, Hereford. It would continue as the Cam family home for over a century and is still a doctors' surgery. They were associated with the General Infirmary from its opening in 1776 at 162 Eign Street, when a John Cam, possibly a son of the above John, was among the original doctors. This John was born at Llanwarne and studied medicine at Cambridge. Other original surgeons at the Infirmary were William Cam and Thomas Cam. In 1783 the Infirmary moved to the new General Hospital on the Wye.

Cam, Thomas (1814-90), general surgeon, MRCS, JP, was born in Bath where his father was a surgeon, although the family was an old Herefordshire one. He qualified and returned to Hereford in 1839 to take over his uncle Samuel's medical practice. He was surgeon extraordinary to Hereford Infirmary and chairman of its board of management. An alderman of Hereford Corporation for 30 years, he was twice mayor, and was appointed to the bench as JP (1863-1890). He retired as a physician *c.*1875. A younger brother, Samuel, was also a surgeon at Hereford Infirmary. An earlier family member, Ann Cam (d.1790), left money to found the

Ann Cam School in Dymock. This opened in 1820 and is still the village school.

Camden, William (1551-1623), historian, was born on 2 May 1551 at the Old Bailey in London, the son of Sampson Camden, a painter, and his wife Elizabeth Curwen. He was educated at St Paul's School and Oxford University, with which he maintained a life-long connection, and he developed his interests in history and geography. He taught at Westminster School, where he continued his antiquarian studies. He travelled the country in search of material for his great work *Britannia*, inspired by the geographer and cartographer Abraham Ortellius. The *Britannia* was published in Latin in 1586 and coincided with the foundation of the Society of Antiquaries, which Camden often addressed. The book was an instant success and was reissued in several editions including an English one (1612). Camden combined evidence from coins, old manuscripts, maps and the research of other scholars into a national icon. In it he describes the antiquities and landscape of Herefordshire, where he travelled looking for manuscripts dispersed from the ruin of the monasteries, and observing the towns and countryside. He described the great houses and the customs of the people, the produce of the fields and the disposition of rivers and hills. Of the Golden Valley he says: 'The hills that incompass it on both sides are cloathed with woods, under the woods lie cornfields on each hand and under those fields lovely and fruitful meadows. In the middle between them glides a clear and crystal river.' He derived Leominster from *Llanllieni*, or the church of the nuns, and writing about its St Bartholomew's-tide fair on 24 August he commends its famous wool, *Lemster Ore*. He described the ruins of Kenchester (*Magnis*) with 'a temple, with a niche still standing'; Dore Abbey, not yet the ruin it would be by Lord John Scudamore's (qv, d.1671) time, with the graves of Walter de Plukenet, Ganfrid de Geneville, Walter de Clifford and Roger de Clifford (qqv) still visible. Near Much Marcle he was astonished by a recent landslide: 'The hill which they call Marcley Hill did, in the year 1571, rouse itself as it were out of sleep, and for 3 days together moved on its vast body with an horrible roaring noise.' He wrote a Greek Grammar which continued to be used for many years and a much praised history of the reign of Queen Elizabeth. He was made Clarenceux Herald. He died at Chislehurst on 9 November 1623 and was buried in Westminster Abbey.

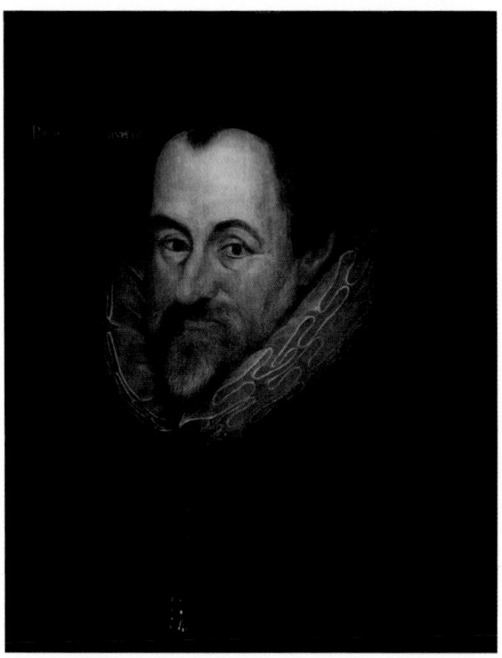

Cameron, George (1884-1975), conductor, was born Basil George Cameron Hindenberg on 18 August 1884 in Reading into a German family. A highly regarded conductor, he was called 'the quiet Maestro', working with the Hallé Orchestra and at the Proms. Before the First World War he used the name Basil Hindenberg but prudently changed to George Cameron when he joined the British Army. He was appointed CBE in 1957. He never married and on his retirement lived in Leominster, dying on 26 June 1975 at the Glendaph Nursing Home, Kingsland.

Campbell, Francis (1724-1804), a Hereford physician who lived at Holmer, was one of the first members of the Society of Tempers. Founded in 1752, the main rule of this popular society was that members should not be offended with each other. They met at the Bowling Green and later the Swan and Falcon (which became the City Arms in 1798). One of their ventures was to lease the Castle Green as a public park from Hereford Corporation. Dr Campbell was first secretary, then long standing president. In 1801 the Tempers celebrated their half centenary with a portrait of him.

Cantilupe, Thomas de (1218-82), St Thomas of Hereford, Bishop of Hereford 1275-82, was the third son of William (II) (qv), born at Hambledon, Bucks. He studied with younger brother Hugh in Paris to avoid riots at Oxford University and was a pupil of the future archbishop John Pecham (qv). He was Chancellor of Oxford University in 1261 during a time of conflict between the barons, led by Simon de Montfort (qv) and Henry III (qv). De Montfort made Thomas chancellor of England during his ascendancy in 1265, causing conflict for Thomas, as his career lay with the king, but he was related to Simon. When Prince Edward (qv Edward I) escaped from Hereford Castle and Montfort was killed at the Battle of Evesham, Thomas discreetly went to Paris, meeting St Thomas Aquinas, and returned at a more settled time. In 1274 he was made a prebend of Preston at Hereford Cathedral and the next year was elected Bishop of Hereford. The diocese had been neglected during the Barons' Wars and he began to restore order. He had been a worldly man but now took his responsibility seriously, combining energetic diocesan work with asceticism. He was firm with the unruly Gilbert de Clare, 'Red Earl' of Gloucester and secured the hunting rights of the diocese in the Malvern Chase from his depredations. He held many offices, benefices and canonries in Herefordshire and elsewhere and travelled constantly around his diocese, which then stretched from Wenlock to Chepstow. He made visitations of parishes, staying in his 21 palaces, a favourite being Stretton Sugwas, close to Hereford, where a stained glass portrait of him in his ordination robes was later placed. The glass was subsequently moved to the east window of St Mary's Church in Ross. Bosbury Palace was especially splendid. Here, on the feast of St Gregory, 3 September 1278, Thomas made a case for possession of land against the see of St Asaph before papal envoys, the minutes being preserved in the cathedral archives. He addressed them in Latin, then in French before they dined. Remains of some of the buildings of the bishop's palace at Bosbury can still be seen along the lane to the east of the church. Bishop Thomas spoke only Latin and Norman French; the Franciscan friar, Henry de Bellington, translated his sermons. In 1282 one of his last acts was to consecrate the new Cistercian Abbey of Dore, dedicated to the Holy Trinity and, as all Cistercian abbeys, St Mary. As the Bishop of St David's also claimed jurisdiction here an armed guard surrounded the abbey while the ceremony took place. A contemporary described Thomas as ruddy-complexioned, a redhead with a temper which he occasionally lost with Archbishop Pecham, who finally excommunicated him. Thomas was visiting Pope Martin IV at Orvieto to have this lifted when he died on 25 August 1282. This last journey with a large retinue was a grand affair and detailed notes of the itinerary have been found in the cathedral archives, giving a glimpse of aristocratic life in the 13th century. But Thomas himself apparently practised self-mortification, according to the testimony of his servant Robert Deynte (qv). His flesh was buried where he died but his bones were returned to Hereford and his heart was buried at the monastery of Ashridge in Buckinghamshire. Archbishop Pecham at first refused to allow his bones into the cathedral as an excommunicate but he was overruled and a splendid shrine was built in the north transept by his successor Bishop Richard Swinfield (qv). The resulting table tomb has six weeping Knights Templar on each side as Thomas was Provincial Grand Master of the Order. On top was a brass of Thomas with two smaller saints, of which only that of St Ethelbert survives. This translation of 1287 was attended by Edward I (qv) and his Court. Miracles of healing were associated with the shrine. His mantle ensured women an easy birth and sea-goers protection from drowning, and silver ships were presented as thank offerings. In 1307 the Pope began collecting information for his canonisation both in Hereford and London; witnesses were called and many details recorded of Thomas's life, the efficiency of his administration, his personal piety and subsequent miracles. The commissioners found his shrine crowded night and day. He was canonised in 1320, the penultimate saint to be created in England and the second most important after St Thomas of Canterbury. An even more splendid tomb was now prepared in the lady chapel and a group from the cathedral toured Britain collecting funds. Indulgences were sold and a scroll in the archives records some of the magnificent gifts, such as the £100 and gold plaque of the Virgin and Trinity given by Hereford canon William Lochard. In the 15th century a separate head shrine was constructed in the north transept while the rest of the saint's remains stayed in the lady chapel. The main shrine was attacked by iconoclasts at the Reformation in 1550, broken up and his bones scattered. Relics were retained, however, and during the plague of 1610 were paraded through Hereford by night. The previous shrine survived, stored away in pieces, and was re-erected in the north transept. When Thomas Dingley (qv) visited the cathedral in 1684 he recorded a painting of St Thomas on the wall behind. In 2009 representatives of the Roman Catholic Church presented relics of the saint, preserved through the penal years, to the Dean and Chapter of Hereford Cathedral in a moving ceremony. They were enshrined in a new feretory on top of the renovated and beautified original shrine. St Thomas is once more enthroned in his diocesan seat, a 14th-century statue stands on the south of the high altar and his arms, three leopards' faces reversed with fleur de lys, are now those of the diocese. His feast day is 2 October.

Cantilupe, William (I) de (d.1239), baron, steward of King John (qv) who in 1204 made him under-sheriff of Hereford, charged with looking after his treasure at Hereford Castle. He oversaw royal forests including the Haye in Herefordshire where forest law obtained. Hereford City was included within this jurisdiction. He entertained John, who loved the chase, at his castle at Kilpeck and founded a Benedictine priory to the east of the village. He married Mazilia and their son William succeeded him; their second son Walter was Bishop of Worcester. He died on 7 April 1239.

Cantilupe, William (II) de (d.1251), was the friend and steward of Henry III (qv), from whom he gained great profit. Like his father William (I) (qv) he was granted lucrative wardships such as that of Alan (II) Plukenet (qv) of Kilpeck and the wealthy heiress Eva, daughter of William (V) de Briouze (qv). He married Millicent, daughter of Hugh de Gournai and widow of Amaury de Montfort (qv Montfort).

Cantilupe, William (III) de (d.1254), eldest son of William (II) (qv) and Millicent, married his father's ward Eva de Briouze, adding greatly to the Cantilupe holdings in Herefordshire and the Marches which brought them increased power.

Capel: Proprietors of How Caple Court from the 12th century. In 1216 William de Capel held the knight's fee from the Bishop of Hereford. The estate passed to Sir William Gregory (qv) in 1672.

Capella, Richard de (d.1127), Bishop of Hereford 1121-7, was a chaplain of Henry I (qv) and keeper of the Great Seal. Henry appointed him bishop and he was consecrated in Westminster Abbey on 7 January 1121. When Henry founded Reading Abbey, Bishop Richard was appointed to assess the revenue of Leominster Priory which would be used to support it. Henry granted him the right to hold a three-day May Fair in Hereford High Town at St Ethelbert's tide. Richard had the first bridge built over the Wye in timber to replace the old ford downstream, a dangerous crossing when the Wye was in spate. This was the precursor of the present 14th-century stone bridge. He greatly expanded Ledbury in 1125, laying out burgage plots along five streets, an arrangement virtually unchanged today. He died at his palace in Ledbury on 15

May 1227, the site now unknown, and was buried in the north choir aisle of Hereford Cathedral. His tomb is in the wall of the Stanbury Chapel.

Caperon: A common name in Herefordshire in the Middle Ages. Agnes Caperon held the gate of Hereford Castle in *c.*1290 for 1d a day. Roger Caperon was a burgess returned for Ledbury in Edward I's Parliament.

Capes, William Wolfe (1834-1914), scholar, was the son of a London bookseller, educated at St Paul's School, London and Queen's College, Oxford, where he studied classics and mathematics. He was an enthusiastic pedestrian at home and abroad. He was ordained in 1868 and appointed rector of Bramshott, Hampshire. He held offices in Oxford University and published work on classical history. He was made a residentiary canon of Hereford Cathedral in 1903 and founded the Cantilupe Society which published the registers of the mediaeval bishops of Hereford. He published several himself, including the *Register of Thomas de Cantilupe* (qv). He was canon keeper of the archives. The chained library had been moved to rooms above the north transept but the manuscripts were poorly kept and regarded and he began cataloguing them. In 1908 he published *The Charters and Records of Hereford Cathedral* with an account of the cathedral's constitution. He died on 30 October 1914 at his home in the cathedral close at Hereford and was buried at Bramshott.

Caractacus or Caradog, (1st century AD), British chieftain, was, with his brother Togodumnus, born in Catuvellaunian territory in the St Albans area of Hertfordshire. Their father Cunobelinus (qv) was an ally of Rome but after his death his sons began to trouble the surrounding tribes, the Trinovantes in East Anglia and the Atrebates in Hampshire. The King of the Atrebates, Verica, fled to Rome, his ally, giving the Emperor Claudius a *casus belli*. An invasion force was sent under Aulus Plautus. At a battle on the Medway Togodumnus was killed and Caractacus fled west to make his stand in, some say, west Herefordshire. Croft Ambrey is one of the fortresses associated with him; British Camp on the Malverns is another, celebrated by Elgar (qv), and yet another is Coxall Knoll Camp by Brampton Bryan Park. Wherever it was, Governor Ostorius Scapula (qv) defeated him at the Battle of Caer Caradoc. He fled north into Brigantian territory but was handed over to the Romans. With his wife and daughter Claudia he was paraded in Rome. Legend has it that Claudia married Linus, a Roman Senator by whom she was converted to Christianity, and persuaded St Paul to send missionaries back to convert the British.

Caradoc (*c.*500-50) was the son of Ynyr Honorius Brenin, King of Gwent, and Saint Madrun (c.430-80) verch (ie daughter of) Vortigern, King of the Britons. He is the ancestor of the kings of Gwent and a descendant of Caractacus (qv), the last British leader to resist the Roman advance – a fabulous parentage but important in the princely Welsh genealogies. He married Enynny verch Cynfarch of the Iceni. In the histories he is called Lord of Hereford and is known as the Elder and Freichfras, 'strong arm'. In the Arthurian romances he is Briefbras or 'short arm', a knight at the Court of King Arthur (qv) whose wife was the only woman at Court virtuous enough to wear a magic mantle. He was said to have lived at Caradoc, Sellack near Ross.

Carausius, Marcus Aurelius Mausaeus Valerius (d.293), usurping emperor (286-293), was a Gaul of humble birth who rose by ability in the western Roman Empire to become commander of the British Fleet (*Classis Britanniae*). Learning of the emperor's order for his execution on a charge of piracy, he declared himself emperor of the provinces of north-western Gaul and Britannia. As a Celt he is likely to have been popular in Britain and legends on the coins he issued express nationalistic sentiments like *Restitutor Britanniae* (Restorer of Britain). More coins of Carausius have been found at *Magnis* (near Kenchester) than of any other emperor, perhaps indicating Carausian recruiting activity in this brief period. Some bear references to messianic texts of Virgil that a golden age has dawned. *Magnis* was a backwater even from a Dobunnic perspective. Constantius Chlorus, official emperor in the west, moved against Carausius and he was assassinated by his minister, Allectus, who then reigned in Britain before himself succumbing to official forces in 296.

Carless, James (fl.1797), huntsman, is mentioned in *The Herefordshire Fox Chase*, a ballad collected by Ella Mary Leather (qv) from Noah Richards of Moorhampton, who remembered Carless. He confirmed that the heroic hunt took place on Twelfth Night 1897 and covered 98 miles of bad ground. Carless with Squire Parry and the dogs picked up the scent at St Margaret's and chased the poor fox across Snodhill Park, through Dorstone and Moccas, Preston Court and Tyberton. Here the Squire stopped for lunch but Carless and his hounds hunted on past Kingstone, down the Golden Valley and all the way to Abergavenny where the fox dropped dead.

> **Carpenter**: A family long settled around Dilwyn and Weobley who held the manor of Hydefield for 500 years.

Carpenter, George (1657-1732), 1st Baron Carpenter of Killaghy, army officer, was born on 10 February 1657 at Ocle Pychard, son of the younger Warncomb (qv under Warncomb Carpenter). He was educated at Hereford Cathedral School and was page to the Earl of Montagu, ambassador to Paris. He campaigned in Ireland and Flanders and on his return in 1693 married Alice (*c.*1660-1731), a wealthy widow, daughter of William Caulfeild, Viscount Charlemont. Their children were George (qv, d.1749) and Alicia. Carpenter bought the forfeited Irish estate of Killaghy and sat as an Irish MP. He was lieutenant-general in the Peninsular wars during the War of the Spanish Succession, where he served with distinction and was wounded. In Britain he was commander in chief of the forces that defeated the Jacobite rising of 1715. He was created Baron Killaghy in 1719 and elected MP for a Hampshire seat. He was Governor of Minorca. He died on 10 February 1732 and was buried at Owslebury, Hampshire.

Carpenter, George (1695-1749), 2nd Baron, was born at Lyvers Ocle, the son of George Carpenter (qv, d.1732). He married Elizabeth, daughter of David Petty of Wanstead, Essex, and their children were George (qv, d.1762) and Alicia. He was MP for Morpeth, then for Weobley (1741-7). Like his father he served in the army.

Carpenter, George (1723-62), 3rd Baron of Killaghy and 1st Earl of Tyrconnell, was born at Lyvers Ocle, a house in the tiny hamlet of Ocle Pychard, north-east of Hereford on 26 August 1723, the only surviving son of George Carpenter (qv, d.1749). In 1774 he married Frances, daughter of Sir Robert Clifton of Nottinghamshire. They had six children, including George (the eldest, qv, d.1805) and Charles (1757-1803), whose son George became 3rd Earl. A daughter, Caroline (*c.*1759-1826), married Sir Uvedale Price (qv). He was created Earl of Tyrconnell with the subsidiary title Viscount Callingford in 1761. He died on 9 March 1762.

Carpenter, George (1750-1805), 2nd Earl of Tyrconnell and Viscount Callingford, was the eldest son of Lord George (qv, d.1762) and Frances. His first marriage to Frances Manners was dissolved and in 1780 he married Sarah Hussey Delaval, the youngest daughter and co-heir of Lord Delaval and they had one child, Susan Hussey Carpenter (*c.*1784-1827), who married Henry de-la-Poer Beresford, 2nd Marquess of Waterford. He was MP for Scarborough and Berwick. He died on 15 April 1805 and was succeeded by his nephew George (1788-1812) as 3rd Earl.

Carpenter, Warncomb (17th century), the sixth son of Thomas Carpenter of the Homme, Dilwyn, was born at Lyvers Ocle and married Eleanor, daughter of William Taylor of Withington and wealthy widow of John Hill. Warncomb fell at Naseby fighting for the king. He had seven children, the oldest being Warncomb (1621-60).

Carrington, Dora de Houghton (1893-1932), artist, was born in Ivy Lodge, Venn's Lane, Hereford on 29 March 1893. She was the fourth child of Samuel Carrington and Charlotte Houghton. The family had moved here from Hornyold House in Bodenham Road where their first three children had been born, and before long they moved again to Belle Vue in Hereford. Later the family moved to Bedford where Carrington, as she preferred to be called, went to school. She was her elderly father's favourite and disliked her mother, whom she saw as shrewish and controlling. She painted portraits of the family while still a child, and went to the Slade Art School where she devel-

oped bohemian habits and was one of the first to bob her hair. She was never a prolific painter, preferring decorative work and using craft materials like silver paper. She was a member of the Bloomsbury circle and had various troubled relationships, resisting Mark Gertler's advances while allowing his influence on her painting. Her strongest relationship was with the writer Lytton Strachey. In 1921 she married Ralph Partridge and in 1924 she, Partridge and Strachey settled into Ham Spray House in Wiltshire. After Strachey died of a stomach cancer she ended her own life in 1932.

Carroll, Lewis see under **Skeffington Hume Dodgson**

Carter, William (1821-96), Mormon, was a blacksmith and glassblower from a poor family in Bye Street, Ledbury. He was a member of the United Brethren, a splinter from the Methodists,

searching for fundamental Christianity. A group of church elders of the Church of the Latter Day Saints, Brigham Young, Willard Richards and Wilford Woodruff, had been sent from the United States by their president Joseph Smith to evangelise Britain. In 1840 Woodruff preached at Hill Farm, Castle Frome and baptised John Benbow (qv) in the farm's pond. He was invited to preach at the Baptist Chapel in the Homend, Ledbury where many were converted, and went on to preach and baptise in the fields and ponds of the area, often to violent opposition. Carter, with many Herefordshire converts, felt called to emigrate to America and trekked to Great Salt Lake Valley, Utah, arriving on 22 July 1847. On the journey Carter married Benbow's two sisters, later taking, in the polygamistic Mormon way, another four wives. Carter was the first man to irrigate, plough and raise a crop (of potatoes) at Salt Lake and became a leading elder in the church, spending time in the County Penitentiary for his polygamy. He died in 1896 at St George, Utah. The pond at Hill Farm where William Carter was baptised is a now a Mormon pilgrimage site.

Cartwright, John (d.1764), forger and quack, lived in the Eardisley area *c.*1730, calling himself a doctor of physic and advertising his patent medicines. He could 'be spoke with every WEDNESDAY at the Red Lion Kington; and on THURSDAY in the Cock in the Hay'. He had acted as scrivener to William Barnsley (qv) of Eardisley Park and knew his affairs and signature. Barnsley's man of business, Mansell Powell (qv), persuaded Cartwright to forge his late employer's will leaving his estates and fortune to him. Cartwright was paid off and moved to London with his family. He squandered his money, left his wife and returned to Herefordshire with a mistress. His angry wife followed, re-igniting the Barnsley family's suspicions, and the case was reopened. The will was found to be a forgery, Powell was convicted and imprisoned, but Cartwright, who had uttered the forgery, was publicly hanged at Tyburn in 1764.

Carver, Thomas (b.1848), stationer, came to Hereford from Kirby Muxloe, Leics. He married Frances from Ludlow and their children were Frank, Irene and Norah. He had premises at 4 & 5 Widemarsh Street at the corner of High Town in Hereford, where he entered a partnership with the printer Edward Jakeman (qv). At the end of the 19th century Jakeman & Carver were major Hereford printers, producing the Woolhope Club *Transactions* and annual trade directories. Carver's stationery business employed 11 men, a woman and a boy.

Carwardine, Penelope (1729-1805), miniature painter, was born at Thinghill Grange, a 14th-century manor house at Withington, on 29 April 1729, the eldest of the six daughters of John Carwardine (b.1703) and Anne Bullock (1700-65) from Preston Wynn. Her mother was a miniature painter and taught Penelope her skills. The family's prosperity suffered from her father's improvidence and Penelope's portraits of neighbours supplemented the family finances. Her fame grew and *c.*1760 she went to London

to study under Ozias Humphrey and exhibited her work with success. In 1763 she married James Butler, organist of St James's, Piccadilly. James Boswell called on her when she was painting Lord Eglinton and thought her a fine-looking woman. She was friends with Sir Joshua Reynolds and his sister Fanny, and Thomas Lawrence painted a portrait of one of her sisters as a gift for her. Her own portrait was painted by Thomas Bardwell. The Wallace Collection has a miniature by her and the National Gallery has mezzotint copies of her portraits, otherwise her work may remain to be discovered in Herefordshire attics. She died a widow with no children.

Cash, John Theodore (1854-1936), physician and pharmacologist, was born in Manchester on 16 December 1854, the younger son of John Walker Cash and Martha Midgley. He studied medicine at the University of Edinburgh and in 1881 married Sophia Bright (d.1924), a fine watercolourist. They had two sons and two daughters. Cash's researches in pharmacology at St Bartholomew's, London led to new remedies, his appointment to a Chair in Aberdeen University in 1886 and election to the Royal Society. His hobby was salmon and trout fishing and he retired to Albyn House on Broomy Hill, Hereford in order to fish the Wye. Here he died on 30 November 1936.

Castle, Edmund (1698-1750), Dean of Hereford 1748-50, was born in Kent on 14 September 1698 and educated at Corpus Christi, Cambridge. He was ordained priest in 1722 and became a Fellow of the college. Castle was appointed to vicarages in Ely and Hertfordshire, and married Susanna. He was rector of St Paul's School and Master of Corpus Christi, serving as Vice-Chancellor of the University of Cambridge in 1746-7. In 1747 he was promoted to a prebend at Lincoln then to the deanery of Hereford. Dr Castle died at Bath on 6 June 1750; his widow survived him by about five years. He was buried at Barley, Herts., where there is a Latin inscription to his memory that describes him as a man of simplicity of manners and great learning.

Cave, Richard (1596-1645), Governor of Hereford, was born at Witney, Oxon the son of Thomas Cave and Katherine Jones. He married Elizabeth (d.1688), daughter of Sir Thomas Bartlett, and they had a son Henry. He was MP for Lichfield in the Short Parliament of 1640 but ejected in 1642 as a Royalist. After Stamford (qv Henry Grey, d.1673) had left Hereford in 1642 it was re-garrisoned by the Royalists and Sir Richard appointed Governor. He vainly tried to organise the defences but the citizens were unrealistic about the threat until, in 1643, Waller's (qv) large force was at the gates. Cave went out to parley with Waller conscious of the weak defences and his forces began to slip away. Bearing in mind that Waller would sack and loot a town taken resisting, he agreed to capitulate. He was imprisoned but escaped and reached Oxford where he was court-martialled for dishonourable surrender. Waller soon gave up Hereford but Cave, although acquitted, felt his disgrace keenly. He tried to retrieve his name with rash fighting at the Battle of Naseby on 16 June 1645 and died from wounds received there. Elizabeth his widow married Dr Thomas Yates (d.1681), principal of Brasenose College.

Cecil: A Welsh family of the minor gentry, originally called Sitsylt, who lived at Allt Yr Ynys (Old Town), in the parish of Walterstone. They had connections with Dore Abbey in the Middle Ages. Their 16th-century manor house with oak panelling and moulded ceilings is now a hotel (Allt Yr Ynys Country Hotel). David Cecil joined Henry of Richmond's (qv Henry VII) army on his march through Wales and fought at Bosworth Field when Henry seized the crown from Richard III (qv). He and his son Richard rose in rank as servants of Henry VII (qv) and VIII (qv), settled at Burghley near Stamford, Notts. and flourished. Richard's son William Cecil (1521-98) became Lord Burghley, Elizabeth's first minister. He built Burghley House and their London house, Theobalds on the Strand. His son Robert Cecil (1563-1612), later 1st Earl of Salisbury, took over his father's position at King James's Court.

Cennick, John (1718-55), Moravian minister, was born on 17 December 1718 in Reading. One of the great evangelical preachers, he travelled widely in England and Ireland, founding the Moravian congregation in South Street, Leominster in 1749. The Moravians were a strongly evangelical Protestant sect from Germany who settled in small numbers in the 1740s. They were noted for the piety of their preaching and hymns, of which Cennick wrote many (qv also Wilkes). He was a contemporary of the Wesleys and George Whitefield (qqv). Cennick married Jane Bryant from Wiltshire in 1747 and they had three children. He died of a fever in London on 4 July 1755 aged only 36 but the Leominster Moravians continue at their chapel in South Street, holding weekly services each Sunday at 4pm.

Chadwick, Elias (early 19th century), a Liverpool cotton merchant of Swinton Hall, Lancashire, had J.T. Brearley of Liverpool build him Pudleston Court (1846-7) near Leominster in the style of John Nash (qv). He was High Sheriff of Herefordshire in 1854. His daughter Frances (d.1892) married Sir Thomas Archer Colt (qv Dutton Colt).

Chambers, William (1723-96), architect, was born on 23 February 1723 in Sweden, where his Scottish parents were on business. He studied architecture in Paris and Italy and came to England. His contacts with Lord Bute and Robert Adam (qv) got him employment with the Royal family at Kew, where he designed the Chinese Pagoda. His architecture is neoclassical in the French spirit, best seen in Somerset House in the Strand, built for the Duke of Somerset (1776-96). Somerset had owned an estate at Vowchurch in the 1730s which later came into the possession of Sir Edward Boughton (qv). In 1780 Boughton used Chambers to build him Poston House, a beautiful, small hunting lodge on his Vowchurch estate. Called a *casino* in the 18th century, it was originally a round, domed room behind a pediment with rounded windows and door. Wings were added in the 19th century and it later became neglected but it has recently been well restored. Poston Lodge passed to the Robinsons by marriage and their daughter married Skeffington H. Dodgson (qv), vicar of nearby Vowchurch and brother of Lewis Carroll. Chambers was a founding member of the Royal Academy in 1768 and it was he who secured the king's participation. He died in London on 10 March 1796 and is buried in Poets' Corner in Westminster Abbey.

Chandler, Thomas (*c.*1417-90), Dean of Hereford 1481-90, was born at Wells, Somerset. He was the son and brother of clerks, one becoming Bishop of Salisbury. He imbibed the new learning at Winchester School and was an outstanding scholar at New College, Oxford, where he became Doctor of Theology. He was warden of both Winchester and New College and Chancellor of the university from 1457 to 1461, maintaining stability in the university during a turbulent period. He was a leading humanist and a conscientious teacher, training many of the distinguished politicians and churchmen of the next generation. He was a chaplain to Edward IV (qv). He drew well, wrote a fine humanist hand and produced learned Latin plays. He became Dean of Hereford in 1481. At Oxford he had been a founder of Duke Humphrey's Library and he brought innovations to Hereford Cathedral library, then housed in a room above the west range of the cloister, such as lecterns to read on. Chandler died at Hereford on 2 November 1490 and is buried in the south-east transept, where his brass can be seen.

Chandos, John (d.1428), the son of Sir Thomas Chandos (d.1375) and grandson of Sir Roger de Chandos (qv), was Sheriff of Hereford in 1382. He was a colleague of Sir John Oldcastle (qv). In 1402 Henry IV (qv) ordered him to defend Snodhill Castle against Glyn Dŵr (qv); repairs were effected and the Welsh resisted. Sir John died childless on 16 December 1428. With the marriage of his niece Alice to Sir Thomas Brugge (or Brydges) the Chandos name passed to the Brydges family (qv). In 1554 John Brydges (d.1557) was created Baron Chandos by the second creation and it was John's second son, Charles Brydges (qv), who bought Wilton Castle from his uncle William Grey (qv). Snodhill Castle was fortified during the Civil Wars when it was bombarded by the Parliamentarian army and the stone subsequently robbed for work at Snodhill Court farmhouse nearby. A legend promises treasure buried in the castle mound 'no deeper than a hen could scratch' and Leland (qv) says there was a quarry for marble here. The ruins are now in poor condition.

Chandos, Robert de built Snodhill Castle near Peterchurch in the early 12th century and the castle remained in Chandos hands for the next 300 years.

Chandos, Roger de (d.1266) was granted the right to hold a fair at Fownhope by Henry III (qv). His son Robert (d.1302), fought in Edward I's (qv) Welsh wars.

Chandos, Roger de (d.1353), son of Robert (qv), served in Edward II's (qv) Scottish wars and was knighted by him. Edward III (qv) made him Sheriff of Hereford in 1321 and governor of Hereford Castle. He sat in Edward's Parliaments from 1337 to 1353 as Baron Chandos. A legend relates that Hugh Despenser (qv), who was in hiding at Mordiford in about 1320, and planning an attack on Hereford, saw Sir Roger's daughter, Isabel, coming down the Wye in a boat. They fell in love and he confided his plans to her, asking her to flee with him after the battle. Isabel felt obliged to warn her father, who was governor of Hereford, and he promptly fell on Despenser's forces, captured him and put him cruelly to death in Hereford. Isabel, forced to watch her lover die on the scaffold, became distraught and took to sailing by their Mordiford meeting place until she finally drowned in the turbulent confluence of Lugg and Wye. Her ghostly skiff can still be seen off Mordiford Bank, as can the ghost of the Mordiford Dragon (qv Garson).

Chapman, D.R. (19th century), was curator and librarian of Rankin's new library in Broad St, Hereford. He wrote *Hereford, Herefordshire and the Wye* (Jakeman & Carver, 1882). It was dedicated to Rankin (qv) and had a preface and photographs by Alfred Watkins (qv).

Charles I (1600-49), King of Great Britain 1625-49, was James I and VI's third child. Frail and with a stammer, he found himself in line for the throne when his older brother Henry died of smallpox. He was a shy individual but high-minded, combining his father's belief in a divine right to rule with the inability to do so. He came to the throne in 1625 and was faced with 15 years of conflict with an unyielding House of Commons. He married the 15-year-old French princess Henrietta Maria (1609-69) in 1624 and they had seven children. His Puritan Parliaments thought his Arminian Anglicanism papistical and executed his supporters Buckingham and Laud (qv). His attempt to rule without Parliament was a failure and unpopular taxes like Ship Money seemed unfair to inland counties like Herefordshire, which had its rate lowered by reassessment twice before refusing to pay altogether. His concessions were seen as

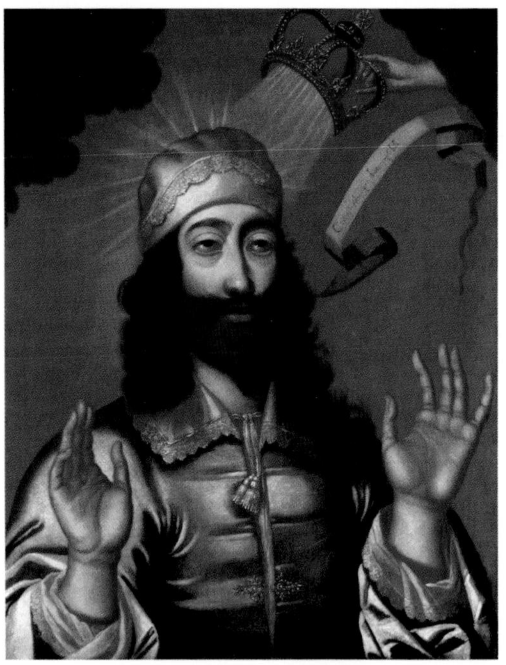

weakness and his resolve autocracy. His disastrous attempt to arrest opponents, invading Parliament with a band of swordsmen, enraged the Commons and he fled London, raising his standard at Nottingham, in effect declaring war on Parliament. He was in Herefordshire several times. In 1630 he had sold the manor of Ledbury to a consortium, including Ambrose Elton (qv), Thomas and Stephen Skinner and William Hooper. The Marches were good recruiting grounds and strongly Royalist. While Charles was staying at Much Birch in 1642 he was sent a cutting of the Holy Thorn of Glastonbury which he planted at King's Thorn, where a descendant can still be seen. In 1644 he was at Bromyard and on 8 May ordered that Hereford's fortifications be repaired and a mint set up in the castle to pay the garrison. He was in Hereford on 19 June 1645 after his defeat at Naseby where he heard of another defeat at Stokesay on 8 June and of the death of his able commander Sir William Croft (qv, d.1645). The Scottish Army besieged Hereford on 31 July 1645 but fled when Charles approached with a large force. He stayed in the bishop's palace, in the mayor's chamber in Church Street and on 3 September at the Unicorn in Broad Street. He showed his gratitude for Hereford's loyalty by augmenting the coat of arms with the three lions of Richard I (qv) beset by ten Scottish saltires, signifying Leslie's (qv) Scottish regiments, and adding the rare lion crest on top of the coat of arms signifying 'defender of the faith' and the helm, found only otherwise on the arms of the City of London. He gave the motto *Invictae fidelitatis praemium* (the reward of unconquered fidelity). He went on to beat the Parliamentary garrison out of Leominster and stayed at 'The Throne', Weobley. But Parliament's forces, pious and professional under commanders like Cromwell, gradually defeated the Royalists. Charles was held by the Scots whilst trying to negotiate and imprisoned in Carisbrooke Castle. There was a show trial at Westminster. Parliament had been purged of moderates like the Harleys (qv) who would have supported the king and Charles was executed on Tuesday 30 January 1649. Cromwell allowed him burial at Windsor.

Charles II (1630-85), king in name when his father was executed, was invited back to Britain from his continental exile in 1660. He visited Hereford in the winter of 1680. On his way he stayed at Eye Manor (qv Gorges). Another connection with Herefordshire is his favourite mistress Nell Gwynne (qv).

Charlton, Lewis (d.1369), Bishop of Hereford 1360-9, was the son of John Charlton, Lord of Powys, and nephew of Bishop Thomas (qv). Other brothers also held high office in the church. He was educated at Oxford and was a learned theologian. The lodgings that he shared with his brothers in Oxford came to be known as Charlton's Inn. He was made a canon by his uncle the bishop, and prebend in 1336, and he moved to Hereford. He received other benefices including a portion of Ledbury Church. In 1360 the Pope at Avignon was persuaded to make him Bishop of Hereford and he was consecrated there. His arrival at Hereford was only 20 years after the Black Death and a fresh outbreak soon occurred. Charlton closed High Town market in 1362 and moved it out to Whitecross, a mile west of Eign Gate. The Cross is his memorial to the Plague and his rampant lion can be seen on it. He toured the diocese tirelessly maintaining discipline and giving heart. He died on 23 May 1369, bequeathing books to the cathedral library with instructions that books should be chained, in anticipation of the later system. He was buried in the cathedral where his effigy remains. He now lies against the north wall of the south-east transept, built by him, in a 19th-century canopied tomb provided by descendants, on which large cherubs hold books and a mitre.

Charlton, Thomas (*c.*1290-1344), Bishop of Hereford 1327-44, was from Shropshire. His brother John (d.1353), 2nd Lord Charlton of Powys (*c.*1300-53), helped Thomas rise in the service of Edward II (qv). Thomas was made Doctor of Laws at Oxford and was given offices and benefices by the king. He became a canon of Hereford in April 1317. King Edward recommended him to the Pope for the see of Hereford but Adam Orleton (qv) was chosen. When Orleton was translated to Worcester Pope John XXII appointed Charlton Bishop of Hereford as a safe pair of hands in the troubled Welsh Marches. He and his brother in Powys and Hereford had major roles during the problems with the Welsh. When Roger (V) Mortimer, Earl of March (qv) ruled England the Charlton brothers conformed themselves to his regime, Thomas becoming chancellor. They were related to Roger (V) Mortimer as their nephew John had married Roger's daughter Matilda. They were quick to trim, however, after Edward III's coup of 1330. Thomas was a conscientious bishop and when away from his diocese appointed effective surrogates. Edward III showed his trust by appointing him Chancellor of Ireland, initially with another brother John. Charlton died in Hereford on 11 January 1344 and was buried in a canopied tomb below the north transept window, close to the feretory of St Thomas de Cantilupe of Hereford (qv).

Cheers, Henry Arthur (1853-1916), architect, was born in Cheshire and articled in Liverpool, where he set up his practice in 1880 and married Isabella Anson. He moved to Twickenham where he had success as an architect of public buildings. He later won the contract to build Hereford Town Hall in St Owen Street to provide much needed space for the expanding council. Officers like John Parker (qv) were housed in cramped quarters at the Guildhall Chambers in Widemarsh Street, with overspill in the Mansion House. The flamboyant Town Hall in a baroque style was finished in 1904, way above estimate at £24,000, by a local builder, James Bowers (qv). It was clad in highly ornamented, pollution-resistant terracotta, lit by electricity from the new generator in Widemarsh Street. Its main staircase and first-floor hall show civic magnificence. Cheers also built Oswestry Town Hall. He died on 15 January 1916 and is buried in Twickenham cemetery.

Chell, William (c.1500-59), priest and musician from the Malverns, was educated at Oxford University where he was ordained and began teaching. Appointed a vicar choral of Hereford Cathedral in 1518, he was succentor by 1526, canon in 1533 and precentor 1554-6. He was a prebendary of Eigne (1533), then (1545) Eau Withington, and jointly registrar with William Turner. He was rector of St John's (qv) at the cathedral and of Colwall. His friend Bishop Booth (qv) left him some silver spoons in his will. His special interest was church music and he wrote settings for the mass; a manuscript survives in the cathedral archives showing his familiarity with contemporary music theory. Chell was deprived of his offices when Queen Elizabeth (qv) came to the throne and he died soon after.

Chick, William (1829-92), known after 1879 as Cheiake, surveyor and architect, was born in Dorset where his father was a builder. He was apprenticed to Henry Woodyer (qv) in London and married. He worked on Woodyer's projects and was introduced to George Gilbert Scott (qv), who appointed him his clerk of works at Gore Ouseley's (qv) church and choir school at Tenbury Wells. When Scott got the important commission to restore Hereford Cathedral in 1854 he trusted Chick as his clerk of works, with daily responsibility for the work. Chick's first job was to underpin the walls of the eastern parts of the cathedral which were without foundations. Scott and he were more sensitive to the ancient fabric than the Cottinghams (qv), and, with help from Havergal (qv), recovered and restored old monuments and the choir stalls which his predecessors had discarded. Chick and his wife moved to Hereford; he laid out Hafod Road where he built himself a house. He had an office at 25 Castle Street and later at 23 East Street. He carried out much work in the county over the next 30 years and was appointed surveyor for the cathedral and County Surveyor. He restored Ocle Pychard and Thruxton churches. In Ledbury he renovated the Market Hall in 1866 and then built the north end of Ledbury Almshouses, completing Smirke's (qv) row. He built the vicarage at Pipe and Lyde in 1868 for the vicar Revd F.T. Havergal (qv), who was a friend of Scott's, and the same year attractively restored Norton Canon Church for Revd C.J. Robinson (qv) and also built the vicarage here inn 1866. He worked at St Mary's Church, Little Birch in 1869 and substantially restored St Peter and St Paul, Eye which had become dilapidated. He designed Ledbury Girls and Infants National School (1879). Aged 50 he changed his name to Cheiake. He restored St Mary Magdalene, Stretton Sugwas 1877-80 and designed the staircase at Whitfield Court for the Clive family (qv). Later he worked on E.W. Pugin's (qv) Convent of Our Lady at Bartestree. He retired to Woodville, Sutton, which he bought from the Unett (qv) family, and here he died in 1892 and was buried in Hereford City cemetery.

Christian, Ewan (1814-95), architect, was born on 20 September 1814 in London. He studied at the Royal Academy School of Architecture and under the architects William Railton and John Brown of Norwich. He set up his own practice in London in 1842. In 1848 he married Annie Bentham (a relation of Jeremy) and they had three daughters. He was a dependable, prolific architect who built to a strict budget and designed churches for

evangelical use rather than ritual, such as St Matthew's, Cheltenham. He was President of the RIBA and produced many new churches for the ecclesiastical commission. He made sensitive restorations to Herefordshire churches. In 1863 he was commissioned by William Perry-Herrick to reconstruct the church of St Mary Magdalene at Eardisley. He rebuilt the chancels of Kimbolton and Kingstone churches. He built a vicarage at Little Dewchurch in 1863; his 1865 vicarage at Bullinghope is an example of a good Victorian house. His vicarage at Much Birch is now the Pilgrim Inn. The pews in this church were made by Christian for his radical Cheltenham church St Matthew's. In 1871 he rebuilt the chancel at Bosbury and that of St Mary's, Brilley in 1881. In 1875-8 he restored St Bartholomew's, Much Marcle, rebuilding all the roofs. He made a thorough restoration of Clifford Church in 1888, rebuilding the north aisle. Christian lived in Well Walk, Hampstead in a house of his own design, and died there on 21 February 1895.

Clanvowe, John (1341-91) was a poet of Hergest and Yazor, of a Welsh family which had served the English Crown for several generations. Sir John was in the service of Edward III (qv), his Lollard sympathies shared by younger members of the Court, and a knight of the chamber of Richard II (qv). He was a friend of Chaucer and is thought to have written *The Cuckoo and the Nightingale*, once ascribed to Chaucer. There is a family connection with the Skidmores (qv Scudamore).

Clanvowe, Thomas (d.1410), son of Sir John (qv), was a JP and an MP in the Parliaments of Richard II (qv). In 1392 he married Peryne Whitney (qv), and they were both much at Court, receiving pensions from Queen Anne and, Clanvowe being a king's knight, two tuns of wine a year. Sir Thomas was Richard's Sheriff of Hereford for two terms in 1397-9. Like other royal servants he was able to transfer service to Henry IV, his grants were confirmed and he was involved in the Scottish campaign of 1400. With his Whitney father-in-law (qv Robert, d.1402) he fought at the disaster at Pilleth, was captured and ransomed. Sir Thomas and Lady Peryne were buried in St Mary's Church, Yazor. The will he made in English at Yazor, like his wife's later, shows Lollard sympathies: he stipulated an unceremonious disposal of the body with no mass, and he left money to improve the filthy Herefordshire roads to market towns. A daughter of his married into the Perrot (qv) family. There are still Clanvowes in the area.

Clare, Richard de (*c.*1130-76), 'Strongbow', 2nd Earl of Pembroke and Lord of Goodrich, was the son of Gilbert 'Strongbow' de Clare (d.*c.*1149), and a supporter of Stephen (qv) in his wars against Matilda; Stephen created him Earl of Pembroke. It may have been for this support that Henry II (qv) withheld Strongbow's titles and took his lands into his own hands. His success fighting in Ireland, however, caused the king to acknowledge his position. He married Eva, daughter of his ally the King of Leinster; they had a son, Gilbert (1173-*c.*89), and a daughter, Isabella, who married William the Marshal (qv). The central keep of Goodrich Castle is possibly Strongbow's. Gerald of Wales (qv) left a critical account of him. His legendary deeds are celebrated in an old French poem, *The Song of Dermot and the Earl.*

Clarke, Hester (fl. before 1735), was a philanthropist who left money for the almshouses in Bargates, Leominster in 1735 for four poor widows, who were allotted £5pa each and a garden. The houses were rebuilt in 1874, keeping the effigy of a man on the gable, naked but for a cocked hat and a piece of cloth. He once held a hatchet and illustrated the verse carved below him:

He that gives away all before he is Dead
Let em take this Hatchet and knock him on ye head.

Clarke, Robert (1847-1915) and **William** (1853-1923), were architectural sculptors, sons of Edward Clarke of Llandaff. Kempson (qv) met the Clarke family while working with John Pritchard in Llandaff and brought Robert and William to Hereford to work on the library and museum he was building in Broad Street; they carved the exterior decorative features. They settled in Hereford where Robert opened an architectural workshop, the Phoenix Works, in Commercial Road. With his son William Ernest (qv) he made decorative architectural pieces like the fountain (1903) on Castle Green that incorporates a 14th-century head of St Ethelbert (qv). He made the pulpit and reading desk in St Bartholomew's Much Marcle to a design of Havergal (qv). He also carved some of the details during his restoration of the Old House in High Town (1883). He was an active member of the Woolhope Club and secretary from 1912 until his death on 11 February 1915.

Clarke, William (fl.1885-97) was an engineer on the Ledbury, Newent and Gloucester Railway. He built the stations at Rowden Bridge, Bromyard and Fencote, Hatfield and the Skew Bridge at Ledbury.

Clarke, William Ernest H. (fl.1930), architect, son of Robert Clarke (qv), set up in architectural practice with John Nicholson (qv). His is the war memorial at Tarrington, and he restored the wonderful rood screen at St Margaret's.

Clarke-Whitfeld, John (1770-1836), composer and organist, was born on 13 December 1770 in Gloucester, the son of John Clarke (d.1802) of Malmesbury and Amphillis Whitfeld. He was educated at Oxford (B.Mus.1793), and was organist at Ludlow, Armagh and Dublin, then at Trinity and St John's Cambridge where he became professor of music. He published *Services and Anthems* (1800-1805) and set poems to music. He was an advocate of Handel and introduced his oratorios to the English public. In 1820 he was appointed organist and choirmaster of Hereford Cathedral with responsibility for the Three Choirs Festival. In 1822 he conducted his own oratorio *The Crucifixion* and, at the following festival in 1825, his *Resurrection*, and composed complete services in C and F. In 1832, his health frail, he was induced to resign by the new Dean Merewether, who replaced him with the brilliant but unreliable Samuel Sebastian Wesley (qv). Clarke-Whitfeld died at his home in Holmer on 22 February 1836 and was buried in Hereford Cathedral where there is a plaque to him. His widow Susanna died on 18 April 1845.

Clayton, John (1819-61), architect, was born and educated in Hereford and at 18 moved to London to study at the Royal Academy School of Architecture under Professor C.R. Cockerell. In 1846 he published *Ancient Timber Edifices of England*, measured drawings of significant timber buildings, with special reference to those of John Abel (qv). He presented his study of the bishop's palace in Hereford before the RIBA, of which he was made Associate, becoming a Fellow in 1858. In 1846 he moved to Withington with an office in Hereford. His designs for Hereford Central Railway Station (on the Hereford to Newport line) were exhibited at the RA and he built Barton Station (1853), now demolished. He made some alterations to Reavely's (qv) Kinnersley Castle (1857). He restored Eaton Bishop Church (1859). He won the competition to design the Buttermarket in Hereford's High Town (1861) with its Wrenaissance façade in Cotswold limestone and figures of abundance above the entrance carved by William Boulton of Lambeth, who also worked for Cottingham (qv) in the cathedral nave, making the reredos, for example. Clayton had studied Wren and his churches. The Redstreak (qv) Inn was demolished to make way for it. Clayton's Hereford practice received many commissions for Church of England schools, building those at Eardisley (1856) and Kinnersley (1859) for instance. He died on 14 September 1861.

Clayton and Bell (fl.1855-1993) were prolific 19th-century stained glass manufacturers: John Richard Clayton (1827-1913) and Alfred Bell (1832-95). Early examples of their glass can be seen in St John the Baptist, Upton Bishop, and the choir north aisle window to John Hunt (qv) in Hereford Cathedral. These were made in Heaton and Butler's workshops, which they shared until setting up their own successful manufactory in Regent Street, London. Here they made the glass commemorating Wesley, Townshend Smith and Langdon Colborne (qqv), organists of Hereford Cathedral, now placed in the north transept clerestory windows. A late work is the cathedral's great west window of 1902 celebrating the reign of Queen Victoria. Their glass and decorative work is in many Herefordshire churches; see especially their rose window at Canon Frome (1862) where they also made the reredos, and the chancel and west windows at Welsh Bicknor. In St James, Bartestree theirs is all the marble and mosaic work, the painted ceilings and the stained glass for Nicholson & Son (qv), installed when they rebuilt the church in 1888.

Clerke, Clement (d.1693) was an iron founder and entrepreneur from Warwickshire. He was created a baronet at the Restoration and married the heiress Sarah Talbot, who brought him wealth and estates in Leicestershire. He set up a foundry in Herefordshire, at Linton-by-Ross, in competition with the Foleys. Paul Foley (qv) demolished his own furnace in the Forest of Dean to stop Clerke making use of it. He smelted iron, copper and lead here and at other works in London and Coalbrookdale. Clerke and his son Talbot introduced the more efficient reverberatory furnace which used reflected heat. Despite his innovations and entrepreneurial energy he died in debt in 1693. His son Sir Talbot Clerke was more successful. George Skippe (qv) invested in Clerke's rackety schemes. One was to improve the navigation of the Worcestershire Stour, but they only managed to connect Kidderminster with Stourbridge. Skippe, who bought Clerke out of debtor's prison and never recovered his great debts, wrote of him in his diaries as 'that false man'.

Clifford: The family claimed descent from Duke Richard of Normandy, an ancestor of the Conqueror. In Herefordshire Richard fitz Pons (fl.1130), forebear of the Cliffords, was the steward of Clifford Castle, built by Earl William fitz Osbern (qv) 1069-71. After the rebellion of Earl William's heir the castle was granted to the de Tosnys, who appointed fitz Pons steward. He married Maud daughter of Walter of Gloucester, and was a supporter of Bernard de Neufmarché, Lord of Brecon who granted him the castle of Bronllys to hold at a knight's fee. Subsequently fitz Pons and Walter his son asserted their independent control over the castle, by simply refusing to move out, through strategic marriages and, frankly, by the pimping of Walter's daughter, fair Rosamund (qv), with Henry II. As sign of their permanence they adopted the name 'de Clifford'. The settlement that grew under the shadow of the castle became one of the largest in the county in this early period. Cliffords continued to control the castle, despite Henry II's disfavour, until 1311 when it passed to the Mortimers and fell into disuse. Association with a castle was essential in attracting a title and they were made Lords of Clifford in the intervening years. They became Barons of Westmorland in the 14th century and their base moved to Westmorland.

Clifford, Drogo de (d.1127) was, according to legend, one of the two fighting knights depicted on the font in Eardisley church, the other knight, so the story goes, being his son-in-law Ralph (I) de Baskerville (qv).

Clifford, Henry Morgan (1807-84), MP, eldest son of Morgan (qv) and Sophia, lived at Perrystone Court and Llantilio. He married Catherine, daughter of Joseph Yorke. He was MP for Hereford 1847-65. In 1865 he sold Perrystone to George Clive (qv), who converted it into a mock Elizabethan mansion, but it burnt down in 1959 and has been replaced by a new house.

Clifford, Lewis de (*c.*1359-1404), knight, was the son of Roger de Clifford of Westmorland and Maud de Beauchamp, daughter of the Earl of Warwick. He had an estate at Ewyas Harold. He fought in France with Henry V and was made Knight of the Garter. His will shows clear Lollard tendencies, requiring no burial pomp for the 'stinking carrion' of his body, nor any gifts to the church.

Clifford, Lucy de, daughter of Walter, married Hugh de Say (qv Richard Scrob) of Richard's Castle in the 1150s. They owned Stokesay Castle, which is named after Hugh.

Clifford, Morgan Morgan (1780-1814), of the Penallt Morgans, married Sophia Willington and they lived at old Perrystone Court near Foy with its landscaped grounds. Their daughter Emily (1814-68) married Philip Yorke (qv). Morgan was followed at Perrystone by his brother William Morgan Clifford (d.1850).

Clifford, Nicholas (d.1595), son of Henry Clifford and Anne Devereux, daughter of Walter, 2nd Viscount, was MP for Haverfordwest and in the service of his cousin Robert Devereux (qv), 2nd Earl of Essex, who knighted him for gallantry at Rouen in 1591. He married Frances, daughter of Sir William Drury. At Court he enraged Queen Elizabeth by wearing the French Order of St Michael. 'My dogs wear my collars', she shouted, imprisoned him, and made him return it. He was killed off Puerto Rico on Drake's last voyage.

Clifford, Richard fitz Pons (fl.1130s), steward of Clifford Castle for the de Tosnys (qv), married Maud daughter of Walter of Gloucester.

He was a supporter of Bernard de Neufmarché, Lord of Brecon, who granted him the castle of Bronllys to hold at a knight's fee.

Clifford, Robert de (1274-1314), 1st Baron de Clifford, son of Roger (II) de Clifford (qv under Roger (I)), was born at Clifford Castle. He was heir to his paternal grandfather's Herefordshire estates and also in 1308 to his maternal grandfather's castle at Appleby in Westmorland, becoming one of the most powerful barons in England and warden of the Scottish Marches. Thus ennobled, the Cliffords were now based in Westmorland and Yorkshire. They would be Earls of Cumberland and hereditary royal champions.

Clifford, Roger (I) de (d.1286) son of Walter (III), married Sybil daughter of Robert de Ewyas (qv under Ewyas), widow of Robert (I) de Tregoz (qv under Tregoz). As a punishment for rustling cattle and ill-treating the bishop's servants he was made to walk barefoot through the streets of Hereford and was chastised with a rod at the high altar of the cathedral by Thomas de Cantilupe (qv). He was buried in Dore Abbey where his effigy survives. His son, Roger (II) de Clifford, married Isabella de Vipont (d.1291), whose father was Baron of Appleby in Westmorland. He predeceased his father, dying in 1282.

Clifford, Rosamund (*c.*1140-76), fair Rosamund or *rosa mundi*, daughter of Sir Walter (qv) and Margaret, was Henry II's (qv) mistress, living in Woodstock Palace while Queen Eleanor was kept confined (see Henry II for more about this). Henry met Rosamund while campaigning against Rhys ap Gruffydd (qv). Her status is attested in a grant of the manor of Corfham by the king to Walter Clifford 'for the love of Rosamund his daughter'. Woodstock was Henry's favourite palace and he had many delightful features built there for her. In the 17th century John Aubrey (qv) sketched what was left of the pavilions and gardens. Rosamund died young and she and her mother were buried in the convent of Godstow near Oxford, which Henry enriched in her memory. Legend speculates that she was murdered by the jealous queen. Gerald of Wales (qv) called her *rosa immundi,* the flower of unchastity. Her tomb was later despoiled by a sour prelate.

Clifford, Walter de (1113-90), or Walter fitz Richard, was born at Clifford Castle, the son of Richard fitz Pons and Maud. He married Margaret, daughter of Ralph de Tosny (qv under Ralph de Tosny), who brought him the ownership of Clifford, which became the family name. Their children were Walter II (qv), Richard, Rosamund (qv), Amice and Lucy (qv).

Clifford, Walter (II) de (1160-1221), son of Walter (qv), was born on 17 January 1160. He married Agnes Cundy of Kent and had sons Walter (III), Roger, Hugh and Reginald and daughters Maud, Basilia and Cecilia. He was Sheriff of Hereford. Although he kept aloof from William (III) de Briouze's (qv) rebellion against King John (qv), John didn't trust him, and appointed his son Walter (III) (qv) to the barony in his place. His son Roger founded the northern branch of the family.

Clifford, Walter (III) de (d.1263), the son of Walter (II) de Clifford (qv) and Agnes, became Baron Clifford in 1208 on the disgrace of his father. His second wife, Margaret, was the daughter of Prince Llywelyn ab Iorwerth (qv). He rebelled against Henry III (qv) but the king subdued him by besieging Clifford Castle, and Walter joined with him against his father in-law at Brecon. In the 1250s Walter again offended Henry, apparently by making a royal messenger eat his message along with the huge wax seal. He had one daughter, Matilda, with Margaret, who, having been abducted, wrote to the king for help. Henry III set out to her assistance but was met by another message saying she had decided to marry her abductor.

Clissett, Phillip (1817-1901), chairmaker, was born in 1817 in the Worcestershire village of Birtsmorton and apprenticed as a *bodger* – a maker of rustic chairs. He set up his workshop

in Bosbury when he was 21 and married a local girl. Their son William died tragically on the eve of his wedding. Clissett's chairs were made from green wood using ash for the frames with elm seats, the wood coming from nearby Childer Wood on the Hopton (qv) Estate. He turned the wood on a pole lathe – a pliable ash pole attached to a treadle which spun the pole he was carving back and forwards. He made a chair a day, singing as he worked. James MacLaren (qv), discovered Clissett while he was working at Ledbury Park nearby and commissioned work from him. He introduced him to Ernest Gimson (qv) and Ernest Barnsley, both working at nearby Kempley Church. Gimson spent time with Clissett learning his skills. Clissett became well known, and by the turn of the century his chairs were being sold in Heals, and ladderback, rush-seated chairs became familiar Arts and Crafts items. Cheltenham Museum has a collection of Clissett's chairs and there are examples in Hereford Museum and Ledbury.

Clive, Archer (1800-79), a son of Edward Bolton Clive (d.1845, qv) and Harriet, was rector of Solihull, Warks. He lived at Whitfield and was JP and Deputy Lieutenant of Herefordshire. He married Caroline Wigley (qv Caroline Clive).

Clive (née Wigley), Caroline (1801-73), novelist and poet, was born at Brompton, London, on 30 June 1801, the second daughter of Edmund Wigley (1758-1821), who later changed his surname to Meysey-Wigley, and his wife, Anna Maria Meysey (d.1835). Caroline, who was disabled by childhood polio, inherited her father's wealth and married Revd Archer Clive (qv), whom she had long admired, on 10 November 1840. They lived at Whitfield with their children from 1847. When Hereford's Market Hall was demolished in 1861, eight columns were re-erected in the grounds of Whitfield. Caroline wrote poems which were quietly noticed, then *Essays on the Human Intellect as Constructed by God,* published in 1827 under the pseudonym Paul Ferroll. She was a friend of Elizabeth Barrett (qv). Later poetry was well received, the most admired being her satire *The Queen's Ball: a Poem by V* (1847). Her pseudonym 'V' stood for Vigolina, her husband's translation of Wigley. Her novel *Paul Ferroll* (1855, recently reissued) was thought immoral. It brought her celebrity and was translated into several languages. In a sequel, *Why Paul Ferroll Killed his Wife* (1859), V tried to introduce an acceptable motive. Later novels and poetry were less popular and her health suffered from accidents and a stroke. She died of burns after her dress caught fire in the library at Whitfield House, on 14 July 1873. The Clive family still live at Whitfield and have lately improved both house and park. In 1865 a relation, George Clive, bought Perrystone Court from the Cliffords (qv).

Clive, Edward (1704-71), judge, the eldest son of Edward Clive of Wormbridge and Sarah Key, daughter of a Bristol merchant, was educated at University College, Oxford and Lincoln's Inn. He was called to the bar in 1725, became Steward of Newcastle, Deputy Justice of Carmarthen in 1741 and MP for Mitchell

in Cornwall. He resigned in 1745 when he was appointed to the Bench, and was made a Baron of the Exchequer and knighted. He married Elizabeth daughter of Richard Symons (qv) of Mynde Park. After her death in 1762 he married Judith (d.1796), the daughter of his cousin Revd Benjamin Clive of Wormbridge where they lived. There were no children from either marriage. He is said to be the subject of Hogarth's satirical engraving *The Bench* (1758). Sir Edward retired from the Bench with a large pension and died the next year on 16 April 1771. He has a memorial in St Peter's, Wormbridge. Wormbridge House passed to Robert Clive, a distant relative. It was demolished in 1800; the present Wormbridge Court has been developed out of the stable block.

Clive, Edward Bolton (1765-1845) was the son of George Clive of Wormbridge, a partner of Gosling's Bank and cousin of Lord Clive of India. He bought Whitfield Court near Allensmore from Lady Stanhope (qv) in 1798, altered the house and laid out the park with his friend Uvedale Price's (qv) advice. He was a captain in the Foot Guards and married Harriet (d.1816), Lord Archer's daughter. He was chief steward of Herefordshire, Sheriff (1802-3) and MP for Hereford between 1826 and 1845. He was a Whig pressing for reform of pocket boroughs like Weobley, and in 1821 presided over a public dinner for the radical Joseph Hume (qv) in Hereford. He died on 22 July 1845, the same year as a son, and both have a monument in St Peter's Church, Wormbridge. Harriet has a wall tablet by William Theed Senior (qv).

Clive, Geoffrey de (d.1119), Bishop of Hereford 1115-9, was a chaplain of Henry I (qv), who appointed him bishop after Reinhelm's (qv) death. He was consecrated at Canterbury on 26 December 1115, accompanied by Adam de Port (qv) the Sheriff of Hereford. According to William of Malmesbury (qv) he was a country man interested in agriculture, close-fisted and intent on improving his manors to mend the waste of Bishop Reinhelm's (qv) days. He died on 2 February 1119 and was buried in Hereford Cathedral, commemorated by a 14th-century effigy in the north choir aisle.

Clodock or Clydawg (6th century), the pious King of Ewyas, was a son of King Brychan, many of whose 24 sons and 24 daughters were saints. He was murdered near the River Monnow by one who envied his sanctity. As his body was being carried in a cart across the river, the oxen stopped at the ford and here he was buried. Miracles occurred at the spot and a church was built. That the present 12th-century church dedicated to St Clodock is still more ancient is shown by a 9th-century inscription (qv Guindda). St Clodock's feast day is 3 November.

Clowes, John bought Burton Court, Eardisland in 1863 and had Kempson (qv) enlarge the service wing (1863-5). He was a Doctor of Law and a JP and was charitably involved in the area, giving a reading room to the parish. In 1895 he gave the estate to his son Col Peter Legh Clowes as a wedding present on his marriage to Miss Warren, daughter of the proprietor of the Warren Steamship Company. In 1914 Clough Williams-Ellis (qv) was commissioned for some sensitive refacing, retaining the house's glory. Their son was killed on the Western Front in 1918.

Clowes, Josiah (1735-94), civil engineer, the greatest of the early canal builders, surveyed and constructed the Hereford and Gloucester Canal as far as Ledbury. His 2,192-yard tunnel at Oxenhall, for which he brought in gin wheels from a previous tunnel, was commended by other engineers. He was born and died in north Staffordshire.

Clynton: Ivo de Clynton is recorded as the proprietor of Castleditch, Eastnor, in 1261 and in the next century a John Clynton was licensed to celebrate mass in a chapel there. In the 15th century William Clynton is recorded as possessing the house, gardens, orchards and a mill. His descendants continued to live there until about 1600 when Ivo de Clynton's son-in-law, a Reade, sold the estate to Richard Cocks (qv.1623).

Cobbett, William (1763-1835), journalist and farmer, was born on 9 March 1763 in Farnham, Surrey, the son of a farm labourer. He was an irritation to the government with his popular weekly newspaper *The Political Register* (later *Hansard*) which reported parliamentary debates. He produced popular books: an *English Grammar* for the apprentice and the plough boy and, his best known, *Rural Rides* (1830), which is still in print. On the first of his rides round the kingdom he stayed with a Mr Palmer at Old Hall, Orcop and enjoyed a day's hare hunting with his hounds. On his return to Herefordshire in September 1826 he was surprised to find the country people contented and polite at a time of national upheaval. He thought Hereford cattle 'the finest and most beautiful of all horn cattle' and was similarly impressed by the Leicester breed of sheep he found. He sat for various Parliamentary seats and died on 18 June 1835.

Cockerell, Frederick Pepys (1833-78) FRIBA, architect, designed Ledbury Cemetery (1861), its funerary chapels, walls and gates.

Cocks; Somers/Sommers: The Cocks, later the Somers Cocks, were a prosperous family of London merchants who retired to a manor house in Eastnor and started to buy up the farms around them. Two strategic marriages made them very wealthy: Charles Cocks married Mary, sister and heiress of William III's Lord Chancellor John Somers; then John Somers Cocks married the daughter of the rich antiquarian Dr Treadway Nash (qv). They formed a partnershp with Ledbury neighbours the Biddulphs (qv) to found the successful bank Cocks, Biddulph & Co. Aided by these ventures, the Somers Cocks, as they now were, became barons, then earls, and replaced their manor house with the present fairy-tale castle. The current proprietors, the Hervey-Bathursts, are descendants of the Somers Cocks dynasty.

Cocks, Arthur Herbert Tennyson Somers (1887-1944), 6th Baron Somers, was the only son of Herbert Haldane Somers Cocks (1861-1944) and his wife, Blanche Clogstoun (d.1895, qv G.F. Watts), daughter of Major Herbert Clogstoun. His grandfather, Arthur Herbert Cocks, was born at Freshwater on the Isle of Wight where Alfred Tennyson stood godfather. He succeeded his great-uncle (Philip Reginald Cocks, qv under Charles Somers Cocks) as Baron Somers in 1899 aged 12. He fought with the 1st Life Guards through the First World War, becoming commander of the 6th Battalion in the first tank regiment, and was awarded DSC, MC and the Légion d'Honneur. He inherited Eastnor Castle in 1922 and was Lord Lieutenant of Herefordshire. He was Chief Scout of Great Britain, a Freemason and the Empire and Governor of the State of Victoria, Australia. Lord Somers married Daisy Finola Meeking in 1921 and had an only daughter, Elizabeth Verena, (1922-86), who married

Major Benjamin Alexander Frederick Hervey-Bathurst (1920-97), second son of Sir Frederick Edward William Hervey-Bathurst, 5th Baronet. At the death of the 6th Baron the barony died out, leaving the Eastnor estate in the hands of the Hervey-Bathurst family.

Cocks, Charles (1642-1727), youngest son of Thomas (I) (qv) and Elizabeth, married Mary, daughter of John and Catherine Somers of Whiteladies, Worcester. Mary's brother, John Somers (b.1651) was an attorney who rose after the Glorious Revolution to be Attorney General and Lord Chancellor as Baron Somers of Evesham. He amassed property including Somers Town at St Pancras, London, given to him by a grateful King William. At his death Elizabeth and Mary, Charles Cocks' wife, were co-heirs, and Charles and Mary gained possession of half the Somers fortune. They moved to Worcester where Charles was MP first and then for Droitwich. Their second son John married his cousin Mary Cocks (qv Thomas (III) Cocks), heiress of Castleditch, linking the Somers' fortune and the Cocks' Eastnor estate.

Cocks, Charles (1725-1806), 1st Baron Somers of Evesham, was born on 29 June 1725 at Castleditch, Eastnor, eldest son of John and Mary Cocks. He was educated at Westminster and St Alban's Hall, Oxford and married Elizabeth Eliot (d.1771). Their daughter Anna Maria (d.1835) married Revd Philip Yorke (qv). Cocks was MP for Reigate, where the Cocks family had property, and in 1784 was rewarded for supporting the Hanoverians with the title Baron Somers; a title revived from his great-uncle, John Somers, King William's Lord Chancellor (qv under Charles Cocks, d.1727. He sat in both houses of parliament for 58 years and greatly extended the Eastnor estate. After Elizabeth's death he married Anne Pole (1752-1833). There were children from both wives. He died on 30 January 1806, his heir being his eldest son John. His third son James (1790-1856), a prebendary of Hereford Cathedral, died unmarried at Mathon and was buried at Eastnor.

Cocks, Charles Somers (1819-1883), 3rd Earl Somers, was born on 14 July 1819, the son of the 2nd Earl (John Somers Cocks, d.1852, qv). In the 1860s he employed G.E. Fox (qv) to fashion the library at Eastnor. He was government whip in the House of Lords in Lord Aberdeen's coalition government and, from 1855-7, in the Liberal government of Lord Palmerston. In 1850 he married Virginia, the daughter of James Pattle, and they had three daughters, the eldest being Lady Isabella Caroline (qv). Another daughter was Julia Margaret Cameron, the photographer. At the 3rd Earl's death on 26 September 1883 without male issue, the earldom ceased and the junior title of Baron Somers was inherited by his cousin, Philip Reginald Cocks. Countess Somers died in 1910. The 3rd Earl's effigy in the family chapel in Eastnor Church was designed by Fox.

Cocks, Isabella Caroline Somers (1851-1921), married name Lady Henry Somerset, was born in London on 3 August 1851, eldest daughter of the 3rd Earl (Charles Somers Cocks, qv). In 1872 she married Lord Henry Richard Charles Somerset (1849-1932, qv), the Duke of Beaufort's second son. The marriage failed when Lord Henry's homosexuality became evident, and after the birth of a son, Henry Charles Somers Augustus Somerset (1874-1945), he left the family and moved to Italy. Lady Henry retired from the disgrace and engaged in good works from her family homes, Eastnor Castle and Reigate Priory. After her father's death in 1883 she devoted the Somers Cocks fortune to the temperance movement as well as women's causes including female suffrage and the housing and employment of poor girls and women. She built a Home for Girls on the Eastnor Estate (1899) and commissioned estate cottages from the Arts and Crafts architect James MacLaren (qv), as well as a girls' school from Edmund Fisher. She was head of the British Women's Temperance Association and turned the Somers Arms at Eastnor into a temperance hotel. Her friend, the American Temperance activist Frances Willard (qv), often stayed at Eastnor with her. She was involved with the poor and inebriate of Ledbury and provided

the corrugated iron Mission Halls in Bye Street and in Hollybush. The well she had built on Eastnor village green has terracotta reliefs she designed and modelled in an Italian Renaissance style, and her churchyard seat with five terracotta reliefs shows the influence of her mother's admirer G.F. Watts (qv). She wrote a novel *Under the Arch of Life* and other books such as *Our Village Life*, which she illustrated herself. She died on 12 March 1921 after an appendix operation and was buried in Brookwood Cemetery, Surrey.

Cocks, James (b.1734), born on 22 June 1734, was the younger brother of Sir Charles (qv, d.1806). He married Martha Watson in 1772 and they had four sons and four daughters. In 1757 James was invited by Francis Biddulph (qv) to be a founding partner of the banking house Cocks, Biddulph & Co., which was capitalized with Cocks funds. His son James was also a partner in the bank.

Cocks, John (*c.*1690-1771) was the second son of Charles Cocks (qv, d.1727) and Mary. He was educated at Merton College, Oxford. In accordance with Revd Thomas (III) Cocks' will he married his cousin Mary Cocks on her father's death in 1724; an arranged but happy marriage. They lived at Castleditch and had many children: Charles (qv, d.1806), John (b.1731), a clergyman, Joseph (1732-75), James (b.1734), a banker, Philip (1735-97), a clergyman and Thomas Sommers [sic] Cocks (qv). Joseph has a splendid monument in Eastnor Church, designed by James 'Athenian' Stuart and cut by Thomas Scheemakers. John Cocks was High Sheriff of Herefordshire in 1732. He died on 24 June 1771 and Mary on 4 February 1779. Her epitaph reads 'There never was a better mother of children, she taught them all to read herself, and trained them ... by example as well as by precept ... No-one throughout life was more beloved.' Her letters illustrate her nature.

Cocks, John Somers (1760-1841), 1st Earl Somers, was born on 6 May 1760 the eldest son of Sir Charles (Charles Cocks, qv, d.1806), whom he succeeded as 2nd Baron Somers and from whom he inherited great wealth. He was educated at Westminster and St Alban's Hall, Oxford. In 1785 he married Margaret, daughter of Treadway Russell Nash (qv), who brought him more wealth, and they had three sons and one daughter. Old Castleditch was considered unsuitable, despite the Georgian wing that had recently been added, and Sir John commissioned a romantic castle from Robert Smirke (qv) on higher ground above the old house. The result, Eastnor Castle, was a Regency confection in a pre-Puginian mix of styles. Lord John laid the foundation stone on 23 June 1812 and work proceeded quickly. The estate provided all the timber but the roof trusses were of cast iron. The castle was built with great speed and the costs became astronomical. The west wing was up by 1813 and the family were able to move in soon after, although the place continued to be a building site for another ten years. In 1818 Castleditch Manor was pulled down and the valley dammed to provide the 7-acre lake. The park was famed for specimen trees, especially conifers, planted by the first two head gardeners Mr Deakin and William Coleman, who between them were in office for almost a century. In 1812 Somers put up a monument in the Park to commemorate his family: the Lord Chancellor; his eldest son Edward Charles Cocks, who had died aged 26 before the walls of

Burgos during Wellington's Peninsular War; and his brother James Cocks who had died young on an earlier French battlefield. From 1817 to his death he was Lord Lieutenant of Herefordshire and in 1821 he was created Earl Somers. His wife Margaret died in February 1831, and in 1834 he married his cousin Jane, daughter of his uncle James Cocks. The 1st Earl died at the peak of the family's prosperity on 5 January 1841 and was buried in the family vault in Eastnor Church. He was succeeded by John (qv, d.1852), his second son. Jane, Countess Somers died in November 1868.

Cocks, John Somers (1788-1852), 2nd Earl Somers, was born on 19 March 1788. He was Viscount Eastnor between 1821 and his father's (John, qv) death in 1841, becoming heir when his older brother Edward (see under John Somers Cocks, d.1841) was killed in the Peninsular War. He went to Westminster School and also served in the Peninsular War. He succeeded Edward as MP for Reigate, 1812-8. He married Lady Caroline Harriet, daughter of Philip Yorke, 3rd Earl of Hardwick and was MP for Hereford between 1818 and 1832. On succeeding to the earldom he assumed the name Somers Cocks. From 1846-9 A.W.N. Pugin (qv) and J.G. Crace (qv) created the castle's dining room with its coved ceiling and ornate fireplace: featuring a painted genealogical tree and Minton tiles which bore Somers' heraldic emblems. Some of Smirke's original furnishings have survived. Despite massive expenditure, the family fortunes flourished and the estate exceeded 13,000 acres; with the agricultural depression of the 1870s, however, a decline set in. His daughter, Lady Harriet Catherine, married Francis Wegg-Prosser (qv). Earl Somers died on 5 October 1852.

Cocks, Philip James (1774-1857), was born on 2 December 1774, the third son of Charles (qv, d.1806) and his second wife Anne. He married Frances Herbert (1782-1870) and they lived in Colwall. He was MP for Herefordshire, filling the seat vacated by his half-brother John (qv) on his elevation as 2nd Baron, and he was lieutenant colonel in the army. He died in Hereford on 1 April 1857.

Cocks, Richard (1564-1623), third son of Thomas Cocks (d.1601) of Bishop's Cleeve, Gloucs and Elizabeth (d.1605), was an apprenticed grocer in London. He became a wealthy merchant, an alderman and one of the founders of the East India Company. He married Judith Elliot (d.1638) in 1598 and they had eight sons and six daughters, living in Maiden Lane in the City of London. In *c.*1601 he bought the 16th-century manor house, Castleditch at Eastnor; by 1616 he had retired there and become High Sheriff of Herefordshire. It was to be the family home until Eastnor Castle was built. He and Judith were buried in St Mary's, Eastnor. The three youngest sons, John, Henry and Charles, were educated at the Inns of Court and became lawyers in London.

Cocks, Richard (d.1684), 1st Baronet, was the second son of Richard (qv) and Judith and married Susanna Elton, sister of his brother's wife Anne. They lived in Ledbury initially. Richard later joined his uncle, Christopher Cocks, on a diplomatic journey to Russia. Richard (d.1669) their son predeceased Sir Richard, so his son, also Richard, inherited the baronetcy.

Cocks, Thomas (I) (1599-1649), Richard's (qv, d.1623) eldest son, married Anne Unett (qv under Unett family), the widowed daughter of Ambrose Elton (qv), and lived at Massington, a Cocks property near Colwall, with their sons Thomas, John and Richard. When Anne died Thomas married Elizabeth Gower and they had two sons, Henry and Charles. After his mother Judith's death the family moved to Castleditch. During the Civil War this house was attacked by Captain Hopton (qv) and the family fled for a while.

Cocks, Thomas (II) (1629-1704), the eldest son of Thomas (I) Cocks (qv) and Anne, succeeded to the Castleditch estates aged 20. He married Mary Hackett (d.1675), daughter of the rector of Ross. Their sons were John, Thomas (III) (qv), Charles and Seth, and they also had four daughters, Elizabeth, Dorothy, Frances and Mary, all of whom married. Cocks senior was High Sheriff of the county in 1663 and '69.

When Mary died he married Frances. Thomas and Mary are buried in Eastnor Church. His eldest son John, whose portrait survives in Eastnor Castle, inherited Castleditch but died unmarried.

Cocks, Thomas (III) (1666-1724), clergyman, the youngest son of Thomas (II) Cocks (qv) and his wife Mary, inherited Castleditch on his brother John's death in 1718 (qv under Thomas (II) Cocks), when he was rector of a Leicestershire parish. As a condition of his will his daughter Mary was required to marry his closest male relative, John, second son of Charles Cocks of Worcester (qv, d.1727), to keep the estates in the family.

Cocks, Thomas Sommers (1737-96), was born on 3 December 1737 at Castleditch, youngest child of John (Cocks, d.1771, qv) and Mary. He was a partner of the Cocks, Biddulph Bank. He married Anne Thistlethwayte (d.1818) in 1768 and their son Thomas worked at the bank. Thomas Sommers lived in London whilst working at the bank but also had rooms at Castleditch. In 1774 he bought the Bronsil Castle Estate from the Reeds (qv). Like his mother, he was a charming letter writer. He died on 15 November 1796. His son Thomas's children were Thomas (b.1782) and Reginald. They did not live in Herefordshire but were the ancestors of future Somers Cocks.

Coffin, Isaac (1759-1839), baronet and admiral in the Royal Navy, was born in Boston, Massachusetts and was involved with all of the naval actions of the late 18th century; he achieved high rank and was created baronet. He married Elizabeth (1771-1839) daughter of William and Elizabeth Greenly of Titley Court in 1811. When her father died in 1835, aged 93, Sir Isaac and Lady Elizabeth lived at the Court. Coffin experimented with aspects of food preparation and invented an industrial oven for baking biscuits for sailors. He presented J.G. Cotterell's (qv) prize Hereford bull, called *Sir Isaac* after him, to a Massachusetts society to encourage the breeding of Herefords in America. Coffin's wife died before him and is

buried in St Peter's Church, Titley where there are inscriptions to her and her parents. Coffin, who was said to be distraught at her death, died soon after her and was buried in Cheltenham.

Coke, George (1570-1646), Bishop of Hereford 1636-46, was born at Trusley, Derbyshire on 3 April 1570, younger brother of Sir John Coke (qv). He was educated at St John's Cambridge. Coke was appointed Bishop of Bristol and in 1636 was translated to Hereford, 'this place of tryal', where he was surrounded by 'men who were too strong and cunnying for me'. He was in trouble with Archbishop Laud (qv) who accused him of nepotism; indeed, his son Richard was vicar of Eastnor and Chancellor of Hereford; John a prebend and rector of Ross and Whitbourne, and William a prebend, vicar of Bosbury and a portionist of Bromyard. In 1641 Coke was one of the 12 bishops who petitioned Parliament and were imprisoned in the Tower. In Hereford, the city was taken by Parliamentary forces; his palace was used as governor's residence and the soldiery were loose in the cathedral. They withdrew, but when Hereford was taken by Col Birch (qv), Coke, with other prominent citizens, was arrested and imprisoned, first in Gloucester and then in London. His house, Queest Moor, Eardisley was sequestered for the use of Birch, who

kept most of the cathedral's revenue for himself. Coke was finally allowed to return to relatives at Eardisley, where he died, exhausted and impoverished, on 10 December 1646. He was buried in St Mary Magdalene, Eardisley. At the Restoration an ornate monument was erected to him in the cathedral showing him in the wide lawn sleeves of the period; it fell into disrepair and in the 19th century relatives restored it to its present form.

Coke, John (1563-1644), politician, was born on 5 March 1563 in London, the son of Richard Coke and older brother of George Coke (qv). He was educated at Westminster School and Trinity College Cambridge, where he lectured in rhetoric. In 1604 he married Marie, daughter of John Powell of Preston near Ledbury and their love letters survive. He was out of favour with James I (qv) and sought retirement in Herefordshire. While living with Marie's parents at Preston he bought a nearby estate at Kynaston and built the house, Hall Court, which is still substantially to be seen. Coke's letters show concern at Marie's personal involvement in the building of the house, her management of the agricultural estate and the education of the children while he was away at Cambridge. Their letters and other material were brought to Hall Court from Cambridge by the carrier Thomas Hobson (qv). Coke was collector of taxes and subsidies from the Radlow and Greytree (i.e. his local) hundreds. In 1618 his career improved and the family moved to London. Here however Marie died (1624) and, left with five children, Coke married Joan, daughter of Sir Robert Lee, alderman of London. Through the patronage of Buckingham he was made chief commissioner of the Navy and appointed one of King Charles' Secretaries of State. He was elected MP throughout the 1620s and was knighted in 1630. In 1628 Coke sold Hall Court for £3,000 to Dr Samuel Fell (qv). Sir John's family was split in the Civil Wars with one son for the King and one for Parliament, a predicament that exemplified the times. He was thought delinquent by Parliament but made his peace through the Earl of Essex (qv Devereux). He died at the height of the conflict.

Colborne, Langdon (1835-89) was born on 15 September 1835 in Hackney near London. He studied the organ under George Cooper, an organist of the Chapel Royal and assistant organist at St Paul's. Colborne was organist at various churches including Sir Frederick Ouseley's (qv) St Michael's College, Tenbury. In 1877 Ouseley was developing the musical life of Hereford Cathedral as Precentor and had Colborne appointed organist and choir master after the death of Townshend Smith (qv). Colborne had trouble with choir discipline and found Ouseley a useful ally. He introduced oratorios into services – Bach at Christmas and Handel at Easter. He died in 1889 and was buried in the cathedral, where he is commemorated in a north transept clerestory window by Clayton and Bell (qv).

Coleridge, Samuel Taylor (1772-1834), poet and philosopher, was born on 21 October 1772 in Ottery St Mary in Devon where his father was vicar and headmaster of the grammar school. He was inordinately precocious. The book of verse he produced with Wordsworth (qv), *Lyrical Ballads*, marked the start of the English Romantic movement. He loved the Wye Valley and with and without the Wordsworths often walked there. During one tour in 1794 he stayed at the King's Arms in Ross and wrote *Lines written at The King's Arms, Ross, formerly the House of the Man of Ross*:

> *Richer than miser o'er his countless hoards,*
> *Nobler than kings or king-polluted lords,*
> *Here dwelt the man of Ross.*

He died in Highgate, London on 25 July 1834, his health undermined by his opium addiction.

Colles: From the 16th century proprietors of the manor of Hatfield, where they built Hatfield Court *c.*1590, selling their old manor of Leigh in Worcestershire to Sir Walter Devereux. Hatfield was previously owned by the Pauncefoots (qv). In the late 16th century Jane Colles married Roger Dansey (qv). Sarah Colles (1650-72), daughter and heiress of Timothy Colles (d.1669), married Thomas Geers (qv, d.1700) and died following childbirth. There are memorials to Timothy and Sara in St Leonards, Hatfield, one of the oldest churches in the county. Hatfield Court was rebuilt in the 1850s.

Collins, John (1741-97) was a Shakespearean scholar and rector of Ledbury. Born in Cornwall, he was educated at Eton and Queen's College, Oxford and took holy orders. He married a Cornish cousin, Mary Kendall (d.1781), and they had six children. He drew vitriolic attacks from George Steevens in his 1773 edition of Shakespeare with his defence of Edward Capell, who had refuted Steevens' views. Collins had Capell's edition of Shakespeare criticism *Notes and Various Readings to Shakespeare* (2 vols.) published after Capell's death and later his *The School of Shakespeare* became the focus for further attacks from Steevens and Dr Johnson too. His wife and his friend Capell both died in 1781 leaving Collins in an anxious state and increasingly penurious. He was seen by ecclesiastical patrons as too somnolent a cleric for further advancement and spent his last 30 years in Ledbury rectory. Poor Collins continued to be attacked by Steevens in further editions of Shakespeare and he died at Penryn, Cornwall, on 20 March 1797.

Collins, William (fl.1910) 'of Hereford', author, sometimes signed himself A.L.O.H. He wrote a series of books and pamphlets published by Jakeman & Carver (qv) such as *A Short History of Hereford*, dedicated to Charles Anthony (qv) and a series of 'short history' pamphlets about Hereford churches: *All Saints, St Peter's, St James's, St Nicholas's* and *St Francis Xavier's*. Other works include *The Mayors of Hereford*; *Modern Hereford* and *The Anglican Churches of Hereford*.

Combe, Martha Howell Bennett (1806-93) was the eldest of the five daughters of John Edwards, ironmonger of Widemarsh Street, and his wife Martha, who were all born and educated in Hereford. She was schooled at Miss Croucher's Academy of Drawing at the Gate House in Widemarsh Street, where she had drawing classes from David Cox (qv), who taught there 1814-9. The family moved to High Street, Oxford in the 1830s and Martha did parish work in St Mary's under the vicar J.H. Newman's direction, and was mentioned in his *Letters & Diaries*. In 1840 she married Thomas Combe (1796-1872), prosperous printer to the Oxford University Press and High Churchman, and they lived in a house at The Press. Combe was an early supporter of the Pre-Raphaelites, and especially of their founder, Holman Hunt. In 1850 he paid 150 guineas for *A Converted British Family* by Hunt, who stayed with Martha and Thomas in 1852. It was the Tractarian atmosphere with its mediaeval air that drew Burne-

Jones (qv) and Morris to Oxford, where they met with the Combes. Combe also collected David Cox's (qv) work. Following her husband's death, the widowed Martha continued adding to the Combe art collection, which she presented to the university; she gave Holman Hunt's *Light of the World* to Keble College.

Combe, William (1741-1823) wrote *The Three Tours of Dr Syntax,* illustrated by Thomas Rowlandson. This satirical poem appeared in Ackermann's *Political Magazine* between 1809 and 1811. The first tour is of relevance to Herefordshire, where Dr Syntax, 'in search of the Picturesque', satirises Price and Knight (qqv) and the fad of Wye tourism. Dr Syntax was a great celebrity but Combe, an indefatigable hack and raconteur, spent the last part of his life in debtors' prison. He died on 19 June 1823.

Comper, John Ninian (1864-1960), architect and designer, was born on 10 June 1864 in Aberdeen, the first of the seven children of Revd John Comper and Ellen his wife, both English Tractarians. He studied art at the Ruskin School at Oxford. His father showed him St Michael's, Camden while it was being built by George Bodley (qv), a relation, and his experience of its proportions and purity converted him to the study of architecture. Bodley took him on as an apprentice and he and John P. Seddon (qv) were abiding influences. Comper's first completed building was the Church of the Holy Name in Malvern Link (1893), which shows Bodley's influence. He believed in a simple, integrated design with the focus on the altar. At St George's, Brinsop he designed a gold and alabaster reredos under a ceilure. He carved the rood figures, rebuilt the east window and designed the stained glass which bears his mark, a strawberry plant, in the corner. One window commemorates the Wordsworths (qv). In 1890 he married Grace Bucknall and they had a son, Nicholas. Comper was knighted in 1950. He died on 22 December 1960 and his ashes are buried beneath the windows he designed in Westminster Abbey.

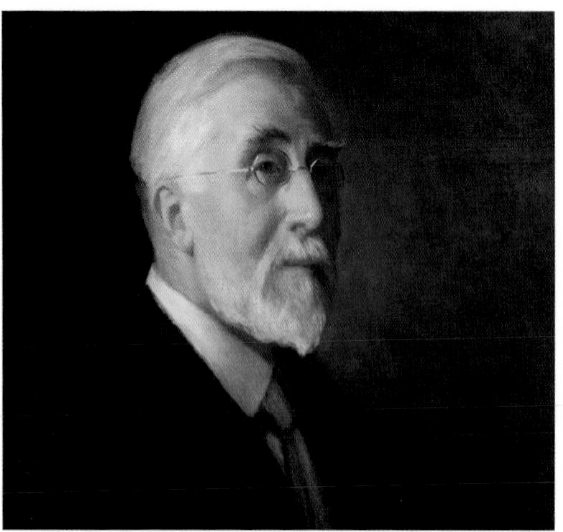

Conan Doyle, see under **Doyle, Arthur Ignatius Conan**.

Concun, see under **Mailseru**.

Coningsby: The family moved into Herefordshire from Herts. in the 16th century when they bought Hampton (later Court), south-east of Leominster. Their arms show three coneys. They were JPs and MPs in Herefordshire until the 18th century, vying with the Crofts and Scudamores to be the senior knights of the shire. They tended to be choleric: outstanding even by Coningsby standards were the corpulent Sir Thomas (qv, d.1625), whose long-running feud with Sir James Croft (qv, d.1590) involved serious violence; and Thomas 1st Earl (d.1729), who fought a duel with Lord Chandos, ran off with a Scudamore wife and eloped with another colleague's daughter. But he was highly valued by William III and perhaps saved his life. Humphrey, who died in 1610 (or at least disappeared then), left a cabinet of curiosities including a sea-horse-tooth hourglass and an anthology of the poetry of the famous Elizabethans he had known. The first and only earl lost his heir tragically and his titles became extinct. Hampton Court passed to his daughter Frances and her husband Charles Hanbury Williams, then to their daughter, who married the Capel Earl of Essex, who sold the estate to the Arkwrights.

Coningsby, Fitzwilliam, (*c.*1596-1666), only surviving son of Sir Thomas (d.1625, qv) was educated at Hereford Cathedral School and Lincoln College, Oxford. He was High Steward of Leominster in 1605. In 1617 he married Cecily (*c.*1604-after 1652), the daughter of Henry Neville, 7th Lord Abergavenny and Lady Mary Sackville, and they had three sons and two daughters. He was MP for Hereford in 1621, and with brother MP Francis Smalman (qv) attempted to clear the weirs along the Wye, which impeded trade. He was returned as the Royalist member in the Parliament of 1640, with Robert Harley (qv, d.1656). He was the leader of the Royalist party in Herefordshire and one of the Nine Worthies (see index).

Coningsby, George Capel (1757-1839), 5th Earl of Essex, was born George Capel, Viscount Malden, at Cassiobury near Watford on 13 November 1757. He was the son of William-Anne Capel, 4th Earl of Essex and Frances Williams, the daughter of Sir Charles Hanbury Williams (qv). He was a friend of the Prince of Wales, who trusted him, in 1797, with his declaration of love to 'Perdita', Mrs Robinson. Essex took her on as his own mistress after the prince's passion had cooled and proved her friend by negotiating a settlement from the prince. Capel adopted the surname Coningsby when he inherited Hampton Court from the Countess of Coningsby. He was High Steward of Leominster in 1802 and Lord Lieutenant of Herefordshire 1802-17. He died at Cassiobury on 23 April 1839. Hampton Court and the Coningsbys' Herefordshire lands were sold to John Arkwright (qv).

Coningsby, Humphrey (1516-59), son of Sir Thomas Coningsby (qv, d.1527) of Hampton, was born on 1 March 1516. He was brought up by his grandfather, Sir Humphrey, after his father's death, but was still a minor when his grandfather died also. A servant of Thomas Cromwell, he was a steward of Leominster and a JP in the county. He married Anne daughter of Sir Thomas Englefield, his father's colleague on the King's Bench. They had two sons and three daughters. He was a gentleman pensioner in Mary's reign and elected knight of the shire. He bought church lands at Bodenham and buildings of Leominster Priory, and acquired the Hereford Blackfriars, which had passed through the hands of the Scudamores since the Dissolution. In 1557 he was licensed to build two woollen mills with 40 broad cloth looms. He was re-elected to Westminster in 1559 but died that year. Anne his widow married their neighbour Sir John Hubaud (qv). Anne and Humphrey are buried in St Mary's Church, Hope under Dinmore, where their monument remains.

Coningsby, Humphrey (1567-1610/11), traveller and collector of poems, was a son of John Coningsby and cousin of Sir Thomas (qv, d.1625). A resident in Shropshire, he was close to the family at Hampton. He compiled an anthology of contemporaries, including Queen Elizabeth, Sir Philip Sidney etc. He disappeared on his way to Venice in 1610, leaving his cabinet of curiosities, which included a sea-horse-tooth hour-glass, to his cousin Thomas. His splendid memorial is at Neen Sollars in Shropshire.

Coningsby, Humphrey (1622-92), eldest son of Fitzwilliam Coningsby and Cecily, was baptised on 22 September 1622 at Hampton. He married Lettice, daughter of Sir Arthur Loftus and had issue Elizabeth and Thomas. He was Royalist MP for the county until 1644 when he was evicted.

Coningsby, Thomas (d.1527), knight, was a son of Sir Humphrey Coningsby, a Justice of the King's Bench and MP in Henry VIII's time and Alice Ferebie. He married Cicely, daughter and co-heiress of John Salwey of Stanford, Worcestershire. In 1510 he bought Hampton, later Court, from the Leinthalls (qv).

Coningsby, Thomas (1550-1625) was born at Hampton on 9 October 1550, the second son of Humphrey Coningsby (qv, d.1559). His older brother Edward died shortly after their father and Thomas succeeded as a minor. He also owned lands at Bodenham, Pencombe and Orleton. He was introduced at Court by

his patron the Earl of Leicester and travelled with Philip Sidney, Leicester's nephew, on his European tour in 1573. He married Philippa, daughter of Sir William Fitzwilliam and his wife Anne, who was a Sidney. They had ten children. Coningsby was at the siege of Rouen, where he was knighted by Essex, and wrote a memoir of the campaign. After Essex's fall he succeeded him as steward of Leominster. As Deputy Lieutenant he was often at odds with the leading figure in the county, the prickly Sir James Croft (qv, d.1590). They were opposed in religion, Coningsby being Calvinist while the Crofts were Catholic, and abuse and affrays occurred between their servants in Kington, Leominster and Hereford markets. There was even more serious feuding between Sir Thomas and Croft's stepson Thomas Wigmore (qv). John Aubrey (qv) tells of a Mr Brown, brother-in-law of Coningsby, who was murdered and whose ghost returned many times to declare the fact. After Croft's death, Coningsby was senior knight of the shire in Elizabeth's later Parliaments, although his poor health and great corpulence made it increasingly hard for him to get there. His wife brought him the remains of the preceptory of the Knights of St John of Jerusalem off Widemarsh Street as her dowry. In 1614 he converted the conventual buildings of the Blackfriars which his father had bought into Coningsby's Hospital for old soldiers and serving-men with 12 cottages for them. He instituted rules that provided for a chaplain to preach a sermon and march the servitors to the cathedral each Sunday, and for the senior resident to be known as Corporal Coningsby. The almshouses, chapel and chaplain survive today. Sir Thomas, an increasingly difficult man, is said to be the model for Sir Puntarvolo in Ben Jonson's *Every Man in His Humour*. Sir Robert Harley (qv, d.1656) gave up his negotiations for the hand of his daughter Anne because of his impossible conditions. She eventually married Sir Richard Tracy of Hatfield, Herts. Katherine married Sir Thomas Morgan (qv, d.1679) and Elizabeth Sir Humphrey Baskerville (qv, d.1647) of Eardisley Castle. Sir Thomas died on 30 May 1625 and was buried next to Philippa at St Mary's, Hope under Dinmore.

Coningsby, Thomas (1656-1729), 1st Earl of Coningsby, was born at Hampton (Court) on 2 November 1657, the only son of Humphrey (qv, d.1692). He studied law at Lincoln's Inn in 1671 and was called to the bar. He married Barbara, daughter of Ferdinando Gorges (qv); they had three sons and four daughters, though they later divorced. He was MP for Leominster from 1679-1710, a Whig and an ally of Lord Scudamore (qv John, d.1697), whose wife, Lady Frances, he seduced and abducted. Scudamore pursued them, bringing her back at pistol point. In 1698 Coningsby was found *in flagrante* with the wife of another colleague, Richard Jones, Earl of Ranelagh. In the same year he married Jones's daughter Frances (1674-1715), who was promptly disinherited by her angry father. Their son died aged two in 1708 by choking on a cherry stone. This is alluded to on their monument in St Mary's, Hope under Dinmore, the Coningsby church, in which the boy holds the fatal cherry. Coningsby owned the monastic buildings at Leominster Priory, which he converted into the town gaol. He was paymaster of King William's army and was with the king at the Battle of the Boyne in 1690 when William was shot in the shoulder; Coningsby staunched the blood with his handkerchief. He stayed on in Ireland to round up James II's army and put William's conciliatory measures into effect, for which he was made Baron Coningsby of Clanbrassil in the Irish Peerage. Back in London Coningsby looked after William's affairs in Parliament and sat in his inner cabinet formulating policy. His attachment to the king was such that he added Court to Hampton as a reference to the king's palace. Sir Thomas had a choleric temper and pursued feuds with the Crofts, the Harleys (Lord Oxford and the Bishop of Hereford) and Robert Price (qqv). Robert Harley's rise under Queen Anne led to Coningsby's decline and he retired to his Herefordshire interests as Lord Lieutenant. Under King George, Harley's nemesis, he fared better, and in 1719 he was created Earl of Coningsby. In 1697 he fought a duel with Lord Chandos (qv James Brydges, d.1714) about the chief stewardship of Hereford. He was at odds with his tenants and published a pamphlet attacking the Lord Chancellor, for which he was punished with six months in the Tower of London. Leominster Corporation complained through Lord Chandos to the Privy Council about his tyrannical activity as steward and Coningsby was ejected. He was not on terms with either of his fathers-in-law and excluded his sons by Lady Barbara from their inheritance: he settled the title and estate on Margaret and Frances, his daughters by his second wife. Frances married Sir Charles Hanbury Williams (qv). Margaret became Viscountess Coningsby of Hampton Court in 1717 and it was she who erected the monument in St Mary's to her mother and brother. When the Duke of Marlborough died in 1722, Coningsby, aged 65, proposed to his widow, who presumed he was mad. He died at Hampton Court on 30 April 1729 and was buried with his ancestors in

St Mary's, Hope under Dinmore. His Irish and English baronies became extinct soon after his death and the Hampton Court estate passed to his younger daughter Frances and her husband Charles Hanbury Williams (qv). There is a beautiful estate map in Hereford Record Office of *c.*1720 showing the Coningsby lands around Marden.

Constantine (6th c.), King of Ergyng (ie Archenfield). In the century after the Romans had left their civil settlement at *Ariconium* (near Weston under Penyard) King Constantine authorised the refounding of the Romano-Christian church in the town to a safer place at Garthbenni on a hill above the Wye, later to be the site of Goodrich Castle. His bishop, Dyfrig (qv Dubricius), consequently founded a monastery and bishop's house here which flourished until Viking and Welsh incursions sacked many churches in western Herefordshire. The *Book of Llandaff* names six 'bishops in Archenfield' following Dyfrig: Inabwy (6th c.), Ufelfwy (early 7th c.), Berthwyn (early 8th c.), Tyrchan (mid 8th c.), Nudd (late 9th c.) and Cyfeiliog (d.927). With the troubles of the 11th century Bishop Herewald of Archenfield moved Constantine's church again, combining it with the 'church of the 12 saints' at Welsh Bicknor. This church came by a confused memory to be known as St Constantine of Bicknor.

Cooke, Charles Walwyn Radcliffe (1840-1911), politician and promoter of cider, was born on 16 January 1840 at Hellens, Much Marcle. His father was Robert Duffield Cooke (1796-1882) and his mother, Mary Anne (1798-1871), was the daughter and heiress of Edward Walwyn (qv), from whom Hellens descended. He was privately educated and at first practised law until he inherited Hellens, where he took up farming on a small scale. He was active in the Conservative Party and secured a seat in a south London constituency (1885-92). In 1893 the Liberal MP for Hereford resigned and Cooke was elected. He became known as the 'member for cider' because of the support he gave to the Herefordshire cider industry. In letters to the press and speeches to the House he advocated state aid for the industry. This led to the founding of the National Fruit and Cider Institute at Long Ashton, near Bristol in 1903, whose experimental work produced a great resurgence in fruit growing. In his *Book about Cider and Perry* (1898) he showed how cider was a perfect crop for small growers, stressing the need for scientific methods and development of the market. His efforts led to increased consumption of cider but to the neglect of his own business, and increasing financial problems led him to lease out Hellens (qv Abercrombie). He died on 26 May 1911 from heart disease and was buried at St Bartholomew's, Much Marcle, where his memorial reads 'he restored a principal industry of his native county'. Hellens passed via Lady Gleichen to the Munthes (qqv).

Cooke, Robert (*c.*1535-93), herald, from Cheshire, was educated at St John's College, Cambridge. He became Rose Blanche pursuivant and later Clarenceux King of arms. He was assiduous in his visitations of families wishing to register pedigrees and coats of arms and was notoriously prolific in those he allowed. He investigated his entire province of the south of England. His visitation of Herefordshire was conducted in 1569 and was printed by Frederick William Weaver in 1886, supplemented by later visitations and other sources such as Revd Robinson (qv).

Cooke, William Henry (1811-94), judge and antiquary, took over John Duncumb's (qv) *Collections towards the History and Antiquities of the County of Hereford.* He finished the second volume with an index in 1866 and volume 3, Greytree parish, in 1882. In 1892 he published volume 7, which dealt with the Hundred of Grimsworth. After Cooke's death, work was continued by Revd Morgan Watkins (qv) and John Mathews (qv). Cooke wrote biographies of all vicars choral from 1660 to 1823 and bought the Revd C.J. Bird's (qv) collection of antiquarian writings. His papers were eventually deposited in Hereford Record Office.

Cooper, Edward (d.1596), Archdeacon of Hereford 1565-78 and Treasurer 1583-96, was custodian of the Hospital of St Ethelbert in

Hereford. It originally stood in Broad Street; he assisted in the move to its present site in Castle Street, by the Castle Gate. He restored St Mary's, Stoke Edith in 1575. He was Master of St Katherine's Hospital in Ledbury and extended the Master's House there – his initials 'EC' and the date 1588 appear on an overmantel in the panelled room. This 13th-century group of hospital and chapel is unique. He left money for the building of Ledbury's Market House in his will. There is a memorial slab to him on the north wall of St Anne's Chapel in Ledbury Church, with an incised black line portrait. His career and our future are summarised:

Edward Cooper, grave, learned and wise,
Archdeacon of Hereff canon erst here lies.
Of Ledburies Hospital maister in his life.
The poor did protect, theyr land rid from strife.
He deceased the XVI day of July 1598
The time will come that you shall be as I am now.

Cooper, John (fl.1616-27), 'stationer of Hereford', was apprenticed to William and Mary Cooper, his father and mother, in 1616 for seven years and then made free of the Haberdasher and Stationers' etc Guild of Hereford. His widowed mother mentions that he was their joint apprentice in a later testimonial of John's 'serviceableness' to her, implying she was equally involved in the trade. The Coopers must have been preeminent as they were chosen to rebind books for the cathedral library (some 380 volumes can be traced) when presses were set up in the lady chapel. John Cooper's name appears on invoices for the years 1625, '26 and '27 when the books were returned to Dr Best (qv) at the library. Many had been in poor condition. Some which had lain flat in presses were unable to stand upright on the new shelving. John Cooper's accounts mention staining the page edges with vermillion, clasping and stringing the books as well as binding them and repairing pages. One important book rebound by Cooper at this time was Hereford's 8th-century *Anglo-Saxon Gospel Book.* John married an Eleanor and their son, also John (d.1671), was apprenticed to his father in due course and practised as a stationer, bookseller and binder in Hereford. He must have been successful as at his death he left his widow much property in Hereford, Hampton and Yazor, and Eleanor, the wealthy widow, remarried. John Cooper's story was discovered by the cathedral's honorary librarian Penelope E. Morgan (qv F.C. Morgan).

Cooper-Key, Henry (1819-79) was the rector of Stretton Sugwas, a keen astronomer, who with his friends William Webb and George With (qqv) developed optical viewing equipment in Herefordshire.

Cornewall: The family were descended from Richard Earl of Cornwall. They acquired the estate at Eye and Berrington (also called Beritune or Beriton) some time in the 14th century from the Beringtons (qv), with castles north of the present Berrington Hall and at Moccas. Two distinct branches of the family formed at these focuses with the Berrington and Eye branch dropping the central 'e' to distinguish them from the Moccas branch. Sir John Cornewall (d.1443) fought at Agincourt and in 1433 was created Lord Fownhope by Henry V. Sir Edmund Cornewall (fl.1450), Baron Burford, married as his second wife Elizabeth daughter of Thomas de la Barre (qv, d.1420) and their daughter Eleanor married Sir Richard Croft (qv, d.1509). There are alabaster effigies of Sir Rowland Cornewall (*c.*1520) and Sir Richard and his wife (a sister of William Rudhall, qv) of *c.*1540 in St Peter and St Paul Church, Eye. Both branches of the family produced celebrated naval officers. In 1775 the Berrington and Eye estates were bought by Thomas Harley (qv, d.1804), who built Berrington Hall near the Cornewalls' castle. The Amyand family married into the family and took the Cornewall name as baronets. There was a Cornewall Bishop of Hereford. The baronetcy continued into the 20th century.

Cornewall, Edward (fl.1650) was a younger son of the Berrington branch. He and his older brother Humphrey fought for the king in the Civil Wars. In 1650 he married Frances, the rich widow of Henry Vaughan (qv under Roger Vaughan, d.1643) and daughter of Sir Walter Pye (qv). He had been imprisoned for poaching in Moccas Deer Park when Frances saw him. They fell in love, married and had a son, Henry (qv).

Cornewall, Folliott Herbert Walker (1754-1831), Bishop of Hereford 1802-8, second son of Frederick Cornewall (qv, d.1788), was born at Delbury, Shropshire. His mother was a Herbert of the Earls of Powis. He was educated at Eton and St John's, Cambridge and ordained. His cousin Charles Wolfran Cornwall (qv) found him a chaplaincy in the Commons and a canonry at Windsor. He married Anne Hamilton, daughter of a brother canon at Windsor, and they had two sons and two daughters. He was Dean of Canterbury and then Bishop of Bristol, which he exchanged for the diocese of Hereford in 1802. In 1808 he was translated to Worcester where he was bishop, until his death on 5 September 1831, living at Hartlebury Castle. He was buried in the family vault at Delbury Church.

Cornewall, Frederick (1706-88), cousin of James Cornewall (qv) and son of Charles Cornwall (qv), was MP for Montgomery. He was also in the Navy and despite being severely wounded himself took over his cousin's command after his death at the Battle of Toulon. He later commanded the *Revenge* in the action off Minorca in 1756. He died in 1788.

Cornewall, Frederick (1752-83), the older brother of Folliott (qv), was MP for Leominster from 1776 to 1780 and for Ludlow from 1780 until his death in 1783.

Cornewall, Geoffrey (1869-1951) was 6th Baronet. He was an archer who took part in the 1908 Olympics in London. He was a JP and Deputy Lieutenant for the county, and was appointed High Sheriff of Herefordshire in 1913 and Vice Lord Lieutenant in 1934. His brother William Francis Cornewall (1871-1962) was 7th Baronet.

Cornewall, George (1748-1819), Baronet, MP for Herefordshire, was born on 8 November 1748, the son of Sir George Amyand, a banker of Huguenot descent. He was educated at Eton and Christ Church, Oxford and joined his father's banking firm. He succeeded to his father's Amyand baronetcy. In 1771 he married Catherine Cornewall (baptised 17 November 1752, died 17 March 1835), daughter of Sir Velters (qv, d.1768). He assumed his wife's surname by royal licence and successfully contested her father's Herefordshire seat in 1774. He improved his Moccas estate, commissioning a survey and plan from Lancelot 'Capability' Brown (qv) for £100. Brown landscaped the grounds running along the Wye with The Scar rapids nearby, and the famous Deer Park, retaining the ancient trees which Kilvert (qv) admired and which still stand. James Lees Milne thought it 'the loveliest view of England I could ever expect to find'. Sir George, who lived in the old house near the church, brought in the fashionable architect Robert Adam (qv) to design Moccas Court for them but quickly replaced him with the cheaper local architect Anthony Keck (qv), who used Adam's decorative features. Keck put up other buildings on the estate, in 1784 rebuilding Home Farm, which was equipped for the latest agricultural methods. The lawns in front of the house were laid out by Humphry Repton (qv) assisted by Cornewall's son George (qv, d.1835), himself a noted gardener and landscape architect. In 1792 the porch was added to the house below the fine Venetian window, and the distinctive estate lodges were built in 1801 and 1804 to designs of John Nash (qv). Sir George also bought Monnington Court across the River Wye from descendants of the Tomkyns family (qv Uvedale Tomkyns). The banks of the Wye were covered with cider orchards, eventually bought by Bulmers (qv). Sir George was a member of the commission which launched an inquiry into the Rebecca Riots (qv Thomas Reynolds) in Herefordshire, which were occasioned by changes in the Poor Law, rises in tithes and toll gate charges. His Jamaican sugar plantations became less productive as a result of French-inspired slave risings. Sir George's correspondence with his managers about production and slave conditions are found in Hereford Record Office. Sir George was MP for Herefordshire in the Whig interest from 1774 to 1796 and, having been displaced for six years by Robert Myddelton Biddulph (qv, d.1814), from 1802 to 1807, and he served in the Herefordshire Militia, becoming colonel in 1805. He died on 26 August 1819 and was buried at Moccas. His eldest daughter, Catherine Frances (b.1774), married Samuel Peploe (qv) of Garnstone Castle, who was his widow Lady Catherine's executor. A younger sister, Frances Elizabeth (b.1783), married Henry Devereux (qv), 14th Viscount Hereford in 1805; and Harriet (b.1787) married Thomas Frankland Lewis, whose son George assumed the name Cornewall Lewis (qv).

Cornewall, George (1774-1835), 3rd Baronet, was born on 16 January 1774, the son of Sir George (d.1819, qv) and Catherine, and was educated at Christ Church, Oxford. He married Jane Naper of Co. Meath, Ireland in 1815 and their children were Velters (d.1768, qv) and George Henry (qv). Following his father he became a colonel in the Herefordshire Militia. He died at Moccas Court on 27 December 1835. There is a fine portrait of him by Sir Thomas Lawrence.

Cornewall, George Henry (1833-1908), 5th Baronet, younger brother of Velters (d.1868, qv), was born on 13 August 1833. He was educated at Rugby and Trinity College, Cambridge, was ordained and became rector of Moccas. He married Louisa Frances (d.1900), daughter of Francis Bayley.

Cornewall, Henry (*c.*1654-1717), of Bredwardine Castle (his mother's Vaughan property), was the son of Edward (qv) and Frances (qv under Walter Pye). He was page of honour to the Duke of York and an equerry to Princess Mary, and rose to be colonel of the Horse Guards in the 1680s. He raised a regiment in Herefordshire to oppose the rise of the Duke of Monmouth. He was MP for Weobley and Hereford at various times and a JP in the Marches. He married first Margarita Huyssen of Zeeland and they had a son Henry (d.1756) who was Whig MP for Hereford in 1747; and secondly Susanna Elham of Kent and they had children James (qv) and Velters (qv, d.1768). He was uneasy with the Glorious Revolution settlement and was elected MP for Hereford as a Tory (probably a Jacobite). He died on 22 February 1717 and is buried in Westminster Abbey.

Cornewall, James (1698-1744), of Moccas Court, naval officer and politician, was a son of Col Henry Cornewall (qv) and the second son of Henry's second wife Susanna, baptised on 17 November 1698 at Moccas. He was Whig MP for Weobley 1732-34. He followed his uncle into the Royal Navy. His legs were shot off with chain-shot at the Battle of Toulon (11 February 1744) and he died of his injuries. He was voted a hero's monument in Westminster Abbey, designed by Sir Robert Taylor (1755).

Cornewall, Velters (1695-1768), of Moccas Court, son of Col Henry Cornewall (qv, d.1717), was educated at Christ Church, Oxford. He was Tory MP for Herefordshire seven times over 46 years, aided by the patronage of his cousin Robert Harley (qv, d.1724), Earl of Oxford. He was instrumental in the repeal of the Cider Tax, to the delight of the county. He was known in the House for his odd humour. He married Catherine the heir of William Hanbury of Little Marcle, who was woman of the bedchamber to the Princess of Wales. He died on 3 April 1768 and was buried in Hereford Cathedral, where there is a memorial to him. The Cornewall estate passed to his daughter Catherine and her husband Sir George Amyand (qv George Cornewall, 1748-1819). There is a portrait of Velters by Gainsborough in Hereford Museum, and one of his daughter Lady Catherine by Reynolds.

Cornewall, Velters (1824-68), 4th Baronet, was born on 20 February 1824. The eldest son of Sir George (qv, d.1835), he was aged 9 at his father's death and the Cornewall estates were held in trust. Sir Velters was educated at Christ Church, Oxford, and in 1847 was High Sheriff of Hereford. He was a friend of Johnny Arkwright (qv, d.1905) and best man at his wedding at Hampton Court. He was a major in the Herefordshire Militia and died on 14 October 1868.

Cornewall Lewis, George, 2nd Baronet (1806-63), was born in London on 21 April 1806, the son of Sir Thomas Frankland Lewis of Harpton Court, Old Radnor, and took his mother's name, Cornewall. He was educated at Eton, Christ Church, Oxford and the Middle Temple and was called to the bar in 1831. He had a wide knowledge of languages and published various literature including a glossary of local Herefordshire words. He married Lady Theresa Lister (1803-65) in 1844, a daughter of the Villiers Earls of Clarendon, who brought him three children from her first marriage. Their country seat was Harpton Court, now largely demolished. He was editor of the *Edinburgh Review*. His father had been involved in the inquiry into the Rebecca Riots (qv Thomas Reynolds). He himself worked on various commissions such as that for the Poor Law and represented Herefordshire in Parliament as Liberal MP from 1847-52. He lost the seat and on the death of his father succeeded to the baronetcy and became MP for Radnorshire (1855-63). As Chancellor of the Exchequer he financed the Crimean War, and was Home Secretary and Secretary for War in Palmerston's administrations. He died on 13 April 1863 and he and his wife are buried in the Lewis family vault in Old Radnor Church, part of the diocese of Hereford until 1920. Walter Bagehot, in his *English Constitution*, saw him as the ideal responsible country squire. The year after his death two large monuments were erected in his memory – the bronze statue by Marochetti outside Hereford's Shire Hall and a Gothic monument in New Radnor by John Gibbs.

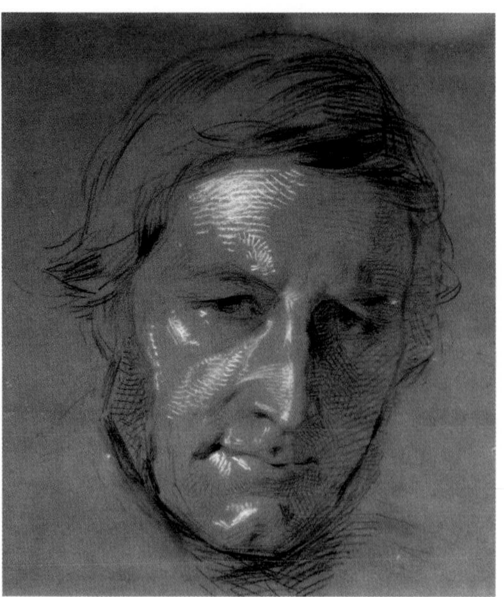

Cornwaille, Richard (fl.1384) was appointed regent master of Hereford Cathedral School in 1384 by Bishop John Gilbert (qv), succeeding Lelamour (qv). He reorganised the school, which had become defunct, for the bishop. One of the school's four houses, Cornwall House, is named after him.

Cornwall, Charles (1669-1718), naval officer, was born at Eye on 5 August 1669 the son of Robert Cornewall (1646-1701) of Berrington and his wife Edith Cornwallis (d.1696). He married, as his second wife, Dorothy Hanmer and they had many children. During a lengthy career in the Navy he rose to the rank of rear-admiral, then commander-in-chief of the Mediterranean fleet, negotiating with the Emperor of Morocco. He played a prominent part in the naval battle off Cape Passaro on 31 July 1718. He was MP for Bewdley (1709-10) and for Weobley from 1715 until his death. He was considered a peppery man, often at odds with colleagues, and he could not get on with Robert Harley (qv, d.1724) in government. He died at Lisbon on 7 October 1718 and was buried in Westminster Abbey. He omitted the 'e' from his name to distinguish his branch of the family.

Cornwall, Charles Wolfran (1735-89), Speaker of the Commons, was born at Berrington on 15 June 1735 the only son of Jacobs Cornwall (qv) and Rose, named after a naval uncle. He was educated at Winchester, Lincoln's Inn and Gray's Inn and was called to the bar in 1757. His cousin Charles Jenkinson, later Earl of Liverpool, son of Colonel Charles Jenkinson and Amarantha Cornwall, found him legal office and he married Jenkinson's sister Elizabeth (1730-1809). He was MP for Grampound, Cornwall, then for Winchelsea and finally Rye, and crossed the floor to take up a lucrative Treasury post with the East India Company offered by Lord North. In 1780 he became Speaker of the Commons. He was a Chief Justice and sworn a Privy Councillor. Cornwall died in Whitehall on 2 January 1789 and was buried in St Cross Hospital, Winchester where there is a monument to him.

Cornwall, Jacobs (1710-36), only son of Charles (qv) and Dorothy, was born at Berrington. He married Rose (1707-83), the daughter of Robert Fowler of Barton Priors, Hampshire.

Cornwall, Richard (*c.*1480-1533), the son of Sir Thomas Cornwall of Berrington, married Jane, daughter and co-heir of Simon Milbourne of Tillington. He was Sheriff of Herefordshire 1506-7, 1519-20 and 1526-7, one of Henry VIII's (qv) spears by 1510, and steward of the lordships of Clifford, Eardisland, Fencote, Mansell Lacy, Orleton, Pembridge and Winforton from 1510 to his death. He was present with the king at various ceremonial occasions, including the Field of Cloth of Gold and fought in Henry's French wars. He was knighted in 1522. He was MP (knight of the shire) for Herefordshire in 1523 and 1529. He was buried at Eye Church.

Cornwall, Robert (1700-56), eldest son of Vice-Admiral Charles Cornwall (qv), was born at Eye. He inherited his father's estates in 1718 and proceeded to style himself Sir Robert de Cornwall, claiming that George IV had promised his father a baronetcy. He served with the Dragoon Guards, and was made High Sheriff of Radnorshire (1738). After several attempts he was elected MP for Leominster (1747-54), and was provincial grand master in the Freemasons. He is said to have predicted the date of his death, which occurred on 4 April 1756.

Cosmas and Damian (d.287 AD), twin saints from Syria, martyred under Diocletian, are, with St Peter (qv), patrons of Stretford Church. Stretford is a double-naved church with a double-niched shrine at the east end for their images. They were popular in the Middle Ages as patrons of doctors and healing, and pilgrims would sleep in the church to be healed. They are depicted in art replacing a man's diseased leg with one from a recently dead Ethiopian. In 1282 Edward I (qv) granted Leominster the right to hold a fair on Cosmas and Damian's feast day, 26 September and the four days following.

Cotterell, John Geers (1757-1845), 1st Baronet, MP, was born on 21 September 1757. He was the son of Sir John Brookes Cotterell and Anne Geers (qv under Thomas Geers, d.1675), heiress of Garnons at Mansell Gamage, which passed into the Cotterell family. He inherited the estate in 1790 and the next year married Frances Isabella, daughter of Henry Evans. He was Tory MP for Herefordshire for nearly 30 years (1804-31) and a colonel in the Herefordshire Militia. He was created 1st Baronet Cotterell of Garnons in 1805. He was an active JP and a member of the Hereford Gaol Committee that brought in Robert Smirke (qv) to build Hereford's new gaol. While involved with the restoration of Hereford Cathedral he met the architect James Wyatt (qv). Impressed, Cotterell commissioned him to build a house at Garnons. His neighbour William Parry (qv) at New Weir nearby recommended Humphry Repton (qv), who produced a *Red Book* showing in watercolour how Garnons Hill would look around Wyatt's planned, but never built, house. Repton's recommendations were carried out and the mature results can now be seen. In 1815 William Atkinson (qv) built a Regency-gothic house, renovated by Arthur Blomfield (qv) in the 1860s. The Elizabethan house has sadly been demolished. Cotterell was a keen breeder of Hereford cattle and in 1824 his prize bull *Sir Isaac*, named after Admiral Sir Isaac Coffin (qv), was presented to the Massachusetts Society, leading to the enormous success of the Hereford breed as the premier American beef cattle. Cotterell died on 26 January 1845.

Cotterell, John Richard Geers (1866-1937), 4th Baronet, was born on 13 July 1866, the son of Sir Geers Henry Cotterell and Katherine Airey. He married Evelyn Amy, daughter of Charles Lennox, 7th Duke of Richmond, in 1896. He served in the Life Guards, was High Sheriff and in 1904 became Lord Lieutenant of Herefordshire. He succeeded to the title of 4th Baronet Cotterell of Garnons in 1900. He died on 13 November 1937.

Cottingham, Lewis Nockalls (1787-1847), architect, was born at Laxfield, Suffolk, on 24 October 1787 into a farming family. He trained with an Ipswich architect-builder, setting up his own business in London in 1814. In 1822 he married Sophia Cotton, an architect's daughter and they had two sons and a daughter. He was fascinated by mediaeval architecture and the problem of employing it in the contemporary world, and became known for combining archaeological and engineering skills. He published descriptions and plans of old buildings, made models and casts of monuments and collected fragments from demolished structures. His London house was a museum of ancient arms and armour, which brought him to the attention of Meyrick (qv) who brought him to Herefordshire. His sensitivity to ancient buildings was unusual before Pugin (qv), and Dean Merewether (qv) thought him the ideal man to restore Hereford Cathedral. In 1842 the dean found that the cathedral's central tower was about to collapse and he tasked Cottingham with stabilizing it. When Cottingham first saw the problem he burst into tears. He had previously stablised cathedral towers but this was the first time the great columns had been replaced under the tower. Restoration meant swingeing replacement of any untidy or irregular stonework; this was Merewether's brief to Cottingham, to the chapter's consternation. Havergal (qv) noted that once, when Cottingham's men had uncovered pristine polychrome Norman work it was cut out and replaced with a more acceptable 19th-century version. He saw the mediaeval choir screen as modern work and pulled it down. Cottingham had been increasingly ill during his years at Hereford and his eldest son Nockalls Cottingham (qv) supervised the work for him. He restored St Mary's, Kilpeck, bringing his antiquarian knowledge to bear on this important church, although he did remove some corbels, considering them to be indecent. He died in London on 13 October 1847 and was buried in Croydon.

Cottingham, Nockalls Johnson (1823-54), Lewis's (qv) eldest son, was trained in his father's office and took on the supervision of the work at Hereford. He also made the eccentric but charming wall plaque to Richard Jones Powell (d.1834), now in the cloisters, and on the death of Dean Merewether (qv) designed the stained glass in the lady chapel, made by Charles Gibbs (1847-51), as a memorial to him. He carried out his father's commission to renovate Ledbury chapter house and unearthed fragments of a 17th-century font which he restored. Funds had run low for the final work at the cathedral. When more money was raised Nockalls absconded to America with it, but drowned when the steamship he was on, *The Arctic*, sank off Cape Cod on 27 September 1854.

Courtenay, William de (1342-96), Bishop of Hereford 1369-75, was a younger son of Hugh de Courtenay, 10th Earl of Devon, and Margaret, daughter of Humphrey (VII) de Bohun (qv), 4th Earl of Hereford. He was educated at Stapledon Hall, Oxford and became Chancellor. His noble connections ensured him livings and prebends and in 1369, aged only 27, he became Bishop of Hereford, requiring papal dispensation as he was under age. He displaced Thomas Brantingham whom Dean Birmingham (qv) and his chapter had already elected. Bishop Courtenay was frequently absent during his six-year tenure but was quick to defend the rights of his diocese. In 1375 he became Bishop of London and in 1381 Archbishop of Canterbury. He officiated at the wedding of Richard II (qv) and Anne of Bohemia and at Anne's coronation. He reproved Richard for his extravagance. He knew John Wycliffe at Oxford but was later active against the Lollards. He died at Maidstone on 31 July 1396 and has a monument in Canterbury Cathedral.

Courtney, Catherine (1847-1929), social worker, was born on 4 April 1847 at Gayton Hall near Ross. She was a daughter (another was Beatrice Webb) of Richard Potter, of a wealthy Northern Unitarian family and with a strong social conscience, who had campaigned for the Reform Act of 1830. Catherine was tutored at home and, imbued with the family ethics, she left to work with the poor of East London. She married Leonard, later Lord Courtney of Penwith.

Cove, Morgan (1753-1830), pamphleteer, the son of a clergyman, was educated at Trinity Hall, Cambridge, taking an LLB in 1776 then becoming ordained. As a vicar he wrote pamphlets on church reform which attracted the notice of Bishop Butler (qv) of Hereford who presented him to the rectory of Eaton Bishop in 1799 and the next year made him prebend of Withington Parva in Hereford Cathedral, then Gorwall and Overbury. He was Chancellor 1828-30. He contributed to the debate of tithes and died at Hereford on 9 April 1830.

Cox, David (1783-1859), artist, was born on 29 April 1783 in Harbourne on the outskirts of Birmingham where his father was a blacksmith. Laid up with a childhood illness, he found he was skilled in painting. He trained under Joseph Barber and quickly excelled. He moved to London and painted theatre sets, sold watercolour landscapes and married his landlord's daughter, Mary Agg. Despite hard work, a prolific output and teaching he wasn't able to support his family and in 1814 answered

Mrs Croucher's advertisement for a drawing-master in her girls' school at the Gate House at Widemarsh Gate, Hereford. His salary was £100 p.a. for two days a week teaching. One of his pupils, Charlotte Price, was a niece of Uvedale Price (qv), who was a great influence on him. From 1815 he also taught at Hereford Grammar School where he met his favourite pupil Joseph Murray Ince (qv). The Coxes lived first at Lower Lyde, then on Aylestone Hill, then in George Cottage at Baynton Wood, before moving to Parry Lane in Hereford, where he added a studio. In 1824 he built Ash Tree House. Cox was now more comfortably off with time to paint and he made painting tours in the Herefordshire countryside, down the Wye and Severn valleys and through Wales. He was inspired by the landscape of Herefordshire and Wales and interested in Uvedale Price's picturesque theories. He developed an impressive body of work, showing the influence of J.M.W. Turner (qv), and was elected to the Society of Painters in Water Colours in London; he exhibited regularly both there and at the Royal Academy. He began painting larger work in oils and attracted patrons. He was chosen to contribute to *The Hereford Guide* (1827), a prestigious album of Herefordshire scenes and other similar books. In the 1820s the Hereford art collector Charles Spozzi bought his work, to be seen by another Birmingham artist, the young Burne-Jones (qv) when he stayed there 30 years later. In 1827 Cox travelled on the Continent, painting with his son David and developing new ideas. Under the influence of Richard Parkes Bonnington and Constable he developed a broken tint style to produce the quality of landscape described by Uvedale Price (for whom he painted *Scene at Foxley Park*). Cox's new work looked forward to Impressionism but was felt by critics such as Ruskin to lack the smooth finish demanded at the time. Cox retired to Birmingham with Mary, leaving their son David painting in London, and painted his finest landscapes which won establishment approval. He died on 7 June 1859 and was buried beside Mary under a chestnut tree in St Peter's churchyard, Harbourne. He was much loved on his summer painting tours and known as 'a sort of little king at Bettws'. He is considered, with Bonnington, Constable and Turner, as a leading painter of his age, the golden age of watercolour.

Cox, David (1809-85), watercolour artist, the only son of David (qv) and Mary Cox, was born on 9 July 1809 in south London. At the age of five he moved with the family to Hereford, where he was educated at the Cathedral School and taught by his father to draw and paint. At 18 he exhibited his *Cottage in Herefordshire*. In south London David married Hannah

Blunt and the couple had four children. When Hannah tragically committed suicide David married Elizabeth Newton and they adopted a cousin. He was fond of travelling and made painting tours to the Continent. He lived in the Dulwich and Streatham areas all his life and continued exhibiting with the Society of Painters in Water Colours. There are examples of both Coxes' work in Hereford Museum and Art Gallery.

Crace, John Gregory (1809-89), interior decorator, was born on 26 May 1809 in London, one of the famous Crace dynasty of decorators. He worked with his father Frederick Crace on George IV's palaces. In 1833 he married Sarah Jane Hine (1815-94) and they had a large family. On taking over the firm from his father, now J.G. Crace & Son, he introduced mid 19th-century French taste and became the most fashionable London decorator of his time, employed by Prince Albert and by the Duke of Devonshire on his library at Chatsworth. He formed a partnership with A.W.N. Pugin (qv) from 1844 to Pugin's death. Pugin's gothicising taste became evident in Crace's style and can be seen in their work at Eastnor Castle on Lord Somers' (qv, d.1852) library in 1849-50. As with Hardman (qv) Pugin transformed Crace's business with a flood of orders, especially for the new Palace of Westminster. Crace was an early photographer and, after handing over the firm to his son, travelled widely recording monuments. He died on 13 August 1889 and ten years later his son wound the business up. Crace's drawings and photographs can be seen in the Victoria and Albert Museum.

Cranston, James (1748-1835), nurseryman and landscape gardener, trained with James Lee of Hammersmith and worked for Sir Uvedale Price (qv) at Foxley in 1771. He married Elizabeth Barrett of Yazor in 1785. They moved into Archenfield House and he extended his father's (John, qv) nursery on the King's Acre site at Breinton. He developed a prize-winning onion, Cranston's Excelsior, and planted cedars around Hereford. He supplied trees to Herefordshire estates and helped Repton (qv) at Garnons. Price recommended him to Sir George Beaumont for whom he worked at Coleorton. He established a partnership with James Douglas of Ludlow and opened a shop in High Town, Hereford.

Cranston, James (II) (fl.1819-42), surveyor and nurseryman, was Thomas's son (qv under John Cranston). He managed King's Acre Nursery.

Cranston, James (III) (d.1871), an architect with a practice in Birmingham, built Leominster Town Hall (1855) in brick with Bath and Grinsel Stone in an Italian style, to house the County Court, Council and Magistrates' Rooms. Over the Council Chamber entrance is a portrait of Sir Charles Hanbury Williams (qv) and a halberd which Sir Thomas Coningsby (qv, d.1625) gave in 1618. Cranston was also involved with the flourishing family business, the Kings' Acre Nursery, now trading as Cranston and Mayo. The Coach and Horses Inn next door was purchased as club house and reading room for the gardeners. Cranston was a founding member of the Hereford Rose Society (1867) and used the title *Rosarin*. The nursery at this time developed the two apples *King's Acre Bountiful* and *Pippin* and was consulted by Revd Bulmer (qv). Cranston arranged for subscriptions to be collected for the rebuilding of St Michael's Church, Breinton (1870) by Kempson (qv). On his death a window was dedicated to him in the north nave and he and other Cranstons are buried in the churchyard. The nursery now trades as Wyevale.

Cranston, John, nurseryman from Glasgow, founded a large nursery at King's Acre, Breinton with his two sons Thomas and James (qv).

Crawford, Lawrence (1611-45), Parliamentarian army officer, was born near Glasgow in November 1611. He fought in Denmark and Sweden until the outbreak of civil war in England when he returned, serving under Manchester and Cromwell in 1644. He was known as a quarrelsome officer; after Marston Moor he transferred to the Western Association under Massey (qv) and was with Alexander Leslie (qv) at the siege of Hereford, where, on 17 August 1645, he was killed by a shot from a Royalist sniper's rifle. He was buried in Gloucester Cathedral on 5 September under a monument which was removed at the Restoration.

Cray, Christina (fl.1294) was a swineherd who kept pigs at Withington. When a stray pig got amongst her herd and was sold along with the rest, she was arraigned before Hereford Assize at Whitsun 1294 and sentenced to be hanged. The sentence was carried out and at vespers her friends were allowed to take her body away for burial but, seeing signs of life, they gave her a warm drink and she revived. She took sanctuary in St Martin's Church, outside Wye Bridge Gate and eventually presented herself to the Justices in a penitent's dress with a cross and foreswore the kingdom. She was allowed to leave Herefordshire and live in London.

Cristall, Joshua (1767-1847), artist, was born on 18 December 1767, either in London or Cornwall as his father was a mariner. Joshua's artistic abilities were fostered by his mother but his father, mistrusting art as a career, had him apprenticed to a dealer in china. He worked at this trade, sketching all the time until, at 25, he enrolled at the Royal Academy Schools in London. He lodged with his sister in London, making a very poor living until his parents died and left him a small amount of money. He made connections with other artists such as the Varleys with whom he sketched and exhibited at the Royal Academy. He was interested in watercolour and was a founder and first president of the Society of Painters in Water Colours. By his 40s his talents were being recognized and he was praised for his landscapes and for his skill with the human figure. In 1812 Cristall was living in Middlesex near his friends Cornelius Varley and William Sawrey Gilpin, and here he met and married Elizabeth Cossins (*c.*1771-1839). Her dowry and sophistication aided Cristall's career; their house became the resort of artists and musicians and he was elected President of the Old Watercolour Society. Cristall felt the need for rural inspiration; the couple had no children and Elizabeth had been looking after the two daughters of Edward Walwyn (qv) of Hellens at Much Marcle, which encouraged them to move to Herefordshire. They bought Granton Cottage at Goodrich which had a room for a studio. The Wye was particularly attractive to Cristall as fashionable tourists were being attracted to the area by the writings of the Revd William Gilpin (qv), his friend William Sawrey

Gilpin's uncle. Here he produced his best work and showed the results in Ross at the first exhibition of its sort in Herefordshire. The next 20 years in Herefordshire were his happiest and most productive: he founded an art circle of like-minded friends who met to sketch and criticise each other's work and exhibit annually in London. Elizabeth died in 1839 and Cristall, in his 70s, returned to London, where he was welcomed but sidelined as old-fashioned. He was cared for by two old servants from Herefordshire, Mary Cox and Sarah Woore. Cristall died on 18 October 1847 in St John's Wood but was buried beside his wife in St Giles's churchyard, Goodrich, where their grave may be seen. His paintings failed to sell at his studio sale and much was lost, but in the next century his reputation revived as contemporary artists found his ideas influential. His paintings, both the watercolours he delighted in and his larger oils, are held at Hereford Museum.

Croft: The family traced their pedigree back through King John to Cadwalader, their motto being *esse quam videri*, i.e. 'to be rather than to be seen'. They fought at Hastings and are named as at Croft in the Domesday record. In the Middle Ages Croft fortunes were closely linked with the Wigmore Mortimers (qv). The Battle of Mortimers Cross (1461) was fought on Croft lands not far from the castle. Crofts represented either the borough of Leominster or the shire of Hereford as members of parliament from 1307 to a hiatus in 1617 when Herbert Croft (d.1629) converted to Roman Catholicism. His grandson the Bishop was also persuaded to convert but was recovered for the Anglican Church. Charles II admired Bishop Croft's preaching but not his attacks on his morals. His son Archer found the transition from James II to William and Mary hard but formally associated himself with the loyal address to William and was elected as a Court Whig in 1690. Early Crofts were knights and in 1671 the Croft baronetcy was created and is still extant. Croft Castle was sold to pay debts in the 18th century, bought back later and finally made over to the National Trust, but Crofts still maintain a presence there.

Croft, Archer (1683-1753), 2nd Baronet, was the eldest son of Sir Herbert (qv, d.1720) and Elizabeth. He married Frances Waring. He was MP for Leominster; a member of Sir Robert Walpole's government, and became Governor of New York. He lost money in the South Sea Bubble and, with mounting debts, was forced to sell Croft Castle to Richard Knight (qv) of neighbouring Downton, and the family moved to Dunston Park in Berkshire. Sir Archer's son Sir Herbert Croft (d.1816) commissioned a writing-table and filing cabinet from the firm of Seddons (qv J.P. Seddon), an innovation known as 'a Croft' which can be seen in Croft Castle today.

Croft, Bernard de (11th century), known as 'the bearded', is recorded in the Domesday Book as a royal tenant in the Leominster area and elsewhere. His son Jasper fought in the Crusades and was knighted by Godfrey de Bouillon at the taking of Jerusalem.

Croft, Edward (d.1547), knight, eldest son of Sir Richard (qv, d.1509) and Eleanor, was seven times Sheriff of Herefordshire and counsel to Princess Mary. He restored St Michael's Church at Croft (1515) with a splendid east window, and was responsible for his parents' tomb, probably at his mother's direction.

Croft, Edward (d.1601) was educated at the Middle Temple and was MP for Leominster. He married Anne (d.1575), daughter of Thomas Browne of Attleborough, Norfolk. In 1589 he was accused of causing the death of Robert Dudley, Earl of Leicester through witchcraft, allegedly an act of revenge for a slight against his father, and he was even tried in court for the offence. He was excluded from his father's (James, qv, d.1590) estates in Herefordshire which were held in trust for his eldest son Herbert (qv, d.1629). His brother James (qv, d.1624) was gentleman commoner at Court until his death in 1624.

Croft, Herbert (1566-1629), eldest son of Edward (qv, d.1601), was educated at Christ Church, Oxford and the Middle Temple. He served with the Earl of Leicester in the Netherlands in the 1580s and on his return married Mary (1573-1659), daughter of Anthony Bourne of Holt Castle, Worcs. They had four sons and five daughters. His patrons Henry Herbert, Earl of Pembroke, Robert Devereux, Earl of Essex and Sir Robert Cecil (qqv) introduced him at Court. The Croft estates in Herefordshire were transferred to him, at the exclusion of his father, and in 1594 he succeeded his grandfather James (qv) at Croft. James I knighted him on his accession. He represented Herefordshire in parliament, where he was an active committee member and recovered some of the lost Croft lands. In the year of the Gunpowder Plot (1605) he placated the protagonists of the 'Whitsun riot' at Allensmore (qv Alice Wellington) with his known Catholic sympathies. In 1617 he converted to Roman Catholicism and entered a monastery at Douai where he died. His sister Mary married the Catholic John Davies (qv), writing master of Hereford. Sir Herbert's pike still stands in the hall of Croft Castle.

Croft, Herbert (1603-91), Bishop of Hereford 1662-91, third son of Sir Herbert (d.1629, qv), was born on 18 October 1603 at Great Milton, Oxfordshire, during his mother's journey to London, and was raised and educated in Hereford. His father persuaded him to convert to Catholicism and he trained as a priest at a Jesuit college. On his return to England, however, he was recovered for the Church of England, according to Pepys, by Archbishop Laud (qv) and he then continued his studies at Christ Church, Oxford. He married Anne, daughter of the dean Jonathan Brown (qv). When his brothers died he inherited the Croft estates and began to rebuild the castle in a mediaeval style with battlements. He extended the formal gardens and had the Jacobean tower placed on St Michael's Church. In 1640 he was made Chaplain to King Charles and in 1644 followed his father in-law as Dean of Hereford. He was soon deprived of his appointments, however, when Hereford fell to Parliamentary forces. He is said to have bravely berated Birch's (qv) sacrilegious troopers in the cathedral from a pulpit which can still be seen. They raised their muskets at him but were stopped by Birch; a roundel on the west front depicts this event. Croft was evicted from the deanery, which was bought cheaply by Birch, and in 1649 cathedral offices were abolished. At the Restoration Dr Croft was reinstated as dean while Nicholas Monck (qv) was made bishop, after Richard Baxter had refused the post. Monck soon died and Croft succeeded him, to great rejoicings in Hereford. He lived at Croft Castle rather than the palace and distributed a weekly dole at the gates. He conducted triennial visitations throughout his tenure. He was the author of several celebrated polemical pamphlets such as *The Naked Truth, or the True State of the Primitive Church* (1675),

although Anthony Wood, the 17th-century antiquary and gossip, thought his divinity was poor. He was a great lover of music and enjoyed the new organ at the cathedral. Late in his life he faced another revolution when William replaced James as king. After serious contemplation he swore the necessary oath to the new regime. He died in his palace on 18 May 1691 and was buried on the right of the high altar. In 1692 his close friend Dean George Benson (qv) was buried next to him. When Lewis Cottingham (qv) displaced many monuments during his renovations Croft and Benson's ledger stones went astray, but Lord Saye and Sele (qv Frederick Fiennes) found them dumped in the cloisters and paid to have them resited in the south-east transept where they now lie, joined by clasped hands (see page 36), not divided by death, as the Latin inscription reads.

Croft, Herbert (1652-1720) eldest son of Bishop Croft (qv, d.1691) and Anne, was created 1st Baronet Croft in 1671 as a reward for the family's tribulations in the Stuart cause. In 1675 he married Elizabeth (d.1709), sister of the architect Thomas Archer, and they had 11 children. He was elected MP for the county in 1679, 1690 and 1695. During the scare of

Monmouth's rebellion, he commanded the Herefordshire militia. He was High Steward of Leominster from 1704 to his death.

Croft, Herbert (1838-1902), 9th Baronet, returned the Croft family to Herefordshire after a century's absence and settled at Lugwardine Court where he became MP for Leominster, as his ancestors had before him. His son Herbert was killed at Gallipoli and Herbert's younger son, James, inherited the baronetcy as a child. It was James's trustees who decided to buy back Croft Castle, a process that was to lead to the castle's being presented to the National Trust, while the Croft family continued to occupy a wing.

Croft, Hugh de (fl.1243) is said to have rescued Prince Edward (qv Edward I) from Hereford Castle, a feat also ascribed to Maud de Briouze (qv Maud de Mortimer).

Croft, James (1518-90), the eldest son of Sir Richard (qv, d.1562) and Katherine, rose to prominence under Edward VI. He was a renowned soldier and fought in France under William Grey (qv). He lost two brothers at the siege of Boulogne as well as his own arm. On his return Edward VI knighted him, appointing him Lord Deputy of Ireland. He fought under Grey, who specifically asked for him, in the Scottish war of 1560. He was Knight of the Shire in 1542, Burgess of Leominster and represented Herefordshire in every Parliament from 1563 till his death. Queen Mary's marriage to the Spanish King Philip led him to join Wyatt's rebellion of 1554 to put her younger sister Elizabeth on the throne. He raised a force of 12,000 men from Herefordshire and the Marches but they were dispersed by Sir Richard Walwyn (qv, d.1573). Sir James was arrested at Croft Castle and sent to the Tower of which he had been deputy constable. He was pressed to implicate Princess Elizabeth in the plot but withstood questioning, earning her gratitude. He was eventually released with a fine and sequestration and a magnanimous King Philip later granted him a pension. He married Alice, daughter of Richard Warnecombe (qv)

and widow of William Wigmore of Shobdon, and they had three sons, including Edward, the eldest (qv, d.1601) and James (qv, d.1624) and four daughters, of whom Eleanor married John Scudamore (qv, d.1623) and Margaret married William Rudhall (qv, d.1626). Alice died in 1573 and he married Katherine daughter of Edward Blount (d.1623, qv under Blount family). He rebuilt Croft Castle in a more comfortable Elizabethan style. He served a grateful Elizabeth in various matters and was granted lands that had belonged to Leominster Priory. He was often in disgrace because of his prickly nature and was involved in a long-running, often violent, feud with Sir Thomas Coningsby (qv, d.1625). He died on 4 September 1590 and was buried in Westminster Abbey. He left an autobiography.

Croft, James (c.1550-1624), third son of Sir James Croft (d.1590), was educated at Grays Inn. He served in Ireland under Sir William Drury, whose widow, Margaret (d.1588), he eventually married; she was a daughter of Thomas, Baron Wentworth. He returned to her estates in Oxfordshire and was introduced at Court. He was knighted by James I and returned MP for Brackley, Northants. He continued a pensioner at Court throughout his long life.

Croft, John de (1372-1419), knight, married Janet (qv Monington), a daughter of Owain Glyn Dŵr (qv) and added the *vulned wyvern* to his arms after Glyn Dŵr's defeat. He was imprisoned for his Lollard sympathies in 1394-5. He died in Leominster.

Croft, Richard (1430-1509), knight, was a minor at his father's death and became the ward of Sir Walter Skull. He married Eleanor (d.1520) in 1460, a Cornewall (qv under Cornewalle family) and the widow of Sir Hugh Mortimer of Kyre, Worcestershire. They had three sons, Edward, John, and Robert, and five daughters, and Sir Richard had a bastard, Thomas (qv, d.1509). Eleanor was reputed to be a warlike lady who led a force against a neighbour in a feud. The Crofts were clients of the Mortimers alongside whom Sir Richard fought at the Battle of Mortimers Cross in 1461, the battlefield being on Croft lands two miles west of the castle. In 1487, having made peace with the Tudor regime, Croft fought at the Battle of Stoke where the supporters of the pretender Lambert Simnel challenged Henry VII in the last battle of the Wars of the Roses. Sir Richard was Henry's treasurer and steward to Prince Arthur. Bishop Audley (qv) appointed him warden of Malvern Chase. He was knight of the Shire, JP and Sheriff of Hereford. He died on 29 July 1509 and is buried beside Eleanor in St Michael's Church, which they rebuilt at the foot of Croft Castle. Their alabaster effigies seem to be portraits, Sir Richard with gaunt face. There are many saints and little weeper figures, uniquely unvandalised.

Croft, Richard (d.1562), son of Sir Edward (qv), married as his second wife Katherine the daughter of Sir Richard Herbert of Montgomery. He was esquire of the body to Henry VIII and knighted.

Croft, Thomas (*c.*1435-88) was the son of William Croft (d.1439, qv) and his second wife Isabella. He served Richard, Duke of York, at Ludlow in 1454 and fought in the battles of the Wars of the Roses in the 1460s. Under the Yorkist kings he held lucrative customs posts at Bristol, where he was involved in transatlantic exploration in the years before Columbus, searching for 'the Isle of Brasile'. In 1472 Thomas married Elizabeth (d.1500), heiress and daughter of John Wysham. Thomas Croft was MP for Leominster in 1478. He offered timely support to Henry Tudor (qv Henry VII) and made a successful transition to the new regime but died soon after.

Croft, Thomas (d.*c.*1509), a bastard son of Sir Richard Croft (qv, d.1509), fought for Henry Tudor at Bosworth and later at the Battle of Stoke in 1487 and was rewarded by Henry VII with property in Hereford; however, he later committed a murder in Hereford and as a result it was confiscated. He was dead by 1509.

Croft, William (b.*c.*1398-1439) of Croft Castle was the son of John de Croft (qv) and Janet ferch Owain Glyn Dŵr (qv). He married Margaret Walwyn (qv under Thomas (II) Walwyn) and their children were John, Richard and Agnes who married Philip Domulton (qv under John Domulton) of Brockhampton. He later married Isabella with whom he had another Richard and Thomas (qv, d.1488). He and his eldest son John died in 1439.

Croft, William (1593-1645), knight, eldest son of Sir Herbert (qv, d.1629), was a Commissioner of Array, one of the ablest of the Royalist Commanders in the county and counted one of the Nine Worthies of Herefordshire (see index). Croft Castle was initially held by Parliament but Sir William rendered it indefensible to prevent it from being of use to the enemy; however, it was then looted by his own unpaid Irish levies. His London house was sequestered by Parliament. After the Royalist defeat at Stokesay on 6 June 1645 he was chased from the field to his own Croft park gates where he was shot. The sad news of his death was conveyed to King Charles at Hereford who regarded him highly. He never married and was succeeded by his brother James, who lived in London and also died childless in 1659.

Cromwell, Oliver (1599-1658), Lord Protector, was born in Huntingdon on 25 April 1599 into a middling gentry family descended from the Tudor statesman Thomas Cromwell. He was MP for Cambridge in Charles's Short and Long Parliaments. At the age of 40 the crisis between Parliament and Charles I induced him to take up arms. He proved such a brilliant strategist, called 'old ironsides', that he rose in position from troop commander to creator of the New Model Army, to Lord Protector of the Commonwealth, defeating Charles I's armies and managing the king's execution. He was a pious man who believed the English revolution was ushering in the rule of the saints. During 1645-6 Cromwell was campaigning in the West driving garrisons from Exeter, Basing, Bristol etc. He passed through Herefordshire and is said to have to have stayed at the Pandy Inn in Dorstone, built by Richard de Britto (qv) in the 12th century. He died at Whitehall Palace on 3 September 1658, leaving an ineffective son, and the Stuart dynasty was restored less than two years later.

Crowley, Robert (1517-88), archdeacon of Hereford 1560-65, author and printer, was born in Gloucestershire and educated at Magdalen College, Oxford. He was an early supporter of the Protestant revolution and during Mary's return to Catholicism went into exile at Frankfurt with other reformers. He returned in Elizabeth's reign and became canon and Archdeacon of Hereford in 1560, with a house in the cathedral precinct. He had a printing press in London and in 1549 printed the first metrical version of the psalter. He produced polemical pamphlets and the first printed edition of Langland's (qv) *Piers Plowman*. He called for control of the new landlords of church property who were raising rents and evicting the poor for sheep runs. He was a severe critic of Romish practices such as ritual and vestments in the church. He attacked pluralism of benefices, although he held several himself. He was so strident that Archbishop Matthew Parker imprisoned him, and his benefices, including the archdeaconry of Hereford, were withdrawn. In time he was restored to his rectory of St Giles, Cripplegate, where he was buried on 18 June 1588 under the same stone as his friend John Foxe, author of the *Book of Martyrs*.

Croxall, Rodney (1702-54), Samuel's (qv) younger brother, was educated at Eton and Lincoln College, Oxford. He was ordained and he was married by his brother at St Mary

Monthalt, his London living. He had two further wives in quick succession; the middle wife, Ann, was buried in Hereford Cathedral. He was also found office by Bishop Egerton (qv), who made him vicar of Sellack, vicar of Madley with Tyberton, prebendary of Moreton Parva and treasurer of Hereford Cathedral. He died and was buried at Madley in 1754.

Croxall, Samuel (1689-1752), poet and clergyman from Surrey, was educated at Eton and St John's College, Cambridge. He wrote Whig pamphlets, translated Ovid and an erotic poem based on the Song of Solomon (*The Fair Circassian*) as well as producing an edition of Aesop. The court rewarded his anti-Tory poems with office and livings. His schoolfriend Henry Egerton (qv), Bishop of Hereford, made him prebend of Hinton and later of Moreton Magna and he used his consecration ceremony to attack the government. He was a canon residentiary, treasurer and chancellor of the Cathedral from 1738 until his death, and archdeacon of the Shropshire part of the diocese (1732-8). He was a portionist of Bromyard and rector of St Mary Somerset and St Mary Monthalt, the chapel of the London house of the bishops of Hereford. He spent his last decades in Hereford. After his wife Philippa Progers died in 1745 he lived with his housekeeper Hester Hooper. He was noted for having a fine library. He was Bishop Egerton's surrogate in old age and managed the diocese. He was a supporter of the Three Choirs Festival and preached on music in religion. He died at Hereford on 13 February 1752 and was buried in the north transept.

Crummer, Esther (1783-1858) was the daughter of William Davies of Bronllys Castle, Breconshire and sister of James Davies, solicitor of Kington, James Crummer's (qv) partner. She married Crummer in 1811, bringing him a large dowry. After her husband's death she became a partner in the Kington Bank, which opened a branch in Knighton in 1838. She was involved with the Kington Bank until her death. The bank traded successfully for more than 100 years as a private partnership until in 1910 it was absorbed

by the Metropolitan Banking Co., subsequently part of the Midland Bank.

Crummer, James (1749-1821), steward, was the son of Christopher Crummer and his second wife Mary of Ballina, Co. Mayo, Ireland. He was the Harley family's steward and trusted friend, managing their estates in Herefordshire and the Marches. After Lord Harley's death in 1804 (qv Thomas Harley), Lady Rodney (qv) continued to employ him as agent of the Berrington estates. He lived at Kington and the Kington Tramway Company negotiated their transit of Harley's lands with him. He was a friend of James Watt (qv) whom he met through Francis Garbett (qv). In 1808 he was one of the founders of Kington Bank. Aged 63, in 1811 he married 28-year-old Esther Davies (qv Esther Crummer). He was a Herefordshire magistrate, a trustee for turnpike roads and High Sheriff of Radnorshire in 1820.

Cunobelinus (fl.43 AD), called King of the Britons by Suetonius, was a Trinovantian ruler. When he and his sons invaded his neighbours' territory the Romans had their *casus belli* for invasion. His son Caractacus (qv) made his stand against the legions in the Herefordshire area. Copper coins of Cunobelinus have been found at *Ariconium*, a substantial industrial settlement near Weston-under-Penyard.

Curley, Timothy (d.1882) was a surveyor and civil engineer of Broomy Hill, Hereford. In 1848 a Mr Rammell, a sanitary commissioner, reported on the high mortality rate in Hereford City and the horrifying public health problems including blocked drains, sewers and cess pits, wells contaminated by over-full graveyards and pollution from abattoirs causing diseases like smallpox and typhoid. Curley, who had been working on the Abergavenny to Hereford railway, was appointed City Engineer and asked by Hereford Corporation to suggest solutions to the commission meeting in the Guildhall, Widemarsh Street, in January 1853. Curley wrote, 'I witnessed such scenes of filth and uncleanliness in this city as I did not before believe could exist in a civilised community.' The life expectancy of a working man was under 40 years and only one in four children survived infancy. 'Behind the White Lion in Maylord's Lane, we saw a stagnant pool of water in a high state of decomposition, which ... flows into the well that supplies the house and adjoining premises, in which are situated the Times printing offices, a large school and many superior private houses.' When the councillors enquired as to who owned the White Lion they found that they did. Curley's report led to the Hereford Improvement Act of 1854. As a consequence he was asked to draw up plans for a new waterworks on Broomy Hill, a new cemetery and a drainage system with sewers. In 1855 he produced his detailed map of Hereford, which can be seen in the foyer of the Town Hall, and in 1858 he drew a map showing geological sections for the new works. In 1856 the new livestock market Curley designed opened in Newmarket Street. At its height in the next century this was handling almost half a million beasts. As a result of these changes between 1851 and 1871 the population of Hereford rose from 12,000 to 18,000. Curley was a Fellow of the Geological Society and a founding member, and President, of the Woolhope Naturalists' Field Club.

Currey, Ada (1852-1913) was born and lived in Weybridge, Surrey all her life. She trained at art school locally and worked for Powells (qv John Hardman Powell) during the last years of the century making stained glass and mosaics, about 120 of which are attributed to her in Powells' records. She created the golden mosaic of Christ Pantocrator over the altar of St Catherine's, Hoarwithy – a wonderful work, the focus of the church. Powells' archive shows she was paid 1s 8d per hour for the 193 hours the work took her. She was also responsible for a stained glass window of the Resurrection in the north aisle at St Dubricius, Whitchurch. She never married.

Curtis, Lionel George (1872-1955), writer and public servant, born near Derby on 7 March 1872, was the youngest of the four children of Revd George James Curtis (d.1904), rector of All Saints, Coddington near Ledbury and his wife, Frances (d.1913), daughter of John Carr, another local clergyman. He grew up at Coddington rectory and was educated at Malvern and Haileybury Colleges and New College, Oxford. His ideas were influential in the transition of Empire to Commonwealth which he believed could form the basis, joined with America, of a future world government. He worked in South Africa for the federal self-government of its states and was influential in the transition of India to self-government. He published books on his ideas.

Cuthbert (736), previously an abbot in west Mercia, was made Bishop of the Magonsaete 736-40 by King Æthelbald of Mercia (qv) and he erected a memorial to his three predecessors. In 740 he was appointed Archbishop of Canterbury. He called a synod at Clofesho somewhere in Mercia in 747, attended by King Æthelbald (qv), to tackle abuses such as lay ownership of religious houses. He had the relics of the Herefordshire princess St Mildred (qv) translated to Canterbury, where her cult became an important one in mediaeval England. Cuthbert died on 26 October 760, popularly acclaimed a saint.

Cuthfleda, accounted a saint in Herefordshire, was the abbess of the Mercian monastery for religious women at Leominster. Founded by King Merewalh (qv) in 660, its first head was Edfrith. The *Anglo-Saxon Chronicle* says the relics of St Cuthfleda and St Ethelbert (qv) were venerated at the House. The foundation was closed after the abduction of its last abbess Eadgifu (qv) by Swein Godwinson (qv) in 1046.

Cynidr (5th century), saint and Bishop of Brycheiniog, was the son of St Ceingar (one of the 24 saintly daughters of Brychan Brycheiniog). His feast day is 8 December. Kenderchurch took its name from him and he is connected with Winforton. His mother St Ceingar may be the founder of Kentchurch although her sister St Keyne (qv) is also given. Legend involves Cynidr with King Arthur. His grave in Glasbury is commemorated by a holy well.

D

Daniel, John (*c.*1252-1326), son of a Derbyshire lord and Cecily le Seculer of Herefordshire, inherited lands in the Wormelow area from his mother's brother Nicholas. He raised troops in the county for Edward II's (qv) Scottish war and when Roger (V) de Mortimer (qv) was in exile he was given his manor of Pembridge. The king further gave Daniel charge of Mortimer's mother Margaret's castle of Radnor, for which she had to pay him (qv under Edmund (I) de Mortimer). Mortimer consequently had a great hatred of Daniel and after his coup captured him with Arundel (qv Edmund Fitzalan) and Robert de Micheldever and beheaded them summarily in Hereford on 17 November 1326. Daniel, bishop Orleton and Edward II (qqv) all gave land for the building of the Blackfriars Monastery in Hereford.

Dansey, Richard (1670-1740) was born at Brinsop Court. He fought in Marlborough's Peninsular wars, under Lord Peterborough and was celebrated in James Payne's (qv) song:

A braver soldier ne'er sure fought
Than gallant captain Dansey,
He trimmed the jackets of the Dons
In battle at Almanza.
His sword at Brinsop's to be seen
A blade both true and trusty,
The Spaniard's blood was ne'er wiped off
Which makes it look so rusty.

He inherited estates at Lower Eaton from his brother William. He died unmarried. Brinsop Court was sold to David Ricardo (qv) in 1814.

Dansey, Roger (1584-1658) was born at Brinsop the son of William Dansey (1545-1628) and Jane Colles (qv under Colles family). Danseys had lived in the picturesque 14th-century manor house Brinsop Court from the 15th century. He married Anne Smyth of Credenhill and they had some 16 children. He was High Sheriff of Hereford. In his 60s he fought for the king in the Civil Wars. Lady Dansey was a friend of Joyce Jefferies (qv) and gave her a cat. Dansey died at Little Hereford on 25 August 1658 where he is buried at St Mary Magdalene.

Dare, Charles James (d.1820) was organist at Hereford Cathedral 1805-18. Dare was appointed by the Dean and Chapter when the incumbent, Miles Coyle, who had been organist since 1789, became too elderly to perform his duties. An advertisement was placed in the London newspapers – the first time this had been done – and Dare, assistant organist at Westminster Abbey and organist to the Margaret Street Chapel, applied. He came as a celebrity, the organist's stipend was increased, the organ augmented and Dare married the daughter of George Carpenter in Hereford. But Dare failed to perform his duties at the cathedral satisfactorily, duties which included instructing the choristers. Warnings and fines were made to no avail and despite publishing books of his glees for the Three Choirs Festivals, he was eventually dismissed, replaced by Aaron Hayter (qv). Dare died in 1820.

Darnall, John (d.1706), son of Ralph Darnall of Loughton's Hope, Pembridge, was educated at King's College, Cambridge and Gray's Inn (1662). The Darnall family were Roman Catholics with interests in Maryland. John's sister Mary was the first wife of Charles Calvert, 3rd Baron and proprietor of Baltimore. Darnall was Serjeant-at-law in 1692 and defended Peter Cooke, who was charged with conspiring to assassinate the king in 1696. In 1698 he was King's Sergeant. He was knighted in 1699 and lived at Canon Pyon and in London where he died on 14 December 1706.

Darnall, John (1673-1735), lawyer, son of Sir John (d.1706, qv), was born at Canon Pyon and educated at King's College, Cambridge and the Middle Temple. Called to the bar in 1695, he was Serjeant-at-law in 1715 and was knighted in 1724. As judge in the court of Marshalsea he was required to judge whether George II or his son, the Prince of Wales, had the right of custody of the Prince of Wales' children, the king's grandchildren. His judgment was that royal grandchildren belonged to the Crown. He married Margaret (d.1741), daughter of Sir Thomas Jenner, and they had two daughters. He died in Petersham, Surrey on 5 September 1735.

Davey, George, Major, leased Kinnersley Castle from the Reavely (qv) family and lived there with his wife and their daughter Doreen. In 1931 he was represented at the funeral of his friend Tom Dew (qv) and in 1938 he invented the Davey Fire Escape (1938), a cable with two belts for lowering people from upper windows. Doreen landed the biggest ever rod-caught Wye salmon in March 1923. She caught it after a long fight, helped by her father, in Cowpond Pool on the Wye at Ballingham on 13 March 1923; it weighed 59lbs 8oz – a record which is apparently unbeaten.

David, patron saint of Herefordshire churches. St David (or Dewi) of Wales (6th century) is the legendary founder of Leominster Minster (but qv Etfrid). There was a later shrine to him at the minster claiming to have his arm bone as a relic. Pilgrimages made to it on 1 March, his feast day, secured papal indulgence, and two such visits were worth one to Rome. St David's church at Kilpeck may refer to a local holy man of this name. Kilpeck derives from the Celtic Kil Peddeg - the cell of Pedic, presumably referring to a local hermit. It stood in the small Welsh Marches kingdom of Ergyng (known as Archenfield to the Angles). When the church was rebuilt by Hugh de Kilpeck (qv) *c.*1240, as part of a Benedictine Abbey, St Mary joined St David as co-patron. St David is also patron of Much Dewchurch (i.e. Dewi's Church) and Dewsall derives from Dewi's well.

Davies, Archibald John (1878-1953), stained glass artist, was educated and trained in Birmingham. He set up his studio in Moseley, Birmingham but was persuaded by Walter Gilbert to move to Bromsgrove in 1906 to work with the other craftsmen of the Bromsgrove Guild of Applied Arts (fl.1898-1966), an Arts and Crafts movement founded by Gilbert. He set up his stained glass studio and worked at the Guild until his death in 1953. Here he made glass for Bromyard Church (1925) and for St James's Cradley, the beautiful east window of St Margaret's Church (1926) in St Margaret's village, and six windows for St Andrew's How Caple, three to the design of Lennox Lee (qv). The Stanbury Chapel windows in Hereford Cathedral are the best of his work in the county, showing scenes from Bishop Stanbury's (qv) life.

Davies, Edward 'Celtic' (1756-1831), poet, was born on 7 June 1756 in Llanfaredd, Radnorshire. He was brought up a Welsh speaker and went briefly to Christ's College, Brecon. He was ordained, taught a little and married Margaret Smith of Whittington. He was a curate in Gloucestershire and Herefordshire where he wrote poems, plays and studies of the Celtic language. His epistolary novel *Eliza Powell* (1795) is said to be the first novel to be written in Welsh. His writings on mythology influenced William Blake but he was uncritical of sources and subject to literary frauds. In 1823 he was made a Companion of Literature. He was an advocate for Herefordshire cider. He died on 7 January 1831, rector of Bishopston on the Gower, where he is buried.

Davies, John (1565-1618), poet and writing-master, is known as 'John Davies of Hereford' to distinguish him from the contemporary poet, Sir John Davies. He was born into a Roman Catholic family from Wales with two brothers and two sisters who settled in Hereford. Although not educated at the university, for a while he lived at Oxford, where he taught handwriting. Thomas Fuller (qv), in *Worthies of England*, called him 'the greatest master of the pen that England in her age beheld' and Pepys possessed a sample of his writing. By 1605 he had moved to London. He taught Prince Henry (the elder son of King James I) and others of the nobility and apparently knew everyone – Donne, Jonson, Inigo Jones, Shakespeare. He married well: first the Catholic Mary Croft (d.1612, qv under Herbert Croft, d.1629), of Croft Castle, with whom he had a son, Sylvanus; then Juliana (d.1614), widow of Sir Amyas Preston. His third wife, Margaret, brought him plate and jewels. He wrote of his wives:

He that would faine reduce an high-borne Wife
Unto the Compasse of his meane estate,
Must not at first stick for a little Strife.

He wrote turgid, derivative verse in every form – love sonnets, satires, epigrams and eclogues – and addressed epigrams to everybody in Jacobean London. Best remembered is his *Microcosmos* (1603) and *The Writing Schoolmaster or The Anatomy of Fair Writing*, published posthumously. Davies died on 6 July 1618 and was buried with his first wife Mary in the church of St Dunstan-in-the-West, London. Fuller (qv) says Davies had a pupil from Hereford called Gittings who was equally good.

Davies, Sneyd (1709-69), poet, was born on 30 October 1709, second son of John Davies, patron and rector of Kingsland and prebendary of Hereford, with two brothers and a sister. His mother, Honora Sneyd, was a cousin of John Dryden. He was educated at Eton and King's College, Cambridge. On the death of his father, who owned the living, he was ordained and continued at Kingsland rectory; a contented, unmarried recluse, he composed poetry in English and Latin, and saw only his companion, Revd Timothy Thomas, vicar of Presteigne. He published no work but had admirers such as Anna Seward, a close friend of his sister, who wept at the reading of his verse. He was chaplain to the Bishop of Lichfield and acquired other remunerative offices but was not absent from Kingsland for long. He died of a stroke on 20 January 1769 and was buried in St Michael's Church, leaving the living of Kingsland to Revd Richard Evans (1710-97). A life with a selection of his verse was written by George Hardinge (1743-1816).

Davies, Thomas (1763-1835), printer from Carmarthen, moved to Hereford in 1788 and worked as a printer on the *Hereford Journal*. In 1795 he established a printing and bookbinding business at 1 High Town, on the corner of Widemarsh Street, where he also sold stationery, books and music, pharmacy and insurance, and later traded with his son Thomas Theophilus Davies (1793-1887) as T. Davies & Son. He wrote ballads, one of which – *The Enchanted Piss-Pot* – was found buried in the wall of a house near Rhayader in 1991.

Davis, David (1745-1827), Welsh poet and dissenting minister, was the nephew of Joshua Thomas (qv) and lived with him as a child in Leominster, where he went to school.

Davis, Hugh (d.1644) was an organist and choirmaster at Hereford Cathedral. He was trained as chorister and organist at Hereford by William Inglott (qv) before he matriculated at New College, Oxford. He took over when Inglott returned to Norwich in 1611, and in 1637 he was appointed *custos* of the college of vicars choral. He died in 1644 before Hereford Cathedral and its offices were disbanded by the Parliamentarian administration.

Davis, John Scarlett (1804-45), painter, was born on 1 September 1804 at 2 High Street, Leominster, the second of the five children of James Davis (1775-1828), silversmith and watchmaker, and Ann Scarlett. The family, tallow chandlers and soap boilers, came to Leominster from Neath in Glamorgan in the 16th century. He went to Leominster Grammar School and learnt Latin and Greek. He drew well and won prizes as a child, and the *Hereford Journal* pronounced him a genius at 12. While still a schoolboy he painted a series of portraits of local citizens for £1 each. He took lessons from David Cox (qv) in Hereford and became friends with Ince (qv). He went on to a painting academy in Hackney and at 16 entered the Royal Academy Schools where he exhibited. He was successful in London with his watercolour landscapes and distinctive interiors and was especially noted

for his portraits. In 1832 he married Elizabeth Abbott and a son and two daughters survived him. He attracted patrons, one John Hinxman owning 489 of his works, but was always indigent and Hinxman once rescued him from a debtor' 'prison. Davies travelled through Britain and the Continent sketching. In 1845 he was in Leominster and stayed with his brother Edmund, curate of St Faith, Bacton. He suffered with diseased lungs and died in London on 29 September 1845, and was buried in Kensal Green Cemetery. The curator of Hereford Art Gallery, F.C. Morgan (qv), collected Davis' paintings, and many may be seen there, including his last oil, the large *Interior of St Peter's with Figures* which he painted in Rome in 1842. More are held in Leominster Museum.

Davis, Richard (1550-1623), Roman Catholic priest, was born in Leominster and educated at the Grammar School. He trained as a priest at Douai and returned to England on mission. He helped Father Nicholas Wheeler (qv) during his short life as a Jesuit priest in England and acted as guide to the famous Jesuit Fathers Edmund Campion and Robert Parsons. Fr Davis' ministry was in Wales and the Marches. He was arrested and questioned several times but convinced his interrogators of his innocence. He was in prison in Hereford in the years 1581-5 but escaped. He was arrested in 1591 and again escaped. In 1615 he was arrested for the third time but seems to have been released as he is recorded as having died in Holborn, blind, in 1623.

Dawes, Richard (1793-1867), Dean of Hereford 1850-67, was born in Yorkshire and educated at Trinity College, Cambridge, where he was known for radical ideas on education. In 1838 he married Mary Helen Alexander and became vicar of Kings Somborne in Hampshire, where he began to try out his ideas. In 1850 he succeeded John Merewether (qv) as Dean of Hereford, to the relief of Bishop Hampden (qv). He was known as a tolerant, affable Whig but he could be determined and forceful. He set about completing the restoration of the cathedral started by the Cottinghams (qv) and brought in the brilliant George Gilbert Scott (qv). Dawes approved the magnificent crossing screen designed by Scott (qv) and dedicated in 1863. This was sadly dismantled a century later and put into storage, but it has now been reassembled in the V&A Museum. In 1864 Hardman's (qv) great north transept window was installed. Dawes and Scott got on well and the restoration was completed on 30 June 1863. It was inaugurated with celebrations and crowds, lit by 500 gas jets. Dawes hated the crowds that flocked to the Three Choirs Festival at Hereford, especially with the advent of the railway connection, refer-

ring to it as the 'abominable festival'. He was a friend of Revd C.J. Robinson (qv), author of books on the mansions and castles of Herefordshire, providing him with the living of Norton Canon in 1865. Dawes supported the Blue Coat and Foundation schools in Hereford and was a patron of the National Schools work in Ledbury where he founded a free primary school (now Sheltered Housing flats called Dawes Court). George Eliot said she thought children would grow good merely by looking at his face. He was Master of St Katherine's Hospital in Ledbury. He died in Hereford Deanery on 10 March 1867. His friend Scott (qv) designed the marble chest-tomb for him, now in the north transept. The effigy was carved by Matthew Noble (1817-76) and the chest by Brindley and Richards.

Day, Charles (fl.1830s), architect, was born in London the son of a surveyor and was apprenticed to the architect Thomas Allason. He set up his practice in Worcester in the 1830s where he built the Shire Hall and was appointed County Surveyor. Day was commissioned to build St Francis Xavier (1839) in Broad Street, Hereford, whose large Doric portico shows Allason's classical influence and that of Smirke (qv). Ionic pillars surround the altar (by Scoles) with a dome above to light it. He also designed Stanbrook Abbey chapel. Day's son Henry took over his Worcester Office and built Lloyds Bank in Corn Square, Leominster in 1866.

Day, Ernest Hermitage (1866-1946) editor of the *Church Times* (1915-24), ran an aggressive but unsuccessful campaign opposing the selection of Henson (qv) as Bishop of Hereford, who was believed to be liberal. Day lived outside Hereford and wrote a number of books on church architecture.

Dee, John (1527-1609), alchemist and astrologer, was born on 13 July 1527 into a Radnorshire family probably in London, where his father was at the Court of Henry VIII. He was educated at St John's College, Cambridge and elected to a fellowship at Trinity College. He was ordained and held various livings, and travelled widely, as

well as teaching and collecting antiquities. He amassed one of the largest libraries in Europe and was awarded the degree of Doctor of Medicine at the University of Prague. He returned to his mother's house at Mortlake, Surrey where he installed his library and alchemical equipment. He had several children by his third wife Jane Frommonds, the best-known being the eldest, Arthur Dee, whose godmother was Blanche Parry (qv). A celebrated mathematician and scientist, Dr Dee had popular notoriety as a magician and necromancer. In his attempts to 'skry' or communicate with spirits he was the dupe of his medium Edward Kelley. He recorded one of his visits to the Marches in 1574, when he stayed with his friends Dr William Aubrey and John Prise, son of Sir John Prise (qv, d.1555), both of them relations, and bought some ancient documents from the latter. He visited Presteigne with Prise on 30 August and next day they explored Wigmore Abbey, which had been dissolved and despoiled 30 years before. He met Thomas Harley (qv, d.1631) of Brampton Bryan, who showed him such of the abbey's records that had been saved, and he seems to have unearthed others in a ruined chapel. On 1 September he describes Hereford Cathedral, noting the dilapidated state of the library. He and Prise were especially interested in ancient British history and its monuments, as witnessed by Dee's choice of name for his eldest son, Arthur. The next day he rode over to Ledbury to meet his old friend Dr Threlkeld, prebend of Hereford, and they climbed Wall Hill to investigate the remains of the earthworks. Dee was consulted by monarchs throughout Europe and was a confidential adviser to Queen Elizabeth and King James. Rumours about dealings with spirits caused his house at Mortlake to be ransacked, books carried off and equipment spoiled. At the end of his life he and his wife experienced poverty and he was appointed warden of Manchester College as a form of assistance. He died in 1609 and was buried in Mortlake Church.

Defoe, Daniel (*c.*1660-1731), author, was born in Cripplegate, London. He is known for his innovative novels *Robinson Crusoe* and *Moll Flanders*, his journalism and his travel writing. His *Tour Through the Whole Island of Great Britain*, still in print, records his view of Hereford in 1725:

> *A large and a populous city, and in the time of the late Rebellion was very strong, and being well fortify'd and as well defended, supported a tedious and very severe siege ... It is truly an old, mean built and very dirty City, lying low and on the bank of Wye, which sometimes incommodes them very much by the violent freshes that come down from the mountains of Wales ... The great Church is a magnificent building however ancient, the spire is not high but handsome, and there is a fine tower at the west end, over the great door or entrance.*

This tower was soon to collapse. He admired the countryside and, like Celia Fiennes (qv), especially appreciated the fruit trees. He found he liked the cider: 'We could get no beer or ale in their publick houses, only cyder ... so very good, so fine, and so cheap ... Great quantities of this cyder are sent to London, even by land carriage tho so very remote, which is an evidence of the goodness of it.' He mentions the Wergin Stones that stand near Sutton St Nicholas, that moved and had to be dragged back by a team of oxen. Just one remains now, stationary by the Hereford Road. Defoe died on 24 April 1731.

Delamaine, Richard (1627-57), son of Richard Delamaine, mathematician of Holborn, had a conversion experience in his teens and travelled to Hereford with a Mr Hill. In Bredwardine he was taken up by a group of pious women and preached in Hereford, where he attracted the approval of Parliamentarian Governor Wroth Rogers (qv) with whom he became friends. Delamaine married Rogers' wife's servant Mary and they called their son Wroth, with Rogers standing as godfather. He was appointed Master of St Ethelbert's Hospital in Castle Street, was licensed to preach in the cathedral and was granted the benefices of Aymestrey, Little Hereford and Longtown. He was seen as an ignorant charlatan by many, however, and in 1654 was anonymously attacked in a Hereford pamphlet *Impostor magnus: the legerdemain of Richard Delamain, now preacher in the city of Hereford. Being a narrative of his life and doctrine since his first coming into that county.* The author, Commissioner Silas Taylor (qv), a moderate Presbyterian who was often at odds with the governor, accused Delamaine of ignorance of the Gospel and stirring the people up with his 'frenzy'. Delamaine had astrological signs painted on the cathedral stalls: Taurus for Governor Rogers, Aries for the Garrison Commanders and Gemini for Mayor and Aldermen. He died in the summer of 1657.

Denis or Dionysius, a 3rd-century saint sent from Rome to convert the Gauls, was executed on Montmartre, which is named after the event, and became the patron saint of Paris. He is one of the 14 Holy Helpers who were venerated together in medieval times (and still are in the Roman Catholic Church) as especially efficacious in curing diseases. St Denis cured possession by the devil and headache: he is generally depicted holding his severed head. Henry I contributed to the popularity of his cult in England when he founded a priory in Southampton in memory of his son William, who had drowned in the sinking of the *White Ship*. There is a St Denys at Pencoyd, and he was patron of the now deconsecrated chapel at Harewood nearby. In 1227 Henry III (qv) granted Bishop Hugh Foliot (qv) the right to hold a fair in Hereford at St Denis' tide, on 9 October, harvest time. The bishop would collect tolls at the city gates (Way Gate, Bishopstreet Gate, St Owen's Gate, Zizene Gate [Eign Gate], Widemarsh Gate and the Wye Bridge Gate). Such tithes supported St Ethelbert's Almshouses in Castle Street. There is still a fair in Hereford at this time of year.

Denton, Anne (1548-66), heiress, was born Willason and inherited her father's Sugwas estate. She married Alexander Denton but died in childbirth in 1566 aged only 18. She is shown lying beside her husband on their alabaster tomb in the south transept of Hereford Cathedral, her baby beside her. The tomb was made for her grieving husband by Richard Parker of Burton on Trent in 1566. Alexander himself died in 1578 and was buried at his Buckingham seat. Scott (qv) restored Anne's tomb in consultation with Havergal (qv), having found it in pieces after Lewis Cottingham's (qv) work at the cathedral.

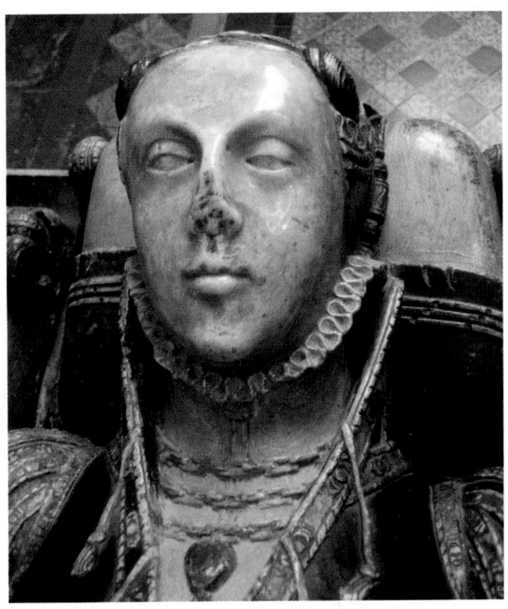

Despenser, Edward (1336-75), 1st Baron le Despenser, was born at Essendine, Rutland, on 24 March 1336, the son of Edward le Despenser (1310-42) and Anne Ferrers of Groby, and grandson of Hugh the younger (qv). The remaining Despenser lands were put in the hands of Hugh de Burghersh during Edward's minority and, on gaining livery of them, he married Elizabeth (*c.*1342-1409), his guardian's daughter, *suo jure* Baroness Burghersh, who brought him the Marcher lordship of Ewyas Lacy, where she had been born. He fought beside the Black Prince (qv Edward of Woodstock) in the French wars and was later in the Pope's service, building a reputation for chivalry and appearing, splendidly arrayed, in a mural of *c.*1368 in St Maria de Novella, Florence. He fought in France with Edmund (III) Mortimer (qv), but he died on returning home on 11 November 1375, leaving an infant son Richard. Richard (1373-1400) supported King Richard II (qv), and gained titles and lands, but, involved in the abortive Epiphany rising against Henry IV (qv), was executed on 13 January 1400 aged 27. He had married Constance daughter of Edmund of Langley. Their son died childless extinguishing the line; their daughter, Isabel (1400-39), married Richard Beauchamp (qv), the Earl of Worcester, and after his death his cousin, Richard Beauchamp, Earl of Warwick (1382-1439).

Despenser, Hugh the younger (*c.*1287-1326), royal favourite of Edward II (qv), was the son of courtier Hugh Despenser, Earl of Winchester (1261-1326) and Isabel (d.1306) daughter of William de Beauchamp of Elmley Castle, Worcs. He married Eleanor, daughter of Gilbert de Clare, Earl of Gloucester and granddaughter of Edward I. He married his daughter Isabel (1312-56) to Arundel's son Richard (qv under Edmund Fitzalan). He and his father replaced Piers Gaveston (qv) as royal favourites and were given wealth, titles and land, including Huntington Castle. They flaunted their wealth and abused their powers, antagonising the barons who ravaged their lands and had them exiled. But Edward revoked their exile and went on the offensive, killing Humphrey (VII) de Bohun (qv), the Earl of Hereford, in 1322. Edward's Queen Isabella (qv) and Roger (V) Mortimer (qv) crossed from France and pursued and captured the Despensers. They were condemned as traitors. Hugh the younger was taken to Hereford, his sentence to be hanged for robbery, drawn for treason and decapitated for crimes against the church. On 24 November 1326, he was stripped, reclothed with his arms reversed and crowned with nettles outside Hereford city walls, then drawn on a hurdle to a 50 foot high gallows where he was hanged, cut down and disembowelled and finally beheaded. There is a miniature by Jean Froissart of this event, which took place beside Hereford Castle. His head was fixed on London Bridge while his father's was sent to Winchester. Four years later Eleanor de Clare was allowed to collect her husband's remains to be interred in Tewkesbury Abbey, which the Despensers had remodelled, where she commemorated him with members of her own family in some of the best stained glass in England in the high chancel windows. Legends arose, one linking him with Isabel Chandos (qv Sir Roger de Chandos, d.1353) at Mordiford.

Devereux: Robert d'Evreux from Normandy fought at Hastings and was granted lands in the Weobley and Bodenham area as feudal tenant of Roger de Lacy (qv). He held Lyonshall Castle for the de Lacys and had land along the Frome Valley. There is an effigy of a Devereux Templar Knight in St Mary's Church, Bishop's Frome of *c.*1300. In 1338 a Walter Devereux married a de Lacy girl and came in possession of Weobley Castle (now just earthworks), which remained the Devereux seat for 300 years. They were granted the barony of Ferrers and in the mid 16th century became Viscounts of Hereford, the premier viscountcy, and then Earls of Essex. But Robert, 2nd Earl, famously pushed Queen Elizabeth too far and was executed. The 3rd Earl was restored to royal favour but repaid it by leading the Parliamentary opposition to King Charles. On his death the earldom and barony became extinct; the viscountcy continued but based in Montgomeryshire.

Devereux, Dorothy (1600-36), poet, daughter of Robert (qv, d.1601) and Frances, was born on 20 December 1600 at Walsingham House, Seething Lane, London. She married Sir Henry Shirley at 15; both were strong Catholics but the marriage ended with Sir Henry's adultery, disgrace and death. Charles, the Shirley heir, was brought up by Dorothy's brother the 3rd Earl. Lady Dorothy was said to be the fairest, wittiest widow of the age. She was a writer and dedicatee of verse in a Catholic circle of poets. She next married William Stafford (*c.*1604-37) of Blatherwyck, Northamptonshire in a Catholic ceremony. She died on 30 March 1636 at Blatherwyck.

Devereux, John (1464–1501), 2nd Baron Ferrers of Chartley, was the son of Walter Devereux, (qv, d.1485). He married Cecily (d.1493), granddaughter of William Bourchier (qv) and Anne of Gloucester (qv in Humphrey IX de Bohun). Devereux was allowed by Henry VII to recover lands lost after Bosworth.

Devereux, Robert (1565-1601), 3rd Viscount Hereford, 2nd Earl of Essex, KG etc., son of Sir Walter (qv, d.1576), was born on 19 November 1565 at Netherwood, the old Mortimer house at Collington north of Bromyard. He was a cousin of Queen Elizabeth and her favourite. He married Frances Walsingham (1569-1631) daughter of the queen's minister

and previously wife of Sir Philip Sidney. His heir was Robert (d.1646, qv) and there was a daughter, Dorothy. Michael Drayton (qv) dedicated *Poly-Olbion* to Lady Devereux. Robert Devereux was politically ambitious; like his father he did badly in Ireland in 1599 and returned against the queen's instructions, for which he was arrested. In 1601 he attempted a coup against her and he was executed for treason in the Tower on 25 February 1601. He is known to have stayed at Hellens, Much Marcle where material connected with him is shown.

Devereux, Robert (1591-1646), 3rd Earl of Essex and 4th Viscount Hereford, was born on 11 January 1591 in his mother's property Walsingham House in London. He was a friend of Henry Prince of Wales and James I restored his

titles. His marriage to Frances Howard was brief and unconsummated and ended in divorce. Later he married Elizabeth (d.1656), the daughter of Sir William Paulet. An heir, Viscount Hereford, resulted but soon died, and Elizabeth became involved in an adulterous affair. During the Civil Wars he was Chief Commander of the Parliamentary Army from 1642-46, an erratic leader, and his failings caused Oliver Cromwell to form the New Model Army. He resigned his commission and died on 10 September 1646; without an heir the line ended. He was grandly buried in Westminster Abbey but the tomb was defaced at the Restoration. His daughter Frances left the old Devereux seat of Weobley Castle to Thomas Thynne, who had married her granddaughter. The castle has disappeared but Silas Taylor (qv) made a sketch of it in 1655. The Thynne family represented Weobley in Parliament for many years. The viscountcy of Hereford was subsequently held by distant relations until the 14th Viscount Henry Fleming Lea Devereux (1777-1843) married Frances Elizabeth (1783-1864, qv under her brother, George Cornewall, d.1819), fourth daughter of Sir George Amyand, later Cornewall (qv) of Moccas Court. Their second son Robert became the 15th Viscount Hereford and his second son, Henry de Bohun Devereux, was a pupil of Kilvert (qv).

Devereux, Walter (d.1402) was the son of Sir Walter and Maud Devereux of Bodenham. His father was a servant of the de Bohuns (qv) and Sheriff of Hereford, an MP, a JP for the county and a friend of Edward the Black Prince (qv Edward of Woodstock). He married Agnes (1371-1436), the 11-year-old daughter of Thomas Crophill of Weobley. He was governor of Builth Castle during the minority of Roger (VII) Mortimer (qv). When his wife's grandfather, John Crophill, died he inherited great estates including the manor of Weobley which he made his main residence. He was a member of Richard II's (qv) council and was knighted in 1391. Sir Walter was killed fighting Glyn Dŵr at the bloody Battle of Bryn Glas at Pilleth in 1402.

Devereux, Walter (1387-1420) of Bodenham was the son and heir of Sir Walter Devereux (qv, d.1402) and Agnes. He was knighted by Henry IV in 1403 and retained by the king. He fought at Agincourt with his brothers Sir John and Sir Richard. In 1409 he married Elizabeth, daughter of Sir Thomas Bromwich, and they had a son, Walter Devereux (qv, d.1459), and a daughter, Elizabeth.

Devereux, Walter (1411-59), knight, was born in Bodenham, the son of a Walter Devereux (*c.*1387-1420) and his wife Elizabeth, a relative of the Oldcastles (qv). He married Elizabeth (1412-38), daughter of John Merbury (qv), a Herefordshire landowner and they lived in Weobley Castle. They had sons Richard (b.1426), Thomas (b.1428) and Walter (qv, d.1485). Their daughter Anne married William Herbert (qv) in 1449. Another daughter, Catherine, married James Baskerville (qv, d.1494). Devereux supported the Yorkists in the Wars of the Roses and was knighted by the Duke of York during an expedition to Normandy in 1441. With William Herbert (qv) he dominated the Marches for the Yorkists. In 1454 he was at the Battle of St Albans, a Yorkist victory, and died on 23 April 1459.

Devereux, Walter (*c.*1432-85), 7th Baron Ferrers, was Sir Walter's (qv, d.1459) third son. He married Anne (1438-69) daughter and heir of Sir William Ferrers of Chartley, Staffordshire in 1446. He escaped from the defeat at Ludford Bridge outside Ludlow at the start of the Wars of the Roses and was pardoned with a fine, eventually recovering his properties. When Yorkist influence was strong again he was appointed a JP and he and his brother-in-law William Herbert (qv) represented Herefordshire in Edward IV's (qv) Parliament. He was the Herefordshire steward of the Duchess Cecily, the king's mother, and lived at Weobley Castle. After the Battle of Towton, King Edward IV knighted him and created him Baron Ferrers of Chartley, in succession to his father-in-law. He was a loyal supporter and counsellor of Edward. He continued to support Edward's brother Richard III (qv) and fell fighting for him at Bosworth on 22 August 1485. He had married a second wife, Joan, widow of Thomas Ilam and their heir was John (qv). He had a house in Castle Street, Hereford and paid for the vicars choral to move from that street to their new residences at the cathedral.

Devereux, Walter KG (1489-1558), son of John (qv) and Cecily, succeeded his father as 3rd Lord Ferrers in 1501 and in 1550 was created 1st Viscount Hereford, the premier viscountcy. He married Mary (d.1538) daughter of Thomas Grey, Marquess of Dorset, and served Henry VIII (qv) in his first Parliament, both diplomatically and militarily. His seat was Weobley Castle, at the centre of his estates in Herefordshire and the Marches, and he was steward of royal lordships in the area and of Princess

Mary's household at Ludlow. He was a member of the coup which ousted Protector Somerset, Edward Seymour. Queen Mary (qv) imprisoned him but later pardoned him. After Mary's death he married Margaret (d.1599), daughter of John Garneys of Kenton in Suffolk and had a son, Edward, who was to be the father of the 5th Viscount Hereford. Devereux died on 17 September 1558 at his home, Chartley, Staffordshire and was buried in Stowe Church. His oldest surviving son, Sir Richard Devereux KG, died 13 October 1547. He had married Dorothy Hastings and their son, Walter succeeded. Another son, William (*c*.1525-79), married Jane, daughter of John Scudamore (d.1571). His daughter Anne married Henry Clifford (qv under Nicholas Clifford) and Elizabeth married Sir James Baskerville (qv, d.1572).

Devereux, Walter KG (1541-76), 2nd Viscount Hereford, 10th Baron Ferrers of Chartley and 1st Earl of Essex, was born on 16 September 1541 at Chartley, the son of Sir Richard and Dorothy (see under Walter Devereux, d.1558). He was a prominent nobleman and adventurer at the Court of Queen Elizabeth and married Lettice, daughter of Sir Francis Knollys. Their eldest child, Penelope (1563-1607), was intended to marry Sir Philip Sidney (qv) and inspired his sonnet sequence *Astrophel and Stella* but he died before she was of age. Instead she married the Baron Rich and, divorced from him, Baron Mountjoy, Earl of Devonshire. Queen Elizabeth sent Devereux to put down a rebellion in Ulster in 1569, and created him a Knight of the Garter and 1st Earl of Essex in acknowledgement of his Bourchier and Bohun (qv) ancestry. He died campaigning in Ireland on 22 September 1576.

Dew, Armine (1826-54) a younger brother of Henry (qv) was a captain in the Royal Artillery, killed in action, as his memorial in Whitney Church relates, on 20 September 1854 at the Alma in the Crimea. His grandson Lieutenant Colonel Sir Armine Brereton Dew (1867-1941) served in the British Indian Army, becoming Chief Commissioner of Baluchistan.

Dew, Henry (1819-1901), son of Tomkyns (qv, d.1853) and Margaret, was born on 18 March 1819 at Whitney Court and was educated at Rugby School under Dr Arnold. He was rector of Whitney on Wye from 1843 till his death. In 1845 he married Mary Monkhouse (1822-1900), a relative of Wordsworth's wife Mary (qv). Kilvert (qv) was fond of Revd and Mrs Dew, their children and sister Fanny (1818-88) and often dined and stayed at the Whitney rectory.

Dew, Thomas Millet (1859-1931), married Margaret (d.1901), daughter of Revd Henry Blisset of Letton Court, where the Millets lived. In 1907 he married Alice, daughter of Charles Sysum. Dew was a county magistrate for 26 years, a rural district councillor and a member of the local Board of Guardians. Letton Court was burnt down in 1924, the fire having been started by a builder's blow-lamp while he and Alice were away and they lost everything.

Dew, Tomkyns (1720-99), of Whitney Court, Lord of the Manors of Whitney and Clifford, married Sarah Thornborrow in 1759. He was an attorney of the Court of Common Pleas with a London house at Marylebone, Middlesex. In 1783 and 1799 he was High Sheriff of Herefordshire. Sarah died in 1789 and aged 70 he married Anne Styleman (1760-1823) and they had three children. The Dews owned the ferry crossing from Whitney to Clifford but the Wye in spate often prevented the crossing. There were calls for a bridge from farmers with lands on both sides of the Wye and from the Welsh drovers that crossed here, driving great herds of cattle to Hereford market. In 1774 plans were made to build a toll bridge and an Act of Parliament was secured in 1779. Dew allowed them to extract free materials for the bridge from his estate for three years. A stone bridge and toll house was built but soon destroyed by floods of great ferocity. In the great flood of 1735 Whitney Old Court and Church were washed away and were rebuilt in 1740 higher up the bank. A second bridge was built but was also carried away, as were those at Hay and Glasbury. In 1782 the consortium built an especially robust third bridge of five arches of 30 feet each, standing 15 feet above river level and 12 feet wide and Wathen (qv) painted it in 1787. This stood until February 1795 when there were catastrophic floods across the county and it and many other bridges were swept away, leaving just the piers. It was his son, also Tomkyns (qv, d.1853) who solved the problem of the Wye crossing. Dew's wealthy young widow Anne remarried a Col Thomas Powell but they later separated.

Dew, Tomkyns (1791-1853), son of Tomkyns (qv, d.1799) and Anne, was born on 9 July 1791 in Roehampton, Surrey and educated at the Inner Temple. He married Margaret Napleton (1794-1877) in 1813 and they had 14 children. The problem of the Wye crossing with which his father struggled continued. John Philips of Hay, financed by the Brecon carrier Longfellow, came forward suggesting a lighter, open-work construction of oak better to withstand the force of the Wye. An Act of Parliament was secured allowing for this change and a new bridge was built in 1802; this, much repaired, has survived. Pevsner called its open cutwaters 'rough work'. A charge is still levied at the Toll House from travellers seeking to cross the Wye at Whitney. Dew died at Roehampton but was buried in Whitney churchyard where there is an inscription.

Deynte, Robert (fl.1275-82), servant of Thomas de Cantilupe (qv), had served the future saint in his pantry and buttery throughout his life and, by the time of Bishop Thomas's last journey to see the Pope at Orvieto in Italy, he had risen to be his chamberlain. He was one of the three people crammed into the tiny tower room as Thomas lay dying in Ferento and later told the commission enquiring into Thomas's sanctity that he had confessed to his chaplain and received absolution. He remembered that he customarily wore a hair shirt next to his skin for mortification, and that Thomas often dealt with diocesan matters in bed, keeping Robert, who shared his room, awake at night; and that although he had a splendid bed he slept on straw that was crawling with lice as further mortification.

Diamond, Harry (1874-1907), musician, was a widely popular singer and banjo player in minstrel shows in fashionable summer resorts; he spent the winters at Ross where he gave banjo lessons. Here on 18 May 1907 he died of heart disease. His gravestone can be seen in St Mary's churchyard, Ross.

Dickens, Charles (1812-70), the most celebrated novelist of his time, was born in Portsmouth on 7 February 1812 and brought up in increasing insecurity in London. His strong views on social inequity were based on his own experiences at the hands of a feckless father. His strong blend of sentiment with forceful characterisation may have been forged during his time as a parliamentary reporter. It is known that in 1867 he stayed at the Royal Hotel, Ross, built 30 years before to cater for the booming Wye tourist trade, and a plaque commemorates the visit. He came up by the London train to meet his man of business George Dolby, who stayed at Wilton House, across the Wye, with Dickens' friend and biographer John Forster (qv) to discuss funding a tour to America. He gave Dolby's children the present of a donkey, which was bought locally.

There is a story that Dickens got the idea for his novel *Bleak House* from a celebrated legal battle lasting 34 years over a disputed will concerning Eardisley Manor, owned by the Barnsley (qv) family. Dickens died on 9 June 1870.

Dinabo (6th-7th centuries) was a saint, known as Junabius with many variants, a cousin of St Dubricius (qv). Llandinabo Church is dedicated to him, the churchyard being the circular *llan* of Celtic Christianity. It has a beautiful Welsh oak chancel screen of the early 16th century covered with scrolling decoration. The saint is pictured in a Kempe (qv) window at Much Marcle.

Dingley, Thomas (d.1695), antiquary, son of Thomas Dingley, controller of customs at Southampton, was educated at the dramatist James Shirley's school in Whitefriars, London and at Gray's Inn. He lived at Dilwyn in Herefordshire, travelling widely on the Continent and in Britain making antiquarian notes and sketches, some later published as *Travails through the Low Countreys* (1674) and *Observations in a Voyage in the Kingdom of France* (1675). In 1684 he accompanied Henry Somerset (qv, d.1700), 1st Duke of Beaufort, Lord President of the Council, through Herefordshire and the Marches, recording and sketching antiquities. Some of these were published in 1805 and 1809 by Theophilus Jones in *A History of the County of Brecknock* but many remain unpublished. His diary was printed in 1864 as *Notitia Cambro-Britannica* for the 8th Duke of Beaufort. Another manuscript, *History from Marble*, shows antiquities which caught his eye in the churches and country houses of Herefordshire and formed the basis for Richard Rawlinson's (qv) *History and Antiquities of the City and Cathedral Church of Hereford* (1717). It was published for the Camden Society in 1866. One of his drawings depicts the cloister of the vicars choral with a great oak in the garth and a stag quietly grazing, and records the *custos* in 1684 as Richard Cox. He also shows the Blackfriars preaching cross in its original state. Another sketch of this time is the earliest depiction of Hereford's Market Hall, now gone. He drew John Birch's (qv) new house at Garnstone, Weobley and the old house at Newport, Almeley before Paul Foley (qv, d.1739) rebuilt it. In Ledbury Church he recorded brasses which are now only partially intact: William Calwe (qv) with the now-missing St Peter; Robert Preece, chaplain of the Trinity chapel, now missing. Dingley died in May 1695 while on a trip to Louvain. He was unmarried and his niece Eliza Melling inherited his papers.

Dodgson, Charles Hassard Wilfred (1876-1941), son of Lewis Carroll's brother Wilfred Dodgson, lived in Breinton House and is buried at St Michael's, Breinton.

Dodgson, Skeffington Hume (1836-1919), vicar, was the second son of the 11 children of Charles Dodgson (1800-68), rector of Croft-on-Tees, Yorkshire and his cousin Frances Jane Lutwidge (1803-51). He was younger brother of Charles Lutwidge Dodgson, better known as Lewis Carroll. Educated at Christ Church, Oxford, he was ordained and, in 1880, married Isabel Mary Cooper (1848-1937). Their children were Amy, Irene, Hume (1884-1980), who was to marry into the family at nearby Poston Hall (qv Boughton), Charles Lutwidge (1885-6), Winifred Mary (b.1888) and Zoë Frances (b.1890). He was vicar of Vowchurch from 1895 until 1910 when he retired to Warlow House, Ewyas Harold. He died in 1919 and was buried in St Bartholomew's churchyard, Vowchurch.

Domulton, John, descended from the original Brockhampton family (qv), acquired the estate of Brockhampton by Bromyard from Robert de Furches (qv) in 1403 and built the 15th-century black and white, half-timbered house so admired today within its moats. There is close timber studding on the hall and its roof is supported by base crucks – long curved timbers that end at rafter level, joining onto collar beams and giving extra height and width to the hall. This was up-to-date technology for such an isolated manor house. The small gatehouse standing over the moat is of the next century. The ruined Norman chapel adjacent is witness to the antiquity of the site. A Philip Domulton married Agnes daughter of William Croft (qv, d.1439) *c.*1430.

Dowding, John Benjamin (1860-1945), embezzler, was born in Leominster and attended a school in the Bargates and Grange House Academy. At 14 he started work in a local solicitor's office and rose quickly with his energy, flair and ability. He soon managed everything – charities, the Free Library, the council – and was Mayor four times in succession from 1917 to 1924. In 1924 he declared himself bankrupt and was found to have been embezzling money on a large scale for which he was imprisoned. His wife Hannah died in 1935.

Doyle, Arthur Ignatius Conan (1859-1930), author, was born on 22 May 1859 in Edinburgh, where he qualified as a physician at the university medical school – said to have provided him with the characters for both Holmes and Watson in his 60 or so Sherlock Holmes stories. He stayed in Herefordshire and knew the county well. *The Boscombe Valley Mystery* is set near Ross, which Watson describes as 'a pretty little Market Town'. Holmes and Watson travel there by railway and Holmes takes a train to Hereford to interview a man in prison. *The Hound of the Baskervilles*, while not set in Herefordshire, draws on names and legends of the county. Dr Mortimer has a very Herefordian name and the storyline follows the local tale of Black Vaughan (qv Thomas Vaughan, d.1469) of Hergest Court near Kington and his ghostly hound. Stapleton, the botanist in the story, takes his name from a village not far from Kington. The Baskerville (qv) family is an ancient Herefordshire one, intermarried with the Vaughans, who once had a castle near Eardisley, also in the Kington area. Conan Doyle wrote much else: the Professor Challenger tales, stories of mediaeval adventure and tracts on spiritualism etc. He campaigned against capital punishment, was an advocate of racial equality, attempted to right miscarriages of justice, and was knighted. He died of a heart attack aged 71 in his Surrey home on 7 July 1930.

Drayton, Michael (1563-1631), writer of verse and plays of an allegorical, historical and geographical nature, was born at Hartshill in Warwickshire. He wrote a verse epic on Roger (V) Mortimer (qv) and the Barons' Wars against Edward II in 1596 called *Mortimeriados*, later reworked as *Barrons Wars*. His best known work

is *Poly-Olbion or a Chorographical Description ... of Great Britain* (1612), which praises the nymphs of the hills and rivers of Herefordshire. He describes the Battle of Wakefield and John Clifford's murder of Edmund of York and shows the 'Wonder' landslip at Marcle. Drayton's verses celebrate the variety of English counties. He was a friend of Shakespeare; both were leather workers' sons from Warwickshire and Shakespeare is said to have died from the effects of a 'merrie evening' in Stratford with Drayton and Ben Jonson. One of Drayton's plays was *Sir John Oldcastle* (qv). Drayton died in December 1631 at his London house and, as poet laureate, was buried in Westminster Abbey.

Droffner, George Egroeg (*c.*1790-1856), was the pseudonym of George Hanford from Leicestershire, where he had a wife, Mary Pryor, and a daughter. He had a spiritual experience and vowed not to sleep in a bed, drink alcohol, shave or wash but to devote himself to the welfare of working people. He took up an itinerant life peddling goods and giving lectures on self-improvement. On entering Herefordshire in 1836 his appearance was enough to have him arrested in Dilwyn for a murder but he managed to prove his innocence. He invented a sort of hurdy-gurdy and in 1838 a lithograph was published in Hereford showing him playing it. He lectured frequently at Hereford, Leominster, Kington, Ross and Hay, and founded Mechanics' Institutes wherever he went for the working man's self-improvement. He was reportedly an inspiring speaker: witty, pithy and lucid but malodorous. He kept a journal, now lost, which dealt with the benefits of the itinerant, mendicant life. He died on 20 January 1856 in the Madeley workhouse, Shropshire.

Dubricius (fl.475-525), saint, Dyfrig in Welsh and Devereux in Norman French, had a cult in Herefordshire and Gwent. His mother was Efrddyl, an unmarried daughter of King Peibio (qv) of Ergyng, a region of Herefordshire later called Archenfield. When Peibio discovered Efrddyl was pregnant he tried to drown then to burn her, but she was miraculously protected

and in the morning she was found sitting in the ashes at Madley with the baby Dyfrig. Peibio suffered from leprosy which the baby miraculously cured with a kiss, securing his grandfather's forgiveness. Peibio gave him the Madley area, called Ynys Efrddyl, to govern as bishop and saint. Madley Church was built on the site of his birth and originally dedicated to him. He founded a monastic settlement at St Dubricius in the Hentland. An angel subsequently told St Dyfrig to establish a monastery where he would find a white sow with her piglets and on finding them he named the place 'Mochros', the moor of the pigs, later known as Moccas. In the Book of Llandaff, he is King Constantine's (qv) 'Bishop in Ergyng'. Bishop Mayo (qv) offered an indulgence to pilgrims visiting a now vanished shrine miraculously built by the saint near Woolhope where miracles were reported. He is the Archbishop of Caerleon who crowned King Arthur (qv) in 518 on St Weonards (qv) Tump. In Tennyson's *Idylls of the King* he is 'Dubric the high saint, chief of the Church in Britain'. There were many churches dedicated to him in Herefordshire: Moccas, Hamnish Clifford, Hentland,

Whitchurch, St Devereux, and others that have been re-dedicated like Preston on Wye which is now St Lawrence's. C.E. Kempe's (qv) south transept window in Hereford Cathedral shows him. His feast day is 14 November.

Duckham, Thomas (1816-1902) cattle breeder, architect and politician, was born on 26 September 1816 at Shirehampton near Bristol. The family moved to Baysham Court, near Ross to farm and Thomas went to school in Hereford. He was a noted breeder of Hereford Cattle at Baysham Court and from 1846 kept the Hereford Herd Book, in which he recorded the line and purity of the breed. In 1845 he married Anne (d.1894), née Morgan, the widow of John Yeomans (qv), a fellow breeder of Herefords, and they lived at Holmer with their daughter, Ellen. He also set up in Hereford as an architect in around 1840, and with William Hayley of Manchester built St John the Baptist, Newton (1842), later returning to effect renovations. In partnership with the builder Thomas Trehern he put up St Nicholas (qv) Church in Friars Street and Hereford Gaol (both 1842). He built the rectory at Ewyas Harold (1845) and renovated the pews in the church. In 1857 he built the rectory at Stoke Prior. In 1873-4 he built Vowchurch School and the master's house, and in 1877 Pencoyd School. He founded the Central and Associated Chambers of Agriculture of which he was chairman, and was secretary of the Herefordshire Agricultural Society (qv Duncumb). He was JP for Herefordshire and the last MP for the Shire before the Redistribution of the Seats Act of 1885 after which he was MP for Leominster. He was an Alderman of Hereford Council, a member of the Ross Board of Guardians and chairman of the Ross Highway Board. He died on 2 March 1902.

Dugdale, William (1605-86), antiquary and herald, was born on 12 September 1605 at Shustoke rectory, Warwickshire, the son of the rector John Dugdale. After his marriage he returned to live at Blyth Hall, Shustoke for the rest of his life. His antiquarian studies were encouraged by Robert Burton, who had written a county history

of Leicestershire. He gathered monastic papers which had been scattered at the Reformation, borrowing Edward Harley's (qv, d.1700) records of Wormsley Priory, and compiled *Monasticon Anglicanum*. This contains a 1665 illustration of Hereford Cathedral with its Norman west front – the earliest known – which he paid Wenceslas Hollar £5 to engrave. He describes Leominster Priory, Dore Abbey, Wigmore Priory, Shobdon Church and Craswall Priory and records charters of the latter. In 1677 he was appointed Garter King of Arms. One of Dugdale's daughters married Elias Ashmole and his papers went to the Ashmolean Museum in Oxford. Dugdale died on 10 February 1686, St Scholastica's Day.

Duncumb, John (1765-1839) topographer and historian, was born at Shere, Surrey and educated at Trinity College, Cambridge. In 1788 he moved to Hereford to edit and print the *Hereford Journal*, resigning his editorship in 1791 when he was ordained. In 1792 he married Mary Webb from Holmer and they had three children: Thomas Edward (d.1823), William George (d.1834) and a daughter. He published a sermon in 1796. In 1797 he became the first secretary of the Herefordshire Agricultural

Society and began publishing books on the agriculture of the county, including *A General view of the agriculture of the county of Hereford* (1805). He was a Fellow of the Society of Antiquaries. He is best known for *Collections towards the History and Antiquities of the County of Hereford*, commissioned by Charles Howard (qv), 11th Duke of Norfolk, who paid him 2 guineas a week and presented him to the rectory of Abbey Dore. Uvedale Price (qv) found him the living of Mansell Lacy. *Volume 1: a General History of the County and a Description of Hereford City* appeared in 1804, but his parish by parish study of the rest of the county was halted by the death of Howard. His research material was seen as the late duke's property and was locked up in a London warehouse. Duncumb lived at Abbey Dore until retiring in 1835 to Hereford, where he died on 19 September 1839. He was buried in Dore Abbey, where there is a monument to him. His manuscript collections were sold by his widow to a local bookseller. The history was only gradually brought to completion long after his death by W.H. Cooke (qv) and other hands. It is still immensely useful, and was reprinted in 1996.

Dunstaple, John (*c.*1390-1453) was a musician and the most important composer of the Courts of Henry IV and V. He is probably the 'John Dunstapylle' who was appointed a canon in Hereford by Bishop Lacy (qv) in 1419, as music at Hereford Cathedral was of a high standard at this time. He originated a 'sweet new English style'. He was also a mathematician and astrologer and royal patronage brought him great wealth. He died in London on 24 December 1453 and was buried in St Stephen Walbrook.

Duppa: They were landowners in the Whitney and Pembridge areas and sheriffs of Hereford in the 15th and 16th centuries. A Mary Duppa married the wealthy ironmaster Ralph Knight (qv). Later Duppas lived in Kent, but a Revd J. Wood Duppa was a magistrate of Pudleston Court in the 19th century.

Duppa, Brian (1588-1662), Bishop of Winchester, was born on 10 March 1588 at Lewisham where his father Jeffrey Duppa was rector. His father was from Pembridge, where he had built the row of black and white cottages still known as Duppa's Almshouses. Jeffrey's other son James was a brewer notorious for 'Duppa's stinking beer', which caused sickness on the voyage to relieve the Jamestown colony in Virginia in 1613. Brian was educated at Westminster School and Christ Church, Oxford. He was a fellow of All Souls and in 1632 Vice Chancellor. With Laud's (qv) patronage he was made Dean of Christ Church and chaplain and tutor to the Princes Charles and James. Laud further rewarded him with the bishoprics of Chichester and Salisbury. He accompanied Charles I (qv) to Carisbrooke Castle where he read the manuscript of *Eikon Basilike* to him. At the Restoration he was made Bishop of Winchester and he celebrated in Herefordshire by rebuilding his father's Pembridge almshouses, where a plaque names him as benefactor. He died on 26 March 1662 and is buried in Westminster Abbey. His daughter married the son of his friend Sir Justinian Isham, an ancestor of the Barnsleys (qv).

Duppa, Thomas (1619-94), born at Eardisley on 2 April 1619, was the son of John and Dorothy Duppa and nephew of Bishop Brian Duppa (qv), who introduced him at Court. He married Joan Wheeler and they had two sons and seven daughters, all baptised in Eardisley Church except for Thomas (1663-1704), who was baptised at St Margaret's, Westminster. Sir Thomas served the Stuart kings, then William and Mary. He was knighted in 1683 and was made Gentleman Usher of the Black Rod (1683-94). The ebony rod with its gold lion is still in the family. He died on 25 April 1694 and is buried in Westminster Abbey, where his monument may be seen. He owned much land at Whitney and his arms may be seen in the church quartered with the Whitney (qv) family.

Dutton Colt, John (1643-1722) was the son of George Colt and Elizabeth Dutton. His father drowned on 20 January 1659 while in exile with Charles II. He was six times MP for Leominster and lived in a Tudor building called Stafferton House on the corner of Etnam Street, Leominster from 1670. This was renamed Dutton House when it was refaced in the 19th century. Dutton Colt's opposition to James II involved him in a trial for treason in 1684 and he was fined £10,000. He tried to hide in a secret chamber in the fireplace, still to be seen, but was detected and imprisoned. On his release he fled to the Continent and worked for the accession of William of Orange, with whom he returned. His first wife was Mary Booth (qv under William Smalman) and they had a son John (1673-1731) who was Sheriff of Herefordshire in 1719. Their fourth son, Harry Dutton Colt (1683-1746), lived at Letton Court and was buried in the church at Letton. John Dutton Colt's second wife, Margaret (d.1730), daughter of Edward Cooke of Highnam Court, Gloucs, had previously been married to John Arnold, and her daughter with Arnold, Mary (d.1761) married John Dutton Colt jr. Their son was Revd Sir John Dutton Colt (d.1809), rector of St Mary Magdalene, Willersley (now a private house) and nearby St John Baptist, Letton. He succeeded to the title of 2nd Baronet Colt of St James's in 1731. The 7th Baronet, Sir Thomas Archer Colt (1615-93), married Frances, the daughter of a wealthy Lancashire cotton manufacturer Elias Chadwick (qv).

Dyer, John (1699-1757), poet and painter, was born in Carmarthenshire at Llanfynydd, the second of the four sons of attorney Robert Dyer. His mother Catherine was from the Cocks (qv) family. At Westminster School he was friends with the Wesleys (qv). He studied law at home, where he also painted and wrote poetry. In 1720 he went to London, where he met artists and writers. In 1724 he travelled in Italy painting and wrote poems about the Carmarthenshire landscape, notably his most famous *Grongar Hill*, set near Aberglasney in the vale of Tywi, and the equally fine *Country Walk*. In 1725 he went home to publish his first book of verse. Between 1730 and 1738 he took over his aunt's farm, Mapleton at Norton near Bromyard, which was in a poor condition, and he lived there from 1734. He took advice from his neighbours and recorded their comments in notebooks which survive today and are a good source of local 18th-century agricultural customs in Herefordshire. The farm was near Withington Court where John Phillips (qv) had written *Cyder* – a great influence on Dyer's own poetry. He married Sarah Hawkins *née* Ensor (1712-68), said to be descended from Shakespeare's brother, and they had four children. They moved to other farms in Worcestershire and Dyer attempted sheep farming, about which he wrote his long georgic *The Fleece*. He was ordained and was rector of successive Leicestershire and Lincolnshire livings. Dyer died of consumption in Coningsby rectory, Lincolnshire in December 1757 and was buried in the church there. A few of Dyer's paintings survive. His poems were influential and popular: Wordsworth (qv) enjoyed him and wrote a tribute to the 'Bard of the Fleece' (1811). Edward Thomas (qv) brought out an edition of his poems in 1903.

E

Eadgifu Anderes (11th century), last Prioress of Leominster Priory, was abducted by Earl Swein Godwinson (qv Swein) as his concubine, perhaps to secure the priory's lands. There was an outcry, Eadgifu was rescued and Swein exiled. The priory was dissolved in 1049 and its estates given to Queen Edith, Swein's sister. Eadgifu was retired on a pension and lived on for many years at the manor of Fencote, where she is recorded in Domesday at 1087. She has been identified, without much evidence, as the mysterious lady of the Bayeux Tapestry, one of the three women shown in the tapestry. Leominster Priory was re-founded as a monastery in 1123 by Henry I (qv) as a dependency of his abbey at Reading.

Eagles, John (1783-1855), art critic and poet, was born in Bristol into a Monmouthshire family. He painted landscapes and wrote throughout his life for *Blackwood's Magazine*, notably a series called *The Sketcher* which he published as a book. He was a curate at various parishes including Kinnersley. One of his rectors was Sydney Smith (qv). He retired to Bristol where he died leaving a large family.

Easton, John (fl.1822-34) was a shipbuilder and timber merchant of Hereford with shipyards and warehouses by the Wye. In February 1822 3,000 people gathered to see his first sea-going ship *The Hereford* launched in the Wye – a 47-foot, 80-ton sloop. Other boats he built there were the *Champion* (124 tons), the *Collinoque* (140 tons) and the steam tug *Paul Pry*. The *Water Witch* built in Hereford in 1834 was still at work recently in South Africa. Such large boats must have passed down the Wye slowly and only partially constructed to the Severn at Chepstow and on into the Bristol Channel. Shallower draught barges were also being built at various places along the Wye such as at Holme Lacy, Fownhope and Wilton.

Ecroyd, William Farrer (1827-1915), worsted manufacturer and politician, was the eldest son of William and Margaret Ecroyd, born 14 July 1827 at Lomeshaye near Burnley, Lancashire. He was educated at a Quaker school and joined the family's worsted manufacturing firm, becoming a partner in 1841. As a Quaker, Ecroyd did much to improve conditions for his workers and those living locally. In 1851 he married Mary (d.1867), daughter of Thomas Backhouse of York, relations of the Backhouses of Herefordshire (qv), and they had three sons and six daughters. After her death he married Anna Maria (1831-1913), daughter of George Foster. He bought an estate at Credenhill in 1880, later to become the Special Air Services camp, and farmed there, building model housing for his tenants. He was Conservative MP for NE Lancashire from 1881 and had a strong interest in tariff reform. He campaigned with Revd Bulmer (qv) to promote cider and was a benefactor of the local church and school. He was a JP and Deputy Lieutenant of Herefordshire. He died at Credenhill on 9 November 1915. Ecroyd believed his name was derived from a Mercian king, Croyda, and connected with Credenhill.

Edefen, Maud de (early 14th century) is the subject of an inscription in St Michael's Church, Edvin (or Edwyn) Ralph, which offers remission from Purgatory for prayers said for her soul: 60 days from the Bishop of Hereford and 30 days from the Bishop of Worcester. There are other Edefen monuments in the church. A romantic legend grew up about Maud who was said to have been killed in attempting to part her two duelling suitors, the lords of Edvin Loach and Edvin Ralph. A much later mournful ballad describes the encounter.

Edfrith or Etfrid (fl. 660), a sainted missionary monk from St Columba's, Northumbria called 'the presbyter' and not to be confused with the

Bishop of Lindisfarne. The foundation legend of Leominster Priory tells how he was inspired to travel to heathen Mercia to convert King Merewalh (qv). Arriving in Herefordshire at night he sat on a hillside to eat his bread when a fierce lion appeared. The saint offered bread to the beast which meekly accepted it. Meanwhile King Merewalh had dreamed of two terrifying dogs from which he was saved by a man with a golden key. St Edfrith was brought before the king to interpret his nightmare and reassured him that he could be saved from the hell of his dream by adopting the faith of St Peter (qv) his rescuer. Merewalh, abjuring his paganism was baptised and ordered a church to be built on the spot, where Leominster Priory was later founded. This legend is referred to in carvings of lions on the west door jambs of the Priory, and lions are offered as the origin of the 'leo' element in the town's name, although others cite their patron Leofric (qv) and others again derive it from the Welsh *Llanlieni*, meaning 'church amongst streams'. St Edfrith was long revered at Leominster Priory as its founder and his feast day, 26 October, was anciently the date of Leominster's autumn fair, confirmed in a grant of Henry III (qv) in 1290. Edfrith's life was included in a collection made for Bishop Adam Orleton (qv) in the 14th century as part of St Mildburg's (qv) biography. In the 16th century John Hakluyt (qv) wrote Edfrith's life, drawing on older versions. St Edfrith and St Peter are the supporters on Leominster's Arms.

Edith (901-37), the sainted daughter of King Edward the Elder, is associated locally with the well at Stoke Edith. She is said to have helped the builders of the church there, and where she sank down exhausted a spring burst forth. Her feast day is 15 July.

Edith (961-84), another sainted contender for the patronage of the well at Stoke Edith (qv Edith, d.937), was the natural daughter of King Edgar and Wulfrida. She entered the nunnery at Wilton where she led a pious life, and at her early death was widely regarded as having miraculous powers. She was venerated in Herefordshire and the healing waters of her well at Stoke Edith cured eye problems up to the end of the 19th century. The well, which may still be seen to the south of St Mary's Church at Stoke Edith, was caged in by Lady Emily Foley (qv) to discourage superstition. Edith died on 16 September 984, a date once celebrated in Herefordshire.

Edith (*c.*1030-after 1066), Queen of England, consort of Harold II, was the beautiful daughter of Ælfgar (qv) Earl of Mercia and his wife Ælfgifu. She married Gruffydd ap Llywelyn (qv), her father's ally. Their daughter Nest married Osbern fitz Richard (qv). Gruffydd was killed by her husband-to-be, Earl Harold Godwinson (qv), later Harold II, on his reprisal raid into Wales in 1063. At Harold's death at Hastings Edwin and Morcar, her brothers, took her to Chester for protection. She may have had a son with Harold, also called Harold. She is another contender for patron for St Edith's well and village of Stoke Edith (see two Edith entries above).

Edith (*c.*1025-75), Edward the Confessor's queen, was a daughter of Earl Godwin (qv) and well educated at Wilton Abbey. She was probably forced on Edward by the powerful Godwin as, during the Godwin family's exile, Edward rejected her – but he did value her as an astute adviser. She commissioned a life of her husband – the *Vita Edwardi* – and may have been the patron of the Bayeux Tapestry. Amongst other property she had a great estate at Leominster which included lands granted her after Leominster Priory had been dissolved (qqv Swein and Eadgifu). Its extent is described in the Domesday record as requiring 260 ploughs, and to manage it eight reeves, eight beadles, eight knights (*radcnichts*), 238 villeins, 75 cottagers and 82 slaves. The villeins – free labourers – had to plough 140 acres of the queen's land and sow it with their own wheat seed; they paid her 11 pounds and 52 pence annually. The eight officials paid her 14 shillings and 4 pence and three jars of honey from the land she allowed them. There were eight mills in this land of waters that were worth 73 shillings and 30 sticks of eels (a stick is 25). Woods on the estate yielded 24 shil-

lings and food for the pigs. Queen Edith died at Winchester on 18 December 1075 and was buried in Westminster Abbey.

Edric (d.1017) called Streona or *grasper*, was the son of Æthelric. Chroniclers write of his low birth, effrontery, skilful speech, treachery and murderous rapacity. Siblings were Brihtric, Ælfric, Goda, Æthelwine, Æthelweard and Æthelmær. Ælfric's son was Edric the Wild (qv); Æthelmær was the father of Wulfnoth who was the father of Godwin, King Harold's (qqv) father. Edric married Eadgyth, daughter of Ethelred the Unready, who made use of his services and made him Ealdorman of Mercia in 1007. He treacherously hindered the English resistance to the Danish attacks in Ethelred's reign and took the opportunity to murder opponents and ravage neighbours' lands. The *Anglo-Saxon Chronicle* holds him responsible for the failure of resistance to the Danish invasions. When Edmund Ironside succeeded Ethelred in 1016, one of Edric's sons is supposed to have assassinated him, and Edric defected to the Danish side with some English ships. Cnut restored him as Earl of Mercia and he is recorded as leading the Magonsaete, his own people in south Herefordshire, in battle. Cnut realized the extent of Edric's treachery, however, and had him beheaded in 1017.

Edric the Wild (fl.1067-72), or Eadric Cild, was a son of Ælfric the brother of Edric Streona (qv) with lands in the Wigmore area. He had submitted to the Normans and was holding Harold's recently fortified city of Hereford for them in January 1067. He was offended by Richard Scrob (qv) and the Norman garrison however and left in rebellion that August. He is remembered in Domesday as Edric *salvage* or *silvaticus* or one of the forest dwellers. He ravaged western Herefordshire with Kings Bleddyn of Gwynedd (d.1075) and Rhiwallon of Powys (d.1070). He attacked Hereford Castle but was beaten off by Ralph (I) de Mortimer (qv), who now held Edric's lands, and retreated into Wales from whence he continued to harass the Normans. In 1069 during unrest in the north he attacked Shrewsbury with King Bleddyn and King William led an army out against him personally in 1070. He was captured by Richard fitz Osbern (qv) but William, recognizing his abilities, pardoned him and included him in his invasion of Scotland. Further, some of his lands seem to have been restored as he later held estates from Robert de Losinga (qv), Bishop of Hereford. There were many legends about Edric including one that Walter Map (qv) relates in his *De nugis curialium* that Edric took a fairy bride called Godda. Their son Alnoth was miraculously cured of paralysis at the shrine of Saint Ethelbert (qv) at Hereford, indicating some restoration after the sack of 1055. At Domesday, Siward, a cousin of Edric's, was still holding what were probably old family lands, now as a feudal tenant of Roger de Lacy, Osbern fitz Richard Scrob, Ralph de Mortimer (qqv) and Earl Roger de Montgomery. A family called Savage later held lands in the area and could be his descendants.

Edward I (1239-1307), called 'Longshanks', King of England 1272-1307, was born at Westminster on 18 June 1239 the eldest son of Henry III (qv) and Eleanor of Provence. At 14 his father married him to Eleanor of Castile. He grew up with his mother's Savoyard relations during increasing baronial unrest which found effective leadership on the arrival of Simon de Montfort (qv). Sympathising initially with the barons and their call for reforms, he was later reconciled with his father. In 1264 he and King Henry were captured at the Battle of Lewes, eventually being held at Hereford Castle. But Edward, allowed to exercise on Widemarsh Common, one day simply galloped off, outpacing his captors. In the contemporary Chronicle of Robert of Gloucester Edward calls back to his pursuers thus: 'Lordlings, I bid you good day. Greet my father well and tell him that I hope to see him soon, and release him from custody.' One source has Maud (qv Maud de Mortimer), wife of Roger (III) de Mortimer, who was Edward's cousin, as originator of the escape plan. Her men met him and conducted him to the safety of Wigmore and then Ludlow Castle. Later, with Edward's effective leadership restored, the barons were defeated at Evesham. Edward spent the next few years in the Holy Land on Crusade, returning as king in 1272 on the death of his father. From 1277 to 1282, based at Hereford, he campaigned in Wales against Llywelyn ap Gruffydd (qv), bringing the royal apartments in the castle into good order and building a new chapel. In 1282 he granted Leominster a fair to be held on the feast day of Saints Cosmas and Damian (qv), and the next year, also at Leominster, he gave free warren to Eustace de Whitney (qv). He granted the boroughs of Weobley, Bromyard, Ledbury and Ross the right to return two members each to Parliament, the two for Weobley being Adam Sagoun and John Compaygnoun. In the next century these four boroughs requested the right be withdrawn, finding the honour too expensive, leaving Leominster and Hereford alone represented. In 1287 Edward was in Hereford with his Court for the translation of the remains of Bishop Thomas de Cantilupe (qv) to his tomb in Hereford Cathedral. Edward completed the subjugation of Wales and created his son Prince of Wales. He built several magnificent, impregnable castles including Caernarfon. Edward then turned his attention to the Scots and Hereford lost its strategic importance. Despite minor repairs the castle fell into disuse. Edward expelled the Jews from the country, including the important settlement at Hereford (qv Hamo) and a smaller one at Weobley. He died on 7 July 1307.

Edward II (1284-1327), Edward of Caernarfon, King of England 1307-27, was born on 25 April 1284, the youngest and probably 16th child of his 43-year-old mother Eleanor of Castile, at Caernarfon Castle, which his father was building. His favourite sister, Elizabeth of Rhuddlan, married Humphrey (VII) de Bohun (qv). He married Isabella of France and his son and heir Edward was born in 1312. Lavish expenditure and reliance on favourites were his downfall. His first favourite was Piers Gaveston of whom a contemporary said that as soon as Edward saw him he 'felt such love ... that he entered into a covenant of constancy, and ... indissoluble love'. His reliance on Gaveston's counsel and other abuses raised increasing opposition amongst the nobility headed by Humphrey (VII) de Bohun (qv), Earl of Hereford, but the king ignored their warnings. During the ensuing conflict Gaveston was caught and executed by Hereford and Warwick. Edward's next favourites were the Despensers (qv Hugh Despenser the younger), a family more politically astute than Gaveston, who through abuse and extortion built up great estates across England and Wales, drawing the barons together in united opposition, including William (VII) de Briouze, Humphrey (VII) de Bohun Earl of

Hereford, Roger (V) Mortimer of Wigmore, Hugh Audley and Adam Orleton, Bishop of Hereford (qqv). They exiled the Despensers but Edward negotiated their recall and went on the offensive, killing the Earl of Hereford and other barons. Queen Isabella, in France ostensibly on an embassy, joined up with Mortimer and they returned in 1326, capturing the king and executing the Despensers. Edward was taken to Berkeley Castle, staying overnight at the bishop's palace in Ledbury. At Berkeley he is believed to have been cruelly and ingeniously murdered. His corpse was bravely taken in by the Abbot of St Peter's, Gloucester, where his beautiful effigy still lies under its decorated gothic canopy, the focus of pilgrimage which paid for the modernisation of the eastern parts of the abbey. Another account has Edward escaping into exile and living for many years as a monk on the Continent, where his son visited him secretly.

Edward III (1312-77), King of England 1327-77, was crowned on 25 January 1327 aged 15, after his father's murder. For the first three years of his reign Roger (V) de Mortimer (qv) and Isabella, the Queen were de facto rulers of England. At 18, encouraged by followers, he secretly entered Nottingham Castle where the two were staying and surprised them. Despite Isabella's plea to 'spare gentle Mortimer' he hanged him summarily at Tyburn and confined his mother in a nunnery. He married his second cousin Philippa of Hainault with Papal dispensation. He and his Court was present at the consecration of the Blackfriars' Church just outside Hereford, his father having granted the friars land here. The remains can still be seen off Widemarsh Street. Edward's long reign was later seen as a golden age with the Hundred Years War in France to occupy the barons, and Arthurian Romance at home. Hereford became a backwater, until fresh rebellions and Welsh incursions reminded monarchs of its strategic importance.

Edward IV (1442-83), King of England, was born on 28 April 1442 at Rouen, a Plantagenet of the Yorkist branch. His father Richard Duke of York was the son of Anne Mortimer, daughter of Roger (VII) Mortimer (qv), and his mother was Cecily Neville. Edward and his brother Edmund were brought up at his father's castle at Ludlow. He was Earl of March and after his father's death at the Battle of Wakefield, Duke of York. He was tall and well built with golden red hair, features passed on to his Tudor descendants. He knew Herefordshire and hunted in Bringewood Chase and Deerfold Forest. Edward was part of his father's struggle with those around Henry VI from a young age and was only 18 when he fought and won the decisive battle at Mortimers Cross on St Blaise's Day, 3 February 1461. Edward met the Lancastrian forces under Jasper Tudor on the River Lugg south of Aymestrey, the Yorkists using Aymestrey Church as stables and store. On the misty morning of the battle the opposing armies saw the apparition of three suns called parhelion, which Edward interpreted as the Holy Trinity blessing his own victory. After this the 'sun in splendour' became Edward's personal symbol, together with the white rose of York. A monument to this 'obstinate, bloody and decisive battle' was erected at Kingsland in 1799 to commemorate 'The great Slaughter on both Sides'. Many Herefordshire and Marcher men were present at Mortimers Cross: William Herbert and his half brother Thomas Vaughan of Hergest, his brother Roger Vaughan, Walter Devereux of Weobley, Herbert's father-in-law

John Lingen, Richard Croft of nearby Croft Castle, Lord Reginald Grey of Wilton, Lord Audley, Lord Fitzwalter, Humphrey Stafford, Richard Hakluyt (qqv) etc. The Scudamores of Kentchurch fought for Lancaster. After his victory Edward declared King Henry unfit to rule and was crowned in his stead, destroying Henry's larger army at the Battle of Towton on 29 March 1461. Although Henry's redoubtable wife Margaret of Anjou managed to wrest the crown back briefly for Henry, Edward went on to reign until his death on 9 April 1483. He was magnanimous in his treatment of old enemies: he sought to bring peace to the riven country and married the Lancastrian widow Elizabeth Grey (née Woodville). The Wars of the Roses had a final act to play however when Henry Tudor (qv), son of Jasper and grandson of that Owen (qv) who had been executed at Hereford, seized the throne for Lancaster from Edward's brother Richard III on Bosworth Field. Henry VII (qv) finally resolved the dynastic rivalry by marrying Edward's oldest daughter Elizabeth of York, a marriage of Houses symbolised by the white and red Tudor rose.

Edward the Confessor (*c*.1003-66), King of England (1042-66), was a son of Ethelred the Unready and Emma of Normandy. He had spent his youth in exile in Normandy during the reign of Cnut and his sons. On his recall to reign he

was increasingly under the sway of Earl Godwin (qv) and his sons and married Edith his daughter. He was fond of the chase and frequently visited Hereford with its extensive royal forests running away to the south. He would have stayed in his nephew Ralph de Mantes' (qv under Ralph) new castle, possibly sited on Hogg's Mount in the north-east of Castle Green. The Domesday Book records that Hereford men were to be the king's beaters at the hunt, and the men of Kingstone were tasked with bringing the kill back. A confessor is a saint who died of natural causes and Edward was canonised by Pope Alexander III in 1161. Henry III (qv) had a special devotion to the Confessor, naming his son after him, building him a splendid shrine at Westminster Abbey and being himself buried near him.

Edward the Elder (*c*.870-924), King of the Anglo-Saxons, succeeded his father Alfred the Great in 899. His mother was Ealhswith, a Mercian noblewoman. He married twice and had about 14 children, five sons became kings after him and several of his daughters married into Continental royal houses. He vanquished the Danes of East Anglia, succeeded his sister Æthelflad (qv) to the throne of Mercia and pacified the Danes up to the Humber. He followed his father's policy of building fortified *burhs* and fostering a spirit of preparedness in defence. He strengthened his sister's *burh* at Hereford in 908 and placed a mint within. In 914 when a Viking army from Brittany sailed up the Severn, a force of Hereford and Gloucester men defeated it. Edward died on 17 July 924 succeeded by his eldest son Æthelstan (qv).

Edward the Martyr (962-78) was a King of Wessex reigning from 975 to his death. He was murdered at Corfe Castle, Dorset by, it is said, his stepmother Ælfthryth, and buried at Shaftesbury Abbey where a cult grew up around him. Relics of Edward found their way to Leominster Minster, perhaps through the agency of Æthelstan (qv), that inveterate collector of relics, and were installed in a splendid shrine above the high altar at Leominster. The enormous collection of relics made by the nuns of Leominster was largely pillaged by Reading Abbey at the 12th-century refounding of Leominster as a priory.

Edward of Woodstock (1330-76), the Black Prince, the eldest son of Edward III (qv), was born on 15 June 1330. He was a friend of Sir James Audley (qv) and was said to have dined with him at Hellens, Much Marcle, where the fire mantle has his motto 'ich dien' with the three feathers. He was a great military leader, winning memorable victories over the French at Crécy and Poitiers and was the first Knight of

the Garter. He governed Aquitaine with his wife Joan at a Court held to be the most brilliant in Europe. He suffered from a debilitating disease, perhaps multiple sclerosis, and died on 8 June 1376, predeceasing his father and leaving the throne to his young son Richard II (qv).

Edwi (11th century), a Mercian earl, is recorded in Domesday Book as holding Eardisley and other Herefordshire manors. He probably fell with Harold (qv) at Senlac and his lands were granted to the Lacy (qv) family by the Conqueror. His son Aylwin was allowed to keep two of his father's manors in west Herefordshire as Walter de Lacy's tenant.

Edwin (d.1039), or Eadwine, Leofwine's (qv) son, acted as Earl Ranig's (qv) deputy in Hereford after Cnut had distributed the shires amongst his Danish followers. He was killed at the Battle of Rhyd-y-groes in 1039.

Edwin, Humphrey (1642-1707), a London merchant, was born at Hereford, the son of William Edwin, a Hereford hatter. The family were dissenters and his father was an alderman and twice mayor. Humphrey was apprenticed to a Hereford tailor, then moved to London and traded in Bishopsgate as a wool merchant. He married Elizabeth, the daughter of a wealthy merchant, and they had at least ten children. He gained wealth and high office in the City of London and was knighted by James II. He transferred allegiance easily to William III and outwardly conformed to the Established Church, but caused scandal when Mayor of London by attending a dissenting service in full state with the City Sword. He retired to his house at Llanfihangel where he died at on 14 December 1707.

Egerton, Henry (1689-1746), Bishop of Hereford 1724-46, was born on 10 February 1689, the third son of the Earl of Bridgewater. His older brother, Scroop, was 1st Duke of Bridgewater. He was educated at Eton, studied law at New College, Oxford and was ordained and presented to several lucrative livings, including a canonry at Christ Church, Oxford. In 1720 he married Elizabeth, daughter of William Bentinck, 1st Earl of Portland and their eldest son was John Egerton (qv). At 35 he became Bishop of Hereford through family influence at Court. His friend Samuel Croxall (qv) attacked Robert Walpole and the Tory government in his consecration sermon. He renovated the bishop's palace and annoyed antiquarians by destroying the 11th-century bishop's chapel built by Robert de Losinga (qv). He had poor relations with his dean John Harris. Egerton got into more trouble by abusing a carter who had got in his way. The Tory opposition arranged for the carter to sue and he won substantial damages, and press vilification for the bishop. He is also remembered for attempting in 1741 to prevent the performance of Handel's *Messiah,* which he considered sacrilegious. George II intervened on the side of the oratorio. He died of tuberculosis and was succeeded as bishop by James Beauclerk (qv).

Egerton, John (1721-87), Dean of Hereford 1750-56, was Bishop Henry Egerton's (qv) eldest son, born on 30 November 1721 in London and educated at Eton College and Oriel College, Oxford. He married his cousin Lady Anne Sophia de Grey (d.1780) and they had a daughter

and three sons, two of whom became the 7th and 8th Dukes of Bridgewater. He was ordained in 1745 and his father appointed him rector of Ross-on-Wye with Cublington prebend; he was later appointed Dean. His happiest days were at Ross where he was an early promoter of tourism on the Wye, later popularised by William Gilpin (qv). He took guests on pleasure cruises between Ross and Chepstow to sketch the picturesque banks. He was a chaplain to George II. In 1756 he became Bishop of Bangor, moving on to the see of Lichfield and Coventry and finally to Durham. Egerton was generous, conscientious and eirenic, noted in Durham for his conciliatory skills.

Egerton, William, Henry's (qv) younger brother, was a prebendary of Canterbury and chancellor of Hereford. His daughter Jemima (1728-1809) married Edward Brydges (1712-80) from a family with strong Herefordshire connections. Their poet son Sir Egerton Brydges (1762-1837) founded the Roxburghe Club which printed fine editions of neglected works of literature. Sir Egerton became disastrously obsessed with proving his connection to the Chandos barony. A daughter of his, Jemima, married Edward Quillinan (qv) who vainly tried to help his father-in-law. The Egertons were relations of Jane Austen's friend Ann Lefroy and were acquainted with the Austen family.

Elgar, Edward William (1857-1934), composer, was born on 2 June 1857 at The Firs, Broadheath, Worcestershire, now the Elgar Birthplace Museum. His father William Elgar (1821-1906) was, although a Protestant, organist at St George's Roman Catholic Church in Worcester. His mother, Ann Greening (1822-1902), was the Catholic daughter of a Herefordshire farm-worker. There were six other children and it was agreed that the boys would be brought up as Protestants and the girls Catholics. Elgar's father sold musical instruments and sheet music and tuned the pianos of the local gentry, including Queen Adelaide, William IV's widow, at Witley Court. Edward's love of literature and nature came from his mother and he explored the countryside far and wide by bicycle. His younger brother Joe was seen as the musical one, but when he died aged seven Edward took on the mantle. He helped his father tune pianos and enjoyed playing on the wealthy customers' instruments. In 1885 he took over from his father as organist at St George's and took pupils, one, Caroline Alice Roberts, becoming his wife in 1889. With Alice's encouragement Elgar began to compose seriously. His first Three Choirs Festival was at Worcester in 1878 as a viola player. He was a friend of Dr Sinclair (qv), organist of Hereford Cathedral, the dedicatee of his *Te Deum and Benedictus* and whose bulldog Dan features in variation XI of his *Enigma Variations*. Elgar's mother, then living at Colwall, suggested the idea of the oratorio *Caractacus* (1898) but the piece was poorly received. The Elgars with Carice their daughter lived in London for a while but, despite the success of the *Enigma Variations* (1899), were forced for economic reasons to move back to Worcester-

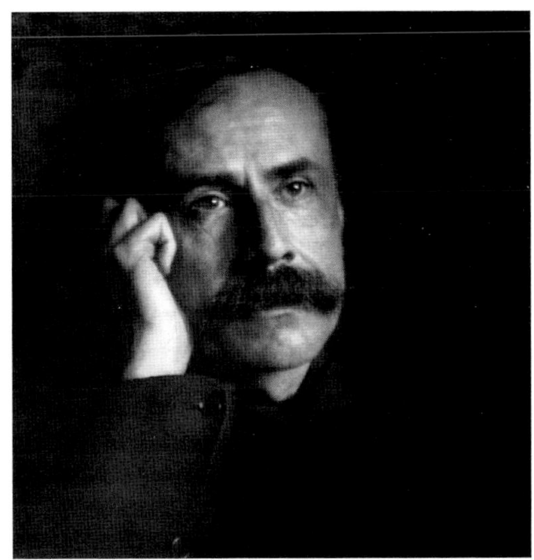

shire. They lived at 86 Wells Road, Malvern. The house was called Craeg Lea, made up from letters from family names (Elgar was fond of anagrams). In 1904 Elgar was knighted and moved to the newly built Plas Gwyn, Hampton Park Road, Hereford, now divided into flats. Here he wrote important works such as the two symphonies, the violin concerto and *The Kingdom*. The Festivals of the 1920s and '30s were dominated by such works as *The Dream of Gerontius*, *The Apostles*, and *The Kingdom*. In 1924 he was appointed Master of the King's Music and in 1931 created a baronet. The last concerts he conducted were performances of *The Kingdom*, *Gerontius* and the cello concerto at Hereford in 1933. Elgar is also remembered for the five *Pomp and Circumstance* marches, concertos for violin (1910) and cello (1919), two symphonies (in A-flat of 1908 and E-flat of 1911), the *Cockaigne* overture *(In London Town* 1901), *Falstaff* (1913), *Salut d'amour*, some chamber compositions and piano pieces, songs and music for church and stage. After Alice died in 1920 Elgar's creativity waned. He died on 23 February 1934, one of the greatest English composers for choir and orchestra, and was buried in Alice's grave in St Wulstan's Church, Little Malvern. There are statues of him in Worcester and Great Malvern and one with his bicycle outside Hereford Cathedral by Jemma Pearson. He was the first major composer to have his work systematically recorded.

Elias of Bristol (fl.1230) was born in Bristol the son of Durand and became a canon and prebend of Hereford and a canon of Salisbury. He founded St Ethelbert's Hospital (*c*.1225) in a corner of Hereford Cathedral's graveyard, later moved to the south side of Castle Street. It was placed in the charge of the Dean and Chapter of the cathedral. In 1230 he left money to provide bread and beer to the occupants of the almshouses.

Elizabeth I (1533-1603), Queen of England 1558-1603, was born at Greenwich Palace on 7 September 1533, the only child of Henry VIII and Anne Boleyn. She survived the dangers of her father's, brother's and sister's reigns and constant plots in her own. After Mary's return to Catholicism she re-established a moderate Protestant religion. Her first appointment to the depleted bench of bishops was Scory (qv) to the see of Hereford in 1559. In a charter of 1576 she reaffirmed Hereford city's market rights in a splendid document illuminated with a miniature of the queen on show at Hereford Town Hall. She also granted a Cap of Maintenance to be worn by the Sword Bearer on civic occasions. Hereford is one of only ten cities with

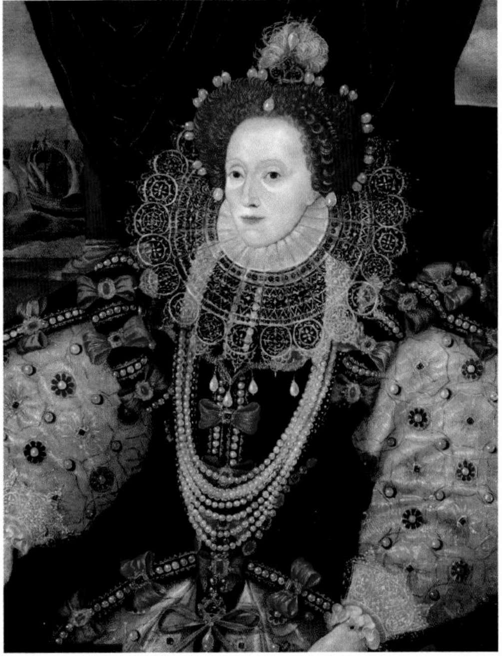

this symbol of authority. Proud of these rights, Hereford built a new Town Hall in the middle of High Town, sadly demolished in the 19th century. Two annual fairs were held here in Elizabeth's time: St Ethelbert's in May and St Denis's (qqv) in October, on Saturdays and Wednesdays. Elizabeth cannily induced Bishop Scory to part with church property, halving the revenue of Hereford diocese. This property, including the manor of Ledbury, was later sold by Charles I (qv) to the profit of local families with capital. Elizabeth's Commission of 1582 sent officials to inspect Hereford Cathedral library and found the books in a shocking state, mouldering in a damp room over the cloister. Instructions were given for its proper organisation and improvements instituted. Two of her ladies, Blanche Parry and Margaret Hawkins (qqv), were Herefordshire women. It is said her undergarments were made from Ryeland (qv) wool from Leominster. She died on 24 March 1603 at her palace of Richmond and is buried in Westminster Abbey.

Elizabeth (fl.1517), 'Holy Maid of Leominster', is recorded by Sir Thomas More as living in a cage on top of the rood screen in Leominster Priory. She was 'a strange wench ... sent hither by God, and would not lie out of the Church', living only on the consecrated wafer which rose mysteriously to her as if carried by angels from the altar. Pilgrims crowded the nave to see her and left offerings. She came to the attention of Margaret Beaufort, Henry VII's mother who had the matter investigated. The cage was found to be full of meat bones and communicated with the prior's quarters. She admitted to pulling the host up with hairs tied together and to being the prior's concubine. They were given a public penance and made to abjure the land. She is later recorded living in English Calais laughing about these events.

Elizabeth of Rhuddlan (1282-1316), born on 7 August 1282, was the eighth daughter of Edward I (qv) and Eleanor of Castile, her brother Edward II's favourite sister. On the death of her first husband, the Count of Holland, she married Humphrey (VII) de Bohun in 1302 and they had some 12 children.

Ellis, Alice Blanche (1848-1918), artist and botanist, lived in Hereford. She was a gold medallist from Bloomsbury School of Art. With Henry Bull's (qv) daughter Edith she illustrated the Woolhope Club's lavish *Herefordshire Pomona*, working in the Bulls' front room on College Green. Between 1876 and 1885 they made watercolour paintings of all the apples and pears grown in Herefordshire. These were reproduced by a new chromo-lithographic process. 600 copies were produced in a two-volume edition by Jakeman & Carver (qv) of Hereford, one copy being in Hereford Library. Today there is an online version.

Ellis, John was Dean of Hereford 1560-75. Dean Ellis and Bishop Scory (qv) were appointed at the same time and immediately fell out. Scory's visitation was, as was traditional, rejected, and the permission the bishop wanted to pull his palace down and build a more commodious one withheld, despite Scory's grumble that he had hired his workmen. On Dean Ellis's death John Watkins (qv) was appointed dean and continued and intensified the resistance to Bishop Scory.

Elmslie, Edmund Wallace (fl.1862), architect, designed Whitbourne Hall in north-east Herefordshire (1862) for the Worcester banker Edward Bickerton Evans (qv). The Palladian portico with its six giant Ionic columns based on the Erechtheum on the Acropolis was Evans' idea. The great hall has a unique blue and white glass ceiling, thought to be the largest in Britain, and some public rooms still have original decoration. The partnership of Elmslie, Franey and Haddon (qv Haddon) designed a range of buildings from churches to the tiger house at London Zoo. In Hereford he and Haddon built much of the suburbs. He built the National Provincial Bank in Broad Street, Hereford (1863) and buildings in Malvern such as the Imperial Hotel, now St James Girls College, and the railway station (1862). In 1867 he built The Grove in Avenue Road, Malvern as his own home but sold it as his practice expanded in London. Later The Grove was part of a girls' school where Elgar (qv) and G.B. Shaw performed.

Elton, Ambrose (1572-1659) JP, of the Hazle, Ledbury, was born on 1 March 1572 the son of Anthony (qv) and Alice and was educated, as founder's kin, at Brasenose College, Oxford. His was one of the prosperous Ledbury families that bought up church lands that had passed to the Crown after the Reformation. He owned Hazle Farm and 'the lease of' Lower Hall, Ledbury which brought with it a portion of the living of Ledbury Church. He married Anne (1589-1660), daughter of Sir Edward Aston of Charlecote, Warks and Anne Lucy (qv Charles Lucy). They had three sons and 14 daughters. One daughter, Anne, married first a Unett (qv Unett family) then Thomas (I) Cocks (qv) of Castleditch; another, Susanna (1605-89), married Thomas's brother Sir Richard Cocks. Elton supported Parliament and was a commissioner for taxing and sequestrating his Royalist neighbours' property. He was High Sheriff of Hereford in 1618 and 1646. He died on 19 February 1659 and Anne on 5 February 1660. Their memorial in Ledbury Church gives Elton's birth as 1578 and says they lived to see 120 descendants.

Elton, Ambrose (b.*c.*1604), of the Hazle and Upper Hall, Ledbury was the son of Ambrose (qv) and Anne. In about 1630 he married Mary Bray (b.*c.*1608) and their children were Bray (1630-97), John and Anne Elton. In 1720 The Hazle passed to Jacob Tonson (qv).

Elton, Anthony (1544-87), son of William (qv) and Margery was born in Ledbury and married Alice Scudamore (qv under John Scudamore, d.1593). He died on 13 September 1587.

Elton, John (fl.1529) was the son of William Elton of Elton, Cheshire and Anne Willason who settled in Ledbury. He was a canon of Salisbury then chancellor of Hereford. In 1529 he donated funds for the tuition of his family at Brasenose Hall, Oxford. Richard Pearle (qv) was another Herefordshire founder of Brasenose. Their funds provided scholarships for the youth of the county, such as Thomas Traherne (qv).

Elton, William (*c.*1516-58), brother of John (qv), married Margery Carew (*c.*1520-45). Their daughter Anne married her cousin Richard Willason (qv), and their daughter, also Anne, (qv Anne Denton), something of an heiress, married Alexander Denton. Another of Elton's daughters, Elizabeth, married Richard Seaborne of Sutton. William Elton was buried in Ledbury Church on 15 August 1558.

Ernle, John (1647-86), was born at Calne, Wiltshire, eldest son of Sir John Ernle, Chancellor of the Exchequer 1676-89, and was educated at Exeter College, Oxford. After his marriage to Vincentia, daughter and co-heiress of Sir John Kyrle (qv, d.1680) he lived mainly at Homme House, Much Marcle. He was a naval officer commanding a ship of the line during the Battle of Solebay (1672) and a cornet in Prince Rupert's Horse. He was wounded at Texel in the Third Anglo Dutch War. His exploits are mentioned by John Aubrey (qv), but Pepys dismisses him as one whose rank was due to money. However he was valued by Prince Rupert as a brave and effective soldier, and was knighted in 1673. From 1681 Sir John was a conservator of the Forest of Dean, a JP for Gloucestershire and Herefordshire from 1689 and MP for Calne in 1685 (James II's Parliament). He is buried in St Bartholomew's, Much Marcle. He had two children: Hester (1676-1723) and John Kyrle Ernle (1682-1725), who married Constantia Rolt (*c.*1687-1755). Their daughter Constantia, having no issue, made the child of Hester, Elizabeth her heir. Elizabeth married a Francis Money of Wellingborough and their son James Money (1724-85), after long law suits, inherited both the Ernle and Kyrle estates.

Ethelbert (780-94), patron saint of Hereford, King of the East Angles, is said to have been a relative of Offa's (qv) and may have been a client king. He succeeded his father Ethelred as King of the East Angles in 792 and travelled to Offa's Court at Sutton Walls seeking the hand of his beautiful daughter Ælfrida (or Ælfthryth). In the saint's legend his journey to Herefordshire was attended by omens and visions. At Sutton Ethelbert was murdered by Offa, some say by his Queen

Cynethryth. His decapitated body was later discovered in a marsh at Madley where, as an act of expiation, Pope Adrian required Offa to build a church. The spring that rose from the ground where his body had lain still flows from under the east end of Madley Church. His remains were taken to Hereford Cathedral and more springs appeared where the cart stopped. One of these sites is St Ethelbert's Well in the north wall of Castle Green, which has a 14th-century head of the saint from the west front of the cathedral built into it. In Leland's (qv) time in 1540 the spring here flowed freely within the castle walls. Miracles occurred at Madley and at his costly shrine in Hereford Cathedral, which became a major pilgrimage centre throughout the Saxon period, second only to Canterbury. When Hereford was sacked in 1055 the saint's bones were scattered and the shrine looted, but fragments were collected and his severed head was sent to Westminster Abbey, then under construction. Gerald of Wales' (qv) 12th-century biography of St Ethelbert gave fresh impetus to devotions and an altar was dedicated to him in the central eastern apse of the cathedral. Offerings increased and paid for a great rebuilding of the whole east end of the cathedral with the replacement of the three eastern apses by an ambulatory behind the high altar. Lives were also written by Osbert de Clare, Matthew Paris and Roger of Wendover. The Hospital of St Ethelbert was founded by Bishop Hugh Foliot (qv) in Castle Street, Hereford. There is a carved seal above the entrance showing the saint blessing. In 1117 Henry I (qv) granted Bishop Richard de Capella (qv) a licence to hold a May Fair at St Ethelbert's tide, which lasted for nine days, until in 1838 the city council took it over and reduced it to three. St Ethelbert's story has been depicted at the entrance to the lady chapel. He is still patron of 15 churches in the county, old Leominster Priory was dedicated to him with St Cuthfleda (qv), and he is co-patron, with the Blessed Virgin Mary, of Hereford Cathedral. His feast day is 20 May.

Ethelred (fl.675-716), sainted King of Mercia, was a son of Penda who followed his brother Wulfhere to the throne. He married Osthryth, the daughter of King Oswiu of Northumbria. He had the reputation of being a pious monarch and founded many churches in Mercia, but he ravaged Kent and burned the cathedral at Rochester, driving its bishop, Putta (qv), to seek safety in Hereford. He inflicted a substantial defeat on the Northumbrians and brought the Hwicce under his hegemony. In about 680 Archbishop Theodore divided the vast see of Lichfield into five dioceses, one of which was Hereford. In 697 Queen Osthryth was murdered and was buried in Bardney Abbey in Lindsey, which she and Ethelred had founded. In 704 Ethelred resigned his throne to his cousin Coenred and retired to Bardney. After his death in 716 he and Osthryth were accounted saints. Relics of Ethelred were venerated at Leominster Priory.

Etheridge, Robert (1819-1903), geologist, was born at Ross on 3 December 1819, the elder of the two sons of Thomas Etheridge, a Gloucester shipper, and his wife Hannah Pardoe. He was largely self-taught although he went to school briefly in Ross. He worked in the family business in Bristol and built up a museum of local natural history specimens. He married Martha Smith from Shropshire in 1845 and their son Robert also became a palaeontologist. He worked as a curator for local institutions, met Murchison (qv) at the Cotteswold Naturalists Club and became expert in geology and palaeontology, especially of the Jurassic Period, gaining notice and awards. He was appointed assistant keeper in the department of geology at the British Museum, as later was his son. He lectured in geology and published the course as *Stratigraphical Geology and Palaeontology* (1887). He was elected FRS in 1871 and was president in 1881. He died on 18 December 1903 at his home in Chelsea, London.

Eure, Sampson (d.1659), Royalist MP from 1621 to 1643, was the son of Sir Francis Eure of Upper Heyford, Oxfordshire. He was educated for the law and became Kings Attorney for Wales in 1622 and Examiner in the Court of the Marches of Wales in 1625. In 1640 he was King's Serjeant. In November 1640 he was elected MP for Leominster in the Long Parliament and next year was knighted. He joined King Charles at Oxford when the Civil War broke out and was made Doctor of Civil Law and Speaker of his Parliament there. He lived at Gatley, Park, Leinthall Earls near Aymestrey which he bought from the Croft family (qv) in 1633 and where he died in 1659. After his son John died, in 1679 his widow sold Gatley Park to Philip Dunne, whose descendants live there still.

Evans, Edward Bickerton (d.1892) was a banker and part owner of the Hill Evans Vinegar works in Worcester. Founded by his father, it was the biggest vinegar producer in the world. He was an amateur archaeologist who led the investigations at Palmyra in what is now Syria. He commissioned E.W. Elmslie (qv) to build Whitbourne Hall (1860-2) for £21,500 using the Erechtheum on the Acropolis as the model for the great Ionic porch. He had Robert Roumieu add the elegant Palm House (*c.*1870) but the glass was taken out in the last war. His Herefordshire estate was over 2,500 acres in its 1876 heyday. After his death his widow Margaret Evans lived in the Hall until she died in 1909. The family eventually sold the Hall for conversion to private residences in 1980.

Evans, Philip (1645-79), Jesuit saint, born in Monmouthshire, was educated at the English College at St Omer and in 1665 entered the Society of Jesus. He was ordained at the English College at Liège and sent to the Jesuit College at Cwm, Llanrothal to serve in that area. During the hysteria of the Popish Plot of 1679 Evans was arrested at a house in Glamorgan and imprisoned in Cardiff Castle. Under a law of Queen Elizabeth's a practising priest was guilty of treason and Evans, with Father John Lloyd, was hanged, drawn and quartered. Pope Paul VI canonised Evans on 25 October 1970 as one of the 40 martyrs of England and Wales. St John Kemble (qv) was martyred in the same year.

Evans, Thomas (fl.1865-87) and his wife were munificent parishioners of St Andrew, Moreton on Lugg, paying for the rebuilding of the church by W.H. Knight of Cheltenham. The chancel is paved with Godwins' (qv) encaustic tiles which also clad the east wall on each side of the altar with a design of Seddon's (qv), exhibited at the Paris Exhibition. The stained glass was by George Rogers (qv) and there is glass and mosaic work by Salviati (qv). The Evanses also paid for the parochial school. A relative of the architect, J.H. Knight, built Moreton Court for the Evanses in the 1860s, in an Elizabethan style. The mansion has been demolished but a lodge by Knight survives nearby.

Evans, William Edward (1801-69), clergyman and naturalist, was born on 8 June 1801 at Shrewsbury, son of John Evans MD. Educated at Shrewsbury School and Clare College, Cambridge, he was ordained and became curate of Llanymynech, the family's home village. Here he married his cousin, Elizabeth Evans and was presented to the perpetual curacy of Criggion, Montgomeryshire. In 1832 he resigned this to live at his wife's property, Burton Court, Eardisland, which brought with it the living of Monkland where he was vicar for 18 years, succeeded by Sir Henry Baker (qv) in 1859. He then became vicar of Madley with Tyberton. He was a good preacher and in 1841 was appointed prebendary and prelector of Hereford Cathedral and in 1861 made a canon. An angler and naturalist, he wrote *The Song of the Birds or Analogies of Animal and Spiritual Life* (1845) and an open letter to the Bishop of Hereford about education in Herefordshire. Burton Court was sold to John Clowes (qv) in 1865 and he lived in Hereford Cathedral Close until his death on 22 November 1869. He was buried in the cathedral. He left a daughter and three sons. Commemorative windows were erected to him and his family in Llanymynech, Shropshire where his father had been vicar.

Evelyn, John (1620-1706), diarist and writer on horticulture, was born on 31 October 1620 into a wealthy family at Wotten, Surrey and educated at Balliol College, Oxford. He was a pious, quiet man and after an appearance at the Battle of Brentford absented himself during the Civil Wars and travelled on the Continent, where he married Mary Brown, the daughter of

the ambassador to Paris. They returned to live at Sayes Court, Mary's father's house at Deptford, and Evelyn, a founding member of the Royal Society, pursued the life of a *dilettante.* His motto was *Omnia explorate; meliora retinete* 'explore everything, keep the best' (from I *Thessalonians* 5, 21). He was particularly interested in gardening and lavished much care on his estates at Sayes Court and later at Wotten. He wrote learned books about horticulture and silviculture drawing on his own practical knowledge and that of other experts. His diaries, which cover most of his life, are a lengthier, more formal, less indiscreet record of 17th-century England than Pepys's. His book *Sylva* (1664) contained the division *Pomona* on orchard trees which was co-written with John Beale (qv). In it he praises the orchards of Herefordshire as 'a Pattern for all England', 'Herefordshire has become ... an entire orchard'. In the following centuries T.A. Knight (qv) and also Bull and Hogg (qqv) of the Woolhope Club wrote treatises based on Evelyn's. Evelyn's *magnum opus* was *Elysium Britannicum* in which he draws on the help of learned friends like Sir Thomas Browne and Beale to describe how the horticulturist's art must conform with and develop the genius of the place. He uses as his example Backbury Hill near Hereford on the Stoke Edith estate, a place which Beale had described to him in a letter of 1659. Evelyn's principles in this book are Beale's and his ideas would influence future theorists of the picturesque in landscape design: Uvedale Price, Richard Payne Knight, Repton and Nash (qqv). Evelyn's *Parallel of the Antient Architecture with the Modern* (1664) which influenced Restoration architecture, was formed from the ideas of Hugh May (qv) as seen in the south and east façades of Holme Lacy House which May built for Sir John Scudamore (qv, d.1697). Evelyn died on 27 February 1706.

Evesham, Epiphanius (fl.1570-1623) was born in Wellington near Hereford on the feast of the Epiphany, 6 January, the youngest of the 14 children of William Evesham of Burghope Hall and his wife Jane, daughter of Alexander Haworthe of Burghill. They were a recusant, gentry family related to the Boyle Earls of Cork, who were Evesham's patrons. He trained as a sculptor, painter and metal engraver in London with Richard Stephens, an alabaster worker in the Southwark style. His first recorded work, an engraved brass sundial plate dedicated to his brother John, is in Hereford Museum. Another early work is the carved tomb to John (d.1587) and Dorothy Farnham in Quorn Church, Leics. Dorothy was the daughter of Sir Richard Walwyn (qv, d.1573) of Much Marcle. Evesham had a studio in London and worked for a while in Paris. He was the foremost sculptor-engraver of his age. His greatest work is considered to be the tomb of Christopher Roper, Lord Teynham (d.1622) at Lynsted, Kent.

Ewyas, Harold de (late 11th century), Ralph de Mantes' (qv under Ralph) son, was brought up at Court by his great-aunt Edith (qv), Edward the Confessor's queen. He inherited his father's estates and lived at Ewyas Harold Castle, which was named after him. He was granted some of Alfred of Marlborough's (qv) lands in Herefordshire after Alfred's death. His son was Robert fitz Harold de Ewyas (qv).

Ewyas, Robert de (c.1140-98) was born at Ewyas Harold Castle, son of Robert fitz Harold (qv). He married Pernel (b.c.1152) and their daughter Sybil de Ewyas (b.*c.*1182) married Robert (I) de Tregoz (qv) in about 1197, then Roger (I) de Clifford (qv). A later Lord Robert's effigy has survived the ruin of Dore Abbey alongside that of his relation Roger de Clifford.

Ewyas, Robert fitz Harold de, (*c.*1094-*c.*1166), lord of Ewyas Harold, youngest son of Harold de Ewyas (qv), was a friend of King Stephen (qv) and a follower and constable of the powerful Roger (qv Miles) Earl of Hereford. He founded the Cistercian monastery of Dore Abbey in 1147. He had met the abbot of Morimond Abbey in France on the Second Crusade and Dore became a daughter abbey of Morimond which sent monks over in 1147 to erect the original wooden buildings, for which they were allowed timber from Robert's Ewyas estates. The monks dug a channel from the River Dore to run beneath their monastery for fresh water and to drive the mill. Bishop Peter de Aquablanca offered an indulgence to those who contributed and the abbey was consecrated by Bishop Thomas de Cantilupe (qv), Robert's brother-in-law and future saint, under armed guard as the Bishop of Menevia or St David's claimed the territory as part of his diocese. The first abbot was Adam (qv). As founder Robert would have been buried at his abbey and annually remembered. The abbey was M.R. James's (qv) favourite place.

Eye, Osbert de (or Eia) is recorded in a charter of 1145 and lived at what was to be Eye Manor. The Eye family (12th-15th centuries) took its name from this area north of Leominster. In the 13th century a Walter de Eye lived here and his son Philip went on Crusade; he was clerk to Richard Plantagenet, Henry III's brother and treasurer to Edward I. In the mid 15th century John de Eye's daughter married John Blount (qv under Blount family) and the manor passed to him.

F

Falkner, Thomas (1707-84), Jesuit, son of Thomas Falkner (or Falconer), a Manchester apothecary, born on 6 October 1707, was educated at Manchester Grammar School. He studied medicine in London and physics and mathematics under Isaac Newton. He was advised that sea travel would benefit his health and joined a ship going to Buenos Aires as surgeon. Here he was converted to Catholicism and became a Jesuit. He worked with the Indians studying their herbal medicines for the Royal Society. He was professor of mathematics at Cordoba and on his return to England was chaplain to the Beringtons at Winsley House, Hope under Dinmore, and other Catholic families in the area. He died on 30 January 1784.

Fell, Samuel (1584-1649), Dean of Christ Church, Oxford, was born in London and educated at Westminster School and Christ Church. He became Doctor of Divinity in 1619. He married Margaret, daughter of Thomas Wyld, of the Commandery, Worcester. Their son John Fell (1625-86) followed his father as Dean of Christ Church, and was Bishop of Oxford. Anthony Wood accused Fell of being a cringing creature of Laud's (qv) and he accumulated many livings and offices, including Dean of Christ Church following Brian Duppa (qv). However he was frequently censured by Laud for his laxness. He was the first known delegate for the Oxford University Press, another position he passed on to his son. He received favours from Sir John Coke (qv) from whom he bought Hall Court, Kynaston, near Much Marcle. He was briefly arrested by Parliamentary officers and ejected from his Oxford deanery in the 1640s but managed to remain unmolested at his rectory of Sunningwell, Berkshire throughout the Civil Wars, dying there in 1649. It is his son Dean John Fell who is remembered by the imitation of Martial's epigram made on him:

I do not like thee, Doctor Fell,
The reason why - I cannot tell;
But this I know, and know full well,
I do not like thee, Doctor Fell.

Felton, William (1715-69), composer, was born at Market Drayton, Shropshire and educated at St John's College, Cambridge. He was ordained at Hereford Cathedral on 11 August 1742 and became a vicar choral in 1743 and *custos* of the college in 1769. He married Anna, daughter of Revd Egerton Leigh. Hereford MP Velters Cornewall (qv, d.1768) gave him the rectory of Moccas, and in 1749 the chapter appointed him rector of Norton Canon. He was a steward at the Three Choirs Festivals at Hereford and Gloucester. He was a skilled harpsichordist and wrote concertos for harpsichord and organ, a set of which he dedicated to Cornewall. Handel and Charles Burney admired and subscribed to his concertos. The manuscripts are in the cathedral library. Felton revived Hereford's Musical Society and the vicars choral college hall was rebuilt for their concerts (1753). In 1769 he became chaplain to the Princess of Wales and received the benefice of Preston and Blakemere. He died at Hereford on 6 December 1769 and was buried in the lady chapel. His memorial in the bishop's cloister reads *Vir animose justus et rerum musicarum peritissimus*, 'A just and courageous man, supreme in the art of music'.

Fermor, William (1648-1711), Baron Leominster, art connoisseur, was born on 3 August 1648 the son of William Fermor and Mary Perry. He was educated at Magdalen College, Oxford and succeeded as 2nd Baronet on the death of his father in 1661. In 1692 he married, as his third wife, Lady Sophia Osbourne daughter of the Duke of Leeds (he was her second husband), who secured for him the higher rank of Baron Leominster in 1692. Nicholas Hawksmoor built

Easton Neston House (1702) for Sir William in his native Northants and he bought the collection of ancient Greek statuary known as the Arundel marbles to adorn it. His son Thomas Fermor (1698-1753) succeeded as 2nd Baron Leominster on his death on 7 December 1711, and in 1721 was created Earl of Pomfret.

Field, Theophilus (1575-1636), Bishop of Hereford 1636, was baptised on 22 January 1575 at St Giles Cripplegate, London where his father John Field was a preacher, and educated at Pembroke College, Cambridge, graduating DD in 1611. After ordination he had livings in the Home Counties, attached himself to the Duke of Buckingham in his ascendancy and became one of the king's chaplains. In 1619 he was appointed Bishop of Llandaff. He married his wife Alice in 1621 and they had six children. He was brought before the bar of the Commons on a charge of bribery and reprimanded in Convocation. He sought the richer see of Hereford from his patron but had to make do with St David's in 1627, hardly richer than Llandaff and too 'steep, craggy, and welshly tedious' for him. He did eventually get to Hereford but only lived six months to enjoy it, dying on 2 June 1636. Alice survived him. He was buried in the north chancel aisle of the cathedral where there is a Latin inscription with his effigy which translates as:

> *The sun is set that lit 3 churches; the Field is buried in a grave. But the sun shall rise again and the Field renew its flowers.*

Fiennes, Celia (1662-1741), tourist, was born on 7 June 1662 in Newton Toney, near Salisbury, the daughter of Col Nathaniel Fiennes, a son of Viscount Saye and Sele, a supporter of Parliament during the Commonwealth. Celia started taking short trips around Hampshire on horseback for air and exercise and, finding she enjoyed it, ventured further afield. In 1697 she went on a longer journey from Cornwall to Newcastle and found the experience so delightful she started to keep a record and advised others to do the same. She visited Herefordshire in 1696, seeing it first on a June day from the top of the 'Mauburns', which she thought '2 or 3 miles up'. 'Herrifordshire' on the 'Weltch' side seemed 'like a country of gardens and orchards ... being very full of fruit trees'. She stayed in New House, Stretton Grandison with her cousin Col John Fiennes, one of Cromwell's commanders, who died later that year. She noted Lady Susanna Hopton's (qv) house at Canon Frome, and went on to 'Herriford town', 'a pretty little town with timber buildings, the streets are well pitched and handsome as to breadth and length'. The Wye was 'much disturb'd', fast-running and yellow. She called on Paul Foley (qv) at Stoke Edith, staying in the Elizabethan mansion while he was starting to build his new house. She was more interested in the different ways people lived than in antiquities or beautiful landscapes, enjoying novelty, busy places and their trade and industry. When shown round stately homes she noted the living arrangements rather than the paintings. In 1702 she wrote up her notes to entertain her relatives, a matchless social history of her time, unprinted until 1888 when it was published as *Through England on a Side Saddle*. She died, unmarried, on 10 April 1741 in Hackney, probably in the home of one of her nieces, and was buried in Newton Toney.

Fiennes, Frederick Benjamin Twisleton-Wykeham (1799-1887), 16th Baron Saye and Sele, was born on 4 July 1799. He was rector of Broadwell and Adlestrop in Worcs, a residentiary canon at Hereford Cathedral from 1840, archdeacon from 1847 and treasurer for over 60 years. He slept through sermons with a scented handkerchief over his face. Kilvert thought him eccentric and muddled and found his sermons worse than Bishop Hampden's (qv). He was master of the cathedral library with F.T. Havergal (qv) his effective deputy. A keen antiquarian, he was president of the Hereford Natural History, Philosophical and Literary Society. His family seat was Broughton Castle near Banbury, Oxfordshire, which was in a ruinous state until Fiennes had Sir George Gilbert Scott (qv) restore it. Fiennes and Scott had become friends at Hereford Cathedral. He died on 26 May 1887. Ranulph Fiennes is his great-grandson.

Fills, Robert (1521-78), clergyman from Lancashire, was educated at St Alban's Hall, Oxford and ordained whilst still under age. Under the new dispensations of Edward VI's reign he was able to marry one Rose. Queen Mary returned priests to celibacy and he went into exile at Geneva. Here he heard Knox and Calvin and returned with translations of Calvin's sermons which he published. He had met John Scory (qv) too who, on his return as Bishop of Hereford, made Fills prebend of Bromyard in 1562 and rector of Kingsland. Fills continued translating radical works of Genevan Protestantism, but found Hereford sadly lacking in the spirit of reform. His patron Robert Dudley, Earl of Leicester made him rector of Pembridge (1567) and his chaplain. The rectories of Kingsland and Pembridge brought him £67 pa. In 1576 the Archbishop of Canterbury appointed him a commissioner for his visitation of Hereford Cathedral. Fills died on 16 October 1578 and was buried in the chancel of St Michael's, Kingsland. In his will Revd Fills mentions a 'Paracelsian Still' so he presumably made alchemical experiments at Kingsland rectory. He left many learned books.

Finch, John (I) (1594-1664) was a bell founder of St Peter's parish Hereford. The Hereford Bell Foundry produced some 50 bells. In 1626 he cast one for All Saints, Hereford and in 1628 bells for Hentland and Holmer; there is a sanctus bell by Finch still ringing at Foy Church. St John the Baptist, Yarkhill still has a tenor bell cast by him in 1636 – Yarkhill being the home of Fabian Stedman (qv), the 17th-century bell-ringing theorist. At St Lawrence, Preston-on-Wye bells 4 (*c.*1625) and 5 (1641) are by Finch (with the 3rd by Abraham Rudhall qv). They were rehung as six bells in 1994 and are now ringing again. An old treble bell of 1325 still hangs above them. In the 1640s and '50s production ceased, recommencing at the Restoration to cater for the celebrations.

Finch, John (II) (1622-65), the son of John Finch (qv) was baptised on 13 July 1622. In 1649 he was married at St Peter's and had sons Richard and John. Both John Finches are buried in the Cathedral Close. His son, also John (1649-1705) was rector of St Nicholas, Hereford.

Fitzalan, Edmund (1285-1326), 9th Earl of Arundel, was originally one of the Lords Ordainers opposed to Edward II's (qv) rule, but drew closer to the king when his son Richard married Isabel, the daughter of Hugh Despenser the younger (qv). As a supporter of the king and his hated favourites, and because of some disputed territories in Powys, Fitzalan attracted his cousin Mortimer's enmity. Following Roger (V) Mortimer's (qv) coup against Edward II Fitzalan was beheaded without trial in Hereford on 17 November 1326, with John Daniel (qv) and Robert de Micheldever. His son Richard's marriage to the nine-year-old Isabel Despenser was annulled and Richard married Eleanor of Lancaster. Their daughter Joan married Humphrey (IX) de Bohun (qv). A century later his descendant Lady Margaret Fitzalan married Sir Rowland Leinthall (qv).

Fitzroy-Scudamore, see under **Scudamore**

Flaxman, John (1755-1826), sculptor and the son of a minor Yorkshire sculptor, was a sickly, hunchbacked boy who could draw brilliantly from an early age. The family settled in London where John made a name for himself and exhibited at the Royal Academy. In London he was influenced by William Blake's poetic idealism. He worked for Wedgwood where his knowledge of the antique, facility with the neo-classical style and general virtuosity astonished. His work can be both heroic (viz. his statue of Nelson in St Paul's Cathedral) and intimate. In Herefordshire he made the beautiful monument for William Miles (d.1803) in Ledbury Church, using the simple symbolism of a mourning woman with a book by a broken column, and there is another moving wall monument of 1814 in King's Caple Church. In 1810 he was appointed first professor of sculpture at the Royal Academy. He died in London on 7 December 1826 and is buried in St Pancras churchyard.

Flitcroft, Henry (1698-1769), architect, was the son of Jeffrey Flitcroft, garden labourer at the royal palace of Hampton Court. He was a carpenter for Lord Burlington who, noticing his talent for design, secured him a position in the Office of Works. Dicky Bateman (qv Richard) employed him on renovations at old Shobdon Court and probably gave him charge of the mansion he was building there and at Shobdon Church. He worked for the Foleys (qv) at Stoke Edith Church (*c.*1740) and at their Worcestershire mansion Witley Court. He was employed by the Harleys (qv Edward Harley, d.1741) on their London houses.

Foley: A Presbyterian family from Dudley. Richard Foley (1580-1657), son of a nail maker, set up as an iron-master, introducing the 'slitting mill' which manufactured nails industrially. Moving to Stourbridge, he created a virtual monopoly on nail making and amassed a fortune. His son Thomas (d.1677) established and expanded this, built Witley Court and entered Parliament. The dynasty was continued by his sons: Thomas, Paul the 'Speaker' and Philip, who each inherited a third of the business. Their father, Thomas, bought the Stoke Edith estate from the Lingens in the 1670s and gave it to his son Paul, who got licence to impark 500 acres around the old Elizabethan manor house Stoke Court, which he rebuilt completely. Paul entered Parliament and proved an active Whig MP for Hereford. He was meticulous at the business of the House, known as 'Heavy Paul' for his gravity, and was consequently chosen Speaker for the last four years of his life. He forged marriage alliances with the Harley family and there were subsequently many Foley and Harley relations in Parliament. The Foley barony was created for Paul's son Thomas (d.1733) in recognition of his father's merits. The last Foley, Lady Emily, was a strong force in the county for half a century; after her death the Stoke Edith estate was auctioned off, and in 1927 the great house was destroyed by fire.

Foley, Edward (1747-1803), was the second son of Thomas (qv, d.1777) and Grace, inheriting the Stoke Edith estate. He married Anne Margaret daughter of the 6th Earl of Coventry. Divorced from her he married Eliza Maria Foley Hodgetts (d.1805), a descendant of Paul Foley's brother. Their children were Edward Thomas Foley (qv), Anna Maria (d.1857), who married Sir Henry Lambert, and Elizabeth Maria (d.1857), who married Henry 4th Viscount Gage. He had Repton (qv) landscape Stoke Edith Park in 1799. He was a Whig supporter of Fox with a scandalous reputation. The statue of him in St Mary's Church was designed by Charles Tatham (qv) and executed by Edward Blore (qv). Edward and his brother Thomas (qv, d.1793) were great spenders and out of their large inheritance left only debts.

Foley, Edward Thomas (1791-1846), heir of Edward (qv) and Eliza was born on 21 December 1791. He graduated Doctor of Civil Law and was MP for Herefordshire. He married Emily Graham in 1832. He was lord of Great Malvern Manor and died on 29 March 1846 without issue, leaving Emily a 54-year widowhood.

Foley, Emily (1805-1900), the fourth daughter of James Graham, 3rd Duke of Montrose, married Edward Thomas Foley (qv) on 16 August 1832 and lived at Stoke Edith Park. After Dr Foley's death Lady Emily became a prominent force in the counties of Hereford and Worcester, planning the layout of Malvern for instance. There was a local station at Stoke Edith but she preferred to alight on the east side of the Malvern Hills to avoid the tunnels and had her own waiting room at Malvern Station, now Lady Foley's Tea Room. She was prominent in the civic affairs of Hereford and in 1898 opened the Victoria Suspension Bridge that crosses the Wye from Castle Green. She was a keen archer and a member of the Hereford Bowmeeting which often met in Stoke Edith Park. She sold the Newport estate to James Watt Gibbs Watt (qv) in 1863. After her death on 1 January 1900 a large part of the Foley estate was auctioned off at the Green Dragon, Hereford by her heir Paul Hodgetts Foley. The Foley Library had found its way into the Hereford Cathedral collection by 1925. In 1927 Stoke Edith House burnt down although lodges and evidence of landscaping remain.

Foley, Paul (1645-99), 'Speaker Foley', was the second son of Thomas Foley (1617-77), a prominent ironmaster of Stourport and later Witley Court, and Anne Brown. His brothers were Thomas (*c.*1641-1701), Nathaniel and Philip. Although of Presbyterian sympathies the Foleys supplied ordnance to both sides in the Civil Wars. Paul was educated at Magdalen Hall, Oxford and the Inner Temple, and took over his father's ironworks in the Forest of Dean, his brothers running those at Stourport. He also had an interest in furnaces at Llancillo, Peterchurch, Pontrilas and St Weonards. The Foley business continued to expand. He married Mary daughter of John Lane in 1668 and they had two sons Thomas (qv, d.1733) and Paul (qv, d.1739). Daughters Elizabeth (d.1691) and Sarah married Robert and Edward Harley (qqv). His father Thomas bought the Stoke Edith estate from the trustees of Sir Henry Lingen (qv) in 1670 and lands of the bankrupt Thomas Prise (qv) and settled them on Paul. He sat as MP for Hereford regularly until his death. He headed the country Whigs with Harley and was fiercely anti-Catholic during the Popish Plot hysteria, bearing some responsibility for the execution of Father Kemble (qv) in 1679. He became Speaker of the Commons and engineered the exclusion of the Duke of York (qv James II), later heading the coup to replace him with the Protestant Prince William of Orange. While Speaker he promulgated the Act of 1695 to provide for free navigation on the rivers Wye and Lugg, which were then clogged with weirs, eel traps etc. But his politics were unpopular in Hereford and there was a reaction against his influence. He was ejected from Hereford Council and in 1683 he and Sir Edward Harley (qv, d.1700) were imprisoned in Hereford Gaol. Foley was locked up again during Monmouth's rebellion. He tightened his alliance with the Harleys by marrying two of his nieces to Edward Harley's sons. When a Hereford mob threatened to

pull down his house and jeered at his family, he leased Stoke Edith out for a while. At the end of the century he replaced his Elizabethan mansion with a modern house. Celia Fiennes (qv) stayed with him in 1696 and they discussed his architectural plans. On her next visit in 1698 she noted the building progress. He obtained a royal licence to create a deer park. He died on 13 November 1699 of a gangrenous foot, the result, he claimed, of being jostled at Court. He was buried in St Mary's Church, Stoke Edith where his monument can be seen. At the time of his death there were five Foleys in the House of Commons and business benefited from government contracts for iron.

Foley, Paul (1688-1739), Paul Foley's (qv, d.1699) second son, was a barrister educated at the Inner Temple. He failed to be elected MP for Weobley in 1715. His wives were Susanna Massingberd and then Susanna Hoare. He bought the well-wooded Newport estate near Almeley in 1712 with an eye for the timber for his furnaces and built Newport House (*c.*1718) on the site where Sir John Oldcastle may have once lived.

Foley, Thomas (1673-1733), 1st Baron Foley, was born on 8 November 1673, son of Paul (d.1699, qv). His sister Elizabeth married Robert Harley (qv, d.1724) and he entered Parliament, with his brother-in-law's patronage with the Tories. In 1702 he married Mary Strode, a wealthy heiress. In 1712 he was created Baron Foley of Kidderminster. He died on 22 January 1733 in London and was buried in Great Witley Church.

Foley, Thomas (*c*.1695-1749), was married five times. His first wife Hester Andrews was the mother of his heir Thomas (qv, d.1766); his second, Mary Warter of Barbados, gave him Robert Foley, Dean of Worcester; the third, Elizabeth Worstenholme produced Paul Jermyn Foley; the fourth wife was Elizabeth daughter of Robert Unett (qv Unett family) of Birchend, and the last was Catherine Gwyn.

Foley, Thomas (1703-66), 2nd Baron, eldest son of Thomas (qv, d.1749), inherited great estates and iron furnaces in three counties. He was a fellow of the Royal Society and rebuilt Great Witley Church in memory of his father. He died without issue, ending the barony of this creation. His heir was his cousin Thomas (qv, d.1777).

Foley, Thomas (1716-77), was born on 8 August 1716, the son of Thomas (qv, d.1749) and his first wife Hester. He was heir of Thomas, 2nd Baron and became 1st Baron Foley of Kidderminster of a new creation in 1776, inheriting both the Great Witley and Stoke Edith estates. He married Grace daughter of George Granville, Baron Lansdowne in 1740 and they had seven children. He was MP for Herefordshire 1768-76 and died on 18 November 1777.

Foley, Thomas (1742-93) 2nd Baron Foley, eldest son of Thomas (qv, d.1777) and Grace, was born on 24 June 1742. He received the Great Witley estate from his father and married Henrietta daughter of William Stanhope, 2nd Earl of Harrington in 1776. He was MP for Herefordshire between 1767 and 1774 and after for Droitwich. A stout man, he was known as Lord Balloon. He died on 2 July 1793.

Foliot, Gilbert (*c*.1110-87), Bishop of Hereford 1148-63, was a Benedictine monk of Norman origins: his father was steward to King David of Scotland and his cousinage was extensive. He studied canon law at Bologna and Robert de Béthune (qv) appointed him Abbot of St Peter's, Gloucester. In 1148 he was made Bishop of Hereford, proving a dedicated diocesan administrator. He expected to be made Archbishop of Canterbury but was passed over for Thomas Becket (qv) and was given the diocese of London in 1163 as recompense. He opposed the low-born Becket's election saying he 'always was a fool and always will be'. He was excommunicated by Becket although this was later lifted. When Henry II regretted making Becket archbishop he used Gilbert to negotiate his possible deposition with the Pope and Foliot suffered from the backlash against Becket's murder on 29 December 1170. Foliot died on 18 February 1187, blind but still pursuing his studies. He commissioned an astrological treatise from Roger of Hereford (qv). Walter Map (qv) remembered him with affection.

Foliot, Hugh (*c*.1150-1234), Bishop of Hereford 1219-34 and a relative of previous Foliot bishops, was born in Northants a son of Roger Foliot and his wife Roheise. Robert made him a canon at Hereford and Archdeacon of the Shropshire part of the diocese. He acted as the Pope's judge-delegate (deciding cases of Church law) and was favoured by King John who gave him the living of Colwall. When Bishop Hugh de Mapenore (qv) died in 1219 Hugh was elected to succeed him, while keeping his other offices. He made his younger brother Thomas precentor of Hereford. In 1221 he went on pilgrimage to Santiago de Compostela, appointing Ralph de Maidstone (qv) the first Dean. With William Pembrugge (qv Pembridge) he founded the Franciscan friary outside the walls of Hereford near Greyfriars Bridge (1228). He was a friend of the great Robert Grosseteste (qv). In 1223 he received the surrender of Hereford Castle from Hubert de Burgh (qv) and in 1227 Henry III granted him the right to hold a fair in Hereford at St Denis's tide (qv), 9 October, a popular time for fairs coinciding as it did with harvest. He was involved at this time in investigating the extent of forest law in Herefordshire, which at one time

covered Hereford City. In 1233 he founded the Hospital of St Katherine at Ledbury for pilgrims and poor travellers, placing it in the charge of Dean and Chapter, as it still is, and appointed its first Master. The land on which it was built faces Ledbury Market and is a possible site for the bishop's palace. A 1588 copy of a portrait of Hugh still hangs in the hospital chapel. He was also involved in the founding of St Ethelbert's Hospital in Hereford (qv Elias). Hugh died at his palace in Ledbury on 7 August 1234 and was buried in Hereford Cathedral. He kept a trained staff of clerks, and many charters survive showing Hugh's concern for the cathedral's estates.

Foliot, Robert (d.1186), Bishop of Hereford 1173-86, Gilbert Foliot's (qv) nephew, was born in Oxfordshire. His uncle made him a prebendary of Hereford. He was a learned advisor to Thomas Becket and clerk to his relative the Bishop of Lincoln, where he was a prebendary. As Archdeacon of Oxford, in the diocese of Lincoln in 1151, he attended many papal commissions including the third Lateran Council of 1179. He was appointed Bishop of Hereford after a seven-year gap that followed the death of Becket. In Hereford he found many of the clergy were married. Pope Alexander III tolerantly advised him not to interfere because of the barbarity of the area, but requested him at least to stop priests bequeathing their churches to sons. Either he or his successor William de Vere (qv) replaced Bishop Robert de Béthune's (qv) palace with a large timber hall, using the massive oak timbers which are still to be seen when the palace is open to the public. It is one of the oldest surviving timber structures in Britain, dated by dendrochronology to a felling date of 1179, but Robert left much timber available for use by de Vere. Bishop Robert had a Roman gemstone as his seal and gave a purple and gold cope to Wigmore Abbey when he dedicated the church. He died on 9 May 1186 leaving money, lands and books to Hereford Cathedral and was buried in the south choir ambulatory. His papers and correspondence are in the Bodleian.

Forster, John (1812-76), biographer, was born on 2 April 1812 in Newcastle. He was briefly at Cambridge and the Inner Temple but preferred journalism. He became a confidential friend of Dickens, contributed to his (qv) periodicals and wrote biographies of Goldsmith, Swift (qv) *et al.* He is remembered for his life of Dickens: for 40 years he was Dickens' literary, business and legal adviser and is said to have suggested the death of Little Nell in *The Old Curiosity Shop*. Dickens based the character of Podsnap in *Our Mutual Friend* on him. He married later in life and often stayed in Herefordshire, in the house beside Wilton Castle on the Wye opposite Ross, now the Castle Lodge Hotel. He died in London on 2 February 1876 and is buried in Kensal Green Cemetery.

Fosbroke, Thomas Dudley (1770-1842), antiquary, was born in London on 27 May 1770 and educated at St Paul's and Pembroke College, Oxford. He was ordained and became curate of

Horsley, Gloucs where he married Mary Howell. He published a series of antiquarian works, viz. *British Monachism* (1802), the *Encyclopedia of Antiquities* (1824) and a history of Gloucester. In 1799 he was elected a fellow of the Society of Antiquaries. He was curate of Walford in 1810, then vicar. Revd Fosbroke was Provincial Grand Chaplain of Herefordshire Freemasons. He wrote his popular guide *The Wye Tour* (1818) to serve the lucrative tourist excursions centred on Ross. Fosbroke was a friend of Dr Edward Jenner (qv), discoverer of vaccination. He died on 1 January 1842 and was buried in his church at Walford where there is a memorial to him in the chancel.

Foster, Alice (d.1932), daughter of Ebenezer Jordan of Boston, Mass., married Revd Arthur Wellesley Foster (1855-1929) in the late 1870s. As a wedding present her parents bought them the 18th-century Upper House at Brockhampton by Ross. In 1893 they rebuilt the house as Brockhampton Court (architect George Faulkner Armitage) in a grandiose Tudoresque style, full of rich decorative detailing with Morris wallpapers and stained glass. They commissioned W.R. Lethaby (qv) to build All Saints Church (1902) nearby in memory of Alice's parents. The resident clerk of works was Arthur Randall Wells (qv) and the style was Arts and Crafts. The Fosters were dissatisfied with the building work and Lethaby waived his fee and never built another church. Pevsner thought it the best church of its date anywhere. It has two tapestries made by Morris and Co. to designs by Burne-Jones (qv) and stained glass by Christopher Whall (qv).

Foulger, Emma (1841-55), aged 14, was shot and killed by her brother as she was coming downstairs. He stumbled when entering the house with a loaded rifle. The family were farmers at Aylton Manor, near Ledbury and her ghost is said to haunt the spot where she died. Thomas and Eliza Foulger, her parents, put up a gravestone in Aylton churchyard with an affectionate inscription but soon after the burial, body snatchers stole her body.

Fox, George (1624-91), founder of the Society of Friends, was born in July 1624 at Fenny Drayton in Leicestershire, the son of a pious weaver. He was a devout youth and considered training as a priest but at 19 he felt urged to wander, telling people of the Christ within and warning them of the dead religion of the steeple house. He was in constant trouble with authorities throughout his life. He was persecuted in the Commonwealth, although Cromwell respected his conscience, and things worsened under the restored Anglican Church. In his leather clothes he crossed the British Isles, Holland and America teaching that the word of God was within each person and not the monopoly of the priest. In 1655 two Quakers, Thomas Goodaire and George Scarfe, preached Fox's beliefs in St Mary's Church, Ross. In his journal for 1663 Fox records large meetings in Herefordshire, one in Ross and another 'in the Inn' at Hereford. This was judged an illegal assembly by Hereford magistrates who tried to apprehend him but 'the Lord so arranged things that I escaped their hands'. In 1667 he presided over open-air meetings in the Leominster area and the next year he held a meeting at James Merrick's house at Ross. In 1669 he married one of his followers, Margaret Fell. There was much antipathy to his controversial views and he was beaten and jailed many times. Quakers were widely persecuted and mocked for their refusal of

GEORGE FOX,
Founder of the Society of Friends.

'hat-service' and the swearing of oaths. Thomas Traherne (qv) wrote that he would like to live on little and wear leather in the manner of Fox. Fox's journal gives a vivid account of his tribulations and confidence in the directing Spirit and has never been out of print. The Friends are still moved to independent thought and fearless humanitarian activity. There are several Meeting Houses in Herefordshire.

Fox, George E. (fl.1860-80), decorator, was working at Eastnor Castle during the 1860s after Pugin's death. Here he decorated the Staircase Hall and the Great Hall with frescos and the library rooms in an Italian Renaissance style. He worked from a turret room off the library called 'the fox's den' by the family. In the 1880s he organised the decoration of St Catherine's Church, Hoarwithy for Seddon (qv). He brought in the Italian firm of Salviati (qv) to provide the mosaics in the chancel, and Powell's mosaicist Ada Currey (qv) to create the Christ Pantocrator in the eastern apse.

Foxe, Edward (1496-1538), Bishop of Hereford 1535-8, was born in Dursley, Gloucs the son of William and Joanne Foxe, and educated at Eton and King's College, Cambridge (where he was later provost). He was Cardinal Wolsey's (qv) secretary and involved in Henry VIII's divorce of Catherine of Aragon. He wrote *The Difference between Kingly and Ecclesiastical Power* to justify Henry's assumption of ecclesiastical power and was made, amongst other offices, archdeacon of Leicester (1531), Dean of Salisbury (1533) and Bishop of Hereford in 1535. He visited Luther and helped Cranmer write the *Ten Articles* of 1536, the first steps towards Protestantism in England. He was active in suppressing the monasteries of which there were 18 in Hereford Diocese, Wigmore and Leominster being initially excepted. Foxe died on 5 May 1538 at Monthalt House, the London house of the bishops of Hereford, and was buried in its chapel.

Francis, Reginald Cyril (1884-1975), Hereford GP, was educated at Christ's College, Brecon and qualified as a physician at Guy's Hospital. He worked at a Ross practice briefly before serving as a medical officer in the First World War. He was a practising Hereford GP from 1925-75, known for riding to his calls around Hereford in a pony trap. After his death his carriage was donated to Hereford Museum, where they also display Jimmy, a pony that Queen Victoria gave to his mother. The stuffed Jimmy was popular with Dr Francis's children and long stood in his hall.

Freeman, John (1689-1764), lawyer, of Huntlands near Whitbourne, a farmhouse with a 15th-century cruck hall at its core. He made some renovations here when he married Abigail Jones. Their daughter Betty married Bartholomew Barneby Lutley (qv) of Brockhampton Park. In 1732 Freeman inherited neighbouring Gaines with its extensive park and orchards built by his ancestor Bellingham Freeman in the 1680s. He connected the two mansions with a tree-lined avenue and brought in Barneby's architect T.F. Pritchard (qv) to extend the house, and Thomas Leggett, landscape designer, to unify the estate.

Freeman, John (1731-1801), Worcester lawyer, made further improvements to the Gaines-Huntlands houses and combined estate. In 1832 a John Freeman of Gaines was High Sheriff of Hereford. Freeman ownership of the greater estate continued into the 20th century.

Freer, Richard Lane (1804-63), was the son of Revd Thomas Lane Freer of Handsworth near Birmingham and Sarah Wetherell, whose father was Dean Wetherell (qv) of Hereford. He was educated at Westminster and Christ Church, Oxford and ordained in 1829. He was vicar of Bishopstone cum Yazor in 1839 and in 1847 prebendary of Hereford. Next year he married his cousin, the daughter of Canon John Clutton. In 1852 Bishop Hampden (qv) appointed him archdeacon. He was a member of the Diocesan Church Building Society and organised much church rebuilding, including his own dilapidated church at Bishopstone and that at Yazor begun by Uvedale Price (qv). He was Deputy-Provincial Grand Master of Hereford Freemasons. He published various devotional works and his memoir of a journey to America was brought out posthumously in 1876. He died on 11 August 1863. His memorial is the large three-light window of 1864 by Hardman (qv) in the north wall of the cathedral's north transept. It cost £1,316 and is thought to be the finest Victorian glass in the building.

Fresne, Hugh de (fl.1294) was licensed to fortify his manor house at Moccas near the present deer park in 1294. The manor passed to the Vaughans (qv) who let it fall down and lived at nearby Bredwardine Castle.

Fresne, Richard de (d.1375) was a Knight Templar. On his death the de Fresne estates were divided between his father's three sisters. The effigy in St Dubricius Church at Moccas may be of Sir Richard. The Fresne arms are a helm with two green birds.

Fresne, Simon de (fl.1198-1201) or Freine, poet and canon of Hereford, called *Fraxinetus* or Ash, was brought to Hereford Cathedral by Bishop William de Vere (qv). He persuaded his friend Robert Grosseteste (qv) to join the brilliant circle that formed around the bishop and when Abbot Adam (qv) of Dore attacked Gerald of Wales (qv) Simon wrote a poem in his defence, boasting of Hereford's learning and philosophy and summoning Gerald to join them. His other poems include a version of Boethius' *Consolations of Philosophy* and a life of St George.

Fresne, Walter de (11th century), a knight of William the Conqueror, succeeded Nigel the physician (qv) as Lord of Moccas. A mound in the east of the deer park marks the site of his castle. Walter's name appears in the margin of the Domesday Book as 'de Mocres'. The estate had originally been the property of St Guthlac's (qv) Priory in Hereford. A descendant, Hugh (qv), was licensed to fortify a manor house at Moccas in 1294.

Frowcester, Edmund (d.1529), Dean of Hereford 1513-29 under bishops Mayo and Booth (qqv), succeeded Wolsey (qv) at the request of Henry VIII. His brass shows him with both of Hereford's saints, Ethelbert and Thomas (qqv), and a Latin eulogy. He greeted Henry VIII (qv) on his visit to Hereford in 1528 and died on 16 May 1529, leaving his library to the cathedral.

Frowde, James Henry (1831-99), clown, was born in Portsea, Hants into a German family: his mother was a Hengler of the famous 19th-century circus dynasty. The family moved to Gloucestershire where James learnt the traditional skills of a clown and *equilibrist*, travelling with Hengler's Circus as Frowde the Proud. The circus played regularly in Herefordshire and Frowde earned a great deal of money. He had been left Hayes Farm at Pool Hill, near Newent and also bought nearby Walden Court. He married twice and had four children. He sought respectability as a gentleman farmer and was licensed as a lay reader. He held rank in a Gloucestershire Regiment and was a prominent Freemason in Newent and Ledbury Lodges, becoming Worshipful Master with Grand Provincial Rank. His Ledbury Lodge met, as they do now, at the Feathers Hotel. He died in Westgate Street, Gloucester on 28 August 1899.

Fuller, Thomas (1608-61), clergyman and author, was the son of a Northants parson, educated at Queens College, Cambridge and ordained. He married and wrote many books. His *Holy State*, biographies of historical characters, was an early success and a major work *Speculum Anglorum: A History of The Worthies of England* or *Fuller's Worthies*, was edited and published after his death by his son John. It describes the quirks and oddities of the English counties and their character. Herefordshire he calls *Pomerania*, showing its contemporary reputation for apples. This was the first biographical dictionary and advanced the writing of biography in Britain considerably by treating the psychology of his subjects. His constant message was individuality within an ordered state. He was a tolerant man who preached an accommodation between King and Parliament which earned him distrust both at Court in Oxford and in Parliament. His property was sequestered and he stayed with friends, still preaching in London and writing texts for the times, steering between Laudianism and Independency. He died on 16 August 1661.

Furches, Robert de (fl.1283), bought Brockhampton Manor near Bromyard from the Brockhampton (qv) family in 1283. Others of this name are found on Bishop Swinfield's Ledbury rental of 1288. His family owned the estate until 1403, when it was sold to John Domulton (qv).

G

Gadwgan was Bishop of Bangor until 1236 when he became a monk at Dore Abbey. He wrote a book of homilies called *A Looking Glass for Christians* and a *Tract on the Blessed Virgin Mary*. The abbey was to become a centre for learning and music in the next century (qv Richard Straddell).

Gallet, Jane (1644-1749) of Tarrington was recorded in the Parish Register as 105 at her death. She could remember the great wind of 1658 that marked the death of Oliver Cromwell.

Galliers, William (1713-79), was a breeder of Hereford cattle at his farm Wigmore Grange. He was a friend of Richard and Benjamin Tomkins (qqv) with whom he consulted. He left his herd to his sons John and William who continued to develop the breed. William the younger won 13 cups for his cattle from the Herefordshire Agricultural Society between 1802 and 1815.

Gamage, Albert Walter (1855-1930), department store owner, born in Hereford on 14 July 1855, was the 17th child of Henry Gamage, plumber and glazier and Tryphina Carr. After leaving the local school he was apprenticed to a draper at Winslow, Bucks. Then, leasing a small hosiery shop in Holborn, he learnt to buy cheaply in bulk what people wanted. He achieved great success by focusing on small profits, sourcing new goods from America and the Continent and undercutting competitors. His store, Gamage's in Oxford Street, sold everything from cars to toys and at Christmas was a child's dream. Other innovations were large scale advertising and mail order buying. His only rival was William Whiteley. He married in 1888 and passed on the business to his son Eric. He died on his Buckinghamshire farm on 5 April 1930.

Garbett, Edward (1817-87), clergyman and journalist, sixth son of Revd James Garbett the prebend (d.1857, qv), was born at Hereford on 10 December 1817. He won a scholarship at Brasenose College, Oxford, was ordained priest in 1842 and was his father's curate at Upton Bishop. The next year he went to St George's, Birmingham as curate of his cousin John Garbett. In 1844 he was vicar of St Stephen's, Birmingham and five years later minister of St Bartholomew's, Gray's Inn Road, London. He was editor of *The Record* from 1854 and published many works of evangelical piety. From 1877 to his death on 10 October 1887 he was rector of Barcombe, Sussex. He was survived by his wife Elizabeth, a son and a daughter.

Garbett, Francis (1743-1800), was the only son of Samuel Garbett (1716-1803), a Birmingham assayer. Francis married Elizabeth Walsham (qv under John Walsham, d.1648), heiress of Knill Court. He was the secretary of Lord Lansdowne and High Sheriff of Radnorshire in 1790. He had a son, John (qv John Garbett Walsham), and a daughter, Anne (1785-1818), who married Lansdowne's friend Sir Samuel Romilly (qv) in 1798. His father had a hand in coal mines where he employed Watt and Boulton steam engines. Francis was friendly with Watt jnr (qv) in Herefordshire and with Lord Harley's steward James Crummer (qv).

Garbett, James (1775-1857) prebendary of Hereford, was *custos* of the vicars choral at Hereford Cathedral and vicar of St John the Baptist, Upton Bishop, where Hardman Powell's (qv) east window commemorates him. He was married with six sons.

Garbett, James (1802-79), theologian, eldest son of Revd James Garbett (d.1857, qv) was, with all his brothers, a pupil at Hereford Cathedral School and won a scholarship at Brasenose

College, Oxford, where he was a noted classical scholar. He was elected professor of poetry and became archdeacon of Chichester. He died at his home in Brighton on 26 March 1879.

Garbett, John (1771-1819), see **John Garbett Walsham**

Gardiner, Richard (1591-1670), clergyman, was born in Hereford, educated at the Cathedral School and Christ Church, Oxford and was ordained. He impressed James I with his preaching and acquired offices and livings. He became Charles I's chaplain and graduated DD. His support for Laud (qv) and the High Church made him unpopular in the 1640s and he was ejected from his livings and his property sequestered. He continued to publish in favour of King and Church however, e.g. *Sermon Preached ... on the Anniversary Meeting of Herefordshire Natives, June 24 1658*. At the Restoration his livings and his canonry at Christ Church were returned to him and he was made *custos* of the vicars choral at Hereford Cathedral. He paid for the building of the present vicars choral hall where a plaque dated 1670 puns on his name: *Hortulanus rigat dat fructum Deus* – 'the gardener waters but God gives the fruit'. The plaque shows a cloudy hand holding a watering can in the sky watering a formal garden under a blazing sun. Gardiner died at his college on 20 December 1670 and was buried in Christ Church Cathedral.

Garrick, David (1717-79), actor, was born on 19 February 1717 in the Angel Inn, Maylord Street, Hereford, where a plaque commemorates him. He was the third child of Peter Garrick (1685-1737), an army officer whose family was of Huguenot origin and his wife Arabella (d.1740), daughter of Anthony Clough, a vicar choral of Lichfield Cathedral. He was baptised in All Saints Church on 28 February and the family returned to Lichfield where he grew up. He discovered his acting skills at the schools he attended, one of which was run by Samuel Johnson. This was the start of a life-long relationship between the two men and in 1737 they set out together for London and their futures.

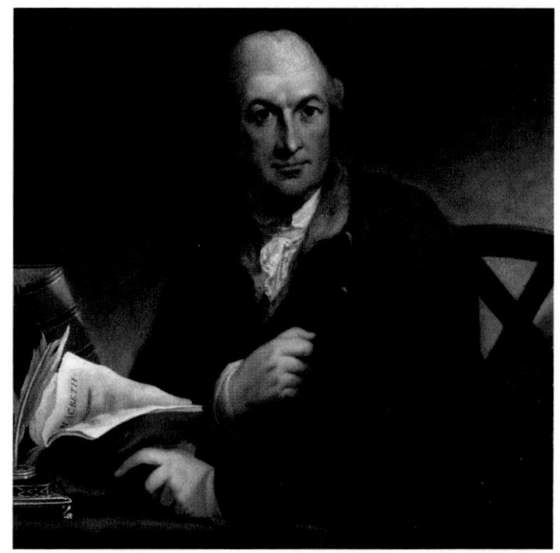

Garrick ran his brother Peter's wine business and developed contacts with the theatrical world. He burst onto the world as Richard III in an unlicensed theatre, with a mesmerizing performance and a naturalistic technique new to audiences used to a formal, static delivery. In 1749 he married the dancer Eva Maria Veigel, a protégé of the Burlingtons with whom they often stayed. The marriage was long and happy but childless. Garrick took on management and introduced new fashions and modern techniques to the stage, innovative lighting and props, using a hair-raising wig when playing Hamlet for instance. He raised standards of morality, probity and professionalism. His special interest was Shakespeare. He restored the texts and helped create the legend of a national Bard, making himself a fortune. He bought a summer house west of London, employing Capability Brown (qv) on the gardens, Robert Adam (qv) to construct a temple of Shakespeare and Roubiliac (qv) to make the statue of the Bard now in the British Museum. He gave his final performance at 60 and died of kidney blockage on 20 January 1779. His widow lived on for another 43 years. Hereford Record Office has an extensive archive of Garrick material.

Garson, a convicted criminal, was promised his life if he killed the Mordiford Dragon, denizen of the marsh of Mordiford. It would sport at the confluence of Lugg and Wye and in Haugh

Wood above, blighting the land around with its poisonous breath and eating people. Garson hid in a cider barrel in the Lugg and shot the beast through a bung hole when it came down to drink, but was incinerated by its dying breath. There was a painting of the dragon on the west gable of Mordiford Church until an 18th-century vicar cleaned it off. Thomas Blount (qv) preserved the inscription:

This is the true Effigies of that Strange
Prodigious monster which our Woods did range
In East Wood it was by Garson's Hand slain
A truth which old mythologists maintain.

Gaunter, John (fl.1154), chief bailiff of Hereford, wrote out the *Ancient Customs of Hereford*, a 17th-century copy of which is held in the town hall strong room. The original is said to have been of 1154.

Geers, Elizabeth (1682-1747), daughter of Thomas (qv, d.1700) and Elizabeth, was born in November 1682 and married William Gregory of How Caple, then Richard Hopton (qv, d.1764), the proprietor of Canon Frome. She died on 3 September 1747.

Geers, Thomas (fl.1600-31) of Batton, Shropshire bought an estate at Bridge Sollers. His son William Geers married Elizabeth, daughter of Thomas Spratt and died at Bridge Sollers in 1631. William added the Elizabethan mansion Garnons to the Geers estates and his son Francis (1588-1658) lived there with his wife Susan Cannock of Essex.

Geers, Thomas (1614-75) 'of the Marsh', eldest of the four sons of Francis and Susan (qv under Thomas Geers, d.1631), married Sarah (d.1693) daughter of Thomas Snowdon of London. Their second son Francis (1645-1721) was a physician in Hereford. In 1724 Francis's son, John (1698-1762), married Anne at Stretton Grandison where her father Revd James Poole was minister. Their daughter, Anne, married Sir John Brookes Cotterell (qv), into whose family Garnons passed.

Geers, Thomas (1643-1700), Serjeant-at-Law and MP, was the eldest son of Thomas (qv, d.1675) and Sarah. He was a bencher at the Inner Temple and married Sarah, daughter of Timothy Colles (qv) of Hatfield; he married his second wife, Elizabeth, widow of Thomas Whitney (qv, d.1670), in 1676 and had a daughter Elizabeth. Both wives were heiresses. Sergeant Geers was MP for Hereford in 1685 and deputy high steward and lived at Canon Frome House which he leased from his friend Susanna Hopton (qv), who tried to convert him to her non-juring beliefs (i.e. not swearing allegiance to William III in place of James II). Thomas and Elizabeth are both buried in St James, Canon Frome.

Geers, Thomas (1672-1750), the son of Thomas (d.1700, qv) and Sarah, married Mercy daughter of Henry Winford of Worcs. Their eldest son Thomas (1697-1753) assumed his mother's name Winford and left the county. A son, Timothy (1699-1750), was vicar of Bishop's Frome and another, Henry (1702-64), of Bridge Sollers. Their youngest daughter, Mercy Beata (1714-72), married James Brome (qv under William Brome) of Eau Withington.

George (d.303), patron saint of England, was a Roman soldier converted to Christianity in times of persecution. Before his martyrdom, it was told

in Herefordshire, he killed a dragon at Brinsop, and there is a lively carving of the struggle on the tympanum of St George's Church there by the Herefordshire School of Sculptors (qv). Nearby is Dragon Well. St George is one of the 14 Holy Helpers; his feast day is 23 April.

Geraint (6th century), hero, son of Erbin, founded a church at Caerfawydd, the old Welsh name for Hereford meaning 'the place of the beeches'. He features in the Arthurian romance *Geraint and Enid* and is found in the *Red Book of Hergest* (qv Vaughan). An old Welsh poem celebrates his deeds at the Battle of Llongborth and also mentions King Arthur (qv). Geraint's love and trials are the subject of two sections of Tennyson's *Idylls of the King*. Old histories give Gerren Llyngesoc, King of Dumnonia, as the founder of the church at Hereford; others King Gerascenus of Ergyng.

Gerald of Wales (*c.*1146-*c.*1223), author and ecclesiastic, born in Manorbier Castle of Norman and Welsh parentage, was the son of William de Barry, a knightly vassal of the Earls of Pembroke, nephew of the Bishop of St David's and a cousin of the Prince Rhys (qv). He studied at Paris and entered royal service. Henry II (qv) sent him to Ireland with Prince John (qv King John) against the over-mighty Hugh de Lacy (qv, d.1186) and Gerald reported on John's high-handed mismanagement of the campaign. Gerald was attracted to the learned court of Bishop William de Vere (qv), joining the group of brilliant canons at Hereford under Dean Richard (qv). The dean commissioned him to write a life of the cathedral's patron St Ethelbert (qv); he drew on William of Malmesbury and gave fresh impetus to the saint's cult. Gerald acted as Archbishop Baldwin's guide when he travelled through Wales in 1188, preaching the Third Crusade. They set out from Hereford and stayed at Leominster Priory – Gerald's *Leonis Monasterium* in the *Itinerary* he wrote of the journey. He made fruitless trips to the Pope in Rome in his attempt to become Bishop of St David's. At Bronllys he relished the unshriven death of Mahel (qv Miles). The next year, after Henry's death, Richard I sent Gerald to south Wales to pacify his cousin Prince Rhys. Gerald's death in Hereford was certified by Dean Thomas of Bosbury (qv). He left many writings, poems, accounts of saints' lives and a description of the world perhaps based on Hereford's own Mappa Mundi.

Gerard (d.1108), Bishop of Hereford 1096-1101, came to England from Rouen as Duke William's chancellor. He was present at the Conqueror's death bed in 1087 and was made Bishop of Hereford in 1096 by William II. He introduced liturgy from Rouen Cathedral which is later referred to as according to the *Use of Hereford*. The rebuilding of the cathedral started by Bishop Walter (qv) seems to have lapsed during his time. He was in the hunting party in the New Forest when William II was killed. Erudite and eloquent, he was, after some pressure, made Archbishop of York by Henry I and was succeeded, after a hiatus, at Hereford by Reinhelm (qv). He died on 21 May 1108.

Gethin, John (1757-1831), bridge builder, was born and lived in Kingsland. His father, also John Gethin (d.1791), a stonemason, maintained and rebuilt the bridges over the Lugg and Arrow upstream of Leominster: in 1782 he rebuilt Noke Bridge over the Arrow near Pembridge which still stands. Gethin junior built bridges in stone, wood and iron, some of which remain. In 1795 he and his son Benjamin built the three-arched stone bridge at Aymestrey (reconstructed in 1932) and *c.*1800 rebuilt Laystone Bridge, Marden. In 1799 he was appointed Surveyor of the county's bridges and in 32 years built 66 bridges for the county and further afield, that at Vowchurch (1815) across the Dore being a survival. He married Esther Gould of Kingsland and they and their family lived at Brick House, Cobnash near Kingsland. Later in the century John Gethin's grandson John, Emily his wife, their two young children Lorna and John, the children's nurse Eliza Preston and family friend Jemima Peace were drowned when the steamship *Drummond Castle* foundered off the island of Ushant near the coast of France on 28 May 1896. John was an architect based in Cardiff who was taking his family to South Africa for Emily's health. The tragedy raised questions in the House of Commons and Queen Victoria sent a telegram of condolence. There are many Gethin gravestones in Kingsland churchyard and the latter family are commemorated by a plaque in the church.

Gibbings, Robert (1889-1958), author and artist, was born in Cork on 23 March 1889; he learnt wood engraving at the Slade and served in the First World War at Gallipoli. He bought the Golden Cockerell Press and as director and designer revitalised it, attracting such as Eric Gill and David Jones. The press collapsed in the

1930s but he continued to design and illustrate books. He wrote his eight river books, including *Coming Down the Wye* about his rambles in Herefordshire in which he also used his own illustrations. He described his walks to Goodrich and Symonds Yat, the Courtfield and Wormelow Tump, and dined in the Booth Hall, Hereford. He met F.C. Morgan (qv) at Hereford Museum and looked round Herefordshire churches. His anecdotal, humorous manner recalls John Taylor (qv) of 200 years before. He died on 19 January 1958 after the publication of his walk up the Thames, appropriately called *Till I End My Song*.

Gibbons, Grinling (1648-1721), wood carver, was born on 14 April 1648 in Rotterdam to English parents. He was drawn to Britain by

the building boom after the Great Fire of 1666, being famously discovered in a Deptford hovel by John Evelyn (qv). Because of his astonishing facility at carving he was employed at Court and by grandees. He knew Paul Foley (qv, d.1699) who used him at Stoke Edith and commissioned him to carve the Royal Arms of William III in St Peter's Church, Hereford, of which Foley had the advowson. He also carved those of William and Mary in How Caple Church. He worked at Holme Lacy for the Scudamores (qv), carving woodwork, much of which is now in Kentchurch Court.

Gilbert, John (d.1396), Bishop of Hereford 1375-89, was an eloquent Dominican friar who had been Bishop of Bangor from 1372-75. He reorganised the Cathedral School in Hereford which seems to have been in disarray and in 1384 appointed Richard Cornwaille (qv) regent master to take charge of it. He was Richard II's chancellor and in 1389 was translated to the see of St David's where he died on 28 July 1396.

Gilden, John (fl.1573) (also written Guldo or Gulden), mason and sculptor of Hereford perhaps of Flemish origin, produced monumental tombs in a Renaissance style which he, uniquely at that time, signed and dated, such as that to John Harford (qv) in Holy Trinity, Bosbury (1573) and to Richard Willason (qv) at Madley (*c.*1574). He also made tombs at Abergavenny and Astley in Worcs.

Gilden, John (fl.1600), muralist, lived and worked in Hereford in the late 16th century. His two painted panels, illustrating passages from Genesis, can be seen in the Old House in Hereford High Town. One presumes a connection with the earlier mason of the same name.

Giles (7th century), a hermit saint popular in the Middle Ages as protection against the Black Death, lived in a forest near Arles and died shielding a deer from hunters. His symbols are a deer and arrow. He is the patron of Acton Beauchamp, Downton, Goodrich and Pipe Aston churches. St Giles' Hospital in St Owen Street was originally a house of the Knights Templar. The Norman chapel, which had the Templars' typical circular nave, was rediscovered when the road was widened. Its tympanum has been built into the west wall of the present almshouses, a worn example of the Herefordshire School of Sculptors (qv) depicting Christ blessing. It is interesting that St Giles, Pipe Aston also has a tympanum by the Herefordshire School. The original almshouses were intended to accommodate five poor men; the paupers were provided with a small garden each and a suit of clothes every three years. The almshouses were rebuilt in 1682 and again in 1927. St Giles is one of the 14 Holy Helpers; his feast day is 1 September.

Gillys (10th century) was the first named moneyer at Hereford. He struck pennies in the reign of King Edgar with the king's portrait.

Gilpin, William (1724-1804), writer on art, was born on 4 June 1724 at Scaleby Castle near Carlisle, Cumberland, the son of Captain John Gilpin, an amateur painter who taught Robert Smirke (qv). He was educated at Queen's College Oxford and ordained. He wrote a *Dialogue upon the Gardens of the Right Honourable the Lord Viscount Cobham at Stowe* (1748) considering the moral effects of a landscape. He married his cousin, Margaret Gilpin and they ran Cheam School and published guidebooks to help tourists find picturesque views. The first of these, *Observations on the River Wye relative chiefly to picturesque beauty* (1782) with aquatint reproductions of his pen-and-wash drawings, brought tourists to the area to sketch and he became famous, parodied by Jane Austen in *Northanger Abbey*. His influence was felt by Richard Payne Knight and Uvedale Price (qqv), by Nash and Repton (qqv), and by Revd John Egerton (qv) who organised sketching cruises on the Wye. Other guide books followed. Gilpin inspected John Kyrle's (qv, d.1724) landscaped walks around the Prospect in Ross-on-Wye, finding them amusingly unpicturesque. In 1777 he became vicar of Boldre in the New Forest and funded two village schools there out of his profits. He wrote on religious topics: 'I have figured so much lately as a picturesque man, that I should be glad to redeem my character as a clergyman.' The influence Gilpin had on the Romantic sensibility, on landscape artists and writers, Constable, Turner and Wordsworth (qv) among them, is great. At the time of his death at Boldre on 5 April 1804 there were eight boats for tourists who plied the Wye in search of the picturesque.

Gimson, Ernest (1864-1919), architect and designer, was born on 21 December 1864 in Leicester. He was apprenticed to J.P. Seddon (qv) through whom he met Ernest Barnsley and learnt craft techniques of furniture making. He set up his workshop with the Barnsley brothers in the Cotswolds (Ernest Barnsley's lectern can be seen in St Edward, Kempley, where Gimson supplied the candlesticks). In Bosbury he was introduced to the 'bodger' or rustic chair maker Philip Clissett (qv) by James MacLaren (qv) and stayed with him for a few weeks in 1890 to learn traditional skills such as pole lathing. He was the most influential Arts and Crafts maker of the turn of the 19th century. He died on 12 August 1919.

Girtin, Thomas (1775-1802), artist, was born in London on 18 February 1775. A childhood friend of J.M.W. Turner, he was an early painter of landscape in watercolours, and helped perfect the use of the medium. In Herefordshire he painted an oil of Mordiford Bridge and Church (*c*.1790) which can be seen in Mordiford's Holy Rood Church, showing the church before Kempson's (qv) rebuild. He died in London on 9 November 1802.

Gleichen, Helena Emily (1873-1947), painter, was a grand-niece of Queen Victoria. Lady Helena and her family lived at Hellens in the 20th century. Her sister Hilda married Axel Munthe (qv), to whom the house passed.

Gloucester, Lucy of, daughter of Miles of Gloucester (qv under Miles) married Herbert fitz Herbert of Winchester, Lord Chamberlain, by whom she had issue. She is buried at Llanthony Secunda.

Gloucester, Margaret of, daughter of Miles of Gloucester (qv under Miles) married Humphrey (II) de Bohun (qv).

Gloucester, Miles of, see under **Miles**

Glover, John, the last prior of the Benedictine priory of Leominster, was evicted with his monks in 1539 at the Dissolution of the Monasteries. The priory survived a few years longer than other religious houses.

Glover, Sarah Ann (1786-1867), music teacher, was born on 13 November 1786 at Norwich where her father Revd Edward Glover was vicar of St Lawrence's, Norwich. She lived at Cromer, Reading and latterly in Hereford with her sister Christiana. She developed a system of music teaching known as the Norwich or Tonic sol-fa which became very popular and is the basis of a song in *The Sound of Music*. She died on 20 October 1867 and is buried in Hereford.

Glyn Dŵr, Owain (*c*.1359-*c*.1416), also *Owain ap Gruffydd Fychan*, was celebrated by the bards as of princely pedigree on both sides of his family, in England as in Wales. He married Margaret daughter of Sir David

Hanmer. Richard II held much land in Wales and the change of regime to Henry IV probably loosened loyalties, which were exacerbated by Henry's heavy taxation. Glyn Dŵr declared himself Prince of Wales on 16 September 1400. Despite initial setbacks his followers captured Conwy Castle. His victory in the Plynlimon Hills in 1401 drew Welsh scholars from the universities and labourers from English farms to his standard – a golden dragon on a white field. His forces were active throughout Wales in 1402 culminating in the victory at Bryn Glas near the village of Pilleth where the English force, including Sir Walter Devereux (qv, d.1402) and Sir Robert Whitney (qv, d.1402), was destroyed, and Sir Edmund (IV) Mortimer (qv) was captured. The Welsh archers in the English army had apparently joined Glyn Dŵr during the battle. The victory greatly heartened the Welsh and more flocked to the dragon banner. The Marches were largely in Glyn Dŵr's hands. Mortimer was taken to Glyn Dŵr's fastness in Snowdonia where an alliance was made, sealed by Mortimer's marriage to Glyn Dŵr's daughter Catherine. They had a son Lionel and several daughters. The next year Glyn Dŵr married another of his daughters, Alice, to John Scudamore or Skidmore (qv Skidmore under John (I) Skidmore), and a third, Janet, to Sir Richard Monington (qv Hugh de Monington). Then Harry 'Hotspur' Percy, acting in concert with the Welsh, rebelled in the north. There was an alliance with Charles VI of France and an agreement with the Pope at Avignon. In 1404-6 the rising was at its most successful with the Marcher Lords' revenues and castles falling to the rebels. Cardiff was taken and western Herefordshire devastated in the summer of 1404, with Welsh forces raiding up to the walls of Hereford and Worcester. Bishop Mascall (qv) wrote that 52 churches had been sacked in the diocese of Hereford, damage that can still be seen. With French assistance Glyn Dŵr took Haverfordwest in 1405, and announced a Tripartite Indenture which divided Britain into spheres of influence between Glyn Dŵr himself, Mortimer and Henry Percy, Earl of Northumberland. Hereford was to be a Welsh province and its cathedral a suffragan of the metropolitan diocese of St David. Successes continued between 1406 and 1412 but the rebellion lost momentum. Henry of Monmouth (qv Henry V), calling himself Prince of Wales, secured the March from his base at Hereford, also using a fortified Leominster as a base. The winter of 1407-8 was a severe one in war-ravaged Herefordshire. Prince Henry's campaigns in Wales began to take back territory and he was able to write to his father from Hereford that a large force had been defeated at Campstone Hill near Grosmont. The end came with piecemeal action from garrisons and by a desire for settled life throughout the region. In 1409 Harlech was in English hands as were some of Glyn Dŵr's family; the Percies were defeated. Glyn Dŵr had retired from active leadership by 1415 and his son Maredudd ab Owain assumed the role. He is assumed dead by 1416, and St Matthew's Day, 21 September 1415, has been given as the date of his death. An alternative end has Glyn Dŵr in hiding with his daughter Alice and her Scudamore husband at his houses of Monnington Straddel in the Golden Valley and in the tower at Kentchurch. There is a portrait at Kentchurch either of him or his bard Sion Cent (see page 173 and qv Jack o' Kent). Kilvert (qv) thought Glyn Dŵr's grave was at Monnington Church, west of the porch.

Godiva and **Wulviva** (11th century), were Anglo-Saxon noblewomen, sisters with estates in the east and west midlands. They presented manors at Norton Canon, Canon Pyon, Woolhope and Preston in Herefordshire to the cathedral to provide the Canons Dole in which corn was given to the poor on 15 January each year. The dole survived as a distribution of bread in Herefordshire parishes until 1856. Godiva, or Godgifu (d.1067), was the wife of Leofric (qv), Earl of Mercia and mother of Ælfgar (qv).

Her sister has given her name to Woolhope which means 'Wulviva's valley'. Lady Godiva is remembered in a 17th-century ballad for her naked ride through Coventry, a creative riposte on her husband's swingeing taxes. Coventrians were instructed not to look but peeping Tom did and was struck blind. There are 19th-century stained glass windows in St George's, Woolhope to the sisters.

Godwin (d.1053), Earl of Wessex, was the son of Wulfnoth of Sussex and a descendant of Edric Streona (qv). He married Gytha a relation of King Cnut and became Earl of Wessex, Cnut's right-hand man, governing England during his absence. He had eight or more children whom he placed in powerful positions. The oldest, Swein (qv) he made Earl of Hereford, an earldom he created out of greater Mercia. The next, Harold (qv), the future king, also became Earl of Hereford. Godwin married his daughter Edith (qv) to Edward the Confessor (qv) in 1045 and his three sons Tostig, Leofwine and Gyrth were all made earls. At Cnut's death Godwin supported Cnut's sons Harthacanute and Harold Harefoot while preparing for the return of the atheling Edward (the Confessor) from his exile in Normandy in 1042. His power was great during the Confessor's reign and, although exiled at one point, he and his family returned in 1052 *de facto* rulers of England. He died from a stroke at Easter 1053.

Godwin, Francis (1562-1633), Bishop of Hereford 1617-33, mathematician and theologian, was born in Northamptonshire the son of Thomas Godwin, Bishop of Bath and Wells. He was educated at Christ Church, Oxford where he met prebendary Herbert Westfaling (qv). He became Bishop of Llandaff in 1601 and was translated to Hereford in 1617. He married the daughter of the Bishop of Exeter and found all his sons livings, although one was later ejected as unsuitable. He married his daughter to his archdeacon Dr John Hughes (1623-46). He was a keen antiquarian and went with his friend William Camden (qv) into Wales looking for material for Camden's *Britannia*, finding an Anglo-Saxon charter for him. He spent much

time writing at his palace of Whitbourne, now Whitbourne Court, and left diocesan matters to his deans. He published a *Catalogue of the Bishops of England* (1601) and wrote a history of the Tudors. But it is for *The Man in the Moone* that he is remembered, in which his hero Domingo Gonzales harnesses birds to his chariot and flies to the moon. Here he comments on the manners of its inhabitants, a satire that looks forward to Swift's (qv) *Gulliver's Travels* and much science fiction. He died on 29 April 1633 and is buried in the chancel of Whitbourne Church.

Godwin, William (1813-83) and **Henry** (1828-1910), ceramics manufacturers. William Godwin with his wife, three daughters and two sons moved into Woodbine Cottage, Lumber Lane, Bartestree in 1849 to open a ceramic works at Lugwardine, having previously run a brickworks at Ledbury. He made bricks, quarry tiles and drainpipes and added fashionable encaustic art tiles to the range. In 1852 he brought his younger brother Henry into the business to exploit this market more effectively. Henry Godwin had become familiar with art tiles during his apprenticeship to Henry Maw of Worcester and brought expertise to their manufacture. By 1856 these tiles were such a success that the brothers decided to separate tile making from the brick and drainpipe part of the business based at Ledbury. William bought Porch House in Lugwardine for his expanding family and in 1861 acquired a clay bed at Withington where he built a large, rationally designed factory connected to the new railway line, and extended the range and quality of the tiles. Henry built his house Mayfield near the works in 1863. The brothers' relationship became tense, and in 1876 Henry left to set up the Victoria Tile Works which, with his flair, became the more successful. Their rivalry took the form of aggressive advertising campaigns and undercutting ventures. In 1880 William built two flamboyantly gothic houses in Bartestree for his son William Henry and himself which can still be seen with their cladding of Godwin tiles, one, by Lewis Powell (qv), now the New Inn, the other by George Haddon (qv). William died in 1883 aged 70 and was buried in a vault in Lugwardine Church. He left the Withington works, Godwin and Sons, to his son William Henry, under whose management it declined until bought out by Tom Davies of Fair Tree Farm, Ledbury, who was developing fruit and preserves in the area and ran down the ceramics side. Henry's Victoria Tile Works continued to prosper until fashions changed in the 1890s and demand ceased, at which point he turned to cider making. He was just as successful at this and the firm flourished until bought by Bulmers (qv). Henry died in 1910 and is buried in Tupsley churchyard. Godwin Tiles are to be found in churches, public and private buildings around the world. There are good examples in the Woolhope Room in Hereford City Library and in the chancel pavement at All Saints, Hereford; they are further to be found in Hereford and Gloucester cathedrals and Belmont Abbey. In Hereford Cathedral they made the chancel pavement to Scott's design: the roundel of Saint Ethelbert is typical of the firm's popular pictorial style. Work here was finished by 1857 and cost £600. George Gilbert Scott (qv) thought their tiles more mediaeval than Minton's and especially admired Godwins' green. Later when Scott was restoring Gloucester Cathedral he used them in the choir and presbytery. William was proud of his achievement at Gloucester and is quoted, in his obituary in the *Hereford Times* (25 August 1883), as remembering how at the beginning of his career he made the bricks for the warehouses on Gloucester Docks.

Goff, Edward (fl.1780), philanthropist, was a humble labourer who went to London where he shovelled coals. Careful and industrious, he returned rich and established free schools. The first was Goff's Endowed Day School at Middle Hengoed, Huntington near Kington in 1781, with a Congregational chapel added in 1828. The first pastor was Revd Thomas Rees (d.1858). Goff went on to build other free schools.

Good, Thomas (1610-78), college head, from Tenbury Wells, was educated at the King's School, Worcester and Balliol College, Oxford where he became a tutor. He was ordained and appointed minister of St Alkmund's, Shrewsbury. He was ejected during the Commonwealth but unlike other ejected ministers he thrived, becoming rector of Bishop's Castle, then Wistanstow (both in the diocese of Hereford) and acquiring further benefices. He supported Richard Baxter in his search for a middle way and they worked for the support of clergy in the west midlands during the Commonwealth. At the Restoration he graduated DD and was appointed canon residentiary of Hereford with the golden or most desirable prebend. During his last years he was Master of Balliol, saving the college from bankruptcy. He died at Hereford on 9 April 1678 and was buried in the cathedral.

Goodere, Edward (1657-1739), 1st baronet, was the son of John Goodere, once deputy governor of Bombay, who had bought Burghope House, Dinmore Hill in 1670. Edward was educated at Christ Church, Oxford and married Eleanor, daughter and heiress of Sir Edward Dineley of Charlton, Worcs; they had three sons, Henry, who was killed in a duel, John and Samuel (qqv), and a daughter, Eleanor. He became an alderman in Worcester through his father-in-law's patronage and was created baronet in 1707.

He was elected MP for Evesham 1708-15 and for Herefordshire 1722-27: he was active in the parliaments of Anne and George, trimming between Whig and Tory interests. He died on 29 March 1739 and is buried in Wellington Church.

Goodere, John Dineley (*c.*1680-1741), 2nd baronet and **Samuel** (1687-1741) 3rd baronet, were sons of Edward (qv) and Eleanor Goodere. John Goodere inherited the baronetcy on the death of his father. Samuel had a career in the British Navy, fighting through the War of Spanish Succession, but was dismissed at a disciplinary hearing. However by 1741 he was again at sea as captain of the *Ruby*. The brothers had fallen out violently over their inheritance. Things came to a head when John decided to cut Samuel out of the entail completely and leave everything to the sons of his sister Eleanor. At this Samuel decided to murder Sir John. He had his brother kidnapped in Bristol and held him on the *Ruby*, moored nearby, where John was murdered. Samuel's crime was soon discovered, however, and on 15 April 1741 he and his accomplices were sentenced at Bristol assizes and hanged. There was confusion about the possession of the baronetcy, some regarding Samuel as heir with his sons Edward and John becoming the 4th and 5th baronets. His son Edward died insane and John (1729–1809), eccentric and destitute, was pensioned as a poor knight of Windsor, where he died. The title may have become extinct at the murder of Sir John, but certainly did on Edward's death. The murder was the notorious subject of woodcuts and ballads; Burghope House, deserted and widely thought to be haunted, gradually fell down.

Goodwin, Meg (before 1502-1609), Morris dancer of Eardisland, could, in her last years, remember the death of Prince Arthur over a hundred years before in 1502. She danced a Morris in Hereford in 1609, a celebrated dance that was performed before James I (qv) by 12 mummers with a total age of over 1,200 years, in which Meg, at 109, played Maid Marion to a Robin Hood by John Mando of Cradley aged only 100. The event took place on the corner of Widemarsh Street and High Town and the crowd was controlled by four whifflers or marshals who were all over 100 years old. In his *Worthies*, Fuller says it was arranged by Sergeant Hoskyns (qv) to entertain King James.

Gordon, William (1794-1836), was the grandson of Michael Biddulph (qv, d.1800). His uncle John Biddulph bought him Haffield at Donnington and, in 1817, he had Smirke (qv) design a new house. He brought in Donald Beaton (qv) to lay out his gardens. Gordon married Mary Wingfield. He was a magistrate for Hereford and High Sheriff in 1829.

Gorges, Ferdinando (fl.1670s-'80s) was the grandson of Sir Ferdinando Gorges, the father of the English colonisation of America and proprietor of Maine. He was a rich London merchant and sugar planter with slave plantations in Barbados who bought Eye Manor from another merchant in 1673, who had in turn had it from the Blounts (qv). In 1680 he rebuilt the mediaeval mansion in brick with splendid plasterwork ceilings, said to be the best of their date in England. He beautified Eye Church and married Meliora Hilliard: the joint Gorges and Hilliard arms and crest are seen in the plasterwork. Their son Henry married Elizabeth Pye (qv) of The Mynde at Much Dewchurch and was MP for Weobley in 1708. Their fifth son, Richard, also an MP, died at Eye in 1743. Barbara, a daughter (*c.*1658-97) married Thomas Coningsby (qv, d.1729) of Hampton. Charles II stayed at Eye Manor in 1680 on his way to Hereford. The Eye estate was bought by Thomas Harley (qv, d.1804) in 1786. Christopher Sandford (1902-83), the proprietor of the Golden Cockerell Press, lived at Eye in the 20th century.

Gour, John (14th century), was the steward of Roger (VI) Mortimer, managing his estates after his death and during his son Edmund's minority (qv Edmund (III) Mortimer).

Gower, John (fl.1665), schoolmaster and churchwarden at Monkland Church, came before the Consistory Court in 1665 charged with unlicensed teaching at Monkland. The court sat in the south transept of Hereford Cathedral. Bishop Croft (qv) dismissed the case and allowed Gower to continue teaching, a judgement preserved in the cathedral archives, dated 6 March 1665. Gower was a common name in 17th-century Monkland.

Gower, Stanley (1600-60), clergyman from Derbyshire, was educated at Trinity College, Dublin. In 1634 he moved with his wife Sarah to Brampton Bryan, where he was appointed rector by the patron Sir Robert Harley (qv, d.1656). Two of the Gowers' children were named Robert and Brilliana after the Harleys. Gower, a Presbyterian like his patron, was noted for long sermons. He sent news of scandalous ministers, the 'devil's orators', of Herefordshire to Sir Robert at Westminster. In 1643 he moved to the more sympathetic churches of London to work on the Presbyterian settlement following the abolition of bishops. His sermons before the Long Parliament were printed. He was appointed minister of puritan Dorchester where he died in 1660.

Grandison: the family originated in Savoy and came to England in the train of Henry III's queen, Eleanor, and acquired estates across the country. In Herefordshire they owned land at Stretton Grandison and Ashperton.

Grandison, Peter (d.1357), eldest of William Grandison's (qv) sons, married Blanche (qv Blanche de Mortimer, 1316-47), daughter of Roger (V) Mortimer (qv). Her effigy in St Bartholomew's Church, Much Marcle, is of great realism and delicacy. She is telling a rosary; the hem of her gown falls casually over the end of the tomb she lies on with sophisticated naturalism. An unnamed kinswoman of hers is carved in a similar style in Ledbury Church. Sir Peter sat in Edward III's parliaments for Herefordshire. His tomb is on the north side of the lady chapel in the cathedral where St Thomas de Cantilupe's (qv) shrine had been moved, showing the cathedral to now be outranking

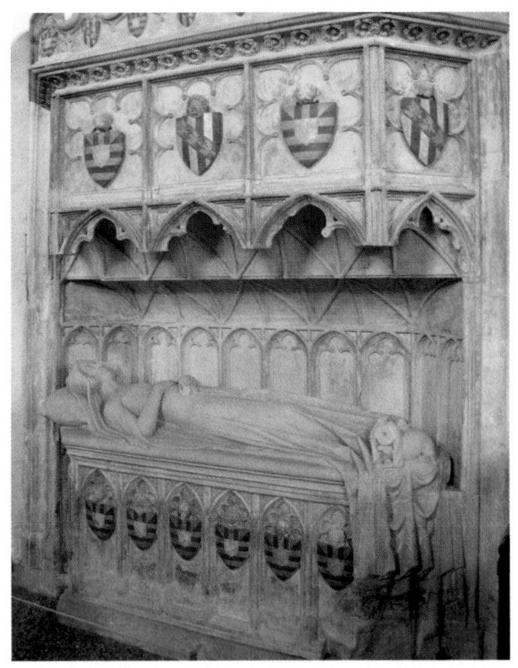

Dore Abbey. Cottingham (qv) reconstructed Grandison's tomb with headless figures he found behind the choir screen during his work at the cathedral. More recently heads and bright colour have been added to the six figures on top:

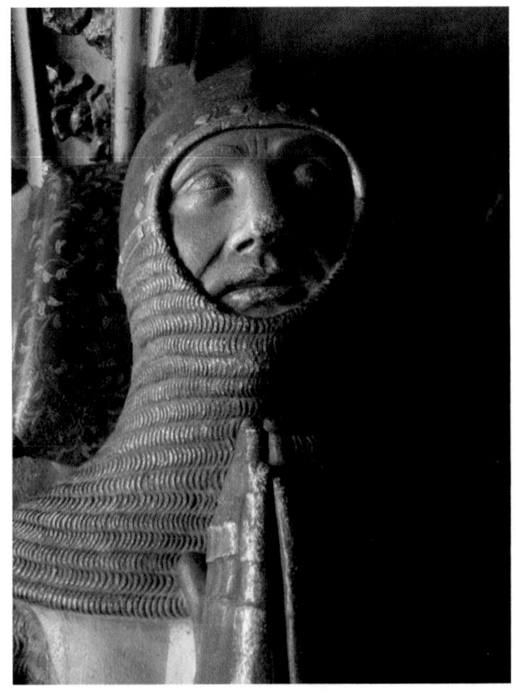

a central coronation of the Virgin with saints Ethelbert, John the Baptist, Thomas of Canterbury and Thomas de Cantilupe, Sir Peter's great-uncle. John Grandison (1292-1369), Bishop of Exeter, and Sir Otho were sons of William, born at Ashperton Castle.

Grandison, William (d.1335), 1st Baron Ashperton, was a relative of Bishop Thomas de Cantilupe (qv). In 1292 he was licensed to crenellate a castle at Ashperton by Edward II. Now only the moat remains, still holding water, to the west of the church. He increased his lands by his marriage to Sybil, co-heir of Sir John Tregoz (qv), a name preserved in Eaton Tregoz where he built a castle in 1309. Five sons and three daughters were born to them at Ashperton (qv Montagu, Countess of Salisbury, for Katherine, the youngest, who married William Montagu). Sybil was a benefactress of St Bartholomew's Church near the castle and work from her time is still to be seen there. She died on 21 October 1334 and William on 27 June 1335. In 1321 he presented a relic of the True Cross to Dore Abbey, in gold and jewels, and Lord and Lady Grandison were buried there.

Gray, Thomas (1716-71), poet, was born on 26 December 1716 in Cornhill, London. He was educated in Cambridge where he spent the rest of his life in literary and antiquarian pursuits, among friends who included Horace Walpole (qv). His poems, such as *Elegy in a Country Churchyard,* won him fame. He travelled abroad and in Britain and in 1770 visited Ross for a trip on the Wye looking for the picturesque: 'a succession of nameless beauties', he called it. He published a book of poems about this, adding to the area's celebrity; the book influenced Gilpin (qv), who was also visiting the area that year. Gray died in Cambridge on 30 July 1771 and was buried in the churchyard at Stoke Poges which he had made famous.

Greening, Thomas (1684-1757), one of a dynasty of gardeners to George I and II, was employed at old Shobdon Court (qv Bateman). He grafted new fruit trees, some of which he supplied to his neighbour Paul Foley (qv, d.1739) at Newport House, Almeley. His son Thomas Henry was royal gardener at Windsor and was knighted. His son Henry Thomas Greening (1730-1809) changed his name as condition of the will of his cousin Mary Gott to Henry Thomas Gott. He was gardener to George II at Windsor and was knighted in 1774. Sir Henry's daughter Sarah married first Robert Whitcombe and secondly Sir Harford Jones-Brydges (qv).

Greenleaf, William (1849-1921), bell hanger from Scotland, trained at the Whitechapel Foundry in London. In partnership with Thomas Blackbourn of Salisbury, he was contracted to rehang the ten bells at Hereford Cathedral and those of St Nicholas, and he subsequently settled in Aubrey Street, Hereford. He joined the cathedral bellringers and restored order and system to their ringing. One of the band, John Tristram, became a partner of his firm and they rehung the bells of some two dozen belfries in Herefordshire and many more elsewhere. Because of the accuracy of his ear and painstaking work he was acknowledged the best in his field. After 20 years work in the county he retired to New Zealand where he died.

Greenway, Richard and **Maud** (15th century) are commemorated on a gravestone in St Mary's Church, Stretton Sugwas that asks us to pray for their souls. Maud died on 27 March 1473, Richard was still alive in 1476. She was the daughter of John Harper of Wellington, who fought on the Yorkist side at Mortimers Cross in 1461 and was rewarded by Edward IV with minor office; he had a son who was a priest. Richard and Maud's son, Richard Greenway, was Sheriff of Hereford in 1491 and '98. Another relative, John Greenway, was a prebendary of Hereford Cathedral.

Gregory, William (1625-96), judge, was born at Fownhope vicarage on 1 March 1625. His father Robert (d.1643) was vicar of Fownhope where the family had been settled for a century, and rector of Sutton St Nicholas. William was educated at Hereford Cathedral School, Gray's

Inn and All Souls College, Oxford. He hedged his bets through the Civil Wars, building up a lucrative barrister's practice and assisting on the Herefordshire County Committee. He was steward of Herefordshire families like the Scudamores (qv) and acquired much property in the county. He was deputy steward for Hereford and a JP at the Restoration. In 1675 he was elected MP for Weobley and in 1679 he was Speaker of the Commons. He was blamed by some in Hereford for his part in the surrender of the City of Hereford's Charter (qv Elizabeth I), as some considered that ancient rights had been eroded by Charles II. It was re-incorporated in an Act of William III (qv). He was knighted as a Baron of the Exchequer, ejected by King James but reinstated under William of Orange. Sir William acquired estates at How Caple and Hope Sollers from the Capel (qv) family in 1672, and rebuilt How Caple Court with its terraces. He restored St Mary's Church, presenting the royal arms and screen. He died on 28 May 1696 and was buried in that church, where there are several monuments to the Gregory family.

Grey, Edward (1782-1837), Dean 1831-2 and bishop 1832-7 of Hereford, was born in Northumberland on 25 March 1782, fifth son of General Charles, 1st Earl Grey. He was educated at Christ Church, Oxford. In 1809 he married Charlotte (d.1821) daughter of James Croft of the Herefordshire Croft family who were then living in Berkshire (qv Archer Croft), and they had seven children. There were two subsequent wives, Elizabeth Adair and Eliza Innes, each with issue. In 1831 his older brother Charles, 2nd Earl Grey (after whom the tea is named) was Prime Minister and nominated Edward as Dean of Hereford and next year as bishop. Merewether (qv) followed him as dean and when Grey held a visitation in 1835 problems were caused by the new dean's reforming zeal and the chapter's resistance arose. Grey died in office on 24 July 1837 and was buried in the cathedral choir.

Grey, Henry (1594-1651), 10th Earl of Kent, was the proprietor of Goodrich Castle. He sat in Parliament as Lord Ruthin in 1640. After his death the dowager countess Amabel received £1,000 compensation for the slighting of her castle, following the siege of 1646 (qv Henry Lingen). As the patron of Credenhill living she granted the rectory to Thomas Traherne (qv) fresh from Brasenose in 1656. Amabel, widow of Anthony Fane and daughter of Sir Anthony Benn, was Grey's second wife. Their son Anthony inherited the title. The Greys were to sell Goodrich to Admiral Griffin (qv) in the next century.

Grey, Henry (*c.*1599-1673), 1st Earl of Stamford, Parliamentarian army officer from Leicestershire, was educated at Trinity College, Cambridge and Gray's Inn. When the Civil Wars broke out he was initially for the king but feeling slighted joined the Earl of Essex's army (qv Devereux). In September 1642 he was ordered to march on Hereford with his regiment of 900 foot and three troops of horse, joined en route by Colonel Robert Kyrle (qv), Edward Massey (qv) and Sir Robert Harley (qv, d.1656) with his eldest son. Despite the king's instructions that Hereford should strengthen its defences, it was unprepared for resistance and on 2 October Stamford was able to establish himself as governor with headquarters in the bishop's palace. Stamford's poorly paid troopers were ill-disciplined, disrupting cathedral services and plundering the citizens. He thwarted a Royalist plan to eject him at the end of October but by 3 December the animosity of the townspeople made his position untenable and he retired to Gloucester and Bristol, ending the first occupation of Hereford. Herbert's Royalist army immediately occupied Hereford and Sir Richard Cave (qv) was left in charge. Royalists then ransacked and garrisoned Sir Richard Hopton's (qv) home at Canon Frome. Disabled by gout, Stamford's subsequent war was a poor one with a disastrous campaign in the west. His son was a radical member of the purged Parliament, the only aristocrat to sign the king's death warrant, to Stamford's sorrow. He became disillusioned with the Commonwealth and in 1659 was part of an abortive uprising. Charles II pardoned him at the Restoration and he died on 21 August 1673.

Grey, Jane (1537-54), queen of England for nine days, was the daughter of Henry, Marquess of Dorset and Frances, daughter of the Duke of Suffolk, and therefore Edward VI's (qv) cousin. In Holinshed and Foxe she is a Protestant martyr. She was highly educated and when the scholar and tutor Roger Ascham called on her, aged 13, he found her reading Plato's *Phaedo* in Greek; she could read the Old Testament in Hebrew. She was married to Guildford Dudley, son of the Duke of Northumberland in 1553, the pair being pawns in their parents' attempt to seize power and keep the Catholic Princess Mary from the throne. She was a favourite of her cousin King Edward and was persuaded to accept the crown to exclude the Catholic Mary to preserve the fragile Protestant settlement. Consequently the sickly Edward was persuaded to make a will passing over his sisters. But little enthusiasm was shown in the country and when support for Mary began to gain ground Jane and her husband were arrested. Counter uprisings broke out in her favour, such as that by Sir Thomas Wyatt in London. A rebellion in Herefordshire on her behalf was put down by Richard Walwyn (qv). Twelve thousand men had appeared in arms, raised by Sir James Croft (qv) who was believed to be the main instigator of the rebellion. Mary had been inclined to clemency but the uprisings sealed Jane's fate and she and her husband were executed on 12 February 1554 in the Tower.

Grey, John de (d.1323), 2nd Baron Wilton, Reginald's son (qv), inherited extensive lands, and by the time of his death owned land in 26 counties, including Wilton Castle and Kempley. He married Anne de Ferrers, and then Maud Basset. Serving the Crown on the field and in council, he was one of the Lords Ordainers appointed to reform Edward II's (qv) administration and contain his favourites. In 1315 he was a justiciar and keeper of the king's castles in north Wales. He died on 28 October 1323. His eldest son was Henry, 3rd Lord Grey of Wilton (d.1342) but his favourite Roger (d.1353) by his second wife Maud inherited most of the lands, causing contention. The Greys were to hold Wilton Castle for the next 300 years. Their barony of Ruthin and their estates in Buckinghamshire were always more important to them, however, and Wilton lost its strategic importance.

Grey, Reginald de (d.1308), son of John and Emma de Grey of Shirland, Derbyshire, married Maud de Longchamps (qv), heiress of Wilton, in 1248 and moved with his father into her castle on the Wye. The king granted Reginald the right to hold a market and fair at Wilton on the same terms as Maud's father and created him Baron Wilton. The Greys continued the Longchamps' work of strengthening Wilton Castle against the threat of Welsh incursions at this important Wye crossing and were granted oaks from the royal forest at St Briavel's. Reginald's father John de Grey was made constable of Hereford Castle in 1260 and was High Sheriff the following year. In 1263 he was captain of the royal forces mustering in Herefordshire to oppose Llywelyn ap Gruffydd (qv). Reginald died at his castle of Ruthin, Denbigh on 5 April 1308.

Grey, William (1508-62), 13th Baron Grey of Wilton, 'flower of soldiers', was the fourth son of Edmund Grey, 9th Baron Grey of Wilton. Despite his title he lived in Buckinghamshire. He fought in defence of Calais and Boulogne and in the Scottish wars. He was rewarded with the grant of Brampton manor (near Ross) by Henry VIII in 1546. The next year he was made a Knight of the Garter. However, when he was captured at the fall of Calais he was forced to sell Wilton Castle to Charles Brydges (qv, d.1619) to pay the 25,000 crowns outstanding on his ransom. He was probably the most competent soldier in Britain in the mid 16th century.

Griffin, Thomas (1692-1771), admiral, in 1740 bought Goodrich Castle, as a ruin, from Henry Grey (qv under Henry Grey, d.1651), Duke of Kent, whose family had owned it, though never lived in it, since the 16th century. Griffin made renovations but kept it as a picturesque ruin. He commanded in the Royal Navy for half a century and ended as MP for Arundel. His descendant Catherine Griffin refused Meyrick's (qv) offer to buy the castle. To her (and Wordsworth's [qv]) annoyance he built his vast Goodrich Court on a hill overlooking it.

Griffiths, Sylvanus (*c*.1576-1624), Dean of Hereford 1617-24 was born in Herefordshire. He graduated at Brasenose and took the degree of D.D. at Christ Church, Oxford. In 1604 he was appointed canon and the treasurer of Hereford Cathedral. He was archdeacon in 1604 and next year received the rectory of Kingsland. When the recently installed dean Richard Montague resigned in 1616 Griffiths was elected in his place. Francis Godwin (qv), his bishop, was frequently absent and Dr Griffiths and his chapter had untroubled control in the diocese.

Grismond, William (d.1650), murderer, was hanged on 12 March 1650 for the murder of a girl in Leintwardine. He was the subject of a popular ballad collected in John Masefield's (qv) *A Sailor's Garland*. In the ballad Grismond killed his fiancée 'with my accursed knife' and attempted to flee to Ireland, but the ship refused to carry him and he was caught. Masefield says he was hanged at the scene of his crime in Leintwardine.

Grosseteste, Robert (1170-1253), theologian and scientist from a poor family in Suffolk, was one of the great thinkers and scientists of his age. He was educated through local philanthropy at Oxford, studying law, medicine, the sciences and the liberal arts. He was attracted to the court of William de Vere (qv), Bishop of Hereford, who had built up a congenial circle of intellectuals in Hereford engaged in scientific studies. These included Roger Infans (qv Roger of Hereford) and Gerald of Wales (qv). They studied chronology, astrology and astronomy, and Grosseteste wrote on all these subjects. He was interested in the natural sciences and the theory of scientific knowledge and was the first in mediaeval Europe to write a commentary on Aristotle. His treatises include *On the Calendar*, *On the Movements of the Planets*, *On the Origin of Sounds*, and works of astronomical calculations. He was a friend and adviser to the young Henry III (qv) and is said to have had a library of some 900 books. He took advantage of the Latin capture of Constantinople in 1204 to familiarise himself with Greek learning. When the bishop died Grosseteste hoped to replace him but was passed over for Gilbert de Briouze (qv). He spent some 25 years in administrative work in the diocese. In 1225 he returned to teach at Oxford, attracted by the new Franciscan ideas. In 1229 he was archdeacon of Leicester and in 1235 Bishop of Lincoln, the largest diocese in England which included Oxford. He died on the eve of St Denis (qv), 9 October 1253. His reforming ideas and attacks on papal corruption influenced Wycliffe.

Gruffydd ap Llywelyn (*c*.1010-63), King of Wales 1055-63, was the eldest son of Llywelyn ap Seisyll, the ruler of Gwynedd and Powys. He gradually assumed control of the principalities of Wales and was sole ruler by 1055. In 1052 he attacked Herefordshire, clashing with a force of Saxons and Normans at Llanllieni (Leominster). In 1055 he allied himself with Ælfgar (qv) the son of Earl Leofric (qv) and sealed the alliance by marrying Ælfgar's daughter Edith (qv); their children were Maredudd ap Gruffydd, Idwal ap Gruffydd and Nest verch Gruffydd (qv). Their combined armies marched into Herefordshire and drove off a force under Ralph (qv), Earl of Hereford. Hereford was undefended and on 24 October 1055 Gruffydd and Ælfgar sacked and looted Hereford and burnt Bishop Æthelstan's (qv) recently completed cathedral. Three canons – Eilmar, Ordgar and Godo – and Eilmar's four sons made a stand at the west doors but were cut down. Saint Ethelbert's (qv) rich shrine was looted and his relics dispersed. After another victory over the English forces at the Battle of Glasbury Gruffydd became sole ruler of Wales, the only Welsh prince to achieve this. In the 1060s Harold Godwinson and his brother Tostig (qqv) made a concerted attack on Gruffydd by sea and land and, on 5 August 1063, he was killed by his own men in his Snowdonia fastness. His head was sent to Harold as was his widow, Edith, whom Harold married. Gruffydd's two sons fought to retain their father's kingdom but both were killed and Wales reverted to its traditional principalities.

Guillim, John (1565-1621), antiquarian, was born in Herefordshire and educated at Brasenose College, Oxford where there were scholarships for Herefordshire students. He was introduced to heraldry by his father and wrote the *Display of Heraldrie*, published in 1610 and reprinted many times. He was appointed Portsmouth Pursuivant of Arms and eventually the Rouge Croix Pursuivant. He married Frances daughter of Richard Siston and had a son, St John Guillim. He died on 7 May 1621.

Guindda (9th century) is buried in St Clydawg, Clodock (qv). She is remembered by her husband on a plaque in the church with an intimate Latin verse:

Hoc tumulum retinet
Membra pudica mulieris
Guindda carae coniugis
Quae fuit ipsa ibidem.

The last line is obscure and the translation contested but a possible interpretation is: 'This mound holds the part of my dear wife Guindda that was most herself'.

Gunter, Edmund (1581-1626), mathematician, was born in Herefordshire although his father was from Gunterstown, Brecknockshire. He was educated at Westminster School and Christ Church, Oxford, where he showed mathematical ability and began to devise mathematical instruments. He received his BD degree in 1615 and was ordained, becoming rector of St George's, Southwark and St Mary Magdalen, Oxford. He was one of the first to observe temporal magnetic variations and was an early user of logarithms, publishing the first tables of sines and tangents. Other mathematical innovations were Gunter's Scale, a precursor of the slide rule for use at sea, and Gunter's Chain for land surveying: a chain 22 yards long with 100 links, ten square chains making an acre. In 1620 he was appointed professor of astronomy at Gresham College, London, the forerunner of the Royal Society. He died on 10 December 1626 at Gresham College and was buried the following day at St Peter-le-Poer, Old Broad Street.

Guthlac (672-714), saint, was the son of Penwald, a Mercian nobleman. He fought in King Ethelred's (qv) army while young but experienced a religious conversion and entered a monastery at Repton. Then, seeking greater austerities, he set up his cell in the wild fens of Norfolk. He was a kinsman and close friend of Æthelbald (qv) and prophesied that he would become King of the Mercians. After Guthlac died on 11 April (his feast day) 714, Crowland Abbey was built on the site of his cell. He was a popular English saint and in Saxon times there was a Benedictine monastery dedicated to him in Hereford on Castle Green, predating Hereford Cathedral and Castle. The walls of the small chapel can be traced in the grass of Castle Green on dry summers. St Guthlac's body was buried at Crowland where his cult developed, but he was revered throughout the Middle Ages at Hereford, which also claimed to have relics presented by Ethelbald. Castle walls were later built around the monastery's precinct and it found itself inside the Norman castle bailey. During the siege of Hereford by Miles of Gloucester (qv) in 1140, buried corpses of the brothers were exhumed and thrown at the attackers and the community were anxious to move. It was first linked with St Peter's new church in Hereford, then Bishop Robert de Béthune (qv)

found them a site outside Bishop's or Byster's (Bye Street) Gate, where the County Hospital now is and in 1143 they were refounded under a prior combining St Peter's (qv) community as St Peter, Paul and Guthlac. St Guthlac's played an important part in Hereford life until the Dissolution of the monasteries in 1539: it was the custom for the bishop to proceed from the priory to his enthronement at the cathedral, through Bishop's Gate, bare-headed and barefoot. One of its properties was St Guthlac's Church at Little Cowarne, the only dedication in the county now, and that restored to it in 1992. In 1535 Leland (qv) calls the old priory 'a faire chapell' and Duncumb (qv) describes it, when Sir John ap Rhys (qv Prise) bought it at the Dissolution, as having great, stately chambers and a large, melancholy chapel, standing in a spacious garden and orchards through which the Eign stream ran. Tunnels are believed to have run from it over a mile down to the Wye. Later, Nash (qv) built Hereford Gaol on the site and in 1836 the county workhouse was sited here. A gable cross and the 15th-century stalls from the priory are now in St Peter's Church, Hereford, and there is some old stonework in Stonebow Road.

Gwillim, John (fl.1823), a merchant apothecary, was elected a Tory member of Hereford corporation in the early 19th century and was Mayor in 1823.

Gwillim, John ap (*c*.1490-*c*.1552), MP, was from a Llangarron family and Gwillims were known in this part of Herefordshire from the Middle Ages (qqv William and Thomas Gwillim). He married Joan, daughter of Robert Powell of Whitchurch and they had four sons, including John his heir, and five daughters. He built a cruck-framed house at Much Fawley near Ross, still substantially to be seen. He entered Henry VII's (qv) service and was Sergeant at Arms by 1514, steward of Fownhope lordship. He held other county offices including duties at the gaol at Hereford Castle. He was returned to Parliament as junior knight for Herefordshire in 1547 and was a magistrate in the county.

Gwillim, Thomas (d.1762), lived at Old Court, Whitchurch, a splendid 17th-century house in the meadows by the Wye south of Ross. He was lieutenant colonel in the Militia and married Elizabeth Spinckes. They had a daughter Elizabeth (qv Simcoe), but Thomas died before her birth and Elizabeth as a result of it.

Gwillim, William (fl.1695) rebuilt Langstone Court at Llangarron which Pevsner calls the best house of the late 17th century in the county.

Gwladus ferch Llywelyn (d.1251) called *Ddu* or dark, was the daughter of Llywelyn ab Iorwerth (qv) and Joan, daughter of King John (qv). She married Reginald de Briouze (qv) in 1215 as part of her father's border alliances and they had a son William. Two years after Briouze's death in 1228 she married another great Marcher lord, Ralph (II) de Mortimer (qv), who was vying with her father for control of the Welsh Marches. They had a son, Roger (III) (qv), and a daughter, Isolde, who married Walter de Balun (qv) and, after his death, Hugh Audley (qv). Gwladus was buried at Wigmore Abbey beside Ralph five years after his death.

Gwyer, Charles James Paul, bought Eywood Hall, Titley from the Harleys and rebuilt it in 1898 (architect: W.O. Milne). He was High Sheriff in 1907 and JP.

Gwynne, Eleanor (Nell) (1651-87), actress and royal mistress. A plaque in Gwynne Street, Hereford indicates the site of her birth, although Oxford and London also claim her. David Garrick (qv) on a visit to Hereford said she had been born in the Royal Oak in Pipe Well Lane. The inn, which had backed on to the wall of the bishop's palace, was pulled down shortly after his visit and the road renamed in her honour. The family was Welsh and Nell told Pepys she had been brought up in a bawdy house. Evidence in favour of Hereford is that her eldest son with King Charles II, Charles Beauclerk, 1st Duke of St Albans, had a son (Lord James Beauclerk qv) who was created Bishop of Hereford while young but received no further advancement. There is a legend that when King Charles was founding Chelsea Hospital he consulted Nell about the Chelsea Pensioners' livery and she chose the red coats she remembered being worn by the pensioners of Coningsby Hospital of her Hereford childhood. The Hospital in Coningsby Street has a display that supports this attractive notion. Nell first appears aged 12 selling oranges outside the King's Theatre where her sister Rose was acting. On 3 March 1665 'pretty, witty Nell' is spotted by Samuel Pepys, a reliable witness of beauty, in the audience of the Duke's Theatre in Lincoln's Inn Fields. Two years later he sees her again, standing at the door of her lodgings in Drury Lane, 'a mighty pretty creature'. Pepys didn't think much of her in serious roles but in 'mad parts' she was inimitable. She was slight and fair and famed for her repartee and it is likely that her royal lover was as much entertained by her scabrous wit as her physical allure. She had the 'smallest foot in England' and 'perfect legs' of which the king was a connoisseur and which we can admire in Lely's portrait. Charles, pleased to share his pleasure, paid for skirts for Nell to wear on stage which swung up revealingly. She poked fun at her ennobled rivals who, unlike her, tried to conceal their origins, and was especially rude about the Roman Catholic Duchess of Portsmouth. She is said to have quietened an angry mob at the time of the Popish Plot by assuring them that she was the 'Protestant whore'. Charles's queen, Catherine of Braganza, tried to befriend Nell and gave her presents but this did not protect her from her railery. Nell was proud of her common touch but it stopped her from getting a title. Charles bought her a grand house though, at the fashionable west end of Pall Mall where her terrace overlooked St James's Park. Here John Evelyn (qv) observed the king chatting over the wall with her. He also bought her a house by Windsor Castle. Charles's death-bed request, 'Let not poor Nelly starve', was heeded by his brother James II and her pension continued, her debts were paid and her property was assured. She called James 'dismal Jimmy'. She herself was always generous, one of her bequests being to the poor Roman Catholics of the area 'to show my charity to those who differ from me in religion'. She survived her royal patron by two years, dying young on 14 November 1687 and is buried like her mother in St Martin's in the Fields.

H

Haddon, George Cowley (1839-86), architect, was born in Crick, Northants and married Anna Crofield (1840-98) of Great Malvern. They lived, and he had his office, in Bridge Street, Hereford, and he kept another office in Malvern with his brother, Henry Rockliffe Haddon (fl.1868-91). The partnership Elmslie (qv), Franey and Haddon built and restored many schools and churches in Herefordshire and Worcestershire. He built the Baptist chapel at Ross and rebuilt Dulas Church. In Ewyas Harold he rebuilt the church, restored the churchyard cross and built the school. He also built schools at Dilwyn, Ivington, Kingsland etc. He provided the reredos at Pipe and Lyde Church for his friend Revd F.T. Havergal (qv). His new churches were often distinctive, like the gothic Eignbrook Congregational Church (1872) on Eign Street and the Italianate Baptist chapel built with John Johnson on Commercial Road (1880). He had antiquarian interests and published a facsimile of the Mappa Mundi (1868) with Havergal and *Fasti Herefordensis* (1869) on the antiquities of Herefordshire. His partnership was declared bankrupt in 1881 and thereafter he practised alone. His brother Henry built the attractive Cottage Hospital in Ledbury's Homend (1891).

Hadley, Isaac (fl.1700) bell founder of Leominster, cast many Herefordshire bells, such as those on Hereford old Town Hall of 1710. They were rung by two quarter jacks now in the Old House in Hereford High Town.

Haemma was the first abbot of the reformed Benedictine Priory at Leominster. St Haemma's bones were revered at Leominster Priory along with those of its founder St Edfrith (qv) until it was dissolved in the 11th century.

Haggard, Henry Rider (1856-1925), novelist, son of William Rider Haggard, Squire of Bradenham, Norfolk, was sent out to work for Sir Henry Bulwer, Governor of Natal, and quickly rose in the state's judiciary; his experiences in Africa would later inform his novels. On his return home he married and was called to the Bar. He determined to be a writer and soon had success with *King Solomon's Mines* (1885) and *She* (1887), finding a winning formula that produced a book a year for the rest of his life. His wife brought him a farm at Ditchingham, Norfolk and he began collecting information about agricultural problems for his book *Rural England* (1902). He often visited Herefordshire for research, staying with his sister, Ella Doveton, and her husband Revd Charles Maddison Green, rector of St Michael's, Ledbury and Master of St Katherine's Hospital. In 1896 he opened the Barrett-Browning Institute in Ledbury. He visited the cider mill which Radcliffe Cooke (qv) ran at Hellens, admiring

Cooke's tireless advocacy of the beverage and laughing at his advice to eat six unpeeled apples and drink a pint of cider each day. In 1912 he was knighted and in 1919 appointed KGB. Sir Henry died in London on 14 May 1925 and was buried in Ditchingham Church, Norfolk. His autobiography *The Day of My Life* was published in 1926.

Hakluyt: Originally from Radnorshire, the family became associated with Eaton Hall, south of Leominster and Yatton in the south-east of the county. They were servants of the Mortimers (qv).

Hakluyt, John (fl.1647), antiquarian of Eaton Hall, wrote a life of St Edfrith (qv) of Leominster. He made records of Herefordshire antiquities, recording a now lost plaque to Kenelm (qv, d.1060) for instance. In 1647-8 he was living in London where he wrote polemical pamphlets and published *Mercurius Melancholicus*, a news book of Royalist propaganda for which he was imprisoned.

Hakluyt, Leonard (*c.*1352-1413), attorney, was the son of Sir Edmund Hakluyt, who lost his Radnor lands when he sided with Prince Llewelyn (qv), but acquired Longworth Manor in Lugwardine. He was the Mortimers' Herefordshire attorney and followed Edmund (III) Mortimer (qv) Earl of March and Ulster to Ireland to secure his estates. After Edmund's death he returned to Ireland again with Roger VII (qv) in 1394. He married Margaret Longland from South Brent, Somerset. He was MP for Herefordshire in Richard II's Parliament of 1385 and in his Merciless Parliament of 1388, after which he was knighted. He later represented Somerset, where his wife had lands. As JP he was involved in the prosecution of Walter Brut (qv) and his supporters. He was sheriff in 1402 and 1409 and escheator for the county, responsible for collecting taxes. A William Hakluyt of Eaton Hall, perhaps his son, fought at Agincourt with Henry V and brought a lucrative French prisoner called St George home for ransom.

Hakluyt, Richard (*c.*1552-1616), geographer, was born about 1552 at Eaton Hall. Both his parents died when he was young and he was brought up by his cousin, another Richard Hakluyt, in London. He was educated at Westminster School and Christ Church, Oxford where he met Philip Sidney (qv). The love of exploration and navigation he felt when his guardian showed him a map of the world and read him Psalm 107 never left him: 'They that go down to the sea in ships, that do business in great waters; these see the works of the Lord, and his wonders in the deep.' He was ordained in 1580 and was chaplain to grandees including Sir Edward Stafford, English Ambassador in Paris, and met Walsingham, Drake, Raleigh, Cecil etc. He told the queen about regions 'in America that are base and barren, and only bear a name for the present [but] may prove rich places in future time'. He was generous in helping others like John Florio with their books, and produced his own great work, *The Principall Navigations...*, which detailed British maritime achievements (1589 and 1600). After his death Samuel Purchas continued to expand the work. Hakluyt accumulated prebends and benefices and grew prosperous, inheriting the Herefordshire estate of Eaton after the death of his older brother Thomas. He married twice and was survived by a son. He died on 23 November 1616 and is buried in Westminster Abbey. There is an active Hakluyt Society.

Hakluyt, Sergeant (fl.1640s) was seconded from Col Massey's (qv) division in 1643 to take charge of Lady Brilliana Harley's (qv) garrison at Brampton Bryan Castle. A 'brave and able soldier', he was a veteran from the German wars.

Hall, Elizabeth (1659-1708), second daughter and co-heiress of Francis Hall of Ledbury, was a descendant of the Skinners (qv). She endowed a school in Ledbury's South End with a mistress to teach 24 girls domestic crafts, including sewing, knitting, washing and cooking. Basic reading, writing and numbers were to be taught to other poor children, eight of whom were to be taught higher skills by a master. Children could have a school dinner for a ha'penny: pea soup on Monday, rice pudding on Tuesday, Irish stew on Wednesday, boiled beef and suet pudding on Thursday and pea soup again on Friday. The school was rebuilt in 1910 in an Arts and Crafts style with funds from John Michael Gordon Biddulph (qv). It is now offices, and the mistress's splendid high chair, which bore Mrs Hall's arms and had been long preserved in the building, has disappeared.

Hall, Henry (*c.*1656-1707), cathedral organist, was taught by John Blow at the Chapel Royal with Henry Purcell. He was organist at Exeter Cathedral and wrote the popular anthem *By the Waters of Babylon.* He was a vicar choral at Hereford Cathedral and in 1679 became assistant organist. In 1688 he replaced John Badham (qv) as organist. He lived with his wife Catherine Woolmer (d.1690) and their sons William (d.1700) and Henry (1690-1717), both musicians, in vicars choral quarters. Hall wrote distinguished church music that is still played and much verse. He drank at the Black Lion, Bridge Street, where his verse, which characterises him as a convivial man, was sung, and arranged popular concerts for the vicars choral in their recently refurbished hall, which can still be seen. He later married Anne Gower. He died on 30 March 1707 and was buried in the vicars cloister, succeeded as organist by his younger son Henry, who was to be buried near his father. William was a violinist and musician in ordinary to the king.

Hall, James Wallace Richard (1799-1860), lawyer and philanthropist, was the son of Revd John Hall of an old Ross family who had retired to live at Much Birch. Wallace Hall set up as a solicitor with offices in Hereford and Ross. He made many improvements to early 19th-century Ross, founding the Ross Dispensary, establishing a new school and pressing for a Ross to Hereford railway connection. His marriage to Mary Bernard brought him property in Little Birch. His second wife was Frances Clifford of Much Birch, where he paid to have the Church of St Mary and St Thomas of Canterbury built by Foster and Okely of Bristol (1837). After his death on 1 July 1860 Frances installed the east window in his memory (Clayton and Bell [qv] 1864). A gothic monument to him beside Ross station was dismantled for road widening but has recently been reassembled through public subscription and now stands at the junction of Smallbrook Road and Station Approach.

Hall, William George Glenvil (1887-1962), politician, descendant of James Hall (qv) and generations of Quaker farmers in the Ross area, was born at Spearmarsh Villa, Almeley. He joined the Independent Labour Party in 1905 and rose to be MP for Portsmouth then Colne Valley, Yorkshire. In the post-war Labour government he was financial secretary to the Treasury and chairman of the Parliamentary Labour Party. He died at his Kensington home on 13 October 1962.

Hamo (d.1232) and his large family were at the centre of Hereford's Jewish community in the St Thomas's area, now Maylord Street. On Isaac Taylor's (qv) 18th-century map this is still called Jewry Lane, and in the 13th century the area was one of the largest such communities in England. Hamo was an important financier nationally at this time and one of the wealthier merchants. He financed the barons de Lacy, Clifford and Marshal (qqv) and this was continued after his death by his sons Ursell and Moses (d.1253). The Jews were an important source of credit at this time and were under the protection of the Crown: for instance, they appealed to King John (qv) to recover Walter de Lacy's (qv) large debt. Henry III (qv) taxed them heavily in the 1240s and put them under the protection of his brother Richard Duke of Cornwall. In 1275 Hereford's Jewry was swelled when Worcester's Jews were moved there. There was also a community at Weobley. Then in 1290 Edward I (qv) expelled the Jews from the kingdom. (Their Hereford synagogue was at the eastern end of St Owen Street, outside the city walls.)

Hampden, Renn Dickson (1793-1868), Bishop of Hereford 1848-68, was born in Barbados on 29 March 1793 the son of Renn Hampden. Educated at Oriel College, Oxford and elected Fellow, he was one of the Noetics concerned with demonstrating the reasonableness of Anglicanism, that nature and scripture were both capable of intellectual investigation. He was ordained and in 1816 married his cousin Mary Lovell (d.1865) and they had four children. As professor of moral philosophy he wrote tracts which drew a storm of protest, exacerbated by his urging the admission of dissenters to the universities. Even Newman attacked him and the eirenic Hampden abstained from further polemic. In 1847 he was elected Bishop of Hereford, following the popular Musgrave (qv), to much protest. The press hounded him as a heretic, but when Dean Merewether (qv) complained to the Prime Minister he was curtly overruled. Hampden retreated into his diocesan duties. He died in London after a stroke on 23 April 1868 and was buried at Kensal Green cemetery, and there is a bust of him in Hereford Cathedral. His mild manner and the formidable nature of his wife are said to have been the models for the bishop and his domineering wife Mrs Proudie in Anthony Trollope's *Barchester Chronicles*.

Hanbury, Thomas (1633-1708), born at Preston the son of a Worcestershire iron master, was a Royalist commander in the second Civil War and was knighted at the Restoration. In 1670 he bought the manor of Little Marcle from the Bodenhams (qv) and lived at Little Marcle Court with his second wife Anne (d.1705), daughter of Sir Nathaniel Powell. Sir Thomas was Sheriff of Herefordshire in 1682. Their son Thomas was ordained and made vicar of Little Marcle Church, which the parishioners rebuilt for him. He married Ursula of the nearby Walwyn family (qv) in 1692. William Hanbury, possibly a son of Sir Thomas of Little Marcle, had a son Thomas (d.1742) and a daughter Catherine, co-heirs. Catherine married Velters Cornewall (qv, d.1768).

Hanbury Williams, Charles (1708-59) KB, MP for Leominster, was born Charles Hanbury on 8 December 1708. He was educated at Eton and went on the Grand Tour. His father, John Hanbury of Pontypool, Monmouthshire, was left great wealth by his friend Charles Williams in gratitude for his help, the condition of his will being that all beneficiaries adopt the name Williams, which Charles did in 1729. In 1732 he married Frances (1709-81), youngest daughter of Thomas, Earl of Coningsby's (qv, d.1729), and they had two daughters, Frances (1735-59) and Charlotte (1738-61). He was *custos rotulorum* in 1741, Lord Lieutenant of Herefordshire from 1741-47, High Steward of Leominster in 1744 and MP for Leominster from 1754, having previously represented Monmouthshire. He was a supporter of Walpole's administration, known for his satirical verse which attacked political enemies. The king created him Knight of the Bath. His last five years were spent on diplomatic work in the courts of Poland, Germany and Catherine the Great in Russia. He was infected with syphilis as a result of his extra-marital affairs and Frances left him, taking their children, to whom he was devoted. His illness developed into its tertiary form and he was committed as a lunatic, dying on 2 November 1759. At this time his favourite daughter Frances, who had married William-Anne Capel, 4th Earl of Essex, died of puerperal fever giving birth to a daughter. Their son, George Capel (qv George Capel Coninsgby), Lord Malden, inherited Sir Charles' estate. Charlotte married Robert Boyle Walsingham, a son of the Earl of Shannon, in 1759 but she also died soon afterwards. Lady Frances, Sir Charles' widow, inherited her father's Coningsby estates, including Hampton Court.

Hardman, John (1811-67), manufacturer of stained glass and ecclesiastical furnishings, was baptised on 9 August 1811 at St Peter's Roman Catholic Church in Birmingham and educated at Stonyhurst College. His father had a manufactory in Birmingham making decorative metalwork items such as buttons. He was a friend of Pugin (qv) and absorbed his radical idea of a Christian architecture in a Gothic style. Pugin, impressed by Hardman's ability to meet his demanding design requirements, took him into partnership and encouraged him to make stained glass and his sister Lucy to embroider his textiles. The firm expanded and began to tackle everything ecclesiastical, satisfying a growing market and turning Pugin's dream into objects. When Pugin was asked to furnish the new Palace of Westminster, Hardman made the furnishings, fittings and nearly all the stained glass, and he made the objects for Pugin's prize-winning Medieval Court at the Great Exhibition of 1851. The splendid wrought-iron chancel gates at Chick's (qv) St Mary, Little Birch may be Hardman's last work as, worn out by the strain of unremitting labour, he died on 29 May 1867 and was buried in Pugin's new Catholic cathedral of St Chad in Birmingham.

Hardman Powell, John (1827-95), the son of John Hardman's (qv) sister Lucy, became chief designer in metalwork and glass from 1852, while Hardman's sons took over the firm. All stained glass design produced by the firm from the 1860s is his. He had been trained by Pugin at his home in Ramsgate, recording his

memories in *Pugin in his Home* (1889) and marrying Pugin's eldest daughter Anne in 1850. The great north transept window of 1864 at Hereford Cathedral is by him, arguably the best 19th-century glass in the county. It was made in memory of Archdeacon Lane Freer (qv), and cost £1,316. Now all Herefordshire churches wanted Hardman glass, and east windows were supplied to St Giles, Goodrich (1875); All Saints, Monkland; St James, Tedstone Delamere; and St John the Baptist, Upton Bishop, where there is also an attractive south window of the Good Samaritan and a brass by him. Much of the glass in Belmont Abbey is by him. His earliest glass in the county is a circular window in Yarkhill School. Powell died on 2 March 1895 and was buried in Pugin's chantry at his home in Ramsgate. The firm of Hardman, under different ownership, continues to specialise in stained glass.

Hardwick, Philip (1792-1870), architect, the second son of Thomas (qv), was apprenticed in his office. He is remembered for the iconic Doric Arch at Euston Station of 1836-40, which was scandalously demolished in 1961. He was consulted by Thomas Musgrave (qv), Bishop of Hereford, about alterations to the palace and prepared a survey of the structure in which he emphasised the importance of its 12th-century features, and subsequently effected renovations. He was asked by Dean Merewether (qv) to report on the state of the lady chapel in Hereford Cathedral and drew attention to its dilapidated condition. Cottingham (qv) was chosen as the architect of the cathedral's restoration work, however. His son Philip Charles Hardwick was also an architect and remodelled Madresfield Court near Malvern in the later 19th century.

Hardwick, Thomas (1752-1829), architect, was born on 22 May 1752 in Middlesex, the only child of architect and mason Thomas Hardwick. His grandfather, another Thomas Hardwick, had been a mason at Weston-under-Penyard, where the family had long been settled. They left the area after an altercation with neighbours, and the young Hardwick moved to Credenhill where, in 1783, he met and married his cousin Jane Hardwick. He studied under William Chambers (qv) and in the RA Schools, where he developed skills as an artist of architectural drawings and landscape. He was a conscientious, conservative exponent of the neo-Palladian style. He was a friend of Sir John Soane and at one time had as a pupil J.M.W. Turner (qv), whom he advised to give up architecture for a career in painting. In 1806-1809 he designed and built the Nelson's Column that stands in Castle Green, Hereford. It was to have had a statue of Nelson on top but money ran out and an urn was substituted. He retired in 1825 when his son Philip took over the practice, and died at his home in St Marylebone on 16 January 1829.

Harford, John (1504-59) of Bosbury invested in church property at the Dissolution, buying chantry land from Henry VIII's agents. He married Anne, daughter of Sir John Scrope. He took over the bishop's palace at Bosbury which had been leased to the Mortons (qv), and he and his son Richard were successive stewards of the bishop's manor. He leased the Crown, an old house still standing in Bosbury. Harford died on 30 August 1559 and a splendid monument was erected to him dated 1573 in Holy Trinity Church, Bosbury, signed by John Gilden (qv) of

Hereford, the earliest known signed sculptural monument in the country.

Harford, Richard (1526-75), John's (qv) son, married Martha Fox, and extended the Crown at Bosbury, where a panelled room bears his and Martha's initials and the date 1571. A table also with their initials and dated is now in the Old House, Hereford. Their more rustic monument in Bosbury Church faces his father's, with its giant figures and his and his wife's effigies. His grand-nephew Dr Bridstock Harford was a physician of Hereford and his name was added to the monument. His son, Bridstock Harford (d.1683), was a barrister and MP for Hereford in 1660. He married Elizabeth, the widow of John Dannett (qv) of Bosbury. Their descendants were the Jones-Brydges family (qv Harford Jones-Brydges) of The Whittern, Lyonshall. There were also Harfords at Temple Court, a former preceptory of the Knights Templars in Bosbury parish. Edna Lyall (qv) used Harford as a character in her Civil War romance of Herefordshire.

Harley: A Marches family, originally from Harley in Shropshire, who acquired Brampton Bryan through marriage to the Bramptons (qv) in 1309. Ralph de Mortimer (qv) is recorded as feudal lord in Domesday when the Bramptons were his vassals. The Harleys extended the works they found there, and the castle gatehouse, now the best preserved part, was built or renovated in the early 14th century as ball flower decoration shows. The Harleys were MPs for the Shire throughout and from then there are 12 generations of direct descent father to son to the 1st Earl of Oxford and Mortimer. In the Civil Wars the Harleys stood out as Parliamentarians in a Royalist county. While MP Robert Harley was at Westminster his brave wife Brilliana resisted two sieges of her castle until weakened by privations she died. Her letters to her son, 'dear Ned', survive. The Harleys knew great power and wealth in the 17th and 18th centuries. They were great collectors: the Harleian collection forms a cornerstone of the British Library's manuscript holdings, and the Brampton Bryan estate papers are lodged with Hereford Record Office. Harleys still live at Brampton Bryan and boast that the house has not been bought or sold since Domesday. The present resident, Edward Harley, is High Sheriff of Herefordshire for 2015-16.

Harley, Alfred (1809-53), 6th Earl of Oxford and Earl Mortimer, was born on 10 January 1809 and succeeded as the last earl in 1849 on his father's death (Edward Harley, qv, d.1849). He married Eliza Nugent in 1831 but there were no children and the title ceased with his death on 19 January 1853. There is a large monument to him in St Barnabas' Church, Brampton Bryan.

Harley, Brilliana (1598-1643), was named after the Dutch town of Brill where her father, Edward Viscount Conway, was governor. She was fortunate in her town of birth as her sister was called Helegenwagh, albeit known as Wacke by the family. In 1623 Brilliana married, as his third wife, the 44-year-old Sir Robert (d.1656, qv) and they had three sons and four daughters. She was a well-educated Presbyterian, able to teach her children Latin when no tutor was available. She sent her young sons off to fight for Parliament under Sir William Waller, writing hundreds of letters, still extant, to them and her husband at Westminster, keeping them informed of events in Herefordshire. She describes the insults offered to her servants and herself when they went to market in Ludlow, and of her household's increasing isolation and vulnerability in the generally Royalist county. She gave the family plate for the war effort and collected information about unsatisfactory clerics for a Parliamentary committee. Col Massey (qv) sent her the experienced veteran Sergeant Hakluyt (qv) to improve the fortifications and command and stiffen her garrison, helped by the family physician Dr Nathan Wright. In July 1643 Sir William Vavasour (qv) called on her to hand the castle over to his Royalist force and when she refused besieged her. She directed a heroic resistance for seven weeks until the Royalist besiegers were called away. Then, ignoring her husband's anxious instructions to flee to safety, she went on the offensive, plundering those who had supported the siege and attacking the Royalist

base at Knighton. The siege was renewed under Harry Lingen (qv) and, weakened by her privations in the increasingly ruinous castle, her strength gave out and she died of pneumonia on 29 October 1643. The castle inevitably fell after bombardment had destroyed the village and out-houses, and the little garrison was treated with some cruelty. The castle was razed, leaving the massive gatehouse and fragments of ancient stonework which can be seen in the gardens. Hakluyt, Wright and three younger Harleys were imprisoned at Shrewsbury.

Harley, Edward (1624-1700), politician and Parliamentarian army officer, was born at Brampton Bryan Castle on 21 October 1624, the oldest surviving son of Sir Robert (d.1656, qv) and Lady Brilliana (qv), the 'dear Ned' of his mother's letters. He was a pious Puritan, educated at Magdalen Hall, Oxford and Lincoln's Inn. At 19 he was commanding the regiment he had raised and fought off the Royalist Horse at Redmarley near Ledbury on 27 July 1644, capturing their Foot. In 1645 he was given command in the New Model Army and was present at the fight at Ledbury when Prince Rupert (qv) surprised Massey (qv) on 22 April 1645. He commanded the garrison at Canon Frome and was appointed General of Horse for Hereford and Radnor. In 1654 he married Mary (d.1661), daughter of Sir William Button of Devon, with whom he had four daughters. Like his father he was MP for Herefordshire, filling the place of the purged Humphrey Coningsby (d.1692, qv) and beating Col Birch (qv) who also stood. He and his father were ejected from the Commons as moderate Presbyterians and imprisoned for their refusal to support the regicides. They favoured accommodation with the king and a system of limited monarchy, and as such neither were employed by the Cromwellian regime. Brampton Bryan, the house, its farms and parks were ruined. When the property of Sir Henry Lingen (qv) was confiscated and given to Sir Edward in reparation for the family's great losses (estimated at £60,000), he gallantly restored it to Lady Alice Lingen. After his father's death in 1656 Sir Edward commemorated his memory by rebuilding the ruined St Barnabas' Church at Brampton Bryan. At the Restoration he built Brampton Bryan House by the castle ruins and restored the devastated park. His interest in antiquarianism led him to excavate a round barrow at Walford near Leintwardine, where he found an urn with ashes. He was recalled to the Long Parliament at the Restoration and made a Knight of the Bath. In 1661 he married Abigail Stephens with whom he had four sons and two daughters, and was appointed governor of Dunkirk. He and his family refused to take the oath of allegiance to James II and he tried to prevent Bishop Croft (qv) from reading it out. At the Revolution of 1688 he and his son Robert (d.1724, qv) raised a troop and rode to secure Worcester for the Prince of Orange, although he was later disillusioned with William's ruinous Continental wars. He represented Herefordshire in 1693-95 and, with his sons, improved navigation of the Wye and the poor roads of the county. He died on 8 December 1700 and was buried in St Barnabas' Church. A Presbyterian within the Church of England, he enjoyed Baxter's sermons and wrote tracts himself.

Harley, Edward (1664-1735) was born at Eywood, Titley on 7 June 1664, second son of Sir Edward (d.1700, qv) and the brother of Robert, the 1st Earl (d.1724, qv). He was educated at Westminster and the Middle Temple but, as a Presbyterian, was barred from the universities. He married Sarah Foley (qv), sister of Robert's wife Elizabeth, in 1683 and they had three sons and a daughter. Edward, his father and brother were involved in the bringing over of William of Orange. He and Col Birch (qv) went to welcome William on Salisbury Plain in 1688 as representatives of Herefordshire and he organised the army's approach to London. He was closely associated with Leominster, as recorder 1692-1732, and MP 1698-1722. He was the sponsor of the Wye Navigation Act in Parliament (1696) which greatly improved trade in Herefordshire, and bought much property in the counties of Hereford and Radnor. He rebuilt Eywood in 1705; it was demolished in the 1950s, the stables alone surviving. He was close to his brother and managed his Herefordshire interests while he was away. He died on 30 August 1735 and is buried at St Peter's, Titley.

Harley, Edward (1689-1741), 2nd Earl of Oxford and Earl Mortimer, was the eldest son of Robert (qv, d.1724) and Elizabeth. In 1731 he married Henrietta Cavendish Holles (1694-1755), daughter and heir of the Duke of Newcastle, who brought him wealth and castles in Derbyshire and Northumberland and Welbeck Abbey in Nottinghamshire, which became their country seat. Their daughter Margaret (1715-85) married William Bentinck, Duke of Portland, and, as the richest woman in Britain, she gained a reputation as a great collector of natural history and fine art. She was known as an intellectual and was a member of the Bluestockings Club. The 2nd Earl amassed an art collection in his London house. He was a connoisseur of books and manuscripts and extended his father's famous library, buying rare manuscripts across Europe. He was a friend of Pope (qv), Swift (qv) and Matthew Prior and of the Herefordshire antiquary William Brome (qv), who supplied him with treasures. He has a splendid monument in St Barnabas' Church at Brampton Bryan. He had no male heir and after his death his daughter sold his library cheaply to the British Museum as the Harleian collection.

Harley, Edward (1699-1755), 3rd Earl of Oxford and Earl Mortimer, cousin of Edward (qv, d.1741), married Martha Morgan in St Anne's, Soho. He auctioned his cousin's huge collection of paintings and sculpture in a sale that lasted many days, as described by Horace Walpole (qv). He died at Bath on 11 April 1755.

Harley, Edward (1726-90), 4th Earl of Oxford and Earl Mortimer, eldest son of the 3rd Earl (Edward Harley, qv, d.1755), was born on 2 September 1726 at Brampton Bryan House. His title from 1741-55 was Lord Harley. He was elected MP for Herefordshire in 1757 and served until succeeding to the earldom in 1755, when he became High Steward of Hereford. He appears as such on Isaac Taylor's (qv) 1757 map of Hereford, which is dedicated to him. He married Susannah Archer (1728-1804) but they had no children. He was Lord of the Bedchamber and Lord Lieutenant of Radnorshire until his death on 11 October 1790.

Harley, Edward (1773-1849), 5th Earl of Oxford and Earl Mortimer, was the son of Bishop John Harley (qv, d.1788). He married Jane Elizabeth Scott (qv) in 1794 and they had seven children but were estranged. In 1835 Harley's daughter, Jane Elizabeth, married Henry Bickersteth, his medical attendant and protégé. Bickersteth auctioned the tithes of Ewyas Lacy in 1804. Harley commissioned work from Robert Smirke (qv), then engaged at Eastnor Castle. Harley's youngest daughter Frances Vernon-Harcourt (qv) supplied the sketches for Robinson's (qv) *Castles of Herefordshire* and *Mansions and Manors of Herefordshire*.

Harley, Jane Elizabeth (1774-1824), Countess of Oxford, was the daughter of Revd James Scott, vicar of Itchin, Hampshire, and married Edward Harley (d.1849, qv) in 1794, her father officiating. It was not a happy marriage: she was a radical Whig with sympathies for the French Revolution and took lovers from the Reform Party where she was known as Aspasia. Her seven children were called by some the Harleian Miscellany. She and Harley lived separately, she at the Harley residences Kinsham Court and Eywood. She was a friend of the Princess of Wales. Lord Byron (qv) was her lover in 1812-13 and she encouraged his radicalism. Richard Payne Knight (qv) advised her on the picturesque possibilities of Kinsham, seeing the Dingle at Kinsham as an example of the sublime. Florence Nightingale (qv) visited Kinsham as a child.

Harley, John (d.1557), Bishop of Hereford, was educated at Magdalen College, Oxford and ordained a priest. He was noted for Protestant piety and learning, which brought him to the attention of Edward VI and Protector Somerset. He was rector of Upton on Severn and made a Royal Chaplain. He was consecrated Bishop of Hereford a month before Queen Mary's accession and the return to Catholicism in June 1553. Harley, being both a Protestant and married, was deprived and imprisoned. When released he lived a wandering life in which he ministered to villagers from the reformed prayer book.

Harley, John (1728-88), Bishop of Hereford in 1787, was born on 29 September 1728, second son of the 3rd Earl (Edward Harley, qv, d.1755). He was educated at Christ Church, Oxford and became Dean of Windsor. He married Roach Vaughan and they had a son, Edward (d.1849, qv). In December 1787 he was made Bishop of Hereford but died immediately after. He was buried on 7 January 1788 in the family grave at Brampton Bryan.

Harley, Robert (d.1349) was the son of Sir Richard Harley, who was the first to be elected Knight of the Shire (for Shropshire in 1300). Sir Robert married Margaret (1286-1349), daughter of Bryan de Brampton (qv) in 1309, thus acquiring Brampton Bryan.

Harley, Robert (1579-1656), politician, son of Thomas (d.1631, qv) and Margaret, was educated at Oriel College, Oxford and the Inner Temple. His first wife Ann Barrett died in childbirth but with her dowry Harley bought Wigmore Castle, previously the seat of the Mortimer family (qv), giving him status in Herefordshire. He was made a Knight of the Bath at James I's coronation in 1603. His Presbyterian beliefs put him at odds with his conservative father and when he installed the Puritan clergyman Thomas Pierson (qv) as rector of Brampton Bryan his father complained to Bishop Bennett (qv). Thomas Cole (1628-97), another independent minister, was brought to Brampton by Sir Robert's son in 1659 after he had been ejected from Ewelme, Oxon. Sir Robert lost his second wife and in July 1623 married Brilliana (qv) daughter of Viscount Conway, Secretary of the House of Commons. He was elected burgess for Radnor in 1604 and later remembered being in the House at the time of the Gunpowder Plot. At this time he became JP for Herefordshire and keeper of the

forests of Bringewood and Prestwood. In 1624, '26 and '40 he was returned MP for Herefordshire in the Long Parliament. Following an Act of 1641 for the Destruction of Idolatrous Relics, and assisted by Sir Robert Pye (qv), he oversaw the removal of images, altar rails and church furnishings, such as the great mediaeval embroidered hanging from Canterbury Cathedral which he had burnt in the street. He also supervised the smashing of all the stained glass in St Margaret's Westminster, replacing it with clear glass. In Herefordshire he destroyed Wigmore Cross and burnt the rood of Leintwardine Church, remnants of which can still be seen. In January 1644 he called down the Scottish army to assist in England against Royalist forces, seeing a model for English religion in their Presbyterianism. In 1647 he presented Parliament with the moderate party's grievances but found himself left behind by events as the Army and the Independents effected a coup. Harley was accused of favouring the king and when Parliament was purged by Col Pride, Sir Robert and his son Edward (qv, d.1700) were ejected and imprisoned. He retired in dejection, distrusted by both sides, and retired to his Brampton Bryan estate where he died on 6 November 1656.

Harley, Robert (1661-1724), 1st Earl of Oxford and Earl Mortimer, was born in London on 5 December 1661, the eldest son of Sir Edward (d.1700, qv) and his second wife. He married Elizabeth Foley (d.1691) (qv Paul Foley, d.1699) of Great Witley, and they lived at Brampton Bryan where they raised four children. After her death he married Sarah Middleton (d.1737). In 1689 he was returned Whig MP for Tregony, Cornwall and the next year for New Radnor. He helped plan the Hanoverian succession. The Whigs were a spent force under Queen Anne and Harley crossed to the Tories. He was Speaker of the Commons from 1701-1705, Lord Treasurer and Chief Minister. In 1711 he was created Earl of Oxford and Earl Mortimer (his grandfather had bought the old Mortimer seat of Wigmore). He launched the notorious South Sea Company to repay the national debt. On the accession of George I, Harley retired to Herefordshire and his many enemies in the House contrived to have him impeached for high treason and he was imprisoned in the Tower of London for two years until charges were dropped. He employed Defoe (qv) and Swift to write pamphlets in support of the administration. He was a patron of writers of the age such as Pope (qv) and collected manuscripts, amassing a famous library which was inherited by his son Edward (qv, d.1741) and later sold to the British Museum as the Harleian collection. He died in London on 21 May 1724 and was buried at Brampton Bryan.

Harley, Robert (1838-1910) succeeded his father Alfred (qv) as 7th Earl of Oxford and married Lady Elizabeth of Devonshire, and their son Alexander (1865-1930) succeeded in his turn as 8th Earl. Alexander married Anne Marie Johnson, daughter of the Duke of Stafford, changed his name to Hartley and moved to Chile, where he started a business. Their sons were George, Edward and Philip. George Hartley, who succeeded as 9th Earl of Oxford and Earl Mortimer, then moved to Peru, where he married Raquel de Gamio y Romaña.

Harley, Thomas (1543-1631), of Brampton Bryan Castle, married Margaret, daughter of Sir Andrew Corbet of Moreton Corbet, Shropshire. He met Dr Dee (qv) on his visit to Herefordshire in 1574 and showed him the ruins of Wigmore Abbey and the abbey records. He was Sheriff of Herefordshire in 1604. Robert (qv, d.1656) was their sole surviving son.

Harley, Thomas (1667-1738) was born at Kinsham Court, the son of Thomas Harley, who was a son of Sir Edward (qv, d.1700) and Abigail Stephens. He was a life-long supporter of his cousin Robert Harley (qv, d.1724), with whose aid he was elected Tory MP for Radnor in 1698. He lost his seat under George I, however, and was briefly imprisoned. He was Deputy Lieutenant of Herefordshire in 1694 and retired to Kinsham Court where he died in 1738, leaving it to his cousin's son Edward (qv, d.1741).

Harley, Thomas (1730-1804), third son of the 3rd Earl (Edward Harley, qv, d.1755), was a wine merchant in the City of London and MP for London. He spoke in the House against the Cider Tax, which was finally repealed through the agency of his family's rival, Velters Cornewall (qv, d.1768). He grew wealthy as a banker and as a government contractor supplying pay and clothing to the British Army in America. In 1752 he married Anne (d.1798), eldest daughter of Edward Bangham, who further increased his fortune. When Lord Mayor of London in 1767 he quelled serious rioting and was sworn of the Privy Council. In 1776-1801 he was MP for Herefordshire and held offices in Leominster, Shrewsbury and Radnorshire. He bought the Berrington estate near Leominster from the Cornewall (qv) family in 1775, including Eye Court. He commissioned Capability Brown (qv) to lay out the park at Berrington and Brown's son-in-law Henry Holland (qv) to build him the striking neo-classical mansion Berrington Hall (1778-81). Harley, now short of money, had to sell farms through his agent James Crummer (qv), some to James Watt (qv). In 1781 his daughter Anne married George, son of Admiral Lord Rodney (qv), and when Harley died at Berrington Hall on 1 December 1804 Anne, now Rodney's widow, and their son inherited Berrington.

Harold de Ewyas, see **de Ewyas, Harold**

Harold II (1022-66), Harold Godwinson, King of England, was the second son of Godwin (qv) the powerful Earl of Wessex and Gytha his wife. He had some five children with his handfast (i.e. common law) wife, the rich and beautiful Edith 'Swan-neck' (*Swann Hnesce*, 'the gentle swan'). It was Edith who recognised Harold's body on Senlac field. Harold, with his cousin Beorn Estrithson, absorbed his brother Swein's (qv) earldom of Herefordshire when Swein was exiled and became the senior family member as his father's influence waned. Harold's sister Edith (qv, d.1075) had married Edward the Confessor (qv) and the Godwin family effectively controlled the king. When things turned against them briefly they were exiled and Edith placed in a nunnery; but by 1052 they were back in power with Edith again queen. For 13 years Harold was *de facto* ruler of England, becoming extremely rich with his brothers all earls. He had extensive estates, with Herefordshire now the focus of his power; he was later found to be holding much of the Bishop of Hereford's lands. When in 1055 Gruffydd ap Llywelyn and Ælfgar (qqv) raided Herefordshire, burning Leominster and Hereford, Harold reorganised the defences, rebuilding the walls and castle at Hereford and those at Huntington, Ewyas Harold and Longtown. He made his warlike chaplain, Leofgar (qv), Bishop of Hereford and with his brothers co-ordinated a punitive attack on Wales from land and sea. The Domesday Book says there were 27 men in Hereford who owed him burgess duties. Harold fell into the hands of Duke William of Normandy after a shipwreck and it seems he swore fealty to him as King Edward's successor, as shown on the Bayeux Tapestry. On returning home Harold took another Edith (qv, d.after 1066), widow of Gruffydd ap Llywelyn (qv), as his lawful wife and they may have had a son, Harold Haroldson. On Edward's death in January 1066 Harold was acclaimed king by the Witan and anointed, despite his oath and there being a prince of the royal blood available, Edgar Ætheling. Harold had several challenges during his 10-month reign. Harald Hardrada, King of Norway, with Tostig, Harold's disgruntled brother invaded and were beaten at Stamford Bridge. Then came Harold's nemesis Duke William with his famous victory near Hastings, which left Harold and his brothers Leofwine and Gyrth dead. Harold's body is said to have been taken by Edith to his beloved abbey of Waltham Cross where a minor cult grew up. During Harold's reign the names of ten moneyers are recorded at Hereford: Ægelric, Ælfwig, Eadwig, Earnwi, Edric, Edwi, Leofnoth, Ordric, Raedulf and Wulfwine. His image is seen on the coins he minted and on the Bayeux Tapestry, which calls him Harold Rex Anglorum.

Harris, Charles (1865-1936), rector of Colwall 1909-29, wrote the music to J.S. Arkwright's (qv) *The Supreme Sacrifice* ('O Valiant Hearts') in commemoration of his son, killed in Mesopotamia in 1917. It was originally set to a traditional tune by Vaughan Williams (qv) but Revd Dr Harris's has subsequently proved the favourite.

Harris, John (d.1738) was Dean of Hereford 1729-36 while Dr Henry Egerton (qv) was bishop. He was from Pembrokeshire and educated at Jesus College, Oxford and a fellow of Oriel. He graduated DD in 1728. He was made Dean of Hereford and Bishop of Llandaff as were the two previous deans (John Tyler and Clavering) to give him an adequate income. Dr Harris resigned both in 1736 when he became Dean of Wells.

Harris, Renatus (*c.*1652-1724), organ builder, was born in Brittany the son of Thomas Harris, organ builder, a recusant Catholic in exile during the Commonwealth. They returned to Britain with the Restoration and found much work in the music-starved cathedrals of England. Renatus married and had many sons and daughters. He was a skilled and inventive craftsman who built 17 organs and restored 14 or so others. There was great rivalry with the Protestant organ builder Bernard Smith, and Harris, a skilled and inventive instrument builder, was a litigious man. Dean Thomas Hodges (qv) raised funds for Hereford's Harris organ, assisted by a gift from Charles II, said to mark his affection for Nell Gwynne (qv). It stood on the pulpitum, the crossing wall that divided the chancel from the nave. Harris was called back to Hereford in 1707 for repairs and the organ was maintained by the Harris family throughout the 18th century. Later improvements were made when Samuel Sebastian Wesley (qv) became organist at the cathedral in 1832. In 1841 the cathedral tower was found to be structurally unsound and pulpitum and organ below were dismantled. The organ that replaced it, by Henry Willis (qv), includes some of Harris's original gilded pipes and a carved lion from the royal arms. Harris lived and died in Bristol where he was buried in September 1724.

Harry, John ap (d.1420), of Poston Court, Vowchurch, MP, was the son of Henry ap John ap William of Oldcourt (d.before 1377) and Eva, daughter of Ievan ap Rhys ap Ievan of Elfael, Radnorshire. He married (before 1399) Elizabeth (d.1420), daughter and co-heir of Sir Hugh Waterton (qv) of Eaton Tregoz and they had two sons, Hugh and Richard. Like his father-in-law, he was a servant of Henry Bolingbroke, and after Bolingbroke's usurpation as Henry IV (qv) he, Waterton and other Marches servants of Lancaster flourished – safe hands in a troubled area. He fought with the English against Glyn Dŵr's rising, although his brothers Thomas and Gruffydd (*c.*1370-after 1404) of Newcourt, Bacton joined with the rebels. He was made Sheriff of Herefordshire 1399-1400, and MP for Herefordshire 1406, '07 and '19. He was escheator for Herefordshire and the Marches and a circuit justice. Through the Glyn Dŵr uprising John, with his associate Sir John Oldcastle (qv), the future heretic and his kinsman and neighbour, garrisoned Clifford Castle for the English and other Mortimer castles across the border. While Oldcastle was on the run he secretly collected his rents for him, despite being bound over not to succour him; many of the king's servants in west Herefordshire were secret Lollards. He was involved in the arrest of Walter Brut (qv) and his adherents although he was a kinsman by marriage. He put down a local uprising by Richard de la Bere (qv under Kynard de la Bere) in 1414 and the next year followed the king to France with a band of Herefordshire bowmen and fought at Agincourt and in subsequent campaigns. On his return he stood surety for a Sir John Mortimer who was a prisoner in the Tower. This Mortimer escaped but was caught and executed, but is not otherwise identified. John ap Harry held lands in the Golden Valley at Vowchurch, Turnastone and Oldcourt and an interest in the lands of Edmund (IV) Mortimer, Earl of March (qv), during his minority. After Edmund's defection to Glyn Dŵr he was granted some of his confiscated lands.

Hartree, John (1869-1948), architect, lived at Eign Croft, an Arts and Crafts house on Vineyard Road, Hereford which he built himself. He worked with John Nicholson (qv) on Holy Trinity Church, Whitecross Road and restored many other Herefordshire churches and built the Old Vicarage at Eardisland.

Harvey, Christopher (1597-1663), clergyman, was from Bunbury, Cheshire where his father had been headmaster. After his father's death the family moved to Brampton Bryan and Christopher was sent to Brasenose College where there were bursaries for Herefordshire scholars.

He was ordained and worked in Whitney parish where he attracted the patronage of the Whitney (qv) family: Sir Robert appointed him headmaster of Lady Hawkins (qv) Grammar School at Kington, rector of Whitney in 1632 and vicar of Clifton-on-Dunsmore in Warwickshire. He was a published poet and one of his verses was included in his friend Izaak Walton's *Compleat Angler*.

Harvey, Joseph (fl.1670-85) was headmaster of Hereford Cathedral School, rector of Weston-under-Penyard and a prebend and chancellor of the cathedral. He was appointed after the previous head, Mr Wakefield, resigned, being unable to take communion as the dean instructed. Harvey married William Brome's (qv) sister. In 1716 Brome, too, was ejected from his offices and cure, unable to swear allegiance to William III, declaring himself and Harvey nonjurors. He was succeeded by Thomas Bisse (qv).

Hastings, Selina (1707-91), countess of Huntingdon, was born on 24 August 1707 at Ashby de la Zouch, Leics, daughter of Washington Shirley, 2nd Earl Ferrers and Lady Mary Levinge. In 1728 she married Theophilus Hastings, 9th Earl of Huntingdon. She became a Methodist in 1738, joining with John Wesley and George Whitefield (qqv) in the revivalist movement. Like Wesley she would have preferred to stay within the Anglican church but this became impossible and she joined with dissenters, founding the Countess of Huntingdon's Connexion chapels all over the country, such as that at Kenchester. She dedicated all she had to evangelical and anti-slavery causes. After her death in London on 17 June 1791 her chapels tended to associate with Congregationalist communities. She was buried in Bunhill Fields in London.

Hatton, Brian (1887-1916), artist, was born at Carlton Villas, Whitecross Road, Hereford on 12 August 1887, the son of Amelia and Alfred with two sisters Ailsa Marr (b.1893) and Marjorie (b.1895). The family claimed descent from Sir Christopher Hatton the Elizabethan financier. They moved to Mount Craig, Broomy Hill, Breinton when Brian was 8 and already a prolific artist, and he painted the Warham landscape. He was frail, subject to asthma and epilepsy, and was sent to live with his doctor's relations at Swansea for his health. He won competitions from an early age and was praised by royalty and artists like G.F. Watts (qv). Watts and his wife met Brian and his mother several times and were encouraging and supportive. After leaving school Hatton spent a year at Trinity College, Oxford but dreaming of being an artist he went to train at a Scottish art school. Returning to Hereford he set up a studio in the coach house at Mount Craig and painted portraits of family and local people like Bishop Percival (qv). In 1908 he sketched in Egypt with Sir Petrie Flinders' archaeological expedition and in 1910 studied in Paris at the Académie Julian. Hatton shared a studio in London and concentrated on portraits. By 1914 he had work accepted at the Royal Academy Summer Exhibition, was nominated for the Royal Institute of Oil Painters and commissioned to illustrate Masefield's (qv) *The Everlasting Mercy*, staying with a relative in Ledbury for local colour. With the First World War Hatton joined the

Worcester Yeomanry and married his Hereford sweetheart Lydia May Bidmead, Biddy, a dancer. She went to live with his family in Mount Craig and gave birth to their daughter Mary Amelia in 1915 just before he was posted as a signaller to Egypt, where he was killed in action on Easter Monday 23 April 1916. In his brief life as an artist Hatton produced over 1,000 works: watercolours, oils, drawings, prints. Brilliantly precocious as a child, Watts thought he would develop into the greatest artist of his generation. His portraits were remarkable but his passion was for horses and scenes of country life like *Duck Shooting on the Lugg*. The bulk of Hatton's work was presented to Hereford Museum by his widow and his sister Marjorie devoted her life to its care, being instrumental in setting up the Brian Hatton Gallery in Churchill Gardens, Hereford. Although this has since closed, Hatton's work is on show at Hereford City Art Gallery. His widow lived on in Hereford, marrying another Hereford man, Angus Wilson, in 1930, and eventually moving to America with her daughter, Mary Hatton, who became a famous ballet dancer.

Havergal, Francis Tebbs (1829-90), cleric and author, was born on 27 August 1829, the youngest son of the six children of William Havergal, rector of Astley. He was educated at New College, Oxford and deeply influenced by Tractarianism. He married Isabel, daughter of Colonel William Martin, to whom he was introduced by his colleague Sir Frederick Ouseley (qv). He was a vicar choral at Hereford from 1853 and vicar of Pipe and Lyde from 1861 to 1874, in which year they moved to Upton Bishop, where he wrote *Records Historical and Antiquarian of Upton Bishop* (1883) and they brought up their five children; Isabel's parents moved nearby. Bishop Atlay (qv) called their eldest, Bertha, 'the best curate in Herefordshire'. His twin sons Ethelbert and William were educated at the Cathedral School. He was a patron of architects: Kempson made extensive renovations to St Peter's, Hereford and Chick built the attractive rectory at Pipe and Lyde for him; and at Upton Bishop, George Haddon (qv) rebuilt his vicarage. He designed the pulpit and reading desk at Much Marcle Church for Robert Clarke (qv) to make. He held Colwall prebend and was the deputy, and effective, librarian of the cathedral library under the master, Lord Saye and Sele (qv Fiennes). He studied the antiquities of the cathedral and published books on it

and its music and on aspects of Herefordshire life such as *Herefordshire Words and Phrases* and *Memorials of the Rev Sir Frederick Arthur Gore Ouseley* (1889). When the Becket (qv) casket was returned to the cathedral, it was Havergal's learning and connoisseurship that confirmed its authenticity. He was editor of the Mappa Mundi facsimile project (1869) and a noted folklorist. His sister Frances Ridley Havergal (1836-79), poet and hymn writer, often stayed with the family and gave a watercolour by Turner (qv) of the cathedral to the Dean and Chapter. On her death her brother presented a bell to Upton Bishop Church that still rings to her memory. New College made him DD towards the end of his life. Revd Havergal died on 27 July 1890 and is buried at Upton Bishop.

Hawes, Richard (1603-68), clergyman, was born in Suffolk and educated at Corpus Christi College, Cambridge. He was vicar of Humber from 1627 to 1636, then of Kenderchurch and Llangua, marrying a local girl. In the 1640s he had a Puritan conversion and was imprisoned and abused by the Royalist garrison of Hereford, but was freed when Birch (qv) became governor. Sir Edward Harley (qv, d.1700) gave him the living of Leintwardine and he became well known as a preacher, impressing Herbert Croft (qv). At the Restoration Sir Henry Lingen (qv) prosecuted him but Lingen died and charges were dropped. Hawes was unable to conform to the restored church and was ejected from his living, although Bishop Croft was sympathetic to him. He lived with his daughter Grace and her husband Nicholas Billingsley, who was vicar of Weobley, from 1657 and then was a teacher at Abergavenny. The family finally moved to Awre in Gloucestershire where Hawes died in December 1668. The bishops of these dioceses recognised Hawes' skills and allowed him to preach.

Hawker, Mary Elizabeth (1848-1908) (pseudonym Lanoe Falconer), writer, was the daughter of Major Peter William Lanoe Hawker. The family lived abroad and Mary first wrote for their entertainment but then began to have work published. On returning to England she had success with sensational romances such as *Mademoiselle Ixe* (1890), *Cecilia de Noël* and collections of short stories. She contracted consumption and retired to her sister's house Broxwood Court, near Pembridge, where, in 1908, she died. She is buried at St Michael's, Lyonshall.

Hawkins, Margaret (*c.*1550-1619) was the daughter of Charles Vaughan (qv Vaughan family) of Hergest Court. She was a Lady of the Bedchamber to Queen Elizabeth (qv) and a friend of Blanche Parry (qv). In 1591 she married the naval commander Sir John Hawkins (1532-95) as his second wife. After his death at sea on Drake's last voyage she had a school built at Kington, the town of her childhood. She lived in St Dunstan's parish in London where she was buried. In her will she left £800 to generate annual income for the grammar school, its master and usher. The rules for the school remain in the cathedral library: boys from Kington, Huntington and Brilley were admitted by entrance exam. John Abel (qv) built the original school for £240 and it opened on 29 September 1630. Its first headmaster was Revd Christopher Harvey (qv). It is still known as Lady Hawkins' School. In 1978 it transferred 260 antiquarian volumes from the school library to Hereford Cathedral's collection.

de la Hay: Lords of Urishay Castle, south of Peterchurch, knights of the shire and magistrates through the Middle Ages and after. The Haye was a royal hunting park stretching from Hereford to the Forest of Dean.

de la Hay, Thomas (d.1440), of Urishay and Arkstone, Kingstone, was MP for Herefordshire in 1413, '23 and '31 and Sheriff of Hereford in 1434. In 1420 he was acting as trustee for the lands of his neighbour John ap Harry (qv). The family were feudal tenants of the Mortimers and in 1398 Thomas's father John de la Hay paid Roger (VII) Mortimer (qv) a fourth of a knight's fee or 25s for Urishay Castle. Thomas fought against Glyn Dŵr alongside neighbours and associates such as Sir John Oldcastle and

John ap Harry (qqv). He stood surety for the latter's attendance at Parliament in 1407 and was a feoffee of his lands at his death. He was involved in affrays against neighbours with a kinsman Thomas de la Hay of Hentland. His eldest son Richard predeceased him; he had married Sir Thomas de la Barre's (qv, d.1420) daughter Margaret. He was survived by his widow Joan and his second son and heir Urian (b.1410).

de la Hay, Thomas (fl.1680s) married Blanche the widow of John Brewster (qv) and they lived at Urishay Castle, then rebuilt as a 17th-century manor house, now ruins.

Hayter, Aaron Upjohn (1799-1873), organist at Hereford Cathedral 1818-20, was born in Dorset and became assistant organist at Salisbury Cathedral. He was appointed organist after the dismissal of the unsatisfactory Charles Dare (qv). Hayter and his brother were implicated in two arson attacks at the college of vicars choral in 1820; there was an outcry in Hereford and he was dismissed. He went on to be organist of Brecon Cathedral, and died in Boston, USA.

Hearne, Thomas (1678-1735) was born at White Waltham, Berks in July 1678 where his father George was parish clerk. He was educated at St Edmund's Hall, Oxford where he developed antiquarian interests and became associated with the Bodleian Library. He had Jacobite sympathies and as a non-juror was debarred from office. He knew and visited the Herefordshire non-jurors William Brewster, William Brome, George Hickes and Richard Rawlinson (qqv), but was scathing about Bishop Henry Egerton (qv). He died on 10 June 1735.

Hearne, Thomas (1744-1817), artist and antiquary, was born in Gloucestershire and grew up near Malmesbury in Wiltshire. He was apprenticed to his uncle who was a pastry cook in London but was inspired by the prints in a nearby shop to become an artist. His skill attracted the support of Sir George Beaumont (Constable's patron). He recorded life in the Leeward Islands and travelled widely in

Britain, often accompanied by George Beaumont, painting in Herefordshire and elsewhere, and publishing the results in *The Antiquities of Great Britain* (1778-1806) engraved by William Byrne. This sold well and Hearne was elected to the Society of Antiquaries in 1793. He illustrated popular books of the period. Like Constable he was ambitious that landscape painting be the equal of history painting in the hierarchy of the arts. R.P. Knight (qv) commissioned him to record his Downton estate and from 1784 to 1786 he produced 12 watercolour studies to illustrate his ideas of the picturesque and painted *An Iron Work at Downton* (1798). George Cornewall (qv, d.1819) commissioned watercolour views of Moccas Park and he made paintings and aquatints of Herefordshire scenes including *Goodrich Castle on the Wye* of 1794 and a view of Mordiford that shows the Mordiford Dragon (qv Garson) on the gable of Holy Rood Church. His painting of Hereford Cathedral with the west front down (1786) is in Hereford Museum and Art Gallery's collection as is his drawing of Snodhill Castle near Peterchurch. His drawing *The Remains of the Chapter House of Hereford Cathedral* (1784) suggests the form of that debated structure. He went out of fashion and became poor but continued to receive Beaumont's support. He died, unmarried, on 13 April

1817 in Soho, London. His work is represented in the V&A, in private collections and in Hereford City Art Gallery.

Heath, Charles (1761-1830), printer, writer and radical, was born at Hurcott near Kidderminster, apprenticed printer in Nottingham and set up his press in Monmouth. He wrote and printed various books of history and topography including the guide *Excursion down the Wye*, a copy of which he presented to Nelson (qv) on his visit to Monmouth in 1801. He was a correspondent of Coleridge (qv) who consulted him about his plans to found a community in America. Heath was twice mayor of Monmouth. He was buried in St Mary's, Monmouth.

Heather, Charles (d.1845), architect-builder, was John Nash's (qv) assistant at Garnstone Castle (qv Peploe) and builder of Robert Smirke's (qv) Shire Hall. He rebuilt the Old Rectory at Withington (1827) and added the gothic porch to St Peter's Church, Hereford (1831) and restored St Mary, Much Cowarne.. He built the Alcove on Castle Green as a house for the constable of the green, which can still be seen although the once open arcade is now filled in. He probably also built The Fosse (*c.*1840), the *cottage ornée* that overlooks Castle Pool. He was county surveyor in 1825 and succeeded John Gethin (qv) as surveyor of bridges from 1831, which involved much work for poor remuneration. Hereford had no livestock market, cattle being sold in the streets in increasingly insanitary conditions, and there were outbreaks of typhoid fever (qv Curley). Heather owned land on the Portfield in Hereford where in 1812 he built himself a villa. He sold the land to Hereford Corporation which built the Municipal Livestock Market on the site, opened to the public on 17 October 1856. In 1857 his villa became The Old Market Inn on Newmarket Street, more recently Zizzi.

Hedley, John Cuthbert (1837-1915), Roman Catholic Bishop of Newport, was a doctor's son from Northumberland, born on 15 April 1837. He studied and taught at the Benedictine community at Ampleforth and was ordained priest. He later became a professor at Belmont Abbey, the house of studies and novitiate for English Benedictines, where he taught philosophy and theology from 1862-81. He was appointed Bishop of Newport at Cardiff where he died on 11 November 1915.

Helyon, Walter de (*c.*1318- after 1357), franklin, son of Hugh de Helyon, was the Audleys' (qv Hugh Audley) franklin at Much Marcle and lived at Hellens, the manor house later named after him. He is said to have travelled to the Holy Land and returned with medical knowledge previously unknown in Herefordshire. He married Agnes Welsh and they had a daughter, Joan. There is a wooden funeral effigy of Walter in St Bartholomew's Church, with accurately depicted clothing: a tight, closely buttoned tunic, wallet and sword with hair and beard cut short.

Henry I (1068-1135), called Beauclerc, King of England 1100-35, was born at Selby in 1070, the youngest son of the Conqueror, succeeding his brother William II in 1100. He built the great Benedictine abbey of Reading as his memorial, lavishing money on it through his life. To fund it he refounded Leominster Priory as a daughter house, with its prior subordinate to the abbot of Reading. Reading's annual revenues from Leominster were initially £666 19s

8d. Leominster's first prior was Hugh who, in 1123, received the Confirmation Charter from Richard de Capella (qv), Bishop of Hereford. Henry corrected William II's abuses by filling vacant bishoprics and reforming the exchequer. He granted a nine-day fair at St Ethelbert's (qv) tide to Hereford, the tolls going to the bishop. His son William was drowned when the *White Ship* sank in 1120. Henry died on 1 December 1135 and was buried at Reading Abbey.

Henry II (1133-89), King of England 1154-89, called Curtmantel and Fitz-Empress, was born on 5 March 1133, the son of Matilda the Empress (as she had been married to the Holy Roman Emperor) and Geoffrey of Anjou. His accession was agreed after Stephen and Matilda had fought themselves to a stalemate through a decade of anarchy. He was the first ruler of the Angevin dynasty, known as Plantagenet from the broom sprig (or *planta genista*) his father wore in his cap. He married Eleanor of Aquitaine, the divorced wife of Louis the French king, and they had eight children. His heir, Henry, was crowned during his lifetime in the Capetian fashion but he predeceased his father and his next son, Richard the Lionheart, succeeded him. Henry's sons were unruly and Eleanor, who tended to support their rebellions, spent much of her life under house arrest while Henry consorted with mistresses including Rosamund Clifford (qv). Henry was reported to be an exhaustingly active man, well educated in law and languages, and had a good memory. He was stubborn, with a furious temper, and often at odds with his wife, his children and, famously, his archbishop Thomas Becket (qv), for whose murder he accepted responsibility. Henry was often at Hereford Castle, with Hereford his base in the Marches; it saw constant activity and increased importance. He confirmed Hereford's charter and allowed it a guild of merchants and a corporation. He granted Leominster a fair in 1170. His policy toward Rhys ap Gruffydd (qv) the strong Prince of Deheubarth was initially to support his Marcher lords, the Cliffords, Scudamores and Mortimers (qqv) in order to contain him but later, fearing their strength, he found it politic to support Rhys as a balance. He died on 6 July 1189 and was buried with his queen in Fontevraud Abbey.

Henry III (1207-72), King of England 1216-72, was born on 1 October 1207 at Winchester, the eldest son of King John (qv) and Queen Isabella of Angoulême. Succeeding to the throne aged 9, he was crowned at Gloucester and the realm was governed during his minority by a regency council headed by William Marshal (qv). Magna Carta was reissued in revised and expanded form at this time in order to appease the barons. This more important second edition of November 1217 was sent out to important centres including Hereford. It can be seen in the cathedral archives with the letter instructing the Sheriff of Hereford how it was to be promulgated in the shire by 12 knights. This version of the great charter became statute law in 1297. It guaranteed liberty to the individual from arbitrary interference and to trial by his peers according to the laws of the land. Henry was a regular visitor to Hereford, maintaining his father's castle and in 1240 adding massive works including the high stone tower within a wall

with ten turrets that was to be Hereford's trademark for five centuries, as shown by Speed (qv) in 1606. Henry also built royal apartments with painted walls in the bailey and a new chapel. He was present in Hereford early in his reign when he dealt with the incursions of Llywelyn ab Iorwerth (qv) and chastised Richard Marshal (qv), besieging the castles at Hay and Ewyas which the Marshals had occupied. (The siege began under William (II) Marshal and ended under Richard.) He came to Hereford on 23 March 1227 and granted citizens the right to hold an autumn fair at St Denis' tide, 9 October. Henry visited the bishop in his palace on the Prospect at Ross in 1236 and 1252. In 1236 he married 12-year-old Eleanor of Provence and in her train came many Savoyard kinsmen and dependents, some of whom, like Peter de Aquablanca (qv), were found offices in Hereford Cathedral. In 1264 Henry renounced his agreements with the barons, causing them to rise in rebellion. At the subsequent Battle of Lewes he and Prince Edward (qv Edward I) were captured by Simon de Montfort (qv), ending up finally at Hereford Castle. Edward escaped by a ruse, promising to release the king, but Henry was still a prisoner of Montfort's when the latter was killed at the Battle of Evesham. The old king was preoccupied with completing Westminster Abbey in his last years, including a splendid shrine to his patron saint St Edward the Confessor (qv), but he was becoming increasingly senile. At his death his body was buried at the high altar of Westminster Abbey; amongst the mourners was the elderly Humphrey (IV) de Bohun (qv), 2nd Earl of Hereford.

Henry IV (1367-1413), King of England 1399-1413, the only son of the dynast John of Gaunt (qv), was born in Bolingbroke Castle, Lincolnshire and was heir to his Lancaster estates. He was Earl of Derby in his own right and was the cousin and childhood playmate of Richard II (qv). He married Mary (d.1394), second daughter and co-heir of Humphrey (IX) de Bohun (qv), 7th Earl of Hereford, and assumed the earldom and the Bohun estates in Herefordshire. Henry joined the Lords Appellant rebellion against Richard in 1387 but later, with his father John of Gaunt, helped the king to reassert himself and was created Duke of Hereford. Henry was involved in accusations of treachery for which Richard exiled him and, on the death of John of Gaunt, confiscated his

estates. In 1399 Henry returned, ostensibly to recover his own, crossing Herefordshire that August with his army and capturing Richard in Conwy Castle. Richard was induced to abdicate and Henry declared himself king. Almost at once Glyn Dŵr's (qv) rebellion broke out, threatening his Herefordshire estates. Henry dealt with it initially through the Mortimers, the Percies and his son Henry of Monmouth, from bases in Shrewsbury and Hereford. When Edmund (IV) Mortimer (qv) was captured by Glyn Dŵr he and Harry Percy joined with the Welsh prince with the aim of dividing the country between them, but they were eventually defeated. During Henry's reign the movement for reform in the Church known as Lollardy became particularly strong in Herefordshire, Sir John Oldcastle's (qv) home. With Henry ill at the end of his life, his sons Henry and Thomas the Duke of Clarence took on the government. Henry died on 20 March 1413 and was buried in Canterbury Cathedral. His reign has been praised for increasing constitutionalism, the flourishing of poets such as John Gower and Sir Thomas Clanvowe (qv) of Herefordshire, and a growing use of English. Henry's will was written in English and he owned an English Bible.

Henry V (1386-1422), King of England 1413-22, was the eldest son of Henry Bolingbroke (qv Henry IV) and his first wife, Mary de Bohun (qv Humphrey (IX) de Bohun). He was known as Henry of Monmouth because of his birth in the gatehouse tower of Monmouth Castle (then within Hereford county) and was created Prince of Wales. After his mother's death he and his brothers were brought up by his grandmother Joan de Bohun, the Countess of Hereford at the Courtfield (then known as Greenfield), Welsh Bicknor. His nurse, Joan Waryn, was allowed an annual pension of £20 for life. When Glyn Dŵr (qv) rebelled, Prince Henry led the opposition from Hereford. He introduced efficiency into royal government and was known to favour reform in the Church, associating with the leading Lollard Sir John Oldcastle (qv) – Shakespeare's Falstaff. By the time his father died in 1413 Henry was an experienced ruler and soldier. He thwarted a plot to replace him with Edmund (V) Mortimer (qv) and asserted his rights to the French throne. His victory at Agincourt led to a brilliant campaign in France and, with English forces at the gates of Paris, the Treaty of Troyes in 1420. This gave Henry the hand of Catherine de Valois, daughter of the French King Charles VI, and recognised their future children as monarchs of France. On his return to England Catherine was crowned queen and they toured England, staying en route at Hereford. Henry returned to France to complete his pacification but died of dysentery on 31 August 1422 without having seen his baby son, Henry VI, the future King of England and France.

Henry VII (1457-1509), was born at Pembroke Castle on 28 January 1457, the son of Edmund Tudor, 1st Earl of Richmond (*c.*1430-56) and Margaret Beaufort (1443-1509), a great-great-granddaughter of Edward III (qv). His paternal grandparents were Owen Tudor (qv) and Catherine de Valois, widow of Henry V (qv). When Edward IV (qv) usurped the throne in 1461 he placed Henry in the wardship of the Herberts of Raglan Castle. William Herbert (qv) was executed after the Battle of Edgecote when Henry was 12 and he was taken by Herbert's widow to live in Weobley Castle with her Devereux kin (qv Walter Devereux, d.1485). At Henry VI's brief readeption Henry stayed with his uncle Jasper in Pembroke Castle but on Edward's return they had to seek asylum in Brittany. Henry was now the chief Lancastrian claimant to the throne and challenged Edward's brother Richard for the crown at Bosworth Field in 1485. His marriage to Elizabeth of York, also a descendant of John of Gaunt, united the antagonists of the Wars of the Roses, founding the stable Tudor dynasty. His sons and grandchildren showed the vigour and golden-red hair of their York inheritance. In 1486 Henry toured his kingdom, checking rebellions and showing himself. He visited Hereford, where he was received with a pageant; he stayed in the dilapidated Hereford Castle and renewed his acquaintance with Weobley. In the following year die-hard Yorkists declared the 10-year-old

Lambert Simnel king and raised an army which was beaten at the Battle of Stoke. James Baskerville (qv, d.1494) of Eardisley Castle, fought for Henry and was afterwards created knight banneret. Another insurrection was raised by Perkin Warbeck, who claimed to be Richard, the younger of the Princes in the Tower. Henry died at Richmond on 21 April 1509.

Henry VIII (1491-1547), second son of Henry VII, visited Hereford in 1528, where he was greeted by Dean Frowcester (qv). He presented the King's Steel or Mourning Sword to the city in memory of his great-grandfather Owen Tudor (qv) who was executed there, a sword that had been recovered from the site of the Battle of Mortimers Cross. It is housed in the town hall vaults and carried in procession in Hereford on the death of a reigning monarch or the death of a mayor in office.

Henson, Herbert Hensley (1863-1947), Bishop of Hereford 1918-20, was from a Plymouth Brethren family in Kent. Despite his father's disapproval of education he won a fellowship to All Souls, Oxford and made his mark as an erudite historian. He was ordained and married Isabella Denistoun. He was known for his preaching and work amongst the poor of London as vicar of Barking, then became Dean of Durham in 1912 and in 1917 was nominated Bishop of Hereford by Lloyd George, against church advice. Resignations were threatened and the *Church Times* under the editorship of E.H. Day (qv) ran a fierce but unsuccessful campaign against him as a liberal who, it was alleged, didn't believe in the Virgin birth or the Resurrection. Bishop Henson mollified his Hereford prebendaries and his archbishop and refrained from controversy to focus on his pastoral duties. He was a fine scholar and published many books including his memoirs *Retrospect of an Unimportant Life*. In 1920 he became Bishop of Durham. He retired in 1941 and died at his Suffolk home on 27 September 1947.

Herbert, George (1825-94), Dean of Hereford 1867-94, was born on 25 November 1825 the son of Edward Clive (later Herbert), 2nd Earl of Powis, and Lady Lucy Graham. The Herberts were an old Marches family. He was educated at Eton and St John's, Cambridge and married Elizabeth, daughter of Sir Tatton Sykes. He was vicar of Clun and, in 1867, Dean of Hereford in succession to Richard Dawes (qv). With Bishop Atlay (qv) he reigned over a long period of quiet at the cathedral with the return of regular services after Scott's (qv) restoration. After his death on 15 March 1894 a large stained glass memorial was commissioned from C.E. Kempe (qv) in his memory for the south transept window, which depicts the company of saints praising God, amongst them locals Dubricius, Ethelbert and Thomas Cantilupe (qqv). He is buried in the lady arbour beside Elizabeth his wife, who had died in 1883.

Herbert, William (*c.*1423-69), 1st Earl of Pembroke, was the son of Sir William ap Thomas (d.1445) of Raglan and Gwladus (d.1454), daughter of Dafydd Gam (d.1415) and widow of Roger Vaughan (qv, d.1415) of Bredwardine. He assumed the noble name Herbert and married Walter Devereux's (qv, d.1459) daughter Anne in 1449. He was an anarchic force in Herefordshire and Wales and was imprisoned for a time in the Tower of London. In 1456 he, his brother-in-law Walter

Devereux (qv, d.1485) and the Vaughan brothers (qv) led 2,000 men of Herefordshire to capture Carmarthen and Aberystwyth Castles for York, imprisoning Henry VI's half brother Edmund Tudor. Their lawlessness brought Henry VI with Queen Margaret to Hereford to try them in person. The Yorkist success at Mortimers Cross in 1461 restored them to power, however, and under Edward IV Herbert and Devereux represented Herefordshire in Parliament. He accumulated honours, was created KG in 1462 and became virtual master of Wales. Warwick, now supporting the Lancastrians, captured him and his brother Richard at the Battle of Edgecote on 26 July 1469 and they were executed and buried at Tintern Abbey. His widow Anne retired to her brother Walter Devereux's manor at Weobley, where they were able to give refuge to the young Henry Tudor, later Henry VII (qv). Herbert's eldest son, William the 2nd Earl, lacked his father's forcefulness and at his death on 16 July 1490 the Herbert empire had collapsed and the earldom in this creation became extinct. His daughter Margaret married Thomas Talbot, 2nd Viscount Lisle (qv under John Talbot, d.1453).

Hereford: The Herefords have lived at Sufton near Mordiford from 1140 to the present day. By tradition they held it of the king for the fee of a pair of gilt spurs to be paid every time the monarch crossed Mordiford Bridge. The Herefords were known Lollards in the 14th and 15th centuries. Old Sufton, the half-timbered 16th-century house, the original home of the Herefords, still stands, with Wyatt's Sufton Court, where they live now, to the south.

Hereford, Bertha de (b.*c*.1130) or Bertha de Pitres, married William (II) de Briouze (qv) and conveyed her father's (Miles of Gloucester, qv under 'Miles') castles on the Marches (such as Hay) into Briouze ownership.

Hereford, Henry fitz Miles de, son of Miles of Gloucester (qv under Miles), Baron Abergavenny in 1141, died 12 April 1165.

Hereford, James (1713-86) commissioned James Wyatt (qv) to build Sufton Court, a Palladian mansion, on his estate at Mordiford in 1788. Wyatt designed the interiors; the finest that survives being the music room. Sufton Park, the picturesque parkland overlooking the rivers Wye and Lugg, was laid out by Repton (qv), who made the most of the house's situation; his *Red Book* of drawings for the scheme survives.

Hereford, James (d.1843) is the subject of a handsome wall tablet by Peter Hollins (qv) in Mordiford Church.

Hereford, Mahel de (d.1164), younger son of Miles of Gloucester (qv, under Miles), was Constable and Lord of Abergavenny from 1163 and attended the Council of Clarendon in 1164. That year Gerald of Wales (qv) says Mahel was killed by a falling stone at Bronllys Castle, Breconshire. Gerald records with relish how Mahel died full of remorse for harassing the Bishop of St David's, Gerald's uncle. He was buried at Llanthony Priory.

Hereford, Nicholas de, son of John of Hereford (1272-1337), Lord of Sufton, and Matilda (d.1362), was born at Old Sufton. In 1363 he married Isabel Helton at Mordiford and they had a son Roger (qv). Nicholas was educated at Oxford, and was a Fellow of Queen's College, a theological scholar and advocate of reform in the Church. He graduated as a doctor of theology in 1382 and was chancellor of the University. At Oxford he met John Wycliffe and developed Lollard ideas. Wycliffe and he translated the Bible into English, Nicholas possibly making the greater contribution. His lectures caused tumults in Oxford and he was summoned to London and excommunicated on 1 July 1382. He went to Rome to appeal but was imprisoned there. Escaping, he returned to England where he was again imprisoned, harshly treated and his writings burnt. He recanted and was made chancellor of Hereford (1384). He was required to judge others convicted of Lollardy and he and other prosecuted Lollards were forbidden by the Church to preach Lollard ideas, although there were sympathetic elements at court. In 1417 he retired to Coventry as a Carthusian monk where he died. A copy of his Bible, known as the Cider Bible because of his Herefordian translation of 'strong drink' as 'sidir', is held in the cathedral archive. It is the first complete rendering into English but little known at the time, as possession of the Gospels required a licence for the laity.

Hereford, Roger (1364-1427), Lord of Sufton, son of Nicholas (qv), married Margery Preston and had a son, Thomas.

Hereford, Walter de (d.1160), a younger son of Miles of Gloucester (qv, under 'Miles'), succeeded to the titles and estates but was prevented by the king from using the title of earl. He was Sheriff of Gloucester from 1155 to 1157 and of Hereford 1155-59. Henry II recovered the rest of his Herefordshire manors including Hereford Castle. Walter died in the Holy Land and the family's Marches empire was divided up amongst his heirs:

Hereford, William de, son of Miles of Gloucester (qv, under 'Miles') died before 1160 without issue.

The Herefordshire School of Sculptors were a 12th-century group of craftsmen with a distinctive, intricate and wholly original style, working probably out of Leominster and Hereford. The work of two masters has been recognized: typical features are horizontal, concertina-like folds of dress, long-clawed and beaked birds, distinctive lions, Norman knights struggling in foliage and swooping angels. The origin of their style, nothing similar to which exists in Britain, has been debated. Oliver de Merlimond (qv), who commissioned their early church at Shobdon, had been on pilgrimage to Santiago de Compostela, past the church of Parthenay-le-Vieux in south-west France where there is similar carving. There is further local Celtic and Scandinavian influence. The School's Shobdon Church was pulled down but distinctive work from it was gathered and re-erected as the Shobdon Arches on the hill above (qv Richard Bateman), now a little worn. A cast was taken of their Christ in Majesty for the Great Exhibition of 1851, however, and this is now in the V&A. The same subject appears well preserved on the tympanum at Rowlestone. St David's at Kilpeck shows something of what Shobdon must have been like and remains the School's *chef d'oeuvre*. G.R. Lewis (qv) made engravings of details here before restoration. Other work includes the monumental Virgin and Child (or the Trinity?) on a tympanum at Fownhope and the Castle Frome font with its extraordinary revelation of the baptism of Christ. The tiny Church of St Giles, Pipe Aston has a tympanum by 'the Aston master' also known at Shobdon: an *agnus dei* supported by the symbols of Saints Luke and John, with dragons. Inside is a further piece, now inverted, of a coiled dragon – perhaps a cross base. There are carvings at Bridge Sollers, Brinsop, Eardisley, Orleton, Rowlestone and Stretton Sugwas. There is a tympanum from St Giles' Chapel, St Owen Street, Hereford and small pieces (including Samson and the lion and angels) on the west doorway at Leominster Priory. Capitals by the workshop are preserved in Hereford Cathedral behind the high altar screen. An ivory book cover in the V&A also shows their distinctive style and hints at great versatility.

Hereford white-faced cattle were pre-eminent among British cattle. The breed derived from the small red cattle of Roman Britain mixed with the large Welsh breed once common in the Marches, and they became the draught oxen of the Middle Ages. Lord Scudamore (qv) is known to have brought some red cattle over from the Netherlands in the previous century. The Hereford became one of the world's most important beef cattle. Their stamina is legendary: when a ship carrying a herd of Hereford cattle was torpedoed in 1940 they were able to swim some distance to the Irish shore. They were first exported to North America in 1817 and in 1825 to Australia, where they became dominant. A herd book recording the breeding details was first kept by Thomas Duckham (qv) and is maintained by the Hereford Herd Book Society.

Herl, Andrew (*c.*1354-92), of Allensmore, was a knight of the shire in Richard II's time who married Juliana le Rouse (12 June 1358-*c.*1422) of Duntisbourne, Gloucestershire. They are also known as Herley. Their remarkable memorial in St Andrew's, Allensmore is a floor slab inlaid with their images, of Herefordshire make; other examples of this style are found at Canon Pyon, Dilwyn and Hereford Cathedral. Their clothes are beautifully observed: Juliana's pet dog is at her feet with a bell on his collar; Sir Andrew has a lion. The inscription reads 'Sir Andrew Herl gist ycy et Julian sa femme dieu de lour almes eyt mercy'. Their daughter Alice married John Pauncefoot (qv) whose arms (three lions) are included on the brass. Their own arms show three ducks around a star in coloured inlay. The church vestry was once the Herl (or Herley) family chapel.

Hervey, John was Dean of Hereford (1491-1501) during the episcopate of Bishop Audley (qv). He is remembered in a brass on the south wall of the south-east transept of the cathedral.

Hewins, William Albert Samuel (1865-1931), economist and politician, was born on 11 May 1865 near Wolverhampton and educated at Pembroke College, Oxford, where he read mathematics. He considered going into the Church but decided on studying economics and politics. He was elected Unionist MP for Hereford in 1912 with an interest in tariff reform. He became a Roman Catholic in 1914 and married Margaret Slater (d.1940) of Walsall. Lloyd George appointed him Under-Secretary of State for the Colonies in 1917 but his ideas on the Empire and protectionism were seen as wild and in 1918 he was dropped as candidate for Hereford. He detailed his ideas in a lengthy autobiography and wrote books on the future of the Empire. He died in London on 17 November 1931.

Heywood, Thomas (1797-1866), antiquary, was born in Manchester on 3 September 1797 the son of Nathaniel Heywood, a banker. He was educated at Manchester Grammar School and became a partner in his father's bank. In 1823 he married Mary (d.1870) daughter of John Barton of Swinton, Lancashire. After ten years at the bank he retired and in 1828 bought the Hope End estate near Ledbury from Edward Moulton Barrett (qv). Here he and Mary brought up their son and two daughters, the younger of whom was Mary (qv Mary Sumner), founder of the Mothers' Union. Heywood had made an important local history collection which entered Chetham's Library in Manchester, and wrote antiquarian articles. He was High Sheriff of Herefordshire in 1840. He died at Hope End on 20 November 1866 and was buried at Wellington Heath.

Hickes, George (1642-1715), non-juring bishop and scholar, was born in Yorkshire on 20 June 1642. He was educated at Oxford at St John's and Magdalen Colleges and became a Fellow of Lincoln College, Oxford where he was an Anglo-Saxon scholar and philologist of note. He married Frances Marshall (*c.*1633-1714) in 1679. Hickes was a chaplain to Charles II and Dean of Worcester. He was sensitive about his loyalty to the Stuarts as his father had been a supporter of Cromwell and his brother was executed for his part in Monmouth's rebellion. After the ejection of James II, clerics of the Church of England who felt unable to forswear their oaths formed a group of non-juring clergy who were hunted down by William's government. When Hickes was suspended as dean in 1689 he went into hiding and, with others, secretly visited the exiled James II at St Germaine and was appointed bishop by him. On his return, ill and persecuted, Hickes hid in the houses of sympathisers. In Herefordshire, where support was strong for the Stuarts, he and his wife were hidden by Lady Susanna Hopton (qv). He was later to publish a book written by her and, perhaps, Thomas Traherne (qv), and provided a foreword himself. He spent 1697 in William Brome's (qv) Eau Withington house. As the regime became more secure he was allowed freedom to offer pastoral support to the non-juring community and became its leading figure; in 1713 he consecrated more non-juring bishops. Despite illness and proscription he was the greatest Anglo-Saxon scholar of his age, publishing in 1703 his great treatise of comparative philology *Linguarum Veterum Septentrionalium Thesaurus* (Treasury of Northern Languages). In 1714 his wife Frances died and on 15 December 1715 he followed her. They were buried in St Margaret's churchyard, Westminster.

Higgins, Edward (1808-84), was born at Eastnor where the family is recorded for centuries. He was educated at Brasenose College, Oxford, (the college frequently associated with scholars from Herefordshire) and ordained. He married an Eastnor girl, Georgiana Esther Gray. They had a daughter, Ellen Gray (1833-1910), and at this time Revd Higgins bought Bosbury House just north of Bosbury which he rebuilt, laying out gardens round the house and landscaping the park, now restored and often open to the public. Here he lived for 50 years, collecting early printed books, MSS, drawings and engravings. The family were known to Disraeli who refers to Higgins in letters as 'the Squier'. Revd Higgins was JP for Herefordshire and Worcestershire and DL for Herefordshire. Their daughter Ellen Gray married Robert Baskerville Rickards Mynors (qv). Bosbury Church has a monument to Higgins and the stained glass in the east window here (qv Wailes) is dedicated to him.

Higgins, Henry (1817-90), a wealthy industrialist from the north, bought a 200-acre estate at Withington where he built Thinghill or the Withington Tower (architects Speakman and Hickson of Manchester, 1871), a large mansion in a Scottish baronial style, and laid out a park. He was a JP and in 1887 High Sheriff of Herefordshire. The Higgins family sold the estate in 1899, and the house was demolished in 1929. A lodge on the Bromyard Road and a cottage remain.

Higginson, Edmund (1802-71) was born a Barneby (qv), which family owned Brockhampton and Bredenbury. He changed his name when his great-uncle William Higginson left him the Norton Farm Estate with old Salt Marsh House, north of Bromyard, shown on Taylor's (qv) map of 1786. The estate, which had been owned by the bishops of Hereford, passed through the Coningsby (qv) family to the Capel earls of Essex from whom William Higginson bought it in 1799. Edmund added to the estate and had W.A. Nesfield (qv) lay out terraces and walks. He imparked acres of farmland, removing the field boundaries and planting thousands of trees. Most of the old castle, anciently the seat of the Coningsbys (qv), was pulled down in the 1840s and in 1846 Higginson built Saltmarshe Castle where he hung his important collection of paintings. He devised winding paths, streams, cascades and lakes stocked with fish in the estate. He had new schools built for 66 children at Bromyard, and left money for the rebuilding of the churches at Tedstone Wafre and Edvin Loach. On his death in 1871 the estate passed to his nephew William Barneby (qv).

Hill, E.F.F. (1896-1954), philosopher, born in Devonport, Devon, was privately educated and went to Birmingham University. He was ordained a priest in 1925 and held various livings in the Midlands until, in 1939, in poor health he moved to the little parish of Hollybush near Ledbury in the south Malverns. In 1952 he was also rector of Birtsmorton until his death. Revd Hill set out his apocalyptic philosophy in a series of brilliant, disturbing essays *Apocalypse and Other Essays: The Crisis of Spirit in a Demonic Age*, later published by a friend in the small Cornish Deucalion Press in 1989.

Hill, James (1697-1727), antiquary, was born on 7 February 1697, the third son of John and Mary Hill of St Nicholas parish, Hereford. A brother was a schoolmaster in the county. James was educated at Trinity College, Oxford, and the Middle Temple. His planned history of Herefordshire was never completed. He was FSA and FRS while still only 21 and began to compile observations of national antiquities. He catalogued Lord Oxford's (qv Edward Harley, d.1741) collection of Saxon coins, and also made his own collection. He was interested in the Roman remains of Herefordshire and made a survey of *Ariconium*. He was a friend of William

Stukeley (qv) and a member of his society of Roman Knights, discussing ancient Rome under his name 'Caradoc'. He lived for a while in London but had returned to Hereford before his early death in August 1727 and was buried in Hereford Cathedral. Most of his proposals, including a long poem on Roman Britain, were left incomplete. His papers were bought by Isaac Taylor and John Allen (qqv) read through them; they were acquired by Thomas Bird (qv), then by Robert Phillipps (qv) who bequeathed them to Belmont Abbey Library, from whence they finally arrived at Hereford Record Office, where they may now be studied.

Hinch, Edward (fl.1870s), builder, was John Arkwright's clerk of works at Hampton Court. He lived at Isle of Rhea Cottage, near Leominster and built the church school and house (1874-75) at Risbury, Humber.

Hoadly, Benjamin (1676-1761), Bishop of Hereford 1721-3, was born on 14 November 1676 the son of a Kent schoolmaster. Treatment for smallpox as a child left him crippled. He was educated at St Catharine's College, Cambridge and ordained. His younger brother John became

primate of Ireland. Hoadly met Sarah Curtis (*c.*1676-1743), a portrait painter trained by Mary Beale, who lodged in the same house near Covent Garden as his sisters, who were mantua-makers. He gave up his college fellowship and they married. Sarah continued to paint portraits of friends and relations after marriage and despite childbirth. Hoadley was musical and a great polemicist and attracted the patronage of the Duchess of Marlborough through his defence of the Revolution of 1688 and his Whig pamphlets. He was rewarded with livings and, in 1716, after the Hanoverian succession, which he supported, was appointed Bishop of Bangor. His Whig record made him unpopular and he was assaulted in Brecon. In 1721 he moved to Hereford, where he was also unpopular: his books were burnt in High Town. He entered into controversy with High Churchmen and non-jurors like Hickes (qv). He made his brother John and his brother in-law, Thomas Wishaw residentiary canons. In 1722 he carried out a visitation, needing assistance as he walked with crutches, but in 1723 he was translated to Salisbury and ten years later to Winchester. Sarah died on 11 January 1743 and Hoadly, aged 68 and very disabled, married Mary Newey, daughter of his dean. He died on 17 April 1761. His portrait was painted by Hogarth.

Hoadly, Benjamin (1706-57), physician and playwright, the eldest son of Benjamin (qv) and Sarah Hoadly, was born in the family home in Broad Street, London on 10 February 1706. They were an artistic family; his father was a musician and his mother painted. He was educated at Corpus Christi College, Cambridge, and elected FRS in 1726. His father appointed him registrar of Hereford Cathedral. He married Elizabeth, daughter of Henry Betts of Suffolk and on her death Ann, daughter of General Armstrong. There were no surviving children. He lived in London where he was elected fellow of the Royal College of Physicians and was physician to St George's Hospital and later to Westminster Hospital. In 1742 he was physician to the king's household and in 1746 to that of the Prince of Wales. He wrote some successful plays for Covent Garden theatre, the most popular being *The Suspicious Husband* (1747) in which David Garrick (qv) acted. It was dedicated to George II who liked it and sent him £100. He died at the house he had built in Chelsea on 10 August 1757.

Hobson, Thomas (1545-1631), was a carrier and the son of a successful Lincolnshire carrier. A carrier transported every sort of goods in wagons pulled by six or seven horses, and Hobson also hired out horses, making sure they were let on a strict rota, hence the expression 'Hobson's choice': you had the next in line. The family moved to Cambridgeshire in 1561 and Thomas became the carrier of choice to the university, achieving celebrity and wealth. His business took him into Herefordshire and Sir John Coke (qv) for one sent letters to his wife via Hobson, receiving Marie's post back and produce from their estate. He continued his business into advanced age and is remembered in two poems by Milton, in the water supply he funded in Cambridge – Hobson's conduit – and in a street named after him there.

Hoby, Philip (1505-58), diplomat, eldest son of his father's first wife, was born at Leominster where his father William Hoby (d.*c*.1532, qv) of Radnorshire had settled. He was a protégé of the Protestant reformer Thomas Cromwell and became one of Henry VIII's trusted officials. As a strong linguist he was sent on sensitive embassies, such as the king's quest for a wife, and to the Holy Roman Emperor Charles V, who liked him. Holbein drew his portrait and that of his wife, Elizabeth Stoner. Elizabeth was a confidante of Queen Catherine Parr. He was appointed the woodward of Ashwood, Leominster. He kept a Protestant chaplain, a Thomas Parson, in 1543 before it was safe to do so and was imprisoned in the Fleet, but was released through his wife's influence. He fought at the siege of Boulogne and was knighted. He was sent on several important embassies to the Continent under Edward VI (qv) and was appointed to the Privy Council. He secured several church properties at the Dissolution;

his favourite was Bisham Abbey, Berkshire. He was at Edward VI's Court at Christmas 1550 and was sent to France in 1551 with his half-brother Thomas in the train of William Parr, Marquess of Northampton, to invest the French king with the Order of the Garter. He managed the troubled transition to Mary's reign well, keeping clear of Wyatt's rebellion. As a reward for Leominster's loyalty to Queen Mary he was named the main burgess, but despite this Philip and Thomas went into exile until their safety was assured. He died at his Blackfriars house on 9 May 1558 and was buried under a magnificent tomb in Bisham Church which was erected by Thomas's wife.

Hoby, Thomas, (1530-66), writer and diplomat, son of William Hoby's (qv) second wife, was educated at St John's College, Cambridge and studied under John Cheke. In 1547 he went to stay with Martin Bucer in Strasbourg, where he studied classics and theology and translated *The Gratulation of M. Martin Bucer unto the Church of England* (1549). He accompanied his half-brother on embassies and went with him into exile during Mary's reign. He wrote about the foreign courts he had visited in *Travels and Life* and translated Castiglione's *The Courtier* (1561), a model of polite behaviour for the Tudor middle classes which is still in print. He inherited Bisham Abbey from his brother and married the brilliant Elizabeth, daughter of Sir Anthony Cooke and friend of Queen Elizabeth. They had two sons. He was knighted in 1566 and sent as ambassador to France, where he died on 13 July that year; he was buried in Bisham Church, Berkshire.

Hoby, William (d.*c.*1532) was the son of Walter Hoby of Radnorshire, who claimed descent from Rhys ap Tudur. He had settled at Leominster by 1505 and married first Catherine Foster, with whom he had a son Philip (qv) and secondly Katherine Forden, the mother of Thomas (qv).

Hodges, Mary (fl.1662), ale house keeper and widow of Hereford, is recorded in Hereford City Rolls for 1662 as charged with witchcraft, an offence that carried the death penalty until repealed by an Act of 1736. Her accuser Richard Benny described her as swearing and blaspheming and keeping a disorderly ale house. He claimed she had cursed him while he was shovelling muck at his father Philip's house in Hereford, causing his father's horse to die and bewitching his cattle. Benny said 'shee falles downe uppon her knees and useth some prayers of witchcraft' and claimed to have seen her at her spells in her garden at night. However the court found that she was a common scold and bound her over to keep the peace.

Hodges, Thomas (*c.*1600-72), was the first Dean of Hereford appointed after the Restoration (1661-72), his predecessor, Jonathan Brown, having been dismissed 18 years before. Hodges was educated at Christ Church, Oxford and was a rector in London parishes before the Civil Wars. At Hereford he oversaw the re-establishment of his chapter and raised funds to restore the essentials of Anglican worship in the cathedral – the philanthropic John Scudamore (qv, d.1671) made a large donation. He had a Renatus Harris (qv) organ erected on the pulpitum, the screen across the east end of the nave, where it stood until Lewis Cottingham's (qv) restoration work in the 1840s. He died on 22 August 1672 and was buried in his Kensington parish church. George Benson (qv) succeeded him as dean.

Hodgkinson, John (fl.1803-11), civil engineer and surveyor, was engaged in the Marches building canals and tramroads. In 1803 he was consulted on difficulties with the Leominster to Stourbridge canal which was to move agricultural goods out and coal into Herefordshire. This was never completed but finally sold to a railway company. In 1811 he was the engineer on the Hay railway, a narrow gauge plate-way for horse-drawn traffic, and for the tramroad that linked Kington to the Burlingjobb quarries (qv James Watt).

Hogg, Robert (1818-97), pomologist, was born on 20 April 1818 at Duns, Berwickshire, the son of nurseryman Robert Hogg. He went to London to work at a Brentford fruit nursery and in 1844 married Caroline, daughter of Charles Milligan, a grain dealer whose partner he became. Hogg was an expert on apple production, an area he felt was neglected, and he published *British Pomology* (1851) and a *Fruit Manual* (1860). He helped to establish the British Pomological Society in 1854, and in 1858 he was secretary of the Horticultural Society's fruit committee. In 1861 he took the degree of LLD. The recently founded Woolhope Naturalists' Field Club had formed a Pomona Committee and asked for Dr Hogg's help in recording the county's varieties of cultivated apples and pears. He wrote the technical notes for each variety, and two lavish volumes of *Herefordshire Pomona, or The Apple Trees of Herefordshire* were published between 1878 and 1885. Hogg died at his London home on 14 March 1897 and was buried at Woking. The Royal Horticultural Society's Hogg Medal for exhibits of fruit commemorates him.

Holford, Thomas (d.1588), martyr, son of the rector of Aston in Cheshire, was also known as Thomas Acton. He was tutor to Sir James

Scudamore's (qv, d.1619) children at Holme Lacy where a priest called Davis converted him to Catholicism. He went to Rheims for ordination in 1582 and returned a Catholic priest. He was banished in 1585 but again returned. The Armada scare in 1588 caused a hardening of the authorities' attitudes to Catholic priests in the country and many were caught and executed; Thomas was hanged at Clerkenwell. They are known as the London Martyrs with whom the blessed Thomas Holford is grouped. Their feast day is 28 August.

Holgot, Philip (d.1404), MP and lawyer of Hereford, was steward of the Mortimer estates and acted as their lawyer throughout his career, particularly for Edmund (III) Mortimer (qv) and the Countess Philippa, and for others including Sir Richard Baskerville (qv). He was a JP in the county from 1380 to his death and served as an escheator 1400-1401. He was MP for the county in 1402. He was associated with Richard and James Nash, Thomas Oldcastle (qqv) *et al.* The ability of the usurping Henry IV to take over the government of Richard II so smoothly must owe something to MPs and lawyers like Holgot, the Nashes, the Oldcastles (qqv) *et al.* especially when one remembers that Edmund (IV) Mortimer (qv) had a better claim to the throne than he. Holgot was probably in his 60s at his death.

Holland, Henry (1745-1806), architect of Berrington Hall, was born in Fulham on 20 July 1745 the son of a London builder with whom he learnt the trade. His father was a partner of Capability Brown (qv) and responsible for his building work. Henry took over this position and married Brown's eldest daughter Bridget. He built Claremont House, Esher in Surrey for Robert Clive on his return from India and took advantage of the expansion of fashionable west London, building terraces and such landmarks as Brooks' Club in St James's and a Palladian mansion for himself and his family in Mayfair. The Prince of Wales commissioned Carlton Palace on Pall Mall from him and Thomas Harley (qv, d.1804) in 1778 had him

The late HENRY HOLLAND, Esq.
View Hans Place

build Berrington Hall: severely neo-classical in local red sandstone with a massive Ionic portico. Holland decorated the interior in the French style with painted ceilings, ornate plasterwork and a high cupola above lighting a spectacular staircase. He employed French decorators and imported fine French furniture for Harley. It cost a fortune and was completed in 1783. Sadly, George IV pulled down Holland's Carlton House but had him remodel Buckingham House at the other end of the Mall. Holland rebuilt the king's favourite house in Brighton, remodelled Windsor Castle and did much work for Whig grandees. He died in London and was buried at All Saints, Fulham.

Holland, Henry Scott (1847-1918), theological writer, was born on 27 January 1847 at Underdown, Ledbury and educated at Eton and Balliol College, Oxford. He was ordained in 1872. He was a friend of Jenny Lind (qv) at Colwall and wrote her biography after her death. In 1884 he became a canon of St Paul's, and was involved with the poor of London's East End. In 1910 he was appointed Regius Professor of Divinity at Oxford. He wrote hymns and books of sermons and the much quoted lines 'I have only slipped away into the next room ...'. He slipped away himself on 17 March 1918 in Oxford.

Hollins, Peter (1800-86), son of William Hollins, architect of Birmingham, was a monumental sculptor whose work, in a neo-classical style, was of great beauty. He produced two funerary monuments in the county: an excellent one for Sarah Freer (qv Nathan Wetherell) at Bishopstone Church, and a wall tablet for James Hereford (qv, d.1843) at Mordiford. There are two monuments by him in Malvern Priory.

Hood, Robin (1160-1247), outlaw born at Locksley, Nottingham in 1160, was noble by birth and called Robert Fitzooth, Earl of Huntingdon. He is the subject of many ballads; that linking him to Herefordshire is recorded in Thomas Bulfinch's *Mythology* and called *The Bishop of Hereford's Entertainment.* In 1245 Robin and his men, hearing that the hated Bishop Peter de Aquablanca (qv) was passing that way, roasted the king's venison by the path 'in merry Barnsdale'. When the bishop tried to arrest them they turned out in force and carried him to their camp, robbing him of his gold. Robin died at the hands of a relative, the prioress of Kirklees Nunnery, to whom he went to be bled. She bled him to death on 18 November 1247. His grave in Kirklees was drawn by William Stukeley (qv).

Hop (or perhaps **Hope), John and Joanna de** (late 14th century), left provision for the founding of a chantry to St Anne in Ledbury Church. Their executors retained William Calwe (qv) as chantry priest from 1384. In 1395 Bishop Trefnant (qv) ordained a John de Hop of St Giles, Hereford.

Hopkins, Gerard Manley (1844-89), Jesuit priest and poet, was born on 28 July 1844 at Stratford, Essex and wrote poetry and painted from an early age. He was educated at

Balliol College, Oxford where he was converted to Roman Catholicism. A further step was taken in Herefordshire while he was on a walking holiday with his friend William Aldiss in 1866. They stopped at the Roman Catholic cathedral (now abbey) of Belmont near Hereford where Dom Paul Raynal spoke to them about the priesthood and Hopkins consequently trained as a Jesuit priest. He stopped writing poetry for some years under obedience but his ideas matured as he studied philosophy, thought deeply and observed closely. He described his developing ideas in letters to his friends, rejecting the blandness of contemporary verse and evolving a 'sprung rhythm' which sought to show the 'instress' or essential individuality of things. The poetry he then wrote was rejected by friends and publishers. He died on 8 June 1889, exhausted by uncongenial work in Dublin, his poetry unappreciated. After his death his friend Robert Bridges apologetically published the poems which had been sent to him, believing them to be interesting failures. But they were hailed as works of genius and F.R. Leavis called him 'one of the most remarkable technical innovators that ever wrote'. Much loved poems include *The Windhover* and *Pied Beauty* and the masterpiece *The Wreck of the Deutschland.*

Hopton: Their main seat was at Hopton Castle in Shropshire. The Hereford branch, recorded since 1408, was of lesser account. Sir Richard Hopton's (qv, d.1653) marriage to his cousin Elizabeth brought Canon Frome Court to him, or The Strong House as it was then called. Hoptons were active on both sides in the Civil War. The passionate Susanna (qv) was active as a lover, a writer and a religious. The 18th and 19th century produced a line of rectors and JPs. Canon Frome Court, originally a monastic building, was the seat of the Hoptons until the 20th century. The house and its grounds were sold as a commune in recent times, and an old portrait of Susanna Hopton that hung in the hall was stolen.

Hopton, Anne (1561-1625), was born in The Strong House or Canon Frome Court. She married Henry, 3rd Baron Wentworth and after his death Sir William Pope of Wroxton, 1st Earl of Downe.

Hopton, Edward (1603-68), second son of Sir Richard Hopton (qv, d.1653) was born at Canon Frome Court. He was a clerk in the East India Company at Surat until recalled by his father to replace his older brother, who had married badly, as his heir. He initially supported Parliament in the county's struggles, as did two brothers, but, escaping from his difficult father's influence, sided with the King. He was lieutenant colonel of foot in 1643-4 and colonel until 1646. He was created knight banneret by Charles I in 1645 and became MP for Hereford in 1661. On 22 July 1645 Canon Frome was damaged by the besieging Scots army and some of the garrison killed. Sir Edward married Deborah Hatton (d.1702) in 1654 and began to restore the damaged house. The ruined church had to wait until the 19th century. Sir Edward died on 1 April 1668 but Deborah lived on until 1702 at Canon Frome and was buried with him in St Lawrence, Stretton Grandison, where one of his gauntlets still hangs.

Hopton, Edward (1837-1912) was the son of Revd William Hopton (d.1841), vicar and patron of Canon Frome, and a Diana. He was educated at Eton and joined the Army in 1854. He fought in the Crimean War, at the siege of Lucknow and in the Zulu Wars. Sir Edward was Lieutenant Governor of Jersey before returning home as Deputy Lieutenant of Herefordshire. In 1874 he married Clare Ellen Trafford and they had two sons and two daughters. He died on 19 January 1912. There is a portrait of Sir Edward of 1880 in Hereford Museum (above).

John Hopton (1782-1870), clergyman and JP, son of Revd William Hopton, lived at Canon Frome Court as rector and patron of the living. He and his son John Hopton JP commissioned Bodley's (qv) rebuilding of St James' Church by the Court in 1860.

Hopton, Richard (1570-1653), was the second son and heir of William Hopton (b.*c*.1550) of Rockhill, Burford in Shropshire. He married his cousin Elizabeth, daughter of John Hopton and heir to her uncle Michael Hopton, a rich London merchant who owned Canon Frome Court, once a house of Augustinian canons. They lived there and had five sons: William, Edward Walter, James and Richard. Sir Richard was High Sheriff of Herefordshire in 1610. Sir Henry Lingen (qv) called him the ringleader of the opposition to Charles' Ship Money in the county. In 1642, when the Earl of Stamford (qv Henry Grey) marched on Hereford, Hopton raised a force for Parliament together with Col Robert Kyrle (qv), Edward Massey (qv) and Sir Robert Harley (qv, d.1656).

Hopton, Richard (*c.*1610-96), was Sir Edward's (d.1668, qv) brother and Sir Richard's (qv, d.1653) fifth son, born at Canon Frome. He trained as a lawyer and became chief justice of the North Wales circuit. During the Commonwealth he acted as a secret Royalist agent assisted by his impetuous wife Susanna (qv). He died at Kington on 28 November 1696.

Hopton, Richard (1685-1764) of Canon Frome married Elizabeth Geers (qv) in 1705. He was MP for Herefordshire 1715-22.

Hopton, Susanna (1627-1709), devotional writer, was born in London and baptised on 27 October 1627, the daughter of Sir Simon Harvey, who died when she was a baby. When her mother Ursula remarried Susanna reacted strongly to her stepfather's Presbyterian views and converted to Catholicism under the direction of Father Henry Turberville (who dedicated his *Manual of Controversies* to her in 1654). She fell in love with Richard Hopton (qv, d.1696) 'truly and passionately', as she told George Hickes (qv). Her attentions must have been unsettling to Hopton as he issued an affidavit to stop her molesting him. However, he spent time recovering her for the Church of England and they married in 1660, in London. They lived at Gattertop at Hope under Dinmore and after 20 years moved to Kington. Their marriage was long and happy but childless. She regretted her lack of formal education and made a determined study of the best authors and is said to have belonged to the devotional circle of Thomas Traherne (qv); her niece married his brother Philip (qv). A manuscript later published as *Meditations & Devotions* (1717) was found among her papers after her death. It was given a preface by Dr Hickes (qv). Passages are said to be by Thomas Traherne, and Part II, *The Soul's Communion with her Savior*, had previously been published by Philip Traherne in 1685. She published devotional books such as *Daily Devotions*, an anthology of religious texts, and devoted herself to daily religious discipline, rising at 4am, worshipping five times a day, fasting, giving alms and writing religious poetry. She had strong objections to the supplanting of James II (qv) and supported proscribed non-juring clergy, hiding Bishop Hickes (qv). Hickes published his memories of her, considering her 'very apt to be abused by crafty flattering Folks abt. her'. She tried to convert her friend and tenant at Canon Frome Serjeant Thomas Geers (qv) to her non-juring principles. Another non-juring friend was William Brome (qv), who said 'her Discourse & Stile upon serious matters was strong eloquent & nervous: upon pleasant subjects witty & facetious: & when it required an edge was as sharp as a Rasor'. Her reputation as a devotional writer was great in the 18th and 19th centuries. At her death on 12 July 1709 she was living in St Peter's parish in Hereford. She was buried beside her husband in Bishop's Frome Church, where their inscriptions may be read. She left money to support the non-juring community.

Hopton, William (before 1765-1841), clergyman, born Parsons, married Deborah Hopton of Canon Frome and assumed her name. The Hoptons were patrons of the living and Revd (Parsons) Hopton was himself rector.

Hoskyns, Anthony (1568-1615), Jesuit priest, was born in Hereford of a good family. He went to the English College at Douai in 1590 and then on to Valladolid in 1593 to train as a Jesuit; he then taught in Spanish seminaries. His return to England on mission in 1603 was uneventful and in 1610 he was recalled to the Spanish Netherlands where he was vice-prefect of the English mission. Here he published some polemical papers and an exemplary translation of Thomas à Kempis' *Imitatio Christi* (1611). He died at the English College at Valladolid, where he was rector, on 20 September 1615.

Hoskyns, Bennet, (1609-80), 1st Baronet, judge and politician, was the eldest son of Sir John Hoskyns (d.1638, qv). He was entered at the Middle Temple in 1620 when only 11 and called to the bar in 1631. He married Ann, daughter of Sir Henry Bingley, an auditor of the exchequer. Hoskyns was returned MP for Buckinghamshire in the Short Parliament of 1640 when his Herefordshire neighbours Sir Walter Pye and Sir Robert Harley (qv, d.1656) were in the House. He tried to keep both sides happy and was a committee member for both King and Parliament at different times. He was accused in Parliament of raising troops for the king in Hereford and during the siege of Hereford by the Scots army in 1645 he fled to Hay. His father's name protected him and he was returned MP for Herefordshire to the Long Parliament of 1646 but rumours of Royalist sympathies caused him to retire in 1647. With Harley's support he was elected to the Rump Parliament of 1649 for Herefordshire and again in 1656-59, and was appointed judge on the Carmarthen circuit in 1654. He was active on committees of legal and religious reform. He was included in Cromwell's funeral procession and sat in Richard Cromwell's Parliament. He was not re-elected after the Restoration but worked quietly in his chambers in the Middle Temple. He bought Harewood Park which had been built on the ruins of a preceptory of the Knights Templar of Garway and purchased the baronetcy of Harewood from Charles II in 1676. On the death of Ann he married Dorothy daughter of Francis Kyrle (qv) of Much Marcle, the widow of John Abrahall (qv under John Abrahall). He died at Harewood on 10 February 1680.

Hoskyns, Chandos (1720-73), 5th Baronet, was Sir Hungerford's (qv, d.1767) son – his forename indicating his mother's family. He married Rebecca May. His heir Sir Hungerford (d.1802) was 6th Baronet.

Hoskyns, Chandos Wren (1812-76), agriculturalist and author, was born on 15 February 1812, second son of Sir Hungerford (d.1862, qv). He was educated at Shrewsbury and Balliol College, Oxford and the Inner Temple and practised as a barrister. In 1837 he married Theodosia, daughter and heiress of Christopher Roberts Wren of Wroxall Abbey, Warwickshire, a descendant of Christopher Wren, and changed his name to Wren Hoskyns by royal licence. They lived in Madeira for the sake of his wife's health and had one child, Catherine. When Theodosia died he married Anna Fane in 1846 and they had a son and two daughters. He was a Woolhope Club member and president in 1868. From 1869 to 1874 he was MP for Hereford and JP. He was interested in land law and agricultural development and was an advocate of free trade, writing persuasive articles for *The Agricultural Gazette* from its founding in 1844 and books on agricultural matters. He rebuilt the chapel of St Denis (qv) by Harewood End in his father's memory. The house was demolished although the chapel remains. The estate was bought by the Duchy of Cornwall in 2000, with Prince Charles personally interested in its development. Hoskyns died in London on 28 November 1876.

Hoskyns, Hungerford (*c.*1677-1767), 4th Baronet, Sir John's (d.1705, qv) eldest son, joined the Army during the War of the Spanish Succession but resigned on his succession to the baronetcy. In 1720 he married Mary daughter of Sir Theophilus Leigh and his wife Mary Brydges (qv under James Brydges d.1714). The Brydges had been ennobled as Dukes of Chandos. A younger son was Philip Hoskyns who lived at Bernithan Court near Ross and whose daughter Jane (d.1768) married William Matthews (qv).

Hoskyns, Hungerford (1776-1862), 7th Baronet of Harewood, was High Sheriff of Hereford in 1785. He married Sarah Phillips (d.1860) and their daughter Sarah married John Arkwright (qv, d.1858). Their eldest son Hungerford was 8th Baronet and their youngest John Leigh Hoskyns (1817-1911) the 9th.

Hoskyns, John (1566-1638), poet and lawyer, was the son of John (*c.*1530-1607) and Margery Hoskyns who farmed at Monkton near Llanwarne. He was educated at Winchester, where he was called the flower of his time, and New College, Oxford, and began to write the satirical poetry which caused him trouble. He went to the Middle Temple where he met Ben Jonson and John Donne and was introduced at Court where he met William Herbert, 3rd Earl of Pembroke, who appointed him recorder of Hereford. He married Benedicta (d.1625) the wealthy daughter of Robert Moyle and widow of Francis Bourne (a colleague at the Middle Temple), and bought a grand house in Hereford. One of their daughters, Mrs Markey, told Aubrey (qv) that Herefordshire fairies left silver as a reward for her clean hearth. In 1604 he was returned to Parliament for Hereford City, and became known for indiscreet satires such as on 'the fart in the parliament house' of 1607. When the king found a suggestion of treason in one of Hoskyns' speeches to Parliament he was stripped of his offices and sent to the Tower, where he is said to have helped Raleigh complete his *History of the World*. On his release in 1616 he was elected Mayor of Hereford but James I had the appointment annulled. He was once more brought before the Privy Council for a libellous poem and had to pull strings to escape punishment. Hoskyns, perhaps thinking of his family, now kept his head down. He became Sergeant-at-Law in 1623 and is usually known as Sergeant Hoskyns. Contacts found him remunerative office in the Middle Temple; he was appointed a circuit judge, and bought the Morehampton estate in Herefordshire. His wife died in 1625 and he married Isabel Barrett (d.1634), a rich widow. He was again MP for Hereford in 1627 and was active on committees. He wrote many poems including an anthem for Hereford Cathedral which survives; his son Bennet (qv) lost a thick manuscript of his writings according to Aubrey. He was famed for his learning, was Doctor of Divinity and a canon of Hereford. Hoskyns died at Morehampton on 27 August 1638 of a gangrenous toe and was buried in Lord Scudamore's (qv) recently renovated church at Abbey Dore. There is a miniature of Hoskyns with a self portrait sketched on the back showing him with Benedicta and their children.

Hoskyns, John the younger (1581-1631), clergyman and author, was the Sergeant's (John Hoskyns, d.1638, qv) younger brother, also confusingly called John. Aubrey (qv) knew Sir John's son Bennet (qv) and recorded stories about the two Johns; that the younger was jealous of his brother's learning and 'would not be quiet but he must be a Scholar too', teaching himself Latin and Greek at the age of 10 and following him to Winchester and New College. Ordained, he became vicar of Ledbury, obtained prebendary stalls at Hereford and was chaplain to his friend Bishop Bennett (qv). He married Frances Bourne (fl.1601-32) and they had four sons and a daughter. In 1613 he was made Doctor of Laws. He was a noted preacher and his memorial on the south chancel wall at Ledbury, paid for by his son Charles, shows him preaching from books under a canopy.

Hoskyns, John (1634-1705), 2nd Baronet, lawyer and MP for Hereford, was born on 23 July 1634 at Bernithan Park, Llangarron, the eldest son of Sir Bennet (qv) and Ann. He inherited Harewood and Morehampton Parks. Aubrey (qv) regarded him as one of his 'chiefest friends'

or *amici* and stayed with him regularly at Harewood. He married firstly Jane, daughter of Sir Gabriel Lowe, in 1671. In 1676 he was knighted and from 1676 to 1703 was Master in Chancery. He was MP for Hereford from 1685-7. He was a scientist who experimented with the grafting of plants and their refrigeration and was one of the original fellows of the Royal Society of London, succeeding Christopher Wren as president in 1682, after which he was secretary. Aubrey said of him:

He was hard-favoured, affected plainness in his garb, walked the street with a cudgel in his hand, and an old hat over his eyes. He was often observed to be in a reverie: but when his spirits were elevated over a bottle, he was remarkable for his presence of mind, and quickness of apprehension, and became the agreeable and instructive companion.

Hoskyns died on 12 September 1705 and was buried at Harewood. A portrait survives by Robert White.

Hoskyns Abrahall, John (1692-1765), Sir John Hoskyns' (qv, d.1705) third son lived at Ingestone near Foy and was rector of Peterstow from 1727 to his death. He assumed his extra surname in compliance with the will of his cousin Mary Abrahall and married Anne (1725-86), the youngest daughter of Theophilus Leigh and Mary Brydges (qv Sir James Brydges, d.1714). Their sons were James and Revd John Hoskyns Abrahall (1773-1840), who was rector of Peterstow after his father.

Howard, Charles (1746-1815), 11th Duke of Norfolk, born on 15 March 1746, was brought up a Roman Catholic and spent much of his youth in France. At the time of the Gordon Riots he conformed to the Church of England. His first wife, Marion Coppinger, died in childbirth. A widower at 22, he married Frances Fitzroy-Scudamore (qv under Scudamore) in 1771, but she became insane and was cared for at Holme Lacy. Howard took a mistress, Mary Gibbon, niece of the historian Edward Gibbon, with whom he had several children. He was styled Earl of Surrey from 1777, and Earl of Norfolk on his father's death in 1786. He was MP for Hereford in 1784, High Steward in 1794 and President of the Society of Arts. Although he spent much of his time in London and at Arundel Castle, his main seat, he was often in Herefordshire and took a great interest in local history. He commissioned John Duncumb's (qv) *Collections towards the History and Antiquities of*

the County of Hereford. He kept a town house in Broad Street, Hereford, where, on 28 August 1802, Nelson (qv) and his wife stayed. It later became the City Arms and is now Barclays Bank. Howard was a clumsy, slovenly man and, with his friend the Prince of Wales, a heroic drinker. He died at Norfolk House, London on 16 December 1815 and was buried at Dorking, Surrey, with his first wife. Poor mad Frances survived him by five years and was buried in St Cuthbert's at Holme Lacy where both their hatchments still hang.

Howorth, Epiphanius (1566-1647) married Blanche, daughter of Griffith Jones (d.1577) of Llowes, Radnor and Jane Parry. Jane was the daughter of Symond Parry (qv) and thus the Parry property of Whitehouse, near Vowchurch, passed to the Howorths. Their sons were Rowland, who married Francis Smalman's (qv) daughter Jane, Richard and Humphrey. Howorths lived at Whitehouse for the next 300 years.

Hubaud, John (d.1583), knight, was Robert Dudley, Earl of Leicester's high steward in Herefordshire. He was a neighbour of the Coningsbys and after Sir Humphrey Coningsby's (qv, d.1559) death married his widow Anne (d.1564); then after her death Mary Throckmorton of Coughton. His family home was at Ipsley, Worcs.

Hues, Robert (1553-1632), mathematician and geographer, was born at Little Hereford and educated at St Mary Hall, Oxford where he was a noted Greek scholar. He studied mathematics under Thomas Allen (qv) and knew the geographer Richard Hakluyt (qv), Master of Christ Church, and Sir Thomas Browne who remembered discussing Ptolemy, Euclid and Aristotle with him. Hakluyt introduced Hues to his friend Sir Walter Raleigh and the great navigators and scientists of the day. He went to sea and made astronomical observations, circumnavigating the globe with Thomas Cavendish (qv Robert Masters) in 1586-88 and again in 1591. His experiments in the variations of the compass at different latitudes using accurate globes, published in *Tractatus de globis et eorum usu*, were essential in the ensuing age of exploration. Hakluyt printed an account of his travels in his *Principall Voyages*... of 1589. Hues retired to Oxford and died on 24 May 1632. He was buried in Christ Church Cathedral.

Hughes, Elizabeth (1755-1849), 'the Kingsland doctoress', discovered she had powers of healing after the death of a child in 1802. She dispensed her gift freely to all comers although her vicar dismissed her as a fraud. In a letter to the *Hereford Times* she is remembered as a respectable woman.

Hungaria, Hugo de (12th century) was a canon of Hereford. He is mentioned in a poem of Hue de Roteland (qv). The deaths of his mother and father are listed in the cathedral obit book in the 1190s.

Hume, Joseph (1777-1855), 'the people's MP', was honoured on 7 December 1821 when he was representing Aberdeen Burghs with a public dinner in Hereford for his efforts to cut taxation and stem electoral corruption in boroughs like Leominster and Weobley. E.B. Clive MP (qv) presided and David Ricardo (qv) spoke for an extension of the franchise to the whole people. Hume was presented with a silver tankard and a hogshead of Hereford cider. Thomas Ballard's (qv) portrait of him is now in Hereford Museum.

Humphreys, Humphrey (1648-1712), antiquarian and Bishop of Hereford 1701-12, was born in Merioneth on 24 November 1648. His father was a Royalist army officer. He was educated at Jesus College, Oxford, ordained and served in parishes in Wales. He married Elizabeth, daughter of the previous Bishop of Bangor, Robert Morgan. He was the chaplain to the new bishop and succeeded him in 1689. He was skilled in the Welsh language and antiquities and his visitation of his diocese was conducted in Welsh. He compiled a life of St Beuno (qv) and other Celtic saints and traced the roots of Anglicanism to the pre-Augustinian church. He had English religious material translated into Welsh and supported the bards and Welsh historians. His writings were published by Thomas Hearne (qv, d.1735). He worked on a revision of the Prayer Book and produced a Welsh edition. He took the oath to King William but was acquainted with non-jurors, his daughter marrying into a non-juring family. He was translated to Hereford in 1701. He attended Parliament and supported Lord John Somers (1651-1716) during his impeachment. Despite poor health he was an active bishop and conducted a visitation in 1710. His favourite residence was Whitbourne, which had been recovered from John Birch (qv), and he died there on 20 November 1712. He was buried in Hereford Cathedral where his memorial is now in the south-east transept. He was preceded as bishop by Ironside and followed by Bisse (qqv).

Hunt, John (1806-42), organist and composer, was born in Dorset on 30 December 1806. He learnt to sing and play the organ at Salisbury Cathedral. He was choragus or choirmaster of Lichfield when Dean Merewether offered him the position of organist at Hereford Cathedral in succession to Samuel Sebastian Wesley (qv) in 1835. Hunt stayed at Hereford until, on 17 November 1842, he tripped over a food trolley at dinner in the vicars choral cloister and died. His nephew James, who was a chorister at the cathedral, died of shock when he heard the news. A memoir with a collection of his songs was published in 1843 and a commemorative stained glass window, an early work by Clayton and Bell (qv), was placed in a north choir aisle window.

Huntingford, George Isaac (1748-1832), Bishop of Hereford (1815-32), was born at Winchester on 9 September 1748 into a farming family and educated at Winchester and New College, Oxford. After ordination his first cure was at Compton near Winchester. He was appointed Bishop of Gloucester (1802-15) through the patronage of his friend Prime Minister Henry Addington, then translated to Hereford where, despite continuing to be warden of Winchester College, he began the renovation of the bishop's palace. He kept in touch with his diocese through his nephew Revd Thomas Huntingford, who was precentor. He died in his rooms at Winchester College on 29 April 1832 and was buried in Compton Church, Surrey.

Husbands, John (1706-32), clergyman, born at Marsh Baldon, Oxfordshire, on 29 January 1706, was the son of Revd Thomas Husbands (1677-1728), vicar of Canon Pyon and chaplain of New College, Oxford, and his wife Elizabeth. John was educated at Mr Rodd's school in Hereford and Pembroke College, Oxford where he was elected Fellow in 1728 and was ordained. He published a volume of poems at Oxford about ancient Hebrew poetry and was writing more when he died on 21 November 1732 in Compton Bassett, Wiltshire. His mother and father were both buried at Canon Pyon Church.

Hutchinson, Emma Sarah (1820-1905), lepidopterist, moved to Herefordshire with her family aged 12. She met and married Revd Keys, vicar of Kimbolton, and they had three sons and four daughters all of whom were naturalists. She was a keen botanist and mycologist who, with Henry Bull (qv), organised the Woolhope Club's first fungus forays. As women were not admitted to Woolhope Club meetings until 1954 her research was presented by her husband. She was a lepidopterist of national repute and found moths that were otherwise unknown in Herefordshire, one of which was named after her. She left her collection to the British Museum.

I

Ince, Joseph Murray (1806-59), painter, was born in London but his family moved to Presteigne while he was young and he was educated at John Beddoes Free School. In Hereford he was taught by David Cox (qv) and met John Scarlett Davis (qv). In 1826 he went

to London, where he exhibited at the Royal Academy, the British Institution and the Society of Artists. He built up a successful career, had a house in London and spent his summers travelling in Wales and Herefordshire, based at his parents' Presteigne house. He was celebrated for his watercolour landscapes of Herefordshire and Radnorshire and his work may be seen in the V&A, the British Museum and Hereford Museum, which has one of his sketch books. He died at his London home, 9 George Street, Portman Square, on 24 September 1859, and was buried in Kensal Green Cemetery near his friend Scarlett Davis. There is a monument to him in Presteigne.

Inglott, William (1554-1621), organist and composer, was the son of Edmund Inglott (d.1583), choirmaster at Norwich Cathedral. William succeeded his father at Norwich and then moved to Hereford Cathedral as organist (1597-1610), training the choristers and arranging and conducting the music. He composed celebrated pieces for the virginal. After returning to Norwich he was replaced at Hereford by Hugh Davis (qv), one of his choristers. He died in December 1621.

Ingram, John (1565-94), martyr, from Stoke Edith, was educated at New College, Oxford. He converted to Catholicism and studied for the priesthood at the English College, Rheims, from where he returned on mission as a Jesuit but was apprehended and tortured. He wrote 20 Latin epigrams in prison. He was executed at Gateshead on 26 July 1594. His feast day is 24 July.

Ironside, Gilbert (1632-1701), Bishop of Hereford 1691-1701, was born at Winterbourne Abbas, Dorset, the third son of Gilbert Ironside, Bishop of Bristol. He was educated at Wadham College, Oxford, and on ordination succeeded his father at his Dorset living. He was warden of Wadham and chancellor of Oxford University. He was rewarded for his resistance to James II with the bishopric of Bristol, then on the death of Bishop Croft (qv) was translated to Hereford. He died in London on 27 August 1701 and was buried in the chapel of St Mary Somerset at the Bishop of Hereford's London house Monthalt, which disappeared in the Great Fire of 1666 and was rebuilt by Wren in 1694. His remains and the black marble tombstone were removed to Hereford Cathedral in 1867 when the chapel was demolished and can be seen in the south-east transept. When his body was inspected at the transfer it was found to be perfectly preserved although his outer silver coffin had been stolen. He followed Herbert Croft and was succeeded by Bishop Humphreys (qqv).

J

Jack o'Kent is a legendary Herefordshire trickster and wizard, credited with cheating the devil, moving stones etc. The name is similar to that of Glyn Dŵr's (qv) chaplain and bard Sion Cent, of whom there may be a portrait at Kentchurch Court where Glyn Dŵr is said to have hidden (see page 173). One of the ancient trees here is called Jack o'Kent's oak. The name may also refer to a 15th-century vicar of Kentchurch, John Kent or John Caerleon, a poet and theological writer who died at Hereford *c.*1482.

Jackson, Basil (1795-1889), military surveyor, was born in Glasgow. Commissioned at Sandhurst to the Royal Staff Corps in 1811, he was on Wellington's quartermaster-general's staff at the Battle of Waterloo, then accompanied Napoleon to St Helena until 1819. In 1828 he married. He rose to the rank of lieutenant colonel and spent the remainder of his working life lecturing at the East India Company's college at Addiscombe. He retired to Glewstone Court, near Ross in 1857, and later moved to Hillsborough, a house in Ross. He published books on surveying and *The Military Life of the Duke of Wellington* (1840). He died on 22 October 1889 and is buried at St Giles, Goodrich.

Jackson, John (1817-91), clergyman, was born in Cumberland and educated at St John's College, Cambridge. He was ordained in 1841 and inducted rector of Ledbury in 1860 and master of St Katherine's Hospital, a role in which he acted as bishop's surrogate in the diocese. He was accused of fathering illegitimate children in the town and suspended in 1869 pending an enquiry. The bishop cleared him of misconduct in 1871 and he was reinstated, but many of his parishioners boycotted services at St Michael's and attended either a makeshift rival church nearby (now converted into an undertaker's premises) or churches in nearby villages. In his idle moments Jackson carved an ornate wooden pulpit and lectern which are still in St Michael's Church. He was the subject of ribald ballads in London. He died on 23 July 1891 in his rectory at Ledbury.

Jakeman, Edward K. (b.1835), printer, was born at Forthampton, Gloucs and married Mary Alice from London. They lived at Donnington then moved to The Old Friary, St Nicholas, Hereford, with their 11 children, a nursemaid and governess. Jakeman formed a partnership with the stationer Thomas Carver (qv) and Jakeman & Carver of 4 and 5 Widemarsh Street were major printers in Hereford at the end of the 19th century. In the 1881 census Jakeman employed 40 men and 10 boys; he gives his occupation as printer, postmaster and farmer. They printed the Woolhope Club's *Transactions* and in 1899 were able to include many photographs by Alfred Watkins (qv). The firm is later found trading as Maylord Jakeman Ltd, and in Bannister's (qv) *History of Ewias Harold* their address is given as The Bible and Crown Press, 4-5 High Town, Hereford.

James, Henry (1828-1911), Baron James of Hereford, politician and lawyer, was born on 30 October 1828 at Hereford, the youngest son of

Philip Turner James, a Hereford surgeon and Frances Bodenham from Presteigne. His James ancestors had been surgeons and apothecaries in Hereford since the 18th century. He was Gladstone's solicitor and attorney general but refused the chancellorship and broke with Gladstone over the issue of Irish home rule. He was QC, PC and was made GCVO in 1902. In 1885 he received his barony, which became extinct on his death in August 1911. Descendants still live in the county.

James, Montague Rhodes (1862-1936), author M.R. James, was born on 1 August 1862. He was provost of King's College, Cambridge and of Eton and a director of the Fitzwilliam Museum. His subject was mediaeval history and he produced an authoritative edition of the Latin *Lives of St Ethelbert* (1917) and edited the Latin text of Walter Map's (qv) *De Nugis Curialium.* He wrote *Abbeys* for the Great Western Railway (1926) which includes studies of Leominster, Wigmore and Dore Abbeys – the latter being 'the most surprising and delightful of all the places' he wrote about. He is remembered as a ghost story writer and at least one of his stories, *A View From a Hill*, was set in Herefordshire. Others were written while staying in the county. In his preface to the *Collected Ghost Stories* (1931) he says 'Herefordshire was the imagined scene of *A View from a Hill* – perfect surroundings'. He had in mind the countryside around Woodlands Farm near Kilpeck where he stayed with his ward Jane and her mother Gwendolen McBryde, an author herself, and where he liked to write. He made

references to Alfred Watkins' (qv) *Old Straight Track.* He attended Kilpeck Church, whose *Guide* McBryde illustrated, enjoyed the antiquities and churches of the area, and used the atmosphere in his tales. McBryde published her letters to James in 1956. After 1929 she moved to Dippersmoor Manor nearby where James continued to visit. At Garway, the Templars' old preceptory, he felt he might have offended the spirit of the place: a rum place that needed careful handling, he noted, with the nest holes of its dovecote ominously numbering 666. He died on 12 June 1936.

Jay, James of Litley Court, Tupsley, was an alderman of Hereford. He had land on Eign Hill which was being developed by the building contractors Elmslie, Franey and Haddon (qv) in the 1850s-60s. They won a competition to build St Paul's Church at Tupsley but Kempson (qv) later took over the job and married Jay's daughter Julia.

Jearrad, Robert W. (d.1861), was the architect-builder of St Martin's Church (1840-5) on the Ross road south of Hereford city centre. The mediaeval church of St Martin (qv) stood on the Wye Bridge and was pulled down in 1645 and rebuilt to the south. The Jearrad family was responsible for the development of much of Cheltenham.

Jebb, John (1805-86), clergyman and antiquarian, was born in Dublin; his uncle was Bishop of Limerick. He was educated at Winchester College and Trinity College, Dublin, graduating DD. He married Frances (d.1866), daughter of General Sir Richard Bourne in 1831. In 1843 he was appointed rector of Peterstow, near Ross and in 1858 prebendary of Preston Wynne in Hereford. He was a residentiary canon, prelector of the cathedral from 1863-70 and from 1878-86 chancellor. With Ouseley (qv), Havergal (qv) and Lord Saye and Sele (qv Frederick Fiennes) he studied the manuscripts, musical records and ancient ceremonial and liturgy in Hereford Cathedral's archives to revive their usage, and published a study of comparative cathedral liturgies. He was a much published author on church matters. His sermons and *A Literal Translation of the Book of Psalms* (1846) brought him regard as a hebraist and he was part of a group appointed to revise the Old Testament, but resigned when undue changes were suggested. There is a stained glass window in the south choir clerestory commemorating Jebb, made by Burlison and Grylls. He died at Peterstow rectory on 8 January 1886.

Jefferies, Joyce (d.1648), was the only child of Henry Jefferies of Ham Castle, near Clifton upon Teme, and the half-sister of Humphrey Coningsby (qv, d.1610), who disappeared on his way to Venice in 1610, leaving her a legacy. She owned a large house in Hereford and houses in Widemarsh Street, outside the city gate. She kept an account book where she noted details such as the blue feathers worn by the Royalist garrison in 1642, and detailed her expenditure, such as the bribe she gave a carpenter to overlook material he was supposed to take for the strengthening of Widemarsh Gate. In her accounts book she noted '*I paid John Trahern my sowldier for ye City of heriford 7 daies training with his Captain Mr Rich. Wiggmore.*' This is probably the Traherne mentioned as being captured by the Scots Army in 1645 and ransomed. Could he be Thomas Traherne's (qv) father? Stamford (qv Henry Grey) billeted four soldiers on her. Following his retreat Governor Barnabas Scudamore (qv) ordered her three houses outside the gate in Widemarsh Street to be pulled down, for which she was compensated a risible £17 15s. She recorded the last rent she was paid by Maud Pritchett at Holyrood Day (14 September) 1643. She then gave up, packed her possessions, including the glass which she had paid a man to remove from the windows, and went to stay with her nephew William Jefferies at Ham Castle. She had a cat, given to her by Lady Dansey (qv) of Brinsop, and a little dog whom she called with a whistle at her girdle. She kept a rare ambling nag (a horse trained to walk with two legs at each side at a time, favoured by ladies). Her hobby and weakness, besides expensive clothes, was standing 'gossip', or godmother to countless godchildren, all of whom received generous gifts of silver. She loved charitable giving and supported poor prisoners in Byster's Gate lock-up. She died in her 70s and was buried in St Kenelm, Clifton. Her account book was published in extracts by John Webb (qv) in 1857, and has recently been republished.

Jenner, Edward (1749-1823), surgeon and discoverer of smallpox vaccination, was born at Berkeley, Gloucs. He was apprenticed to a surgeon and set up in a medical practice in Gloucs where he married. Jenner became interested in smallpox which was then treated by variolation (after *variola,* the name of the virus). Matter from a smallpox pustule was injected into the patient, hoping for a mild infection and subsequent immunity. Noticing that farmworkers at home were often immune from smallpox and supposing it was because of their contact with cattle and exposure to the similar cowpox virus, in 1796 he began to experiment with the much safer method of the injection of cowpox matter, which came to be called vaccination (after *vacca* – cow). In this he was encouraged by his London mentor John Hunter, and his friend the Ross surgeon Thomas Paytherus (qv). He wrote up his findings after discussions with Paytherus and Thomas Westfaling (qv) at Rudhall Manor, near Ross, Westfaling's home. Paytherus was parish surgeon in the parish of Kings Caple and made some of the earliest inoculations of cowpox on the poor. Dr Jenner observed a biopsy conducted by Paytherus at Ross and was able to connect *angina pectoris* with the visibly hardened arteries of the subject and published the results. Jenner became a much decorated, international celebrity, patronised by royalty in many countries and his vaccination method was taken up by the British armed forces.

John (1st century AD), evangelist and saint, is said to have preached at the ancient Apostles Farm at Kingswood near Kington. Nearby are Apostles Lane and an Apostles Stone.

John (1167-1216), King of England 1199-1216, was the youngest son of Henry II and Eleanor of Aquitaine. Born at Oxford on 24 December 1167, he was the favourite of his father, who nicknamed him Lackland. He

could be a cruel, arbitrary monarch and in 1215 his barons wrested from him the bill of rights, Magna Carta, a copy of which can be seen in the cathedral archives. John often visited his castle at Hereford. William fitz Osbern (qv) had built a high earth motte with a wooden tower and John added royal apartments inside the bailey, where he stayed. John was fond of hunting and designated large tracts of the county royal forest. He would often stay with John de Kilpeck (qv under Hugh de Kilpeck), keeper of the Haye, a forest south of Hereford. The Domesday Book says it was required that every house in Hereford, which was then subject to forest law, supply a man to help with the hunt. King John was in Herefordshire in 1200 and issued a charter appointing a priest at Holy Trinity, Bosbury after its enlargement by Bishop de Vere (qv); and he was back in the county in 1202. In May 1213, having negotiated the lifting of Pope Innocent's interdict on his kingdom (1208-12), he stayed in Hereford to arrange its defence against Llywelyn ab Iorwerth (qv) and to quash baronial rebellion in the area. In 1215 he confirmed his brother Richard's (qv) charter to Hereford which freed citizens from royal interference and conferred on its merchants the right to associate in a guild for the regulation of trade. In 1216 he stayed at Eccleswell Castle with Richard Talbot (qv), and died later that year on 18 October. He was buried in Worcester Cathedral where his beautiful Purbeck marble effigy can be seen. Workmen removed his thumb-bone when his grave was opened and this is now in Worcester Cathedral archive, with a copy at Hereford. He was succeeded by his 9-year-old son with Isabella of Angoulême, Henry III (qv).

John the Baptist, last Old Testament prophet and first Christian saint, was, with St Peter (qv), popular in Saxon times and is patron of the oldest parish of Saxon Hereford. The Saxon minster and houses of this parish were demolished for the Norman cathedral, provision being made for parishioners within the cathedral. The vicar was chosen from among the vicars choral until, in the 20th century, it became the dean's role. The parish met in the nave, moving in the 13th century into the lady chapel crypt, where the saint's statue still stands. It later moved back up into the cathedral nave, its parochial altar sited at the south end of the pulpitum (the screen that separated choir from nave). In the late 15th century Dean John Prophete (qv) intended to build St John a separate chapel on the south of the cathedral but died before it was created. There were complaints that the parish's services interfered with the main offices of the cathedral but the opposite would have been true. In the 18th century the north transept and the south transept where the consistory court sat were separated off by wooden screens. Bishop Bisse (qv) created such a snug classical room in the choir area that St John's parishioners rented it for their services. The churches at Aconbury, Byford, Yarkhill and the ruined chapel at Yazor are dedicated to St John the Baptist. A carving of St John's baptism of Christ by the Herefordshire School of Sculptors (qv) can be seen on the Castle Frome font. The nativity of the Baptist, 24 June, was a mediaeval quarter day when Dean and Chapter met to allot the tithes of their parishes.

John of Bath (13th century), a monk of Dore Abbey, wrote out Osbert of Gloucester's Latin dictionary for the abbey, now in Hereford Cathedral library. It may have been John who wrote the chronicles of Dore in a copy of Bede, now in the British Library. It was continued through to the next century by a later hand and records three centuries of the abbey's history.

John of Evesham (fl.1359) was a master mason who worked on Hereford Cathedral in Bishop Trillek's time (qv). He is named in a contract of 1359 which mentions a house made available for him in Hereford. He started work on the chapter house, completed by Thomas of Cambridge (qv), probably bringing the plan from Evesham.

John of Gaunt (1340-99), Edward III's (qv) third son, was born on 6 March 1340. He became Duke of Lancaster through his marriage to Blanche, daughter of the 1st Duke, which formed the ground of the subsequent contention between York and Lancaster. He was Duke of Aquitaine and claimed the crown of Leon and Castile, and fought in France during the Hundred Years War.

With the king and his older brother, the Black Prince (qv Edward of Woodstock), increasingly ill he took over the government of England and after their deaths his ascendancy continued through the minority of Edward's grandson Richard II (qv). He was known to favour reform in the Church; he was a friend of John Wycliffe and protected Lollards such as William Swinderby (qv) in Herefordshire. He was blamed for maladministration by the rebels in the Peasants' Revolt of 1381 when the Kentishmen entered London and burnt Gaunt's palace of Savoy; he was fortunate to be in Scotland at the time. He was governor of Hereford Castle which he started to repair, planning to live there, but Richard was wary of his uncle's ambitions and rescinded his governorship and retrieved the castle for himself. Gaunt died on 3 February 1399 and Richard exiled his heir Henry Bolingbroke (qv Henry IV), who was moved thereby to seize the throne. John's descendant through his mistress Katherine Swinfield was to do the same in the next century when Henry Tudor became Henry VII.

Johnes, Thomas (*c.*1721-80), was born at Llanfair Clydogau in Wales. He married Elizabeth, the only child of Richard Knight (qv) who had recently bought Croft Castle from the Croft family (qv). After her father's death the Johnes lived at Croft.

Johnes, Thomas (II) (1748-1816), MP, landscape architect and printer of fine books, son of Thomas and Elizabeth, was born on 1 September 1748 and brought up at Croft Castle. He moved to Cwmystwyth, Ceredigion and established the Hafod Press, printing many beautiful books. He landscaped the estate gardens, advised and encouraged by his cousin Richard Payne Knight (qv) and friend Uvedale Price (qv). These grounds may have been the source of Coleridge's (qv) fantasy, *Kubla Khan*. But the unchecked expense of his grandiose enterprise forced Johnes to sell Croft Castle, where his mother Elizabeth was still living. Hafod House, with his fine printed books, burnt to the ground, then his daughter Maramne died. As a final act in the tragedy the Forestry Commission covered the area with conifers. There are views of Hafod's enchanted landscape in Croft Castle, a landscape which the present Hafod Trust have plans to restore.

Jones, Constance (1848-1922), philosopher and college head, was born on 19 February 1848 at Langstone Court, Llangarron, an important late 17th-century house. A brilliant scholar, she was educated at the recently founded Girton College, Cambridge, where she became involved with the administration and was eventually its mistress. She retired to Weston-super-Mare where she died.

Jones, Edmund (d.1497), prosperous cider merchant, is buried with his wife in Hereford Cathedral crypt. Their effigies have a barrel at their feet where gentry would have had a lion or dog, proudly asserting their involvement in the cider trade. Jones paid for the renovation of the crypt, then in use as the charnel house.

Jones, Harford (1738-90) was born at The Whittern, Lyonshall. His mother was Elizabeth Brydges (qv Richard Harford) of Old Colwall. He married Winifred, daughter of Richard Hooper, and they lived at Boultibrooke near Presteigne. He was High Sheriff in 1778. He died on 26 March 1790.

Jones, Robert (fl.1805), builder, worked for John Nash and Humphry Repton (qqv). He also designed his own work such as the gothic-style St Ethelbert's Hospital in Castle Street, Hereford (1805) in which he incorporated old stones from the cathedral – seen in the garden elevation. Local mason Thomas Wood (qv) carved the convincing-looking seal above the entrance for him. He surveyed sites for Hereford Corporation such as old Hereford gaol in St Peter's Square and St Katherine's Almshouses in Ledbury. It may have been his son Richard Jones of Ledbury who built the Ann Cam School (qv under Thomas Cam) in Dymock in 1825.

Jones, Robert (1857-98) VC, was born on 19 August 1857 at Penrhos near Raglan. Aged 21 he joined the 2nd Battalion, 24th Regiment of Foot. At Rorke's Drift in January 1879 he defended a hospital hut against great odds while the patients were moved to safety and he received the VC for his bravery. After discharge he worked as a farm labourer in Herefordshire, married Elizabeth Hopkins and had five children. He was disturbed, however, by nightmares of the Zulu Wars – to the extent that he was finally driven to shoot himself while working at Peterchurch on 6 September 1898. He is buried in the churchyard at Peterchurch.

Jones, William (d.1790) of Clodock with Sarah Rugg poisoned Jones's wife at Longtown with arsenic in 1790. They were hanged in St Peter's Square, Hereford and Jones's body was returned to Longtown to be gibbeted on the castle green – the last to be so. Mrs Jones's gravestone is still to be seen in Clodock churchyard.

Jones-Brydges, Harford (1764-1847), 1st Baronet, diplomat and author, was born at Boultibrooke on 12 January 1764, the son of Harford. On 4 May 1826 he assumed the additional surname Brydges (qv) to advertise his connection, through his mother's family, with that influential family. He married his cousin Sarah, daughter of Sir Henry Thomas Gott (qv Greening), and through her gained The Whittern, the Lyonshall estate his father had transferred to Richard Hooper. He was a friend of Sir Uvedale Price (qv). His younger daughter, Sarah, married George Bentham (qv); the older, Sarah Laura, married John Lucy Scudamore (qv) of Kentchurch, and Sir Harford, who was interested in architecture, supervised the rebuilding of Kentchurch Court for his son-in-law. He loved the Middle East, was skilled in Middle Eastern languages and published books on Persia. He worked for the East India Company and later in the government diplomatic service where he was the mover of British policy in Persia and the region. In 1807 he was created baronet and sworn of the Privy Council. He was an active Whig in Radnorshire and Deputy Lieutenant of Herefordshire. He died at Boultibrooke on 17 March 1847. With the death of his son Sir Harford James Jones-Brydges (1808-91) the baronetcy became extinct.

K

Keck, Anthony (1727-97), an architect from a gentry background, married in 1761 Mary Palmer from Lugwardine, where he was working for James Walwyn (qv). They settled in King's Stanley in Gloucestershire and had two children. Here he based his workshop, designing and building distinctive houses throughout the region, typically using bay windows and oval forms. He prefabricated work in his yard and assembled it on site. In 1788 he rebuilt Longworth Manor at Lugwardine for Walwyn, an elegant mansion with bow windows rising right up the façade. It has an oval room with curved door and window frames to match. He built Underdown House at Ledbury, also with bow windows, and modernised Kentchurch Court, John (II) Scudamore's (qv) mediaeval manor house in 1773. Sir George Cornewall (qv, d.1819) found Keck a considerably cheaper option than Robert Adam (qv) when he took over the rebuilding of Moccas Court. Other houses are Canon Frome Court, Sufton Court and additions to Castleditch in Eastnor where Smirke later built his castle. He worked at Burghill Court for Lady Catherine Stanhope (qv) and rebuilt Whitfield Court for her *c.*1780. When in 1786 the west front of Hereford Cathedral collapsed Keck was first there with plans and estimates although James Wyatt's (qv) were accepted; and he was involved with Hereford's new gaol. He died on 4 October 1797 and is buried in King's Stanley graveyard.

Kemble, John (1599-1679), saint and martyr, was born at Rhydicar Farm, St Weonards into a family of recusant gentry; the Jesuit college St Xavier's was nearby at the Cwm, Llangarron. His brother George bought and repaired Pembridge Castle. John trained as a Roman Catholic priest in Spain and was ordained at Douai in 1625. He returned to live with his brother at Pembridge Castle where he served as priest, celebrating the mass in the Welsh Newton area for 54 years. His chapel in the castle can still be seen. The authorities initially overlooked his activities in a county with many Catholic sympathisers, but this changed with the Popish Plot of 1678; the Jesuit college was raided and Fr John seized at Pembridge Castle by Captain John Scudamore, whose own wife and family knew the priest. Kemble, accused of implication in the plot, was imprisoned in Hereford Castle gatehouse for three months. Then, aged 80 and in bad health, he was sent to London for investigation and brought back again, spending days in pain on horseback. In Hereford he was tried at the assizes by Lord Chief Justice Scroggs in the Booth Hall, convicted of celebrating the mass and thus of treason under English law, and sentenced to be hanged, drawn and quartered on Widemarsh Common outside Byster's Gate. Before he left his cell for the gallows Kemble drank and smoked a pipe with his jailer, The expression 'a Kemble cup or pipe' was long used in Hereford. He was allowed to die on the gallows. When he was beheaded his left hand was also cut off and preserved as a relic through penal times when Catholics were persecuted; it now rests in St Francis Xavier Church in

Broad Street, Hereford, a source of miracles. It is ironic that at the Battle of Worcester Kemble's cousin, Captain Richard Kemble, had saved the life of Charles II, the monarch in whose name Kemble was killed. It was Captain Kemble who buried his cousin's remains at St Mary's, Welsh Newton under a stone inscribed 'J.K. Dyed the 22 of August Anno Do. 1679'. There is a brass in the church. He was beatified in 1929 and canonised as one of the 40 English Martyrs on 25 October 1970 by Pope Paul VI. Miracles have been claimed at his graveside. His captor's own wife was apparently cured of deafness while praying here and their daughter of throat cancer. A later visitor to the site was Sarah Siddons (qv), the celebrated actress who was his great-great-grandniece. There is an annual pilgrimage to the grave on 22 August from St Mary's, Monmouth.

Kemble, Roger (1722-1802), actor and theatre manager, was born in Hereford on 1 March 1722 into a Roman Catholic family; his father was a barber. An ancestor, St John Kemble (qv), had been executed in Hereford 40 years before Roger's birth. Roger was apprenticed as a wig maker but loved the stage and joined John Ward's (qv) travelling company. He also loved the manager's daughter Sally (1735-1807), and they eloped, and married at Cirencester. They were forgiven and rejoined the troupe, playing *A Bold Stroke for a Wife* at the Swan and Falcon in Broad Street, Hereford. When Ward retired, Roger took over Leominster Theatre, proving a great manager but never a particularly good actor. Sarah was the commercial and artistic genius of the partnership, besides bearing 12 children. She gave birth to their son Stephen George Kemble (1758-1822) after playing Anne Boleyn in *Henry VIII* at Kington Theatre on 3 April. Two of their children, Sarah Siddons (qv) and John Philip Kemble, became the greatest actors of their age, others, John and Charles, were also famous actors. Charles's daughter Fanny Kemble (1809-93) was 'Queen of Tragedy' on the American stage; her daughter Frances married the Dean of Hereford (qv James Wentworth Leigh). As Roger was Catholic and Sarah Protestant they brought up their sons Protestant and their daughters Catholic. When the children and grandchildren were famous on the London stage their parents retired to a cottage in Kentish Town. Roger was said to have exquisite manners and bearing, on the strength of which he was allowed a coat of arms as a gentleman. He died on 6 December 1802 aged 80.

Kempe, Charles Eamer (1837-1907), ecclesiastical designer and stained glass maker, was born on 29 June 1837 at Ovingdean Hall, East Sussex the youngest and seventh child of Nathaniel Kemp, who was 73 when Charles was born. Charles added the final 'e' in the 1860s. He was educated at Rugby and Pembroke College, Oxford, a shy young man with a stammer which kept him from ordination. Rather than serving in the sanctuary he decided to decorate it and was apprenticed to Tractarian architect G.F. Bodley (qv), a family friend. He travelled widely in Europe to study the mediaeval arts that he and Bodley loved and on his return worked for Clayton and Bell (qv), where he received his first commission: the Bishop Hooper Memorial window in Gloucester Cathedral in 1868. Next year he founded the Kempe Studio, later Kempe and Co. in London, which flourished between 1869 and 1934. It was the most distinctive of the stained glass producers at the end of the 19th century, making Kempe extremely rich. His work is unmistakable with its yellow tint, learnt from 15th-century models such as the windows of Malvern Priory – a hue obtained by flashing silver on clear glass during firing. Distinctive features are the strings of pearls that edge the clothing of the saints, the peacock feathers of the angels' wings, and his love of saints such as Polycarp, Chrysostom and Athanasius, all seen in Dean George Herbert's (qv) south transept window in Hereford Cathedral, with Kempe's arms, three wheat sheaves on a red ground, in the tracery. His workshop was increasingly prolific and made glass for the world, signed with a wheatsheaf. After his death his cousin Walter Tower took over the direction of the firm and the wheatsheaf had a black tower added to it. Herefordshire is rich in Kempe glass. Six early Kempe windows and the reredos were made for

St Bartholomew, Much Marcle where Revd Allan Chatfield, vicar 1847-96, had married Anna Sober (d.1881), both of whom were cousins of Kempe. The splendid east window is a memorial to their son George Kemp Chatfield. St Michael, Ledbury has nine Kempe windows. He also designed brass and wood fittings, furniture, rooms and whole buildings. Kempe died unmarried in London on 29 April 1907 and was buried in the family vault at St Wulfran at Ovingdean, Sussex, near the family home.

Kempson, Frederick Robertson (1838-1923), architect, was born at Birchyfields, Bromyard, fifth son of Revd William Brooke Kempson JP, 1839-59, rector of Stoke Lacy where there are Kempson brasses. A brother, Capt Edward Kempson (1836-68) of the 26th Cameronians, died at sea. Frederick was educated at Cheltenham College and articled to architects J.P. Seddon and John Prichard (qqv), both with connections in Wales and the Marches. With Prichard's help he established an office at Llandaff, Cardiff and, optimistically in Gordon Square, Bloomsbury. But his commissions came mainly from Herefordshire and he moved his practice to 18 St Owen Street, Hereford from 1861. One of his first jobs was for a Romanesque-style chancel, nave and aisles at St Mary's, Bishop's Frome, followed by a general rebuilding of St Peter and Paul at Stoke Lacy (1863-4), his father's old church, and then, responding sympathetically to the original Norman work, renovations at St Andrew's, Wolferlow, where he returned for further work in 1890-4. In 1865 he modernised Burton Court, Eardisland for John Clowes (qv), preserving the important 15th-century hall. A major commission came from Sir James S. Rankin (qv) for his large house Bryngwyn at Wormelow (1868). His usual builders were Fowler, Charles Busteed Jory and E. Brindley. He secured the contract to build St Paul's Church at Tupsley for James Jay (qv) of Litley Court who was developing the area. Haddon (qv) had won a competition for this project; perhaps the change of architect may be related to Kempson's engagement to Jay's daughter Julia Madeleine. He and Julia were the first to be married at the consecration of St Paul's in November 1865 and Kempson became a churchwarden. The heads on the label stops could be portraits of Kempson and the Jays. The couple settled at Singleton, Tupsley and had children Eric and Rachel. Eric's daughter was the actress Rachel, who married Michael Redgrave and became the mother of the Redgrave acting clan. Incidentally, Redgrave's mother was a Scudamore. Kempson also built the vicarage and school in Tupsley. He rebuilt St Anne, Thornbury in his Norman style, keeping the 12th-century windows. He rebuilt the tower at All Saints, Coddington, and worked at St Michael, Breinton in 1866-70. He built St Andrew's at Dinedor in 1867 and in 1870 Little Cowarne Church. He added an arcade to St Peter's, Lugwardine and Holy Rood Church, Mordiford. In 1868 he built a new porch at St Peter's, Pipe and Lyde. Rankin, pleased with his house, chose him as the architect for Hereford Library and Museum in Broad Street (1872-4) with its wonderful terracotta decoration of beasts and birds in the spirit of Ruskin. On the attic floor growling dogs lean out to protect the curator's office, and an ape appears to play the cello. The carving was by the Clarke brothers (qv), whom Kempson had known in Llandaff, with the figures of Art and Science at the entrance by Milo Griffith. There are Godwin (qv) tiles in the first-floor fireplaces. Kempson moved to a bigger office at 134 St Owen Street with an assistant, William Martin (qv), who later set up on his own in Hereford. In 1870 he gothicised the Georgian St John Baptist, Grendon Bishop, introducing tiling and wall texts. In 1874 he was again at St Peter's, Pipe and Lyde working for the vicar, Revd F.T. Havergal (qv) and in 1878 he rebuilt St Mary's Church at Hope under Dinmore (1896). He rebuilt St Peter's, Bullinghope, between 1872 and 1880, and in 1880 he was at St Peter's, Grafton working in the 13th-century style favoured by Scott (qv), supplying an unusual font consisting of a kneeling angel holding a shell. He renovated St Andrew's, Allensmore and supplied fittings such as the font. He also built the school and vicarage here. At Ullingswick he rebuilt nave and chancel with a pretty bell tower. Henry Stuart Goodhart Rendel thought his Holy Trinity in the Whitecross Road (1883) the dullest church he had ever seen. The major project of 1881 was the college in Venn's Lane, now the Royal National College for the Blind. In 1887 he built a convent for the Poor Clares on the Holme Lacy Road and one of his last buildings is a chapel at Kington, now St Bede RC Church (1890-1). Two pupils of Kempson's who became noted Herefordshire architects were Edward James Bettington (1867-1939) and Herbert Skyrme (1871-1944). Kempson was FRIBA, put forward by his old master Prichard. He spent his last years in London and died at his home by Trafalgar Square on 8 October 1923.

Kenelm (d.821) was a sainted Mercian king descended from Offa (qv) with a popular cult in mediaeval England (vid. Chaucer's *Nun's Priest's Tale*). St Kenelm was murdered while hunting in the Clent Hills.

Kenelm (d.1060) was a Saxon prince of the Leominster area and a benefactor of the priory. He had a stretch of the River Lugg diverted to form the northern boundary of the priory precinct, called the Kenwater after him. He was buried in the priory, where the plaque commemorating him was recorded by John Hakluyt (qv).

Kent, Nathaniel (1737-1810) was a land agent from Hampshire who had worked in Portsmouth dockyard. The Admiralty made use of him abroad and he studied land management at Brussels. He wrote *Hints to Gentlemen of Landed Property* (1775). Charles Cocks (qv, d.1806), 1st Baron, brought him in to improve the efficiency of the Castleditch estate at Eastnor and he was able to increase Cocks' income. Kent was famous for restructuring wasteful large estates in an age of agricultural reform, and worked on agriculturally-minded George III's royal farms. He was also employed by Uvedale Price (qv) at Foxley. He died in Fulham in 1810.

Kent, William (1685-1748), architect of the Palladian style, attracted the patronage of Lord Burlington for whom he built Chiswick House. He was employed by Alexander Pope (qv) and was probably involved with Horace Walpole (qv) and others in the design of Shobdon Church for Richard Bateman (qv). The polygonal pulpit there is his.

Keyne (d.505) was one of the 24 sainted daughters, not to mention sons, of King Brychan of Brycheiniog. She refused offers of marriage and became an anchorite in Somerset where the town of Keynsham remembers her. Here a legend that she turned the serpents into stone accounts for the prevalence of ammonites. She returned to the Marches of Wales at her nephew St Cadog's invitation and founded churches in the area. Kentchurch takes its name either from her or her sister St Ceingar (qv Cynidr). Her feast day is 8 October.

Kilpeck, Hugh de (12th century), grandson of William fitz Norman (qv) and a relative of Hugh de Mortimer (qv), lived in Kilpeck Castle of which stone walls and earthworks remain. He founded a Benedictine priory at Kilpeck in 1134 which he presented to St Peter's Abbey, Gloucester. He used the workshop that included the sculptors of the Herefordshire School (qv) to rebuild the Saxon church of St David. The distinctive carving round the south door and on the chancel of Kilpeck Church is similar to that at Shobdon and dated *c.*1140. Hugh and Robert de Béthune (qv) helped the monks of Llanthony Abbey in the Black Mountains to move to the greater security of Gloucester where the ruins of Llanthony Secunda remain. Hugh and his son Henry (d.1196) and their descendants were keepers of the King's Forest of Haye, near Hereford. Henry's son John de Kilpeck was a favourite of King John (qv) who stayed with him at Kilpeck Castle to enjoy the hunt. John married a Juliana and they had a son, Hugh (II) de Kilpeck (fl.1231), who was the ward of William (II) de Cantilupe (qv) after John's early death. In 1231 Hugh was a commissioner empowered to discuss peace terms with Llywelyn ab Iorwerth (qv). He had no son and his daughter Isabella and her husband William Walerand, Sheriff of Wiltshire, inherited his estates. Their son Robert Walerand (qv) was next Lord of Kilpeck and lived in Kilpeck Castle. He was the Sheriff of Gloucester and fought against de Montfort (qv) at Evesham. Before his death Kilpeck was granted to his sister's son Alan (II) de Plukenet (qv) and Walerand was given a pension from the estate.

Kilpeck, Joanna de (d.1337), daughter of Alan (II) Plukenet (qv) married first Thomas Corbet and later Henry de Bohun, son and heir of John de Bohun of Haresfield, Gloucestershire, a grandson of Humphrey (IV)de Bohun (qv), Earl of Hereford, d.1275. In 1315 she became sole heiress of the Plukenet estate. She is styled Countess of Hereford by virtue of her Bohun marriage. She presented the living of Lugwardine Church to the Dean and Chapter of Hereford Cathedral and was a benefactor of the lady chapel being built at the east end of the cathedral. She gave funds for mass priests to pray for her family and to say the Lady Mass. Hers is the tomb on the north wall before the altar. It was panelled over in the 18th century when the lady chapel housed the chained library, and was uncovered by Cottingham (qv) during his restoration. A Society of Antiquities report of 1846 describes her bones as decayed but her profuse golden red hair being perfectly preserved though detached from her skull.

Kilvert, Robert Francis (1840-79), clergyman and diarist, was born on 3 December 1840 at Hardenhuish, Wiltshire where his father Revd Robert Kilvert was rector; his mother was Thermuthis Coleman. He had a brother and four sisters and was educated at the village school run by his father, and then at one in Bath run by an uncle. In 1858 he went up to Wadham College, Oxford and gained a third class degree. Ordained, he was curate for his father at Langley Burrell, Wiltshire, then went to Clyro in Radnorshire as Revd R.L. Venables' curate. Venables described him as 'tall with a black beard and moustache'. The Clyro years, 1865-72, were his happiest and

this area is rightly called Kilvert Country. He returned briefly to Langley Burrell to help his father, then received his own parish, first at St Harmon back in Radnorshire, then as rector of St Andrew's, Bredwardine, where he spent his last two years. Kilvert was a keen observer of his parishioners and the countryside and the diaries he kept are unsurpassed. Their fate is almost as sad as his tragically early death. First his widow pruned them of references to their courtship and other personal matters, which left 21 notebooks. These descended to a niece who sent them to a publisher in the 1930s and William Plomer was asked to look through them. Plomer recognized their worth, made a transcription of selected passages that appealed to him then, as war loomed, returned them to her. The niece, thinking Plomer had taken what was valuable and being unhappy about some personal matters, burnt them, with the exception of three earlier ones. Plomer destroyed his own transcript and published excerpts in three volumes. Thus was the bulk of this great work of literature with its peerless descriptions of the Radnor/Hereford March and its people lost. The later diaries ran from 1870 when Kilvert was in Clyro to his death nine years later. He was a sympathetic, acute, humorous recorder of the rural scene in Wiltshire, Radnorshire and Herefordshire, and a conscientious clergyman. He took advantage of his unique position as priest in times of class segregation to mix with high and low and note his observations sensitively. He was a good mixer, popular and welcomed everywhere, but was also fond of solitariness and the deserted road. He admired William (qv) and Dorothy Wordsworth and was impressed by Dorothy's journal keeping. Like them he was a great walker and, although not a robust man, was constantly out on parish calls, climbing hills, botanising and looking at churches. He was fascinated by local speech and customs. Once he went to Dorset to visit the dialect poet Revd William Barnes whose verse he loved. He was given a slip from the holy thorn of Glastonbury in 1878 and had it grafted at Bredwardine, and in the intensely cold winter before his death he was pleased to see it flowering. He frequently stayed with his sister Thersie and her husband Revd William Smith, vicar of Monnington. After often exhausting days out he took pains to write up his thoughts and observations. Once he pondered, 'Why do I keep this voluminous journal? ... Partly because life appears to me such a curious and wonderful thing that it almost seems a pity that even such a humble and uneventful life as mine should pass altogether away without some such record as this.' He had looked forward to being married and having children but was prevented by his poor salary as a curate. He met Elizabeth Rowland (1846-1911) from Oxfordshire on holiday in Paris. They married on 20 August 1879 and honeymooned in Scotland, but on 23 September that year he died of peritonitis in Bredwardine vicarage. He was buried in his churchyard with the inscription: 'He being dead yet speaketh'.

Kinnaird, Charles (1780-1826), 8th Lord Kinnaird, MP, was born in April 1780 and educated at Edinburgh and Cambridge. Elected MP for Leominster in 1802 he was seen in the Commons as a Jacobite and suspected of planning to assassinate the Duke of Wellington, who was in fact a friend of his. When he was elevated to the Lords in 1806 his friend William Lamb (qv), later Lord Melbourne, succeeded him as MP for Leominster. In 1817 he built a Scottish castle at Inchture in the Carse of Gowrie, where he lived.

Kip, Johannes (1653-1722) was a Dutch draughtsman, engraver and print dealer who worked at the Court of William of Orange. He followed William and Mary to England on their accession to the throne and opened a print shop in Westminster. With Leonard Knyff (1650-1721) he published atmospheric bird's eye view engravings in *Britannia Illustrata* (1707) of the houses of the nobility and gentry which included the great Herefordshire houses including Holme Lacy, and churches such as Hereford Cathedral, before the west front collapsed.

Knight: Richard Knight acquired the Bringewood Ironworks (a blast furnace and a forge) about 1695 and he and his sons expanded their interests by buying up other works along the Stour valley. By the 1770s there were 12 water wheels in operation on this stretch of the Stour. His youngest son, Thomas, the rector of Bewdley, had two sons of some celebrity: Richard Payne Knight (qv), a controversial antiquarian, and Thomas Andrew Knight (qv), an experimental horticulturist. The former inherited his grandfather's Downton property and spent most of his life building and altering a fantasy Gothic revival castle there. Downton Castle at Downton on the Rock in north Herefordshire with its grounds by Nesfield (qv) is extant, surprisingly in view of the survival record for country houses in Herefordshire.

Knight, Andrew Rouse Boughton, son of T.A. Knight (qv), inherited Downton and had Samuel Pountney Smith (qv) of Shrewsbury build the new St Giles' Church in 1861-2 to improve the view from the castle.

Knight, Laura (1877-1970), artist, was born Laura Johnson, in Nottingham on 4 August 1877, one of three girls. After their father's death their mother, Charlotte, taught art in Nottingham schools and took in pupils. Laura grew up surrounded by the practice of art and took over the pupils on her mother's death. She attended Nottingham Art School and met her future husband Harold Knight (1874-1961) on holiday near Whitby, where they stayed on, painting the scenery and selling the results. She was proficient in many media, won awards and exhibited at the Royal Academy. She is associated with the artist colonies at Newlyn and Lamorna on the Cornish coast and from this period date distinctive paintings of women and children in strong colour. She and Harold kept studios in Colwall and spent part of most years painting in the area. They were annually invited to the Malvern Festival. She became the first woman to be elected a Royal Academician in 1936. Despite her conservative views on art she experimented with techniques and subjects like the ballet and the circus, and, as an official war artist, was commissioned to record agricultural and industrial subjects. They lived in Colwall throughout the Second World War and in 1946 she went to Germany to paint a pictorial record of the Nuremberg Trials – an emotionally exhausting experience. They retired to Colwall when Harold's health deteriorated and on 3 October 1961 he died at the Park Hotel, Colwall, his favourite place in England he said. Dame Laura, as she now was, continued to paint with vigour and variety up to her death in London, aged 93, on 7 July 1970.

Knight, Richard (1659-1745), a wealthy iron founder of Downton with iron works in Coalbrookdale, was in partnership with the Foley (qv) family at one time. He bought Croft Castle from Sir Archer Croft (qv), and in 1728 an estate at Downton on the Rock, an area rich in coal and iron. He had a gothic façade added to Croft Castle, which he left to his daughter Elizabeth and her husband Thomas Johnes (qv). His sons Edward Knight (1699-1780), who built a plating mill at Bringewood and Ralph Knight (1703-54), who married Mary Duppa (qv), expanded his interests in the west midlands. Edward was innovative in replacing charcoal with coke as fuel. Another son, Revd Thomas Knight, rector of Bewdley (1697-1764) married his servant, Ursula Nash (b.1724) and had sons Richard Payne and Thomas (qqv).

Knight, Richard Payne (1751-1824), antiquarian and landscape theorist, was born at Wormsley Grange in Herefordshire on 11 February 1751, the eldest son of Revd Thomas Knight, rector of Bewdley and Ursula. His grandfather and uncles (qv Richard Knight d.1745) had become extremely wealthy and Richard was their

heir. He was a frail child and educated at home by a private tutor, excelling at Greek and in 1776-9 travelled to Italy to study the Greek antiquities in the south. He revisited later with the painter J.R. Cozens to record details of the Doric temples. In 1773 he started to create Downton Castle on his Bringewood estate, the castellated, asymmetric house that was to be his life's work. The architect Thomas Farnolls Pritchard (qv) assisted him but his constantly developing ideas were his own. The main accent of the house was its large, square entrance tower which led to a domed, circular dining-room based on the Pantheon, which he had recorded in Rome. The castle and estate, which lay in the wooded valley of the River Teme, set a fashion, influencing Beckford's Fonthill, for instance. Knight laid out his grounds in a picturesque manner, influenced by the theories of the German aesthetician Johann Winckelmann and the poetry of Pope (qv) and others. These associations of the ruins of Italy and the landscape with history, literature and philosophical ideas were early stirrings of the Romantic movement. He was creating 'the kind of beauty which is agreeable in a picture' as Gilpin (qv) wrote, like those of Claude Lorrain (Knight had over 150 of his sketches in his collection) and Jacob van Ruisdael. The landscape round Knight's castle was designed to assist an observer moving through it to meditate on classical literature, great paintings and sublime themes, solaced by 'tints, happily broken and blended and irregular masses of light and shadow harmoniously melted into each other'. The scenery of parts of Herefordshire was already 'sublime' and 'romantic' and as Knight's ideas became known he was called to enhance the picturesque quality of the county's estates. His friend Lady Jane Harley (qv) of Kinsham Court made use of him, for instance. He remodelled the grounds of Croft Castle, dismissing nearby Berrington, laid out by the once modish Capability Brown (qv), as unnatural. Knight promulgated his ideas in *The Landscape: a Didactic Poem* (1794). Knight's neighbour Uvedale Price (qv), a rival theorist, responded with *An Analytical Inquiry into the Principles of Taste* (1805). Price felt Knight was politically extreme, Jacobinical and unpatriotic. Knight was an advocate of all things Greek at a time when Rome was the fashion; he published *An Analytical Essay on the Greek Alphabet* (1791) and *Carmina Homerica Ilias et Odyssea* (1808), which claimed that Homer was not the author of *The Odyssey*. He published an illustrated selection of his and his friend Charles Townley's antiquities in 1809 with a commentary and a history of ancient art, followed in 1818 with a second volume: *An Inquiry into the Symbolical Language of Ancient Art and Mythology*. Knight attracted social opprobrium with his ideas on sexual symbolism in the art of different religions, suggesting that the phallus was the origin of the Cross, and was blackballed from Brooke's because of his interest in the priapic rites he had come across in Italy. He was uncompromisingly controversial and always ready to upset an ally. When consulted about the plan to purchase the Elgin Marbles he advised against it, dismissing them as mere Roman copies. He angered the Prince Regent with outspoken contempt for his architectural taste, and criticised his treatment of his wife. In 1780 Knight was returned MP for Leominster and in 1784 for Ludlow, which he represented until 1806. At Westminster he aligned himself with the opposition Whigs against Pitt's government and, controversial as ever, sponsored Charles James Fox, whose principles of freedom he greatly admired. He found metaphors in the landscape for political, moral and aesthetic freedoms, although his stand against oppression and advocacy of freedom of expression did not prevent him, as a magistrate, from calling in the cavalry to break a miners' strike in Shropshire. Knight's political ideas are expressed in his long poem *The Progress of Civil Society* (1796), which traces the development of freedoms in the history of mankind. The epitome of civil society was for him 5th-century BC Greece; modern life was riddled with decadent superstitions and repression. His endorsement of the French Revolution drew further attacks and he was fiercely anti-clerical. He was a trustee of the British Museum, a founder member of the British Institution and the Society of Dilettanti, and a member of the Society of Antiquaries. In 1823 he published his last work, *Alfred, a Poetic Romance*. Having stood down from Parliament in

1806 Knight made over Downton Castle to his brother and his family and retired to Stone-brook Cottage, a modest house on the estate. On 23 April 1824 he died in London of a stroke and was buried at St Mary's, Wormsley, where his grave and that of his brother Andrew can be seen. He bequeathed his unrivalled collections of bronzes, gems, coins and drawings to the British Museum, where they remain. He commissioned landscape paintings from Thomas Hearne (qv, d.1817) to illustrate his picturesque ideas. There are portraits of him in Hereford Museum, the Whitworth Art Gallery, Manchester (Thomas Lawrence, 1794) and Brooke's, the London club which blackballed him, and a bust in the National Portrait Gallery.

Knight, Thomas Andrew (1759-1838), writer and horticulturist, was born at Wormsley Grange, younger brother of Richard Payne Knight (qv). He went to Balliol College, Oxford and educated himself as a naturalist on his father's huge estate. He married Frances Felton in 1791 and they had a daughter Frances, known as Fanny; she married Thomas Pendarves Stackhouse of Acton Scott (qv Stackhouse Acton). The Knights lived at Elton Hall where Thomas experimented with fruit trees: he grew and grafted apple, cherry, plum and pear and crossing cultivars. He published his findings in *Treatise on the Culture of the Apple and Pear* (1797). He was noted for his work on the strawberry, developing varieties called *Downton* and *Elton*, and his development of potatoes, cabbages and peas. He was especially interested in the influence of gravity on the roots of plants and of light on shoots. He was elected member of the Royal Society in 1795 at the president, Sir Joseph Banks's invitation and read his first paper on the grafting of fruit trees. A species of pear he developed was named *Shobdon Court* after his friend Lord Bateman's (qv) house. He had 15 papers printed in all. He assisted his neighbour Samuel Peploe (qv) with his gardens at Garnstone Castle. He was a friend of Humphrey Davy, who consulted him, and of Charles Darwin, who mentions him on the first page of the *Origin of Species*. He was a founder member of the Herefordshire Agricultural Society and wrote *Pomona Herefordiensis* about old cider and perry fruits of the county, published in 10 parts for the Society by W. Bulmer in 1808-11. It had 30 hand-coloured plates of apples drawn and coloured by Elizabeth Matthews (qv) and Knight's daughter Frances. His older brother Richard made over to him the Downton Castle estate, where he engaged in his important horticultural experiments and corresponded with enthusiasts around the world. A shy, reserved man, he died, the most celebrated horticulturist of his age, on 11 May 1838, in his coach on the way to a meeting of the Royal Horticultural Society of which he was a founding member. He is buried beside his brother at St Mary's Church, Wormsley.

Knill: A Marches family, they were lords of Knill throughout the Middle Ages. Sir John de Knill was Lord of the Manor in the 12th century and a John Knill was Sheriff of Radnorshire in 1561. This branch died out after a Francis Knill's only child Barbara (b.*c.*1580) married John Walsham (qv, d.1648) of Presteigne and Knill Court passed to that family. Knills continued to farm and grow fruit in Herefordshire however and a John Knill's niece Jane (1825-1909) married A.W.N. Pugin (qv) as his third wife. The Knills' Tudor house, which stood by Knill Church, burnt down in 1943.

Knox, Edmund George Valpy (1881-1971) was the poet known as Evoe who edited *Punch* between 1932 and 1949, and was one of their great parodists. His brother was Ronald Knox, writer and priest. He spent annual summer holidays with his first wife Christina Hicks and their daughter, the novelist Penelope Fitzgerald (1916-2000), in his cottage at Knill, near Kington. He wrote *Hell in Herefordshire* to ridicule licensing restrictions on the sale of cider.

Kynardsley: A family that owned the manor of Kinnersley and its castle from the 12th to the 14th centuries. Robinson (qv) recounts a legend from the Kynardsley pedigree of John de Kynardsley, with his sons, confronting Domesday officials at his gate with a halberd. The family arms are given as a silver lion on a blue field. A Hugh de Kynardsley was sheriff of Hereford in 1250 and a benefactor of Craswall Priory. He accompanied Prince Edward (qv Edward I) to the Holy Land where he was knighted and allowed a cross on his blazon. In the late 14th century Sybil, daughter of William de Kynardsley, married Richard de la Bere (qv, d.1382), resulting in the transfer of castle and manor to the de la Beres.

Kyrle: An old Herefordshire family whose name is written Crull, a form of Norman origin; there was a Robert de Crull fighting at Hastings. Robert Crull (1295) of Hom Green near Ross married Maud and their only son was William. They were ancestors of the Kyrles of Walford. Walter Kyrle (d.1489) lived at Hill Court, Walford, where he was succeeded by his sons Walter and James, who lived at Walford Court. James's son was Thomas Kyrle, (qv, d.1577). The Kyrle hedgehog or 'urchin', seen in Ross Church, is a rebus of the old name for the area, Archenfield, said to derive from the Welsh Ergyng and perhaps from the Roman town name *Ariconium*. The Kyrles were active in the Civil Wars on both sides, Col Robert Kyrle having a reputation for looting. When Alexander Pope was researching his *Moral Epistles* he heard from Jacob Tonson (qv) at Ledbury and James Scudamore (qv, d.1668) at Holme Lacy about the philanthropy of 'The Man of Ross', John Kyrle. The resultant poem started a tourist craze that came to form part of the Wye Tour. With Sir John Kyrle the 2nd baronet the direct Kyrle line ended, passing to the Ernles (qv), although in the 19th century 'Kyrle' appeared once more as a suffix.

Kyrle, Francis (*c.*1590-1649), Sir John's (d.1650, qv) eldest son, was High Sheriff of Hereford. He married Hester (d.1644), daughter of Sir Paul Tracy of Stanway, Gloucs and they lived at Much Marcle. Of his two daughters Elizabeth married Robert Holmes, MP for Gloucestershire and Dorothy married first John Abrahall of Ingestone (qv), then Sir Bennet Hoskyns (qv). Francis predeceased his father and his son John (qv, d.1680) succeeded to the baronetcy.

Kyrle, John (1568-1650), 1st Baronet, of Homme House, son of Thomas Kyrle (qv, d.1577), married Sybil Scudamore (qv under Philip Scudamore) in 1589. Their daughter Joan married John Nourse in 1617. Kyrle was MP and High Sheriff for Hereford and was created a baronet in 1627. He owned iron foundries around Goodrich and Whitchurch which exploited ore and timber from the Forest of Dean. John and Sybil's tomb, by Samuel Baldwin (qv), fills the Kyrle chapel of St Bartholomew's, Much Marcle

and their gorgeous effigies show his rich armour and her ornamented bonnet, sumptuous dress with slashed sleeves, embroidered petticoat and large lace ruff with chains about her neck. His arms are fleur de lys with a hedgehog and the motto *nil moror ictus* (I do not mind the blows). The Scudamore crest is a bear's paw in a coronet. Their daughter Elizabeth married Stephen Boughton (qv), vicar of St Bartholomew and has a plaque in the church.

Kyrle, John (1619-80), 2nd Baronet, eldest son of Francis (qv) and Hester, married Rebecca, daughter of Daniel Vincent. Their eldest daughter, Vincentia (1651-83), married Sir John Ernle (qv) and their descendants, the Money-Kyrles, inherited Homme House. Rebecca, Sir John's widow, later married Captain John Booth (qv William Smalman).

Kyrle, John (1637-1724), Man of Ross, philanthropist, was the eldest son of Walter Kyrle (qv, d.1660) who died in 1660. Born at The White House, Dymock on 22 May 1637, he was educated at Gloucester and Balliol Colleges, Oxford and the Middle Temple. Retiring to Ross he dedicated the rest of his life to improving his estate, the town of Ross and its poor. His timber-framed house still faces Ross Market House, on the wall of which, facing his window, he had carved his initials entwined with King Charles's around a heart. He never married but lived with a relation called Judith Bubb who helped him with his extensive charities: 'a very good and fine girl and a great', he called her. He declined office, although he was High Sheriff in 1683. He gave free legal advice to the local poor in disputes, made and dispensed medicines and alleviated distress in every form. He arranged for a piped water supply to be brought into Ross, improved roads and had bread baked every Saturday to be distributed to the poor. He designed Hill Court House for a relative, Richard Clarke *c.*1695, and was an early exponent of the picturesque in landscape gardening and loved the Wye – the path along its banks still bears his name. He laid out The Prospect beside the church, overlooking a great sweep of the Wye, and presented

the ground to the town. The elms he planted in the churchyard stood until the outbreak of elm disease and the storm of January 1974. Suckers from these trees grew up inside the north aisle east window in St Mary's Church at Ross as a natural memorial to one who had loved them, and became a tourist attraction. When they died virginia creeper was planted there, still tended in his memory. Behind his house he created a pleasure garden with a rustic gothic gazebo and a mosaic of a swan in horses' teeth which local people brought him. He died on 7 November 1724 and is buried in the chancel of St Mary's Church where there is a wall monument to him. Another memorial is in Pope's (qv) *Epistle to Lord Bathurst* (1730):

Whose Cause-Way parts the Vale with shady rows?
Whose seats the weary traveller repose?
Who taught that heav'n-directed spire to rise?
The man of Ross each lisping babe replies.
Behold the market place with poor o'erspread!
The man of Ross divides the weekly bread.
He feeds yon almshouse, neat but void of state.
Is any sick? The Man of Ross relieves,
Prescribes, attends, the medicine makes and gives.

In 1829 Thomas Mildenhall brought his players to Ross to perform his own play *The Man of Ross* which dramatised Kyrle's life. The Kyrle Society, the first civic amenity trust, was founded in 1877 by Miranda Hill: its purpose to encourage tree planting in towns and preserve Kyrle's memory. Miranda's sister, Octavia Hill was secretary and went on to found the National Trust.

Kyrle, Robert (1618-69), of Walford Court, was the great-grandson of Walter Kyrle of Walford (qv Kyrle family) and the nephew of Walter, MP for Leominster (qv). He married Elizabeth (d.1668), daughter of John Brayne. He was a colonel in Stamford's (qv) army which occupied Hereford in 1642, and was known as 'a stony hearted rebel' after looting the house of Revd Thomas Swift (qv), vicar of Goodrich. He later transferred to the Royalist party as lieutenant colonel.

Kyrle, Thomas (fl.1500), one of the two sons of James Kyrle (d.1489), married Joan Abrahall and they had nine sons and a daughter, Bridget, who married Roger Pye (qv Walter Pye). The eldest son Walter Kyrle (b.1532) married Joan Warnecombe (*c*.1536-95) and their eldest son was Robert Kyrle (b.1558), who married Jane Evans (b.1560). Robert was a High Sheriff of the county; one of his sons was Sir Walter Kyrle (qv, d.1660)

Kyrle, Thomas (d.1577), fourth son of Thomas and Joan (qv Kyrle family), studied at Gray's Inn. He married Frances, daughter of John Knotteford of Malvern and they lived at Homme House, Much Marcle.

Kyrle, Walter (d.1660) JP and barrister, a descendant of Walter of Walford Court, the eldest of Thomas's (qv) sons, was MP for Leominster 1640-8. In 1645 Parliament granted him Rudhall House, where Lady Rudhall (qv under John Rudhall, d.1636) lived. He married Alice, daughter of John Mallet of Berkeley. She was the widow of Walter Carwardine of Madley. Their children were John (qv, d.1724), Walter and Sybil who married a William Scudamore.

Kyrle-Money, James (1775-1843), soldier, of Homme House, Much Marcle, was a son of James Money (1724-85) and Mary Webster of Stockton on Tees. He was descended from the Kyrles through the Ernle line and inherited their Herefordshire interests and arms. His son added the Kyrle name to his in 1809. He was an army officer rising to the rank of Major General in 1838, when he was created 1st (and only) Baronet.

L

de Lacy: Companions of the Conqueror from Lassy in Calvados, Normandy, they were granted extensive lands in Herefordshire and the Marches. Their barony included the large parish of Marcle, where they built a castle. Other castles were erected at Castle Frome, Lyonshall, Weobley and Longtown, which was once called Ewyas Lacy. Through rebellion their lands were forfeited to the Crown and dispersed to its servants: Marcle went to the Mortimers. By the mid 13th century the family was no longer found in the county and place names like Stoke Lacy, Holme Lacy and Mansell Lacy preserve the memory of their vanished might.

Lacy, Edmund (*c.*1370-1455), Bishop of Hereford 1417-20, was the son of Stephen Lacy of Gloucester. Educated at Oxford and ordained priest about 1399, he entered the royal service and was made a canon of Windsor (1401), Hereford (1412) and Lincoln (1414). He was a noted theologian but also active in the world, and was present at Agincourt. Early in 1417 Henry V made him Bishop of Hereford but in 1420 he was translated to the wealthier diocese of Exeter. Hereford archives show him to have been an active bishop. He was interested in music and appointed the composer John Dunstaple (qv) canon of Hereford. He issued a charter freeing John del Wode (qv), a bond-servant who worked in the kitchens at Colwall. He kept the feast day of St Raphael (5 October), the patron of good health, long celebrated at Hereford. His predecessor at Exeter, Bishop Berkeley, had inspired a cult of veneration and a similar cult grew up round Bishop Edmund's tomb there.

Lacy, Gilbert de (fl.1096-1163) was the son of Roger de Lacy (qv), with whom he was exiled in 1096. He was allowed to return by King Stephen in 1136 but many Lacy estates had been granted to others: e.g. to Hugh's (qv, d.1121) niece Sybil and her husband Pain fitz John (qv under Pain); to Miles of Gloucester (qv) and others. He supported Matilda during the Anarchy and was able to recover much of his patrimony. In 1158 he became a Templar knight and travelled to Jerusalem, resigning his lands to his eldest son Robert (d.1162). He was precentor of the Order in Tripoli where he led an army against Nur ad-Din in the Second Crusade. Gilbert is remembered at Hereford Cathedral on 10 November as a benefactor, for lands he presented to Dean and Chapter.

Lacy, Hugh de (*c.*1073-*c.*1121), second son of Walter (qv, d.1085) and 3rd Baron de Lacy, was the patron of St Mary's Church, Kempley, now in Gloucestershire but in Hereford diocese until the 16th century. The two figures in pilgrim dress painted in the mural in the chancel must be Hugh and his father, while the damaged one opposite would be Bishop Richard de Capella (qv). Above on the chancel ceiling is an extraordinary scene of apocalypse. He was a founder of Llanthony Abbey and of St Leonard's, a house of Augustinian canons at Wormsley where he was buried. The Lacy castle at Weobley was built at this time and was still standing in 1540 when Leland (qv) wrote of its dilapidation. Hugh's heir was his niece Sybil (daughter of his sister Agnes and Geoffrey Talbot (qv, d.1129), who married Pain fitz John (qv under Pain); Sybil and Pain's daughter Cecily conveyed the Lacy honour of Weobley to Roger fitz Miles (qv Miles) on her marriage to him.

Lacy, Hugh de (d.1186), lord of Ludlow, Ewyas and Weobley, was son and heir of Gilbert (qv). He accompanied Henry II to Ireland and was granted the kingdom of Meath, building castles and abbeys and warring with local kings. Henry was worried about the power Lacy wielded here and sent his son Prince John (qv) over with a large army; Gerald of Wales (qv) recorded the mismanagement and failure of this campaign. However Lacy, resuming his warfare with the Irish, was captured at Durrow and beheaded on 26 July 1186. He was buried next to his wife, Rohese de Monmouth (d.*c.*1180), at St Thomas's Abbey, Dublin. Henry II took over the honour of Weobley until his son Walter (qv, d.1241) was of age in 1189. His other sons by Rohese were Hugh, Gilbert and Robert. Hugh had a castle at Castle Frome and built St Michael's Church nearby. The splendid font here is a late piece by the Herefordshire School of Sculptors (qv); the bowl, which crushes three slaves, has a relief of the baptism of Christ, who stands in a pool below the hand of God.

Lacy, Roger de (d.1106), 2nd baron, inherited his father's (Walter, qv, d.1085) extensive holdings in the region – some 96 lordships – as chief Marcher lord. Roger rebelled against William Rufus in 1088 and again in 1094; he was banished and his lands in Herefordshire were granted to his brother Hugh (qv, d.1121).

Lacy, Walter de (d.1085), magnate, was prominent at the Battle of Hastings. He was created Lord of Ewyas and given much land in Herefordshire taken from Edwi (qv) and the thegn Eadwig Cild (qv). Walter took over Eadwig's manor at Weobley which he fortified in the Norman fashion. He raised a castle where Holme Lacy House now stands, rebuilt Harold's (qv) castle at Longtown, and nearby Walterstone takes its name from him. He was lord of Eardisley, where the Baskervilles were his feudal tenants. He married Ermeline; their sons were Roger (qv), Hugh (d.*c.* 1121, qv) and Walter, Abbot of Gloucester (1130-39). His daughter Agnes married Geoffrey Talbot (qv). With William fitz Osbern he held the southern Marches, and stayed loyal to William when fitz Osbern's son, Roger de Breteuil (qv), rebelled. Walter and his descendants were generous patrons of the Church, contributing to the building of Gloucester Abbey and St Peter's in the new Norman market area at Hereford. While he was inspecting the work at St Peter's in 1085, he fell from the tower and died. He was buried in Gloucester Abbey chapter house.

Lacy, Walter de (*c.*1170-1241), Lord of Ewyas Lacy, was a minor at his father Hugh's (qv) death in 1186. He eventually succeeded to great estates in England, Wales, Ireland and Normandy, retrieving them with difficulty from the royal grasp. He finally lost his Norman possessions to the French king. Much of his life was spent on his Irish estates and John made him Earl of Ulster. In 1225 he founded St Mary's Priory, Craswall, a rare example of the French Grandmontine Order. He was Sheriff and castellan of Hereford from 1216-23 and custodian of the see of Hereford during the papal interdict of 1208-14 when Bishop Giles de Briouze (qv), his brother-in-law, was in exile, and during the disputed reign of his successor Bishop Mapenore (qv). His marriage to Margaret, daughter of William (III) de Briouze (qv), an alliance of the two biggest families in the Marches and Ireland, allowed them to act in each other's interests. Both families joined with William the Marshal (qv) and Llywelyn ab Iorwerth (qv) in a vain attempt to resist John's exactions. Nevertheless Walter witnessed John's will and acted on the council of Regency for his son Henry III (qv). When Walter died in 1241, the Jews of Hereford (qv Hamo) were among his creditors. Margaret founded a nunnery at Aconbury whose church is extant. Walter's son and grandson had predeceased him and a younger brother Hugh died the year after him. His granddaughters Margaret and Matilda, co-heiresses of the great Lacy estates, were married to royal servants by Henry III.

Lamb, William (1779-1848), 2nd Viscount Melbourne, Prime Minister, was born on 15 March 1779 in Melbourne House (now The Albany), Piccadilly, the centre of a brilliant Whig circle. Lamb was elected MP for Leominster in January 1806, replacing his friend Charles Kinnaird (qv) who had been made a Scottish peer. It was as MP for Leominster that Lamb made his maiden speech. He was the husband of Lady Caroline Lamb and was Queen Victoria's friend and mentor 'Lord M'.

Lambe, William (1765-1847), physician, was born in St Peter's parish, Hereford, on 26 February 1765, son of attorney Lacon Lambe and his second wife, Elizabeth, sister of Bishop Joseph Berington (qv). The Lambes farmed at Bidney, Dilwyn where, *c.*1780, Lacon built Henwood by facing farm buildings with classical façades and laying out the surrounding park and gardens. William was educated at Hereford Grammar School and St John's College, Cambridge, where he was a fellow until his marriage. He married Harriet, daughter of John Walshe and they had six children. Lambe practised as a physician in London and was interested in the properties of water, warning about the effects of lead piping. As a Fellow of the Royal College of Physicians he lectured and published papers. He was a noted vegetarian. He died at Henwood on 11 June 1847 and is buried in St Mary's, Dilwyn.

Lambert, Henry (fl.1785) bought Barton Court near Colwall from the Bishop of Hereford and in 1780-5 rebuilt the ancient farmhouse as a substantial six-bay manor house which still stands on Barton Holloway. He married Jane, heiress of George Prichard of Hope End, who brought this contiguous estate to the marriage. Hope End had come to the Prichards through Jane's mother who was a Skippe (qv) of Ledbury.

Lambert, Susanna Prichard (1767-1817), Henry's (qv) daughter (married name Lady Tempest) lived with her father after her mother's early death. Her property attracted the attention of Sir Henry Tempest (qv) of Yorkshire. He met her at Colwall disguised as a gypsy woman and told her she would shortly meet her future husband; then he appeared at church next day in his own person and proposed. They eloped and were married at Marylebone in London. Sir Henry returned to Colwall to claim Hope End in the right of his wife, evicted her father and, tiring of his wife, her too. Susanna's father refused to receive her and she found refuge with an elderly relative in Worcester. Her ghost haunted Barton Holloway, becoming such a familiar sight that farm boys practised shooting at it. It was successfully exorcized and confined to a pond (cf the exorcizing of Black Vaughan of Hergest, and Lord Beauchamp at Bronsil – qqv). Elizabeth Barrett (qv), Tempest's successor at Hope End, had heard of the ghost by 1830.

Lane, Edward William (1801-76), orientalist, was born in Hereford on 17 September 1801, the son of Dr Theophilus Lane (1764-1814), prebendary of Withington Parva and his wife Sophia Gardiner, who was a niece of the painter Thomas Gainsborough. Edward went to Hereford Cathedral School and then studied with his brother Richard in London, where he discovered an interest in Arabic. Richard James Lane (1800-72), who had been born at Berkeley Castle, was a sculptor and among the first to make lithographic prints. Edward sailed to Egypt to study the antiquities but became interested in contemporary Egyptian culture and wrote his *Manners and Customs of the Modern Egyptians* (1836), which is still in print. To help him investigate women's quarters he sent for his sister Sophia Lane Poole (qv). Another success was Lane's translation of the *Thousand and One Nights* (1840), still a popular version. In 1840 he married Nafeesah, a slave-girl he had bought when she was eight years old. His great work, which he didn't live to finish, was an Arabic–English lectionary. He died on 10 August 1876 at his home in Worthing and was buried in Norwood Cemetery, London. There is a striking sculpture of Edward in Arabic dress by Richard in the National Portrait Gallery.

Langford, Charles (d.1607), Dean of Hereford 1593-1607 and previously vicar of Lugwardine, was a popular dean and there was an attempt to have him succeed Westfaling (qv) as bishop, but the chapter's wishes were ignored and the unpopular Robert Bennett (qv) was appointed. Dean Langford was a benefactor of the Cathedral School, endowing several scholarships for pupils, and one of the school's four houses is still named after him. He died on 28 October 1607 and was buried in the cathedral.

Langland, William (*c.*1325-*c.*90), poet, was probably born at Langlands near Colwall under the Herefordshire Beacon and educated at Little Malvern Priory, though some believe he came from Cleobury Mortimer. The Black Death of 1348 must have had a traumatic effect on the young man. He was a clerk in minor orders able to marry and lived with his wife and daughter in Cornhill, London where he wrote and revised his life's work *The Vision of Piers Plowman*. This now exists in several versions, written in Middle English and set in the Malvern Hills of his youth. The convention of the dream-vision is a popular one (cf Bunyan's *Pilgrim's Progress*): the narrator lies down by a spring, identified with the Putress Spring on the Herefordshire side of the Malverns, and dreams of a field full of folk, half way between a high tower and a low dungeon. He realises the moral and spiritual danger he is in and is shown what a good life might be like, what a better one would be and what the best of

all is. If the poem is autobiographical, Langland was well-educated by his father for the priesthood but wasted his time, made an ill-advised marriage and is now no better than a beggar. The protagonist, Piers, grows through the poem from being an honest ploughman to a personification of the redeemed soul. Langland's psychology and poetic technique are sophisticated and show knowledge of theology and contemporary literature. The poem was written in unrhymed, alliterative English and its influence was great. It was well enough known in 1381 for Piers the Plowman to be used as the rallying cry of John Ball's rebels in the Peasants' Revolt. Its criticism of the Church and use of the vernacular coincided with Lollard calls for reform of the Church, which were strong in Herefordshire (qqv Sir John Oldcastle, and Walter Brut, whom Langland mentions in the poem). His church on earth is a dim image of 'Unity Holychurch' above. After Henry VIII's break with Rome, *Piers Plowman* became a key text of the Reformation and was printed by Robert Crowley (qv).

Laud, William (1573-1645), Archbishop of Canterbury, was born on 7 October 1573, the son of a Reading merchant. He won a scholarship to St John's College, Oxford and was ordained. He was a brilliant scholar and organiser and passed through several bishoprics to the primacy. He disliked Puritanism and set about restoring order in the Church, replacing railed altars at the east end of the church, reintroducing priestly vestments, manual signs and decent music at services, all considered papistical by Puritans. In 1617 he composed for King James *The Book of Sports*, which allowed for maypoles and moderate Sunday recreation. This was reissued in 1633 to great protests, including one from a Ledbury rectory (qv Henry Page). Laud knew Herefordshire through his friendship with Sir John Scudamore (qv, d.1671). He was interested in Scudamore's spiritual welfare and preached at Holme Lacy on Sunday 20 November 1625. He encouraged Scudamore to restore the ruins of Dore Abbey and furnish it as a model Laudian church: the arms of Laud, Scudamore and Charles I are still displayed

here. When Herbert Croft (qv, d.1629) became a Catholic, Laud persuaded him to return to Anglicanism. In retrospect it is clear that Laud's attempts at moderate church discipline in the climate of the polarisation that was occurring in religious life were doomed. In 1640 he was arrested for treason by the Long Parliament and after a show trial, despite a lack of verdict and a royal pardon, executed on 10 January 1645 on Tower Hill. He is buried in his college of St John's.

Lawrence, Stringer (1697-1775), soldier, was born in All Saints parish, Hereford on 24 February 1697, the son of John and Mary Lawrence. He joined the army at 30, served in Spain and Flanders and fought at Culloden. He transferred to the East India Company in 1746 and commanded its forces, European and Indian, at Madras. His disciplining of the garrison there earned him the title 'father of the Indian Army'. He was commander in chief of the Company's forces in India for the next 20 years, with Clive as his second in command. He dominated Madras and the Carnatic region of south-east India, defeating French and Indian forces and leaving the East India Company in sole possession. He died in London on 10 January 1775. Joshua Reynolds painted his portrait and the Company placed his bust in Westminster Abbey.

Lawrence, Walter Roper (1857-1940), civil servant, was born at Moreton on Lugg to George Lawrence and Catherine Lewis. He married Lilian Gertrude (1858-1929), daughter of John Gwynne James of Aylestone Hill, Hereford, and their two sons were Percy and Henry. He served in the Indian Civil Service 1879-89 in the Punjab and as a Commissioner in Kashmir. From 1899-1903 he was Private Secretary to Lord Curzon, Viceroy of India, and was Chief of Staff during the Prince of Wales' visit to India. He was invested KGC in 1906, becoming 1st Baronet Lawrence of Sloane Gardens, Chelsea. Other orders were CB, GCVO and KGStJ. He published books about his experiences of the subcontinent, its culture and geography. Sir Percy Lawrence succeeded his father as 2nd Baronet.

Lawson, Henry (1774-1855) was an astronomer from Greenwich and a descendant of Catherine Parr. In 1823 he married Amelia (d.1855), daughter of Thomas Jennings, vicar of St Peter's, Hereford where he settled and set up his 11-foot refractor telescope (later presented to Greenwich Royal Observatory). His findings excited the curious in Hereford and he helped found the Herefordshire Literary and Philosophical Society, of which he became treasurer. He was elected to the Royal Astronomical Society and elected FRS. He later moved to Bath where he continued his astronomical and meteorological investigations until his death in 1855.

Leather, Ella Mary (1874-1928), folklorist, was born on 26 March 1874 the daughter of James Smith of Bidney, Dilwyn, a well-to-do farmer. She was educated at Clyde House School and Hereford High School for Girls. In 1893 she married Francis Leather, a Weobley solicitor, and brought up a family of three sons. Regretting the loss of country ways she began making records of local stories. A cyclist and keen photographer, she sought out elderly cottagers and workhouse inmates and scoured old sources, then sent her notes to journals including the *Herefordshire Magazine* and had them published by Jakeman & Carver (qv) as *The Folk-Lore of Herefordshire* (1912). With Ralph Vaughan Williams and Cecil Sharp (qqv) she visited gypsy encampments (two of her sources were Esther Smith and Elizabeth Johnson) and workhouses, preserving traditional songs such as *The Herefordshire Fox-Chase* (qv Carless). She recorded and preserved old buildings like Weobley's 17th-century grammar school, which she bought and used as her study, and contributed a paper on Weobley's timber-framed houses for the Woolhope Club in 1926. In 1928 she was President of the Herefordshire Women's Institute but died of a heart attack on 7 June that year in Weobley and is buried in the churchyard.

Lee, Lennox Bertram (1864-1949), textile industrialist, born on 7 November 1864 in Salford, was educated at Eton and travelled in Africa. He joined the Calico Printers' Association and became chairman in 1908; when he retired in 1948 his son succeeded him. He married Edith MacLellan in 1892 and in 1901 bought How Caple Court, where he farmed and redesigned the house, buildings and gardens. Lee was a benefactor of Hereford Cathedral and Herefordshire churches. He died on 14 December 1949 and was buried in St Andrew and St Mary at How Caple, where there are three stained glass windows designed by him and made by A.J. Davies (qv) in 1920.

Lees, Edwin (1800-87), botanist, was born on 12 May 1800 in Worcester, where he ran a publishing business until retiring to devote himself to the study of botany in the Malverns. He married Sarah Wright (1800-78), whom he met through their mutual friends William Samuel Symonds (qv), the rector of Pendock and his wife Hyacinth. He founded the Worcestershire Naturalists' Club and was its first president; the society published *The Botany of Worcestershire* under his direction. He was a fellow of the Linnaean Society. As a member of the Woolhope Naturalists' Field Club he suggested, in 1868, the club's annual fungus forays in Herefordshire. He was a friend of Dr Henry Bull (qv) to whom he dedicated his book *Scenery and Thought in Poetical Pictures ...* (1880). He died on 21 October 1887 and was buried with his wife in Pendock churchyard.

Leigh, James Wentworth (1838-1923), Dean of Hereford 1894-1919, was born in Paris on 21 January 1838, the younger son of Lord Leigh. He was educated at Harrow and Trinity College, Cambridge. He married Frances Butler (1838-1910), the daughter of the actress Fanny Kemble (qv under Roger Kemble) and her American husband Pierce Butler, and his mother-in-law died in his London house in Gloucester Place. In 1894 he was appointed Dean of Hereford following George Herbert (qv). He found the cloisters full of rubbish and the library stored in the dilapidated west range. This he had demolished, bringing in Sir Arthur Blomfield (qv) to build a new library building. He used earth-tremors of 1896 as an excuse to have Wyatt's (qv) unpopular west front replaced with one by Oldrid Scott (qv). A stained glass window in the south nave aisle by Powell and Sons (qv John Hardman Powell) commemorates the dean's wife Frances. It shows at the top a negro child in reference to the anti-slavery activities of Frances and her mother. Leigh was master of St Ethelbert's Hospital in Hereford, a prominent Freemason and Provincial Grand Master from 1906, with a Hereford Lodge named after him. He retired as dean in 1919 and died on 5 January 1923. He was an advocate of teetotalism and with Lady Somerset (qv Isabella Somers Cocks) supported the movement for the provision of temperance cafés.

Leinthall, Rowland (*c.*1390-1450), knight, son of Rowland Leinthall, a noted soldier, was a favourite of Henry IV (qv), who made him his Yeoman of the Robes. He was given estates in the Leominster area marked by the villages of Leinthall Earls and Starkes. His seat was Hampton Richard, later Hampton Court, at the confluence of the River Lugg and the Humber Brook. It had been a Bohun (qv) property and King Henry had already started to build there. Leinthall married Lady Margaret Fitzalan, an Arundel heiress and a relation of the king, then, after her death, Lucy de Grey (b.*c.*1403). Leinthall distinguished himself at Agincourt in 1415 and Henry V (qv) knighted him. With the money raised from ransoming the prisoners he had taken in the battle he funded the completion of Hampton Court (1434). Leland (qv) described its wonders such as running water from a spring-fed header tank. Sir Rowland's daughter and heir married Lord Burford and in 1510 they sold the estate to the Coningsbys (qv Thomas Coningsby, d.1527).

Lelamour, John (fl.1373) was the Master of Hereford Cathedral School. He translated Macer Floridus' *De Viribus Herbarum* into a Herefordshire dialect of Middle English and signed himself 'scolemaister' at the end, which proves the school to be one of the oldest in England.

Leland, John (*c.*1503-52), antiquary, was born in London on 13 September and educated at Christ's College, Cambridge and later at All Souls College, Oxford. He was ordained and held several livings and prebends. He was Henry VIII's (qv) chaplain and the king commissioned him to visit religious institutions before and after their dissolution to assess their manuscript holdings and acquire what he could for the king. During the period 1535-43 he travelled widely in the British Isles, recording the results in his

book the *Laboryouse Journey* – the first topographical study of Britain – which he presented to Henry. He was in Hereford *c.*1540 and described its antiquities: Hereford Castle was 'one of the fairest, largest and strongest castles in England', as big as Windsor, he thought, with its central keep on a great mound and ten-towered curtain wall. There was a bridge across the moat in the north with a great gatehouse, then dilapidated. North of the moat, on the site of the present Castle Hotel and St Ethelbert's Almshouses, there was an ancient market. While in Hereford he wrote commendatory verses on John Harley (qv, d.1557) shortly before he became bishop. He noted the castle at Weobley was 'somewhat in decay'. At the end of his life he became insane. Some of his notes were published by Thomas Hearne (qv, d.1735) as *The Itinerary of John Leland the Antiquary* (1710-12); the rest went largely into the Bodleian collection.

Leofgar (d.1056), Bishop of Hereford 1056, was Harold Godwinson's (qv) chaplain. He succeeded the saintly Bishop Æthelstan (qv), more with the defence of Hereford in mind than the care of souls. Sporting a military moustache, he led a levy of Herefordshire men into Wales to avenge the destruction of Hereford by Ælfgar and Gruffydd ap Llywelyn (qqv) but was defeated and killed with most of his men.

Leofric (d.1057), Earl of Mercia, was the son of Leofwine (qv) and married Godgifu (qv Godiva). He was made Earl of Mercia by Ethelred II and held his title into Edward the Confessor's reign. He was a generous patron of Leominster Priory, decorating it with gold and silver, some of which survived to the 19th century. Thomas Blount (qv) thought Leominster was named *Leofminstre* after him. He owned great estates in Herefordshire before the Conquest and was a valued minister through five reigns. He and Godgifu were buried in the family mausoleum at Coventry. His son Ælfgar (qv) took part with Gruffydd ap Llywelyn (qv) in the sacking of Hereford. Legend says that another son was Hereward the Wake, who resisted King William in the Fens.

Leofwine (d.*c.*1023), son of Ælfwine, was created ealdorman by Ethelred II in 994 and given estates including one at Mathon. King Cnut left Leofwine his possessions, although he seems to have had his eldest son, Northmann, murdered at Christmas 1017. Leofwine's other son Leofric (qv) became Earl of Mercia on the death of Edric Streona (qv) in 1017. Another son, Eadwine (qv), acted as the Danish Earl Ranig's (qv) deputy in Herefordshire.

Leonard (6th century), the patron saint of prisoners and women in confinement, was popular in the Middle Ages. He was a hermit from a noble Frankish family in King Clovis's time. The priory for Augustinian canons at Wormsley, founded in 1214 by Gilbert Talbot (qv, d.1274) and Sir Walter Map (qv under Walter Map), was dedicated to him as was one at Deerfold. He would have had many altars in Herefordshire but now only the churches of Blakemere, Hatfield and Yarpole remain. St Michael's, Walford was dedicated to him from Saxon times until the 1887 restoration. A brass in the south-east transept of Hereford Cathedral shows him with his symbol, broken chains. His feast day is 6 November.

Leslie, Alexander, 1st Earl of Leven (*c.*1580-1661), rose from humble origins through military service in Sweden and Holland. He returned

to Scotland to fight in the Bishops' Wars. Charles I (qv) created him Earl of Leven in an attempt to buy him off but he saw Charles as a danger to the Covenant and when Parliament invited him to assist, although he was then in his 60s he brought an army into England. He besieged Hereford with his ten Scots regiments from 30 July until 30 September 1645 when, on hearing the king was approaching, he raised the siege. His ten regiments are the origin of the ten saltaires that surround Hereford City's arms. The nursery rhyme 'There was a crooked man ...' is said to be about Leslie, sung as a marching song by his troops.

Lethaby, William Richard (1857-1931), architect, was born in Barnstaple, north Devon on 18 January 1857, the son of Richard Pyle Lethaby, a carver and gilder, and his wife Mary. Passionately interested in architecture and the decorative crafts, he went to London and joined Richard Norman Shaw, who acknowledged himself to be more the pupil. In Norman Shaw's office Lethaby met members of The Guild of St George and began to exhibit with the Arts and Crafts Exhibition Society. He joined William Morris and Philip Webb on the committee of the Society for the Protection of Ancient Buildings and was co-founder and first principal of the Central School of Arts and Crafts in London. In 1902 he was commissioned by Alice Foster (qv), owner of the Brockhampton estate, to build All Saints at Brockhampton-by-Ross. He was both contractor and architect as an experiment in direct building by Arts and Crafts principles, unique at the time. His clerk of works was Arthur Randall Wells, later famous for nearby St Edward's, Kempley, and his builders were given freedom to use their skills. But Alice Foster became impatient with Lethaby's problems and with the escalating costs. With his high morals, Lethaby waived his fee and paid for the project's completion out of his own pocket. Pevsner calls it 'one of the most convincing and impressive churches of its date in any country' with its sweeping thatch, hand-worked local materials and great cruck-like arches inside. The ironwork is hand-forged, with charming details such as plaited door hinges. Lethaby built no

other churches and only a few buildings in his life. Examples of his decorative work are held in Cheltenham Museum. He married the American Edith Rutgers Crosby late in life. They had no children and he died in London on 17 July 1931.

Lewis, Allan Leonard (1895-1918) VC was born in Whitney on Wye on 28 February 1895. He enlisted in the 6th Battalion of the Northants Regt during the First World War and on 18 September 1918 at Rossnoy, near Lempire in France he single-handedly captured a German machine-gun post. Three days later Lance-corporal Lewis was killed by shrapnel whilst sheltering his men from heavy machine-gun fire. He was posthumously awarded the VC.

Lewis, George Robert (1782-1871), painter and engraver, was born on 27 March 1782 in London into a family of political refugees from Hanover. His father was a miniaturist and his brothers, a cousin and his son were all artists. He studied under Henry Fuseli at the Royal Academy and exhibited there. He travelled in Herefordshire and the Marches painting landscapes including one called *Hereford, Dynedor and the Malvern Hills, from the Haywood Lodge, Harvest Scene, Afternoon* (1815), an oil now in the Tate. He was influenced by Constable and painted the non-idealised scene *en plein air*, although unlike Constable there is a sharp focus in his style that looks forward to the Pre-Raphaelites. Lewis believed in phrenology and chose his wife on those principles. He followed the dietary laws of Moses and thought Herefordshire with its ancient churches had Old Testament qualities and a profound meaning for those who could decipher it. He produced a series of lithographs in 1842 recording details of the work of the Herefordshire School of Sculptors (qv) at Kilpeck and Shobdon churches that are still widely reproduced. With his brother Frederick Christian Lewis he recorded many Herefordshire churches. His notes passed into the Walter Pilley (qv) collection, now in Hereford Record Office. In 1838 he published a pamphlet in Hereford about his views on education and design. He illustrated books such as J.C. Loudon's (qv) *Arboretum et Fruticetum Britannicum* (1838), which shows a 'weeping oak' from Moccas Park. His *British Forest Trees* contains illustrations of ancient Herefordshire trees. He died at his home in Hampstead on 15 May 1871.

Lewis, Thomas (1689-*c.*1737) was born at Kington, son of Stephen Lewis the vicar of Weobley and rector of Holgate, Shropshire. He and his brothers went to Hereford Free School where a Mr Traherne was headmaster. He graduated from Corpus Christi College, Oxford and was ordained; his younger brother Stephen was at Merton. He promulgated aggressive and offensive pamphlets against those opposed to his high church beliefs. These became so wild that in 1717 he was charged with sedition and had to go into hiding. He wrote about historical matters in an equally combative manner. He sent an autobiography to the antiquarian Richard Rawlinson (qv).

Lewis, Thomas Taylor (1801-58), clergyman and geologist, was born in Ludlow the third child of Edward and Anne Lewis. He was educated at St John's, Cambridge where he developed his interest in mathematics and geology and attended the lectures of Adam Sedgwick. He was ordained and appointed curate of Aymestrey in 1826. In 1827 he married Eliza Penfold of Cheam and looked after William Onneslow's (qv) charity school. On his travels around Aymestrey parish he noticed that there were fossils in the limestone strata but none in the sandstone. He collected examples and worked out a stratigraphic sequence and the organisms' environment. He noticed how the brachiopod *Pentamerus*, which was common in the Aymestrey beds, gradually changed across the stratigraphic succession before Darwin's ideas about evolution of species was published. He showed this to Murchison (qv), who realised the beds could be seen as a system separate from the Old Red Sandstone above and the earlier Cambrian period below and wrote *The Silurian System* (1839), without crediting Lewis. Murchison made use of Lewis and other local men as his research group in the area. They sent crates of fossils and rock to him in London with descriptions of the facies, inclination of beds etc. Lewis was his contact and the most knowledgeable of the group. In 1842 he was rector of Bridstow, where he married his second wife Elizabeth. Her father, Captain Fergusson of Yatton Court, Aymestrey, considered Lewis her inferior in status and cut them. Lewis was a founding member of the Woolhope Naturalists' Field Club in 1851, active in leading geological field trips and its second president. He produced an edition of Lady Brilliana Harley's (qv) letters for the Camden Society. He died in 1858 and was buried at St Bridget's Church, Bridstow.

Lewis Glyn Cothi (*c.*1420-*c.*1489), one of the greatest of the bards, took his name from his birthplace, the forest of Glyncothi, Pembrokeshire. Many of his poems are extant, some copied into presentation manuscripts such as the *Red Book of Hergest* for his patrons the Vaughans (qv). Another compilation, the *White Book of Hergest* (*Llyfr Gwyn Hergest*), was lost in a bookbinder's fire in the 19th century. His favoured form was the eulogy and he celebrated the deeds of the Vaughan family amongst others, singing at Thomas Vaughan's (qv, d.1469) funeral after his death at Edgecote. He supported the Lancastrians in the Wars of the Roses and went into hiding after the Yorkist victory at Mortimers Cross, but the ethnicity of the armies was more important than English politics and he lamented the Yorkist defeat at Edgecote where many Welsh spearmen fell. He celebrated Welshman Henry Tudor's victory at Bosworth.

Ley, Augustin (1842-1911), botanist, grew up in the vicarage at Sellack where he discovered species of mosses new to Herefordshire. With Revd William Purchas (qv) he produced *The Flora of Herefordshire*, he being solely responsible for the mosses. He wrote papers for the Woolhope Club *Transactions* and was perhaps the finest botanist of the Marches. His wife Mary Sibella Ley was a relation of both his mother and father.

Ley, William Henry (*c.*1815-87), vicar of Sellack near Ross, married Mary (d.1844), daughter of Dr James Cowles Prichard (qv) and they had a son Augustin (qv).

Lilly, John (1823-5), archdeacon of Hereford and rector of Stoke Lacy, inherited the estate of Longworth at Lugwardine. He had it gothicised by H.H. Seward, a pupil of Soane) in 1808-10 and it passed to Robert Phillips (qv under Robert Biddulph Phillips).

Lilwall, C.J. of Llydyadyway, Cusop, arranged for the excavation of Craswall Priory in 1904. On Tuesday 28 June while the dig was underway the Woolhope Club visited and were addressed by Lilwall. Several photographs were taken by Alfred Watkins (qv) and the results published in the subsequent *Transactions*.

Lind, Jenny (1820-87), opera singer, known as the Swedish Nightingale, was born and brought up in Stockholm. When her beautiful voice was discovered she was awarded a scholarship at the Swedish Royal Opera School. Her career was worldwide, brilliant and exhausting. She married Otto Goldschmidt and with her voice suffering from strain they moved to England and retired to Wynds Point, Colwall under the Herefordshire Beacon. She extended the little house recently

built on the site of a quarry and created a rocky garden around it, all now preserved. She died of cancer on 2 November 1887 while Otto lived on there until 1907. They were buried together in Malvern Cemetery. H.S. Holland (qv) wrote her biography.

Lindsell, Augustine (1570s-1634), Bishop of Hereford 1634, was born at Steeple Bumstead. He was educated at Clare College, Cambridge, where he was a tutor and Fellow. He was a friend of Nicholas Ferrar and Isaac Casaubon. After his ordination he was made a prebend of Lincoln Cathedral and in 1619 of Durham, where he joined the Durham House Group, the Arminian circle of his patron, Richard Neile, the Bishop of Durham. The group supported the changes that Laud was effecting in the Church and aroused the antagonism of the Calvinists. Arminians advocated a middle path for the Church of England: the use of vestments, the cross and some ritual, with grace available to all. The Puritan victory of the 1640s meant that moderation was doomed in the short term although ultimately to triumph in the Anglican settlement at the Restoration. In 1628 Lindsell became Dean of Lichfield and in 1633 Bishop of Peterborough, where he introduced

conformity with the *Book of Common Prayer*. The next year he was translated to Hereford, where he announced his intention to hold a visitation. This was strongly resisted by Dean Brown (qv) and his chapter, who claimed the precedence of exemption. They refused Laudian alterations such as moving the altar back into an easterly position. Lindsell complained to Archbishop Laud who, with King Charles, took his side. A date was set for the visitation but Lindsell died days before on 6 November 1634 of anxiety and a gallstone. It was to be over 40 years before one was held (qv Bishop Herbert Croft, d.1691). Lindsell was buried in the south-east transept of Hereford Cathedral where only part of his once splendid tomb remains: Duncumb (qv) said it showed Lindsell amongst the chained books of Hereford's library with a view of the heavenly city of Jerusalem.

Lingen: the family claimed descent from Turstin (qv) de Lingen and Agnes, daughter of Alfred of Marlborough (qv).

Lingen, Henry (1612-62), Royalist army officer, was born at Rotherwas on 23 October 1612. His father, Edward Lingen (d.1635) of Freen's Court, Sutton St Michael and mother, Blanche Bodenham, were Catholics. When his father became insane Harry was brought up by Sir John Scudamore (qv, d.1671). In 1626 he married Alice (d.1684), daughter of Sir Walter Pye (qv), and they had eight daughters and a son. On his father's death he inherited much land in Herefordshire and surrounding counties, and bought Stoke Edith from the Walwyns. In 1638 he was appointed Sheriff of Hereford and reported the county's opposition to Charles I's hated Ship Money tax to the Privy Council. He was sheriff again in 1643 and a commissioner to raise forces for the king; he garrisoned Hereford with 700 men. In July 1643 he and Sir William Vavasour (qv) laid siege to Brampton Bryan Castle held by Lady Brilliana Harley (qv). In March 1645 Lingen's house at Freen's Court was attacked by the Clubmen who had marched on Herefordshire in force to protest about looting and requisitioning by both sides. He was wounded at the fight at Ledbury on 22 April 1645 and retired to Hellens with John Walwyn (qv) to recuperate. That July Lingen was knighted when the king visited Hereford after the raising of the Scottish siege and he was present in the city in December that year when Colonel Birch (qv) took it by stratagem. He escaped across the frozen Wye with Governor Barnabas Scudamore (qv) and shut himself up in Goodrich Castle with 200 'bold riders'. They held out, the last Royalist outpost in England, even staging an attempt to recover Hereford in the spring of 1646 but retiring in the face of the citizens' apathy. Birch finally battered Goodrich Castle into submission with 'Roaring Meg' (qv) and Lingen, with representatives of many local families, marched out, colours flying, playing *Harry Lingen's Fancy*, a tune long remembered in the county. Lingen was imprisoned in Hereford Castle for two months; when he compounded for his release he gave his parole not to take up arms against Parliament. Despite this, Lingen swaggered round Hereford wearing his sword, the only man able to get away with this. When

the second Civil War broke out in September 1648 he raised a cavalry troop, joined by some of the county Royalists including members of the Skippe, Croft, Unett and Dansey families,and attacked Sir Edward Harley (qv, d.1700) near Leominster. They took 80 prisoners who were later released by Harley and Richard Hopton (qv, d.1653), and Lingen was taken and held, wounded, in Powis Castle. Parliament offered Lingen's forfeited estates to Harley but he gallantly returned them to Lady Alice. At the Restoration Sir Henry was elected MP for Hereford. He died of smallpox at Gloucester while returning to Stoke Edith from Westminster and was buried at Stoke Edith Church on 22 January 1662. The king granted his widow £10,000 as recompense but little was actually paid. In 1670 Stoke Edith was sold to Paul Foley (qv) and the remains of Sir Henry's estate divided among his daughters. There is a handsome portrait of Sir Henry and Lady Alice hanging over the fireplace in the Old House, Hereford. He was accounted one of the Nine Worthies of Herefordshire (see index).

Lingen, John (*c.*1440-1506), knight, married Elizabeth de Burgh (d.1522). He fought on the Yorkist side at the Battle of Mortimers Cross (1461), where the victor, Edward IV (qv) granted him the addition of three white roses of York for his arms. Sir John and Elizabeth's alabaster effigies can be seen in St John the Baptist and St Alkmund's (qv) Church at Aymestrey. Their daughter and heiress Jane married William Shelley. In the next century a descendant, Jane Shelley (qv), founded the Lingen Almshouses, Hereford, in her will.

Llewelyn, William (fl.1777) was the pastor of a Presbyterian congregation in Burgess Street, Leominster who introduced a form of Sandemanian or Glasite religion to his flock. This was a primitive form of Christianity where all things were held in common. They called themselves Llewelyns or Llewelynites. The congregation continued after his death, and under a later pastor called Taylor they had local builder James Page of South Street erect a new chapel for 250 people on their Burgess Street site costing £1,600; the chapel may still be seen.

Lloyd George, David (1863-1945), Prime Minister, was born on 17 January 1863 in Manchester into a Welsh-speaking family. He had a long career as a Liberal politician, as chancellor laying the foundations of the welfare state and being Prime Minister during the First World War. He often stayed at the Royal George Hotel in Ross to break his journey from north Wales to London. He died on 26 March 1945.

Llywelyn ab Iorwerth (*c.*1172-1240), or Llywelyn Fawr the great, *de facto* ruler of Wales, was the son of Iorwerth ap Owain Drwyndwn (the flat-nosed) and grandson of Owain Prince of Gwynedd. Gerald of Wales (qv) in 1188 reported that Llywelyn was fighting his uncles Dafydd and Rhodri and by 1199 he was prince of north Wales. He came to terms with King John (qv) in 1205 and married John's natural daughter Joan, who was a great political help to him. In 1215 he made an alliance with Giles de Briouze (qv), Bishop of Hereford and the baronial opposition to John, and Reginald de Briouze (qv), Giles's brother, married Llywelyn's daughter Gwladus (qv). Together Llywelyn and the barons extracted Magna Carta from King John and by 1216 the prince was sole ruler in Wales. He concluded a treaty with Henry III (qv) but fought continually with the Marcher lords. In 1228 he captured William (V) de Briouze (qv) and ransomed him for £2,000. Two years later he found Black William, as the Welsh called him, in bed with Joan his wife and hanged him. In 1233 he was in alliance with Richard Marshal (qv), who was fighting Henry, but when the king took back the castles the Marshals had appropriated at Ewyas and elsewhere and Marshal fled to Ireland, Llywelyn agreed a truce. He retired to die at Aberconwy Abbey having taken the Cistercian habit, and on 11 April 1240 was buried there.

Llywelyn ap Gruffydd (1223-82), Prince of Wales or *Ein Llyw Olaf* (our last leader), was the second of Gruffydd ap Llywelyn's four sons and grandson of Llywelyn ab Iorwerth (qv). Llywelyn regained control of Gwynedd, buying off Ralph (II) Mortimer (qv) by ceding lordships in east Wales to him. Gaining strength, he struggled for control of the Marches with Ralph's son Roger (III) Mortimer, he and Roger both being grandsons of Llywelyn the Great, and with other Marcher lords such as Humphrey (IV) de Bohun (qv). He established control over the patrimony of his grandfather in a greater Gwynedd and hegemony over the lords of Wales throughout central and west Wales. The princes of Powys and Deheubarth had given allegiance to him by 1258. While Mortimer and the king were preoccupied he demolished castles and recovered Gwrtheyrnion and other cantrefs. With the English weakened after the Battle of Evesham he was confirmed in his gains, especially at the expense of Roger (III) Mortimer. Under Edward I (qv) concessions were forced from him at the Treaty of Aberconwy (1277) and he made obeisance to Edward, who acknowledged him ruler of Gwynedd across the Conwy. Edward allowed him to marry Simon de Montfort's sister Eleanor (qv under Simon de Montfort) to whom Llywelyn had long been betrothed but who was held in prison by Edward. He was denied a male heir as on 19 June 1282 Eleanor died giving birth to their daughter, Gwenllian. War broke out again and Edward offered Llywelyn an estate in England which he rejected on the grounds of his ancient duties to his people. The most likely story of Llywelyn's death is that he was lured from his fastness in the north, separated from his army and cut down by the men of Edmund (I) and Roger (IV) Mortimer (qv) near Builth Wells on 11 December 1282. His head was sent to Edward and set over the gate at the Tower of London and his body buried at Abbeycwmhir. Most of the princely lineages of Wales were ended in the fighting of 1282-3 and Edward gave his son the title Prince of Wales.

Locke, Matthew (*c.*1622-77), composer and organist, was a Devon man, educated at Exeter Cathedral School, who fled the Commonwealth regime and joined the royal Court in the Low Countries. He returned when things were quieter and meeting the amateur musician Silas Taylor (qv) was persuaded to settle in Hereford. Silas housed him in a sequestered vicars choral house and, in about 1655, he met and married Mary (d.1701), daughter of Roger Garnons, a Herefordshire recusant, indicating that Locke was probably a Catholic himself. Locke was a great find for Taylor, who arranged for him to give concerts in occupied Hereford; these made the authorities nervous with so many Royalist gentry attending, starved of fine music during the Puritan regime. Taylor remembered the anxious soldiery fingering their weapons during the concerts, fearing trouble. Locke seems to have composed much chamber music in Hereford and titles of some pieces are dedicated to Herefordshire families like *The Flatt Consort for my Cousin Kemble*. The Kembles (qv) were another recusant family, relations of his wife, that produced a saint and an actor. Persecution of Catholics continued in Hereford in the 1650s and Locke courageously associated himself in public with one Catholic at the gallows in High Town, leading to his investigation by Hereford authorities. Locke later moved with his wife and children to London and tried to make a living from his music in a music-averse culture. He taught and drank coffee with friends like Silas Taylor, Samuel Pepys and Henry Purcell. With the Restoration he was enjoyed and employed at Charles II's Court, as organist and composer of musical dramas and masques. He was the greatest musician in the country before Purcell. He died in August 1677.

Longchamps, Henry (I) de (1158-1211), Sheriff of Hereford 1189-91, married Maud, sister of William (I) de Cantilupe (qv), steward of King John's household and related to St Thomas Cantilupe (qv). Their sons were Hugh and William. He is responsible for the issue of Hereford's first charter by Richard I (qv). Richard's successor, the unpredictable King John, confiscated Wilton Castle and Henry went on crusade, taking part in the sack of Constantinople in 1204. Home in 1205, Wilton was returned to him and he was granted a weekly market to help him pay off his debts. He succeeded to Adam de Port's (qv) manor of Kington after the latter's disgrace.

Longchamps, Henry (II) de (*c.*1210-37) of Wilton Castle, was the grandson of Henry (I) (qv) and the son of his son Hugh. Left a minor at Hugh's early death, he was a ward of his maternal relative Walter de Cantilupe, Bishop of Worcester. He married twice, to Joan Birkin and Hawise. In 1231 the king confirmed Henry's right to the dues from Wilton Fair. He strengthened the castle in 1234 and in 1236 went on pilgrimage to Santiago de Compostela. His daughter Maud (qv) was his heir. Bishop Walter looked after the castle for her and in 1238 was further strengthening it.

Longchamps, Hugh (I) de (d.1150) built the first castle at Wilton near an important Wye crossing. It was taken from him during the civil wars of Matilda and Stephen and given to Miles of Gloucester (qv), Earl of Hereford.

Longchamps, Hugh (II) de (d.1187), son of Hugh (I) (qv), was in favour with Henry II (qv), who returned Wilton to him. He married Emma de St Leger and had several sons, including William who became Chancellor of England. Hugh died on 25 October 1187 leaving huge debts for his heir Henry and loss of the king's favour.

Longchamps, Maud de (d.1302), heir of Wilton Castle, married Reginald de Grey (qv) in 1248 and he and his father John continued the work of strengthening the castle, now part of the Greys' barony of Wilton.

Longmore, Edward (1732-77), giant, was the son of Edward Longmore, a prosperous cattle breeder of a yeoman family long settled at Adforton, and Mary. He grew to be 7 feet 6 inches tall and left the county to exhibit himself at fairs. He died on 24 January 1777 in London, described in the parish register as 'a giant'. He was buried 15 feet deep and a guard set to prevent the resurrection men taking his body, but by March it had been stolen. He had a common law wife Anne Sears with a daughter Elizabeth (b.1762), and he named William Matthews, a Weobley inn keeper, as a trustee of his will.

Losinga, Robert de (d.1095), Bishop of Hereford 1079-95, was born in Lorraine in north-eastern France and educated at the cathedral of Liège with its reputation for mathematics. He consequently became a mathematician familiar with the abacus before it was generally known. He was in Britain before the Conquest as his friend Bishop Wulfstan of Worcester ordained him, and he knew St Anselm. He succeeded his countryman Walter of Lorraine (qv) as Bishop of Hereford and proved a skilled administrator to William I and II. He was a commissioner of the Domesday Survey and his report for it is extant. The cathedral and city of Hereford had been sacked in 1055 and Bishop Robert found it still in ruins with services held in temporary shelters. Bishop Æthelstan's (qv) Saxon cathedral had been south of the present one, facing a possible street that linked King Street and Castle Street. Robert largely demolished the buildings in the parish of St John's for his cathedral and built a palace and chapel to

the south by the river. The two-storey chapel with its deeply set west door was dedicated to saints Catharine and Mary Magdalen and was based, as William of Malmesbury (qv) thought, on Charlemagne's chapel at Aachen not far from Liège. The antiquarian William Stukeley (qv) drew it on his 1721 visit. The north wall survives in the grounds of the bishop's palace and can be seen from the lady arbour rising over the cloisters. Some carved stones from it can be found piled up in the vicars choral cloisters. His successors Reinhelm and Béthune (qqv) continued building the cathedral on his foundations. St Peter's Abbey, Gloucester was also being rebuilt at the same time and on 29 June 1089 Bishop Robert laid the foundation stone at its dedication. Robert had a vision of his friend Wulfstan, the Saxon Bishop of Worcester, who told him that he, Wulfstan, would shortly die. After his death Wulfstan appeared to Robert with a warning of his own demise, which occurred on 26 June 1095. He is buried in the south choir aisle under the north wall. His 14th-century effigy holds a model of the cathedral.

Loudon, John Claudius (1783-1843) was the Scottish polymath who built Hope End in 1809-15 for Edward Barrett (qv) in what he called his 'Hindoo style' with ogee and minarets and cast iron domes atop, in the style of the Brighton Pavilion. It was damaged by fire and demolished in the next century, although his park design, the stable block and lower lodge remain. Loudon edited a gardening magazine with his wife; they were both botanists. He published a great deal, including a study of Repton (qv) and made perceptive suggestions for the creation of green belts as breathing spaces around towns.

Lowe, William; Primrose, George; Smith, Samuel and **Voyle, William** (fl.1640-50s) were appointed joint Presbyterian pastors to manage services suitable for the new regime at Hereford Cathedral during the Interregnum after the dismissal of bishop, Dean and Chapter. They arranged the preaching or lectures between them and ordained ministers acceptable to the regime. Thomas Traherne (qv) was sponsored by them to attend Brasenose College, Oxford and they approved his subsequent appointment as rector of Credenhill. At the Restoration dissent became illegal. Lowe and Voyle had died and Smith and Primrose were ejected. Smith (d.1685) went to a living in Berkshire but was ejected and returned to Herefordshire, where he is said to have been unkindly treated. Primrose came from Scotland; his mother had been a nurse to Prince Henry, James I's eldest son who died young. He was well educated and a good preacher. He suffered imprisonment after his ejection but Bishop Herbert Croft (qv) liked him and tried unsuccessfully to persuade him to conform. He was able to preach as a nonconformist in Hereford after James II's Act of Toleration in 1687.

Luard, Louise Henrietta (d.1945), daughter of Revd Sidney Smith, treasurer of Hereford Cathedral 1892-1904, lived in the Cathedral Close. She married Lt-Col Edward Bourryan Luard (1871-1916) in 1905 in Hereford; he was killed in action in the First World War. She was the first female mayor of Hereford in 1929, and again in 1936, and added a link to the mayoral chain – a jumping Wye salmon. She was invested MBE and died at Bourryon House, 7 Cantilupe Street, Hereford on 21 June 1945.

Lucy, Charles (1814-73), history painter, belonged to a Ledbury family that claimed descent from the Lucys of Charlecote, whose deer Shakespeare is reputed to have poached. He was born in Hereford and apprenticed there to his uncle who was a chemist. He decided on a career in art and studied in Paris under Paul Delaroche and later at the Royal Academy in London. He married and lived with his son in Hereford but painted in the summers at Barbizon, near Fontainebleau, fashionable for artists like Corot, and regularly submitted work to the Royal Academy. He was well known for large history paintings of 17th-century subjects and was popular in America. There are examples of his work at Hereford Art Gallery. At the end of his life he lived with his son Charles Hampden Lucy in London where he kept a studio. He is commemorated in St Michael's Church, Ledbury where the Lucys have a family vault at the east of the south aisle. Their memorial shows a rebus of three *luces* or pikes. The Eltons (qv) had a Lucy ancestor, Anne (qv Ambrose Elton, d.1659).

Lug, a Celtic deity of the sun and light and artificers, was identified by the Romans with Mercury or Hermes (qv). His name was a common component of place names in the Celtic world and 1 August was sacred to him. It is an attractive notion to associate him with the River Lugg.

Luny, Thomas (1759-1837), painter, was born in Cornwall and apprenticed in London where he settled. He exhibited regularly at the Royal Academy. An important patron was the East India Company, for whom he painted many seascapes. He had himself been to sea as purser. Four oil paintings of the naval victories of Admiral Rodney (qv), painted for his friends the Harleys (qv Thomas Harley, d.1804) of Berrington Hall, show incidents from the Battle of the Saints against the French and Spanish in the War of American Independence and still hang in the dining room at Berrington. He was later crippled by arthritis but continued to paint prolifically from a wheelchair with a brush strapped to his fist. He died on 30 September 1837.

Lutley, see under **Barneby Lutley**

Luxmoore, Charles Scott (1792-1854), eldest son of John (qv), was educated at St John's, Cambridge, a noted classical scholar, and ordained. He was, through the influence of his father, rector of Bromyard and Cradley *inter alia*, a prebend of Hereford and, when his father had become Bishop of St Asaph's, dean there. He died at Cradley on 27 April 1854.

Luxmoore, John (1766-1830), Bishop of Hereford 1808-15, was born in Devon and educated at Eton and King's College, Cambridge and graduated DD in 1794. He was Dean of Gloucester then Bishop of Bristol for a year before moving to Hereford. He supported the improvement of elementary schools in Herefordshire and was patron of the National Church Schools founded in 1811. From 1815 until his death he was Bishop of St Asaph's where his son was dean and where there is a monument to him. He married Elizabeth, niece of Edward Barnard, Provost of Eton and they had a large family.

Lyall, Edna (1857-1903), novelist, is the *nom de plume* of Ada Ellen Bayly. She was born in Brighton, a frail child who never married. She lived with her sisters and their families and a brother, Revd R. Burges Bayly, vicar of Bosbury. She was a religious woman with radical views, a lifelong member of the Women's Liberal Association and a supporter of women's suffrage. She was a friend of the MP and persecuted freethinker Charles Bradlaugh, and contributed to his legal funds and finally to a memorial. Lyall was a prolific writer, producing 19 popular novels: one of her last, *In Spite of All* (1902), a play rewritten as a novel, was about 17th-century Herefordshire and follows the fictional lives of historical characters such as the Harleys and Hoptons (qqv) during the Civil Wars. She made use of names found in Bosbury Church for characters, like the Harfords (qv), and brought historical figures into Herefordshire: Archbishop Laud (qv) sitting in the consistory court at Hereford Cathedral, for instance. When Parliamentary troopers ordered the vicar of Holy Trinity, Bosbury to remove the

churchyard cross, he persuaded them to leave it with the warning added: 'Honor not the X, Honor God for Christ' and these two lines, still seen on the cross today, gave Lyall the idea for her story. She died in Sussex and her ashes were scattered at the foot of the Bosbury Cross. There is a dedication to her on the chancel screen inside the church. In Sussex she presented three bells to a local church called after three characters of her novels: Donovan, Erica and Hugo. She had a Kempe (qv) window installed in St Saviour's Church in Eastbourne where she customarily worshipped.

M

Machen, Arthur (1863-1947), writer, was born Arthur Llewellyn Jones on 3 March 1863 in Caerleon, his father being the vicar of nearby Llandewi Fach. Machen was his mother's maiden name. He boarded at Hereford Cathedral School and received a good classical education. Failing to get into medical school in London, he began to write tales of mystery and the supernatural. He dabbled in fashionable Edwardian mysticism, and the tale of the apparition of the angels of Mons and archers from Agincourt aiding British forces during the First World War came from his stories *The Bowmen and other legends of the war* (1915). He was a prolific jobbing journalist, translated from French, wrote novels and plays and enjoyed acting. He wrote two books of childhood memories: *Far Off Things* (1922) and *Things Near and Far* (1923). He died on 15 December 1947 and was buried near his home in Amersham, Bucks. He had been married twice and left a son and a daughter.

Macky, John (d.1726), spy and writer, was a Scot employed by the government to report on Jacobite activities across the Channel. In 1697 he married a daughter of Sir William Spring of Pakenham, Suffolk and they had a son called Spring Macky. Discredited as a spy and in debt, he took up travel writing and wrote his popular *Journey through England in Familiar Letters* (1714). He called Hereford 'the dirtiest old city I have seen in England', a view supported by Defoe (qv) ten years later and still true at the time of Curley's (qv) report of 1852. Macky died at Rotterdam in 1726. In 1733 his son published *Memoirs of the Secret Services of John Macky*.

MacLaren, James Marjoribanks (1853-90), architect, was born on 12 January 1853, a Scottish farmer's son who did his architectural training in Glasgow. He set up an architectural practice in London, working in an Arts and Crafts style blended with Scottish vernacular, and influenced Charles Rennie Mackintosh. He designed additions to New Place, Ledbury (1886) for Lord Michael Biddulph (qv, d.1923) and the same year designed two tile-hung cottages on the Eastnor estate (*c.*1886) for Lady Henry Somerset (qv Isabella Somers Cocks). In Ledbury he discovered the Bosbury bodger Philip Clissett (qv) and introduced him to Ernest Gimson (qv) and wide celebrity. He died on 20 October 1890.

Maddox, Mary (1793-1853), dressmaker, was the daughter of William Maddox and his wife Elizabeth Lowe of Ledbury. She worked at Hope End for the Barrett family and became a good friend. Mary acted as Elizabeth Barrett's (qv) chaperone when she visited the scholar Hugh Boyd in Malvern and Elizabeth wrote sympathetically about her in her diary, letters and poems. Elizabeth heard of Mary's illness and death with great sadness later in London.

Maidstone, Ralph de (before 1195-1245), was Bishop of Hereford 1234-9. He was treasurer of Lichfield Cathedral in 1219 and in 1222 Archdeacon of Chester, where he wrote a commentary on the *Sentences* of Peter of Lombard which survives. In 1231 he was chancellor of the University of Oxford. Bishop Hugh Foliot (qv) appointed Ralph his dean in Hereford and Ralph eventually succeeded him as bishop. As bishop he was used by Henry III (qv) on diplomatic business. His negotiations with Llywelyn ap Iorwerth (qv) led to a treaty with Henry; and he escorted Eleanor of Provence to England for her marriage to the king. He was a benefactor of the cathedral presenting valuable books. He gave Monthalt House in the City of London to the bishops of Hereford as their London residence. It was on the west side of Old Fish Street, off Thames Street. The small chapel adjoining it became the Church of St Mary de Monthalt (also called St Mary

Somerset) where several bishops of Hereford were buried. Monthalt House burnt down in 1666 and was not rebuilt. Ralph resigned his bishopric to become a Franciscan friar and was sent to Gloucester to help found the community there. He died there on 27 January 1245 and was buried in the chancel of the Greyfriars Church, the ruins of which can still be seen behind the churchyard of St Mary de Lode.

Mailseru, a priest of Lann Timoi (i.e. Foy) in the 860s and **Concum**, a priest of Lann Suluc (i.e. Sellack), witnessed a charter granting land from an Abraham to a Bishop Nudd. In the reign of Edward the Confessor (qv), Bishop Herewald of Llandaff appointed Joseph son of Brein to the church at Lanntiuoi (Foy).

Map, Walter (*c.*1130-1210), archdeacon of Hereford and poet, was from a prosperous Herefordshire family, educated at St Peter's Abbey, Gloucester and in the schools of Paris. He was related to Sir Walter Map, Lord of Wormsley (one of the founders of the priory of St Leonard (qv) of Pyon, Wormsley) and Philip Map, canon of Hereford and chaplain to Bishop Gilbert de Briouze (qv). Walter wanted to be Bishop of Hereford but King John passed him over. He was clerk and justice to Henry III. At Hereford he served Bishop Gilbert Foliot (qv) and was a friend of Gerald of Wales and Hue de Roteland (qqv). He was a celebrated commentator on contemporary events and wrote satirical verses, for example on Henry II's illegitimate son, Geoffrey. His *De nugis curialium* (*Courtiers' Trifles*) retailed Court gossip (qv Pain fitz John for one of his stories). His *Of the King Apollonides* concerned Prince Rhys (qv) of Deheubarth.

Mapenore, Hugh de (d.1219), Bishop of Hereford 1216-19, was the son of Robert de Mapenore, Lord of the Manor of Hampton Mapnors (now Hampton Court), and his wife Matilda. He was William (III) de Briouze's (qv) clerk and appointed dean by his son Giles (qv). When the Briouzes fled to Ireland from King John, Hugh also lay low. At Bishop Giles de Briouze's death in 1215, Hereford Cathedral chapter elected him Giles's successor. King John contested the election but died, the Pope confirmed the election and he was consecrated in Worcester. England had been under papal interdiction during 1208-14 and all church activity stopped. The interdict was lifted in the last year of Bishop Giles's term and Hugh took the opportunity to review liturgical practices, resulting in the *Use of Hereford*, which was to become world famous. Hereford is referred to in the preface of the *Book of Common Prayer* in this context. Hugh was an active bishop, issuing charters and supporting the young Henry III (qv) against rebels and the Welsh Prince Llywelyn ab Iorwerth. He issued writs for the protection of the Jews of Hereford (qv Hamo), who were under the king's protection. He died on 16 April 1219, and was buried in Hereford Cathedral.

Mapson or **Mappeson, Godric** (fl.1086), Saxon thegn, was the eponymous proprietor of Goodrich mentioned in the Domesday Book. He must have had some provision for defending this important crossing of the Wye. The castle is early called Godric's Castle.

de la Mare. The family were possessed of Caradoc Court from at least 1281 when a Robert is recorded there. It was once called Caer Caradoc and is one of the places associated with Caradoc's (qv) last stand against the Romans.

de la Mare, Malcolm (d.1399), son of Reynold de la Mare of Yatton, and younger brother of Sir Peter de la Mare, (qv, d.1387), married Alice, widow of John Romsey of Kidderminster. He was MP for Herefordshire in 1388 and held office in the county as tax collector. He owned family property at Yatton, near Ross and at Little Hereford. Neither he nor his older brother left heirs.

de la Mare, Peter (d.1387) was the son of Sir Reynold de la Mare, and collected taxes from the Forest of Dean's iron mines. He was High Sheriff of Hereford in 1374 and Edmund (III) Mortimer's (qv) steward, accompanying him to Ulster with troops he had raised. With Mortimer's patronage he was a knight of the shire at Edward III's Good Parliament in 1376. As Speaker (the first one named) he was imprisoned for his summary of the House's criticism of the influence of the king's mistress Alice Perrers and the corruption of the Court managed by John of Gaunt (qv). Released the next year on the accession of Richard II (qv), he continued to represent Herefordshire and act as the spokesman of Parliament. During the Peasants' Revolt of 1381 he headed the commission in Herefordshire to resist disaffection and took Hereford Cathedral under his control.

de la Mare, Richard (d.1435) is shown with his wife Isabel (d.1421) in a Hereford Cathedral brass, both in the height of fashion – she with two little dogs pulling at her gown. He was High Sheriff. After his death his home, Caradoc Court, passed by marriage to the Abrahalls (qv under John Abrahall).

Margaret (d.304), virgin martyr, was one of the most popular saints of mediaeval England. She is the patron of Newton St Margaret's Church at the foot of the Black Mountains, and there is a 14th-century mural of her in St John the Baptist, Byford, standing against a background of stars holding a church. There would have been many altars to her and paintings of her standing on her dragon. She was one of the 14 Holy Helpers and her aid was sought by peasants, pregnant women and the falsely

accused. Followers of Alfred Watkins (qv) linked her and other dragon-slaying saints like Michael and George with the fructifying energies of the dragon paths or ley lines. Her feast day is 20 July.

Markham, Gervase (*c.*1568-1637), author, was from a gentry family in Nottinghamshire. He lived in London writing plays, poems and tracts and served for a while in the Low Countries under Sir Francis de Vere (qv). Writing for a Puritan London audience, he mocks country manners in *The Newe Metamorphosis or a Feaste of Fancie* (1600) which describes a journey to Colwall, whose inhabitants 'such kindness shew'd me, I remember't still'. He stayed with one Hartland and laughed at Herefordshire Sabbath-breaking activities such as feasting in the ale-house (which is still next to the church at Colwall) and dancing round the maypole 'with drums and bagpipes and with warlike guns'.

Markye, Clare (17th century), John's (qv) daughter, was intended for a wealthy Rudhall but fell in love with a gardener's boy. They planned to marry quietly but as the day approached the young man found the social pressure too much and drowned himself in the Wye. His body was buried at the Copse Cross in Ross-on-Wye and the path Clare distractedly walked from her home to the grave is known as Old Maid's Walk.

Markye, John (d.1667) built Alton Court, near Ross *c.*1602. There are family memorials in the Markye Chapel in the south aisle of St Mary's Church, Ross.

Marlow, Mary (d.1778), philanthropist, was the daughter of a London jeweller who settled in Townsend House, Green Lane, Leominster from 1765 until her death. In 1771 she paid for Leominster Baptist Chapel with a burial ground behind it and for a minister's house and cottages for two poor Baptist widows, endowing her charities with land at Dilwyn.

Marriott, Catherine (d.1898) was the widow of Major Charles Marriott (d.1848) of Goodrich. As lady of the manor she erected a memorial to her husband at St Swithin's, Ganarew. She paid for George Bodley (qv) to build Christ Church, Llangrove (1854-6), where her life is remembered in the art nouveau reredos.

Marshal, Richard (1191-1234), brother of William Marshal (qv, d.1231), succeeded his brother as 3rd Earl of Pembroke in 1231 and married Gervaise de Dinan. The later Marshals were often at odds with the turbulent Plantagenet kings, and led the barons and Llywelyn the Great (qv) in rebellion. Richard died in Ireland on 16 April 1234 of wounds received at the Battle of Curragh and was succeeded by his brothers Gilbert (1194-1241) and then Walter. Walter died at Goodrich Castle on 24 November 1245 and was succeeded by the youngest brother Anselm, who married Maud, daughter of Humphrey (IV) de Bohun (qv), 2nd Earl of Hereford. None of the brothers had male issue and their estates in four realms were split among the five female descendants and their husbands. One, Eva (d.1246), married William (V) de Briouze (qv) and their daughter Maud married Roger (III) Mortimer (qv) in 1247, making him the greatest lord in the area.

Marshal, William the (1146-1219), 1st Earl of Pembroke, was reputed 'the greatest knight that ever lived'. The hereditary title of Lord

Marshal made him the most powerful man in the kingdom after the king, having risen from the lower nobility through his friendship with Henry II's (qv) son, Henry the Young King (who never actually became king). He assumed, as a new creation, the earldom of Pembroke after his marriage to Isabella, daughter of Richard 'Strongbow' de Clare (qv), 2nd Earl of Pembroke of the previous creation. They had five sons and five daughters. William held great estates in France, Ireland, England and Wales and was Lord of Ewyas where the castle was his Marches base. King John granted him Goodrich Castle, built by his father-in-law, Strongbow, and he extended its defences. He was regent of the young Henry III (qv) after King John's death and supervised the reissue of Magna Carta, which can be seen at Hereford Cathedral. He founded the Knights Templar preceptory at Bosbury 1217-9. He died on 14 May 1219 and his effigy is in Temple Church, London. His son commissioned a verse history of his deeds which describes his death, weeping in the arms of Isabella.

Marshal, William (1190-1231), son of William the Marshal (qv), succeeded his father. In 1214 he married Alice (d.1215), daughter of Baldwin de Béthune, and a relative of the Bishop of Hereford, Robert de Béthune (qv). Ten years later William married Henry III's 9-year-old sister Eleanor, King John's youngest daughter with Isabella of Angoulême. But when William rebelled, being Henry's brother-in-law did not save him, and his castles at Usk, Hay and Ewyas were besieged. He died on 6 April 1231 and was buried beside his father in Temple Church, his legs crossed, resting on a lion. His widow Eleanor, aged 16, made a vow of chastity but later married Simon de Montfort (qv).

Marshall, George JP FSA (1859-1950), eldest son of George William Marshall (qv), was an energetic local historian who preserved and copied parish registers for Hereford Record Office. He was a prominent member of the Woolhope Club, its secretary for 29 years and president in 1922 and 1940, contributing articles to its *Transactions*, including a history of

Herefordshire fonts and a paper on the Norman occupation of the Golden Valley. He presented many of his books to the club's library.

Marshall, George William (1839-1905), genealogist and barrister, was appointed Rouge Croix Pursuivant, an officer in the college of arms, then York Herald. He married, in turn, Alice and her sister Caroline Hall and had several children. He was a Freemason and a member of the Harleian Society for which he published several genealogical works. He bought the Sarnesfield estate from the Webb family (qv under Hugh de Monington) in 1891 and was High Sheriff of Herefordshire for 1902.

Martin (316-97) was patron saint of Tours, the central point on the pilgrimage route to Compostela. A chapel dedicated to him in Hereford stood in what is now Castle Green, south of Nelson's column. It is shown on Speed's map of 1606 and crop marks of the walls can still be seen in dry weather. This was a chapelry of the parish church dedicated to him which stood south of the old Wye Bridge. Its parish is Hereford south of the Wye but included Castle Green. In 1645 the Scots Army fired cannon

into Hereford from the church tower. After their departure the whole church was pulled down. It was rebuilt in 1845 by R.W. Jearrad (qv) on a new site further south on the Ross Road. St Martin's feast day is 11 November and started Advent in the Middle Ages.

Martin (13th century) was a tile maker whose work, a tile showing an angel blowing a trumpet, was found in the Cistercian Dore Abbey. It bears the inscription: *Martin me fecit*.

Martin, Basil Kingsley (1897-1969), journalist and editor, was born at Ingestre Street, Hereford, on 28 July 1897 the son of Basil Martin, a congregational minister, and Charlotte Turberville (qv). Kingsley went, unhappily, to Hereford Cathedral School up to age 16, and in 1913 the family moved to London. Influenced by his father's principled ministry, he was a conscientious objector in the First World War, which he spent as an ambulance orderly, then went up to Magdalene College, Cambridge. He was a Fellow of Magdalene and tutor at the LSE, worked on the *Guardian* but found his forté as editor of the *New Statesman* for 30 years. Here he maintained his reputation as a great journalist and editor although the Labour Party leadership complained of his criticism, and George Orwell accused him of being soft on Stalin. He died of a stroke in Cairo.

Martin, James (1738-1810), banker, was born on 24 May 1738 at Overbury Court, Tewkesbury, the second generation of Martins at the Grasshopper Bank in Lombard Street, London. His father Thomas Martin from Evesham had transformed his goldsmiths' company into the famous banking house of Martins, at the sign of the grasshopper. James learnt banking under his older brother Joseph, became a partner in

1760 and followed Joseph as senior partner in 1775. In 1774 he married Penelope (1740-1830), daughter and heiress of John Skippe (qv, d.1796) who, on the death of her uncle, brought the Upper Hall estate in Ledbury to the Martin family. They had three sons and four daughters. His daughter Margaret married Treadway Nash (qv), the Worcester antiquary. Martin was MP for Tewkesbury from 1776-1807, living in Downing Street next door to his friend Pitt the younger, but his Ledbury house was the family home even before uncle Skippe's death and their children were born there. He died on 26 January 1810 and was buried at Overbury.

Martin, John (1774-1832), banker, was born on 27 November 1774 at Upper Hall, Ledbury, James Martin's (qv) eldest son, the third genera-

tion of Martins at the Grasshopper Bank. He was senior partner from 1807 until 1830 and steered the bank through the financial problems that followed the Napoleonic War, when many banking houses failed. It became the most successful and stable financial institution of the day. In 1803 he married Frances (1770-1862), daughter of his partner Richard Stone and they had two daughters and five sons, three of whom, John (1805-80), James (1807-78) and Robert (1808-97), were partners in the bank. John had the Church of England Boys' School built in Ledbury's Homend in 1868, now rebuilt as sheltered housing. He followed his father as MP for Tewkesbury and owned houses in London and Chislehurst, Kent. He died on 4 January 1832 and was buried in Ledbury Church. Martin's Bank merged with Barclays in 1969 but the sign of the golden grasshopper remains a memorable icon of banking in the City. The Martins lived at Ledbury until Upper Hall was sold to the county council to be used as a school.

Martin, William Edward (1843-1915), architect, born in Cork, had moved to Herefordshire by 1867 and was living in Tillington with Anna his wife and Edward their son. Initially a partner of Kempson (qv), he later developed an extensive practice on his own. He rebuilt St Mary, Elton (1876) and St John of Jerusalem, Bolstone (1876-7). He built the Wesleyan Chapel in Holmer Road (1879) and over-restored St Dubricius, Ballingham (1885), where his is the alabaster reredos of 1893. By 1880 the Martin family had moved into Hereford where he designed and built himself a house in Baggallay Street (now numbers 10 and 12). In 1881 his two-year-old daughter Katherine died and he raised a cross for her in the cemetery on Westfaling Street, with a pretty mosaic. He also worked in London and on the Continent. At the end of his life he returned to Ireland and died in Co. Offaly.

Mascall, Robert (d.1416), Bishop of Hereford 1404-16, was born in Ludlow and educated at Oxford, receiving his doctoral degree in 1393. He was a Carmelite friar and subsequently prior in Ludlow. He assisted Bishop Trefnant (qv) with the trial of the suspected Lollard Walter Brut (qv) in Hereford in 1393 and preached before Richard II (qv). He was Henry IV's (qv) confessor, having shared his exile, and was rewarded with the bishopric of Hereford, although the Pope wanted Adam of Usk (qv). He went to Rome for his consecration on 29 March 1404 but on his way home he was captured by pirates and had to be ransomed. In Hereford he watched as his diocese was devastated by Glyn Dŵr's (qv) raids. He records in his *Register* in Hereford Cathedral archive that 52 churches were destroyed in the deaneries of Archenfield, Weobley, Leominster, Titley, Lyonshall and Kington. He was a conscientious, resident bishop and a good preacher. He died in London on 22 December 1416 and was buried in the Friary Church at Ludlow which he had been rebuilding.

Masefield, John Edward (1878-1967), poet laureate, was born at The Knapp in Ledbury's Homend on 1 June 1878, the third of the six children of George Edward Masefield, a solicitor in Ledbury where the family still practise. John was baptised at nearby Preston Church because of the boycott of Revd John Jackson (qv)

and his Ledbury services. His mother, Caroline Louisa Parker died in childbirth in 1885 and his father, severely depressed, was hospitalised and died in 1890. John was brought up by an aunt and uncle at The Priory by the church; they tried to stop him reading and he was unhappy there. What he remembered about his childhood was the countryside: 'Whenever I think of Paradise I think of parts of this county, for I know no land so full of the beauty and bounty of God.' At 16, at the end of the age of the great sailing ships, he trained to be an officer in the merchant navy in Liverpool. He was shipped back sick from Chile on his first trip; on another trip he jumped ship at New York and spent three years doing menial work and educating himself. He returned home in 1897 with a revolver, saying he would either become a successful writer or shoot himself. *Salt-Water Ballads* was published in 1902, with the memorable *Sea Fever* and *Cargoes*. In London he met W.B. Yeats and J.M. Synge who introduced him to London literary circles, and in 1903 he married Constance de la Cherois Crommelin (1867-1960). Their children were Judith and Lewis. He wanted to write for the common man, like Kipling, and thought of success as live readings in East End pubs. His verse was popular but his drama less so, although his sense of dramatic realism is felt in verse tales like *The Everlasting Mercy* (1911) and *Dauber* (1913) and shocked some. *The Widow in the Bye Street* (1912) set in 'a small Shropshire Town' was really the Ledbury of his childhood. In the First World War he served with the Red Cross in the Dardanelles. He became a successful novelist with *Reynard the Fox* (1919) and wrote children's stories such as the strange *Box of Delights* (1935), also set in a fictionalised Ledbury and the surrounding landscape. The apogee of success came with his appointment as poet laureate in 1930. He was given the freedom of Hereford and made a speech praising Herefordshire. More praise of the county comes in his partial autobiography *Grace After Ploughing* (1966), in which he remembers the land of his childhood. When the public library opened in the Barrett-Browning Institute, Ledbury in 1938 Masefield spoke at the opening ceremony. He was unaffected and affable, refusing honours that might distract from his cherished concern to be a poet of the people, and it was for this reason that he felt he could accept the laureateship. He died on 12 May 1967 at his home at Abingdon and was buried in Westminster Abbey.

Massey, Edward, (*c.*1604-74), army officer, was from a Cheshire gentry family. He joined the Earl of Stamford's (qv Henry Grey) Parliamentary regiment, already with military experience, becoming lieutenant colonel. He believed in good counsel and pure religion and, like many moderate Presbyterians in the Civil Wars, retained a degree of sympathy for the king. In September 1642 he marched with Stamford on Hereford, which fell without much resistance as most of the Royalist gentry had fled. The hostility of the citizens caused them eventually to remove to Gloucester where Massey was appointed governor, repelling Royalist attacks against great odds – a brave, vigorous commander although suspicious of colleagues. His defence of Gloucester was seen as a turning point for Parliament and he was fêted in London. Joining with William Waller (qv) he marched through Herefordshire and they briefly retook Hereford. In 1645 he tried to garrison Ledbury from Gloucester but Prince Rupert (qv) made a surprise attack early on 22 April and drove him out. Rupert and Massey both shot each other's horses from under them. At this time the Clubmen, a neutral force that had taken to arms to defend their fodder and livestock, arrived in the Ledbury area in great numbers. Massey rode out to parley with them and they agreed to disperse under his protection but Prince Rupert then arrived and peremptorily hanged the leaders and ravaged the area. Massey was MP for Wootton Basset, Wiltshire in 1646 but was purged with other moderate Presbyterians like the Harleys (qv Edward Harley, d.1700) and fled to the Netherlands. Here he made his peace with Charles II, fighting for him in the Second Civil War in which he was severely wounded and captured. Tried for treason, he escaped back to Holland but returned again in 1659 to raise rebellion in the West. He failed again and was again taken prisoner but boldly escaped. At the Restoration he was knighted and became MP for Gloucester. Sir Edward bought an estate in Ireland where he died on 6 February 1674.

Masters, Robert (d.1619) is commemorated in the north nave of St Mary's Church, Burghill by a brass of a terrestrial globe of the world with an inscription that describes how he travelled with Thomas Cavendish to Virginia

and afterward aboute the globe of ye whole worlde and after his return marryed Winefrid ye daughter of Thom.s Cornwall of Buckland Gent, by whom he hath 2 sones and 7 daughters. He departed this life the 3 of June Ao 1619.

This voyage, with Hues (qv), Sir Thomas Cavendish and Richard Grenville, was made in 1585. It was only the second circumnavigation by Englishmen and they made their fortunes from plundered Spanish gold. With it Masters bought the manor of Burghill and he and Winifred settled there; the Masters family held it until 1702. Elgar (qv) cycled out to Burghill from Hereford and enjoyed seeing the Masters brass.

Mathews, John Hobson (1858-1914), historian, born at Croydon and educated at Cambridge, moved to Wales and converted to Catholicism in 1877. He trained as a solicitor and married Alice Gwyn-Hughes in 1892 and they had four sons and two daughters. He was archivist to Cardiff Corporation and published many records, including in 1912 *The Vaughans* (qv) *of Courtfield: a study in Welsh genealogy*. He contributed the final volumes, V and VI, to Duncumb's (qv) *History of Herefordshire* and died in Ealing on 30 January 1914.

Matthews, Charles Skinner (1785-1811), tenth child of John (qv, d.1826) and Elizabeth, was born on 26 March 1785. He was a member of Byron's (qv) intellectual, freethinking and libertine côterie at Trinity College, Cambridge, whose behaviour shocked their contemporaries. Byron's journal records a party at Newstead Abbey with Matthews where, dressed in monks' habits, they 'used to sit up late ... drinking burgundy, claret, champagne and what not, out of the *skull-cup* [and] buffoon[ed] around the house'. Byron thought much of Matthews and was devastated when he drowned swimming in the Cam on 3 August 1811. He is buried in St Benet's, Cambridge, where there is a wall plaque to him.

Matthews, Elizabeth (d.1860), artist, eldest daughter of John Matthews (qv, d.1826), drew and painted 27 of the 30 plates for T.A. Knight's (qv) *Pomona Herefordiensis* (1811). They were engraved by botanist William Hooker.

Matthews, Henry (1789-1828), born on 21 June 1789, fifth son of John (qv, d.1826) and Elizabeth, inherited Belmont on his father's death. He was a fellow of King's College Cambridge. In 1821 he married Emma (d.1861), daughter of William Blount (qv under Thomas Blount) of Orleton Manor. They lived in Ceylon where he was Puisne Judge of the Supreme Court and had three children. He wrote *Diary of an Invalid* (1820), a journal of his unsuccessful quest for health, and died in Ceylon on 20 May 1828. Their daughter Mary (1823-90) married Julien de la Chere of Paris and their daughter Alice married Alfred Hornyold, of a Worcestershire Catholic family. There is a portrait of her by Sophie Rude in Sizergh Castle with which the Hornyolds were connected.

Matthews, Henry (1826-1913), Viscount Llandaff of Hereford, was born in Ceylon on 13 January 1826, the son of Henry (qv, d.1828) and Emma, and was educated in Paris and at London University. He was called to the bar, qualified as a barrister and was QC in 1868. His legal career was enhanced by his skilful cross-examination of Sir Charles Dilke in 1885. Dilke had been cleared of a charge of adultery but, sensitive to slurs on his reputation, ill-advisedly reopened the case. Matthews demolished Dilke's case and he was ruined. Matthews had been elected MP for Dungarvan as an Independent Liberal. Queen Victoria, who approved of his part in the republican Dilke's downfall, made him a Privy Councillor and, on his re-election in 1886 as Conservative member for Birmingham East, insisted on his becoming Home Secretary (1886-92) in Lord Salisbury's administration, during the Jack the Ripper murders. An effective administrator he was unpopular in parliament for his cool manner. The Matthews family were Roman Catholics and Lord Llandaff was the first Catholic to hold a cabinet position. He was prominent in the campaign to build Westminster Cathedral. Dying unmarried on 3 April 1913 he was buried in the family vault at All Saints, Clehonger.

Matthews, John (1755-1826), physician and MP, son of William (qv) and Jane, was baptised on 30 October 1755 at Burton Court, Linton. Educated at Merton College, Oxford he graduated MD in 1782. In 1778 he married Elizabeth (1757-1823), daughter and heir of Arthur Ellis at Much Marcle, and they had eight sons and six daughters. A Fellow of the Royal College of Physicians, he was briefly physician to St George's Hospital, London, then retired to the Belmont estate at Clehonger in 1788. Belmont House had been damaged in a fire and Matthews had James Wyatt (qv) rebuild it (1788-90), and Humphry Repton (qv) landscape the grounds along the south bank of the Wye. Several of the cottages on the estate were designed by John Nash (qv). Ten years later he sold Burton Court to Joseph White, and he sold it to Lord Ashburnham. Matthews took a prominent part in county affairs: he was Mayor of Hereford in 1793 and chairman of the quarter sessions for nearly 20 years, colonel of the Herefordshire Militia and MP from 1803 to 1806. In 1794 he published a riposte to Uvedale Price's (qv) theories of landscape design in *A Sketch from the Landscape* and he wrote anonymous verse such as his parody of Pope's (qv) *Eloisa* and a lampoon of Richard Payne Knight's (qv) landscape poem, which he disliked. He also translated poetry and dedicated his version of Fontaine's *Fables* to his friend Dr Paytherus' (qv) daughter Fanny. He advised his neighbour Edmund Pateshall (qv) on the stocking of his lake at Allensmore Court. He died at Belmont on 15 January 1826 and was buried in the south aisle of All Saints Church, Clehonger where there is a monument to him. There is also a monument on the east wall of the cathedral cloisters showing a consoling angel, and there are portraits of Col Matthews and his wife by Romney in the Tate Britain collection.

Matthews, William (d.1799), was the son of William Matthews of Linton near Ross, who bought the Burton Court estate in 1738. William the younger built Burton Court in the mid 18th century. He married Jane (d.1768), daughter of Philip Hoskyns (qv under Hungerford Hoskyns, d.1767) of nearby Bernithan.

Maudslay, Alfred Percival (1850-1931), archaeologist, was born in Surrey on 18 March 1850 and educated at Harrow and Trinity Hall, Cambridge, where he studied natural sciences. Giving up medicine for warmer climes because of bronchitis, he travelled widely and developed an interest in archaeology and the exploration of lost cities in Central America. He had casts made of Mayan sculpture and inscriptions and exhibited them in South Kensington (they are now in the British Museum) with an extensive study of his findings. He married Annie Morris (1848-1926) in 1892 and they retired to Morney Cross overlooking the Wye at Fownhope, where Maudslay translated *The True History of the Conquest of New Spain*. After Annie's death he married a neighbour, Alice Purdon (d.1939). He died on 22 January 1931 and was interred in Hereford Cathedral crypt.

Maxwell Fry, Edwin (1899-1987), modernist architect, built Warham Ash at Breinton for A.M. Hudson Davies in 1938, an example of modernism unique in the county.

May, Hugh (1621-84), architect, was born in October 1621 at Mid Lavant, near Chichester. His family served the Court in exile during the Interregnum and May was appointed surveyor of the royal palaces at the Restoration and was involved in the rebuilding of London after the Great Fire. One of his major works was the rebuilding of Holme Lacy House in 1674 for Sir John Scudamore (qv, d.1697), with Anthony Deane his builder. It has been altered subsequently but May's work on the south and east façades looks forward to the restraint of the 18th century and shows the Dutch influence of his years of exile. Examples of his vigorous carving survive inside. May's work has been overshadowed by Wren and Hawksmoor and his importance as creator of the Restoration house is neglected. He was a friend of Peter Lely, with whom he travelled in the Netherlands, and helped John Evelyn (qv) write his comparison of ancient and modern architecture. May died on 21 February 1684 and was buried in Mid Lavant Church, Sussex.

Maylord – three mayors of Hereford: John Maylord in 1560 and 1574, his son William Maylord in 1585 and William's son Thomas in 1591. Dr William Brewster (qv) and a later John Maylord bought the Blewhouse in Widemarsh Street, renamed the Mansion House. A street is named after them, as is Hereford's Maylord shopping centre.

Mayo, also **Mayhew**, a common name in Herefordshire spelled variously.

Mayo, Herbert (1720-1802), clergyman, born in Hereford the son of Charles Mayo, was educated at Brasenose College, Oxford and married Mary (1733-1824), daughter of George Coldham, surgeon-extraordinary to the Prince of Wales. They lived in London where their eldest son Paggen William Mayo (1766-1836) followed the family tradition and became a physician. His younger brother Charles Mayo (1767-1858) was a noted Old English scholar.

Mayo, John (1761-1818), physician of Hereford, was born on 10 December 1761, the son of a Thomas Mayo. He was educated at Brasenose and Oriel Colleges, Oxford. He married a Jane Cock and they had a son Thomas. Having qualified in medicine, he was appointed physician to the Foundling Hospital (1787) in London, and physician to the Middlesex hospital in 1788. He was physician in ordinary to Caroline of Brunswick, Princess of Wales. He did not return to Herefordshire, but practised latterly in Tunbridge Wells where he died. There is a plaque to him there.

Mayo, Richard (1440-1516), Bishop of Hereford 1504-16, was born in Wiltshire and educated at New College, Oxford, where he became a Fellow and was ordained priest. In 1480 he became the first president of Magdalen College, laying the cornerstone of the tower, and was Archdeacon of Oxford. He was employed on diplomatic work by Henry VII and escorted Catherine of Aragon to Britain as Prince Arthur's bride – the unwitting nemesis of Mayo's church. He arrived in Hereford as bishop in grand style; already Chancellor of Oxford and Almoner to the king, he was accompanied by a retinue of knights and followers. Mayo knew Wolsey (qv) at Magdalen and in 1512 made him his dean. In 1514 he issued an indulgence to pilgrims visiting St Dubricius' (qv) shrine at Woolhope. He presented an organ to the lady chapel in the cathedral, sited in the upper room of the Audley

Chapel. Mayo was buried, as he wished, by the statue of St Ethelbert on the south of the high altar where his effigy remains under its high canopy. His episcopal ring is sometimes shown in cathedral exhibitions.

Mayo, Thomas (d.1625), lived at Bodenham with his wife Catherine and their children. He died on 22 January 1625 but Catherine and her son Thomas suffered sequestration at the hands of the Parliamentary commissioners at Hereford (qv Silas Taylor) in the Interregnum. She died in September 1653. Their monument was seen in Bodenham Church by Thomas Dingley (qv).

Meg (founded 1646), a heavy mortar popularly called Roaring Meg, was one of the largest to be cast in Britain at that time, on the orders of Col Birch (qv), Governor of Hereford. It was made in a Forest of Dean foundry specifically for local siege work in 1646 and cast missiles of 2cwt. It was difficult to move; Birch had it positioned on a rise overlooking Goodrich Castle, which was garrisoned for the king by Sir Henry Lingen (qv). Birch pounded Goodrich into submission and the Royalist garrison surrendered. Meg was then hauled off to subdue the garrison of Raglan Castle. Birch was proud of Meg and later drew her through Hereford in triumph. Then for two centuries she served as a bollard on the corner of Gwynne and Bridge Streets, giving her name to a pub. From 1839 she stood on Castle Green under Nelson's Column, then she was sited in Churchill Gardens on Aylestone Hill. She is now on show at Goodrich Castle.

Melun, Robert de (*c*.1100-67), Bishop of Hereford 1163-7, philosopher, logician and theologian, was considered a great teacher at the school of St Geneviève, a forerunner of the University of Paris. His name came from a small town nearby although he was an Englishman. He wrote an influential book, *Liber Sententiarum*, and was a friend of Peter Abelard and John of Salisbury. Thomas Becket (qv), another friend, had Henry II summon him to England to be Dean of Oxford, and for the last four years of his life he was Bishop of Hereford, the city at this time being a centre of thinkers and scientists. He was present at the stormy meeting between Henry and Becket at Northampton in 1164 and tried to wrest the crozier from

Becket's hands, after which the archbishop fled into exile. He was present again at Clarendon when Henry issued the constitutions that made clear the differences between him and Becket, particularly his requirement that 'criminous clerks' be tried in civil courts. In 1167 on the Pope's instructions he tried to visit Becket in exile to attempt to reconcile him with the king, but Henry prevented him going. He returned to Hereford where he died on 27 February 1167, it is said of grief at his failure to heal the rift between king and archbishop. He is buried in the south choir aisle of Hereford Cathedral under the south wall, the most easterly of the row of bishops sited here in the 14th century. Another memorial to Robert in the cathedral is the 12th-century reliquary showing the murder of St Thomas Becket which he may have commissioned.

Merbury, John (d.1438), MP of Lyonshall and Weobley, had family on the Cheshire/Shropshire borders with a castle at Lyonshall which was to come to him. He started out as an archer and entered John of Gaunt's (qv) service. He married Alice, daughter of Sir John Pembridge, who was the widow of Edmund de la Bere and Thomas Oldcastle (qv). Their daughter was Elizabeth, who married Walter Devereux (qv, d.1459) *c.*1432, and her son Walter Devereux (qv, d.1485) would be created 7th Baron Ferrers of Chartley. After Alice's death he married the even richer Agnes née Crophill, widow of Sir Walter Devereux, (qv, d.1402). She brought him Weobley Castle, which became his home. His two lucrative marriages made him one of the wealthiest gentlemen in the county. He was MP for Herefordshire between 1419 and 1427, and was the most important Lancastrian servant in the area, being Sheriff of Hereford in 1406, 1415, 1419-1421, 1422, 1426, 1430 and 1434-35 – possibly a record of shrieval tenure. He was Justiciar of South Wales 1421-3; Steward of Brecon (1414-29) and Kidwelly (1417-23) and the escheator for Herefordshire and its Marches (1416-30). During Glyn Dŵr's rebellion his military experience in the Marches was invaluable and he acted with others like John ap Harry (qv) to restore order. He was tasked with the capture of the outlawed Sir John Oldcastle (qv) but despite a reward seemed not to notice that he was in hiding nearby at Almeley. If this was loyalty to a friend and relative it was a feeling common to all Oldcastle's neighbours, many of whom had Lollard sympathies. Bishop Mascall (qv) appointed him steward of church property in the wider see of Hereford. In 1434 he was managing all the old Mortimer estates now in the hands of Richard of York. He is buried in Weobley Church beside his second wife Agnes with fine alabaster effigies, she in a horned head-dress. In his will he left 100 marks for a chantry in Weobley Church for prayers for his family's spiritual welfare – not a Lollard trait – and enormous sums as dowries for his daughters.

Mercury, a god of the Roman pantheon: a herald, a trickster and god of commerce and boundaries, is depicted in a small bronze statue that was found on the site of the Eignbrook Chapel, Hereford, but that probably came from *Magnis* (Kenchester). The statue has winged sandals and cap and holds a caduceus. The Romans may have seen him as the same as the Celtic Lug (qv).

Merewalh (*c.*625-85), was appointed regulus or sub-king of the Magonsaete by King Penda of Mercia, who was possibly a relation. The name Merewalh means *illustrious Welshman*. The Magonsaete were originally known as the Western Hecani and their territory was coterminous with the Diocese of Hereford. Merewalh was converted to Christianity by St Edfrith (qv). As his second wife he married Domne Eafe, later sainted, a Kentish princess, and their sons Merchelm and Mildfrith (qv) succeeded him. Their saintly family included Mildburg, Mildred, (qqv) and Mildgytha. Merewalh is the traditional founder of St Peter's Priory in Leominster (660). Leland (qv) said Merewalh's palace was on a hill east of Leominster, later called Comfort Castle, where the inhabitants of Leominster held their annual sports.

Merewether, John (1797-1850), Dean of Hereford 1832-1850, was born at Marshfield, Gloucestershire and educated at Queen's College, Oxford, where he received the degree of Doctor of Divinity. As a curate in the home counties he attracted the attention of the Duke of Clarence (later William IV), who appointed him chaplain to his wife, later Queen Adelaide. With this patronage he was presented to the living of New Radnor in 1828, became vicar of Madeley in Shropshire but within the diocese of Hereford, and was then appointed Dean of Hereford, succeeding Edward Grey (qv), who had become bishop. He married Mary Baker and they had nine children. Merewether, a reforming Tory, hoped to become bishop but was passed over first by Melbourne and then by Peel. He opposed the appointment of Bishop Hampden (qv) in 1847, regarding him as a heretic, and was autocratic with his chapter. He had decided ideas on how an ancient cathedral should look and was unhappy with the 18th-century appearance of Hereford. As the structure, especially of the tower and crossing, was unsafe he raised money for a major renovation and brought in Lewis Cottingham (qv), an architect known for his comparative sensitivity to mediaeval architecture; there was dust and chaos for years. He was also eager to renovate the cathedral music. He attempted to stir up slack choristers in vain, and appointed the brilliant but unreliable organist Samuel Wesley (qv), restoring the old organ for him. Wesley repaid him by eloping with his sister. Merewether was a keen if destructive archaeologist and one month in the summer of 1849 he opened some 35 barrows in Wiltshire, among them West Kennet and Silbury Hill. His archaeological notes were published as *The Diary of a Dean* in 1851. He died on 4 April 1850 at his Madeley vicarage and was buried in Hereford Cathedral's lady chapel. Nockalls Cottingham (qv) designed a stained glass memorial to him in the five lancets of the lady chapel, and John Hardman (qv) made him a monument.

Merlimond, Oliver de (12th century) was steward of Hugh (I) Mortimer (qv), who granted him the manor of Shobdon and appointed him guardian of his son Hugh (II). In order to honour Hugh's deathbed wish to found an abbey, Oliver instructed a Sir Bernard to rebuild the Saxon Church of St John at Shobdon. Oliver went on pilgrimage to Santiago de Compostela in Spain, calling at the Augustinian Abbey of St Victor in Paris to arrange for an abbot and canons to take charge of the new foundation. The Mortimers repeatedly changed their minds about the new abbey, and its monks moved four times before finally settling at Wigmore, where *c.*1172 the abbey was dedicated by Bishop Robert Foliot (qv). For over 200 years it was to be the mausoleum of the Mortimer family. Oliver's new church at Shobdon was consecrated *c.*1140 by Bishop Robert Béthune (qv). It was a showcase for the Herefordshire School of Sculptors (qv) and perhaps their first work. It was demolished by Richard Bateman (qv), but distinctive details can be seen on the Shobdon Arches gathered on a hill nearby. The workshop's visual ideas are thought to have been brought back by Oliver from his pilgrimage in south-west France and other sources. The original font remains at

Shobdon, a large bowl supported by four lions, a beast popular among the sculptors.

Merlin (6th century), wizard and adviser of King Arthur (qv), was originally Myrddin in the Welsh poems, then Latinised to Merlinus by Geoffrey of Monmouth. Herefordshire legend has him buried under Mynydd Myrddyn, the hill to the east of Longtown Castle, Herefordshire. There is a Merlin's Cave and a King Arthur's Cave in the Doward which have yielded prehistoric remains. In the former, two Dark Age burials have recently been exhumed.

Meryk, Richard ap (b.1445), or Ameryke, was born at Bollitree House (now Castle) near Ross. He moved to Bristol and became a wealthy merchant. He sponsored John Cabot's voyage to the New World and his name is a possible origin of the name America.

Meyrick, Gelly or Gelli Meurig (*c.*1556-1601), conspirator, was a Welsh squire of Pembrokeshire, the eldest son of Rowland Meyrick (1505-66), Bishop of Bangor. He owned lands in Herefordshire and was granted Wigmore Castle by his patron, the 2nd Earl of Essex (qv Robert Devereux). He married Elizabeth Lewis of Harpton Court, Old Radnor and their children were Rowland and Margaret. He joined Essex in his raid on Cadiz and was knighted by him. He joined Essex's abortive rebellion of 1601 against Queen Elizabeth, trying to raise support in Herefordshire. On the afternoon before the uprising he commissioned a performance at the Globe of Shakespeare's *Richard II*, which dealt with the overthrow of the monarch; for this he was found guilty of treason and hanged, drawn and quartered with Essex on 13 March 1601. His lands were confiscated by the Crown, but Roland and Margaret later had part of his Herefordshire lands around Eyton and Lucton returned to them.

Meyrick, Samuel Rush (1783-1848), historian and antiquary, was born on 26 August 1783 at Westminster, the only surviving son of John Meyrick and grandson of James Meyrick

of Lucton, descendant of Sir Gelly (qv). Educated at Queen's College, Oxford he was a successful advocate in the ecclesiastical and admiralty courts. His marriage to Mary Parry displeased his father, who cut him out of his will, but as the favoured son predeceased his father Samuel inherited after all. He collected arms and armour, amassing more than he could store in his house in Cadogan Square. He saw Goodrich Castle as a perfect setting for his collection. When the owner, Catherine Griffin (qv), refused to sell he built his own version on the hill overlooking the ruins. His architect was Edward Blore (qv), a colleague from the Society of Antiquaries. The vast Goodrich Court went up between 1828 and 1831 and the collection was installed, filling the purpose-built rooms and long galleries. There were pageants of armed horses and men, an ancient chapel and a complete tournament with mounted knights and heralds. Meyrick was a leading authority on arms and armour, and published learned articles on the subject. He was consulted by Sir Walter Scott on his decorations and purchase of armour at Abbotsford; by the authorities at the Tower of London about the display of their armour; and by George IV and William IV at Windsor, for which work he was knighted. In 1834 Sir Samuel was installed as High Sheriff of Herefordshire with great pageantry. His astonishing castle drew criticism and praise: it spoilt Catherine Griffin's view, and to Wordsworth (qv), a lover of the Goodrich area, it was an 'impertinent structure'. It was, though, an added tourist attraction on the Wye Valley tour. Giddis, the original 17th-century house on the estate, remains. Meyrick died at Goodrich Court on 2 April 1848 and was buried in St Giles churchyard. His heir was his second cousin Lt-Col Augustus Meyrick, whose son sold the collection. Much went to the Wallace Collection and much was bought by Charles Somers Cocks (qv) for Eastnor Castle. Goodrich Court, with the remains of the armour, was bought by George Moffatt (qv). After a spell as a school it was finally auctioned off after the Second World War in stages from the fittings to the stones of the walls. It had been completely demolished by 1950. Blore's Monmouth Gatehouse (1837) remains to give a feel of what the great house was like.

Middleton, John de, Dean of Hereford *c.*1375-82, put in the cathedral choir stalls with their misericords *c.*1380. They were originally sited beneath the tower. Scott (qv), restoring the cathedral in the 1860s, found 40 still serviceable, restored them and added 20 new ones.

Milbourne: Baronets of Tillington Court, Burghill. There are monuments in St Mary's, Burghill, especially an altar tomb with an effigy of Sir John Milbourne and his 12 children. Sir Simon Milbourne (15th century) married Jane Baskerville (*c.*1439-71) and had 13 children: Agnes married Thomas Walwyn (qv, d.1531) of Hellens; Alys married Henry Myles Parry (qv) and Anne married William Rudhall (qv, d.1530).

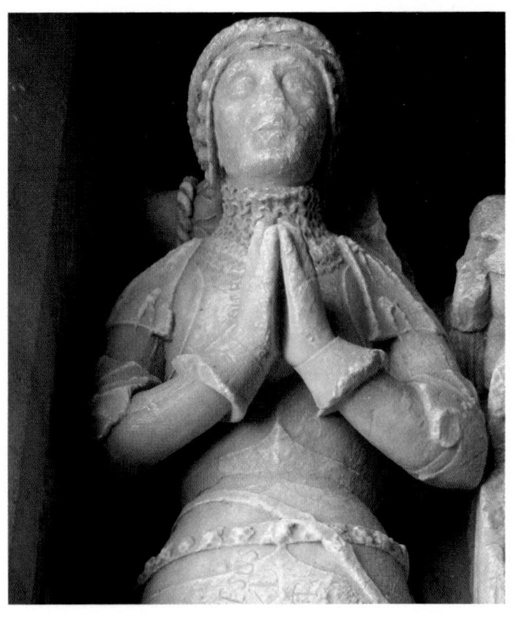

Mildburg (fl.716-33), saint, was the daughter of King Merewalh (qv) and his second wife Domne Eafe. She and her younger sister Mildred were much venerated in mediaeval Herefordshire with another sister Mildgytha. Mildburg, who became the abbess of Much

S. MILBVRGA FILIA MERWALDI REGIS IN ANGLI
Virgo.et Abbatissa Ordinis. S. Benedicti. Feb. 23.

Wenlock in the mediaeval diocese of Hereford, was noted for levitation and control of birds. She had a shrine at All Saints, Coddington, where on the north wall a bracket remains that once held her image. Until recently Milborough, a version of her name, was a common girl's name in Herefordshire. Her feast day, 23 February, was one of the days on which the bishop presided in the cathedral.

Mildfrith (7th century) succeeded his father Merewalh (qv) as subregulus of the Magonsaete under Offa (qv). This small Christian Celtic kingdom between Powys in Wales and the Anglians of Mercia had been absorbed by Mercia. Mildfrith had the body of St Ethelbert buried at Fernley (an old name for Hereford) and built a monastery on the site. He is said to have built the first bridge over the Wye, before which the river was forded opposite the bishop's palace where Neolithic stone tools have been found. In the 8th century Bishop Cuthbert (qv) set up a cross commemorating him and three bishops.

Mildred (d.733), saint, was one of the daughters of Merewalh (qv). Born and brought up in her father's hall at Leominster, she was the pious first abbess of the double monastery at Minster on the Isle of Thanet which her mother had founded. Archbishop Cuthbert (qv) translated her remains to Canterbury where she was venerated above all others until the cult of St Thomas Becket (qv) displaced her in the 13th century. Her remains were later removed to Holland, but have now been restored to her abbey at Minster.

Miles of Gloucester (1097-1143), 1st Earl of Hereford of a new creation, Lord of Brecknock and appointed hereditary Constable of England, was the son and heir of Walter de Gloucester, a Sheriff of Hereford between 1104 and 1121. Miles was a favourite of Henry I, who appointed him Constable of England. He supported Stephen as King Henry's successor but sided with Matilda, Henry's daughter, when she landed, and held Gloucestershire and Herefordshire for her. She confirmed him as Constable of Herefordshire and in 1141 when she was in the ascendant made him Earl of Hereford. The same year he married Sybil, daughter of Bernard de Neufmarché and granddaughter of Gruffydd ap Llwelyn (qv). During the disturbances under King Stephen he allowed the monks of Llanthony Priory, who had found sanctuary with Bishop Robert de Béthune (qv) at Hereford, a hide of land outside Gloucester where they built a safer monastery. Miles was killed on 24 December 1143 while hunting in the Forest of Dean and although he had been excommunicated by Bishop Robert of Hereford, St Peter's Abbey Gloucester and Llanthony vied for his body. He left five sons and three daughters. For Roger, see under fitz Miles; for Bertha, Henry fitz Miles, Mahel, Walter and William, see under de Hereford; for Margaret and Lucy, see under Gloucester.

(fitz) Miles, Roger (d.1155), 2nd Earl of Hereford, eldest son of Miles of Gloucester (qv), was, unusually in this period, literate. He married Cecily, daughter of Pain fitz John (qv under Pain), whose mother was Sybil, niece of Hugh de Lacy (qv, d.*c.*1121). She brought him much land in Herefordshire, including Archenfield and the Lacy honour of Weobley. He succeeded to his father's title in 1143 and supported the Angevin Matilda in the civil wars, helping Duke Henry her son to the throne as Henry II (qv). He was a power in the Marches and made treaties with other Marcher lords like William (II) de Briouze (qv). He was a generous patron of local priories and supported Llanthony in its move to Gloucester, except that when the prior, William of Wycombe (qv) criticised his father he had him exiled. In the aftermath of the civil war Henry II found that Roger had occupied royal castles and lands in Herefordshire, including Hereford Castle, and threatened to reclaim them by force if necessary but Bishop Gilbert Foliot (qv), Roger's kinsman, negotiated a compromise (although involving excommunication at one point). In 1155 Earl Roger retired sick to St Peter's Abbey, Gloucester where he died. The countess lived until 1204.

Minton, Micky Herbert (1883-1957), cyclist called The Little Wonder, was born at Much Dewchurch. His father manufactured bicycles at his Trinity Cycle Works at Whitecross and sold them from his shop: H. Minton's of Hereford. Micky held world records for cycling and in 1912 was champion of England over 440 yards on his fixed wheel Rover bicycle

Moeran, Ernest John (1894-1950), composer, a vicar's son known as Jack, was born on 31 December 1894 at Brentford, Middlesex and studied at the Royal College of Music. He fought in the First World War but was invalided home where he continued his music studies under John Ireland. His brother, Revd (William) Graham Moeran, was vicar of Leominster and a prebendary of Hereford and found Gravel Hill Villa near Kington for the family. Here his mother Esther converted a shed into a studio for Jack, in which he found the peace to compose and inspiration from his walks along Hergest Ridge and through the Golden Valley, writing his best work: *Rhapsody for Piano and Orchestra*, *Overture to a Masque*,

his cello sonata, a cello concerto and a sinfonietta, all in the romantic tradition. Moeran was interested in local folk songs and reflected this in his *Songs of Springtime*. He met the cellist Peers Coetmore at a concert in Leominster and married her at St Mary's, Kington in July 1945, after which his mother sold Gravel Hill and moved to Ledbury where Graham was now rector. The marriage was not a success and 'Cottie' was unable to cope with his drinking and chaotic lifestyle. In Ledbury in 1949 Moeran started his 2nd Symphony but Graham and his mother also found him difficult. During a holiday in Kenmare, Kerry, a spot he loved, on 1 December 1950 Moeran fell off the pier and drowned. At the time of his death a friend thought she saw him in Ledbury High Street. She went to speak to him but he ignored her.

Moffatt, George (1806-78), London tea merchant, was born on 11 May 1806. The prosperous family tea business Moffatt & Co. brought him wealth and he entered politics and travelled widely. In 1871 Moffatt bought Goodrich Court from the heirs of Sir Samuel Meyrick (qv) with the remnants of its great collection of armour, to which he added. A JP and Deputy Lieutenant of Herefordshire, he died on 20 February 1878 and was buried in Goodrich churchyard.

Mogridge, George (1787-1854), writer, was born on 17 February 1787. After the failure of his japanning business in Birmingham, he left his wife and family and stayed with his uncle Revd J.W. Phillips, vicar of Brockhampton by Ross; his vicarage was on the site of the later Brockhampton Court. Revd Phillips was the secretary of the British and Foreign Bible Society and encouraged his nephew to write the short, improving pieces for which he was to became famous. He was accepted by the Religious Tract Society under the *nom de plume* Old Humphrey, amongst over 20 other pen names. He wrote especially for children and the labouring classes. The family was reunited in London and Mogridge wrote prolifically, although never profitably, until his death at Hastings on 2 November 1854. His collected tracts are still published.

Monck, Nicholas (*c.*1610-61), Bishop of Hereford 1660-1, son of Sir Thomas Monck of Devon, was educated at Wadham College, Oxford and ordained in 1631. He obtained a Devon rectory and married Susanna Payne (d.1666). His younger brother George Monck was a Parliamentary general in the Civil Wars and Nicholas took intelligence to him from the exiled king that induced him to switch sides at a crucial moment. This led to a restored, free Parliament which invited Charles II to return. Monck was made Doctor of Divinity and Bishop of Hereford in reward. He never visited his diocese and died in Westminster on 17 December 1661. He was buried in St Edmund's Chapel, Westminster Abbey with a silver mitre and crozier on the coffin, an old tradition revived with him. His grandson added a large monument by William Woodman (qv).

Monington, Hugh de or Moynton (fl.1400) married a daughter of Nicholas de Sarnesfield (qv) and for the next 300 years Moningtons were lords of Sarnesfield and Monnington manors. Hugh's son Sir Richard Monington married Janet, Glyn Dŵr's (qv) daughter, and widow of Sir John de Croft (qv). In the next century Sir Richard's daughter Sybil married Sir Rowland Morton of Bosbury. In 1781 Ann Monington, the last of the line, became a nun and willed the Sarnesfield estate to a relative, John Webb, and in 1891 George William Marshall (qv) bought it. Through penal times Sarnesfield and indeed the whole Weobley area was described as a 'nest of papists', and the Moningtons maintained a Catholic chapel, St Thomas of Hereford (qv Thomas Cantilupe), at Sarnesfield Court. Later the Moningtons were patrons of the parish church of St Mary's where their memorials remain.

Montagu, Katherine (d.1349), Countess of Salisbury, the youngest daughter of William Grandison (qv), was christened in the Grandison family church at Ashperton. She married William Montagu, 1st Earl of Salisbury (1301-44) and they had six children. Montagu played a leading part in the capture of Roger (V) Mortimer (qv) and Queen Isabella and the earl and countess became close friends of the young Edward III. Montagu was prominent in Edward's wars in Scotland and France. Jean Froissart calls Katherine one of the most beautiful ladies in the land. It was her garter which caused Edward III to utter his famous riposte '*honi soit qui mal y pense*' and which became the emblem of the Order Edward founded. The earl died of wounds received at the tournament to celebrate Edward's creation of his knights of the Round Table and Katherine made a vow of celibacy.

Montfort, Henry de (1238-65), soldier, was the eldest son of Simon de Montfort (qv), Earl of Leicester (qv) and his wife Eleanor, King John's (qv) daughter, making Henry III (qv) his uncle. In 1264 during the start of baronial unrest he attacked the Marcher barons who supported the king. He fought at the Battle of Lewes where Henry III and his son Edward were captured and, with his brother Guy, was put in charge of them when they were held at Hereford Castle. He was told to keep a close eye on Prince Edward (qv Edward I), especially. However, Edward was allowed to exercise on the Wide Marsh outside the walls of Hereford and, having asked for a fresh horse he simply galloped off, leaving Henry and other knights behind – an error that led directly to the Battle of Evesham on 4 August 1265 and the deaths of Henry de Montfort and his father. They were both buried at Evesham Abbey. He and his younger brothers Simon and Guy were unpopular due to the favours shown them by their father, an added cause of their father's waning popularity.

Montfort, Simon de (1208-65), 6th Earl of Leicester, was born in France on 23 May 1208, third son of Simon (*c.*1170-1218), Lord of Montfort l'Amaury in the Île-de-France and Alice (d.1221), daughter of Bouchard de Montmorency, and was brought up in Provence during his father's Albigensian crusade. He was related to Henry III (qv) and came to England in 1230 to claim the earldom of Leicester. He married Eleanor, the king's sister who, although only 16, was already the widow of William (II) Marshal (qv). Eleanor had sworn a vow of chastity but broke it on meeting Montfort and they had seven children. (One of their descendants was Elizabeth Woodville, Edward IV's queen.) Their daughter Eleanor married Llywelyn ap Gruffydd (qv) with whom Simon was in alliance. He was a pious man who wore a hair shirt and was keen to reform Church abuse. He went on Crusade, anxious about his wife's broken vow. He was a scholar and friend of the great humanist Robert Grosseteste (qv). He governed Gascony for Henry but was recalled humiliatingly. In 1263 he and other magnates rebelled, seeking rights granted in Magna Carta. At the Battle of Lewes on 14 May 1264 he captured the king and Prince Edward (qv Edward I) securing them finally in Hereford Castle in the charge of his eldest son Henry (qv). Hereford was a particularly strong royal castle which de Montfort was using. Montfort ruled England himself for a year, appointing his relation Thomas de Cantilupe (qv) his chancellor. In this period Montfort called representatives from the shires together as the first elected parliament, earning him the title Father of Parliament. He was popular in the country although the barons saw representative government as an erosion of their prerogatives and opposed him in this. Roger (III) Mortimer (qv) raided Hereford's suburbs but failed to take the castle. Later, as one story has it, Mortimer's wife Maud (qv) managed to secure Prince Edward's escape to Wigmore and Ludlow Castles. He was then able to organize the king's forces, meeting Montfort at the Battle of Evesham on 4 August 1265 where de Montfort and his son Henry were killed. Montfort's head was sent by Mortimer to his wife Maud at Wigmore.

Morcar (d.1087), Earl of Northumbria, son of Earl Ælfgar (qv), had an estate at Kingsland where there was a custom that when Morcar's lady arrived the Reeve would present her and her officials with money. Morcar was appointed Earl of Northumbria in place of Tostig Godwinson (qv under Godwin). He, with his older brother Eadwine, accommodated with the Normans but twice rose against them.

Mordred (fl.500 AD), nephew or illegitimate son of King Arthur (qv), is said to have crossed the Wye at Mordiford, thence named after him, on his way to the last battle, in which Arthur died. The green dragon once painted on the west face of Mordiford church tower was, according to one local legend made widely known by Geoffrey of Monmouth, supposed to be a copy of that on Mordred's banner. The church tower has since been rebuilt by Kempson (qv).

Morgan, Frederick Charles (1878-1978), librarian, was born on 29 June 1878 in Stratford-upon-Avon, where his father was a printer and bookseller and ran a circulating library. He became librarian of Stratford and then of the new Malvern Public Library, where he improved the collections. He married Penelope. In 1924 after service in the First World War he was appointed librarian and curator of art at Hereford Art Gallery and Museum, where he built up the neglected collections. His daughter Penelope E. Morgan (1916-90) followed him as City Librarian. He was a member of the Woolhope Club and president twice, he edited the club's *Transactions* and organised lectures. He wrote over 100 articles and made an extensive photographic record for its archive, illustrating particularly rural crafts, vernacular architecture, agriculture and archaeology in Herefordshire. He was chief steward of Hereford City. With his daughter he made a lifelong collection of children's books which in 1954 they donated to the Morgan Collection of Children's Books in the Baillieu Library of Melbourne University. He was honorary librarian of Hereford Cathedral library, succeeded by his nephew Paul Morgan (a local historian in his own right) and then by Penelope. He died aged 100 in July 1978.

Morgan, Henry Frederick Stanley (1881-1959), sports car manufacturer, was the son of Henry George Morgan, rector of Stoke Lacy, where his grandfather and great-grandfather had also been rectors. He was born in the rectory on 11 August 1881 and went briefly to Marlborough School but was withdrawn and sent to Italy for health reasons. On his return he studied at Crystal Palace Engineering College and was apprenticed with the Great Western Railway Company. He was fascinated by motor cars and drove early models. In 1905 he started his own motor servicing works in a Malvern Link garage with his partner Leslie Bacon from Bromyard and they ran the first motor bus service between the Link and the Wells. A master at Malvern College allowed them use of his well-equipped workshop and they began building their own cars. Their first, in 1909, was the Morgan 3-wheeler Runabout. In 1912 Harry married Ruth Day, their son Peter (1919-2003) subsequently becoming chairman of the Morgan Motor Co. In the First World War they manufactured munitions but continued making luxury sports cars afterwards; business prospered and the present firm developed. He died in Malvern on 15 June 1959. There is a memorial to the four generations of Morgans in Stoke Lacy Church.

Morgan, John (*c*.1650-93), 2nd Baronet, the eldest of Thomas's (d.1679, qv) ten children, married Hester Price of Pilleth, and was MP for New Radnor and for Hereford in 1685, 1689, and 1690-93.

Morgan, John (I) of Arkstone Court, Kingstone, probably son of Sir Thomas Morgan of Pencoed, and his son John (II), both dead by 1572, were MPs for Carmarthen. In the previous century Arkstone had been the home of the de la Hays (qv).

Morgan, Nathaniel (1775-1854) was a Quaker philanthropist and Clerk of Ross Friends' Meeting for 20 years. He founded the Ross and

Archenfield Bank, was thrice Mayor of Ross and strongly supported parliamentary reform. He pressed for the abolition of slavery and better education for the poor, and gave Ross Methodists the site for their chapel. He also organised improvements to Ross amenities, supplying a town clock, improving the road to Hereford, and organising street lighting and the town fire service.

Morgan, Thomas (1604-79), 1st Baronet, army officer, was born at Old Court, Llangattock Lingoed in Monmouthshire on 10 December 1604. At 16, speaking only Welsh, he went to fight on the Continent, returning in 1642 for the English Civil Wars as one of the most experienced Parliamentary officers, much valued by George Monck (qv under Nicholas Monck) and popular with his men. He was small, high-voiced and choleric, barely literate, and had a tendency to gout. He was good at sieges and advised Birch (qv) on the surprise capture of Hereford – a particular blow to King Charles (qv), who had just visited the city and was negotiating with Parliament. The next year Morgan was commanding all Parliament's forces in the west midlands. He married first Katherine, one of Lord Thomas Coningsby's (qv, d.1625) three daughters and after her death, Delariviere Cholmondeley, who brought him Braham Hall, near Knaresborough in Yorkshire. In the 1650s he campaigned in Scotland as major-general and fought with distinction in Flanders, where he was knighted by Richard Cromwell. In Scotland he rejoined Monck, who confided in him his intention to restore the king and, on the achievement of this goal in 1661, he was advanced to a baronetcy. He was in Portugal as part of the deputation making Charles II's marriage arrangements. He bought estates in Herefordshire such as Chanstone Court near Vowchurch and Kinnersley Castle, and recovered his birthplace, Old Court. He never retired to enjoy his property, however, and died whilst Governor of Jersey on 13 April 1679.

Morgan, Thomas (*c.*1685-1716), 3rd Baronet, of Kinnersley Castle, married an Anne Roydhouse of London. The Morgan baronetcy became extinct in 1767 but was revived by distant descendants in 1831 for John James Walsham (qv) of Knill Court.

Mortimer: A dynasty of violent, energetic but generally short-lived Marches magnates, named from Mortimer-en-Brai in Normandy. After the Conquest Ralph was first given lands in Hampshire belonging to Edric the Wild (qv), and within 20 years he had built up extensive holdings in 12 English counties. The three Mortimer lordships, Wigmore, Chirk and Richard's Castle, became distinct lines of the family, with those at Wigmore, the senior branch, granted a barony by Edward I. Wigmore Castle had been built by William fitz Osbern (qv), Earl of Hereford, in the late 1060s and was given to Ralph (I) when William's son Roger de Breteuil (qv) rebelled. In the 12th century Hugh (II) founded Wigmore Abbey, eventually an Augustinian Priory, where Mortimers would be buried and where the monks would keep the Mortimer archive. They struggled with the Welsh for control of the Middle March but were also often in alliance with them against the English king. They intermarried with the Welsh princely houses: Ralph (II) married Gwladus Ddu, Llywelyn's daughter; they were often identified as Welsh heroes themselves, as when Edmund (IV) joined with Glyn Dŵr's rebellion. And Roger (VII)'s deeds were celebrated by the bards. Herefordshire legends of 'Mortimer of Wigmore' were performed by strolling players into the 20th century. The power and pride of the Mortimers at their height made them difficult subjects: Roger (V), 1st Earl of March, overthrew and murdered King Edward II and ruled with his queen, Isabella, as his lover until King Edward III re-established royal command. After this treachery, and because the Mortimers were as close to the throne as subsequent monarchs, they needed cautious handling. There was a plot to put the kindly Edmund (V), the last Earl of March, on the throne, and finally Anne Mortimer, Roger (VII)'s daughter, married Richard of Conisbrough. They were both descendants of King Edward III, and their son Richard, the future Duke of York, made a more serious bid for the throne as part of the Wars of the Roses. Richard's son succeeded in this, becoming King Edward IV. Edward IV's male descendants, the Princes in the Tower, were probably murdered by their uncle, Richard III, who died at Bosworth in 1485. The dynasty seemed short-lived but the successful Lancastrian claimant Henry Tudor (qv Henry VII) married Edward IV's eldest daughter Elizabeth of York and united the warring Houses. Their eldest son Arthur, Prince of Wales, was recognized as a Mortimer descendant and granted title to the Earldom of March, with the Wigmore holdings in Herefordshire. And so through the Tudors the Herefordshire Mortimers continued to occupy the throne. The old castle of Wigmore was bought in the early 17th century by Sir Robert Harley (qv, d.1656) and in 1711 his grandson Robert (qv, d.1724), was created 1st Earl Oxford and Mortimer.

Mortimer, Anne (*c.*1388-*c.*1414), eldest daughter of Roger (VII) (qv), married Richard of Conisbrough, 3rd Earl of Cambridge who was, like herself, descended from Edward III. They met when Richard was fighting Glyn Dŵr (qv) on Mortimer lands. Their son, Richard (1411-60), the future Duke of York, therefore had a double claim to the throne but was killed asserting it at the Battle of Wakefield. His son Edward, however, created Earl of March, became Edward IV (qv).

Mortimer, Blanche de (*c.*1316-47), daughter of Roger (V) (qv), married Sir Peter Grandison (qv) at Wigmore and they had a daughter, Isabella. Blanche's strikingly beautiful effigy (see page 178) can be seen in St Bartholomew's Church, Much Marcle, her dress hanging with fictive realism over the edge of the tomb, her hands telling a rosary. When the tomb was conserved recently a lead coffin was discovered containing her remains.

Mortimer, Edmund (I) de (1255-1304), 7th Lord and 2nd Baron Wigmore, was the son of Roger (III) (qv) and Maud. Intended for minor orders, he abandoned the Church in 1273/4 on the death of his elder brother Ralph, which made him heir; his father died in 1282. He is thought to have been responsible for the subterfuge that trapped Llywelyn ap Gruffydd (qv). Edmund married Margaret (1262-1333), daughter of William (II) de Fiennes and Blanche de Brienne; their children were Roger (V) (qv), Isolde and Matilda, all born at Wigmore. Edmund died on 17 July 1304, wounded during a skirmish near Builth. The widowed Lady Margaret had Edward II's agent John Daniel (qv) imposed on her as manager of the Mortimer estates, including Radnor Castle, during her son Roger (V)'s exile. When he returned he saw Daniel off. Edmund's daughter Isolde married first Walter de Balun (qv) and second Hugh de Audley (qv), Earl of Gloucester.

Mortimer, Edmund (II) de (1302-31), son of Roger (V) (qv) and Joan, was disinherited as the son of a traitor. He and his mother had distanced themselves from Roger, whom he called 'the King of Folly', and the family was not punished further. He married Elizabeth de Badlesmere and they had a son, Roger (VI) (qv). Edmund died in 1331, the year after his father, and his widow Elizabeth married William de Bohun (qv), Earl of Hereford.

Mortimer, Edmund (III) (1352-81), 3rd Earl of March and of Ulster, and eldest son of Roger (VI) (qv), was born at Llangoed in Brecknockshire on 1 February 1352. He was betrothed, aged six, to Princess Philippa (1355-

78), daughter of Edward III's son Lionel, Duke of Clarence. This brought him lands in Herefordshire and extensive tracts in Ireland and showed the extent of King Edward's forgiveness for Roger (V) Mortimer's treachery. He was eight at the time of his father's death and became the ward of William Wykeham, Bishop of Winchester and Richard Fitzalan, Earl of Arundel. The Mortimer lands were in several hands during Edmund's minority but managed by the family steward John Gour (qv). At 17 he fought in the French wars and in 1371 was allowed livery of his estates. He was one of the largest landowners in Britain and summoned to Parliament. In 1379 he went to Ireland with his brother Sir Thomas to secure his lands there. He died at Cork on 27 December 1381 and his body was returned to be buried in Wigmore Abbey. Edmund and the Princess Philippa had three sons, Roger (VII) (qv), John and Edmund (IV) (qv) and two daughters – Elizabeth, who married Sir Harry 'Hotspur' Percy, and Philippa, who married first John Hastings, Earl of Pembroke, son of Agnes (d.1368), daughter of Roger (V) (qv) and Joan. After Hastings' death, Philippa, still only 14, married the great landowner Richard Fitzalan, 4th Earl of Arundel and 9th of Surrey. Fitzalan was fond of the girl and renamed his favourite castle at Shrawardine, Shropshire *Castle Philippa*. Edmund was patron of Adam of Usk (qv), chronicler of the Mortimer family,

Mortimer, Edmund (IV) (1376-1409), the youngest child of Edmund (III) (qv) and Philippa, was born at Ludlow on 9 November 1376, attended, it was later said, by ill portents. When Henry Bolingbroke, Duke of Lancaster (qv Henry IV) was at Hereford on 2 August 1399 in pursuit of Richard II in Wales, Edmund and John Trefnant (qv) Bishop of Hereford made their submission to him although Edmund had better right by descent to the throne. The revolt of Owain Glyn Dŵr (qv) broke out soon after and Edmund and his brother-in-law Henry 'Hotspur' Percy and a force of Herefordshire men moved against him, Edmund's Welsh tenants having joined Owain. On 22 June 1402 Edmund's force was defeated at Pilleth near Knighton with heavy casualties and reports of atrocities committed on the fallen by Welsh women after the battle. Mortimer himself was captured and taken to Glyn Dŵr's mountain lair in Snowdonia, where he was treated courteously. King Henry refused to pay a ransom, concluding that he had defected to Glyn Dŵr, and indeed on 30 November that year Edmund married Glyn Dŵr's daughter, Catherine. Henry confiscated the Mortimer estates and gave them to his own sons. Edmund then publicly declared that he had joined with Glyn Dŵr to reinstate King Richard or give the crown to his nephew Edmund (V) (qv). A later modification was that England and Wales were to be divided between Glyn Dŵr, the Percy family and Edmund himself. Over the next decade Henry overcame the rebellion. Mortimer died in the siege of Harlech in February 1409 but his deeds lived on, in Shakespeare's *Henry IV Part I* and in folk memory and ballads. With Glyn Dŵr's daughter he had a son, Lionel, and several daughters. The family were taken into Henry IV's custody and died in 1413 in London where they were buried at St Swithun's.

Mortimer, Edmund (V) (1391-1425), 5th Earl of March and 7th of Ulster, was born on 6 November 1391 in Hampshire, the eldest son of Roger (VII) (qv). He was the last Mortimer Earl of March at Wigmore. His descent from King Edward III made him heir presumptive to Richard II (qv), and he was perceived as a threat by the usurping Lancastrian dynasty, especially when his uncles Edmund (IV) (qv) and Henry Percy were in rebellion with Glyn Dŵr; Henry IV (qv) thus kept him and his younger brother under close supervision. During the rebellion the Mortimer estates in Herefordshire were devastated and only slowly recovered. After Henry IV's death, Henry V allowed Edmund lands and liberty for a surety of 10,000 marks. He married his cousin Anne (d.1432), daughter of Edmund, Earl of Stafford, with papal dispensation. In 1415, while the king was preparing to invade France, a plot to have Edmund declared king was being hatched by Edmund's brother-in-law Richard of Conisbrough, 3rd Earl of Cambridge. Edmund heard of the plot and informed Henry, who pardoned him and required him to judge the conspirators. A few years later a Sir John Mortimer was held in the Tower; he was probably connected with the Wigmore dynasty as John ap Harry (qv) stood surety for his good behaviour in prison. Despite this he escaped, having boasted to his gaoler that he could raise 40,000 men in the Marches, but he was recaptured and executed. After Henry V's death Edmund was a counsellor of the baby Henry VI, but died of plague while visiting his Irish estates in Ulster on 18 January 1425. He was a kind, pious man whose closeness to the throne was a danger for him. With his death the male line of the Wigmore Mortimers ended, but not the associated Yorkist claim.

Mortimer, Hugh de, (1219-74), Baron Burford, born at Richard's Castle, the son of Robert (qv, b.*c.*1176) and Margaret, was briefly forced to surrender the castle to Simon de Montfort (qv) in 1264. He died on 18 November 1274.

Mortimer, Hugh de (1274-1304), of Richard's Castle, 1st Lord Mortimer and Burford, son of Robert (qv, d.1287) and Joyce, married Matilda (*c.*1272-1308) in about 1290 and their daughters were Joan (b.1291) and Margaret (1295-1345). Joan married Richard Talbot (qv, d.1328), to whom Richard's Castle then passed.

Mortimer, Hugh (I) de (d.*c.*1150), Ralph (I)'s (qv) eldest son, supported Stephen in his struggle with Matilda. He was described as an evil-tempered, choleric, wilful lord given over to pleasure, a quarrelsome neighbour and a lusty warrior. In his will he instructed his steward Oliver de Merlimond (qv) to found a religious house at Shobdon for the expiation of his sins.

Mortimer, Hugh (II) de (d.1181), a son or grandson of Hugh (I) (qv), was brought up by Oliver de Merlimond (qv). He married Matilda, daughter of William le Meschin and widow of Philip de Belmeis and they had four sons: Hugh, Roger (II) (qv), Ralph and William. He established Wigmore Abbey, moving the monks from their original site at Shobdon, eventually, to his grandfather's foundation at Wigmore. It was dedicated in 1179 by Bishop Robert Foliot (qv) of Hereford. Hugh was in rebellion against Matilda's son Henry II who subdued him by besieging his castles. On 26 February 1181 he died at Cleobury Castle, which the king then demolished. He was buried in Wigmore Abbey, the date being commemorated as a feast day in Lent by the Victorine Augustinian Canons until the abbey's dissolution. He was proud, arrogant and hasty, like his father. Hugh, his eldest son, was killed in a tournament and predeceased him and he was succeeded as Lord of Wigmore by Roger (II).

Mortimer, Hugh (III) de (d.1227), son of Roger (II) de Mortimer and half-brother of Ralph (II) de Mortimer (qv, d.1246) served King John and his son Henry III and witnessed the young Henry's reissue of Magna Carta in 1217, a copy of which was sent to Hereford and is still held in the cathedral archives. He lost control of the parts of Powys conquered by his father (Roger (II), qv) to Llywelyn ab Iowerth (qv). He married Annora de Briouze (qv under William (III) de Briouze). Hugh died on 10 November 1227 and was buried at Wigmore Abbey. He was succeeded by his younger brother Ralph (II).

Mortimer, Maud de (1224-1301), Baroness Wigmore, was the daughter of William (V) de Briouze (qv). She married Roger (III) Mortimer (qv), a cousin to whom she had been betrothed since childhood, bringing the honour of Radnor and estates in Ireland as her dower. They had five sons: Ralph (d.1274), Edmund (I) (qv), Roger Mortimer (IV) de Chirk (qv), Geoffrey (d. before 1282) and William, who married Hawise de Muscegros and died before June 1297; and two daughters: Margaret, who married Robert de Vere, Earl of Oxford, and Isabella, who married John (III) Fitzalan and died after 1300. Maud, beautiful and clever, is said to have organised Prince Edward's (qv Edward I) escape from Hereford Castle. She smuggled plans to Edward and on 28 May 1265 a party of horsemen were stationed beyond the Wide Marsh; when Prince Edward was out exercising he called for a fresh mount and fled with his rescuers to Wigmore, where they refreshed themselves, and on to Ludlow Castle. Maud died on 23 March 1301.

Mortimer, Katherine de (d.1369), daughter of Roger (V) (qv) and Joan, was born at Wigmore. She married Thomas Beauchamp, 11th Earl of Warwick (1314-69). They had five sons and two daughters. She and her husband were buried in the chancel of St Mary's Church, Warwick where their splendid alabaster effigies can be seen.

Mortimer, Ralph (I) de (*c*.1060-*c*.1105), eldest son of Roger (I) (qv) and Hawise, was a commander at the Battle of Hastings. He was rewarded with estates in England and after 1075 was granted the Wigmore estate. Becoming one of the largest Norman landowners, he was mentioned in the Domesday Book as the proprietor of Wigmore. Ralph, with other turbulent Marcher lords, was himself often in rebellion against William Rufus but became reconciled with his brother Henry I (qv). He endowed Wigmore Church as a college of canons, dedicated in 1105. He married first Millicent Ferrers and then a lady called Mabel. His daughter Hawise married Stephen, Count of Aumale, the Conqueror's nephew.

Mortimer, Ralph (II) de (d.1246), son of Roger (II) de Mortimer (qv), married Gwladus Ddu (qv), Llywelyn ab Iorwerth's daughter and widow of Reginald de Briouze (qv) in 1230. They had a son, Roger (III) (qv). He was unable to make headway against Llywelyn (qv) for control of the lordships of Maelienydd and Gwrtheyrnion. After Llywelyn's death he induced his grandson Llywelyn ap Gruffydd (qv) to cede them to him and by the time of his death on 6 August 1246 Mortimer control was re-established in the Radnor-Monmouth area. He was buried at Wigmore Abbey.

Mortimer, Robert de (b.*c*.1176) of Attleborough, Norfolk, married Margaret de Say, daughter of Hugh de Say (qv under Richard Scrob) of Richard's Castle, as her second husband in 1210, and assumed the barony of Burford with its nine castles including Richard's Castle and Stapleton Castle near Presteigne.

Mortimer, Robert de (*c*.1252-87), Baron Burford, of Richard's Castle, was the son of Hugh (qv, d.1274). He married Joyce la Zouche and died on 7 April 1287. He was buried at Worcester Cathedral.

Mortimer, Roger (I) de (fl.1054-80), Lord of St Victor-en-Caux in Normandy was one of Duke William's strongest supporters against the incursions of the French king. His wife Hawise owned great estates in Normandy.

Mortimer, Roger (II) de (1155-1214) was described in the *Wigmore Chronicle* as gay, inconstant and headstrong. He was imprisoned by Henry II (qv) when his men killed the Prince of Maelienydd who was returning from Court under royal guarantee. He planted castles in the Marches and attempted to subdue the Welsh. Henry suspected him of conspiring with the Welsh, however, and he fled into exile. His relationship with Henry's son King John (qv) was even worse. Roger married Isabel Ferrers, with whom he had two sons and a daughter. He died in August 1214 and was buried at Wigmore Abbey.

Mortimer, Roger (III) de (1231-82), 1st Baron Wigmore, was the second son of Ralph (II) (qv) and Gwladus. He was a minor at his father's death and in 1247 paid a fine to the king for livery of his lands and married his cousin Maud de Briouze (qv Maud de Mortimer). In 1253 aged 21 he was knighted by Henry III (qv). Like his ancestors he was ruthless and savage in war: 'all Wales feared his power', Dugdale (qv) said. Though originally part of the baronial opposition to the misrule of Henry, Mortimer came to side with the king. Henry granted him some of Montfort's (qv) Herefordshire manors, which he ravaged, holding the bailiff of Dilwyn to ransom. Montfort took some of Mortimer's lands in response, notably Wigmore. In 1262 Peter de

Aquablanca (qv), Bishop of Hereford reported to Henry that the whole area was in confusion. Mortimer and the men of Herefordshire besieged the baronial stronghold of Nottingham Castle and took many prisoners, but Montfort (qv) struck back and at the Battle of Lewes (1264) defeated the royalist army, capturing King Henry III and Prince Edward (qv Edward I) and imprisoning them in Hereford Castle. Mortimer was allowed to return to Herefordshire to defend the March but he refused to comply with his parole conditions and Montfort and Llewelyn's forces sacked the Mortimer lands. Despite blood ties with Mortimer, Llewelyn was often in alliance with Montfort and the barons, which eroded Mortimer's influence in the March. Montfort's power was waning, however, and Mortimer with the Prior of Leominster's men attacked Hereford's suburbs, bombarding the quarter within Byster's Gate, burning houses and looting St Guthlac's Priory. Roger's wife Maud helped their friend Edward escape and he (with Mortimer and Gilbert de Clare) finally defeated Montfort at the Battle of Evesham, where the king was freed. Mortimer is reputed to have killed Montfort himself, and sent his head back to Maud at Wigmore Castle. Mortimer benefited from his support of the throne and his friendship with Edward I, acting as regent during the king's absences. In a stronger position, he resumed his struggle with the Welsh for supremacy on the Marches. He died at Kingsland on 26 October 1282 and was buried at Wigmore Abbey, the ruins of which can be seen at Adforton north of Wigmore.

Mortimer, Roger (IV) de (*c*.1256-1326), of Chirk, was the third son of Roger (III) (qv) and Maud. He married the heiress Lucy, daughter of Robert Wafer, who brought him properties in Wales and Herefordshire including Tedstone Wafre. He campaigned in the Marches where he established a lordship, taking the title 1st Lord Mortimer of Chirk. Archbishop Pecham (qv) on his visitation to Herefordshire accused him of adultery with wives of Marcher lords and of abusing a priest who had imposed penance on him. There were several rebellions in Wales at this time. Roger, with Edmund (I) Mortimer (qv), was a captain of the force which defeated and killed Llywelyn ap Gruffydd (qv); and in 1316, with his nephew, Roger (V) Mortimer of Wigmore (qv) and Humphrey (VII) de Bohun (qv), Earl of Hereford, he was involved with subduing Llywelyn Bren's uprising in Glamorgan. They were also worried about the influence of the Despensers on Edward II and the three of them forced the favourites into exile. Edward marched against de Bohun and the Mortimers, however, and trapped them with the Welsh at their rear. Roger died in captivity in the Tower of London on 3 August 1326. On 14 September 1326 Adam Orleton (qv), Bishop of Hereford, and the prior of Wigmore were allowed to bury his body in Wigmore Abbey beside that of Lucy who had predeceased him.

Mortimer, Roger (V) de (1287-1330), 1st Earl of March, son and heir of Edmund (I) (qv), was born on 25 April 1287 at Netherwood, a Mortimer house at Collington in the north-east of the county. As with many of the Mortimers he was a minor at his father's death and Edward granted his wardship to the favourite, Piers Gaveston, whose ostentatiousness and arrogance were soon to earn him the enmity of the barons of England, and ultimately lead to his death. Roger bought his lands back while still under age and married Joan de Geneville, with whom he had 12 children, including Edmund (II) (qv) and Blanche (qv). Roger was knighted by Edward I and summoned to Parliament. In Edward II's (qv) reign he and his uncle Roger of Chirk (qv Roger (IV) de Mortimer) joined Humphrey (VII) de Bohun's (qv) opposition to the Despensers (qv) but by 1322 they had surrendered to the king's forces at Shrewsbury. They were imprisoned in the Tower of London but Roger (V) escaped to France by drugging the constable, leaving his uncle to die in the Tower. He joined in alliance with Queen Isabellla and Prince Edward in France and they crossed to England with a French force, recruiting men from among Mortimer's tenants in Herefordshire. On 25 November 1326 Mortimer, Queen Isabella and the young Prince of Wales stayed in

Mortimer's castle by the church at Much Marcle while the army camped in the fields around. They cornered Edward II with the younger Despenser in Wales. The king, forced to abdicate in favour of his son, was cruelly murdered at Berkeley Castle and Despenser executed in Hereford with Mortimer savagery. Isabella and Roger ruled England in Edward III's name for three years, increasingly corruptly, until Edward, now 18, surprised them both in Nottingham Castle, entering with a small force through the maze of caves below the castle. Despite Isabella's plea of mercy for 'gentle Mortimer' he was summarily hanged at Tyburn on 29 November 1330 and the great estates the Mortimers had assembled were seized by the Crown. His widow Joan and their children received a pardon in 1336 and she was allowed to retrieve her husband's body for burial in the chantry chapel in St Mary Magdalene, Leintwardine. There is a frequently reproduced 14th-century miniature of Mortimer and Queen Isabella with their host camped outside Hereford.

Mortimer, Roger (VI) de (1328-60), 2nd Earl of March, the son of Edmund (II) and Elizabeth de Badlesmere, was born on 11 November 1328 at Ludlow, as Wigmore had been confiscated with most other Mortimer property at his grandfather's (Roger (V), qv) execution. It was Roger's achievement to reassemble the family estates. He was helped in this by his mother's Bohun husband (qv William de Bohun), a close friend of Edward III, who helped Roger back into royal favour. The king became fond of Roger and restored old Mortimer lands that had been granted out to other noble families including, in 1342, Wigmore. He was able to assume the title as 2nd Earl of March and was a founding knight of the Order of the Garter. He showed off his military ability aged 15 at a great tournament at Hereford in 1344 and distinguished himself in the king's French campaigns. He was knighted by the Black Prince and fought at Crécy. Earl Roger married Philippa, daughter of William Montacute, 1st Earl of Salisbury. Their daughter Margery married John, Lord Audley, and her dower was Marcle, which thus passed to the Audley family (qv). Roger Mortimer died on 26 February 1360.

Mortimer, Roger (VII) de (1374-98), 4th Earl of March, 6th Earl of Ulster, eldest son of Edmund (III) (qv) and Philippa, was born at Usk as was his sister Elizabeth. He was the ward of Thomas Holland, 2nd Earl of Kent, a half-brother of King Richard II, and married Holland's daughter Eleanor (d.1405). They had two sons, Edmund (V) (qv) and a younger brother, Roger, and two daughters, Anne (qv) and Eleanor. On succeeding to his patrimony in 1393 he became, after Richard II, the largest landowner in the region. On a 40-day progress through the Marches and Wales he was fêted everywhere. The Welsh, on the eve of Owain Glyn Dŵr's revolt, expected much of him as a descendant of the Welsh and English royal houses and the bard Iolo Goch wrote a poem in his praise. He was proud of this genealogy and traced his family to Cadwallader and Brutus; his mother was a granddaughter of Edward III. Like his father he campaigned in Ulster (as the king's lieutenant) with his brother Edmund (IV) (qv), and was killed there on 20 July 1398; his body was returned to Wigmore Abbey for burial. He was long remembered in Welsh and English legend. Defoe (qv), travelling through Wales in 1720, found his name in every mouth. His widow Eleanor married Sir Edward Charlton, who had custody of the Mortimer estates until Edmund (V)'s majority.

Morton, Rowland (d.1554), knight, brother of Thomas (qv), married Sybil daughter of Richard Monington (qv under Hugh de Monington). They lived at The Grange, Bosbury and had a son, Richard. In 1503 he and Thomas leased the 13th-century bishop's palace in Bosbury, remains of which lie to the north of Holy Trinity Church. The Bosbury chantry chapel was endowed by Sir Rowland for masses to be said for the family; after the Reformation its revenues were diverted to fund Bosbury Grammar School.

Morton, Thomas (d.1511), archdeacon of Hereford, was an executor of Bishop Stanbury's (qv) will and responsible for the construction of the Stanbury Chapel in Hereford Cathedral, and the similarly fan-vaulted porch of the vicars choral quarters, both of the 1490s. Similar work is seen in the early 16th-century Morton Chapel in Bosbury Church, where the family rebus – a tun with an M – appears on the pendentives. The Bosbury rood screen may also have been presented by the Mortons. His brother was Rowland (qv) and their uncles was Cardinal John Morton (1420-1500), Archbishop of Canterbury and Henry VII's (qv) chancellor. The Morton rebus is seen on his architectural work at Canterbury Cathedral, which must be the inspiration for the Herefordshire work.

Muckleston, Rowland (1812-97), rector of Dinedor 1855-97, was born in Lichfield the son of a canon. He was a fellow and tutor of Worcester College and an examiner for Oxford University. He was largely responsible for rebuilding Dinedor School.

von Munchausen, Karl Friedrich Hieronymus Freiherr (1720-97), fantasist, was born in Bodenwerder, Brunswick, Germany. He is famous for the tall tales he told of his military expeditions in Russia, which were gathered together by Rudolph Raspe. In 1785 Raspe published an English translation with even more astonishing and unlikely tales added and this edition, translated back into German, is the standard one. The tales were an immediate success in Hereford, where readers founded a Munchausen Society to appreciate his tales and compete with them by writing their own.

Munthe, Axel Martin Fredrik (1857-1949), psychiatrist and author, was born on 31 October 1857 in Oskarsham, Sweden. He practised as a physician in Paris, Rome and at the Swedish Court where he was a friend of Princess Victoria of Baden. Whilst travelling in Italy, on a romantic cliff top in Anacapri he found the ruins of San Michele which he rebuilt and surrounded with gardens. In 1907, after the

death of his Swedish first wife Ultima Hornberg, he married Hilda, daughter of John Pennington Mellor (1878-1967) and sister of Lady Helena Gleichen (qv), owner of Hellens, an ancient manor house near Much Marcle. They had two sons, Peter and Malcolm. Hilda brought Hellens to the marriage and another historic house in Southside, Wimbledon, both of which Munthe worked on while Hilda developed the gardens. Munthe built a house in Sweden where the family spent the summers although his favourite home was San Michele. He became a British citizen and served in an ambulance corps in the First World War. His autobiography *The Story of San Michele* was published in 1929 and became a best seller. When Munthe died in Stockholm on 11 February 1949 Hellens passed to Malcolm, who wrote *The Story of Hellens*. Hilda lived on at the house, a familiar guide. Hellens was used as a painting store by the Tate during the Second World War.

Murchison, Roderick Impey (1792-1871), geologist, was born on 19 February 1792. He served in the 36th Regt 'The Herefordshire' at the end of the Napoleonic Wars. In the 1830s he visited the Aymestrey area with Revd T.T. Lewis (qv), who helped him to map the fossiliferous limestone beds exposed there and to decipher the sequences exposed in the Woolhope

Dome. In 1839 he controversially announced a new era called the Silurian system which he fitted into the sequence of geological time after the Ordovician period. He was a founder member of the Geographical Society (1830) and an early member of the Woolhope Naturalists' Field Club in Hereford. One of the most noted geologists of his time, he later proposed that another period of geological time be fitted in between his Silurian and the Carboniferous which he named the Devonian, and in 1841 he proposed the Permian period to follow the Carboniferous. Sir Roderick was an ambitious scientist and not always clear about the debt he owed to humble helpers like Lewis; colleagues called him arrogant and unhelpful, and to Henry Bull (qv) he was 'Old Grumpy'.

Murimuth, Adam (fl.1320s-30s), chronicler and canon of Hereford, was cantor at Exeter Cathedral. He was resident at Hereford in the 1330s and is recorded as the donor of stained glass at Eaton Bishop. One panel shows Saints Michael and Gabriel flanking a Crucifixion, another the Virgin and Child. It is the best glass of its date in Herefordshire, full of feeling.

Murray, Richard Hollins (d.1957) was an accountant and the inventor of a reflecting lens. He sold the patent to Yorkshireman Percy Shaw who produced the cat's eye reflector stud. In 1927 Murray moved from Manchester and bought Dinmore Manor, a preceptory of the Knights Hospitaller. He greatly extended the house in 1929-36 using the Hereford firm Ford and Beddington. A sign pointing to the manor is still picked out in cat's eyes. He wrote *Dinmore Manor and the Commandery of the Knights Hospitaller of St John of Jerusalem* (1936) and in 1922 he published *Income Tax for Farmers*. British Railways named a locomotive Dinmore Manor, recently restored by the West Somerset Railway. There is a 1,200-year-old yew in the manor grounds.

Musgrave, Thomas (1788-1860), Bishop of Hereford 1837-47, was born on 30 March 1788, the eldest son of W. Peete Musgrave, a Cambridge tailor, and Sarah his wife. He was educated at Trinity College, Cambridge, was ordained in 1817 and graduated DD in 1837. He travelled on the Continent and was in Brussels during the Battle of Waterloo. An active Whig, he came to the notice of Lord Melbourne who appointed him Bishop of Hereford in 1837. In 1839 he married Catherine Cavendish (d.1863); there were no children. He was a reforming bishop and during his episcopate 30 new schools were built and many churches. He revived the office of rural dean and tackled the problem of pluralism and non-residency. He was a broad churchman with liberal views but noticed with consternation, as his predecessors had, Romish leanings in the county. His motto, however, was *Quieta non movere* – let sleeping dogs lie, which would have helped him with his dean, the active but difficult Merewether (qv). He had Philip Hardwick (qv) modernise his palace, and the Cottinghams (qv) were restoring the dilapidated cathedral. Musgrave's Whig contacts made him Archbishop of York over the head of more senior candidates, and in York he pursued his interests in education and the adequacy of places of worship. He died on 4 May 1860 at his London home, 41 Belgrave Square, and was buried in Kensal Green cemetery.

Mylling, Thomas (*c.*1430-92), Bishop of Hereford 1474-92, was an acolyte at Westminster Abbey, matriculated at Gloucester College, Oxford and was Doctor of Theology in 1466. He rose to be Abbot of Westminster, where he was a patron of Caxton. Here, in October 1470, he took Edward IV's (qv) Queen Elizabeth and her daughters into sanctuary from Henry VI's vengeful Queen Margaret, a brave act, and, when Elizabeth gave birth to her first son Edward, Mylling stood godfather to him. When Edward IV returned as king after the Battle of Tewkesbury he showed his gratitude by appointing Mylling chancellor and Bishop of Hereford. He was a councillor at his godson's court in Ludlow, in the diocese of Hereford. He was frequently absent from Hereford using Richard Wycherley (qv) as his suffragan. His nephew Thomas Mylling was prebendary at Hereford. Bishop Mylling died in January 1492 at Hereford but was buried in the chapel of St John the Baptist, Westminster Abbey.

Mynors: Baronets of Treago, St Weonards, who were established from the 11th century although little is known until the 15th century. The Mynors crest is a hand with a bear's paw, punning on the French *main ours*. A moated castle dates from the early 14th century although only 16th century work is now visible. The grounds were landscaped in the mid 18th century. The family has usually also resided at Evenjobb, Radnors., where they held county offices such as JP and DL.

Mynors, Arthur Clynton Baskerville (1854-79) younger son of Robert (qv) and Ellen, served as a 2nd Lieutenant in the 3rd Battalion of the 60th (King's Royal Rifle) Regiment. He died of dysentery at Fort Pearson on 25 April 1879, during the Anglo-Zulu War.

Mynors, Richard (*c.*1440-1528), knight, married Joanna, daughter of Gwillym ap Thomas. He was an usher of the chamber to both Edward IV (qv) and Richard III (qv) and collected taxes in Wales for Henry VII (qv). Sir Richard rebuilt Treago Castle. He had three sons, Roger (qv), Reginald and Thomas (qv), and five daughters, the youngest of whom, Alice, married William Scudamore (qv, d.*c.*1520).

Mynors, Robert Baskerville Rickards (1819-89), the son of Peter Rickards Mynors of Treago Castle, was educated at Eton and Christ Church, Oxford. He married Ellen Gray Higgins, daughter of Revd Edward Higgins (qv), and lived at Evancoyd near New Radnor where he was JP, and at the family seat Treago Castle. He was a captain in the Herefordshire Militia, and High Sheriff of Radnorshire in 1856.

Mynors, Roger (before 1478-1537), knight, eldest son of Sir Richard (qv), with two brothers, Thomas and Reginald, married Alice, daughter of Sir William Mill of Harescombe, Gloucs. He was a gentleman usher to Henry VII (qv) by 1509 and attended his funeral. His brother Thomas was also a royal servant. In 1513 he accompanied Henry VIII (qv) on his French campaign and was with the king at the Field of the Cloth of Gold in 1520. He was knighted in 1527 and was a royal nominee to sit in the Commons in 1529 for Derbyshire, where he lived on his wife's lands. He had no issue and his brother Thomas inherited the Treago estate.

Mynors, Roger Aubrey Baskerville (1903-1989), of Treago Castle, a classical scholar, married Lavinia Sybil, daughter of Very Revd Cyril Alington (qv). Sir Roger catalogued the manuscripts in Hereford Cathedral library.

Mynors, Thomas (d.1539), the third son of Sir Richard Mynors (qv) married Catherine, daughter of Watkyn Vaughan (qv, d.1504) and their offspring are found at Treago to the present day. In the 18th century a Theodosia Mynors was sole heir and married a Peter Rickards, but on inheriting Treago they assumed the name Mynors.

Mynors, Willoughby Baskerville (1854-1914), DL, JP, eldest son of Robert (qv) and Ellen, was educated at Christ Church, Oxford and gained the rank of Major in the Shropshire Yeomanry Cavalry. He married Mabel Stevenson and lived at Bosbury House. He was High Sheriff and Deputy Lieutenant of Radnorshire. He formed a celebrated library including mediaeval manuscripts and letters written in Disraeli's own hand to his father.

N

Napleton, John (1739-1817), clergyman and educational reformer, the son of the Revd John Napleton, vicar of Pembridge, was educated at Brasenose College, Oxford with its county connections, offering scholarships to students from Herefordshire, where he graduated DD in 1789. He was one of the best Oxford tutors of his time, and his report into conditions led to reforms in the university examination system. In 1777 he was vicar of Tarrington. When Bishop Butler (qv) was translated from Oxford to Hereford he made Napleton his chaplain and gave him the bishop's prebend (known as the golden prebend as it carried the automatic right of a seat on chapter). In his 50s he married Elizabeth Daniell of Truro. In 1796 he became cathedral chancellor and proved a good manager of the chapter's business, which included financing the rebuilding of the cathedral nave and west front. He was also Master of St Katherine's Hospital, Ledbury, rector of Stoke Edith and vicar of Lugwardine in 1810. Bishop Luxmoore (qv) appointed him prelector of divinity at the cathedral. Napleton died at Hereford on 9 December 1817 and was buried in the cathedral choir. His portrait (see below left) hangs in College Hall at the cathedral.

Nash, James (d.1400) was a lawyer and MP of Nash, near Presteigne, but later lived in Hereford. He was the illegitimate son of Richard Nash of Nash (qv), also a lawyer and MP for Hereford (d.1395). James was a servant of Edmund (IV) Mortimer, acting as his lawyer. He followed his father into King Richard's (qv) parliaments of 1390, '97 and '99, but as Henry IV (qv) appointed him king's attorney on seizing the throne it is presumed that Nash (with his Mortimer master) had been aware of the coup. He also served as coroner. He was associated with the Oldcastles, Hakluyts and Holgots (qqv). He died young, an intestate bastard, and it was found that he owned much property in and around Hereford, including a house in St Peter's Square and shops in 'Cabouchelane', Hereford the income from which were used to provide a chantry for him and his father at the altar of St Stephen in the cathedral.

Nash, John (1752-1835), architect, was born in London on 18 September 1752 into a Welsh family. He was apprenticed to the architect John Taylor and married Jane Kerr in 1775. He designed public buildings in Wales including prisons. In 1793 he was building Hereford gaol, employing his friend Auguste Charles Pugin, the father of A.W.N. Pugin (qv), as draughtsman. The gaol was demolished in 1929 although the governor's house, which Nash added in 1826, survives. In 1793 he worked for Lord Foley

(qv Thomas Foley, d.1793) at Stoke Edith House, where he created an Etruscan parlour. Here he met Humphry Repton (qv) with whom he went into partnership. In 1806-10 he rebuilt Garnstone Castle near Weobley for Samuel Peploe (qv), now demolished, like many of the big Regency buildings in the county. Lord Scudamore (qv John (I) Scudamore, d.1796) asked him to make his 14th-century castle buildings at Kentchurch look more mediaeval: he heightened and castellated the tower and remodelled the rest, consulting Sir Uvedale Price (qv) on its picturesque potential. Only his tower and porch remain now, with paintings to recall how it was. He also built some cottages on the Belmont estate for John Matthews (qv) and Dewsall Lodge. Nash was taken up by the Prince Regent and designed celebrated projects such as Regent's Park and Street with stylish shops and villas; Buckingham Palace; Marble Arch; Carleton Palace; and the Royal Pavilion in Brighton. He died in May 1835 and is buried at St James's Church in East Cowes on the Isle of Wight, his home of many years.

Nash, Richard (d.1395), lawyer and MP of Nash, Herefordshire, was the son of Nicholas Nash (or Ash) of Nash and Lucy his wife. He was MP for Hereford through the 1370s and '80s. With Kynard de la Bere and Leonard Hakluyt (qqv) he was involved with the arrest of Walter Brut (qv) and his adherents. As he himself and many associates were sympathetic to Lollardy, the failure at this time to successfully arrest and prosecute Lollards in the county is well explained.

Nash, Treadway Russell (1725-1811), antiquary and clergyman, was born at Kempsey, Worcestershire on 24 June 1725 and educated at King's School, Worcester, and Worcester College, Oxford. He was ordained and presented to Eynsham vicarage by James Martin (qv) father of his friend John Martin of Ledbury, and married his friend's sister Margaret (1734-1811) in 1758. On the death of his brothers, Treadway inherited the family estates and began his antiquarian researches. He was a Fellow of the Society of Antiquaries, published books of local history and printed an edition of *Hudibras* by Samuel Butler, a Worcestershire man, using John Skippe's (qv, d.1812) engravings. His daughter Margaret (1761-1831) married John Somers Cocks (qv, d.1841) and the Nash wealth helped build Eastnor Castle. Lord Cocks, John's father (Charles Cocks, d.1806) made him rector of Leigh in 1792. He died at Bevere House, North Claines, on 26 January 1811 and was buried at St Peter's, Droitwich, leaving his antiquarian papers to the Eastnor Castle archive.

Nelson, Horatio (1758-1805), naval officer and hero, was born on 29 September 1758, the 3rd son of Revd Edmund Nelson, rector of Burnham in Norfolk. His mother Catherine's family was descended from Sir Robert Walpole and the boy was named after his godfather Horace Walpole (qv). His uncle Captain Suckling, commander of a man of war in 1771, took him to sea aged 13 and by 1777 he was a lieutenant and developing the bold tactics for which he was to become famous. Through daring, bravery, skillful seamanship and an adroit use of publicity Nelson rose in the Navy and in national esteem. He married Fanny Nesbit, whom he met

in the West Indies, and later famously acquired a mistress, Emma Hamilton. He was a friend of Thomas Westfaling (qv) from Rudhall near Ross, whom he met while staying with the Hamiltons in Naples. He stayed with the Westfalings at Rudhall House in 1802 with Sir William and Lady Hamilton. The party lodged at the Swan and Falcon, Ross-on-Wye and went on a pleasure cruise on the Wye, then visited Sir William's estates in Pembrokeshire. On 22 September 1802 Nelson was given the Freedom of the City of Hereford, staying at the town house of the 11th Duke of Norfolk (qv Charles Howard) in Broad Street. Sir Uvedale Price (qv) was for a time his secretary. After Nelson's death on the quarterdeck of his flagship *Victory* at the Battle of Trafalgar on 21 October 1805 the citizens of Hereford raised a subscription for a memorial by Philip Hardwick (qv), who erected a column on Castle Green, 30 years before the one in London. When money ran out a simple urn was substituted for the planned statue. For many years Hereford churches rang their bells muffled on the anniversary of Nelson's death.

Nesfield, William Andrews (1793-1881), landscape architect, turned to painting after a military career and sketched with David Cox (qv) but came to prefer 'painting with nature's materials' or landscape design. With his two sons William Eden and Markham he was the most sought-after landscape artist in Britain. He designed gardens at Stoke Edith House in 1854 and those at Newport House, Almeley for James W.G. Watt (qv) and traces of his work can still be discerned at both. He laid out the gardens by the Victoria Suspension Bridge in Hereford and worked at Saltmarshe Castle for Edmund Higginson (qv), designing terraces and walks (now a caravan park). In 1860 he worked at Shobdon Court, where a terrace of his design has survived the house's destruction. He designed gardens at Garnstone for Daniel Peploe Webb (qv under Samuel Peploe). He was particularly known for his water features, and the heroic fountain at Witley Court (1853) is his.

Nest verch Gruffydd (1039-64) was the daughter of Gruffydd ap Llywelyn (qv), King of Wales, and Edith, beautiful daughter of Ælfgar (qv), Earl of Mercia. After Gruffydd's death, Nest's mother married Harold II and became queen of England. Nest married Osbern fitz Richard (qv Richard Scrob), Lord of Richard's Castle. Their children were Hugh fitz Osbern, Turstin, Simon Scrope and Nesta (or Agnes), who married Bernard de Neufmarché, Baron of Brecon (who became Hugh's heir).

Newman, George (1870-1948), public health reformer, was born at 14 Broad Street, Leominster on 23 October 1870. His father, a Quaker elder and editor of *The Friend*, had been a missionary in India. George originally wanted to be a missionary but decided on medicine and studied at Edinburgh University and King's College, London where he received his MD. He married Adelaide Thorpe in 1898. In 1907 he was Chief Medical Officer to the Board of Education and in 1919 to the Ministry of Health, and he is noted for his work on infant mortality. He was knighted in 1911, and appointed KCB in 1918 and GBE in 1935. His diaries are in the National Archives and the family papers in Hereford Record Office.

Newton, Ernest (1856-1922), architect of small country houses mainly in the home counties, studied under Norman Shaw and was a founder, with his friend Charles Voysey (qv), of the Art Workers Guild. His one Herefordshire house, Brands Lodge, Colwall (1910) for Julia Manning, is typical of his work. He saw house and 20-acre estate as a whole and planned the gardens to suit the house and views. It is not far from Voysey's Perrycroft. He was president of RIBA and published books on the country house.

Newton, John (1621-78), mathematician and clergyman from Buckinghamshire, was educated at Oundle School and St Edmund Hall, Oxford. He wrote books on astronomy and mathematics, advocating the decimal system of accounting. Anthony Wood, the 17th-century Oxford biographer, knew him at Oxford and said he was learned but capricious. He suffered during the Commonwealth, supporting himself by teaching and was recompensed by Charles II with a royal chaplaincy and the degree of DD. He was appointed vicar of Ross, succeeding Revd Philip Price (qv), and then rector of Stretton Sugwas, and had the prebend of Cublington at Hereford Cathedral. He was active in the founding of Ross Grammar School and enthusiastic for the teaching of mathematics to young children. He secured an Act of Parliament (1671) to correct the anomalous position whereby Ross and its chapelries had both rector and vicar, the former taking the great tithes. After the death of John Cooke, the previous rector, Ross, Weston and Brampton each became separate rectories and Newton rector of Ross. He died on 26 December 1678 at Ross and is buried in the chancel of St Mary's.

Nicholas (4th century), patron saint of Christmas, Santa Claus. His feast day is 6 December and in Hereford Cathedral on the nearest Saturday to that date the Boy Bishop Ceremony takes place. The boy, a retired chorister, leads a service the climax of which is the reading of the magnificat 'He has brought down the powerful from their thrones and lifted up the lowly'. The Boy Bishop is enthroned and holds office until Holy Innocents Day, 28 December. The ceremony developed in the 13th century as a period of allowed misrule and is understood in Hereford as exemplifying Jesus's teaching in St Matthew's Gospel, when 'calling to him a child, he put him in the midst of them'. One of the ancient parishes of Hereford is dedicated to St Nicholas. Its mediaeval church, which stood at the junction of King and Bridge Streets, was damaged in the Civil War, restored in 1718, taken down in 1841 and rebuilt by Thomas Duckham (qv) on a new site in 1842. Sutton St Nicholas is also under his patronage.

Nicholson, John Anthony Thompson (d.1942) took over Nicholson & Son after his father's (qv Thomas Nicholson) death. He was also a prolific restorer of churches – St Andrew, Bridge Sollers for example – and worked in partnership with other architects such as John Hartree and W.E.H. Clarke (qqv). He completed Frederick Kempson's (qv) Holy Trinity in the Whitecross Road, Hereford with Hartree – causing, it seems, a rift with Kempson, who accused them of stealing his ideas. Other church restorations include Dewsall, Eardisland, Garway, Hentland and How Caple. The partnership of father and son was the longest and most prolific practice in Herefordshire.

Nicholson, Thomas (1823-95), diocesan architect of Hereford, oversaw much of the county's church restoration work, such as that at St Mary's, Brilley in the 1860s. He rebuilt St John, Pencombe in 1864-5, trying for a historically accurate 'transitional' style. He worked at Fownhope Church in 1873, St John the Baptist, Aymestrey between 1879 and 1886 and St Mary, Burghill. In 1888 he built St James's Church, Bartestree, now a private house, and in 1889 restored the isolated little church of St James, Llangua. In 1891 he rebuilt St John the Baptist, Aston Ingham, merely retaining the chancel arch and the west tower.

Nicoll, Allardyce (1894-1976), literary scholar from Glasgow, was a professor at Yale, then head of the English Department at

Birmingham University. He wrote many books on English literature, notably the *Cambridge History of English Drama*. He retired to Wind's Acre, Colwall where he died on 17 April 1976.

Nigel (11th century), physician, appears in the Domesday survey as 'Nigellus medicus'. He was William the Conqueror's doctor, with lands in the Moccas area granted him from St Guthlac's Priory in Hereford. He was succeeded at Moccas by Walter de Fresne (qv).

Nightingale, Florence (1820-1910), nurse, was born in Florence, Italy on 12 May 1820. She stayed as a child at Kinsham Court near Presteigne on the banks of the Lugg next to Kinsham Church, with her parents' friend Lady Oxford, the estranged wife of Lord Harley (qv Jane Harley, d.1824), and is known to have visited the Barretts (qv) at Hope End. She is celebrated for her reforms of army nursing procedures after the horrors of the Crimean War and persuaded

the public that nursing could be a respectable profession. As the lady of the lamp she became an icon of nursing care. She was an early user of statistical evidence in support of her arguments, demonstrating facts in graphic form. A less certain link with Herefordshire lies with the Davies family of Ivington, whose daughter Florence Nightingale Davies grew up to be a statistician. Florence died on 13 August 1910 and the nation wanted her buried in Westminster Abbey, but she preferred the quiet country Hampshire churchyard of St Margaret's, East Wellow near the family home.

Nollekens, Joseph (1737-1823), sculptor, was born into a Roman Catholic family from Antwerp in Soho, London. His father, 'Old Nollekens', was a painter. An unassuming and notoriously mean man, Joseph became one of the most famous and influential artists in Britain. There is a monument to John 2nd Viscount Bateman (qv) by him in Shobdon Church (1804). He died on 1 May 1823 and was buried in Paddington.

Numerianus, Gaius Marcus Aurelius, Roman Emperor (283-4), is named on a milestone from the Roman town near Kenchester which is referred to on the Antonine Itinerary as *Magnis*. The inscription says it was made by the public office of the council of the Dobunni, the Celtic tribe of southern Herefordshire and Gloucestershire whose cantonal capital during Roman times was *Corinium Dobunnorum*, Cirencester. Numerian was murdered at Nicomedia in November 284, the brevity of his reign enabling this work in far-away Herefordshire to be dated with unusual accuracy. Massive dressed stonework has been found in the Kenchester area from temples and villas; and two altars are known bearing biographical material of Romano-Celtic times (qqv Silvanus and Beccicus).

O'Dare, Josephine (1899-1951), real name Theresa 'Trixie' Agnes Skyrme, confidence trickster, was born on 8 January 1899 at Holmer Cottage, Wellington. She lived at various Herefordshire addresses in Canon Pyon, Sutton St Nicholas, Withington, Tupsley and Barton Road, Hereford, and was involved in crimes of deception until brought before Hereford magistrates. Her brother George was independently convicted of fraud in Liverpool at this time. Trixie avoided prosecution and moved to London, where as society darling Josephine O'Dare she was involved in increasingly outrageous swindles. She became addicted to cocaine and was sentenced for fraud at the Old Bailey. On her release she disappeared from notoriety until her final reappearance as Joan Brooks, dead from a barbiturates overdose in St George's Hospital, London.

Offa (d.796), King of Mercia 757-96, was descended from Penda, who secured the Mercian throne after the assassination of Æthelbald (qv). He absorbed small Marches kingdoms including the Magonsaete and the Hwicce and by the 770s greater Mercia stretched from Shropshire to London, with suzerainty over East Anglia and Kent. His well-made coins circulated throughout England. He agreed his western border with the Welsh by constructing the Dyke that bears his name and which can still be seen in north-western Herefordshire. He was holding court at his palace at Sutton Walls near Hereford in 794 when the 14-year-old King Ethelbert (qv) arrived seeking the hand of his daughter Ælfrida (or Ælfthryth) and, encouraged by his wife Queen Cynethryth, is said to have murdered Ethelbert to secure control of his East Anglian kingdom. In expiation Offa founded the church at Marden where St Ethelbert's body rested and had him buried at Hereford Cathedral.

Ogilvie, Charles Atmore (1793-1873), clergyman from Cumberland, was educated at Balliol, Oxford, becoming a fellow and a university examiner. He was ordained and appointed rector at several parishes and married Mary Gurnell (née Armstrong) in 1838. The next year he was appointed rector of Ross, where he remained until his death. He was a canon of Oxford and the first Professor of Pastoral Theology at Christ Church. He died on 17 February 1873 and was buried in Christ Church Cathedral.

Oldcastle, John (*c*.1370-1417), Baron Cobham, Lollard, was the son of Sir Richard Oldcastle. The Oldcastles were Lords of Almeley Manor where the mound of their castle remains. He was a kinsman of the ap Harrys (qv). He was knighted by 1400 and served on Henry IV's (qv) campaign against the Scots. When Glyn Dŵr's (qv) revolt broke out he commanded the garrisons of Builth and later Hay Castles. He defended Usk when Glyn Dŵr besieged that town and with his neighbour John ap Harry (qv), he was charged with receiving the submission of Welsh rebels; and he was at the siege of Aberystwyth Castle with Prince Henry. Other colleagues with whom he was closely associated during the uprising and in other business were Sir John Chandos and Thomas Walwyn II (qqv).

In 1404 he was elected MP for Herefordshire. He was Sheriff of Herefordshire in 1407. He married first Katherine Ievan, with whom he had two sons, and secondly the heiress Joan de la Pole, who brought him estates from her previous three marriages and from her grandfather Lord Cobham. By right of his wife, in 1409 he was called to the Upper House as Baron Cobham or Lord Oldcastle. Legislation brought forward at this time to disendow chantries and confiscate temporalities (ie those lands dedicated to providing an income for the bishop), presaging the events of the Reformation, are thought to have stemmed from Oldcastle. West Herefordshire was a centre of widespread Lollard ideas. The name of this movement for reform of the church came from the Dutch word for mumbler. Its leader in England was Oxford theologian John Wycliffe, whose patron, John of Gaunt (qv), was sympathetic to the movement and gave protection to his followers. Their ideas look forward to the Reformation of the next century: the primacy of scripture, denial of papal authority, personal responsibility for salvation and the need for general reform of abuses such as the selling of pardons. Sir John had probably been converted when Swinderby (qv) preached at Almeley *c.*1390. Attempts by the church to arraign Oldcastle were defused by Henry V (qv), who described Sir John as one of his greatest and best loved servants. However his continued obduracy lost him the king's support and he was tried and convicted. King Henry obtained a delay for his execution and with help from friends he contrived to escape from the Tower. He went into hiding, planning a Lollard uprising. The king easily thwarted this though and rounded up the rebels. Oldcastle escaped in the confusion and returned to Herefordshire, living openly at Almeley, shielded by sympathetic neighbours. John ap Harry for instance was bound over to deny him help although he is known to have been collecting Oldcastle's rents. Sir John is thought to have also travelled widely seeking support but was eventually arrested and brought to the Bar of the Lords where he gave a sermon describing his Lollard beliefs. He was found guilty and hanged and burned the same day, 14 December 1417, on the 'Lollers Gallows' in St Giles' Fields, London. His widow Joan was released from her detention in the Tower to make her fifth marriage, and Sir John's second son Henry was allowed to inherit his Herefordshire lands. Oldcastle, poet, wit and soldier was much valued by Prince Henry. Shakespeare's Falstaff was originally called Oldcastle but was changed when relatives complained, and the line 'my old lad of the castle' remains in the play as a clue (*Henry IV part I*). There was support for Lollardy at Court, but Sir John's heterodox, increasingly revolutionary views were too much for the establishment. In Herefordshire several suspects were questioned: Nicholas de Hereford, William Swinderby, Walter Brut (qqv), Stephen Bell *et al.* They were more slippery than Sir John and recanted but continued preaching, but Lollardy, nevertheless, was now waning.

Oldcastle, Thomas (d.1398) was the second son of John Oldcastle and Isabel of Almeley, the grandfather of Sir John, (qv, d.1417); Thomas was therefore Sir John's uncle. He married Alice, heir of his neighbour Sir John Pembridge and the widow of his cousin, Edmund de la Bere; the marriage required Bishop John Gilbert's (qv) approval. They lived at Eyton. He was Sheriff of Herefordshire for 1386-7 and 1391-2, escheator in 1388-9, and MP for Herefordshire in 1390 and 1393. He was closely associated with John Merbury (who married his widow Alice), Richard and James Nash, Kynard de la Bere, Philip Holgot and Thomas (II) Walwyn (qqv). Oldcastle's daughter Wintelan (or Wenllian) married Robert Whitney (qv, d.1441).

Olmsted, Frederick Law (1822-1903), journalist and landscape gardener, was born in Hartford, Connecticut on 26 April 1822. He came to Britain in 1850 to consult famous landscape practitioners such as Uvedale Price (qv), whose work at Foxley Olmsted considered seminal. He published *Walks and Talks of an American Farmer in England* (1852). Returning to America, he designed academic campuses and urban parks like Central and Prospect Parks in New York. He was buried in Hartford.

Onneslow, William (fl.1500), left a will in 1516 endowing a charity school for the poor of Aymestrey. It was to be in the sexton's cottage and the original trustees were John Bayley, John Borcard, John Tyler and Richard Gold. The school continued through various vicissitudes of funding and dereliction until the 1960s when the buildings were sold. The sexton, an usher and a dame were variously employed over the years, and the children were provided with slates and testaments and often with clothes too. One of its masters was Revd T.T. Lewis (qv).

Orleton, Adam (*c.*1275-1345), Bishop of Hereford 1317-27, takes his name from the village of this name but was born in Hereford, where his father William Orleton was mayor. He was educated at Oxford, ordained priest and was a doctor of canon law by 1310. He found employment at Court through the patronage of Bishop Swinfield (qv), whose proctor he was, and went on embassies to Rome to forward the canonisation of Thomas Cantilupe (qv) (which was achieved in April 1320). Orleton's abilities secured his succession to Swinfield (qv) and he was consecrated bishop on 22 May 1317 at Avignon, proving an active and effective bishop. He was the uncle of John Trillek (qv), who was brought up in his household and who, through his influence, succeeded him as Bishop of Hereford. Edward II (qv) met him at Hereford and charged him with supporting the barons' rebellion and he was one of three bishops the king vainly asked the Pope to remove. In 1320 Orleton allowed Queen Isabella (qv Edward II) and the 14-year-old Prince Edward refuge in Hereford's bishops' palace when she was uneasy during unrest, and he argued Isabella's case for the throne of France in Paris, as she was the sister of the late King Charles. Orleton's diocese was a Mortimer fiefdom and he supported Roger (V) Mortimer (qv) in his struggle against the Despensers. He helped Mortimer escape from the Tower and negotiated with the French for their backing of Isabella and Mortimer's invasion of England. Orleton joined the queen at Hereford for the condemnation of the younger Despenser (qv), and was prominent in the arrangements for the deposition of Edward II, haranguing him angrily and requiring his abdication. He presented Edward III as king to the lords in parliament on 7 January 1327 and to the enthusiastic Londoners outside. He is supposed by Christopher Marlowe in *Edward II* to have assisted in Edward II's murder. Certainly his support earned him translation to Worcester in 1327. He survived the fall of Mortimer and the queen and moved to Winchester in 1333 against Edward III's wishes. Orleton died aged and blind on 18 July 1345 and was buried in Winchester Cathedral. He commissioned lives of saints including Edfrith and Mildburg (qqv), now in the Harleian collection of the British Library.

O'Rourke, Daniel (fl.1852-3), carrier pigeon, was used by the *Hereford Times* during Charles Anthony's (qv) editorship to bring urgent news to the paper before the advent of the telegraph. Daniel was named after the 1852 Derby winner when s/he brought the welcome news of the winner to Hereford, arriving home on the same day as the race. The racehorse had been named after a character in an Irish fairy story who is carried to the moon by an eagle. The following year the bird brought news of the Act of Parlia-

ment which allowed a rail link to be constructed between Hereford and Worcester, with a consequent drop in commodity prices. Daniel the pigeon may be seen, still on duty, stuffed and mounted in the *Hereford Times* foyer.

Osbern fitz Richard (*c.*1045-88), sometimes known as fitz Scrope or Le Scrope, owned an estate adjacent to that of his father, Richard Scrob (qv) at Richard's Castle. He married Nest verch Gruffydd (qv), the daughter of Gruffydd ap Llywelyn (qv) and Ealdgyth (qv) who was the daughter of Ælfgar, Earl of Mercia (qv). Their children were Hugh fitz Osbern, Turstin (qv), Simon Scrope, Agnes, and Nest (b.1082), who married Bernard de Neufmarché, Baron of Brecon. Osbern inherited his father's great estates and took advantage of the times to amass more: large tracts along the Golden Valley which Harold II (qv) had taken from the Welsh in his recent campaigns; border manors brought to him by Nest; and presents from King William of confiscated Saxon estates. Domesday records him as a major landholder in several shires. Osbern was Sheriff of Hereford in the 1060s, garrisoning the town during the Norman invasion. He led the hunt for Edric the Wild (qv), the local Saxon landowner who later rose against the Normans. When Edric was caught King William rewarded Osbern with more estates in the area. Despite this he joined the Welsh Marcher rebellion of 1088 but fared better than the others and was able to pass on Richard's Castle to his heir Hugh fitz Osbern (b.1078). Hugh married Eustache de Say *c.*1106 and their son Hugh de Say (1118-90) married Lucy de Clifford (qv). Their son, also Hugh de Say (*c.*1156-97), married Mabel Marmion and their daughter Margaret de Say (*c.*1192-*c.*1242) married first Hugh de Ferrières, secondly Robert de Mortimer of Richard's Castle (qv, b.*c.*1176) and third William de Stuteville. Henry III granted William the right to hold a weekly market at Stapleton in 1223. Stapleton Castle later passed from the Mortimers to the Cornewalls and then to the Harleys.

Ottley, Adam (1655-1723), Bishop of St David's, son of Sir Richard Ottley of Pitchford, Shropshire, was educated at Trinity College, Cambridge. He was made rector of Pontesbury, became a prebendary of Hereford and Archdeacon of Shropshire (part of the diocese of Hereford) but was beaten to the bishopric of Hereford by Philip Bisse (qv). In 1713 he was given St David's, which Bisse had vacated, through the patronage of James Brydges (qv, d.1744), MP for Hereford. Ottley was a resident bishop. He funded George Hickes' (qv) great study of Anglo-Saxon, in which he is praised by Hickes.

Ouseley, Sir Frederick Arthur Gore (1825-89), composer and musicologist, was born on 12 August 1825 in Grosvenor Square, London, the fourth and youngest surviving child of Sir Gore Ouseley, a diplomat, and his wife Harriet. He was educated at Christ Church, Oxford where he was photographed by Lewis Carroll, and in 1844 succeeded his father as 2nd Baronet. Precociously musical, he composed throughout his life and became a learned musicologist and professor of music. He founded his own church and college where he could develop the music and liturgy to his liking and built St Michael's Church, Tenbury, devoting his life and fortune to it. He employed Langdon Colborne (qv) and recommended him to Hereford Cathedral as organist. He was canon and precentor of Hereford where he resided for part of the year. He was a friend of Sir Henry Baker (qv), who

shared his ecclesiastical tastes, and, helped by Havergal (qv), designed an organ for Sir Henry. He wrote much church music and collected a valuable library of musical literature and manuscripts at St Michael's College, which were eventually given to the Bodleian. He died in Hereford on 6 April 1889 and was buried at St Michael's, Tenbury.

Owen (*c.*600-684) was the sainted Bishop of Rouen whose cult was brought to Hereford by the Normans, who dedicated a church to him in their new northern suburb of Hereford. His name is preserved in St Owen Street. His feast day is 24 August. There was another St Owen, a Benedictine monk and steward in the household of St Etheldreda who is probably the patron of the small hamlet of St Owen's Cross near Hentland. His feast day is 4 March.

P

Page, Henry (*c.*1604-63), clergyman, was educated at Christ's College, Cambridge and ordained in 1627. He married Alice Gowland, the sister of the keeper of Westminster Library and in 1631 was appointed rector of Ledbury. He was a Puritan and attacked the *Book of Sports* from the pulpit. This was a declaration made by King James in 1617 and written by Archbishop Laud (qv), to allow for recreation after divine service on the Sabbath. Bear-baiting and plays were banned but archery, dancing and harmless sports were permitted, as was the setting up of maypoles and Morris dancing. When it was reissued by Charles I (qv) in 1633 there was Puritan opposition and Page attacked it from Ledbury's pulpit. His congregation was unsympathetic to this 'opprobrious and disgraceful' sermon, however, and reported him to Archbishop Laud and the High Commission, who questioned him closely about his scorn for the royal proclamation. The outcome is not known but Page survived as rector of Ledbury for another 30 years. He witnessed the 'Battle of Ledbury' in April 1645, when his church and rectory came under fire, adapted to Presbyterianism and independency in the Commonwealth (when there were no maypoles in Ledbury) and then to the restoration of the Anglican prayer book (when there were) and passed on his cure to his son. Age taught him discretion and perhaps his wife's family protected him. His son John was rector for only two years, dying in 1665, probably of the plague that swept Herefordshire. In the inventory of his possessions his books are valued at £100. Mrs Page lived on until 1684, leaving two sons, Henry and Peter, to see to her funeral in Ledbury.

Pain fitz John (1096-1137), baron, was the son of John fitz Richard whose father followed the Conqueror from Normandy. His mother may have been a daughter of Ralph (I) Mortimer and one source places his birth at Ewyas Castle. When young he was a body servant of Henry I, and Gerald of Wales (qv) says that he and Miles of Gloucester (qv) were confidants of the king. Pain and his brothers Ralph and William were among Henry's 'new men'. Walter Map (qv) relates that one of Pain's duties was to draw a measure of wine for the king should he wake thirsty at night. As he rarely did Pain drank this himself. Once Henry did wake and asked for wine. Pain confessed, trembling, but Henry was sympathetic and told him to draw two measures in future, one for each of them. Henry rewarded Pain with extensive lands in Herefordshire. Pain married Sybil Talbot, niece of Hugh de Lacy (qv, d.1121) and their daughters were Cecily and Agnes. Cecily's first husband was Roger (qv Roger fitz Miles), son of Miles of Gloucester. Pain was Sheriff of Hereford from 1123-7 and then also of Shrewsbury, probably for the rest of his life; and royal justice in both shires. Henry I consulted Pain on the appointment of Robert de Béthune (qv), prior of Llanthony, to the long vacant see of Hereford. Pain attended Henry's funeral and was an early supporter of the usurping Stephen (qv). Contemporary annals describe Pain and Miles as paramount all along the Marches, with Pain dealing with the Welsh. Pain was killed in a Welsh ambush while pursuing a raiding party, and was buried in Gloucester Abbey. Painscastle in Radnorshire and Painswick in Gloucestershire are named after him.

Painter, Ralph and **Leslie** (fl.1920s) founded the Hereford firm Painter Brothers with their father in the 1920s, making steel towers on the Holmer Road. It became a limited company in 1929. In 1950 they received the prestigious commission to build the Skylon for the Festival of Britain. This icon of modernity hung at the centre of the Festival and wits compared it with post-war Britain, having no visible means of support. The firm still manufactures steel structures as part of the BICC group.

Paish, Frank Walter (1898-1988), economist, born in Croydon, was a professor at the London School of Economics from 1932 and published several books on economics. Later in life he lived at the Old Rectory Cottage, Kentchurch, where he died on 23 May 1988.

Palairet, Charles Michael (1882-1956), diplomat, was born on 29 September 1882 at Berkeley, Gloucestershire, the second of three sons of Charles and Emily Palairet of Westhill, Ledbury, where he grew up. The family had moved to England after the revoking of the Edict of Nantes in 1689. They had cousins who were well-known cricketers. Palairet went to Eton, studied languages abroad and joined the diplomatic service. He married Mary Studd in 1915 and they both became Roman Catholics. In the period before the Second World War he served in Romania, Greece and Austria, observing increasing Nazification. Returning home, he was appointed assistant under-secretary at the Foreign Office dealing with matters involving prisoners of war. He died at his home in Somerset on 5 August 1956. There are memorials and a window (qv Whall) to the Palairets in Ledbury Church.

Palin, Edward (1825-1903), clergyman, was educated at St John's, Oxford, ordained and became perpetual curate of Summerstown. He was appointed vicar of St Mary's, Linton (1865-1903) where he proved a colourful character. He married Britta, an American, and is commemorated by a drinking fountain which he donated to the village in 1880. His great-grandson is the actor Michael Palin.

Palmer, Thomas (*c.*1500-53), soldier, knighted at Calais, was a friend of Henry VIII. He leased Dinmore Preceptory in 1548 after the Dissolution of the monasteries and constructed a house in the preceptory buildings. He gave testimony that proved crucial for the Duke of Somerset's (qv Edward Seymour) fall in 1551. He was implicated in Lady Jane Grey's (qv) bid for the throne, however, and was arrested for treason and beheaded.

Panton, Thomas (d.1685), son of John Panton of Leicestershire, was a colonel in Charles II's lifeguards but resigned following his conversion to Roman Catholicism. He was a skilled gambler but, winning a fortune at a game, was so shaken that he never played again. He married Dorothy Stacy (1641-1725) and bought an estate in Herefordshire. He built houses in Panton Street, London, which is named after him, and he and his wife are buried in Westminster Abbey.

Parker, John (1866-1921), Hereford City Surveyor, was born in Greenock, Strathclyde where he trained as an architect. He practised both in South Africa and in Hereford, where he built the storage tower (1886) for Hereford Waterworks on Broomy Hill begun by the then surveyor George Cole. He tackled Hereford's sewage problem with a treatment centre and refuse incinerator at Bartonsham and built low-cost council housing schemes: 16 houses on St Owen Street and more in Eign Mill Road. He constructed the Electricity Supply Works at Widemarsh (1898), and the same year built the Victoria Suspension Bridge, at a cost of £1,200, to commemorate Queen Victoria's Jubilee. After centenary repairs this attractive footbridge is in good condition. Parker was a Woolhope Club member. He died and was buried in Cape Town, South Africa.

Parker, William (fl.1781-91), a Hereford joiner who became a successful builder-designer, won the contract for the General Infirmary on Nelson Street, Hereford (1781-3) after Thomas Symonds' (qv, d.1791) plans had been rejected. It was built on land donated by Edward Harley (qv, d.1790), Earl of Oxford. This is now converted to housing. He designed and built Hereford Theatre in Broad Street *c.*1789 for J.B. Watson (qv) and was paid from the takings on several benefit nights; and the next year he built the Swan Inn, Hereford. In 1791 he built a house for the Duke of Norfolk (qv Charles Howard) on Broad Street (now Barclays Bank).

Parry: An old Welsh family whose English surname originated in the suffix ap Harry – son of Harry. The family intermarried with the Skidmores (qv) and the Vaughans (qv) and were celebrated in bardic poetry. They were related to the Herbert Earls of Pembroke, the Cecils (qv) and the Oldcastles (qv). With these connections, Parrys found places at the Tudor Court, notably Blanche, Queen Elizabeth's lifelong gentlewoman. Blanche's monument at Bacton Church is one of the sights of the county. Armorial glass of the 15th century showing the Parry arms has been moved to Atcham Church, Shropshire.

Parry, Blanche (1508-90), gentlewoman of Queen Elizabeth, was born at Newcourt, the daughter of Henry Myles (qv) and Alys. She and her sisters were educated by the Augustinian nuns of Aconbury and brought up speaking Welsh. Blanche was introduced at Court by her aunt Lady Herbert of Troy and served Princess Elizabeth from birth, through the vicissitudes of her youth and imprisonment in the Tower. She became chief gentlewoman at Elizabeth's accession in 1558 and keeper of the queen's jewels. Elizabeth's three ladies, another being Lady Mary Scudamore (qv, d.1603), exercised great power – 'a trinity of ladies able to work Miracles'. Beside the jewels Blanche had charge of books presented to the queen and of her wardrobe and linen. She controlled access to the queen, brought her intelligence and wrote her letters. She received great rewards from Elizabeth and douceurs from others and amassed money and lands, but was never allowed to leave the queen. She distributed offices amongst her Herefordshire relatives including her nephew Rowland Vaughan (qv), who became a member of the queen's guard. Long before her death she commissioned the extraordinary monument in St Faith's, Bacton which shows her kneeling before her queen with an autobiographical description of her status and duties at Court, stating how she 'with maiden Queen a maid did end my life'. The queen never let her retire or marry, and when she died on 12 February 1590 she was buried at the queen's cost with the ceremony due to a baroness in St Margaret's, Westminster. It is said that her heart was buried in the monument at Bacton. She rebuilt the west tower at St Faith's and had the Newcourt to Moor road repaired.

Parry, Charles Hubert Hastings (1848-1918), baronet, composer, was the last of the six children of Thomas Gambier Parry of Highnam

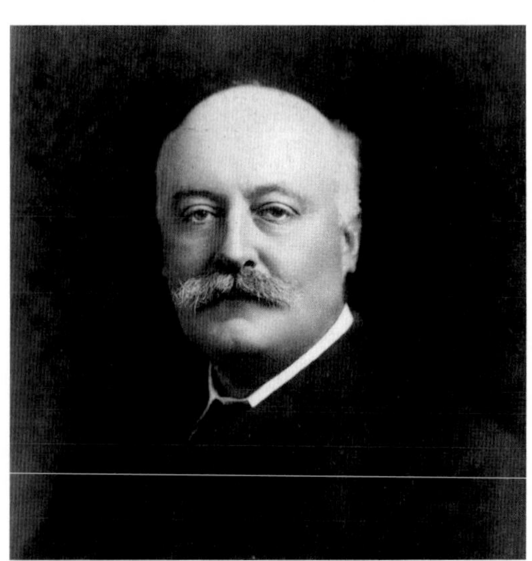

Court, Gloucs. His father built the church by the house, one of the finest ecclesiological buildings in Britain. It was at the Three Choirs Festival in 1861 at Hereford that he first realised the power of music and started his lifelong connection with the festival. He had his first piece conducted at a Gloucester Festival concert by S.S. Wesley (qv). He became a major figure of the musical establishment, composing some symphonic works, though his work was mainly choral on a smaller scale, such as his setting of Blake's *Jerusalem*. He was an academic at Oxford and the Royal College of Music. His last choral work, *Ode on the Nativity*, was produced for the Three Choirs Festival at Hereford in 1912.

Parry, Henry Myles (d.1488) of Newcourt, Bacton was the son of Thomas Aparry, whose monument is in St Mary Magdalene, Turnastone (qv ap Harry). Henry married Alys, one of the 13 daughters and co-heiresses of Simon Milbourne (qv). Theirs was a Welsh cultural environment and Welsh and English were spoken at home. Henry was steward of Ewyas Lacy and of the Cistercian Abbey of Dore and three times High Sheriff of Herefordshire.

Parry, Myles (d.1544) of Newcourt, eldest son of Alys and Henry (qv), married Eleanor, daughter and co-heir of James Scudamore (qv, d.1553) of Kentchurch. Their two daughters, Joan and Elizabeth, inherited both Parry and Scudamore property. They married respectively Watkyn (qv, fl.1550) and Roger Vaughan (qv, d.1607). Myles is buried in Bacton Church.

Parry, Symond (d.1573), Myles' (qv) younger brother, lived at The Moor, later called Whitehouse, near Vowchurch. His daughter the heiress Jane married Griffith Jones (qv Howorth) and Whitehouse passed to him. Symond had three other illegitimate children. Symond is buried next to his brother Myles (qv) in the chancel of Bacton Church, below their famous sister Blanche (qv).

Parry, William (1687-1756), antiquary and poet, was the son of Devereux and Margaret Parry of St John's parish, Hereford. He was educated at Jesus College, Oxford and appointed rector of Shipston-on-Stour, Worcs. He left extensive antiquarian notes and some verse written in a beautiful italic hand. The Parry family were from Wormbridge and produced a Bishop of Worcester in the 16th century.

Parry, William (fl.1788), a descendant of William (qv, d.1756), was a Hereford solicitor who retired to New Weir, a house he had built in 1788 overlooking the Wye near Kenchester. Humphry Repton (qv) advised on the landscaping of the grounds and submitted his customary *Red Book* showing how the estate would look before and after Repton's suggested works. The Weir Gardens are now owned by the National Trust.

Parsons, Richard Godfrey (1882-1948), Bishop of Hereford 1941-8, was born at Pendleton, Lancashire on 12 November 1882. He was educated at Magdalen College, Oxford and ordained priest in London in 1907; he held liberal theological views. He married Dorothy Streeter (d.1953) and they had two sons. He was appointed principal of Wells Theological College, in 1924 he took the degree of DD at Oxford and in 1927 he became suffragan

Bishop of Middleton, then in 1932 Bishop of Southwark, a poor and demanding area of London. In 1941 he was consecrated Bishop of Hereford where he remained until his death in Hereford General Hospital on 26 December 1948. A stone commemorates him in the cathedral crypt.

Partridge, Mary (fl.1927) of Bacton,was the owner of the racehorse Sprig who, ridden by Ted Leader, won the Grand National at Aintree on 25 March 1927 at odds of 8:1. Sprig was trained by Tom Leader, Ted's father, in memory of Mrs Partridge's son Capt. Richard Partridge, who fell in the Great War. The bells of Abbey Dore, Pontrilas, Ewyas Harold and Bacton were rung to celebrate the victory. The race was filmed for Pathé News in the presence of George V and was the first to be broadcast by BBC radio.

Pateshall: The Pateshalls became prominent in the area around the 14th century. A John Pateshall was escheator in 1497, and it was his descendant, also John (qv), who bought Pudleston Hall. In the 18th century Edmund Pateshall (qv) acquired Allensmore Court. A John Pateshall was mayor of Hereford in 1818, and William Pateshall, attorney, was mayor in 1820. A relative, George Pateshall Colebatch, farmer and chemist, was born at Underley, Wolverflow and had a famous son – Sir Harry Pateshall Colebatch (1872-1953). In 1878 the family migrated to Australia where Harry (often known as Hal) became a celebrated journalist and politician. In 1910 Captain Harry Evan Pateshall was lord of the manor of Allensmore. The house has now been demolished and most of the timber felled, but attractive estate buildings and signs of fine gardens survive.

Pateshall, Edmund (fl.1725) of Pembridge bought Allensmore Court in 1725. His daughter Jane had a son, Edmund Lechmere (d.1790), who assumed the Pateshall name and had the Hereford architect Thomas Symonds (qv, d.1791) extend and reface the old Queen Anne house in 1782. His son, also Edmund, continued to beautify the estate with the help of advice from his neighbour John Matthews (qv) at Belmont.

Pateshall, John (fl.1523-64), son of William Pateshall of Ford, bought and beautified Pudleston Court, east of Leominster. John was educated at the Inner Temple and accounted a learned man. He married Eleanor, daughter of James Tomkyns (qv under Tomkyns family) of Weobley. He held county office with duties at Hereford Castle gaol, and was elected to the last Parliament of Queen Mary's reign. He supported Elizabeth's return to Anglicanism, however, and was made JP for the county, dying soon after. In the 1630s a John Pateshall had a house in Bridge Street, Leominster where a break-away group from John Tombes' (qv) congregation met.

Paul, Roland Wilmot (1864-1935), was born at Weston-super-Mare the son of a bank manager. Known for his beautiful architectural drawings, especially of abbeys, he was especially fascinated by Thomas Blashill's (qv) discoveries at Dore Abbey and made many plans and detailed drawings of it, discovering that the 13th-century rebuild, consecrated by Thomas de Cantilupe (qv) in 1282, was unusually sumptuous for a Cistercian abbey. Chosen for a major renovation of the church between 1898 and 1904, he wrote a history of the abbey and, with Blashill, appealed for funds. He repaired roof and walls, renewed choir stalls and traced and excavated the foundations of the ruined abbey buildings, finding and preserving architectural elements, carvings, glass, tiles and the 17th-century woodwork from John Scudamore's (qv, d.1671) restoration. He found the great ceiling boss of an abbot praying before the Virgin and Child which had been preserved at the dissolution of the abbey, then concealed during the 17th century. Other finds included the small figure of Bishop John de Breton (qv) holding his heart (recently stolen) and, in Tan House Farm nearby, the Cistercian abbey's high altar, with its space for a relic and five consecration crosses. Paul was elected FSA in 1900 and left the Society his plans and drawings of Dore and other Herefordshire churches. He rebuilt the chancel and south chapel (1906) at St Mary, Sarnesfield, and was architect for Bristol Cathedral.

Pauncefoot: The family is known to have resided at Cowarne Hall, Much Cowarne, at Hatfield, and at the Netherhall, Ledbury and the nearby Pauncefoot Manor at Munsley. The eldest son was traditionally named Grimbald and a Grimbald de Pauncefoot owned Longworth Manor in the 13th century. He sold it to Sir Edmund Hakluyt (qv Leonard Hakluyt).

Pauncefoot, Grimbald (13th century) of Hatfield married the beautiful Constantia, daughter of John de Lingen. In 1253 whilst on Crusade Grimbald was captured by the Moors. His ransom was 'a joint of his wife', which Constantia paid with her hand, cut off at the wrist. Silas Taylor (qv) in notes for his history of Herefordshire says their effigies in St Mary, Much Cowarne, showed the lady with her right hand missing, but now only Grimbald's battered figure remains. Hatfield later passed to the Colles (qv) family.

Pauncefoot, Grimbald (18th century) is recorded as building the Congregational Chapel in Bromyard, and his relative Laetitia Pauncefoot (d.1753) has a fine wall plaque in St Peter's, Bromyard, by C. Philpott (a Bromyard mason).

Pauncefoot, John (1368-1448), son of Hugh and great-grandson of Grimbald of Hatfield (qv) was knighted by Richard II (qv) and fought in Ireland under Roger (VII) Mortimer (qv). He transferred allegiance to the usurping Lancastrian kings and was wounded when accompanying Henry IV (qv) in Scotland. He married Alice, daughter of Sir Andrew Herl (qv) and they lived at Letton Court. In 1401 he was advised to fortify the house against Glyn Dŵr (qv), but in vain as they were forced to flee his ravaging of the shire. He was at the Battle of Shrewsbury in 1403. He was an MP and JP in Gloucestershire and Sheriff at different times of both Gloucestershire and Herefordshire. Their son John married Margaret Beauchamp of Holt, Worcs. An Alice Pauncefoot was an executor of John de Hop (qv) who supervised the founding of St Anne's Chantry in Ledbury in 1384 (qv Calwe). There is a splendid late 14th-century effigy of a Pauncefoot lady in the north-east chapel (now the vestry) at Ledbury.

Paxton, Joseph (1803-65), landscape gardener and architect, was born on 3 August 1803 at Milton Bryan in Bedfordshire, the youngest child of William Paxton, an agricultural labourer. He was a bright boy and began to make a name as a designer of gardens. He caught the attention of the Duke of Devonshire and became his head gardener at Chatsworth when only 23 and his personal adviser. Paxton married Sarah Brown, a Derbyshire girl. He was known for his radical approach to glass buildings and in 1844 John Arkwright (qv) had him design a conservatory as part of his major rebuild of his newly acquired Hampton Court (near

Leominster). Paxton stayed at Hampton Court for Christmas 1844, and by 1846 the conservatory was in place. It has recently been renovated and is now the tea house. Paxton's most famous glasshouse was the Crystal Palace (1851).

Paytherus, Thomas (1752-1828), surgeon-apothecary, was born in Fownhope into a family of yeoman farmers. He was apprenticed to Richard Browne Cheston, a neighbour and a surgeon at Gloucester Infirmary, and to an apothecary in Gloucester. After further education in London and Edinburgh Paytherus commenced practice as a surgeon-apothecary in Ross-on-Wye, entering into partnership with the elderly, established William Wood (1707-94) and setting up his home in Wilton. A friend of Edward Jenner (qv), he discussed Jenner's ideas about vaccination with him. He invited Jenner to witness a post mortem on a patient who had died from angina, which established a link between angina and hardening of the arteries. Throughout his life Paytherus remained a strong advocate of Jenner's controversial methods. In 1786 Paytherus married Frances Hodges at Bridstow and their children were Thomas, Fanny, Emma and Mary. He took on apprentices; the first, Richard Evans, went on to practice in Ross until at least 1828 and was a strong supporter of vaccination. Paytherus continued surgeon at Ross for 11 years, also taking on the medical care of the poor in Kings Caple. In 1784 he moved with his family to London where he added the manufacture and selling of medicines to his practice. He analysed the mineral waters of Cheltenham and made his up own profitable version – a chalybeate aperient. The business attracted royalty and the fashionable and was exceptionally successful. One of his apprentices in London was John Purchas (qv under Purchas family) of Fownhope. Eventually retiring, Paytherus moved with his family to Abergavenny where he died and is buried.

Pearle, Richard (d.1577) of Dewsall Court bequeathed scholarships to Hereford Cathedral School and Brasenose College, Oxford, and Herefordshire scholars were favoured in this way.

Pearle, Richard (1560-1644), son of Richard (qv, d.1577), was educated at the Cathedral School and Brasenose. He and his wife Dorothy are buried in St Michael's Church, Dewsall. Their son John married a Parry of Aconbury and they had a daughter Mary who married Sir John Brydges (qv, d.1632) and brought Dewsall Court to him as her dowry. Sir John bought Aconbury Priory from the Pearles and converted the conventual buildings into a residence.

Pearson, John Loughborough (1817-97), architect, thoroughly renovated Ledbury Church in 1894-6, supplying all the pews and installing a new heating system. He is best known as the architect of Truro Cathedral (1880).

Pecham, John (*c.*1230-92), Archbishop of Canterbury 1278-92, pious friar, theologian, scientist, writer and diplomat, was one of the great figures of the 13th century. He was a friend of Friar Bacon and Pope Nicholas IV and supported the Friars movement as agents of the Church's ministry at parish level. With Pope Nicholas he preached a Crusade to recover the Holy Lands. He was tutor of Thomas de Cantilupe (qv) but later found him obstinate and excommunicated him. On these grounds he refused Cantilupe's bones burial in Hereford Cathedral until Edward I (qv) insisted. Like Thomas Becket (qv) he loudly championed the Church against the king's encroachment. He made several visitations of Herefordshire. Hearing of Roger (III) de Mortimer's (qv) adultery with Marcher ladies, he confronted him and, from a Hereford base, in October 1282 he visited Llywelyn ap Gruffydd (qv) in his Snowdonia fastness to negotiate an end to his rebellion, but excommunicated him on his refusal. He had the Forbury Chapel built in Leominster to solve the problem of secular access to the priory and dedicated it to St Thomas of Canterbury, clearly a model for him. He is buried in Canterbury Cathedral, in a canopied tomb decorated with the first instance of the Decorated style of architecture in England.

Pede, Richard (d.1481), Dean of Hereford 1463-81, previously Chancellor of Lichfield, was collated Dean of Hereford in March 1463. He supported the vicars choral request for accommodation closer to the cathedral than their quarters at the time which were in Castle Street, and had their present houses built. His bishop, Stanbury (qv), was also in favour and Walter Devereux (qv, d.1485), Baron Ferrers, whose town house was also in Castle Street, put up money. Two canons' houses were pulled down to make way for their houses around the peaceful garth with a covered way to the south door of the cathedral. It was completed in 1481, the year Pede died on 6 March. The cathedral library has a 13th-century Bible presented by Pede which he bought in a Hereford bookshop for five marks or £3 6s 8d.

Peibio (d.585) or Peipiau, King of Ergyng, known as 'Clafrog', the leprous, was a younger son of King Erb of Gwent. When Erb's kingdom was divided up amongst his sons in the Welsh manner, Peibio got Ergyng, which included southern Herefordshire. He married the daughter of King Constantine of Dumnonia and they had four sons: Cynfyn, Gwyddgi, Cynwst and Tewdr and a daughter called Efrddyl. Peibio halted the advance of the Angles into Herefordshire and returning home he found that the unmarried Efrddyl was pregnant and attempted to murder her. She was miraculously preserved, however, and her baby boy Dyfrig (qv Dubricius), on kissing his grandfather, healed his leprosy. Peibio was succeeded as King of Ergyng by his son Cynfyn.

Pember, Robert (*c.*1500-60), scholar and poet from Herefordshire, won a scholarship to St John's College, Cambridge and was a founding fellow of Henry VIII's new Trinity College, a centre of humanist learning. He was skilled in Latin, Greek and Hebrew and taught Princess Elizabeth's tutor, Roger Ascham, to whom he left his extensive classical library. He was reader in Greek at the university, his under-reader being John Dee (qv), and managed to conform to the changing religious requirements of his time. Pember's Latin verse is now largely lost; a piece that survives is dedicated to Martin Bucer. He died and was buried in Cambridge. The name Pember may originate at Pembridge and the family continued to be found at Bodenham. In 1625 Francis Pember was High Sheriff of Hereford despite the reported insufficiency of his estate.

Pembridge (sometimes Pembrugge): The family can be traced in the county to the reign of Stephen and take their name from the village of that name. In *c.*1135 Ralph de Pembridge built Pembridge Castle at Welsh Newton, far from Pembridge village. Pembridge Castle was sold to Walter Pye in 1644. It remains well preserved and in fact has been improved recently. In 1228 Sir William Pembrugge founded the Franciscan Friary at Hereford on lands donated by Bishop Hugh Foliot (qv). Henry de Pembridge (d.1279), and his son Henry after him, held the manor of Gillow in the Hentland. The Gillow estate was sold to the Abrahalls (qv) in 1417.

Pembridge, Anthony (*c.*1567-1610), lawyer, MP, was the fourth son of Thomas Pembridge of Mansell Gamage and Jane, daughter of William Baskerville of Wellington. Pembridge Castle had been sold to Walter Pye (d.1659, qv under Walter Pye). Pembridge was educated at the Inner Temple and married Anne, daughter of John Breynton of Stretton; they had several sons and daughters. He was described by John Hoskyns (qv, d.1638) as 'Little Mr Pembrugge'. He inherited the manor of Wootton, Wellington from his uncle Thomas Baskerville, and was a servant of the 2nd Earl of Essex (qv Robert Devereux, d.1601). He was MP for the county in 1597 and from 1604 until his death. He and Anne were reported for recusancy by Henry Scudamore (qv under Sir John Scudamore, d.1623), who committed 'outrage and riot' against Pembridge. He was removed from the bench by Bishop Bennett (qv), who was of the Scudamore faction, but restored later. In his will he does in fact commend himself to the Catholic

Church. He died on 13 July 1610 of the plague while a sitting MP. His son, also Anthony, was mayor of Hereford in 1633-4. After this the family moved to Gloucestershire.

Pembridge, Richard (d.1345) of Pembridge Castle, represented Herefordshire in the parliaments of 1337 and 1338. He was Lord Warden of the Cinque Ports. He and his wife Petronilla are buried in All Saints, Clehonger where they endowed a chantry chapel in 1342. Their lively alabaster effigies are in the chancel, she with angels at her pillow and a swan which tugs at her cloak and he with detailed contemporary armour and a fine dog.

Pembridge, Richard (d.1375), of Pembridge Castle, son of Sir Richard (qv) and Petronilla, was arrested with some other young men for misdemeanours in the Forest of Dean just after his parents' death. He was knighted by 1340 when he fought at the Battle of Sluys. He is mentioned by Jean Froissart and fought at Crécy (1346) and Poitiers (1356); he profited from these battles and married Elizabeth, formerly the wife of Lord St John and Gerard de Lisle. She brought him lands and he, as a friend of Edward III (qv), received grants of lands and bought up estates. He was the 45th Knight of the Garter, Edward III's new chivalric order, reflecting his wealth and status. Sir Richard was appointed Lieutenant of Ireland but refused to go and lost the king's favour. He died in disgrace on 26 July 1375. His wife and his only son predeceased him, leaving his sisters Amice and Hawise his heirs. Hawise married Sir Thomas de la Barre (qv). The splendid alabaster altar tomb with effigies of Sir Richard and Elizabeth was placed, as he requested in his will, on the south side of Hereford Cathedral before an image of the Virgin. It was damaged by the fall of the nave roof in 1786 and one of Sir Richard's legs and also the shield that had hung above his effigy were lost. He wears a garter on his leg, the first to be depicted, and his feet rest on his lurcher dog. His fashionable armour and wonderful feathered helm are shown with great accuracy and accord with the spirit of chivalric romance at the Court of Edward III.

Penoyre, Francis Rigby Brodbelt Stallard (1767-1866), whose names summarise the recent marriages of the family, extended the park at The Moor and had G.P. Manners rebuild the house (his first work of 1827-9) in a gothic style. It was demolished in the 1950s, like many others with the fanciful styles of this period. Lodges etc remain. He founded the Clifford Endowed National School. The Penoyres arranged for the large parish of Clifford to be divided and Hardwicke Church was built (by Thomas Tudor 1849-51) to serve the new parish. Its first vicar was Revd William Timothy Napleton Stallard Penoyre (1804-56), its second Revd T.W. Webb (qv).

Penoyre, Thomas (1722-66), physician, descendant of Thomas ap Jenkin Penoyre (qv), moved his practice to Spanish Town, Jamaica. He married Sarah Gardner and their daughter Ann (qv Ann Brodbelt) married Francis Rigby Brodbelt, whose son Francis (qv Francis Penoyre) would inherit The Moor.

Penoyre, Thomas ap Jenkin (fl.1500) came to Clifford from Wales and he or his son Howell bought The Moor estate, a mediaeval lordship between Clifford and Cusop; the family were henceforth known as Penoyre of The Moor. Howell married Margaret, daughter of Robert Whitney (qv, d.1541), the substantial landowner of Whitney.

Pentecost, Osbern (fl.1048), was a Norman who accompanied Edward the Confessor (qv) back to England from exile. Edward's relative Ralph de Mantes (qv under Ralph) granted Osbern lands in Herefordshire and he secured these with castles such as that at Ewyas Harold in 1048 and perhaps that at Hereford. The reappearance of the Godwin family (qv) from exile in the 1050s and the English reaction to Edward's foreigners caused Osbern to flee north in 1052.

Peploe, Hanmer William Webb (1837-1923), clergyman, third son of Revd John Birch Webb (see under Samuel Peploe), was born on 1 October 1837 at Weobley before his family moved into his uncle's castle of Garnstone. He assumed the additional surname of Peploe on his father's death. He was an evangelical clergyman, vicar of St Paul's, Onslow Square, London, and a prominent speaker at the Keswick Conventions. In 1887 the estate was sold to the Cheshire salt tycoon Joseph Verdin (qv). Like other grand early 19th-century houses in Herefordshire, such as Saltmarshe and Goodrich Court, Garnstone was demolished in the 1950s. Nash's West Lodge survives as do some of the great trees in the park; the huge ornamental gates from the north ride entrance are now in Calgary, Alberta, Canada.

Peploe, Samuel (d.1845) of Garnstone, Weobley, was born with the surname Birch (qv Sarah Birch), which his father had assumed on inheriting the Garnstone estate through the female line but which Samuel dropped. He married Catherine, eldest daughter of Sir George Cornewall (qv, d.1819). The grounds of Garnstone ran from Weobley Castle mound in the north down through the deer park. John Nash (qv) built Garnstone Castle between 1806 and 1810, leaving the old Tomkyns-Birch (qqv) house on the hillside above, with Charles Heather (qv) his builder. It stood in celebrated gardens with hothouses which saw input from T.A. Knight (qv). Garnstone passed to Peploe's nephew Daniel Peploe Webb (d.1866) who brought in W.A. Nesfield (qv) to add water features, then to his brother Revd John Birch Webb (d.1869). This latter, vicar of Weobley and King's Pyon, married Annie (1805-80) and was a noted religious writer.

Peppercorn, Arthur Henry (1889-1951), chief mechanical engineer of the London and North Eastern Railway, was born on 29 January 1889 in Leominster and educated at Hereford Cathedral School. He was apprenticed with the Great Northern Railway (GNR) and rose to become their last chief mechanical engineer. He designed the Peppercorn Class Locomotives, said to be the best steam engines ever made. He

retired in 1949 with an OBE and died on 3 March 1951. Locomotive Peppercorn Class A2 *Blue Peter* is preserved at the Royal Scot Locomotive and General Trust, near Chesterfield, Derbyshire. A reconstruction engine, *Tornado*, was launched in 2008 by Peppercorn's 92-year-old widow.

Percival, John (1834-1918), Bishop of Hereford 1895-1917, was born in Brough Sowerby, Westmorland on 27 September 1834 and educated at Queen's College, Oxford with a fellowship. He married Louisa Holland in 1862 and they had six children. Ordained, he taught at Rugby School then was the first headmaster of Clifton College, turning it into one of the leading public schools. He returned to Rugby as headmaster until January 1895 when Archibald Rosebery made him Bishop of Hereford, against Queen Victoria's wishes. Percival's wife died after his elevation and in 1899 he married again. He was a liberal, broad churchman in a conservative diocese, contrasting with his predecessor the conservative and 'High' Atlay (qv). He was unpopular in the House of Lords: Edmund Gosse wrote that 'his voice, like the bleat of a sheep upon a hillside, throws everybody into a sort of distress'. He supported the WEA, chairing meetings and dismayed Dean and Chapter by allowing nonconformists to take communion in the cathedral. He criticised the Boer War and the use of concentration camps for Boer prisoners. He discontinued the use of the Athanasian Creed in sung services at the cathedral because of the effect the awful words would have on innocent children, to the horror of the minor canons. He enjoyed the novels of Edna Lyall (qv), whose liberal views he shared, and wrote a letter of condolence to Revd Burges Bayly, her brother in Bosbury, on her death. In 1910 he visited Brian Hatton (qv) in his Hereford studio and had his portrait painted. He was disappointed not to be made Archbishop of York and retired to Oxford where he died on 3 December 1918. He is buried in the chapel crypt at Clifton College.

Perrot: A family based at Moreton on Lugg and Wellington with gentry connections in Pembrokeshire. In the late 15th century a William Perrot married into the Clanvowe family (qv Thomas Clanvowe) and Perrot girls married Vaughans and Bohuns (qqv).

Perrot, Francis (1619-67), son of Robert (qv), fought with the Venetian Fleet against the Barbary Coast pirates. He died at home

in Monnington on 24 October 1667 and was buried in St Mary's, Monnington under a statue bust with verses extolling his valour and capacious mind.

Perrot, Herbert (1617-82), son of Robert (qv) and Fortuna, was born in Wellington and educated at Brasenose College and Gray's Inn. He inherited the title and estate at Haroldstone of the Pembrokeshire Perrots. He was of nonconformist sympathies and supported Parliament throughout the Civil Wars. His support was discreet, though, and he managed the transition to the Restoration well. In 1959 and 1660 he was returned MP for Weobley and was knighted in 1660. He was a receiver of taxes for the area and clashed with John Birch (qv) whose powerbase was at Weobley. In 1666 he was High Sheriff of Pembrokeshire and in 1675 was appointed commissioner for recusants. He was mayor of Haverfordwest in 1677. He married first Jane Lloyd, then Hester Barlow and finally Susanna Norreys. He died on 16 June 1682 and was buried in St Margaret's Church, Wellington where the Perrot heraldic pears are depicted. His son was murdered in a tavern brawl and his daughter Hester inherited the Perrot estates, which went to her husband Sir John Pakington of Worcestershire.

Perrot, Robert (1572-1657), merchant, was born at Moreton on Lugg the son of Richard Perrot and Margaret Bromwich (whose uncle was a Perrot). He was educated at Brasenose College, Oxford and married Fortuna Tomkyns (qv under Richard Tomkyns) in about 1611. He was Mayor of Hereford in 1589. He studied the Perrot pedigree and claimed the arms of the Pembrokeshire Perrots, with its rebus of three pears, but this was challenged in the Heralds' Court.

Peter (1st century), sainted apostle, was allowed out of his Roman prison, on parole, with St Paul according to Herefordshire legend. They sailed to Wales where St Paul stayed but St Peter crossed the Black Mountains to preach in Herefordshire. At Peterchurch he baptised many Britons in a holy well which he blessed, leaving a trout with a golden collar as a symbol of the Christianity he had brought. A fish was caught here in the 16th century and an image of it put up in St Peter's Church. Of the three wells at Peterchurch two cured eye complaints but have been filled in; the third, a Celtic head of St Peter spouting water, cured rheumatism and is now in Hereford Museum. St Peter's in Hereford was originally a collegiate church founded by Walter de Lacy (qv, d.1085). When Bishop Robert de Béthune (qv) resited St Guthlac's (qv) Priory outside the city walls he combined it with St Peter's community as St Peter, Paul and Guthlac, leaving St Peter's Church within the walls as a parish church hosting civic ceremonies. St Peter's Hereford houses some memories of its association with the defunct St Guthlac, in a gable cross and some mediaeval woodwork. A dedication to St Peter is a sign of an ancient foundation as at Bromyard and Leominster. Such ancient dedications have often been changed – St Michael's and All Angels, Ledbury was originally St Peter's. Rain on St Peter's Day, 29th June, blesses apples.

Philips, John (1676-1709) scholar and poet, was born on 30 December 1676, at Bampton, Oxfordshire the son of the vicar Revd Stephen Philips (1638-84). His father was a canon of

Hereford and archdeacon of Shropshire in the diocese of Hereford. His grandfather, also a canon of Hereford, had been vicar of Lugwardine. His great-grandfather was a Ledbury clothier and the family had been Royalist during the Civil War. They owned Withington Court. Phillips was educated at Winchester and Christ Church, Oxford, where the dean and many of the students were from Herefordshire. He was intended to be a physician and studied natural history and botany, but he remained at Christ Church for the rest of his life without taking a degree, reading the classics and writing poetry. He was often at the family home at Withington and with his friend William Brome (qv) at Eau Withington. Here he learned about apple cultivation and cider making. This is clear in *Cyder* (1708), the long poem he wrote about Herefordshire and its traditional drink. It was a burlesque of Virgil's *Georgics* and showed the influence of the blank verse of Milton's *Paradise Lost*, also about an apple. He praised Lord John Scudamore's (qv, d.1671) Redstreak (qv) and the Bosbury perry pear with its great yield but floating lees. He describes local places and legends such as the disappearance of *Ariconium*, near Weston-under-Penyard, which he imagines sinking into the earth to yield huge bones to frighten the ploughman. Jacob Tonson (qv) the publisher, himself to settle in Herefordshire, paid Philips 40 guineas for the poem and he became famous. He retired ill with consumption exacerbated by heavy pipe smoking to his mother's house in Hereford where he died on 15 February 1709 and was buried in the north transept of Hereford Cathedral under Latin lines commissioned by his mother. Such was his fame that he was also given a memorial in Westminster Abbey next to Drayton's (qv), another celebrator of Herefordshire. His influence on poetry was great: on Pope's *Windsor Forest*, on James Thomson's *The Seasons* and on John Dyer (qv) and William Cowper. Dr Johnson wrote his biography in his *Lives of the Poets*.

Phillipps, Robert Biddulph (1798-1864), was the son of Robert Phillipps (d.1822), who had recently acquired Longworth, Lugwardine from his nephew James Walwyn (qv, d.1800). Robert was educated at Trinity College, Oxford and the Middle Temple. In 1834 he married Elizabeth Barneby (qv, d.1852) of Brockhampton, and they lived at Longworth where they had two daughters. Phillipps bought Hagley Court and Lower Bartestree Farm and *c.*1850 ran a carriageway from Longworth to the Ledbury Road with wrought iron gates and lodges in Keck's (qv) style. He collected antiquarian papers, including some from Richard Walwyn (qv, fl.mid-17th c.) and others from James Hill (qv), which he left to Belmont Abbey after his conversion to Roman Catholicism. He donated land from his now extensive estates to the Convent of Our Lady of Charity and Refuge at Bartestree and in 1863 had Edward Welby Pugin (qv) rebuild the old chapel of St James there. One of the four sisters at the convent was his daughter Elizabeth Bulkeley Phillipps (1836-1909), whose name in religion was Sister Mary Peter of Alcantara. He was a JP and Lord Lieutenant of Herefordshire. He died in August 1864 and is buried with his wife and youngest daughter Mary Anne in his restored chapel in the convent. Longworth Hall was sold the next year to Edward Hutchinson.

Phipps, Richard (1838-1910), philanthropist, from a wealthy family of Northants brewers, bought the Buckenhill Manor estate north of Bromyard from Lady Shackleton in 1881 and retired there with Ellen his wife. He converted the manor house into a school for boys from Dr Barnardos. In 1889 he built the Victoria Temperance Hotel and working men's reading and social club in Bromyard and in 1895 the Church Institute Hall. He bought a snow plough to clear the impassable winter streets of Bromyard and supplied food and fuel in times of rural depression. He had piped water pumped into town using power from the Three Mills corn mill. He died in December 1910 at Worcester Station and was buried in St Peter's, Bromyard. Buckenhill Manor was later bought by William Barneby (qv) of Saltmarshe.

Phipson, Edward Arthur (1854-1931), artist, was born on 9 February 1854 in Kings Norton, Warwickshire. As a young man he studied languages and adopted the name 'Evacustes', Greek for good listener. He was a prolific, accurate watercolourist specialising in old buildings, recording the timber-framed buildings of Herefordshire, Shropshire *et al.* In April 1890 he was in Ledbury painting old houses, such as those to be demolished for the Barrett-Browning Institute, and in Church Lane. His work is held in Hereford and St Albans Museums. He died in 1931 at Rye, Sussex.

Picton-Turbervill, Edith (1872-1960), social reformer, was born on 13 June 1872 at Lower House, Fownhope, the daughter of Captain John Picton-Warlow (b.1838), an officer in the Indian army, and his second wife, Eleanor Temple. Edith, her twin sister Beatrice and their siblings spent their early years in Brighton in the care of a maiden aunt while their parents were in India. In 1883 the family moved to the Vale of Glamorgan in Wales. Edith was educated at home and at the Royal School in Bath. In 1892 her father inherited the Ewenni Priory estate and assumed the name Picton-Turbervill. The family grew wealthy but Edith reacted to this and, after a religious conversion, turned to social activism. She worked amongst the poor of Shoreditch and from 1900 did charitable work for the Young Women's Christian Association in India. As a feminist she called for women's ordination and with her partner Emily Kinnaird was friends with leading women activists such as Frances Balfour, Chrystal Macmillan, Lilian Baylis and Cicely Hamilton. She was elected Labour MP for the Wrekin district (1929-31). She wrote *Life is Good* (1939), an autobiography, and latterly lived near Cheltenham, dying in Barnwood Hospital in Gloucestershire on 31 August 1960.

Pierson, Thomas (*c.*1573-1633), clergyman, was born in Weaverham, Cheshire, and educated at the free school in Northwich and Emmanuel College, Cambridge, a centre of Puritanism, where he was ordained. He married Helen, widow of Christopher Harvey and returned to Northwich. In 1612 Robert Harley (qv, d.1656) appointed him rector of Brampton Bryan, where he was at odds with his congregation and frequently reported for nonconformity. Harley protected him from the bishop and he set up Puritan lectureships at neighbouring towns and trained local clerics. He published *The Cure of Hurtfull Cares and Feares* and *Excellent Encouragements Against Afflictions.* He died on 16 October 1633, leaving his large collection of theological books to Harley as a free library.

Pilley, Walter (1848-1913), antiquarian, was born on 18 January 1848 in High Town, Hereford, the son of James Pilley (*c.*1807-49) and Mary Rosser (b.1814). He married Sarah Price in St Francis Xavier in Broad Street in 1871. He was interested in archaeology and investigated the foundations of Hereford Castle, finding skeletons and huge stone-lined drains. He discovered the foundations of the Franciscan friary to the west of Hereford's city walls in 1894. He was Mayor of Hereford in 1910. His collection of historical papers on Herefordshire, now in the Hereford Record Office, includes watercolours by James Wathen (qv) and Samuel Meyrick's (qv) notes on Goodrich Castle. He died at his home 2 Barton Villas, Hereford in 1913 and was buried in Belmont Abbey with an inscription in St Francis Xavier in Broad Street. Hereford has a road named after him.

Pipa was a Saxon saint whose name is preserved in that of the village Pipe and Lyde.

Piper, George Harry (1819-97), antiquary, geologist and solicitor, was born on 8 April 1819 in Marylebone, Middlesex, the son of Edmund and Jane Piper. The family, including several brothers and sisters, moved to Herefordshire while he was young, to Castle Frome initially and then to Ledbury where older brother Edmund set up as a wine merchant in the Homend. He was articled to a Thomas Jones, Attorney of Ledbury, and admitted as a solicitor in 1849. He practised at law throughout his life, based at Ledbury, becoming Registrar and High Bailiff of the Court. He was also the proprietor of the Feathers Hotel in the 1870s and a representative for the London Assurance Co. He studied local historical sources, transcribing original Ledbury parish registers for instance, and was a Fellow of the Geological Society. He helped map the complex geology of the Woolhope Dome and, with Henry Brookes (qv), investigated the upper Silurian beds exposed in the railway cutting at Ledbury noting the key Passage Beds that formed a passage from Murchison's (qv) Silurian into the Devonian Period. The steeply dipping beds are still exposed above the tunnel entrance at Ledbury Station. They found the ostracoderm, an early fish, *Auchenaspis egertoni* and brachiopod or bivalve *Pentamerus knightii* which were indicative of the beds. Piper was president of both the Woolhope and Malvern Naturalists' Clubs. He lived at the Old Court House in the Southend, Ledbury where his sister Mary kept house and where, like Brookes, he had an extensive geological museum. He died on 26 August 1897.

Pipes, Jenny (fl.1809), married name Corran, lived in Leominster Workhouse. She was the last person to be publicly ducked on Leominster's ducking stool in 1809. A Dr Fairchild Watling (Mayor of Leominster in 1839) was present at the ducking and reported her foul language afterwards. The contraption, now kept in Leominster Priory, was the punishment for adulterers of food and, as in Jenny's case, public scolds. There is a women's Morris group in Leominster called Jenny Pipes.

Plowman, John (*c.*1773-1843), architect-builder from Oxford, was the foreman and eventual partner of architect Daniel Harris. In 1836 the Hereford Poor Law Union was formed and the Board of Guardians had Plowman build Hereford Workhouse for 250 inmates in the old grounds of St Guthlac's (qv) Priory on the south side of Commercial Road. The large, plain building contained four yards for women and men, old and young and cost £5,600. Gilbert Harding's mother and father were later managers of Hereford Workhouse and he was born there. The extensive buildings subsequently became the General Hospital. Plowman also built smaller workhouses at Ross and Abbey Dore. He died on 12 August 1843 leaving his sons Thomas and John (1807-71) to continue his practice. The latter worked with his father on the Hereford Workhouse and built the Royal Hotel, Ross-on-Wye (1837).

Plukenet, Alan (II) (d.1298), Plugenet or Plunkett, was the son of Alan and Alice Plukenet. As a minor he was made ward of William (II) de Cantilupe (qv). He was knighted by King Henry III in 1260 at Westminster, and was retained by the king for 20 marks per annum. He fought on the royalist side during the baronial rebellion and was at their victory at Evesham, after which he seized rebel estates. In 1269 he was granted the castle and barony of Kilpeck from the ownership of his uncle Robert de Walerand (qv Hugh de Kilpeck). He fought in Edward I's Welsh campaigns and was created seneschal of west Wales. In 1295 he was called to Parliament as a baron. He married Joan, daughter of Andrew Wake of Somerset and their children were Alan (qv Alan (III) Plukenet) and Joanna de Kilpeck (qv), countess of Hereford. He supported the nuns of Aconbury and was a generous patron of Dore Abbey, where, at Christmas 1298, he was buried.

Plukenet, Alan (III) (d.1325), 2nd Lord Plukenet, was the son of Alan (II) Plukenet (qv). He sat as a baron in Edward I's Parliaments and fought in his Scottish and Gascon campaigns. He was granted the right to hold a market at Kilpeck. He created (and gave his name to) the parish of Allensmore by draining the marshes. He and his wife Sybil were buried at Dore Abbey, leaving no issue. Kilpeck passed to his sister Joanna (qv Joanna de Kilpeck) and from her into Bohun hands.

Polton, Thomas (d.1433), Bishop of Hereford 1420-2, of a Wiltshire family, was educated at Oxford, where he was involved in a student riot that included a murder. He represented Henry V and VI at the Papal Curia and was made Dean of York (1416) and Bishop of Hereford. He probably never visited his diocese and was soon translated to Chichester and then to Worcester. He enjoyed controversy and made enemies easily. He died at the Council of Basel on 23 August 1433 and was buried there. In his will a legatee is named Eve St John, 'whom I commonly call wife'.

Poole, Sophia Lane (1804-91), travel writer, sister of Edward Lane (qv), was born in Hereford on 16 January 1804. She helped her brother with his research into the life of Egyptian women, creating a scandal when she revealed in her publication *The Englishwoman in Egypt* that she had dressed in Turkish trousers and lived in harems. Her marriage to an impecunious clergyman was not a success and she left him to live with her brother and his wife. Her son Edward Stanley Poole was also an Arabic scholar and brought out a new edition of his uncle's *Thousand and One Nights*. Sophia died on 6 May 1891.

Poole, William (1854-1901), vicar of Hentland with Hoarwithy 1854-1901, commissioned St Catherine's Church and the school at Hoarwithy, and St Dubricius, Hentland from J.P. Seddon (qv). Seddon pulled down the recently

built brick church at Hoarwithy in 1843 and built St Catherine's (1874-9). The interior took another 25 years to complete. Poole also had Seddon rebuild his church at Hentland and the vicarage there. He was an eccentric and irascible man; when in a bad mood he would throw the workmen's wages in small change down the steps of the church. St Catherine's was costly: in a neo-Byzantine style it had a tall campanile, semi-cloisters and a reading room on a steep rise above the River Wye. Interior mosaics and fittings are by G.E. Fox (qv), who had been working at Eastnor Castle, and Powell & Co. (qv John Hardman Powell). In 1893 Powell's mosaicist Ada Currey (qv) installed her beautiful gold Christ Pantokrator in the eastern apse. There is glass by Morris and Co. and on Poole's death Seddon supplied the stained glass in the apse in his memory. The church was only finally completed in 1913.

Pope, Abednego (1802-63), dancing master, was born in Bristol and taught dancing in a school near Westbury on Severn, Gloucs. He retired to St Katherine's Almshouses in Ledbury.

Pope, Alexander (1688-1744), poet, was born on 21 May 1688, educated at home and, while denied university as a Catholic, became

the greatest poet of the Augustan Age. He was a close friend of Teresa and Martha Blount of Middlesex and stayed at Orleton Manor, the Herefordshire home of the Blount family (qv), where he wrote in the room over the porch. Pope's major works are: the pastoral *Windsor Forest*, which shows early ideas of the picturesque; the mock heroic *Rape of the Lock*; a verse translation of Homer and an edition of Shakespeare which Jacob Tonson (qv) published. Pope stayed with his friend Tonson at The Hazle near Ledbury, and was an early Wye tourist and a guest of Lady Frances Scudamore (qv under James Scudamore, d.1716) at Holme Lacy House in the 1720s. He gave the word 'picturesque' currency in his *Letter to Caryll* and his ideas can be seen in the grotto at his Twickenham house, ideas that influenced the Herefordshire writers Uvedale Price and Richard Payne Knight (qqv). In his final decade Pope wrote great satires including the *Dunciad*, which lampooned dullness, and *Moral Essays* (1731-35): four epistles, the first of which, the *Epistle to Burlington*, satirised bad taste in architecture and attacked Lord Chandos, James Brydges (qv, d.1744) at Cannons. The second, *Epistle to a Lady*, was written to Martha Blount; the third, *Of the Use of Riches*, addressed to Lord Bathurst, contains praise of the charitable works of John Kyrle (qv, d.1724), 'the Man of Ross' of whom he heard while staying with Lord Scudamore at Holme Lacy. Finally he wrote the *Essay on Man* (1733-34), a philosophical treatise, and *The Imitations of Horace*, a satire on corruption in the England of George II and Robert Walpole. Pope was stricken by a form of tuberculosis and died on 30 May 1744. He is buried in Twickenham Parish Church, where there is a monument to him and his parents.

Port, Adam de (d.*c*.1138), Sheriff of Hereford 1130, was a Norman official whose family, from Port-en-Bessin, Calvados, had come to England after the Conquest. The family had settled at Basing, Hampshire but held manors at Eardisley and Kington in Herefordshire in the reign of Henry I. Adam accompanied Bishop Geoffrey de Clive (qv) to Canterbury for his ordination in 1115 where they were informed by the king that the bishop should recover lands in Herefordshire which had been alienated.

Port, Roger de (d.*c*.1161), Adam's (qv) son, married Sybil d'Aubigny, and their son Adam (fl.1161-74) held extensive estates based on his manor of Kington. This Adam was accused of an attempt on Henry II's (qv) life in 1171 and was exiled. He took part in an invasion of northern England by William the Lion, King of Scots, in 1174 and disappears thereafter.

Porter, William (d.1524), canon residentiary and precentor (1515-24) at Hereford Cathedral, was commemorated by a large brass in the cathedral. It was broken up and dispersed but fragments remain, including the canopy which has an Annunciation of very high quality showing a sturdy young angel flying in to Mary, his hair and robe in the disarray of motion. Mary turns to him from prayer in surprise with her words of humble compliance. Other pieces show Saints Thomas of Hereford and Ethelbert (qqv) and the decollation of John the Baptist (qv).

Potts, Cuthbert (1824-1909), minister, was born in South Shields. In 1868 he was appointed pastor of Ledbury's Congregational Chapel (now the Burgage Hall). He became a dominant force in Ledbury and was active on many committees. He was an advocate of teetotalism, for which he was presented with a purse from the town and from Lady Henry Somerset (qv Isabella Somers Cocks). Revd Potts died on 11 May 1909, having been minister for 41 years.

Pountney Smith, Samuel (1812-83), architect of Shrewsbury, designed and built the new church of St Giles in Downton Castle park for Andrew Rouse Boughton Knight (qv) in 1861. He was known for reliability and good workmanship and used his own contractors. The ruins of old St Giles' Church can be seen nearby. Pountney Smith's new estate church completed the vista south-west of the castle. It has encaustic tiles throughout by Godwin of Lugwardine (qv). He rebuilt the nave at the nearby Church of St George, Burrington in 1855 and restored other churches in north-west Herefordshire.

Powell, Edward (*c.*1580-1653) of Pengethley was created baronet in 1622. He supported Parliament in the Civil Wars. The baronetcy lapsed at his death. Pengethley Manor had been bought by John Powell in 1583.

Powell, Lewis (1836-after 1888), architect-builder, was born in Tarrington. In 1871 he was lodging with his widowed mother Mary in Edgar Street, Hereford. His houses and church restorations are in a vigorous style similar to that of Haddon (qv). He built St John's Methodist Church in St Owen Street, Hereford (1879-80); 15 Aubrey Street (1880) and the store 24 High Town, Hereford (1881); the charming old Hereford Dispensary in Union Street (1881) of badly eroded Beer stone; Bullinghope School (1886); The Ferns (now the New Inn) Bartestree for William Godwin (qv); and villas at Grafton. In 1888 he was declared bankrupt.

Powell, Mansell (1694-1775), a Hereford attorney, was the son of Revd. Roger Powell, rector of Moreton-on-Lugg. He became wealthy and acquired property including the Townsend estate in Leominster and the manor of Wellington. In 1733 he married Martha Hoare of the London banking family and was elected High Sheriff of Herefordshire in 1734, and High Sheriff of Radnorshire in 1740. He was also a Justice of the Peace. However, his image as a pillar of the local establishment was shattered when he became entangled in a legal case which acquired notoriety and may even have inspired Charles Dickens' depiction of the machinations of the Court of Chancery in his novel *Bleak House*. The events that led to this sorry situation began when Powell managed to involve himself in the affairs of a William Barnsley (qv) of Eardisley. Having taken over the whole management of Barnsley's affairs, after Barnsley's intestate death in 1737 Powell produced a forged will (qv John Cartwright) granting the Eardisley estate to himself and Samuel Barnsley, a 'cousin' of the deceased'. Barnsley's vulnerable son was passed over – Powell promised him an annuity but never paid it – and the will was proved. Many years later, however, the case was reopened, and in 1749 a jury found the will to be a forgery and the estate was restored to the son. In the meantime, however Powell had used the property and wealth accruing from the estate to secure his election as MP for Weobley in 1747. A judgment in Chancery required Powell to make restitution to young Barnsley of all costs and rents. Powell was unceremoniously unseated on petition at Weobley and his debts bankrupted him. With his accomplices he was found guilty of forgery and committed to Hereford Gaol, where he died on 5 June 1775, aged 79. He was buried at Moreton-on-Lugg.

Powell, William (*c.*1620-80) of Pengethley, MP, was created Baronet in 1661. His title lapsed at his death. The house passed to the Symonds family (qv Thomas Symonds, d.1760).

Powell, William (1735-69), actor, was born in Hereford and educated at the Cathedral School and Christ's Hospital, Sussex. In London he met Garrick (qv) and started acting. He was a great success but died of pneumonia after only ten years. His bust adorned the pediment of Watson's (qv) new theatre in Hereford.

Pralph, John (*c.*1564-1644), vicar of Tarrington, aged about 80, was accosted by a party of Massey's (qv) Parliamentary troopers at Stoke Edith's well in April 1644, on their way back to Ledbury after harrying the outskirts of Hereford. They asked him who he was for and when he answered 'The king' shot him through the head.

Preedy, Frederick (1820-98), architect, was born at Offenham near Evesham in Worcestershire on 2 June 1820 into a well-to-do family of hosiers; his father and grandfather had been mayors of Evesham. He was apprenticed to an architect in Worcester and set up his own practice at 62 Foregate Street in 1849. In 1852 he was elected a member of the Ecclesiological Society and his designs were published in *The Ecclesiologist*. One of his first contracts was the restoration of St Lawrence, Stretton Grandison where a painted reredos by him has recently been discovered. In 1856 he rebuilt St John the Evangelist, Storridge where the deeply undercut naturalistic foliage on capitals, corbels and font, and the well-carved heads in the nave are all typical of him in his 'early decorated' manner. The stained glass in the east window is considered his best. The next year he designed glass for the north chapel in Ledbury Church, made by George Rogers (qv). He built the little church of All Saints, Hollybush in the south Malverns. He married Mary Morgan and moved to London in 1859, setting up his practice in Baker Street with a stained glass workshop in the garden. In 1869-71 he rebuilt St David's, Little Dewchurch, where the decorative carving, the font with Noah and his ark, the ironwork and stained glass are all by him. It was the rediscovery and conservation of painted zinc panels from behind the altar here that started off the current re-evaluation of Preedy's work. He also built the school at Little Dewchurch. He was a friend of William Butterfield and William Burges, both of whom employed him. He was a prolific designer of stained glass, encaustic and mosaic, and other forms of painting, nearly always in churches.

Price, John (1773-1801), historian of Leominster, published his *Account of Leominster and its Vicinity* (1795), dedicated to Viscount Bateman (qv). For this early work of local history he drew on Thomas Blount's (qv) unpublished papers. In 1796 he brought out *A Historical Account of The City of Hereford.*

Price, Mary (d.1638), founder of Aubrey's Almshouses, Hereford, arranged to have built a group of six timber-framed houses for poor widows on land she had bought, herself a widow, behind the Green Dragon, lying between Berrington and Aubrey streets. The mediaeval Wroughthall House stood on the plot then, with other dwellings and an orchard. Her will required her executor, Charles Booth (d.1678), to provide the homes within two years of her death. She endowed them with £200 to provide for six poor widows or single women of good character aged at least 60. A Mr Elfe later took over the charity. The present name comes from Harcourt Aubrey (qv), who married Mr Elfe's granddaughter Elizabeth; Aubrey was a wealthy landowner from Clehonger, who refounded and enhanced the endowment.

Price, Philip (d.1661), vicar of Ross 1615-61, remained with his congregation in 1637 after his rector and those who could afford to had fled the plague-stricken town. He organised torchlit burials at night for the victims. The plague pit is marked by a cross with the inscription 'Plague Ano Dom 1637 Burials 315. Libera nos Domine'. He imposed a *cordon sanitaire* around the town halting the spread of infection but dooming many in Ross. He visited the sick throughout the pestilence and organised a public act of contrition singing the litany in a procession along High Street, after which the plague abated. He was evicted during the Commonwealth for using the prayer book and replaced by John Tombes (qv) and others. He was welcomed back at the Restoration but died shortly after. His successor, John Newton (qv), was also much loved.

Price, Robert (1655-1732) judge, was from a Denbighshire family, educated at St John's College, Cambridge, the Inner Temple and on his Grand Tour. In 1679 he married Lucy, eldest daughter of Robert Rodd of Foxley, Yazor. When Rodd died Price bought out the other inheritors of the Foxley estate and, in 1717, rebuilt the house – the stables are now all that remain from his time. He became an alderman of Hereford and was steward for Catherine of Braganza, James II's queen. He was a judge in Wales in 1700 and MP for Weobley from 1690 to 1702, when he resigned the seat in favour of his son Thomas (d.1706). Under Queen Anne he was made Baron of the Exchequer and justice of the Court of Common Pleas in 1726. Thomas Coningsby (qv, d.1729) called him the worst of judges. Sir Robert died in February 1733 and his monument has been moved from the old Church of St John the Baptist to St Mary's, Yazor. His younger son and heir Uvedale Tomkins Price (1685-1764) married Anne (d.1741), daughter of Lord Arthur Somerset (qv) and their son was Robert (qv, d.1761). Price's daughter Lucy married a cousin, Bamfylde Rodd.

Price, Robert (1717-61) artist, son of Robert (qv, d.1732) and born at Foxley Hall, went on the Grand Tour and studied drawing in Italy. He returned to Foxley and married Sarah Barrington. He sketched along the Wye; his interest in the picturesque was inherited by his son Uvedale (qv). Hereford Art Gallery has his *Castle Mount at Foxley, 1744*. Gainsborough and Thomas Jones were friends of his. He built The Ragged Castle, a Gothick gazebo in the woods, in 1743 and started to organise his already rugged lands picturesquely. He died at Foxley Hall.

Price, Robert (1786-1857), 2nd Baronet, born on 3 August 1786, the only son of Uvedale (qv) and Caroline, married his cousin Mary (d.1878), daughter of Revd Dr Robert Price, canon of Salisbury. He was MP for Hereford from 1818 until 1841. He was a keen archer of the Hereford Bowmeeting which met in Foxley Grounds. In 1843 Sir Robert had George Moore build a new church, St Mary, at Foxley, Yazor, and transferred to it family monuments and the 14th-century font at which the Prices had been baptised. Sir Robert had invested heavily in the Glamorgan Iron and Coal Co. with Foxley as security but the company failed and Foxley was forfeit. Sir Robert died without issue on 5 November 1857 and the baronetcy became extinct. John Davenport bought the Foxley estate in 1856 and commissioned William Butterfield to restore a transept of the now ruinous St John Baptist as a chapel for the Davenport family. Davenport's son Horatio (d.1919) rebuilt the mansion in an undistinguished fashion. House and grounds were used by the American forces as a hospital during the Second World War and demolished in 1948. A camp for the resettlement of Polish servicemen was sited in Foxley grounds in the 1940s. Sparse ruins of the house can still be seen, and a ha ha that marked off Sir Uvedale's garden, but the world-famous grounds are now covered with commercial forestry.

Price, Uvedale (1747-1829), 1st Baronet, landscape theorist, was born at Foxley Hall, Yazor on 14 April 1747, Robert II's (qv) eldest

son. He was educated at Eton College and Christ Church, Oxford. He was a friend of the radical Whig politician Charles James Fox and toured Italy with him, buying Salvator Rosa's landscapes and calling on Voltaire at Ferney. On his return he continued his father's landscaping and extended the estate, employing Robert Adam (qv) on the house. He married Caroline Carpenter in 1774, youngest daughter of George, 1st Earl of Tyrconnell (qv, d.1762), and their children were Caroline (d.1853) and Robert (qv, d.1857). Price managed his estate for both its economic and aesthetic potential, writing on the unity of the productive and the picturesque in the celebrated *Essay on the Picturesque* (1794). He was the neighbour and intellectual sparring partner of Richard Payne Knight (qv) of Downton Castle, with whom he shared an antipathy for Lancelot 'Capability' Brown (qv) who, they felt, imposed an overall design without reference to local conditions and hid the cottagers from the landlord. Price wanted his picturesque landscape to combine local distinctiveness, economic effectiveness and artistic and literary reference for meditation and appreciation of the sublime. The genius of Britain lay in the local and the diverse. He consulted the spirit of the place, as Alexander Pope (qv) suggested, and looked to Claude Lorrain and Jacob van Ruisdael, Virgil and Homer for painterly and literary references. He set his theories out in *A Dialogue on the Distinct Characters of the Picturesque and the Beautiful* (1801), to which his neighbour R.P. Knight replied with *An Analytical Inquiry into the Principles of Taste* (1805). Price published an exchange of letters about the nature of landscape gardening with Repton (qv) and with Thomas Hearne (qv). David Cox (qv) gave as a reason for living in Herefordshire that it was the home of the picturesque. Cox's 'broken tint' style was intended to reproduce Price's picturesque texture. Price commissioned *Scene at Foxley Park* from Cox and hired him to teach his niece Charlotte Price. John Britton (qv) visited Foxley on a walking tour in 1798 and noted its superiority to Repton's (qv) landscapes. Price was an influence on John Nash (qv) at the start of his career and had him design a house and cottages in the picturesque manner. Nash and J.C. Loudon (qv) went on to develop Price's ideas into the Victorian garden-suburb. Wordsworth (qv) visited Foxley but thought it unreal. Price was an admirer of the poet and they worked together on the design of Sir George Beaumont's garden in Leicestershire. The gardens at Eywood and Whitfield both show the influence of Price. Not everyone was convinced though and Dr John Matthews (qv) of Belmont published his disagreement in *A Sketch from the Landscape* (1794). An unexpected admirer of the 80-year-old Sir Uvedale was young Elizabeth Barrett (qv) who commended his *Essay on the Picturesque* for its clarity and charming style. Price in his turn complimented her on her classical learning and asked her advice on Greek and Latin pronunciation. Price was a member of the Society of Dilettanti and was Sheriff of Herefordshire in 1793. He acted as Admiral Nelson's (qv) secretary at one time. He was a member of the committee to replace Hereford Gaol which appointed John Nash as architect in 1796. In the last year of his life he was created a baronet. Price died at Foxley on 14 September 1829 and Lady Caroline three years earlier on 16 July 1826. They were buried in Yazor churchyard under the east wall of the church, marked by a table tomb. The *Hereford Journal* for 16 September 1829 praised Price's learning, wisdom and taste.

Price, Uvedale Tomkins S. (d.1844) of Yazor has a brass cross in the church designed by A.W.N. Pugin (qv) in 1851 and made by Hardman.

Price, William (d.1642) was Mayor of Hereford when the Earl of Stamford's army occupied the city, without resistance, on 30 September 1642. When the Parliamentarian army withdrew he was accused of treason, imprisoned and threatened with hanging. He died as a result of his rough handling.

Prichard, Edward of Almeley, Roger's son (qv), his uncle John Eckley and four other Quakers were among the 13 signatories of William Penn's 1682 charter for Pennsylvania.

Prichard, James Cowles (1786-1848), physician and ethnologist, was born in Ross on 11 February 1786, to Thomas (qv) and Mary. His paternal grandmother was a Cowles. His brother Thomas emigrated to America to take care of the family's commercial interests in New York. James trained under Quaker physicians in Bristol and studied medicine at St Thomas's Hospital in London and at Edinburgh University. In Edinburgh he met Anna Maria Estlin, sister of a student friend, and they married in 1811 and had ten children. In order to matriculate at Trinity College, Cambridge and St John's, Oxford Prichard conformed to the Church of England. He studied the origin of the races of mankind and their development before Darwin and was known as the father of British ethnology and anthropology. He wrote treatises on the philology of Western languages, on insanity, on the nervous system and on Egyptian mythology. His *Natural History of Man* was much reprinted. He was a Fellow of the Royal Society and president of the Ethnological Society. His daughter Mary married the vicar of Sellack, Revd William Ley (qv). In 1841 after the death of his first wife, he married Emma Henrietta Ley, a relation of his son-in-law Revd Ley. Then, to further unite the families, Revd Ley and Mary's son Augustin (qv) married a cousin, Mary Sibella Ley. Prichard died in London on 23 December 1848 and was buried at Sellack, his son-in-law's church. Other Prichards remained in Ross as practising Quakers. James's younger brother Edward Prichard (1789-1822) was a Ross banker.

Prichard, Roger (fl.1658) was a glover in Worcester and travelled in Ireland where the family may have originated. He settled in Almeley Wootton in the 1660s. He had met Quakers in Montgomeryshire in 1658 and bought The Summer House in Almeley Wootton as a Meeting House for them – one of the earliest in the country. The Quaker elder Richard Davies writes of the Almeley Friends' meetings in his journal of 1669. The house remains a place where Quakers meet.

Prichard, Thomas (1765-1843) married Mary Lewis (1763-99), both Quakers of substance in Ross. He owned an ironworks in Bristol but kept a home in Ross where he retired in 1800. His obituary calls him 'The patriarch of Ross' and 'an ardent friend of education'.

Primrose, George, see under **William Lowe**

Prise, Gregory, the eldest son of the 11 children of Sir John Prise (qv, d.1555), married Mary, daughter of Humphrey Coningsby (qv, d.1559), who owned the church lands contiguous with the St Guthlac estate. He was MP for Hereford and mayor in 1573, 1576 and 1597, dying soon after.

Prise, John (also ap Rhys) (1502-55), humanist scholar, son of Rhys ap Gwilym ap Llywelyn of Brecon, was a Welsh antiquarian who traced his origins to the kings of Brycheiniog. He studied civil law at Oxford and the Middle Temple and came to the notice of Thomas Cromwell. He was a servant of Henry VIII, attending his wedding to Anne Boleyn, and was secretary of the Council in Wales and the Marches. He conveyed ecclesiastical property in the Marches into royal hands for Thomas Cromwell, collecting bargains for himself: he bought Brecon Priory with its valuable library and, in 1540, St Guthlac's Priory, off Commercial Street, Hereford and made his house from the conventual buildings. He was a

JP and knighted by Edward VI in 1547. An MP in Wales, he represented Hereford in the 1553 Parliament and became Sheriff of Hereford in 1554. He married Thomas Cromwell's niece and they had 11 children, including sons Gregory (qv) and Richard. In 1547 he wrote a treatise of advice to priests in Welsh *Yn y Lhyvyr hwnn.* He defended Arthurian legend in his *Historiae Britannicae Defensio* against Polydore Vergil's (qv) attack and his son Richard ensured it was published. He died on 15 October 1555 and left his divinity books to Hereford Cathedral. Another son, Sir John, sold manuscripts to Dr Dee (qv) on his visit in 1574.

Prise, John (*c.*1603-69), MP, was born at Brecon Priory, eldest son of Thomas Prise (d.1654) and Anne, daughter of William Rudhall (qv, d.1626) of Upton Bishop. He was the grandson of Sir John Prise's (qv, d.1555) second son Richard, and he married Mary, daughter of Sir John's eldest son Gregory (qv). His second wife, Anne Chute, brought Wistaston Court, Marden to the Prises. He renovated the 15th-century hall and hung it with family portraits, amongst them one of Joyce Andrews (qv). He was a JP in Breconshire and Herefordshire in 1624-45. During the Civil Wars he was a colonel in the Royalist army and considered one of the Nine Worthies of Herefordshire (see index). He lost much in fines and was poorly rewarded, dying in debt. The family fortunes never recovered.

Prise, John (1674-1738), MP, of Wistaston, Marden, son of Thomas (qv) and his second wife Mary Came, was educated at Magdalen College, Oxford. He was MP for Herefordshire in 1708-12, sponsored by James Scudamore (qv, d.1716) and Edward Harley (qv, d.1735) at different times. He married Elizabeth Prise, a second cousin. In 1712 he was made a commissioner of excise but was ejected at the Hanoverian succession and withdrew from political life. He died on 27 February 1738 leaving Wistaston to his daughter, the wife of Thomas Hayton. He was buried in the family vault of Wistaston Chapel which he had rebuilt in 1715. House and chapel are now ruins.

Prise, Thomas (1629-*c.*99), MP, was born at Wistaston Court, son of John Prise (d.1669, qv). He was JP for the county 1660-89 and MP for Herefordshire in 1661. He was imprisoned by Wroth Rogers (qv) for his part in Booth's Rising of 1659. His wives were reported to be Roman Catholic and he seems not to have been well treated at Court where enemies intrigued against him. Edward Harley (qv, d.1700) thought him a papist. In 1667 when receiver for Herefordshire he was arrested for unaccounted monies and was forced to sell much land to Paul Foley (qv, d.1699). Pepys saw him at the treasury with a hat of the latest fashion. Sir Herbert Prise (1605-78), Thomas's half-brother, was governor of Hereford in 1643 and fought at Naseby.

Pritchard, Edward (*c.*1783-1863), architect and surveyor of Tarrington, was employed by the Foleys (qv Emily Foley) as 'Head Builder' on their Stoke Edith estate 'for upwards of 60 years', as the inscription on his grave in Tarrington churchyard records, and was a man of 'integrity and uprightness'. He built the north aisle at Stoke Edith Church in 1835 and restored Weston Beggard Church in 1826. He died on 23 March 1863.

Pritchard, Thomas Farnolls (1723-77), architect, was born in Shrewsbury on 11 May 1723. He was apprenticed to his father as a joiner but built up an architectural practice in Shropshire and Herefordshire, tackling everything from ornamental details to the Iron Bridge across the Severn at Coalbrookdale (1777-9), the first to be built from cast iron. In Herefordshire he worked at Hill Court near Ross for the Clarke family in the 1740s. He built Brockhampton House near Bromyard for Bartholomew Barneby Lutley (qv) in *c.*1764 and worked at John Freeman's (qv, d.1801) house called Gaines nearby (Freeman had married Barneby's sister), and for another of Barneby's sisters at Suckley, Worcs. In the 1760s he was working at Croft Castle for Thomas Johnes (qv), who had bought it from Thomas Knight. Bishop Herbert Croft (qv) had recast it in a mediaevalising style and Pritchard, taking his cue from

this and perhaps from Shobdon Court, rebuilt the east front in the new gothick manner. The Blue Room (1765) and staircase remain of his work. R.P. Knight (qv), a relation of Johnes, consulted Pritchard about Downton Castle in 1772. Pritchard died on 23 December 1777 and is buried in St Julian's, Shrewsbury.

Prophete, John (*c.*1350-1416), Dean of Hereford 1393-1404, was from Carmarthenshire with family in the Hereford area. He was related to Sir John Oldcastle (qv) the Lollard and moved discreetly in Lollard circles himself. He was educated at Oxford, where he attached himself to William Courtenay (qv), later Bishop of Hereford. He held office under Richard II and his supplanter Henry IV, as secretary and keeper of the Privy Seal. He was a skilled administrator and an indispensable organiser and was made Dean of Hereford to sort out the muddle at Hereford diocese. He corrected abuses at St Katherine's Hospital in Ledbury and instituted responsible management there. He failed to become Bishop of Hereford although the income from all his benefices probably exceeded that of most sees. He was fond of Hereford and had intended to build a chapel for the parish of St John the Baptist (qv), the patron saint of the area in which the cathedral stood but died before he had a chance to do it. He became dean of the lucrative diocese in 1404. He was generous to his relatives and staff and liked by all, although a complaint was made against him by Bishop Trefnant (qv). He has been called the greatest of the mediaeval deans. He died in April 1416 and was buried in St Peter and Paul, Ringwood, Hampshire, one of his many livings, where his brass remains (see above).

Prosser, Richard (1747-1839), clergyman, was baptised on 26 July 1747 at Market Drayton, Shropshire. His father Humphrey

Prosser (1694-1781) and mother Eleanor Witherston (1708-79) are both buried in the church at St Margaret's where their gravestones can be seen. In 1826 Revd Dr Prosser bought Belmont House in Clehonger almost immediately upon the death of its previous owner John Matthews (qv, d.1826), living there and making many alterations, while continuing to visit Durham where he was canon. He died at Belmont on 8 October 1839 and was buried in All Saints, Clehonger where there is a memorial. His heir was his great-nephew Francis Wegg-Prosser (qv).

Pugin, Augustus Welby Northmore (1812-52), architect and designer, was born in Russell Square, London on 1 March 1812, the only child of Auguste Charles Pugin (1768-1832) and Catherine Welby (*c*.1772-1833). He had little formal education but learnt precociously at home, fascinated by mediaeval things. His other passions were the theatre and the sea. From 15 he was designing furnishings for George IV amongst others. In 1832 his first wife Anne died from puerperal fever leaving him with a baby daughter, and both his parents died soon after. He remarried to Louisa Burton, and leaving his baby with her set off in 1833 on a tour of the Wye Valley, visiting Tintern the year after Tennyson. He was looking for great gothic architecture but was disappointed to find Georgian dullness everywhere. Tintern was picturesque but dull when studied as architecture. At Hereford he found the cathedral Georgianised with Wyatt's execrable new west end and wood panels cladding the old walls within and the beautiful lady chapel full of old bookcases. He was impressed by the battered or sloped footings of the lady chapel though, and used the details when inventing his own Early English structures. The Church of England depressed him, and following the Catholic Emancipation Act of 1829 he became a Roman Catholic and found himself in demand for work on Catholic churches and presbyteries. His interiors at Barry's Palace of Westminster are his greatest achievement. There are examples of his and his sons' work in Herefordshire. Dean Merewether (qv) drew on Pugin for the choir

east window in his newly renovated cathedral. Pugin's designs, manufactured by his friend John Hardman (qv), show the Crucifixion, the Resurrection and the Ascension. It was later decided that the window was difficult to see in this position and it was moved to its present site in the south transept east clerestory. He designed stained glass angels and apostles for the aisle windows of St Peter's Church at Pudleston, made by Hardman, commissioned by Elias Chadwick (qv) of Pudleston Court in 1851, who was having the aisles rebuilt. In 1851, his last effective working year, he designed a brass cross for Uvedale T.S. Price at Yazor, also made by Hardman. He designed the apse window at Kilpeck in 1849, the year that Earl Somers (qv John Somers Cocks, d.1852) brought in J.G. Crace (qv) to furnish a gothic dining room in Eastnor Castle. Crace recommended Pugin, who designed the room with a great chandelier and an elaborate fireplace above which was displayed the family tree and portraits of the earl and countess in mediaeval dress. The table, chairs and sideboard are also by Pugin, and made by Crace. Pugin was unaware that Eastnor was of modern Regency date or that it had been built by the despised Smirke, and made the fireplace for massive mediaeval walls when Eastnor's were fairly flimsy. This caused him and Crace trouble and expense, but he was proud of this major work and exhibited the complete room at the Great Exhibition of 1851. The scheme remains unaltered in the castle, one of only two such schemes to survive. Pugin's second wife died and he married Jane, one of the Herefordshire Knills (qv). The energy and anxiety of his unremitting work exhausted him and he became insane and died on 14 September 1852 aged 40. He was buried in the chantry of St Augustine's, the church which he had built by his house at Ramsgate. It was his example and writings, with Ruskin, that changed British Art and Craft more than anything else. He left a young widow and eight children.

Pugin, Edward Welby (1834-75), architect, the eldest son of A.W.N. Pugin (qv), took over his father's practice, aged 18. Later his brother, Peter Paul Pugin (1851-1904), son of his father's third wife Jane, joined him and they traded as Pugin & Pugin. Wegg-Prosser (qv) commissioned him to build the new abbey church and buildings at Belmont and the splendid Church of St Michael and All Angels was erected at Belmont in 1854-6, but building work continued for another 30 years and the crossing tower was completed in 1882 by Peter Paul Pugin. In 1880 the firm made the monument for its first bishop (qv Thomas Brown), and in 1898 Peter Paul Pugin built the beautiful small Church of St Ethelbert's in Leominster's Bargates.

Purchas: An established Fownhope family. In 1810 John Purchas, son of the merchant Nathaniel Purchas, was apprenticed for five years to surgeon Thomas Paytherus (qv) in London for £410.

Purchas, William Henry (1823-1903), was born in Broad Street, Ross, the son of Thomas Whittlesey Purchas, wine merchant and brewer. William helped found a Sunday School at Ross and was secretary of the Church Missionary Society. He worked in the family business until his younger brothers were able to take over. He married a Frances Williams of Cheltenham. Purchas went up to Durham University and was ordained. He was interested in natural history from his earliest days, particularly ferns. Revd Purchas was a member of the Hereford Literary and Philosophical Society and it was after his lecture on Herefordshire ferns that the idea of a more scientific society was discussed, to become the Woolhope Naturalists' Field Club, of which he became an honorary member. He and his friend Augustin Ley's (qv) botanising led in 1889 to the publication of *The Flora of Herefordshire* by the Woolhope Club, and a Herefordshire bramble, *Rubus purchasianus*, was named after him. The geological notes were the contribution of Revd W.S. Symonds (qv), from whose advanced views he distanced himself in the preface. Purchas corresponded with leading botanists and was a member of the Botanical Society of London. His collections were presented to the British Museum.

Putta (d.688) was the first Bishop of the Magonsaete, or the Western Hecani, and later Hereford. A legend has King Gerren Llyngesoc of Dumnonia building a cathedral at Caerfawydd, as Hereford was called in the 6th century. Putta was Bishop of Rochester when King Ethelred (qv) of Mercia ravaged Kent in 674; Rochester Cathedral was burnt and Putta fled into exile. Bede in his *History of the English Church* says that Putta was offered land for a church amongst the Western Hecani by Seaxwulf, Bishop of the huge diocese of Lichfield and this may be the origin of the see of Hereford. Putta was a pious man with an interest in church music and taught the use of Gregorian tones introduced into England by St Augustine. His name appears in contemporary charters but some say there are two Puttas. He heads the traditional list of the Anglo-Saxon bishops of Hereford, most of whom are otherwise unknown. For the full list of bishops, see the index.

Pye: A Herefordshire gentry family who claimed descent from William the Conqueror's Viking mercenaries. In the mid 15th century a John Pye of Saddlebow, Much Dewchurch married Elizabeth, daughter of Sir John (II) Skidmore (qv) and fought in Henry VI's French wars.

Pye, Robert (1585-1662), younger brother of Walter (qv), was baptised on 24 March 1585 at Much Dewchurch and educated at the Middle Temple. He and Walter entered the service of the Duke of Buckingham and Robert was made an auditor of the Exchequer, a profitable office. He was knighted in 1621, bought an estate in Buckinghamshire and married Mary Croker. He sat in Parliament through the 1630s, retained his seat in the Long Parliament of 1640 and joined his old friend Sir Robert Harley (qv, d.1656) on his committee for the destruction of idolatrous church images. With Harley he was excluded in Pride's Purge of 1648 and his estate suffered damage during the Civil War. He conformed to the restored monarchy and died at Westminster on 20 May 1662.

Pye, Walter (1571-1635), lawyer, was born on 1 October 1571 at The Mynde, Much Dewchurch (anciently called Ty'r Groes). He was the eldest child of Roger Pye (d.1591) and Bridget (d.1624), the daughter of Thomas Kyrle (qv, fl.1500) of Walford. He was educated at St John's, Oxford and the Middle Temple and called to the bar in 1597. In 1602 he married Joan (d.1625), daughter of Col William Rudhall (qv, d.1651) and they had 15 children. One of their daughters, Alice, married Sir Henry Lingen (qv), and another, Frances (1613-1701), married first Roger Vaughan of Bredwardine (qv, d.1643), then Edward Cornewall (qv, fl.1650). His sister Joanna married Thomas Beale and their son was

the scientist John Beale (qv). Pye profited from his legal position and gained advancement from aristocratic patrons like Charles Howard, Earl of Nottingham and George Villiers, Marquess of Buckingham, becoming Lord Chief Justice. He was knighted in 1621 and was attorney of the Court of Wards and Liveries. He represented Herefordshire in the Parliaments of 1626 and 1628-9. Pye was a covetous, partial and nepotistic attorney and there were complaints and once even an attack. He died on 25 December 1635, 'the devil's Christmas Pye', contemporaries said, and was buried in St David's, Much Dewchurch, where he is shown on a monument (sculpted by Samuel Baldwin, qv) with his wife and 13 of their children (see above). His eldest son, also Walter (1610-59), took over his parliamentary seat. The Pyes bought Pembridge Castle.

Q R

Quarre, Bernard (d.1252), prior of Champagne, was Bishop Peter de Aquablanca's (qv) chaplain and provost of St Peter's in Hereford. During the bishop's absence in 1252 Hereford citizens broke into the bishop's chapel of St Mary Magdalen where he was saying mass and murdered him. He was buried in St Peter's and transferred to St Guthlac's (qv) Priory when it was granted a new site outside Bishop's or Byster's Gate.

Quillinan, Edward (1791-1851), author and poet, was born in Oporto, Portugal on 12 August 1791. He married Jemima (1793-1822), daughter of Sir Egerton Brydges (qv under William Egerton). Her mother Jemima was the daughter of William Egerton (qv), both families with strong Herefordshire connections. Quillinan had tried to assist his father-in-law Sir Egerton with his affairs. He had got entangled in fraud (Trust funds had been misappropriated) and was only acquitted with expense and difficulty. The Quillinan family moved to Rydal where they were neighbours of the Wordsworths (qv) and de Quincey. His wife Jemima was committed as a lunatic after the birth of their second child, and on discharge was fatally burned when her nightdress caught fire. Quillinan in his grief travelled widely but falling in love with Wordsworth's daughter Dora (1804-47), returned and married her in 1841 – initially against her father's wishes. They often visited Dora's maternal relatives, the Hutchinsons (qv under Wordsworth), at Brinsop Court. He died at Loughrigg Holme, Rydal, on 8 July 1851.

Radegund (*c.*520-86) was a Frankish princess who founded the monastery of the Holy Cross at Poitiers and was canonised in the 9th century. Richard de Clare dedicated a Benedictine nunnery at Usk to her and St Mary Magdalen in the 12th century. The 14th-century chapter house at Ledbury Church was dedicated to her. Her feast day is 13 August.

Ralph (fl.1135-58), first Dean of Hereford, was appointed by Bishop Robert de Béthune (qv) to see to the daily running of the cathedral, the rebuilding of which was completed in his time. It was consecrated at a high mass at Whitsun 1138 at which King Stephen (qv) was seated on the chair known as Stephen's throne, wearing his crown. Subsequently there was civil war between Stephen and Matilda and anarchy in the area. The cathedral was fortified by earthworks when Hereford was taken by Geoffrey Talbot (qv, d.1140) and Miles of Gloucester (qv). After Stephen had evicted them, Ralph effected a restoration and sponsored the combining of St Peter's with St Guthlac's (qqv), which had found its position within the castle precincts untenable. Ralph was said to have been rebellious and to have been deposed by the Pope but his tenure seems to have been a long one.

Ralph de Mantes (d.1057), Earl of Hereford, was the second son of Drogo, count of Amiens and the Vexin, and Godgifu, daughter of Ethelred II and Emma. When his father died on pilgrimage to Jerusalem in 1035, his mother remarried to Eustace, Count of Boulogne (d.*c.*1087). Ralph with other Normans came to England in 1041 in the train of his uncle Edward the Confessor and was given lands in the Sudeley area. On Swein Godwinson's (qv Swein) disgrace the large area he held was broken up and part, including Hereford, granted to Ralph. Ralph gave land to vassals like Osbern Pentecost (qv) at Ewyas, to Richard fitz Scrope (qv under Richard Scrob) in the north of the county and Thruxton in the Archenfield to Robert Fitz Wymarch. In 1052 Ralph built a wooden fort by the Wye at Hereford, enclosing the ancient priory of St Guthlac within the perimeter. Earl Ælfgar (qv), bent on revenge after his exile, invaded Herefordshire in 1055 in alliance with the Welsh Prince Gruffydd ap Llywelyn (qv).

Ralph called out the Herefordshire fyrd, or levy, but he mounted them in the Norman way when they were accustomed to fight on foot and they fled, leaving Hereford undefended. Ælfgar and the Welsh sacked and burnt the city with its new cathedral and Ralph's castle. Hereford didn't recover from this for half a century. The Godwin (qv) family regarded Herefordshire as their own fief and mounted punitive reprisals against the invaders, earning Harold, the future king (qv), the sobriquet *Strenuus* to Ralph's *Timidus*. Ralph died on 21 December 1057, leaving his heir Harold de Ewyas (qv). He was buried in Peterborough Abbey.

Randall Wells, Albert (1877-1942), an architect from Hastings, was the resident clerk of works for Lethaby's (qv) All Saints Church (1901-2) at Brockhampton-by-Ross. Lethaby allowed his clerk and builders freedom to develop the building with a minimum of plans, in the Arts and Crafts style, to the consternation of the patron Mrs Foster (qv). Wells went on to build St Edward at Kempley (1903-4) across the border in Gloucs for Lord Beauchamp, also using direct labour and local materials.

Ranig (1016-42) was a Norse follower of King Cnut, who made him Earl of Mercia. His deputy in the county was Edwin (qv). He was present at the shire gemot or court that sat under Bishop Æthelstan (qv) at Aylton probably in the 1030s (qv Thurkil).

Rankin, James Reginald Lea (1871-1931), 2nd Baronet, Sir James S. Rankin's (qv) eldest son, was educated at Eton and Christ Church, Oxford and called to the bar. He married Nest Rice, daughter of Lord Dynevor. Sir Reginald, a noted eccentric, was a JP and Deputy Lieutenant for Herefordshire, assistant private secretary to the Secretary of State for the Colonies in 1903-4 and a war correspondent. He fought in the Boer War and wrote *A Subaltern's Letters to his Wife* (1901) about his experiences. In 1910 he commissioned Brian Hatton (qv) to paint his portrait with Dervish, his hunter. He also served with the 1st battalion Herefordshire Regiment. He separated from his wife and was estranged from his second son Niall. When Niall wanted to marry, the bride's father, the 12th Earl Stair of Wigtown, insisted on a reconciliation. On meeting his son's proposed bride, Lady Jean Dalrymple-Hamilton, Sir Reginald was so enchanted with her that he left the couple everything. Sir James and Nest's first son was Sir Hubert Charles Rhys Rankin, 3rd Baronet (1899-1988).

Rankin, James S. (1842-1915), 1st Baronet and politician, was born on Christmas Day 1842, the eldest son of Robert Rankin, a wealthy timber merchant and shipowner from Scotland. James read natural sciences at Trinity College, Cambridge. He married Annie Laura Bushell (1844-1920) and they had four sons and four daughters. His father gave the couple the manor of Bryngwyn, Much Dewchurch as a wedding present. Rankin chose Kempson (qv) to rebuild the house and, liking his work, got him the prestigious commission for Hereford's new library and museum opposite the cathedral in Broad Street. Rankin was the prime mover of this project, buying the site and presenting it to the

council in 1871. The building went up in 1872-3 and cost £8,000, most of which came from Rankin. He was a prominent member of the Woolhope Naturalists' Field Club, president in 1868 and 1908, and made it a condition, still met, that the club should have permanent premises in the library. The librarian and curator was D.R. Chapman (qv). The library's external decoration reflects Rankin's love of zoology and is covered with terracotta birds and beasts; he gave papers to the Woolhope Club on zoological subjects. In 1892 he commissioned C.R. Ashbee and the Guild of Handicraft to supply interior decoration for an extension to Bryngwyn as a 21st birthday present for his son Reginald. Rankin was Conservative MP for Leominster for 30 years from 1880-1912 (with a four year break 1906-10 when a Liberal candidate was elected). He was High Sheriff of the county and chief steward of Hereford and in 1898 was created baronet. He was co-founder of the library at Wormelow and a governor of Orcop School. He also served on Herefordshire County Council and as chairman of the education committee lost a battle with local teachers who wanted a proper salary scale. Whilst he built new housing for workers on his estate, he opposed farmworkers' efforts to raise their income when they formed a union in 1912. The Rankin Constitutional Club, in Corn Square, Leominster, is named after him. He commissioned the large stained glass window in the south nave aisle of Hereford Cathedral from Powells & Co. (qv John Hardman Powell), showing King Charles (qv) at the retaking of Hereford in 1645 with many contemporary worthies. He died on 17 April 1915.

Raper, Robert William (1842-1915), university teacher, of Hoe Court, Colwall was born on 9 March 1842. He was educated at Cheltenham College and Balliol where he was a brilliant classics scholar. He was elected to a scholarship at Trinity College where he became bursar and vice president. He founded the first university employment agency. He was a neighbour of Stephen Ballard (qv) at Colwall and with him halted building on the Malvern Hills, setting up the Conservators with an Act of 1884 and presenting land to them. He died on 15 July 1915 and was buried at St James, Colwall.

Rapson, Edward James (1861-1937), student of Sanskrit, was born at Leicester on 12 May 1861. His father, Revd Edward Rapson, was an organist with a music school at 53 New Street, Ledbury and later in Oakland House. He and his wife Eleanor taught at the school attended by Edward and their other children. In around 1880 Revd Rapson became vicar of West Bradley, Somerset and the family moved there. Edward studied classics at St John's College, Cambridge and specialised in Sanskrit. He married Ellen Daisy Allen from his father's congregation. He worked on Indian coins at the British Museum and was Professor of Sanskrit at London University and for 30 years at Cambridge. He was a contributor to the *Dictionary of National Biography* and published books on Indian history. He died at St John's College.

Rawlinson, Richard (1690-1755), antiquarian, was born on 3 January 1690. His father, a staunch Jacobite, was a vintner and Lord Mayor of London. Richard was educated at St Paul's, Eton and St John's College, Oxford. He and a brother collected books and manuscripts and studied Anglo-Saxon. At Oxford he was ordained a non-juring priest, ministering to other non-jurors such as Thomas Hearne (qv, d.1735) and William Brome (qv) of Eau Withington. He made a tour of the Continent visiting the Pretender's Court and studying at Utrecht, Leiden and Padua. On his return he was consecrated a non-juring bishop. He travelled in Britain making antiquarian and topographical notes and recording inscriptions. He brought to print the unfinished work of other antiquarians like Elias Ashmole, John Aubrey (qv), Hannibal Baskerville (qv), Anthony Wood and Thomas Dingley (qv), whose manuscripts of the antiquities of Herefordshire he organised and rewrote as the *History and Antiquities of the City and Cathedral Church of Hereford* (1717). Describing his own visit to the cathedral, he found it covered in the scaffolding of Bishop Bisse's (qv) modernising works. He died on 6 April 1755; his heart was placed in the urn of his memorial at St John's College and his body in St Giles' Church, Oxford. He bequeathed all his historical material to the Bodleian Library and endowed the Rawlinsonian Chair in Anglo-Saxon at Oxford University.

Reavely, Thomas (d.1904) JP, High Sheriff of Herefordshire in 1867 and Deputy Lieutenant, bought Kinnersley Castle from a Mr Clarke *c.*1855 and had John Clayton (qv) make alterations. With it came the living of Kinnersley and he made his relative, Francis, rector. He married Johanna Stiefvater from Hamburg where he had business connections. Their daughter Minna (1851-1933) married George Bodley (qv) who was working at Llangrove nearby and they had a son, George Hamilton Bodley (b.1874). After Bodley's death in 1907 Minna married a Capt. Alan Monypenny.

Reavely, Thomas George Wood (1852-1924), was born on 17 October 1852, the only son of Thomas (qv) and Johanna. He was educated at Trinity College, Cambridge and the Inner Temple, making his money in the Stock Exchange. He married Veronica Stammers (b.1863) in 1889 and they had three sons and three daughters. In the 20th century the Reavely family leased Kinnersley Castle to a series of tenants including a Belgian hospital and Major Davey (qv), eventually selling it to Lord Brockett, who lived there during the Second World War. Reavely died in 1924 at Brighton but is buried at Kinnersley.

Rebecca, Biagio (1735-1808) was an Italian artist who decorated Adam's and Wyatt's (qqv) buildings in a neo-classical style. Adam recommended him to Henry Holland (qv), the architect of Berrington Hall, and in the 1780s Rebecca painted roundels of English authors on the dining room ceiling at Berrington, and a central one of *The Feast of the Gods*, imitating antique bas reliefs. Rebecca was elected ARA in 1771 and granted a pension from the Royal Academy in his impoverished later years.

Redstreak is a cider apple which was developed by Lord John Scudamore (qv, d.1671) in the 17th century by crossing Herefordshire varieties with stock brought back to Holme Lacy from France. John Beale (qv) experimented with it on his Cobhall estate in the 1650s. John Evelyn (qv) in *Pomona* celebrates 'the famous *Red-strake* of Herefordshire, a pure Wilding within the memory of some now living, surnamed the Scudamore's Crab'. It was the premier Herefordshire cider apple and with stronger glass bottles and better corks it was drunk nationally. In the 1720s the Duke of Chandos (qv James Brydges, d.1744) was sending bottles to his agent in Genoa. T.A. Knight (qv) wonders in his *Pomona Herefordiensis* whether 'excellent cider was ever made, in any other country, previous to the existence of this apple'. The Redstreak is much mentioned in literature: William Shenstone writes:

Is not the Redstreak's future juice
The source of your delight profound
Where Ariconium pours her gems profuse
Purpling a whole horizon round?

John Phillips (qv) says in *Cyder*

Let every Tree in every Garden own
The Redstreak as supreme; whose pulpous Fruit
With Gold irradiate, and Vermillian shines.

The Redstreak Inn stood on the north side of High Town in Hereford. It is shown on Isaac Taylor's (qv) 1757 map but had been demolished before John Wood's map of 1836. The Buttermarket was built on the site but its cellars remain below. The popularity of cider suffered from the Cider Tax of 1763 to pay for wars and the Redstreak gave way to other varieties although enthusiasts still grow the Redstreak for cider in the county. Lord Scudamore's contribution and the varieties of Redstreak are discussed and illustrated in *Herefordshire Pomona*, produced by Robert Hogg and Henry Bull (qqv) and published by the Woolhope Club.

Reed: Oliver Reed of New Court, Lugwardine married Margaret, daughter and co-heiress of Richard Beauchamp (qv, d.1503), 2nd Baron Powick, in the 1400s, and lived at Bronsil Castle. They were troubled by Beauchamp's unquiet spirit, unable to rest while his remains were scattered in a foreign land. (The legend was that he had died fighting in Italy – qv Richard de Beauchamp, d.1503.) In the early 17th century Gabriel Reed had his ghost exorcized on the advice of Dr Allen (qv), who told him to collect the bones in a box, which Aubrey (qv) later saw labelled 'Lord Beauchamp's Bones'. Treasure was said to lie buried under the castle, guarded by a raven. In 1637 Elizabeth Reed (d.1667) of New Court, Lugwardine married Thomas Traherne (not the famous mystical writer, but one of the Trahernes of Middle Court, Lugwardine). During the Civil War Bronsil Castle was damaged by a band of Royalists. The Buck brothers (qv) drew the castle in 1771 when Thomas Reed was proprietor and showed an imposing gatehouse with symmetrical walls and towers. The estate was sold to Thomas Sommers Cocks (qv) in 1774, and over the next 200 years Bronsil Castle almost totally disappeared except for the moats and part of a gatehouse which collapsed only recently.

Reinhelm (d.1115), Bishop of Hereford 1107-15, was a priest at Rochester and chancellor to Matilda, Henry I's queen. Henry agreed to Reinhelm's candidacy for bishop but Archbishop Anselm refused to accept him as coming from lay recommendation and there was a five-year delay while peace was made. Reinhelm completed and dedicated the east end of the cathedral in which was the high altar, and is consequently described in charters as the founder. He reorganised the college of secular canons attached to the cathedral. The east wall of the south transept gives an idea of what work of his time looked like and capitals of an early date stand behind the reredos. He was one of the founders of Llanthony Priory

in the neighbouring diocese of Llandaff. He died of gout in October 1115 and is buried in the north choir aisle of the cathedral, where his early 14th-century effigy can be seen.

Repton, Humphry (1752-1818), landscape designer, was born on 21 April 1752 at Bury St Edmunds. He went to the Netherlands for a commercial education, mixed with gentry and sketched in watercolour. He met John Nash (qv) whilst both were struggling and they worked up a lucrative partnership in Wales, though it later soured. Repton, unlike Lancelot Brown (qv), did not concern himself with the practicalities of earth-moving but produced ideas in his coveted *Red Book*, with its before and after panels, a work of art intended for display. Nash introduced Repton to Sir Uvedale Price and Richard Payne Knight (qqv) who advised him and brought him contracts in the county. Repton saw Foxley as less romantic and neater than Downton and thought Knight's idea of the sublime too wild. Between 1790-5 he worked in Herefordshire on some six estates. In 1790 he met Edward Foley (qv) and produced a *Red Book* for Stoke Edith Park in 1792. He also produced one for Garnons, the Cotterells' estate at Mansell Gamage (qv John Geers Cotterell),

showing James Wyatt's (qv) proposed but never built house. Sufton Park at Mordiford is another estate for which a *Red Book* survives, making much of its situation above the Wye and Lugg. George Cornewall (qv, d.1819) employed Repton and Nash at Moccas where Brown (qv) had landscaped the deer park and Repton laid out the lawns around the house. He also designed the riverside gardens at New Weir for William Parry (qv, fl.1788). His standard rate was five guineas a day and throughout the 1790s this brought him in both a large income and access to the houses of the wealthy. At his peak he worked at Woburn and the Prince Regent's Brighton Pavilion. Both Price and Knight published poems criticising his work and Repton responded with his beautifully illustrated *Sketches and Hints on Landscape Gardening*. Commissions declined with the Napoleonic Wars and he fell from fashion. Jane Austen mentions him slightingly in *Mansfield Park* but his ideas were popular throughout Europe. He designed a rose garden to be planted around his own grave in the churchyard of Aylsham Church, Norfolk and died of a heart attack on 24 March 1818.

Reynolds, Thomas and **Baylis, James** (18th century) were rioters caught up in the movement of protest against the exaction of tolls on the Turnpike Roads. Such rioters were known as 'the daughters of Rebecca' from *Genesis* 24:60. Toll gates with a house for the keeper had been erected all over Britain to provide revenue for the maintenance of roads. They were immensely unpopular and rioters disguised in women's clothes and blackened faces attacked the gates. The death penalty for such an offence was introduced in 1734; nevertheless a Turnpike Riot occurred in Ledbury in September 1735 and gates were destroyed. Arrests were made and local men Reynolds and Baylis were held at Justice John Skippe's (qv, d.1764) house, Upper Hall. That night a mob tried to free the prisoners and a battle raged through Ledbury. Skippe read the riot act, issued firearms and fired on the crowd, which eventually dispersed. Baylis and Reynolds were sent to London, where on Monday 5 July 1736 they were sentenced to death. Baylis, who it was acknowledged might have been swept up into the affray, was reprieved but Reynolds had been arrested with blackened face and a woman's dress which, a witness said, he had bought in Ledbury just before the riot. It was the element of disguise that led to his conviction. Reynolds was hanged but revived and was carried off in his coffin by the crowd on a triumphal tour of public houses, which finally killed him. Two other men who were taken into custody, William Bithell and William Morgan, were hanged at Worcester on 9 April 1736.

Rhys ap Gruffydd (*c.*1132-97), Prince of Deheubarth, was the youngest son of Gruffydd ap Rhys (d.1137) and Gwenllian (d.1136), daughter of Gruffydd ap Cynan. With his brothers he retook Ceredigion and part of Powys from the Normans, and with the agreement of Henry II became ruler of Deheubarth until his death 42 years later. In 1186 after the Welsh had raided into Herefordshire Rhys supervised the restoration of peace, celebrating at a banquet in Hereford which is described by Gerald of Wales (qv): sitting amongst his Marcher lord enemies, he charmed them with his wit and courtesy. When Gerald and Archbishop Baldwin travelled to Wales raising troops for the Third Crusade Gerald says he showed them every kindness.

At the end of his life his unruly sons, in concert with William (III) de Briouze and Roger (II) Mortimer (qqv), took some of his castles, but Rhys in a last campaign captured his sons, defeated Mortimer and sacked Briouze's stronghold, Painscastle, at the Battle of Radnor (1196). He was a great patron of poets and musicians and his festival at Cardigan Castle in 1176 is the first recorded eisteddfod. He was the subject of much praise but also of satire in Walter Map's (qv) *Of the King Apollonides* in which Map acknowledges his dislike of the prince but praises him for his excellence and magnanimity. He also features in Hue de Roteland's (qv) *Ipomedon*. Rhys died on 28 April 1197 and was buried in St David's Cathedral. His eldest son and heir Gruffydd ap Rhys II (d.1201) married Matilda daughter of William III de Briouze (qv).

Ricardo, David (1772-1823), MP and economist, was the author of *Principles of Political Economy* (1817). He was present as a supporter of Joseph Hume (qv) and as a Herefordshire freeholder at the public dinner given in honour of Hume in Hereford in 1821, presided over

by E.B. Clive (qv). He spoke on the need for radical reform of boroughs like Leominster and Weobley, for the extension of the franchise and the use of the secret ballot. He was a magistrate in Hereford and Gloucester and died at his house in Bromesberrow. In 1814 his son David bought the manor of Brinsop from the Danseys (qv Richard Dansey).

Richard, Dean of Hereford (*c.*1186-1200), presided with Bishop William de Vere (qv) over a circle of brilliant canons, scholars, mathematicians and philosophers at Hereford and over the rebuilding of the eastern parts of the Norman cathedral. He commissioned a life of St Ethelbert (qv) from Gerald of Wales (qv).

Richard I (1157-99), Cœur de Lion, King of England 1189-99, was born on 6 September 1157 at Oxford, a son of Henry II (qv) and Queen Eleanor. Richard was well educated in Latin, wrote poetry, composed music and appreciated Muslim culture. But he knew no English and was a savage warlord, laying waste parts of western France. Soon after his accession, in order to raise funds for a crusade to relieve the Latin Kingdom of Jerusalem he sold 'Hereford in Wales' its freedom from feudal control in a charter dated 9 October 1189. The citizens were to pay him £40 p.a. and take charge of the fortifications and they would be free from royal interference. Richard's three lions feature in the city's arms, which were granted by Charles I (qv), one of only two cities to use a sovereign's arms. Richard was captured returning from the crusades and money to pay his ransom was collected from his lands, including Hereford. At his early death his younger brother John (qv) succeeded him.

Richard II (1367-1400), King of England 1377-1399, was born on 6 January 1367, the son of Edward the Black Prince (qv Edward of Woodstock) and Joan 'the fair maid of Kent'. The death of his older brother, then of his father and finally of his grandfather Edward III, brought Richard to the throne at the age of 10. He was autocratic, lavish and reliant on favourites, and disaffection built up, finding head in the Peasants' Revolt of 1381 when the 14-year-old king bravely negotiated with the rebels and defused the uprising. A few years later unpopular favourites were arraigned by a group known as the Appellants, which included his cousin Henry Bolingbroke (qv Henry IV), and Richard's chamber knights were executed or exiled. Richard was deeply angered by this encroachment on his prerogative and went on a 'gyration' or progress to build support in the country. He stayed at Hereford and built up a power base in Wales and the Marches. John of Gaunt (qv) wanted the use of the royal castle at Hereford of which he was governor and had started restoration work there, but Richard refused him. The Priory of St Guthlac drew income from Hereford Castle's mill for a thrice weekly mass in the castle chapel and Richard ensured that the prior maintained this. He also made sure there was clear access from the castle gate across the moat to the north into Castle Street. In Richard's time this was one of the centres of mediaeval Hereford and the site of a corn market. He granted timber for the repair of Hereford Bridge. In 1383 Richard ordained that the chief officer of Hereford be called mayor and be addressed as 'right worshipful' rather than the more usual 'worshipful'. Richard confronted his opponents with a force drawn from Herefordshire and the Marches but was defeated in 1387. John of Gaunt, returning with his son Henry, helped Richard reassert himself, exiling and executing his opponents. Henry was rewarded with the earldom of Hereford but was soon again in disfavour with Richard and exiled in 1398. Gaunt died in 1399 and Richard disinherited the absent Henry, giving him reason to return to secure his own. Richard was in Ireland when he landed and England quickly fell to Henry. Richard's army deserted and Henry held him at Conwy Castle, charging him with misgovernment. Richard abdicated and probably starved to death, dying on 14 February 1400. He was buried in a sumptuous tomb in Westminster Abbey next to his much loved Queen Anne. There had been no children and he regarded Edmund (V) Mortimer (qv), Earl of March, as his successor. Sixty years later the Duke of York, a descendant of Mortimer, asserted his right to the throne, and his son became King Edward IV.

Richard of Haldingham, (d.1278) was the creator of Hereford Cathedral's Mappa Mundi, which says in the lower left corner in Norman

French 'Richard of Holdingham [sic] or of Lafford made and drew this history', asking us to pray for him. This Richard may have been the Richard de Bello (i.e. from Battle near Hastings) who was a non-residentiary prebend of Hereford and known to Bishop Swinfield (qv). He, or perhaps a relative, was a prebendary of Haldingham, Lincoln, which is clearly shown on the map with its towers and a street going up the hill. Hereford and the River Wye appear to be later additions to the map. Bishop Swinfield was connected with Lincoln and may have commissioned the Mappa there. It must have been made in the later 13th century as King Edward's new castles at Conwy and Caernarfon are shown. It came to the cathedral at roughly the same time as the inception of the cult of its new saint Thomas de Cantilupe (qv). The Mappa is an encyclopaedia of current knowledge not only of geography but of history, legend and theology, amassed perhaps by Richard from other *mappae* and sources like Orosius who is mentioned in text on the map. Distant places are populated with terrifying peoples and beasts like the sciapod sheltering beneath its huge foot, the anthropophagi eating victims, and the seductive mermaid. Classical legend and scripture coexist, for example Jason's golden fleece and the Cross in Jerusalem. The map was an object of veneration as much as study, housed in a box that opened into a triptych made from dated Herefordshire oaks. On the inside of the doors two angels flank the world, while outside when the doors were closed there was an Annunciation. The doors have disappeared but the back of the box is shown by the Mappa. At the top of the Mappa is the Last Judgement similar to the slightly later stained glass in Tewkesbury Abbey. Christ the Judge is urged to have mercy by his mother, who bares her breasts. The Mappa has survived many vicissitudes. At the Reformation it was hidden under the floor in Bishop Audley's chantry chapel, and it has recently escaped being sold, along with the whole of the chained library, through the munificence of Sir John Paul Getty jr. and housed in its present home.

Richer, John (fl.1800), acrobat and dancer, was a famous tightrope act at Sadler's Wells. He came to Hereford in 1796 to perform at John Boles Watson's (qv) Hereford Theatre where he fell in love with Watson's daughter Louisa. They married in 1800 and moved to Stroud, Gloucestershire where Richer managed Watson's theatre.

Roaring Meg, see under **Meg**

Robinson, Charles John (1833-98), antiquarian clergyman, was a son of Charles Frederick Robinson and Eleanor Rocke of Ashcott, near Glastonbury. After ordination he held London curacies and became domestic chaplain to the Earl of Caithness. In 1865 he was given the rectory of St Nicholas, Norton Canon by his friend Dean Richard Dawes (qv). Here his wife died in childbirth and at the same time he lost both parents; as a distraction he took up local history and wrote *The Castles of Herefordshire and Their Lords* (1867) and *The Mansions and Manors of Herefordshire* (1873) with sketches of some of the sites by Lady Frances Vernon-Harcourt (qv). Both books, recording the history of Herefordshire in terms of its proprietors, their pedigrees and biography, were printed by James Hull of High Town, Hereford. He also wrote 18 notices for the *Dictionary of National Biography*. As the parsonage at Norton Canon was dilapidated his parishioners raised money for William Chick (qv) to renovate it while Robinson stayed at Harewood. He was a friend of Charles Darwin and corresponded with him after the publication of *On the Origin of Species*. He was a member of the Woolhope Club and its president in 1875. In 1877 he moved to Hackney, marrying Emma Crocker with whom he had four daughters.

Robinson, Henry Crabb (1775-1867), diarist, was born in Bury St Edmunds, Suffolk. He was a journalist for the *Times*, one of the founders of the University of London and a practising barrister, and is remembered for the journals he kept recording the sayings of contemporary writers. He visited Coleridge, Southey, Blake, Lamb and others, visited the Hutchinsons with the Wordsworths (qv) at Brinsop Court, and went to see the Wye, a fashionable tourist venue, calling on John Thelwall (qv) in his retreat at Llyswen, where he lost a shoe in a peat bog and had to buy a new pair in Hereford.

Rodd, James Rennell (1858-1941), 1st Baron Rodd, was a politician and poet. The Rodds lived at Foxley until 1679 when Lucy, daughter of Robert Rodd, married Robert Price (qv, d.1732) to whom she brought the estate. James was born on 9 November 1858, the son of James Rennell Rodd of The Rodd near Presteigne, and Cornwall. He was educated at Balliol College, Oxford where he was a friend of Oscar Wilde. He married Lilias Guthrie (d.1951) in 1894 and they had four sons and two daughters. He had various ambassadorial posts and published books of verse. From 1928 to 1934 he was MP for Marylebone. He became Baron Rennell in 1933 and died on 26 July 1941.

Rodney, George Brydges (1719-92), 1st Lord Rodney, admiral, was a family friend of Thomas Harley (qv, d.1804) and frequently visited him at the newly built Berrington Hall. A naval hero, he was victorious at sea against the American rebels and the Spanish. He married Jane Compton, and their son George, 2nd Lord Rodney (1753-1802), married Harley's second daughter Anne (1758-1840). At Harley's death Anne was a widow and her son George, 3rd Lord Rodney, inherited Berrington. The dining room is hung with paintings by Thomas Luny (qv) of Admiral Rodney's naval victories and outside are brass cannon taken from Spanish men-of-war. Eye Court was used as a vicarage by Revd Henry Rodney, vicar of Eye in the 19th century. In 1901 the 7th Lord Rodney sold Berrington to Frederick Cawley, who, in 1957 as Lord Cawley transferred Berrington to the National Trust in lieu of death duties. Eye passed to Christopher Sandford of the Golden Cockerel Press.

Roger fitz Miles, see under **Miles**

Roger of Hereford (fl.1178-98), mathematician and astronomer, was called *Infans* or *Puer* (the child) by his contemporaries. He had studied astronomy at Toledo and was familiar with the new science and Arabic ideas. He was one of the circle of intellectuals that made Hereford a centre for science in England in the 12th century. In 1178 he compiled a set of influential astronomical tables based on the meridian for Hereford and witnessed charters there. He calculated the church calendar for Gilbert Foliot (qv) using Arabic sources, made mathematical improvements to the calculation of horoscopes and wrote on astrology and alchemy. He did much to further the study of the mathematical sciences in England and may have been responsible for attracting Robert Grosseteste (qv) to the bishop's household in Hereford.

Rogers, George (fl.1845-67) of Worcester, stained glass manufacturer, made the Pyndar windows in Ledbury Chapter House, the glass in the transepts and south aisle in St Peter's Bromyard, the stained glass at St Guthlac, Little Cowarne and some glass at Moreton-on-Lugg. He made the early glass that Frederick Preedy (qv) designed, viz. the east window at Mathon, glass at Whitbourne and windows at Stretton Grandison. There is a splendid east window at St Mary de Crypt, Gloucester of 1845 with an early attempt at mediaeval figures by Rogers.

Rogers, Henry (1584-1658), clergyman, the son of a clergyman, was born in Herefordshire, educated at Jesus College, Oxford and ordained. He proceeded BD and in 1637 DD. He became a lecturer at Hereford Cathedral and in 1642 a canon residentiary. In 1616 he received the Hereford prebend of Pratum Majus. He was appointed vicar of Dorstone, rector of Moccas from 1617 to 1636, rector of Stoke Edith from 1618 to 1646, and vicar of Foy from 1636 to 1642. He married an Elizabeth and they had several children. He was an argumentative man and often at odds with Dean and Chapter and with Bishop Francis Godwin and his family. In 1623 he was imprisoned in the Fleet prison. He published *The Protestant Church Existent, and their Faith Professed in All Ages* (1637). He was on better terms with Bishop Coke (qv) and outspoken against the Presbyterians, who called him the devil's orator. When Hereford was taken by Parliamentary forces in 1645 he was imprisoned as a known malignant. On his release, deprived of his livings he was privately supported by Lord John Scudamore (qv, d.1671) and other Royalist gentry. He was buried in St Margaret's, Wellington on 15 June 1658.

Rogers, Wroth (d.1683), Parliamentary officer and politician, was born in Llanvach in Monmouthshire. He served under Cromwell in the New Model Army, rising to the rank of lieutenant colonel by 1649. He was appointed Governor of Hereford by Parliament, initially with John Birch (qv). His Governor's Lodge was in Castle Cliffe with his garrison in barracks on the Castle Green. He was responsible for the subjugation of Royalist Herefordshire and southern Wales and was also Governor of Ludlow. He foiled Sir Henry Lingen's attempt to raise Hereford in 1647 and was appointed president of the commission to appropriate and sell Royalist estates. He was often at odds with Birch and with Silas Taylor (qv), who had a more humane interpretation of their brief. He married twice. He sat in the Rump Parliament until it was dissolved in Cromwell's coup of 1653, and then in the Barebones Parliament, other members for Herefordshire being John Herring and John James. In 1654 he was Sheriff of Herefordshire. Birch was becoming suspect to the authorities and Rogers had him arrested and imprisoned. In 1659 he scotched Booth's Rising, arresting Thomas Prise (qv, d.1699) on his way to a meeting of conspirators at Burghope House. He sat as Knight of the Shire in Cromwell's Protectorate Parliament and was present at his investiture as Protector. He continued as Governor of Hereford to the Restoration when General George Monck (qv under Nicholas Monck) stood him down. He then disappears, perhaps living in Worcester with a third wife and daughters.

Romilly, Samuel (1757-1818), lawyer and politician, was born on 1 March 1757 in Frith Street, Soho the son of French Protestant emigrés. He trained as a lawyer and became a prominent Whig politician and friend of former Prime Minister Lord Lansdowne, interested in reform and the abolition of slavery. He was knighted for his legal work for the Whig administration. He was a politician of great probity but susceptible to mental strain. He met Anne, daughter of Lansdowne's secretary Francis Garbett (qv) of Knill Court, Herefordshire. They married at St Michael and All Angels, Knill in 1798 and lived at the Court, a beautiful spot near

Presteigne, and had seven children including the future Baron Romilly of Barry. When Anne died after a long illness on 18 October 1818 Romilly became depressed and on 2 November 1818 cut his throat. He and his wife were buried at St Michael's, Knill.

Ross, John (1719-92), Bishop of Exeter, was born at Ross on 25 June 1719, the only son of John Ross, attorney. He was educated at Hereford Cathedral School and St John's College, Cambridge, becoming a noted classicist. Ordained in 1746 he accumulated wealthy livings, chaplaincies and offices and rose to be Bishop of Exeter in 1778. He was a Whig in politics and tolerant of dissent. He died on 14 August 1792 and was buried in the south aisle of Exeter Cathedral choir.

Ross, John de (d.1332), Bishop of Carlisle, was the son of Roger le Mercer and Sybil of Ross. He was educated at Oxford and awarded a doctorate by 1300. He was a canon and subdean of Hereford, and later archdeacon of the Shropshire part of the diocese of Hereford, with several prebends and canonries elsewhere. In 1289 Bishop Swinfield (qv) appointed him his proctor at the Roman curia where he forwarded the canonisation of Thomas Cantilupe (qv). He helped raise money for the central tower of Hereford Cathedral which was being built *c.*1307. He was appointed Bishop of Carlisle in 1325 and died there in 1332, but his body was returned to be buried at St Mary's Church, Ross where he had established a chantry in 1330. His house by Ross churchyard was mentioned when Bishop Trefnant (qv) was later combining chantries.

Roteland, Hue de (fl.1175-90), poet and cleric from Rhuddlan, Flint lived at Credenhill, as he says in his poem *Ipomedon* in which he mentions Prince Rhys (qv Rhys ap Gruffydd of Deheubarth). He wrote in Norman French and the poem was translated into Middle English. Another long poem, *Protheselaus*, is dated *c.*1190. He was a friend of Walter Map (qv).

Roubiliac, Louis-Francois (1702-62) sculptor, moved to London *c.*1730. He opened a studio and produced his first major work: a statue of Bishop Hough in Worcester Cathedral. His greatest work is in Westminster Abbey: the Duke of Argyll's monument (1749); Lady Nightingale (1758); and Handel, his last work, made in 1759. Central to Roubiliac's work is the portrait bust, always technically excellent and full of character, combining the animation of the Rococo with the solidity of the Baroque. There are three small examples of his work in Herefordshire: a bust of James Thomas (d.1757) in Hereford Cathedral, standing above the door in the chained library, the remains of a bigger tomb; a bust of a Mrs Esdaile in the south-east transept; and a bust of George Sawyer of 1753 in St Lawrence, Canon Pyon. Wordsworth (qv) said his monument to Newton in Trinity College Chapel, Cambridge showed

... a marble index of a mind for ever
Voyaging through strange seas of Thought alone.

He was a convivial man who retained his French accent. He died in his house in St Martin's Lane, London on 11 January 1762.

Rudge, Mary (1842-1919), chess player, was born in Leominster on 6 February 1842 and lived there until the death of her father Henry,

a surgeon in the town, in 1874. (Her mother, Eliza Barrett, had died in 1863.) She and her sisters were good chess players from an early age, winning local tournaments. She and her sister Caroline moved to Bristol where their brother Henry was a curate and joined the Bristol Chess Association, which had just begun to admit women. Mary was considered one of the best chess players in the country. She suffered from money and health problems throughout her life, and died on 22 November 1919.

Rudhall or Rudhale: In the 13th century William de Roedhale was granted the lease of a mill and land at Brampton Abbotts.

Rudhall, John (1498-1530) was educated at the Inner Temple under his famous father (William Rudhall, d.1530, qv); his mother was Anne Milbourne. He was elected junior knight for Herefordshire in 1529. In this he was supported by Sir Richard Cornwall (qv, d.1533), who had married his aunt, Jane Milbourne; but he died the next year, just after his father.

Rudhall, John (*c*.1587-1636), son of William (d.1626) and Margaret (a daughter of Sir James Croft qv, d.1590), was educated at Christ Church, Oxford and the Middle Temple and travelled in Europe. He was MP for Hereford and appointed Charles I's commissioner to collect the hated Ship Money and royal loans in Herefordshire. Later in life he married a rich widow, Mary Chocke, daughter of Sir William Pitt but died soon after of the plague that was endemic at this time in the Ross area (qv Revd Philip Price). Plague claimed his children and ended the male line. The Rudhall estate was held in trust until 1645 when Parliament seized it, then granted it to MP Walter Kyrle (qv, d.1489), who rented it to Lady Rudhall. Their table tomb in Ross Church (by Samuel Baldwin qv) shows Mary and John's alabaster effigies in the height of Caroline fashion, holding hands. His father and mother also have a wall monument nearby. There is a contemporary memorial

in Ross churchyard with the stark inscription: 'Plague. Ano Dom 1637. Burials 315. Libera Nos' – save us!

Rudhall, Richard (d.1476), archdeacon of Hereford 1446-76, and his brother William, were born at Rudhall House near Brampton Abbotts and Ross in the house built by their father Nicholas Rudhall. Richard studied at Oxford and the University of Padua where he received a doctorate in canon law. He was a canon residentiary and archdeacon of Hereford, and collected books which at his death were presented to the cathedral library, where they remain, showing his marginal comments. A full-length brass in the cathedral's south-east transept shows him in robes of office. He left money for the repair of the chapel of St Katherine's Hospital in Ledbury. William's son John (d.1506) married a Joan; their brasses were in Brampton Abbotts Church but were lost, but hers (with an inscription) has subsequently been retrieved from under the floor.

Rudhall, Richard (fl.1590s), eldest son of William (qv, d.1626), was prominent at the taking of Cadiz in 1596 by Essex (qv Robert

Devereux, d.1601), for which he was knighted. He died young from a fever contracted on a further Spanish expedition. William's second son Gilbert also died young and John (qv, d.1636), the next in line, succeeded to the large estate.

Rudhall, William (d.1530), son of John and Joan Rudhall (qv under Richard Rudhall, d.1476), studied at the Inner Temple and became a prominent bencher. He was elected knight of the shire in the last Parliament of the 1490s, was a JP in Worcestershire and Herefordshire, and became attorney general to Prince Arthur, Henry VII's eldest son. He married Anne, daughter and co-heir of Simon Milbourne (qv Milbourne family) of Tillington and was steward of Herefordshire (1511-2). He enlarged Rudhall House, creating the beautiful building seen today, which encases the older house. Bishop Booth (qv) accused him of extending the Rudhall estates at the expense of the diocese. There are alabaster effigies of him and Anne on an altar tomb in Ross Church with saints, mourners and scenes depicted on the sides – the Annunciation with the family looking on and the Trinity – a rare example of pre-Reformation religious art intact.

Rudhall, William (d.1626) married Margaret, daughter of Sir James Croft (qv, d.1590), and they had 11 children, including Anne, who married John Prise (qv, d.1669), Richard (qv), Gilbert, John (qv, d.1636) and William (qv, d.1651).

Rudhall, William (d.1651), son of William (qv, d.1626), eventually came into possession of the Rudhall estates. In 1602 his daughter Joan married Sir Walter Pye (qv, d.1635). Another daughter Frances married Herbert, son of Bishop Westfaling (qv) and in 1658, Rudhall Manor was conveyed to that family. William Rudhall was one of the Nine Worthies of Herefordshire (see

index) and died in the Civil Wars. His monument in Ross Church shows him in Roman armour.

Rupert, Prince, of the Rhine (1619-82), Charles I's (qv) nephew, was the epitome of the cavalier during the Civil Wars. His dashing cavalry charges, always successful, rarely contributed to the overall battle, as they charged off the battlefield in pursuit of some distant baggage train. He solved the problem of the Clubmen in Herefordshire in 1645 with off-hand brutality, hanging their leaders while they were camped near Ledbury, having been given safe conduct by Barnabas Scudamore (qv). One of his charges took place along Ledbury's Homend on 25 April 1645 when, hearing that Col Massey (qv) had occupied the town, he arrived from Hereford early one frosty morning, surprised the Parliamentary garrison and drove them back to Gloucester. Bullet holes remain in the church doors and in the wall of the Talbot in New Street. He made his headquarters at New Place, Ledbury. He was born in Prague on 17 December 1619 to Frederick V and Elizabeth, daughter of James I. He was a brilliant man, innovative at everything he attempted – general, admiral, governor, scientist, artist. His parents (the 'winter' king and queen of Bohemia) were driven from their kingdom by a Catholic confederacy and he spent his life in exile, mostly in Britain. Rupert continued to oppose the Commonwealth at sea, and after the Restoration fought the Dutch as Admiral of Charles II's (qv) forces. He was an experimental scientist, making several important discoveries and a founding member of the Royal Society. His last days were spent with his mistress, the actress Margaret Hughes and their daughter Ruperta. He died on 29 November 1682.

Rushook, Thomas (fl.1350s-90s), prior, from Rushock, Worcestershire, was prior of the Dominican friary at Hereford (the Blackfriars) in the 1350s and became provincial of the order, archdeacon of St Asaph's, then Bishop of Llandaff (uncanonically for a friar). He had dealings with the Briouze and Beauchamp families. He was Richard II's (qv) confessor and the king made him Bishop of Chichester. The barons regarded him as one of Richard's 'evil counsellors' and exiled him to Ireland where he died. John Gower called him a 'professor of evil' and 'a friar black within and without'. In Rushook's absence the king showed his confidence by taking another Dominican from Hereford Blackfriars, his protégé John Burghill (qv) as his confessor.

Ryeland Sheep, one of Britain's oldest breeds, were bred by the monks of Leominster on the wet pastures where rye was grown, giving the short wool a special strong quality known as 'Lemster Ore'. In 1454 an Act of Parliament fixed the price of Leominster wool at £13 a bag compared with £8 6s 8d for Cotswold wool. In 1783 Ryeland wool was sold at 2 shillings a pound when ordinary wool fetched only 4d. Queen Elizabeth I (qv) would only wear 'Lemster' wool next to her skin. The Parrys grazed and improved Ryelands on their pasture under the Black Mountains and one likes to imagine Blanche Parry (qv) introducing her queen to the wool. The sheep are good eating too: 'the sweet meat of Herefordshire'. There is a Ryelands Road in Leominster. The breed was improved by Benjamin Tomkins (qv) of Kings Pyon.

S

Sabatini, Rafael (1875-1950), novelist, was born in Italy on 29 April 1875. His mother was English and the family returned here. He wrote tales of swash-buckling adventure from an early age and continued with the theme of historical romance throughout his life. His first published novel was *The Tavern Knight* (1904). He took British citizenship, married and wrote a stream of novels on the model of Stanley Weyman. After the death of his first wife he married Christine Wood in 1925, and in 1931 they bought Clock Mills at Clifford. Sabatini became popular and prosperous. The embryonic film industry found his stories translated well onto celluloid and made successful films from his romances including *Captain Blood*, *The Sea Hawk* and *Scaramouche*, some more than once.

The 1940 film of *The Sea Hawk* had a score by Eric Korngold with top stars playing the lead: the young Errol Flynn, Tyrone Power, George Saunders, Flora Robson etc. Sabatini was an active man and enjoyed fishing in the Wye and skiing. It was in a skiing accident that he met his death in Switzerland on 13 February 1950.

Salviati and Co. (fl.1880-1920) were an Italian firm of glass makers and mosaicists based in Murano, one of the islands off Venice, who opened a shop in Regents Street, London. They provided the mosaics in the eastern apse of St Catherine's, Hoarwithy, and in St Andrew, Moreton-on-Lugg G.E. Fox (qv) brought them in to decorate the chancel (1887). The name dates back to the 16th-century painters Giovanni and Francesco Salviati.

Sarnesfield, Nicholas de (d.1394) was a follower of Edward the Black Prince (qv) and held office under Edward III (qv) and Richard II (qv). One of his daughters married Hugh de Moynton or Monington (qv) and Sarnesfield passed to that family.

Sarnesfield, Philip de leased Sarnesfield Manor from its Norman owner Roger de Lacy (qv) in the early 12th century.

Savage, John Boscawen (1760-1843), officer of marines, was born in Hereford on 23 February 1760 the son of Marmaduke Savage from Rock Savage in Ireland. He joined the army but transferred to the marines, seeing action at Cape St Vincent, Gibraltar and with Nelson off Egypt. He married Sophia Cock, and succeeded to the family estate of Rock Savage, Ballygalet, Co. Down. On retirement he had reached the rank of Major General and was appointed CB and KCH. Sir John lived at Woolwich Common, where he died on 8 March 1843. There is a monument to Sir John and his wife in the church there.

Saxton, Christopher (*c.*1542-*c.*1610), the father of English cartography, was a Yorkshireman born in about 1542. He went to

Cambridge University and returned to Yorkshire as an apprentice map maker. He surveyed England and Wales in 1570 with the patronage of Queen Elizabeth and Lord Burghley (qv) who gave him a patent on mapmaking. In 1579 he produced the first accurate atlas with maps based on his own surveying rather than copied – a model for later work including John Speed's (qv). His work put Britain at the forefront of map making and Saxton's outline of the British Isles became the accepted one until the Ordnance Survey mapping of 1801. He surveyed and drew a Herefordshire county map showing much local detail. A copy he presented to Lord Burghley exists with notes in his hand recording landowners' names, such as Skydmor (Scudamore) at Kynechurch (Kentchurch). He records the landslip of 1575 at Kynaston, near Much Marcle, still called 'the wonder' on recent OS maps. Four years before publication an earth movement had swallowed fields along with grazing beasts at Kynaston and the chapel whose bell some say still rings. Saxton is buried in Woodkirk, Yorkshire.

Scapula, Publius Ostorius (d.52 AD), the second Roman governor of the Province of Britannia 47-52, brought the Ordovices and Silures, under the command of Caractacus (qv), to battle in 51. Herefordshire legend places the battle at a ford on the Wye below Capler Camp, which is said to be named after Scapula who, driven off by Caractacus, retreated up the hill and fortified himself there. Scapula's HQ was said to be at *Ariconium*, near Weston-under-Penyard, and Blackwardine has been suggested as the site for another camp. Caractacus was beaten and later captured with his family. Scapula died in post in Britain, worn out, Tacitus says, by his task, and was buried somewhere in south-east Wales.

Schomberg, Reginald Charles Francis (1880-1958), explorer, was born in Kent on 19 September 1880, joined the army and served in India. In 1910 the family, sister Mary and aunts, moved to Chasewood Lodge, Ross, where Schomberg often stayed. He was wounded in

the Middle East in the First World War and awarded the DSO and bar. After retirement he explored and engaged in diplomatic work in central Asia. He wrote several popular books on his adventures: *Peaks and Plains of Central Asia* (1933), *Between the Oxus and the Indus* (1935), *Unknown Karakorum* (1936), and *Kafirs and Glaciers* (1938). Schomberg was a Catholic and became involved with parish work around Ross at the end of his life. He died in Hereford General Hospital on 1 March 1958 and was buried at Belmont Abbey.

Scory, John (*c.*1510-85), Bishop of Hereford 1559-85, was born in Norfolk and joined the Dominican friars in Cambridge just before the Reformation. He was a reformer who surrendered his friary eagerly at the Dissolution and was taken up by Archbishop Thomas Cranmer. He was Bishop of Chichester under Edward VI and his outspoken Protestantism earned him enemies. After an attempt to conform when Mary restored Catholicism Scory went, with his wife Elizabeth, into exile at Emden in Germany where he published a defence of the Reformation. He returned on the accession of Elizabeth and was made Bishop of Hereford – one of her first appointments. He found his new diocese unaffected by the Reformation and considered the whole cathedral staff 'rank Papists'. He vainly tried to have evangelical preachers sent up from London and sympathetic JPs appointed for the prosecution of recusancy. He appointed the firebrand London printer Robert Crowley (qv) Archdeacon of Hereford and made the learned Miles Smith (qv) a canon, giving them both houses in the Cathedral Close. His idealism waned, however, in the unsympathetic environment. He made his wholly unsuitable son Sylvanus a prebendary and gave him a portion of the tithes of Ledbury. John Aubrey (qv) noted that the bishop 'loved him so dearly that he fleeced the Church of Hereford to leave him a good estate', and he provided his wife with the income from three prebendal stalls. On the other hand the bishop left the large sum of £200 to Hereford City to help poor clothiers and other craftsmen to find work. He died on 25 June 1585 at his Whitbourne manor and was buried in St John the Baptist Church, Whitbourne. His unruly son went to the Low Countries as a soldier. His wife Elizabeth died in 1592; 50 years later Isaac Taylor reported seeing her effigy with the Scory arms in the church.

Scott, George Gilbert (1811-78), architect, was born on 13 July 1811 in Buckinghamshire. He drew mediaeval buildings when young and was apprenticed to a London architect, soon designing his own buildings. He married his cousin Caroline Oldrid (1811-72). He was a year older than A.W.N. Pugin (qv), who introduced him to the gothic manner of the late 13th century as the proper style for Christian architecture. He became the Victorian church architect *par excellence* in the Gothic revival style and, with his big office and large output, dominated the architectural scene. He could work in a classical style as at the Foreign Office in Whitehall but is best remembered for buildings such as St Pancras Hotel and the Albert Memorial. One of Scott's early jobs in Herefordshire was to rebuild St John's Church and rectory, Eastnor (1849-52) for Earl Somers (qv John Somers Cocks, d.1852). He re-erected the ancient tower and added the beautiful Somers Cocks Chapel to the chancel, paid for by the vicar Revd William Pulling. After the death of the Cottinghams (qv), Scott was the obvious architect to complete

the restoration of Hereford Cathedral. Dean Dawes and Archdeacon Fiennes (qqv) raised the necessary money and Scott and his clerk of works William Chick (qv) began to renew decayed stonework and underpin the walls. The Cottinghams had left many ancient tombs in the cloisters and Scott and Havergal (qv) identified them and replaced them as close as possible to their original positions – the Denton tomb, for instance (qv Anne Denton). Scott recommended rebuilding Wyatt's (qv) unsatisfactory west front, returning the nave to its original length, restoring the beautiful, crumbling 14th-century tower and rebuilding the ruined chapter house, but none of this could be afforded. He designed an ironwork screen at the crossing to replace the pulpitum that had been removed, built by Francis Skidmore (qv) of Coventry. The gilt ironwork, statues and paste gems in decorated gothic fell victim to 1960s taste, but the screen is now restored and on view in the V&A Museum. Godwins (qv) supplied the floor, with the central image of the patron St Ethelbert. The restored cathedral opened on 30 June 1863 with long queues, and the nave services became very popular. Scott kept in touch, corresponding with his friend Havergal and giving advice. The year before he died he gave a talk to the Woolhope Club about his work in Hereford. He restored St John the Baptist, Upton Bishop in 1862 and rebuilt St Mary's, Edvin Loach. In 1864 he restored the unique Blackfriars' preaching cross in Hereford for John Hungerford Arkwright (qv), who owned the ruins, and the Whitecross (to Alfred Watkins' [qv] displeasure), adding the shaft and head. He restored Leominster Priory, returning just before his death for further work on the south nave and aisle. Scott died on 27 March 1878 and was honoured by a tomb in Westminster Abbey. In 1882 a commemorative tablet was placed in Hereford Cathedral.

Scott, John Oldrid (1841-1913), architect, was George Gilbert Scott's (qv) second son. Wyatt's (qv) west front for Hereford Cathedral was widely disliked and the earthquake of 1896 gave an excuse to replace it. Dean James Leigh (qv) raised funds and Oldrid Scott was chosen for family reasons. His new west front of raw stone and busy detailing went up in 1902-08 in a late 14th-century style, and was liked as little as Wyatt's. One pictorial detail in a roundel shows Bishop Herbert Croft (qv) in his pulpit berating Birch's troopers, one of whom raises his musket at him. He kept the Clayton and Bell (qv) Victoria memorial window.

Scott, Walter (1716-86), benefactor of Ross-on-Wye, went to the Blue Coat School in Ross which was set up to educate 60 poor boys and girls. Walter ran away to London when he was 13, having being caught scrumping, and through diligence made a fortune. At the end of his life he remembered the poor charity school of his youth and left a legacy for its re-endowment. A monument records this in Ross churchyard.

Scrob, Richard (*c.*1020-67), a Norman who accompanied Edward the Confessor (qv) to England, was granted in the 1040s the manor of Auretone, where he built his castle: a mound with a wooden fort on top and bailey known as Richard's Castle. During Edward's reign he married the daughter of another Norman, Robert fitz Wimarc, and they had two sons: Osbern fitz Richard (qv) and William. When the Godwin family (qv) returned in 1052 many Normans fled but Richard was protected by the privileged status of king's housecarl. In 1066 he and his sons rose in support of the invading Normans. He died soon after.

Scudamores, see also under **Skidmore**: A Norman gentry family who were settled at Upton Scudamore, Wiltshire in Edward the Confessor's time. In Domesday a Ralph is recorded at *Sancta Keyna* or Kentchurch. In the 13th century Ralph Scudamore had a fortified manor at Poston near Vowchurch and from the early 14th century a John Skidmore had the manor of Rowlestone. The name also appears at Moccas and Ballingham south of Holme Lacy. Philip (d.1419) is the first recorded Scudamore at Holme Lacy, which became their senior seat. During Glyn Dŵr's (qv) rebellion John (I) Skidmore (qv) was believed to have given succour to the rebel who was a relation by marriage, to the detriment of his career. In the next century Scudamores held positions at Court. They fought on opposing sides in the Civil War, as did many families, and Rowland (qv, d.1645), with the Parliament Army besieging Hereford, was killed returning from a parley with his nephew Barnabas (qv), governor of Hereford. They were at their height with Sir John 1st Viscount, learned and pious, a friend of King Charles I and Archbishop Laud, and restorer of Dore Abbey. Holme Lacy had been rebuilt in brick but now a magnificent palace worthy of their viscountcy was required and Sir John, 2nd Viscount, had Hugh May rebuild it at incalculable cost. Subsequently, despite great wealth there was sad decline, but the family continues at Kentchurch, regularly open to the public; and Holme Lacy, now a hotel stripped of its original furnishings but still with splendid plasterwork, is open for visits.

Scudamore, Barnabas (1609-52), Royalist governor of Hereford, Sir James's (d.1619, qv) ninth son, was baptised on 2 April 1609. He married twice. He joined the king's forces at the start of the Civil Wars and fought at the battles of Coventry and Edgehill. He burnt both Wilton and Eardisley castles in 1644. He was Governor of Hereford in 1644 and later that year Sheriff of the county. He set about strengthening Hereford's defences for the next siege. It was hoped that having a Scudamore as governor would unite soldiers and citizens, but the country people of Herefordshire were tired of military control and billeted soldiers looting their fodder and crops. A large neutral force called the Clubmen was formed in Wales and the west to resist levies and looting. On 19 March 1645 a force of some 16,000 Clubmen marched on Hereford, many well-armed and mounted. Massey (qv), the watchful Parliamentary commander, made contact with the force and tried to enlist them for his cause. This prompted Scudamore to accede to some of their demands and Massey retired to Ross. Bands of dissatisfied Clubmen remained around the Ledbury area, and on 29 March Prince Rupert (qv) dispersed them with a troop of cavalry and hanged the leaders. The Clubmen's demands were not met and, worse, Rupert's and Scudamore's men 'plundered everie parish and howse poor as well as others leavinge neyther clothes or provision'. When the neutral Sir John Brydges (qv, d.1652) refused to allow a Royalist garrison in Wilton Castle, Scudamore (his uncle) with Sir Henry Lingen (qv) burned it down one Sunday morning while the family was at church. Scudamore's strengthened fortifications at Hereford held off the Scottish Army which arrived under its commander Lord Leven at the end of July 1645. Leven made his headquarters at Fownhope and sent a letter to Scudamore asking for his capitulation which was refused. The Scots surrounded Hereford, camping on Bartonsham Meadow and throwing up the earthworks on the south bank of the Wye facing the castle and bishop's palace, still to be seen today, and firing cannon into the city. They tried to undermine the walls at Friern Gate, to the south of Eign Street, but Scudamore countermined their tunnels. At news of the king's approach with a relieving army the besiegers lifted the siege and King Charles (qv) was greeted with rapture. In Hereford Charles knighted Barnabas, but later, in a very cold December, Birch (qv) took the city by stratagem and Sir Barnabas escaped across the frozen Wye. When Scudamore reached the Royalist city of Worcester he was accused of bribery and imprisoned. He never cleared his name despite publishing his *Defence* in 1646. He moved to London but was accused of plotting for the Royalists and died of melancholy in 1652.

(Fitzroy-)Scudamore, Frances (1711-50), Duchess of Beaufort, only child of James Scudamore (qv, d.1716,) and Frances, was born on 14 August 1711. Her inheritance made her highly eligible and on 28 June 1729 she married Henry Somerset (qv, d.1745), 3rd Duke of Beaufort, who took the name Scudamore by Act of Parliament the following year. Frances had an affair with William Lord Talbot and her marriage ended in scandal and separation. She was left with her estates, however, and an illegitimate daughter from the liaison. In 1742 Beaufort started divorce proceedings and when Frances counter-claimed that he was impotent, he apparently disproved it before witnesses. Divorce was granted by Act of Parliament and she married Colonel Charles Fitzroy (1713-82), who assumed the surname Scudamore. Frances died two years later, on 15 February 1750, five days after giving birth to their daughter.

(Fitzroy-)Scudamore, Frances (1750-1820), daughter of Frances Fitzroy-Scudamore (qv, d.1750) and Charles Fitzroy, was heiress of Holme Lacy and the wider Scudamore estates. On 2 April 1771 she married (as his second wife) Charles Howard (qv), later 11th Duke of Norfolk, but descended into mental illness. The duke pressed for an annulment and lengthy legal proceedings followed, much reducing the great estate. Dickens (qv) is said to have used the case for his study of Chancery in *Bleak House*. The duke died in 1815 and the duchess five years later, when this line of the Scudamores became extinct. After lengthy legal proceedings the estate was divided amongst the descendants of the first viscount's eldest daughter. Holme Lacy went to Captain Sir Edwyn Francis Stanhope, who added Scudamore to his name (qv, under Scudamore-Stanhope). His son, Henry Edwyn Chandos, succeeded in 1883 as 9th Earl of Chesterfield.

Scudamore, Henry (d.1461) was a son of Sir John (II) Skidmore (qv), alongside whom he fought at Mortimers Cross. He and Owen Tudor (qv) were captured and both were executed in Hereford on 3 February 1461.

Scudamore, James (1472-1553), son of Thomas Scudamore of Kentchurch, married Joan Baskerville (qv under James Baskerville d.1494) of Eardisley. Their daughters and co-heirs were Joan (b.*c*.1498), the second wife of her cousin Philip Scudamore (*c*.1484-1554) of Rowlestone, who inherited Kentchurch; and Eleanor (b.1501), who married Myles Parry (qv) of Whitehouse. James's younger brother Nicholas was said to be the ancestor of the Scudamores of Llancillo.

Scudamore, James (1568-1619), Sir John's (qv, d.1623) son by his first wife Eleanor, was, like his siblings, brought up a Catholic but renounced this later and became a determined persecutor of the Catholics in the area. On 19 June 1605 he and three other JPs made a surprise descent on Catholic houses along the border, finding much religious material but residents flown. He was a friend of Sir Philip Sidney and made a grand showing as a jousting knight at Queen Elizabeth's Court. He adopted the punning motto *l'escu d'amour*, and was the model for Edmund Spenser's Sir Scudamour in *The Faerie Queene*. He took part in the attack on Cadiz in 1596 under the Earl of Essex (qv Robert Devereux, d.1601) who knighted him. In 1597 he married Mary, daughter of Peter Houghton, a London alderman and, when she died the next year, Mary (d.1632) née Throckmorton, widow of Sir Thomas Baskerville (qv, d.1597). They had nine children, one of whom, Mary (d.1634), married Sir Giles Brydges (qv, d.1637). After the birth of their ninth child, Barnabas (qv), they lived apart. Under Sir James, and his father Sir John, Holme Lacy was 'not onely an Academy, but even the very Court of a Prince'. Queen Elizabeth (qv) is said to have been present at his tilting yard at Holme Lacy, and the war horses trained in their stables were celebrated. Artists and scientists were also drawn to the house: Thomas Bodley, John Dee (qv), Thomas Allen (qv) etc. Sir James died in 1619, before his father, and the Holme Lacy estate went to his first son John (qv, d.1671). There are two suits of his armour, bought from Holme Lacy House, on show in the Metropolitan Museum of Art in New York.

Scudamore, James (1624-68), fourth son of Sir John (d.1671, qv), was born on 26 June 1624 and educated at St John's College, Oxford. He was captured with his father at Waller's (qv) siege of Hereford in 1643. He was a worry to his pious father who had him elected MP for Hereford in 1642-4 and again in 1661-6. From

1644 to '48 he fled abroad from creditors and gambled his way across Europe, into Turkey and Egypt. On his return he married Jane (d.1699), daughter and co-heir of Richard Bennet of Kew and they lived at Cary Cradock (or Caradoc), Sellack. On the outbreak of the Dutch Wars he fought in the Navy. He predeceased his father on 18 June 1668. He and his wife are buried in St Cuthbert's, Holme Lacy – he reclining in Roman dress as on a stage in a sumptuous monument by William Woodman (qv), who made other Scudamore tombs here.

Scudamore, James (1684-1716), 3rd Viscount, eldest surviving son of John (qv, d.1697) and Frances, was educated at Gloucester Hall, Oxford and in 1712 became Doctor of Civil Law. In 1704 he increased his estates by the addition of his cousins' lands at Ballingham and work was done at Holme Lacy, where the chapel was rebuilt and dedicated by Bishop Bisse (qv) on St Luke's Day 1715. He travelled on the Continent and on his return married Frances (1684-1729), daughter of Baron Digby, in 1706. He was disabled by a fall from his horse and later died of smallpox, and the title became extinct. His widow Lady Frances made Holme Lacy famous as a centre for writers and poets including Alexander Pope (qv) and John Gay. She died on 3 May 1729.

Scudamore, John (1486-1571), the son of William (d.*c.*1520, qv), bought up church properties during the Dissolution such as the Dore Abbey lands, Kentchurch Park, the deer park of the Knights of St John, and the Blackfriars in Hereford. In 1511 he married Sybil (d.1559), daughter of Watkyn Vaughan (qv under Thomas Vaughan d.1469) of Hergest with whom he had nine children, including four sons: William (qv, d.1560), Richard (d.1586), who was agent to Sir Philip Hoby (qv), John (qv, d.1623) and Philip (d.1602). His youngest daughter Jane married first John Warnecombe and later Sir William Devereux (qv under Walter Devereux, d.1558). His chief seat was Holme Lacy, which he rebuilt in brick in the 1540s. The chapel was consecrated by Bishop John Skippe (qv) in 1546. He later married Joan Rudhall (qv). He was steward of Hereford and MP for Herefordshire in 1515. He was gentleman usher to Henry VIII and esquire of the body through the influence of his patron Thomas Cromwell, and was appointed his receiver. Queen Mary appointed him to her Council in the Marches and he was JP and *custos rotulorum* for Herefordshire by 1561. He died at Holme Lacy on 25 September 1571 and is buried in St Cuthbert's Church where his and Sybil's splendid alabaster effigies can be admired.

Scudamore, John (1522-93), a younger son of John (d.1571, qv) and Sybil, married Margaret Pollard, and their daughter Alice (1548-95) married Anthony Elton (qv).

Scudamore, John (1542-1623), knight, son of William (qv, d.1560) and Ursula, was born on 1 February 1542. He was a minor at his father's death and Sir James Croft (qv, d.1590) was appointed his guardian. He was educated at the Inner Temple and married Sir James's daughter Eleanor in 1568. She died the next year in childbirth and he married Mary Shelton (Mary Scudamore, qv). Scudamore rose at Court with the patronage of Croft, Comptroller of the Household and Mary's help. He was junior MP for the shire with Croft in the 1570s and '80s, *custos rotulorum* in 1574 and Sheriff in 1581. He was Deputy Lieutenant of Herefordshire but so much at Court that another had to be chosen. He was knighted in 1592. After Queen Elizabeth's death he and Mary retired to Holme Lacy and his county duties. His sister married a recusant and his eldest son John (1567-after 1624) became a Catholic priest on the Continent. His eldest son, Henry, harassed a neighbouring JP, Anthony Pembridge (qv), and complained of him to the bishop as a recusant. Mary died on retirement but Sir John lived another 20 years, surviving his son and dying on 14 April 1623.

Scudamore, John (d.1616) has a monument in St Mary's Church, Kentchurch, erected by his wife Amy Starkie: John and Amy lean stiffly with a row of children and a baby in a cradle.

Scudamore, John (1601-71), 1st Viscount, 'the Glory of our Countrey', eldest son of Sir James (qv, d.1619) and Mary, was born at Holme Lacy on 28 February 1601. Aged 14 he married Elizabeth (1609-52), daughter of Sir Arthur Porter, a wealthy heiress who brought him the lands of Llanthony Secunda at Gloucester. He was educated at Magdalen College, Oxford and the Middle Temple. At Court he was a favourite of Charles I and his grandfather bought him a baronetcy in 1620. He was MP for the shire in the 1620s and high steward of Hereford from 1630. For his defence of the king's friend Buckingham he was rewarded with the Irish baronies of Dromore and Sligo in 1628. He was ambassador to France from 1635-9. After Elizabeth's death he married Jane Bennett of Kew and they had a son John. Scudamore was the wealthiest inhabitant and only resident peer in Herefordshire, a learned, pious man and friend of Thomas Hobbes and Sir Kenelm Digby. He rebuilt decayed churches in the area at the prompting of his friend William Laud (qv) and restored impropriations made at the Reformation. Laud was fond of him, treating him as his son and often visiting him at Holme

Lacy. In 1632 Scudamore commissioned John Abel (qv) to restore the ruined church of Dore Abbey and letters between them survive. Abel's woodwork, still to be seen, includes a screen with the arms of Scudamore, Charles I and Archbishop Laud. He restored the 15th- and 16th-century stained glass in the east window of St Tysilio, Sellack, which he rededicated to 'RS 1630', and his fifth son was christened Rowland at the church that year. Sir John's rivalry with Fitzwilliam Coningsby (qv) in Hereford undermined Sir Richard Cave's (qv) defences allowing Waller (qv) to take Hereford in 1643 and Scudamore spent the next four years under arrest in London. Holme Lacy was looted, his property in Gloucester was destroyed and he was massively fined. On his release he set out to improve his Herefordshire estates. He was noted for the cultivation of cider apples and grafted the Scudamore crab or Redstreak (qv) on a French slip he had brought home and produced cider known as *vin de Scudamore*. He was also a successful cattle breeder and is credited with developing the Hereford breed of cattle (qv). Despite his losses he continued to support impoverished clergy, such as Robert Herrick. He died on 19 May 1671 and was succeeded by his grandson John (qv, d.1697). A brother William married Sybil Kyrle, sister of 'the Man of Ross' (John Kyrle, qv, d.1724).

Scudamore, John (*c.*1650-97), 2nd Viscount, son of James (d.1668, qv) and heir of Sir John, 1st Viscount (d.1671, qv). He inherited great wealth despite all the fines, philanthropy and gambling of his ancestors but the Scudamores were now eclipsed as premier nobility in the county by the Somersets, the Dukes of Beaufort and the Chandos Brydges (qqv). Sir John was educated at Christ Church, Oxford and married Frances Cecil, daughter of the Earl of Exeter. He commissioned Hugh May (qv) to rebuild Holme Lacy in the French style. He was High Steward and a JP in the county and elected to the Cavalier Parliament in 1673. A Coningsby spy heard him and Shaftesbury discussing a revolutionary army to oust James II, although he kept free of actual plots. Sir Edward Harley (qv, d.1700) and other Hereford gentry tried to reconcile the Scudamores and Coningsbys but the feud was exacerbated when Frances Lady Scudamore ran off with Thomas Earl Coningsby (qv, d.1729). Her husband set out after her with armed servants and brought her back at gunpoint. He neither opposed nor supported William of Orange's regime, and died on 2 June 1697.

Scudamore, John (I) (1727-96), first son of Richard Scudamore of Rowlestone, was MP for the county in the Whig interest, 1764-84, a JP and a colonel in the Herefordshire militia. He inherited Kentchurch from his cousin William Scudamore in 1741 and, fond of hunting in the park, died on 4 July 1796 from a chill caught thus.

Scudamore, John (II) (1757-1805), son of John (I) (qv, d.1796), was born on 11 June 1757 in Hanover Square, London. He married Lucy Walwyn (qv under James Walwyn, d.1800) and brought in Anthony Keck (qv) to refashion the old manor house Kentchurch Court. Lucy died at the birth of their son John Lucy Scudamore (qv) in 1798 and John (II) died on 12 April 1805.

Scudamore, John Lucy (1798-1875), son of John (II) Scudamore (qv, d.1805), was born at Kentchurch, and educated at Eton and Brasenose College, Oxford. In 1822 he married Sarah Laura (d.1863), daughter of Sir Harford Jones-Brydges (qv), and they completed the rebuilding of Kentchurch to Nash's plans under the supervision of Sir Harford. He was High Sheriff of Herefordshire and a JP, and like his father held the rank of colonel in the county militia. He was buried at Kentchurch.

Scudamore, Laura Adelaide (1831-1912), was born on 24 April 1831, the eldest child of John Lucy Scudamore (qv). She married Major Fitzherbert Dacre Lucas (1823-57), who added Scudamore to his name. He died at the siege of Lucknow. Their son Lt-Col Edward Scudamore Lucas-Scudamore (1853-1917) was Deputy Lieutenant of Herefordshire and is the ancestor of the present Lucas-Scudamore proprietors of Kentchurch. He lived at Castle Shane, Monaghan, Ireland where he was High Sheriff. He died on 9 March 1917 and was buried at Kentchurch.

Scudamore, Mary (née Shelton) (*c.*1550-1603), Lady Scudamore, was the daughter of Sir John Shelton of Norfolk and kinswoman of Queen Elizabeth's (qv) mother Anne Boleyn. She was called to Court in the 1570s where she became one of the 'trinity of ladies' who, with Blanche Parry (qv) and the Countess of Warwick, were Queen Elizabeth's foremost personal servants and controlled access to the queen. She met and married Sir John Scudamore (qv, d.1623) and the queen, whose temper was legendary, was furious. A maid wrote 'she hath delt liberall both with bloes and yevell wordes' and broke one of Mary's fingers in her rage. The Scudamores had no children but Mary was very fond of her step-children, taking their part in arguments with their father. Their home was Holme Lacy, where Mary died on 15 August 1603. She was buried in St Cuthbert's where there is a monument to her.

Scudamore, Philip (1528-1602), a younger son of John (qv, d.1571) and Sybil, married Joan Warncombe (1536-1635). Their daughter Sybil (1565-1635) married Sir John Kyrle (qv, d.1650) of Homme House, Much Marcle, and her splendid effigy rests in St Bartholomew's Church.

Scudamore, Richard Philip (1762-1831), John (II)'s (qv, d.1805) brother, succeeded to his seat in Parliament, which he held for the next 20 years, quietly opposing the government's socially oppressive measures and supporting the return of *habeas corpus*. He died on 5 March 1831.

Scudamore, Rowland (d.1631), brother of Sir John (qv, d.1623), bought Caradoc Court, Sellack from the Mynors (qv) in 1594 and remodelled it. It remained in the family until the 18th century.

Scudamore, Rowland (1577-1645), grandson of William (qv, d.1560) and Ursula Scudamore – he was a son of their youngest son George – held Parliamentarian sympathies at odds with the strong Royalist beliefs of the rest of his family. He was with Lord Leven's (qv) Scots army besieging Hereford in 1645. He went with a party to parley with his nephew Barnabas Scudamore (qv) in Hereford and was accidentally killed by Scottish fire from his own side.

Scudamore, William (1464-*c.*1520), of Holme Lacy, son of Philip Scudamore (qv under John (I) Skidmore) married Alice Mynors (qv under Richard Mynors) and their son was John Scudamore (qv, d.1571).

Scudamore, William (1514-1560), eldest son of John (qv, d.1571), married Ursula, daughter of Sir John Pakington. Born at Holme Lacy he made his home at Lyvers Ocle, an old Benedictine monastery his father had bought. He predeceased his father, leaving his son John (1542-1623, qv) a minor.

Scudamore-Stanhope, Edwyn (1793-1874), Baronet, succeeded, as a distant relative, to the Scudamore estates at Holme Lacy (see under Frances (Fitzroy)-Scudamore, d.1820), assuming the Scudamore name and making Holme Lacy House his county seat. His son, Henry Edwyn Chandos Scudamore-Stanhope (1821-70), became the 9th Earl of Chesterfield. He married Dorothea, daughter of Sir Adam Hay.

Scudamore-Stanhope, Edwyn Francis (1854-1933), 10th Earl of Chesterfield, son of Henry, 9th Earl of Chesterfield (see under Edwyn Scudamore-Stanhope, d.1874), was educated at Eton and Brasenose. Edwyn was Lord Stanhope between 1883 and 1887 before succeeding as earl. He practised as a barrister and served in Gladstone's government. He was Lord Steward of Queen Victoria's Household and created KG in 1915. He was buried at St Cuthbert's, Holme Lacy; his memorial in the churchyard is a bronze soldier by Gilbert Bayes. His younger brother Henry (d.1935) succeeded him as 11th Earl and is also buried in Holme Lacy churchyard. The 12th and last Earl, their nephew Edward Henry Scudamore-Stanhope (1889-1952), has a tablet in the church by his daughter Evelyn.

Seculer, Nicholas le and Joan his wife were Herefordshire landowners in the time of Henry II (qv). An ancestor, Nigel le Seculer, is recorded in Domesday as having land granted him by the Conqueror. Alexander le Seculer of Sutton St Nicholas is noted as being Henry II's physician in 1247. He and his sister Cecily were given lands in the Wormelow area.

Seddon, John (1725-70), minister, was born at Hereford on 8 December 1725 the son of Peter Seddon, dissenting minister, and his wife Elizabeth Eckley. The family later moved north and John went to Glasgow University. He became a dissenting minister in Warrington, where he continued to be based until his death on 23 January 1770.

Seddon, John Pollard (1827-1906), architect, was born in London on 19 September 1827. His family, well known cabinet makers, invented

a writing-table and filing cabinet in 1780 for Sir Herbert Croft, 5th baronet (1751-1816), a writer who that year published a novel called *Love and Madness*. The writing table designed for him became known as a 'Croft'. John like others of his generation was influenced by John Ruskin's *Seven Lamps of Architecture,* which he read in his twenties, and like Pugin (qv) regarded gothic as the only Christian art. He married Margaret Barber from Yorkshire in 1864 and they had three children. An early job of 1853 was the restoration of the 14th-century church of St Dubricius (qv), Hentland, painting ashlar stonework with flowers on the interior. He was sensitive but not sentimental about the mediaeval fabric and clear that his work was a contemporary interpretation. Frederick Kempson (qv) was a pupil in his London office in the 1850s and Seddon helped him set up his first office. Seddon worked on Kilpeck, supplying pews and pulpit (1864) and rebuilt the small church of St Andrew at Adforton in 1875, supplying the font with its little carved fishes. He was diocesan architect for Llandaff. With his partner John Prichard he built the extraordinary neo-Byzantine church of St Catherine's, Hoarwithy for Revd William Poole (qv). It has a narrow campanile up a steep flight of steps, high on the north bank of the Wye, with an open ground floor from which to enjoy views across the countryside and is connected to the church by a cloister. They built the school at Weston (1865) and rebuilt St Mary's, Kentchurch (1858-9). He also restored St Giles, Goodrich and St Deinst, Llangarron (1901). Seddon was a witty man of pungent articles and satirical lectures. He died on 1 February 1906 and is buried in Fulham cemetery in West London.

Sharp, Bertram (1876-1949), Jack's brother, (qv) played full back for Hereford Town and Hereford Thistle in the Birmingham League. He was signed for Aston Villa, Everton and Southampton, and joined Jack as an Everton director. He played cricket for Herefordshire Cricket Club. On retirement he ran a Liverpool public house.

Sharp, Cecil James (1859-1924), collector of English folk-songs and dances, was born on 22 November 1859 in Denmark Hill, London, the eldest son of John James Sharp, a slate merchant. He was educated at Clare College, Cambridge. He practised law in Australia for 10 years then returned to Britain and married Constance Birch. He taught music and discovered folk music and dancing when he saw a Morris group near Oxford. From then on he collected folk-songs, amassing over 1,500. In 1906 he published *English Folk-Songs for Schools*

dedicated to the Princes Edward and Albert (to whom Sharp was music tutor from 1904 to 1907). He found Herefordshire a good source of old songs and dances, which he collected with Ella Mary Leather and Vaughan Williams (qqv). They found *The Farmer's Curst Wife* and *The Bitter Withy* at Ross Workhouse for instance, recording 67-year-old Thomas Taylor on 10 September 1921. He and Leather believed in the purity of the folk source and saw corruption in the growing popularity of the folk tradition. He regarded the Morris dancing of Herefordshire and the Welsh borders as a corruption of an original style. Herefordshire Morris Men and Women still dance. One group is the Silurian Border Morris Men based at Ledbury. In 1911 Sharp was a founder of the English Folk Dance Society and in 1919 he became its director. He died in June 1924.

Sharp, Jack (1879-1938), sportsman, was born in Eign Street, Hereford and played football locally, winning a reputation as a fast right winger. Jack was signed by Aston Villa and transferred to Everton FC (1899-1910). He played two FA Cup finals, winning in 1906. He was later a director of Everton. He also played cricket for Lancashire (1899-1914) and test cricket for England. After the First World War he was captain of Lancashire 1923-5. There is a plaque to him in Eign Street, Hereford and he featured on cigarette cards of the time. He retired to run a sports shop in Liverpool.

Shelley, Jane (17th century) was connected with Sir John Lingen (qv) through his son-in-law William Shelley. She founded the Lingen Hospital, a Hereford almshouse for six widows in the Whitecross Road, in 1609. She left £30 p.a. from her properties at Kenchester and Haymonds Farm to be divided between the six widows and a further sum for repairs. The cottages were restored in 1801 and again in 1849 but were eventually demolished and replaced by the six houses behind Bricknell Close by the Bricknell Webb Benefaction of 1968.

Sibthorpe, Margaret (1836-1916), feminist, née Shurmer, born in Hereford, married John Sibthorpe in Scotland. She agitated through her journalism for the rights of women, for their education and social standing, for rational dress, and for theosophy.

Siddons, Sarah (1755-1831), actress, was the daughter of Roger (qv) and Sarah Kemble. She was the greatest English tragic actress and her brother John Philip Kemble became one of the greatest actor managers. She was born and baptised in Brecon where her parents' travelling company was appearing, but the Kembles hailed from Church Street, Hereford. She acted in her parents' troupe in the Marches and Midlands and by the age of 12 had performed all the principal female roles in Shakespeare. She married fellow actor William Siddons. Pregnancies didn't interfere with her acting: at Gloucester she went into labour during a performance. David Garrick (qv) encouraged her to go to London where she was initially troubled by the large stages but built up a great reputation and left her feckless husband. Her performances were often accom-

panied by hysterical sobbing from the audience, and her rise from a hypnotic monotone to wild shrieks and frightening rages caused fainting. In her forties Siddons returned to John Boles Watson's (qv) Theatre in Broad Street Hereford for five extremely successful plays and doubled prices; later her brother John Philip Kemble had similar success in *Hamlet* here. Siddons died on 8 June 1831 and was buried in Paddington Green cemetery.

Sidney, Philip (1554-86), poet, courtier and model of Elizabethan chivalry. His *Arcadia* is one of the best poems and *Apology for Poetry* the best work of literary criticism in the Elizabethan period, and his sonnet sequence *Astrophel and Stella* started the sonnet craze of the 1590s. He was born at Penshurst Place, Kent on 30 November 1554 the eldest son of Sir Henry Sidney and Lady Mary Dudley, connected to many of the aristocratic families of England. His uncle Robert Dudley, Earl of Leicester, was Queen Elizabeth's favourite. Sidney went to Shrewsbury School where, aged 12, he was presented to the Moreton Magna prebend of Hereford Cathedral by Bishop John Scory (qv). His tutor at Christ Church, Oxford was Thomas Thornton (qv) and here he met Richard Hakluyt (qv) who urged his involvement with the colo-

nizing of Virginia. He fell in love with Penelope, daughter of Walter Devereux, Viscount Hereford (qv, d.1576) and dedicated *Astrophel and Stella* to her. There was talk of their marriage but, on her father's death, Penelope married Baron Rich. Sidney married Frances daughter of Sir Francis Walsingham, Elizabeth's secretary and spymaster. After Sidney's death Frances became the wife of Robert Devereux (qv, d.1601). Sidney died from a gangrenous leg while fighting in the Netherlands, on 17 October 1586.

Silas, Ellis Luciano (1885-1972), artist, was born on 13 July 1885 in London, son of Louis Ferdinand Silas, artist and designer and Letizia Sara Paggi, an opera singer. He trained in his father's London studio and with Walter Sickert, concentrating on marine painting. He moved to Australia in 1907 to paint coastal scenes and in 1914 joined the Australian army. He was posted to Egypt as a signaller, like Brian Hatton (qv), and in 1915 to Gallipoli but was invalided home with exhaustion and returned to England to convalesce. There are sketchbooks from this period and a book published

as *Crusading at Anzac*. In Australia he worked as a commercial artist and in 1922 travelled to the Trobriand Islands where he sketched and collected ethnographic material which resulted in *A Primitive Arcadia* (1926). Back in England he established himself as a maritime artist in oils and watercolour, illustrating books and posters. In 1927 he married Ethel Detheridge and they lived in London. He made publicity posters for an airline and with the outbreak of the Second World War moved to Hereford where he was employed by Barronia Metals, an aircraft parts factory producing murals, posters and other war publicity. There are photographs and original works in oil and watercolour by him in the Hereford City Art Gallery and his work is represented in the National Maritime Museum. Silas died in London on 2 May 1972, survived by his wife.

Silvanus, a Roman tutelary spirit worshipped in 3rd-century Herefordshire and across the Roman Empire, was the protector of flocks, cattle and field boundaries and delighted in trees – as his name indicates. He was worshipped on the banks of the Wye, as an altar dedicated to him attests. It was found in Broad Street, Hereford but came from a rural temple by the river near the Roman town of *Magnis* (Kenchester). Silvanus loved Pomona, a nymph of the apple tree, and would have enjoyed Herefordshire.

Simcoe, Elizabeth Posthuma (1762-1850), diarist and watercolourist, was the posthumous daughter of Thomas Gwillim (qv). She was brought up by her mother's sister Margaret Spinckes at Old Court, Whitchurch until her aunt married and they moved to Honiton, Devon. Here, aged 19, Elizabeth married her new uncle's godson John Graves Simcoe (1752-1806). He was the first Lieutenant-Governor of the new colony of Upper Canada and founder of Toronto where they made their lives. Simcoe's brilliant career was cut short by illness and death half a century before his wife's. She returned to Devon to further the careers of their 11 children and is remembered for her diaries and paintings. There is a grand, ruinous monument to the family in the graveyard of St Dubricius' (qv) Church, Whitchurch.

Simon, Ernest Emil Darwin (1879-1960), 1st Baron Simon of Wythenshawe, politician, was born in Didsbury, Manchester, on 9 October 1879. His father, Henry Simon (1835-99), a German migrant, owned flour mills in Manchester. Ernest went to Rugby School and Pembroke College, Oxford. He returned to develop the family business and in 1912 he

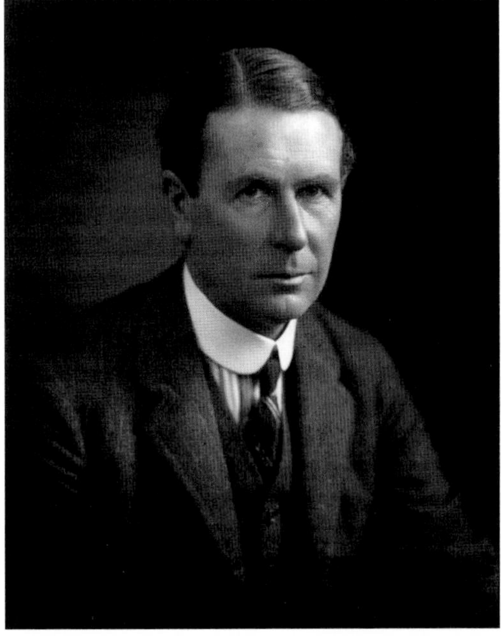

married Shena Dorothy Potter (1883-1972). He became a Manchester City councillor and in 1921-2 was Lord Mayor. Between 1923 and 1931 he was elected Liberal MP for Manchester Withington and was involved with the slum clearance programme there. His son Roger became a solicitor and founder of CND and Brian an historian. He bought the farm Leadon Court near Bosbury where he experimented with methods of pasteurising milk. Here meetings were held to develop Liberal policy on social reform. It was at a meeting at Leadon Court that the Liberal summer school movement began. He was Governor of the BBC and appointed baron in 1947. Lord Simon died in Withington after a stroke on 3 October 1960. Leadon Court is now a care home.

Sinclair, George Robertson (1863-1917), organist, was born on 28 October 1863 in Croydon. He was organist at Gloucester and Truro cathedrals and in 1889 was appointed director of music, organist and master of the choristers at Hereford Cathedral, where he remained until his death. He was involved in the Three Choirs Festival and raised musical standards. Dr Sinclair lived at 20 Church Street, Hereford with his bulldog Dan. He was the dedicatee of Elgar's *Te Deum and Benedictus* and he and Elgar (qv) would walk along the river together opposite the cathedral. Dan's bark can be heard in variation XI of Elgar's *Enigma Variations* as he scrambles out of the river, and his statue stands on the river bank walk. There is an enamel portrait of his master at his organ in the cathedral by Fanny Bunn (qv).

Skidmore, Francis (1817-96), metalworker, was born in Birmingham and moved to Coventry as a child. He was apprenticed in his father's jewellery business but preferring non-precious metals built up his own metal-working firm and in 1859 founded a factory in Alma Street, Hillfields, Coventry. Sir George Gilbert Scott (qv) contracted with him to supply the ironwork for his restoration of Hereford Cathedral. His marvellous crossing screen of 1862 was of gilt cast-iron covered with statues and decorative gems in a middle-pointed style. It was hailed as a masterpiece at the International Exhibition of that year and stood in the cathedral until in 1967 it fell victim to 20th-century distaste for the decorative arts and was dismantled and stored in poor conditions. It was eventually bought by the Herbert Art Galley in Coventry and conserved and reassembled by the Victoria

and Albert Museum where it may once more be seen. Other ironwork by Skidmore in the cathedral remains, such as the gates to the choir aisles and at the entrance to the lady chapel. His work for the Albert Memorial in Hyde Park has also been renovated. Skidmore was not a businessman and his insistence on perfection lost the firm money. Reduced to poverty, Coventry awarded him a pension. He died as the result of a traffic accident.

Skidmore, John (I) (d.1415), knight, was the son of Richard Skidmore alias Ewyas of Rowlestone. He was bailiff of Edmund (III) Mortimer's (qv) lands at Radnor, Comberwyne and Eardisley and keeper of the immense Radnor Forest. At Edmund's death he sat on the jury of inquest into his lands in Herefordshire in 1382. He was commissioned to keep the mills on the River Usk and the fishery there until Edmund's heir Roger (VII) Mortimer (qv) was of age. He was an escheator of Herefordshire and south-east Wales, constable of Goodrich Castle in 1396, Mortimer's constable at Clifford and Henry Bolingbroke's (qv Henry IV) steward at Brecon; he also oversaw the priories of Craswall and Abergavenny. He married first Margaret, daughter and heir of Sir Thomas Brut of Britte Court, Kingsland, and later Glyn Dŵr's daughter Alice. His dealings with Owain Glyn Dŵr (qv) during his revolt were ambiguous and he was removed from his stewardship. There is a Marches tradition that Glyn Dŵr ended his life at either Monnington Straddel in the Golden Valley or in the tower Sir John had built at Kentchurch, a property he had acquired from the Wroth family. Sir John and his son fought at Agincourt, where he was wounded. Many of the bowmen, who contributed greatly to the victory, were from Skidmore's Herefordshire estates. Later, wider knowledge of Sir John's marriage to Glyn Dŵr's daughter caused him to lose his offices, and he retired to Kentchurch.

Skidmore, John (II) (*c*.1396-*c*.1475) of Kentchurch Court, Bredwardine, Moccas and Thruxton, was the son of Sir John (I, qv) and Margaret. He married Joan, daughter of John Parry of Poston. He was at Agincourt with his father, John (I) (qv). His sons and brothers feuded lawlessly with John Talbot (qv, d.1453) in Archenfield, committing murder and kidnap. He was MP for the shire in 1420-21 and thereafter and a knight by 1445. He supported Henry VI in the Wars of the Roses and fought at the disastrous Battle of Castillon in Aquitaine in 1453, where his rival John Talbot (qv, d.1453) fell. He was at the Lancastrian defeat at Blore Heath near Market Drayton in 1459. The Battle of Wakefield (1460) restored power temporarily to Lancaster and Skidmore was ordered to confiscate York's lands in Herefordshire. He took 30 men at arms to Mortimers Cross in 1461, a bloody defeat for Lancaster from which he narrowly escaped to the safety of Pembroke Castle. Edward IV (qv) excluded him from his pardon and, although his life was spared, all his lands were forfeit. He had the attainder reversed in 1472 and died shortly after. They had three sons: John, James and Henry, and four daughters: one, Elizabeth, marrying John Pye (qv under Pye family). His son John married Ellen, daughter of Sir Robert Whitney (qv, d.1441) and their daughter Janet (or Sioned) married Llywelyn ap Gruffydd Fychan of Carmarthenshire. His son James (fl.1441-54) was heir of Kentchurch. James married Maud, daughter of Gruffydd ap Nicholas of Newton, Carmarthenshire. In 1454 his father-in-law was charged at Hereford for assaults but freed through Skidmore interest. Skidmore's last son Henry (d.1489) lived at Moccas and married Elizabeth, daughter of John Chabnor. (Her second husband was Hugh Vaughan.) Skidmore was Sheriff of Herefordshire at the time of his death.

Skidmore, Thomas (fl.1390-1422), alias Ewyas, of Rowlestone, was Sir John's brother. (John (I) Skidmore, qv). He, his brothers and nephews were a source of anarchy in the Archenfield area: in 1398 he attacked Dore Abbey with an armed party, taking away the seal and monuments and imprisoning the abbey's servants. In 1422, with Maurice Skidmore, the terrifying John Abrahall (qv) and 60 men arrayed for war, he broke into the house of Maurice Dawe, a servant of John Talbot (qv, d.1453) and murdered him. At the same time William Skidmore was committing murder and abductions at Aconbury. The inhabitants of Archenfield appealed to the authorities but the lawlessness continued until Lord Talbot eventually prevailed. Thomas was five times Mayor of Hereford (1385-94) where he had a house.

Skinner, Edward (1544-1631), fifth son of Stephen Skinner (d.1557) of The Burtons, Ledbury, was a wool dealer and financier. He married Elizabeth (b.*c.*1548) and they had five sons and five daughters, all seen at prayer in their remarkable monument in the chancel of Ledbury Church, their clothes accurately depicted. In 1592 he and the rector arranged for piped water to be brought into Ledbury by a conduit. He bought estates and houses in the area and in 1595 built what has been called the best black and white mansion in the county, the five-bay New House at Ledbury's Top Cross, which stands in its own deer park (in which the bishops of Hereford hunted). In the next century the mansion was sold to the Biddulphs (qv). A John Skinner was High Sheriff in 1649.

Skinner, John (fl 1650-60s) from Ledbury was the pastor of the 'Gathered' Baptist Church at Weston under Penyard. In 1653 he signed a letter to Cromwell as an Elder of the Gathered Churches. John Tombes's (qv) name is also on the letter. Weston Church was a Chapel of Ease to Ross then and Skinner was ejected from his position at the Restoration.

Skinner, Robert (1591–1670), a relation of the Ledbury Skinners from Northamptonshire, was the Laudian Bishop of Oxford until put out during the Interregnum. At the Restoration Dr Skinner resumed his bishopric and immediately began ordaining priests, amongst them Thomas Traherne (qv), at Launton, Oxfordshire. In 1663 he was made Bishop of Worcester. An Edmund Skinner was rector of Cradley in the 17th century.

Skinner, Samuel (d.1725), naval captain, a descendant of Edward, was 'no mean proficient in naval affairs' as his wall monument in Ledbury Church tells us. This surrounds his portrait with naval implements, guns and sextants, cleverly executed amongst spin-drift and smoke by Thomas White (qv). There are other 18th- and 19th-century Skinner memorials in the chancel of Ledbury Church.

Skip/Skippe: A Norfolk family who appeared in Herefordshire when John Skippe was appointed bishop of the diocese by Henry VIII. His heirs lived at Upper Hall, Ledbury and bought church property cheaply at the Reformation. The Skippes suffered attack during the Battle of Ledbury in 1645. As a magistrate in the next century John Skippe read the riot act from Upper Hall and fired on a mob during the Turnpike Riots. Their time ended with the death of bachelor artist John Skippe in 1812.

Skippe, Edmund (d.1608), as Bishop Skippe's (John Skippe, qv, d.1552) brother, was able to acquire church property. He married Alice Unett (qv) in 1558 and they lived at Upper Hall in Ledbury.

Skippe, Edmund (fl.1650s), of Ledbury, was perhaps Edmund Skippe's (qv, d.1608) son. An ordained minister at Bodenham, he was ejected in the Commonwealth. He was in a controversy with the Quaker Humphrey Smith (qv), who reported that after much anguish Skippe renounced tithes and became a Baptist, publishing the broadside *A Declaration of Several Baptized Believers* (1659).

He had probably been influenced by the Baptist in all but name John Tombes (qv), who preached at Leominster and Ledbury.

Skippe, George (1633-90), son of John Skippe's (qv, d.1684) second marriage, was educated at Balliol and Gray's Inn and lived at Upper Hall. In 1661 he married Sarah (1642-65), daughter of Esa Risby of St Andrew, Holborn. She brought a portion of £2,000 to George but died after only four years of marriage. Her brass is at the south side of the altar steps of Ledbury Church. George invested Sarah's dowry in the farm of alcohol tax for various towns in partnership with her father. In 1669 he married Elizabeth, daughter of Hugh Norris, a London merchant also of Holborn, who brought him a dowry of £3,000. They had several children including John his heir (qv, d.1764). He lent out money on interest and financed business ventures. One partner, Sir Clement Clerke (qv), 'that false man', over-extended himself and Skippe rescued him from debtors' prison by paying his debts. Skippe also funded Clerke's scheme to improve the navigation of the River Stour in Worcestershire, taking the project over when Clerke again failed (it eventually only connected Kidderminster with Stourbridge) and he had to write off much of his investment. His post from London was delivered to the Ram Inn, Gloucester and he paid 10 shillings a year to have it brought to Ledbury, often by foot. Skippe kept a memorandum from 1668 to his death of the books he bought and read, his legal and business dealings, how much his family drank and spent on cider and the details of his planting of gardens and orchards at Upper Hall, including the Redstreak (qv) and several otherwise unrecorded species of peach. He records a drink-driving incident when, out for dinner one evening at the Hoptons of Canon Frome House, their coach hit a pier of a bridge over the Leadon on the way home. In 1683 he noted earthquakes in Herefordshire. The manuscript is in the Woolhope archive at Hereford Library waiting for a publisher. Elizabeth and her son John lived on at Upper Hall after George's death. John married Jane daughter of Thomas Wellington of Whately *c.*1702.

Skippe, John (d.1552), Bishop of Hereford 1539-52, of Norfolk parentage, was educated at Gonville Hall, Cambridge, where he was subsequently master 1536-40. A supporter of Henry VIII's divorce, he was appointed Anne Boleyn's chaplain and was with her at her execution. He

was an early supporter of Protestant reform and involved with Thomas Cranmer in the creation of Edward VI's 1548 prayer book. In 1539 he was made Bishop of Hereford and may have been involved in the end of Wigmore Priory. When Skippe came to Hereford he found many of the clergy in prison and released them. He arranged for the transfer of the Forest Deanery in the south of the diocese to the new see of Gloucester and oversaw the dissolution of 77 chapels and chantries in Herefordshire. He died at Monthalt House, the Bishop of Hereford's London residence and was buried in its chapel, St Mary's. Among his papers was a recipe for apple tart. His sister Alice married John Willason (qv) of Sugwas who leased church property including Upper Hall, Ledbury with its portion of tithes. Their son Richard left the Upper Hall estate with its rights as portionist (i.e. the right to a share of the tithes) to Edmund (qv, d.1608).

Skippe, John (d.1619), son of Edmund Skippe (qv, d.1608), was born and died at Upper Hall. He married Sybil, daughter of John Berington (qv under George Berington). His gravestone can be seen by the altar in Ledbury Church.

Skippe, John (1604-84), son of John (d.1619, qv), was baptised at Ledbury on 8 November 1604. His second wife was Mary, daughter of Thomas Copley of Worcestershire. Skippe's house, Upper Hall, was damaged in Prince Rupert's (qv) attack on Ledbury in 1645 and later that year he was one of Henry Lingen's (qv) garrison at Goodrich Castle when it was besieged by John Birch (qv). He wrote a personal account of this siege which is now lost. He was Deputy Lieutenant of Herefordshire in 1676 and High Sheriff in 1680. He leased his house to the apothecary William Matthews in 1681 and died at nearby Wall Hills in September 1684 and was buried in Ledbury Church. His daughter Margaret married William Skinner of Ledbury Park and their child was Constance. John's other children were Anne, Susan, Mary, Elizabeth, Henrietta and Richard.

Skippe, John (1679-1764) married the heiress Jane, daughter of Thomas Wellington of Whately, Warwickshire, and they lived at Upper Hall. He was High Sheriff in 1706 and JP. Justice Skippe was holding turnpike rioters prisoner at Upper Hall (qv Reynolds and Baylis) when, on the night of 21 September 1735, a mob attacked the house in an attempt to free them. Skippe read the riot act and armed his men who fired on the mob. The battle filled the streets of Ledbury until the rioters were chased off into the countryside.

Skippe, John (1707-96) of Upper Hall, eldest son of John (qv, d.1764), married Penelope, daughter of Thomas Symonds Powell Symonds (qv) of Pengethley Manor. He kept a memorandum book (now in Hereford Record Office) in which he describes a journey through Italy in 1766-7, during which tour he bought Correggio's *Leda and the Swan* for £60. He lists his expenditure on painting materials and his notes on a technique for copying Titian's flesh tints. He was High Sheriff in 1772. His daughter Penelope (1740-1830) inherited Upper Hall after the death of her brother John (qv, d.1812). She married James Martin (qv, d.1810) of the banking family, bringing the estate to him.

Skippe, John (1741-1812), artist and wood-engraver, was born at Upper Hall on 7 July 1741, the eldest son of John (qv, d.1796). He

was educated at Merton College, Oxford, then travelled through Italy with his father making studies from the old masters. He studied under J.B. Malchair and John Baptist Jackson. His engravings were used by the Worcestershire antiquary Treadway Russell Nash (qv) for his edition of *Hudibras*. The British Museum holds drawings and colour engravings after the old masters by him, and there is work in the V&A, the Tate and Hereford Art Gallery. There is a painting by him of Upper Hall in 1790. He died unmarried on 14 October 1812.

Slaughter, Edward (1603-86) of Cheney Court, Bishop's Frome, was the son of George Slaughter (d.1650) and Katherine Arnold. He married Jane Bellingham of Cowarne, and their son and grandson, called Bellingham Slaughter, lived at Cheney Court.

Slaughter, Edward (1655-1729), Jesuit and Hebraist, was born at Cheney Court on 5 January 1655. The family produced other Catholic priests. He became a professor at the Jesuit College at Liège, where he died and was buried. Cheney Court burnt down and the building now called Cheney Court was the Slaughters' home farm.

Slingsby, Henry (1602-58), baronet of Scriven, Yorkshire, sat as MP for Knaresborough in the Parliaments of 1625 and 1640 and raised forces for the king during the Civil War. After Charles's execution Sir Henry retired to his home at Knaresborough and wrote his memoirs. He had stayed at Hereford at some stage and wrote:

This city of Hereford is cituate'd not much unlike to Yorke, and in some parts resembles it very much; for it hath a round tower mount'd upon a hill, like to Cliffords tower, and ye mills near it, with some little works about, having ye river Wye running close by, but ye walls tho' they be high yet are not mount'd upon a rampeir as Yorke walls are.' ['Original Memoirs, written during The Great Civil War Being The Life of Sir Henry Slingsby'].

He became involved in plots against the Commonwealth for which he was executed. His son Thomas succeeded to the baronetcy.

Smalbroke, Richard (1672-1749), librarian and bishop, was born in Birmingham, educated at King Edward's School and Trinity College, Oxford and ordained. He graduated DD in 1709. He was vicar of Lugwardine and a residentiary canon of Hereford where from 1713 to 1724 he was librarian of the cathedral's chained library, then sited in the lady chapel. He presided over a revival of the neglected library a hundred years after its removal to the lady chapel (qv Thornton), dedicating its income (which was being spent on the choir) to maintenance and acquisitions, selling duplicates and encouraging gifts. He wrote a catalogue, listing over 1,000 books and their whereabouts in the chapel. In 1723 he was appointed Bishop of St David's and in 1731 was translated to the see of Coventry and Lichfield. He wrote *A Vindication of the Miracles of our Blessed* Saviour (1729) to refute Thomas Woolston's freethinking views. He married Catherine Brookes and found their children and her relations church offices. He died at Lichfield on 22 December 1749 and is buried in that cathedral.

Smalman, Francis (1565-1633), lawyer, was the son of William Smalman of Ivington Bury near Leominster, a farm he rented from his brother Thomas. Smalman settled as a money lender in Clerkenwell, where he prospered and married twice: Elizabeth (d.1602, buried in Leominster Priory) née Stockmede, widow of George Croft of Clerkenwell, with whom he had a son and two daughters; then Susanna (d.1632) née Fabian, widow of John Clarke of Clerkenwell. In 1618 he bought the newly rebuilt Kinnersley Castle from Roger Vaughan's (qv, d.1607) widow Elizabeth, and with it the manor of Letton. He married his daughter Jane to Rowland Howorth (qv under Epiphanius Howorth) of Widemarsh, Hereford, and another daughter to a Coningsby, and had himself elected MP for Leominster in 1621, partnering Fitzwilliam Coningsby (qv). Together they attempted

the removal of weirs from the Wye. He was a JP and Sheriff of Hereford in 1626-27. He died on 7 September 1633. The superb Smalman wall monument in St James's Church, Kinnersley was erected by his son William (qv). It is by Samuel Baldwin (qv) and shows the family all kneeling at prayer. Smalman left his daughter the enormous sum of £1,000 in his will.

Smalman, William (*c*.1615-43), son of Francis (qv), married Lucy (*c*.1610-73), daughter of Sir Robert Whitney (qv, d.1653) in 1631 – she was named after her mother's family, the Lucys (qv). Their daughter Lucy married James Pytts of Kyre Park, Worcs and inherited Kinnersley. Smalman was elected MP for Leominster in the Short Parliament of 1640, the partner of Walter Kyrle (qv, d.1660). He was one of the Nine Worthies (see index) who formed the Royalist leadership in Herefordshire in the summer of 1642, and he and a son died in the Civil War fighting for King Charles. In around 1648 his widow married John Booth (d.1704) of Durham, a Royalist cavalry captain, and they had a daughter Mary, who married John Dutton Colt (qv). After Lucy's death Captain Booth married Rebecca (née Vincent) widow of Sir John Kyrle (qv, d.1680). Lucy and John Booth were both buried in Hereford Cathedral. Lucy, her daughter, was also buried there with Smalman. Dingley (qv) drew her monument, since destroyed.

Smart, John (d.*c*.1539), last Abbot of Wigmore 1518-39, was educated at St Mary's College, Oxford. He was Cardinal Wolsey's (qv) candidate for abbot and acted as suffragan for Bishop Booth (qv). By the 1530s Wigmore Abbey was dilapidated and burdened by debt. Wolsey tried to have Smart removed but fell from power. Bishop Booth authorised John Lee, a canon of Wigmore and John Cragge, a cathedral prebendary to reform the administration but Smart wrested back authority with the help of Canon Richard Cubleigh. In 1534 Booth also authorised Smart to hold visitations, inspecting the diocese on the bishop's behalf. In 1536 Edward Foxe (qv), the new Bishop of Hereford, sent his vicar-general Hugh Corwen to investigate Wigmore. His report was damning but Cromwell was now closing the monasteries in any event. Smart was pensioned off with £80 p.a. and disappears from history. Recent critics have found him dishonest and ambitious.

Smirke, Robert (1780-1867), architect, second son of the painter Robert Smirke, was born in London on 1 October 1780. He was accomplished in Latin and Greek and loved drawing. He was apprenticed to archi-

tects John Soane and John Dance and studied at the Royal Academy. Other brothers also became architects. In 1799 he toured the classical lands of southern Italy and Greece and watched the Elgin Marbles being crowbarred off the Parthenon and crashing to the ground. In 1812 Earl Somers (qv John Somers Cocks, d.1845) commissioned Eastnor Castle from him – a romantic pile that would cost more than £100,000. Smirke was on site for three weeks initially, returning to develop his ideas and take instruction from Lord Somers, who wanted it done quickly. Smirke was conscientious and his health suffered. The west wing was finished in 1813 and the family moved in, with dust and scaffolding for another ten years and unfinished interiors for decades. Smirke's use of iron trusses in the roofs introduced this new material into domestic use. The castle made his name in Herefordshire and secured him other commissions. Hereford Corporation asked him to build the Shire Hall as a replacement for the inconvenient county courthouse. The old gaolhouse that stood on the site was demolished and Smirke put up the Doric temple we now see. It was based on the Theseum which he had sketched in Athens with a portico of giant columns. In 1817 he designed Haffield, Donnington for John Biddulph's (qv, d.1845) nephew William Gordon (qv). On Castle Green he built Fosse Cottage with a pillared portico which can still be seen. Lord Somers had Smirke design the south range of St Katherine's Almshouses in Ledbury High Street in 1822 (the north range was added 40 years later by William Chick [qv]). In 1845 he built the village school in Eastnor. Smirke was one of the finest architects of the 19th century; his British Museum is one of the great buildings of the world. He died at his home in Cheltenham on 18 April 1867.

Smith, Frederick William Boyton (1837-1911), composer from Dorset, was a boarder at Hereford Cathedral School and one of George Townshend Smith's (qv) organ scholars. He wrote many salon pieces and later set his friend Thomas Hardy's verse to music.

Smith, George Townshend (1813-77), born on 14 November 1813, was appointed organist and choirmaster at Hereford Cathedral in 1843 following the tragic death of John Hunt (qv) and served for 34 years, the cathedral's longest serving organist. He planned the programme and conducted at the Three Choirs Festivals at Hereford and in 1864 introduced chamber recitals. He took organ scholars, one being the composer Frederick Boyton Smith (qv). He died on 3 August 1877, survived by his wife and daughters. A brass plate commemorates him in the cathedral's south choir aisle, and a stained glass window in the north transept clerestory.

Smith, Humphrey (1624-63), Quaker preacher, was born at Stoke Bliss, a parish east of Bromyard, now in Worcestershire. His parents Humphrey and Elianor farmed in north-east Herefordshire and he at Much Cowarne where he married a Jane. He left his farm at the outbreak of the Civil Wars, began to preach and joined the Parliamentary army. Like many at this time he drifted through the sects before joining the nascent Quakers and becoming known to George Fox (qv). He wandered the country preaching as a Quaker, imprisoned and abused wherever he went, dying in a Worcestershire prison. He published spiritual and prophetic writings. His son Humphrey was also a Quaker.

Smith, Isaac Gregory (1826-1920), clergyman, born in Manchester on 21 November 1826, was educated at Rugby and Trinity College, Oxford. He was a Fellow of Brasenose College, was ordained and presented to the college living of Tedstone Delamere. He married Augusta, daughter of Revd G.W. Murray and from 1872 to 1896 was vicar of Great Malvern. From 1870 he was a prebendary of Hereford Cathedral. He wrote books on theology and philosophy and a history of Worcester diocese (1882). He was a diocesan inspector of schools. He died on 17 January 1920.

Smith, Josiah William (1816-87), legal writer from Baldock, Hertfordshire, was born on 3 April 1816. He was a JP in Herefordshire.

As a QC he was County Court judge for Herefordshire and Shropshire, known for his individuality: he once refused leave to appeal in case his judgement was overruled. He wrote books on law which are still standard and religious manuals. He and his wife lived at Athelstan Hall on Aylestone Hill, Hereford. He was buried at Baldock, Hertfordshire.

Smith, Martin Linton (1869-1950), Bishop of Hereford 1920-30, was educated at Hertford College, Oxford and married Kathleen Dewe. He was ordained and worked at Liverpool and Colchester. He won a DSO on the Somme in the First World War and was subsequently raised to the episcopate as suffragan Bishop of Warrington. He became Bishop of Hereford in 1920 and was translated to Rochester 1930-39. His portrait by Francis Dodd hangs in Hertford College.

Smith, Miles (*c*.1553-1624), Bishop of Gloucester, was born in Hereford, the son of a fletcher. He was educated at Corpus Christi and Brasenose Colleges, Oxford and was a noted scholar. He was ordained and in 1580 Bishop Scory (qv) of Hereford presented him to the prebend of Hinton at Hereford in 1580. He became vicar of Bosbury in 1584 and rector of Hampton Bishop in 1587, but as a canon residentiary he lived in a cathedral house. He married Mary Hawkins of Cardiff and they had sons and daughters. He graduated BD in 1585 and DD in 1594. He was a linguist, skilled in Hebrew, Chaldee, Syriac and Arabic, and his study notes and portrait can be seen in the cathedral library. He was a translator of the 1611 Bible, being responsible for several books of the Old Testament and, with Thomas Bilson, Bishop of Winchester, was a member of the supervisory committee which made the final review. He wrote the prefatory address to the 'most dread Sovereign' King James, as a reward for which, in 1612, he was appointed Bishop of Gloucester with William Laud (qv) as his dean, an unhappy pairing of low and high church tendencies. He died at Gloucester on 20 October 1624 and his memorial, between those of his two daughters, can be seen in the lady chapel at Gloucester Cathedral.

Smith, Samuel, see under **William Lowe**

Smith, Sydney (1771-1845), clergyman and wit, spent his early years at the family home of Bromesberrow Place near Ledbury. A founder and lifelong contributor to the *Edinburgh Review*, he is said to have been so amusing that his servants were allowed a quiet rest after serving at table. He was a friend of the Stackhouse Actons (qv Frances Stackhouse Acton) whom he visited at Elton Hall and Downton Castle.

Solers: The family came from Soliers near Caen in Normandy and have given their name to Bridge Sollers and Hope Sollers. A Mary Solers married Simon de Brugge (qv) *c*.1297.

Somerset, Lord Arthur (1671-1743) was a younger son of Henry Somerset (qv, d.1700), and lived at Poston House in Vowchurch with his wife Mary (d.1724), daughter of Sir William Russell of Laugharne. Her mother, Hester, died at Poston House in 1717. Lord Arthur was the dedicatee of Thomas Apperley's (qv) book *Observations in Physic*. His eldest daughter Mary married Algernon Greville, and through their daughter Poston passed to the Boughtons (qv Charles William Boughton). Lord Arthur's second daughter, Anne, married Uvedale Tomkins Price (qv).

Somerset, Henry (1629-1700), Lord Herbert of Raglan, 3rd Marquess of Worcester from 1667, married Lady Mary Capel. He was Lord President of the Council in the Marches (1672-89), and JP in Herefordshire (1663-89). He was created Duke of Beaufort by Charles II. As a non-juror after the Glorious Revolution he was stripped of his offices. His daughter Anne (1673-1763), also non-juring, became the countess of Coventry, a bibliophile, writer and advocate of female education.

Somerset, Henry (1707-45), 3rd Duke of Beaufort, great-grandson of the 1st Duke, had estates in Herefordshire and in 1729 was high steward. In 1729 he married the most eligible heiress in Herefordshire, Frances Fitzroy-Scudamore (qv, d.1750), daughter of James (qv, d.1716) and Frances Scudamore. Somerset took the name Scudamore by Act of Parliament. In 1741 Frances was discovered in an affair with William Lord Talbot and Somerset divorced her. See Frances Fitzroy-Scudamore's entry for more about this sorry affair.

Somerset, Henry Richard Charles (1849-1932), politician and comptroller of the household under Disraeli 1874-79, was JP in Herefordshire and sworn of the Privy Council. Like his namesake Henry Somerset (qv, d.1745), he also made an unhappy marriage in Herefordshire, in this case to Lady Isabella Somers Cocks (qv) in 1872. After having a child they separated and Somerset lived abroad to avoid scandal, Isabella being granted custody of their son.

Southall, Henry (1836-1916), draper, was a Quaker benefactor called the 'grand old man of Ross'. He was one of the Improvement Commissioners for the development of Ross. He managed a meteorological station in the town, for many years recording the weather, and was elected a Fellow of the Royal Meteorological Society, in 1895 producing a paper, *Floods in the West Midlands*.

Southey, Robert (1774-1843), poet laureate 1813-43, was born in Bristol on 12 August 1774. His father was a draper and his mother, Margaret Hill (1752-1802) was from a Herefordshire gentry family. He went to Westminster School where he was flogged and Balliol College, Oxford where he learnt to swim. He was deeply influenced by Coleridge (qv) and they married the Bristol sisters Edith and Sarah Fricker and planned to set up a pantisocratic ('all equal') commune in America. This fell through and they settled in Keswick where they both wrote furiously. When Coleridge left his wife and children, Southey took them in. In 1813 Southey was appointed poet laureate and published his *Life of Nelson*. He met the Wordsworths (qv) at nearby Grasmere and he and his daughter liked to visit Mary Wordsworth's relations, the Hutchinsons, at Brinsop Court (qv under Wordsworth), where Sara Hutchinson acted as his amanuensis. He enjoyed the Wye

valley. After Edith's death in 1837 he married the poet Caroline Anne Bowles. He died on 21 March 1843.

Speed, John (1552-1629), cartographer, was born at Farndon, Cheshire the son of a tailor. His father's trade made him a freeman of the Merchant Taylors' Company who commissioned maps from him. He married Susanna Draper and had 12 sons and six daughters. Inspired by Christopher Saxton (qv), he strove to produce an accurate atlas of the country. He travelled widely with his sons surveying the country, many places (including Hereford) being surveyed for the first time. In collecting his material he was helped by fellows of the Society of Antiquaries such as Robert Cotton and William Camden (qv). He was generous in sharing his own findings, helping Cotton with numismatics. In 1602 he prepared map plates, engraved by Jodocus Hondius, and in 1606 published *The Theatre of the Empire of Great Britaine.* His map of Herefordshire shows the Battle of Mortimers Cross but sites it near Tenbury. The Hereford City map is dated 1610 and shows details like the Whitefriars by the Wye and the Blackfriars with the old preaching cross standing in the fields to the north. The five gates are named, and Hereford Castle is a huge structure with gatehouse to the north and water gate to the Wye, the only part now standing. He shows that the stream that fed the moat was fast enough to drive two mills. Round the edge of his plates runs the story of British history, its battles and institutions and a gazetteer of place names. The work was an instant success in many editions, copied as standard until the 18th century. By 1625 he had become blind but nevertheless he published *A Prospect of the most Famous Parts of the World* (1627), the first world atlas in English, based on text and maps from European atlases. It was later combined with *The Theatre* in a single work. He published works of theology, genealogy and geography such as *The Holy Genealogies of the Sacred Scriptures* (1616) and *A Clowd of Witnesses*, and biography like his life of Chaucer. He was employed by both Elizabeth I and James I and was granted a coat of arms. He died in London on 28 July 1629 and was buried in St Giles, Cripplegate.

Spofford, Thomas (1370-1456), Bishop of Hereford 1422-48, was born in Craven, North Yorks the son of Roger and Celia Spofford. He was a monk at St Mary's Abbey, York and abbot in 1405, with a seat in Parliament. Henry V (qv) made use of his learning and sent him on diplomatic missions abroad, where he was involved in the condemnation of John Huss the reformer. On 24 May 1422 he was consecrated Bishop of Hereford, having previously been intended for Rochester. Hereford had been without a bishop for over four years and discipline was poor. He found that the Hospital of St Katherine at Ledbury was not performing any of its intended functions under its Master Nicholas Lyney but was not able to rectify matters. He did some rebuilding in the cathedral at his own expense and his arms can be seen in the vault over St Anne's Chapel in the south transept. He also beautified his palace at Sugwas. In the 19th century a stained glass window he had installed here was bought by a vicar of St Mary's, Ross and fitted into the east window, but there was room for only four of the five lights and the central Crucifixion panel has disappeared. Spofford is pictured kneeling at the feet of St Anne

and the Virgin, holding his heart in devotion. St Thomas Cantilupe (qv) stands to the right. In December 1448, worn out after his 26 years at Hereford and feeling a 'worthless bishop', he retired to the peace of his abbey in York where he died and was buried.

Spring, Tom (1795-1851) prizefighter, was born Thomas Winter at Rudge End near Fownhope on 22 February 1795, the son of the village butcher, who taught him to box from a young age using a sandbag. The boxer Tom Cribb, who was staying nearby, persuaded him to fight professionally and with Cribb he toured the country giving demonstration fights. He was landlord of the Booth Hall in Hereford and later owned taverns in London. He fought challenges across

the country and of his 12 big fights he lost only one. Not having a strong punch he developed a close defence, nimble footwork – his 'harlequin step' – and sudden left hook, earning him the title of 'lady's maid fighter'. He was universally loved as ballads attest. He employed his good looks and fine physique as a life model at the Royal Academy Schools. He died at his Castle Tavern Inn, High Holborn on 20 August 1851 leaving a wife and son and was buried in West Norwood cemetery where his gravestone remains. An old cider mill has been placed as a monument to him at Rudge End on the road from Fownhope to Woolhope.

St John, Harris Fleming (1833-1903), antiquarian clergyman, descendant of John Fleming St John (qv), was a curate at Kempsford and married Gertrude Ward. He lived at Dinmore from 1878 and restored the dilapidated chapel (architect: J.P. St Aubyn, 1886). He acted as chaplain, designing a series of stained glass windows. He acquired Stukeley's (qv) valuable papers and left them to the Bodleian.

St John, John Fleming (1789-1848), clergyman, bought and restored Dinmore, a preceptory of the Knights Hospitaller. The complex comprises the preceptory buildings where Sir Thomas Palmer (qv) had built his manor house, a ruined chapel, a mediaeval dovecote and an ancient yew.

St Owen, Ralph (fl.1303) of Burton Court, Eardisland, married Alice of the de Briouze family (qv under William (V) de Briouze). The St Owens were lords of Burton Manor in the 14th and 15th centuries and built the early 15th-century great hall that remains at the centre of the house. Thomas Downton was heir to the estate.

Stackhouse Acton, Frances (Fanny) (1794-1882), daughter of T.A. Knight (qv), was born at Elton Hall, where she grew up surrounded by pets and her father's horticultural experiments. When Elizabeth Matthews (qv) fell ill, Fanny finished the 30 plates of apples for her father's *Pomona Herefordiensis* (1808-11), her beautiful work being introduced by her father as by 'a young and inferior artist of my family'. She later presented the plates to Hereford City Library and Museum where they remain. Seventy years later she helped with the plates of the *Herefordshire Pomona* (qv H.G. Bull). In 1812 she married Thomas Pendarves Stackhouse Acton (1778-1835) of Acton Scott, at Downton Church. She left a memoir describing Elton Hall and Downton Castle and the famous people who called, like Sydney Smith (qv) and Humphrey Davy.

Stafford, Henry (1455-83), 2nd Duke of Buckingham, was born on 4 September 1455. He traced his ancestry to Edward III through Thomas of Woodstock who had married Eleanor de Bohun the daughter of Humphrey (IX) de Bohun (qv) Earl of Hereford, and in other ways. He was brought up by Edward IV's (qv) Queen Elizabeth and married her sister Katherine Woodville. On Edward's death Stafford supported Edward's brother Richard III, and is said to have murdered the princes in the Tower in return for Bohun lands held by the crown. He later rebelled against Richard and attempted to raise the Herefordshire gentry at Weobley on behalf of Henry Tudor but, in torrential rain and with rivers flooding, he was captured and executed for treason on 2 November 1483. He had lodged his wife and child with Richard (qv, d.1382) and Sybil de la Bere, who kept them safe at Kinnersley Castle. They survived into Tudor times, Katherine marrying Jasper Tudor.

Stanbury, John (d.1474), Bishop of Hereford 1453-74, was born at Morwenstow in Cornwall. He was a friend of Henry VI (qv) and one of his chaplains. Henry made him Bishop of Bangor in 1448 and moved him to Hereford in 1453. In 1460 he was with the king at his defeat by Yorkist forces under Warwick the Kingmaker at the Battle of Northampton. Warwick imprisoned him, then allowed him to retire to Ludlow. Henry remained nominal king, concerned with religious matters like the founding of King's College, Cambridge and Eton College in which

he was helped by Stanbury. The dean for much of his long reign was Richard Pede (qv). Stanbury died at Ludlow on 11 May 1474 and was buried in Hereford Cathedral. His alabaster effigy on its table tomb stands by the beautiful Stanbury chantry chapel, where prayers were said for the welfare of his soul: a miniature of perpendicular gothic architecture, with fan vaulting and carved emblems. The glass in the windows that shows scenes from his life is by A.J. Davies (qv). When his tomb was opened in the 1840s his sapphire ring was brought out and is now displayed in exhibitions. It is secular and decorative, inscribed *en bon an* – a happy new year.

Standish, Henry (*c.*1475-1535), Bishop of St Asaph's, was from Lancashire but educated in Hereford at a school run by Franciscan friars, and at Oxford where he graduated Doctor of Theology by 1502. His support for Henry VIII was rewarded with the poor bishopric of St Asaph's. The king and Erasmus thought Dr Standish a fool.

Stanhope, Catherine (*c.*1650-1717), daughter of Arnold Burghill (qv) of Thinghall Parva, Withington by his second wife Grizell, co-heiress of John Prise of Ocle Pychard, married Alexander Stanhope, a diplomat, the youngest son of Philip, 1st Earl of Chesterfield. Their son James was born in Paris, fought in the War of the Spanish Succession and was a celebrated Whig politician. He was created 1st Earl Stanhope. She acquired Whitfield Court on James Booth's (qv) death, and had Anthony Keck (qv) rebuild it substantially as it is today. In 1798 it passed to the Clive (qv Edward Bolton Clive) family. The Stanhopes were later to inherit the Scudamore estates (qv Frances Fitzroy-Scudamore, d.1820).

Stapleton, Everard (17th century), is the subject of a legend in which, after his father's death, his mother is persuaded by her unscrupulous steward Morgan Reece that Everard too has died, and Reece hotly presses her to marry him. When she resists he cuts her throat, claims she has committed suicide and seizes Stapleton Castle. He has sent Everard to America but when he returns years later his mother's unhappy ghost tells him what really happened. In a melodramatic dénouement Reece is shot by a trusty retainer of the Stapleton family, Everard assumes his rightful position and his mother's spirit is satisfied by burial in Presteigne Church. This story is recorded by W.H. Howse in his excellent *Radnorshire*. Children in Presteigne are said to sing of her ghost:

Lady Bluefoot all in black
Silver buttons down her back
Harigoshee, harigoshee
Lock the cupboard and take away the key.

Stapleton Castle was in fact owned by the Cornewalls (qv) in the 17th century and was slighted by Parliamentary forces in 1645.

Stedman, Fabian (1640-1713), the father of change ringing, was one of the seven children of Revd Francis Stedman, vicar of St John the Baptist, Yarkhill for 37 years and commemorated on a wall plaque in the vestry. Fabian introduced an order to bell ringing known as Stedman's Method. He began ringing bells while apprenticed to a London printer and published *Tintinnalogia* (1668) and *Campanalogia* (1677) in which he showed the possible complexity of the permutations available to ringers, and gave names to changes, some commemorating him, like *Stedman caters*.

Steer, Philip Wilson (1860-1942), painter, was born in Birkenhead on 28 December 1860, the youngest son of Philip Steer, himself a painter. When Philip was four years old the family moved to Apsley House, Whitchurch. Between 1875 and 1877 Philip followed his brother Henry to Hereford Cathedral School, then went to Gloucester School of Art and the drawing schools of the Department of Science and Art in South Kensington. After failing to get into the Royal Academy Schools he enrolled at the Académie Julian in Paris under the fashionable artist Bouguereau, studied at the École des Beaux-Arts and returned to a studio in Chelsea. While impressionistic in his painterly effects he saw himself as quintessentially English in the tradition of Constable and Turner. He revisited Herefordshire annually for *plein air* sketching campaigns. He taught at the Slade Art School where, with Henry Tonks, he was a memorable figure. During the First World War he was commissioned to paint the British Fleet. In his later life he produced delicate seascapes in

watercolour. He died of bronchitis on 21 March 1942.

Stephen (1092-1154), King of England, was the son of Adela, daughter of William the Conqueror, and Etienne, Count of Blois-Chartres. When Henry I's (qv) son William was drowned in the *White Ship* he adopted Stephen as his heir. However when Henry's daughter Matilda, the widowed Empress of Germany, returned to England, Henry adopted her as his successor and the magnates, including Stephen, swore allegiance to her. In spite of this, on Henry's death in 1135 Stephen crossed the Channel and had himself proclaimed king. This went well until Matilda asserted her rights and civil war ensued. In 1138 Geoffrey Talbot (qv, d.1140) seized Hereford Castle for her but Stephen drove him out and on Whit Sunday 1138 celebrated high mass in Hereford Cathedral wearing his crown, seated on the throne said to be that which is still in the cathedral. He granted Hereford the right to hold a fair and gave charters allowing Bishop Robert de Béthune (qv) to hold a Sunday market in Ledbury at the feast of its patrons Saints Peter and Paul (29 June), and one in Ross. Stephen and Matilda's civil war caused anarchy in England and the powerful were free to ravage the countryside. In 1141 Stephen strengthened Wilton Castle at a strategic crossing of the Wye and used it as an assembly point for his forces in Herefordshire. Here Robert of Gloucester besieged him in 1143. Stephen and Matilda were both captured at different times and it was eventually agreed that Stephen should reign during his life but that Matilda's son, Henry (qv Henry II), would succeed him. Stephen was buried in the new Cluniac monastery at Faversham in Kent alongside his son Eustace and Matilda, who had died two years before. When Henry VIII dissolved the monasteries their tombs were broken up and their bones scattered.

Stephen of Thornbury (fl.1216-47), Dean of Hereford 1234-*c.*1247, was appointed canon in 1216 when Dean Hugh de Mapenore (qv) became Bishop of Hereford and Thomas de Bosbury (qv) dean. Stephen followed Thomas as dean and Peter de Aquablanca (qv) was appointed bishop. Stephen was dead by 1247 when his successor Giles of Avenbury assumed office. He left several valuable books to the cathedral library and these still survive.

Stephens, Charlotte Alice (1874-89), poet, daughter of a Ledbury ironmonger, was born on 15 December 1874. Lottie was a bright, thoughtful girl who died at school in Hereford, to her parents' grief. To commemorate her life they published a little book of her poems and stories.

Stillingfleet, Benjamin (1702-71) was a botanist and friend of Robert (II) Price (qv) of Foxley. Price allowed him a cottage on his Foxley estate and they botanised together.

Stillingfleet, Henry James William (1826-87) was educated at Brasenose College, Oxford. He was ordained and in 1868 became rector of Hampton Bishop. He married Victorine Agassiz of Paris. Their sons Henry and Herbert were drowned in the sinking of the *Knowsley Hall* sailing to New Zealand in 1879.

His friend Henry Graves Bull's (qv) son Alexis went down in the same ship.

Storer, James Sargant (1771-1853), draughtsman and engraver, was born and lived in Clerkenwell. He and his eldest son Henry Sargant Storer (1796-1837) engraved illustrations for such as Cowper, Burns and Bloomfield (qv) and made engravings of British antiquities. They wrote and engraved the *History and Antiquities of the Cathedrals and Antiquities of Great Britain* (1814-9) which gives a detailed plan and description and many large plates of Hereford Cathedral after Wyatt and before Scott (qqv). Pugin (qv) called it the most accurate views of those buildings in existence.

Straddell, Richard (d.1346), distinguished scholar, theologian and diplomat, was abbot of the Cistercian house of Dore. His sermons were admired and anthologised, and he served the Court and the Cistercian chapter on diplomatic missions. The abbey had been founded by Robert fitz Harold (qv) of Ewyas on the banks of the River Dore as a daughter house of Morimond Abbey in France. It had been lavishly rebuilt by Abbot Adam (qv) and consecrated by Thomas de Cantilupe (qv). The relic of the True Cross, presented in 1321 by William Grandison (qv), drew pilgrims and prosperity. The tomb of the pious Lady Matilda de Bohun (qv under Humphrey (VI) de Bohun) was another focus for miraculous healings. The abbey was dissolved in 1536 and bought by John Scudamore (qv, d.1571).

Street, George Edmund (1824-81), architect, was born on 20 June 1824 in Woodford, Essex, third son of Thomas Henry Street, a solicitor. He and Bodley (qv) were pupils in the office of Sir Gilbert Scott (qv). He rebuilt All Saints, Monkland for Sir Henry Baker (qv) in 1865-66 as a setting for high Victorian liturgy, leaving the original Norman windows with their surrounds of local tufa and the 13th-century tower arch. He designed the east window, which was made by Hardmans (qv), and the lychgate. In the following year he restored St

Lawrence, Weston-under-Penyard, conserving the Norman work there too. Street's memorable national work was the Royal Courts of Justice in London. He died at his home in London on 18 December 1881, an early death brought on by hard work and stress, and is buried in Westminster Abbey near Scott.

Stukeley, William (1687-1765), antiquarian, was born on 7 November 1687 in Holbeach, Lincolnshire, the eldest son of John Stukeley, attorney. He was apprenticed at his father's law firm, developed a life-long passion for antiquities and read medicine at Corpus Christi College, Cambridge. After his father's death he practised as a physician at Staples Inn in London, making influential friends including Isaac Newton – it was to Stukeley that Newton told his parable of gravity and the apple. In the 1720s he travelled widely in Britain recording and sketching antiquities, published as *Itinerarium curiosum* (1724). In 1721 he was in Hereford drawing Bishop Robert de Losinga's (qv) chapel, now demolished. He drew the chapter house but the vault had fallen by his time and he wrongly imagined it as having a central column, a mistake that has been hard to shake off. He

confused *Ariconium* (near Ross) with *Magnis* (near Credenhill) which anyway he believed to be Hereford, and noted that gentry like Dansey and Coningsby (qqv) had collected mosaics and coins from the site. He married Frances Williamson and after her death Elizabeth Gale (1687-1757), whose dowry freed him from money troubles. He investigated Avebury and Stonehenge noticing astronomical alignments. He discovered the earthwork avenue and cursus at Stonehenge and coined the word *trilithon*. His sketches record Stonehenge before it was later damaged. His later days were spent as a rector in London, where he died from a stroke on 3 March 1765. Stukeley's antiquarian papers were acquired by Revd Harris Fleming St John (qv) of Dinmore Court, who presented them to the Bodleian Library.

Styrmin, John (*c.*1500-52), Archdeacon of Hereford 1542-51, was educated at Gonville Hall, Cambridge. He subscribed to the Royal Supremacy Act in 1535 and was the college's 14th Master. He was appointed to Eyne and Bartonsham prebends in Hereford and appointed archdeacon by his friend Bishop John Skippe (qv).

Sumner, Mary Elizabeth (1828-1921), founder of the Mothers' Union, was born Mary Heywood (qv under Thomas Heywood) on 31 December 1828 at Swinton near Manchester and the family moved to Hope End, which her father bought from Edward Barrett (qv). Mary was fond of music and her father installed an organ for her. She studied music and singing in Rome where she met her husband George Henry Sumner (1826-1909). They married at St James, Colwall in 1848. George became rector of Old Arlesford and they lived in his family home, Farnham Castle, where they brought up their two daughters. When George became archdeacon of Winchester then suffragan Bishop of Guildford, Mary organised women's groups, locally at first then nationwide, often lecturing to large meetings. A network of mothers' groups was formed for prayer, bible study, and family support. The Mothers' Union crossed

class and denominational boundaries and spread internationally. It remains an effective force. Her husband died in 1909 but Mary continued to develop the MU until her own death on 9 August 1921. The Mothers' Union worldwide headquarters is called Mary Sumner House.

Swein Godwinson (d.1052) or Swegen, eldest son of Godwin and brother of Harold (qqv). Through the influence of his father on Edward the Confessor he was made Earl of the old kingdom of Mercia, which included Herefordshire. From a base at Hereford he campaigned in Wales against Gruffydd ap Llewelyn (qv). He kidnapped the Abbess of Leominster, Eadgifu Anderes (qv), and there was such an outcry that he was exiled. The large earldom was partitioned between Harold and his cousin Beorn Estrithson. Swein persuaded the king to allow him back, however, against Godwin family advice, but soon he had murdered Beorn in Herefordshire. This caused general disgust and he was declared *nithing* or worthless and again exiled, his earldom now split between Harold (qv) and the Confessor's nephew Ralph de Mantes (qv under Ralph). When Swein returned again in 1051 the whole Godwin family were exiled. The unpredictable Swein walked barefoot to Jerusalem in expiation but died on the way back at Michaelmas 1052, perhaps at Constantinople. He had a son called Hakon.

Swift, Jonathan (1667-1745), author of *Gulliver's Travels* etc, was the son of Jonathan Swift (1640-67) and grandson of Thomas (qv). Jonathan senior was born at Goodrich rectory and in 1664 married Abigail Erick. The family moved to Ireland where much of Jonathan Swift junior's life was spent. Jonathan, the author, was educated at Trinity College Dublin and Oxford and ordained. He wrote in support of the Tory administration and was rewarded with the deanship of Dublin although he had hoped for the bishopric of Hereford, which went instead to Philip Bisse (qv). Dean Swift was to dedicate a chalice to the memory of his grandfather in Goodrich Church.

Swift, Thomas (1595-1658), clergyman, the son of Thomas Swift, rector of St Andrew's, Canterbury, was vicar of St Giles, Goodrich from 1624 for over 30 years until deprived of his living in the Commonwealth. He married Elizabeth, niece of Sir Erasmus Dryden, grandfather of the poet Dryden. He was an active Royalist

in the Civil Wars and claimed to have been 'plundred by the roundheads 6 and 30 times' (qv Col Robert Kyrle). He lived at Newhouse Farm which has his initials carved in the porch; its three-winged structure is perhaps a trinitarian symbol. He sold his plate for the king after Naseby and when Charles was resting at Raglan Castle conveyed 300 gold pieces to him sewed into his waistcoat. He died on 2 June 1658 aged 62. His memorial can be seen in the church. St Giles also has a chest with his rebus on it: a pair of stags for swiftness.

Swinderby, William (14th century) was a learned man educated at Merton College, Oxford who preached the heretical ideas of John Wycliffe with eloquence and simplicity in the Midlands and Herefordshire. The Lollard heresy was that Christ was directly available to people without the intervention of a priest and that the selling of pardons and indulgences etc was a form of simony. Chaucer and Langland (qv) attacked corruption in the church at this time and there was sympathy for Lollard ideas at the Courts of Richard II and Henry IV (qqv). Swinderby knew Walter Brut (qv), another Lollard preacher in Herefordshire, and

John Oldcastle (qv). Swinderby was questioned in Leicester and Herefordshire by Bishop Trefnant (qv) but had the protection of John of Gaunt (qv) and others at Court. He went to ground in Deerfold Forest where he was under the protection of the Mortimers, the Crofts and the Whitneys (qv Robert Whitney, d.1402). He is reported as preaching at Whitney in 1390 and had interviews with Trefnant in Kington Church and at his manor of Whitbourne. In 1391 Trefnant arranged for Swinderby to publicly defend his beliefs at Bodenham, where he won over his audience with such pious eloquence that he was allowed freely to depart. Trefnant was censured by the Pope for his leniency and issued a warrant for Swinderby which he eluded, and he was excommunicated. He appealed to the king but the sequel is unknown and Swinderby seems to have lived on in the Deerfold area unmolested.

Swinfield, John (d.1311), brother of Bishop Richard (qv), was precentor of Hereford. His is the tomb by the steps leading up to the lady chapel on the south side; it is covered with pigs eating acorns in a field in punning allusion to his name. The pigs wear little coats bearing the Dean and Chapter's arms.

Swinfield, Richard (d.1317), Bishop of Hereford 1283-1317, was born in Kent, but the family had moved to Herefordshire by the late 13th century as his father Stephen (d.1282) was buried in Bosbury Church where his memorial stone can be seen. In 1264 after university he entered the service of Thomas de Cantilupe (qv), becoming archdeacon of London and finally succeeding him as Bishop of Hereford. He was with Cantilupe on his last journey and with him when he died, ensuring that his bones and heart were returned to Herefordshire. Swinfield reported miraculous healing effected by Thomas's remains to Pope Nicholas IV, who initiated canonisation proceedings. Pilgrims' contributions flooded in, providing for rebuilding: the transepts were finished, the aisles rebuilt and *c.*1310 the great crossing tower was built with a spire, replacing a Romanesque tower. The inner porch was constructed with its frieze of figures, some humorous and indecent. He had connections with Lincoln and may be the link that brought the Mappa Mundi to Hereford; writings in the Mappa's spandrels relates to Swinfield. Changes at the east end of the cathedral facilitated the movement of pilgrims to and from St Thomas's shrine: presbytery aisles were widened and effigies of bishops supplied to line the ceremonial way. In 1287 he had Thomas's remains moved to a new tomb in the north transept and this, recently restored and beautified, now once more holds a relic of St Thomas of Hereford. Bishop Richard did not live to see his patron's canonisation as he died on 12 or 15 March 1317 at Bosbury, his favourite palace, as it had been his master's. He was buried in the cathedral in his ceremonial robes and holding a symbol of his building works. The canopied setting of his tomb has been lost and he now shares a ledge with Bishop Bennett (qv), whose stern Protestant voice of 300 years later would have disturbed the eirenic Swinfield. His tomb was opened during 19th-century works and his crozier, with its beautifully carved crook, was brought out and is occasionally shown. John Webb (qv) edited *A Roll of the Household Expenses of Richard de Swinfield* in 1854.

Symonds: Their arms show a black dolphin with a silver fish in its mouth and their pedigree is posted at the entrance of Pengethley Manor, which was brought into the family by Penelope Powell in the 17th century. The house was formerly in the hands of the Powell baronets (qv Edward Powell, d.1653). There are Symonds family memorials in St Tysilio's (qv), Sellack.

Symonds, Thomas (1685-1760) married Penelope Powell (1693-1773), who brought Pengethley Manor near Ross to the marriage. Thomas Apperley (qv) praised Symonds' medical knowledge and dedicated his book on smallpox to him.

Symonds, Thomas (d.1791), architect, was of a family which had long worked on the cathedral – a John Symonds is mentioned as working on the steeple (since removed) in building works at the Restoration. Thomas was a noted sculptor of funerary monuments and his signature appears on many Herefordshire church wall-plaques and busts. He was employed on architectural and building work: in 1775 he was Richard Payne Knight's (qv) clerk of works at Downton Castle, he worked on the County Gaol and the Infirmary (though his plans for the latter were rejected in favour of those of William Parker [qv]), and extended Allensmore Court for Edmund Pateshall (qv). He repaved Bishop Bisse's (qv) new choir in 1774 at a cost of £92, with a £10 gratuity as he had probably underestimated to get the job. This led to his appointment as surveyor of the cathedral's fabric in 1777 with a workshop in the corner of the chapter house yard. He repaired the nave roof and presented a list of urgent repairs needed on the crumbling north-west tower. He was eventually allowed to get to work at the west end in 1781 and filled in the western nave arcades as better foundations for the tower, but only its complete removal would have saved the structure. Ominous cracks widened, stones fell. Then, on Easter Monday 17 April 1786 the whole west end of the cathedral with its 12th-century arcading collapsed, bringing down a couple of bays of the nave. There were no casualties although James Wathen (qv) had been sketching there shortly before, but the roar was heard and the cloud of dust was seen miles away. The *Hereford Journal* thought the ruins awful and pleasing. Symonds the scapegoat was sacked. After his death in 1791 his widow advertised that his business would continue, employing a man from London.

Symonds, Thomas Powell (1762-1819), of Pengethley Manor, son of Thomas Symonds Powell Symonds (qv), was educated at Trinity College Oxford and rose to become lieutenant colonel of the South Gloucester Militia. He was Sheriff of Hereford in 1798-9 and an MP for Hereford from 1800-1819; in order to secure re-election he was forced to part with valuable timber from the estate to raise the necessary funds. Sir Thomas was secretary of the Woolhope Club, which recorded the size of his ancient oaks before felling. He died on 19 August 1819 and was buried at Sellack Church. He married a Miss Rootes but had no children and Pengethley passed to his nephew Revd Thomas Powell Symonds, son of Revd Joseph Symonds, his younger brother. Revd Symonds had Pengethley rebuilt in 1826 after a fire.

Symonds, Thomas Symonds Powell (d.1793) of Pengethley was the son of Thomas Symonds (qv, d.1760). He married Sarah, daughter of Joseph Chester of Gloucester, and they had eight children. Their eldest son, Thomas Powell Symonds (qv) was heir, and their daughter Penelope married John Skippe (qv, d.1796) of Ledbury.

Symonds, William Samuel (1818-87), clergyman, geologist, novelist, was born in Hereford on 13 December 1818 the eldest child of William Symonds (d.1840) Lord of the manor of Elsdon and Deputy Lieutenant of Herefordshire, and his wife Mary Anne Beale (qv). He was educated at Cheltenham and Christ's College, Cambridge where, in 1840, he married Hyacinth (d.1907) daughter of Samuel Kent of Upton upon Severn. He was ordained in 1842 and appointed to a curacy in Worcestershire, later becoming rector of Pendock near the Malverns. Here he was well placed for the study of geology and met luminaries and enthusiasts: Charles Lyell, Murchison (qv), Joseph Hooker, Revd T.T. Lewis (qv) and Revd Edwin Lees (qv). He studied the outcrops exposed in the railway cutting at Ledbury, discovering fossils which elucidated the transition from the Silurian to the Devonian Era, the 'Passage Beds'. He excavated the deposits in King Arthur's Cave, finding fossil rhinoceros, lion and hyena bones. He helped found the Malvern Naturalists' Field Club in 1853 and became its president. In 1851 he addressed the Literary, Philosophical and Natural History Institution of Hereford, founded in 1836, stirring a desire in his audience for a more scientific club. This led to the founding of the Woolhope Naturalists' Field Club of which he was a founding member, the name referring to the complex geology of the Woolhope Dome area which they hoped to explore. Their first field trip to Tarrington the following May was led by Revd Symonds, but the weather proving bad they looked at fossil bones that had been uncovered by Stephen Ballard (qv) during excavations at Bosbury for his Ledbury to Hereford Canal. After lunch they were shown round Lady Emily Foley's (qv) park at Stoke Edith and investigated quarries in the Woolhope area. In 1853 he was elected a Fellow of the Geological Society and published scientific papers, mainly on palaeontology. He studied 'the wonder', a large land displacement near Much Marcle and addressed his findings to the Woolhope Club in 1878. He was amongst the first to recognise the Pre-Cambrian age of the Malverns and supported Darwin's theories on the development of species, unusual among contemporary clergymen. He retired in 1887 and took in pupils, one being Alice Roberts, the future wife of Elgar (qv). He contributed advanced views on geology to *The Flora of Herefordshire* from which Revd William Purchas (qv) distanced himself. He also wrote popular descriptions of geological processes and successful historical novels such as *Malvern Chase* (1881), which gives a romantic account of the Battle of Mortimers Cross, and *Hanley Castle* (1883), which deals accurately with local history.

Symonds died in Cheltenham on 15 September 1887 after a long illness and is buried in Pendock Church, where the west window commemorates him. His daughter Hyacinth was to marry the botanist Joseph Hooker.

Symons, John (*c.*1708-63), MP, son and heir of Richard Symons (qv), was educated at Christ Church, Oxford and the Middle Temple, and married Anne Colebrooke. He was elected MP for Hereford in 1754, partnering Velters Cornewall (qv, d.1768). They spoke against the Cider Tax which was subsequently repealed. He died, without children, on 30 December 1763.

Symons, Richard (fl.1700-50), a wealthy London merchant, in 1750 bought Mynde Park, Much Dewchurch, an estate which had been owned from ancient times by the Pye family (qv). He left it to his son John (qv). Of his daughters, Elizabeth married Edward Clive (qv) of Wormbridge and Anna Sophia married Richard Peers, an alderman of London.

Symons, Richard Peers (1743-96), MP, son of Anna Sophia and Richard Peers (see under Richard Symons), inherited Mynde Park and a large fortune on his uncle's death and assumed the surname Symons. He was elected MP for Hereford (1768-84) and was a supporter of Pitt. In 1774 he was created a baronet. On his death on 4 July 1796 the title became extinct and the property passed to his nephew Thomas Raymond, who also adopted the name Symons. His descendants inherited in direct male line until Thomas Edward Raymond Symons (d.1928), when Mynde Park went to a fellow army officer, Henry Ambrose Clive, younger son of General Edward Henry Clive of Perrystone Court. Symons memorials can be seen in St David's Church, Much Dewchurch.

Synock: A Weobley family. In 1468 John Synaugh was a Weobley burgage tenant. In 1520 William Synoghe of Weobley married his daughter Eleanor to James Tomkyns (qv under Tomkyns family) of nearby Garnstone. The Synock family have farmed at Weobley for six centuries.

T

Talbot: Earlier spelled Thalebot, they were vassals of the Giffards in Normandy and followed them to England at the Conquest. In Domesday they are recorded at Badlestane, Beds. They appear in Herefordshire through marriage into the pre-Conquest Flaitel family of Linton, near Ross, which became a Talbot base. Here they built Eccleswell Castle where King John, who liked to visit Herefordshire for the hunt, stayed. They were found at Richard's Castle, they repaired and occupied Penyard Castle and they took advantage of the fall of the Despensers to acquire Goodrich Castle. They co-founded Wormsley Priory which became a Talbot mausoleum and later founded Flanesford Priory also. In the 12th and 13th centuries they were at the forefront of most military activities in the area: they backed Matilda in her struggle with King Stephen; they supported Roger (V) Mortimer in his overthrow of Edward II but managed the transition to service under Edward III well. Through marriage and knightly service they rose into the nobility with a barony under Edward III. In the 15th century the brilliant military commander John Talbot (qv, d.1453) was made Earl of Shrewsbury by Henry VI, who relied on him in his French wars, and called him 'our good dog' in reference to the Talbot family badge – a white hound called a Talbot. Father and son fell at Castillon, a grandson was killed in a duel and the line died out in the county.

Talbot, Geoffrey de (d.1129), a son of William de Talbot (qv) and Bastia, married Agnes, daughter of Walter de Lacy (qv, d.1085). Their children were Geoffrey (qv), and Sybil, who married Pain (Payn) fitz John (qv) of Ewyas.

Talbot, Geoffrey de (d.1140), son of Geoffrey (qv, d.1129) and Agnes, took and fortified Hereford Castle in 1138 on behalf of the Empress Matilda as one of the first acts of the civil wars between Stephen (qv) and the Angevins. Stephen called in his feudal vassals, besieged him and drove him out. Talbot and his kinsman Gilbert de Lacy (qv) fled to Weobley Castle but Stephen forced them from there too. Geoffrey returned to fire Hereford, which was still recovering from the sack of 1055. He and Gilbert attacked Bath, Stephen's base in the west, were captured but escaped. In 1140 he was wounded in a battle at Bath and died on 22 August.

Talbot, Gilbert (*c.*1225-74), son of Richard Talbot (qv, d.1234), married Gwenllian (1219-68), daughter of Gruffydd ap Rhys II (qv, d.1201. He was a justice of Hereford and Chester, with a house in Hereford. He founded a priory for Victorine Augustine canons at Wormsley and dedicated to St Leonard de Pyon soon after 1200, with Sir Walter Map (qv under Walter Map). There were several Victorine Houses in the west of Herefordshire and Shropshire (qv Andrew of St Victor). Earthworks are all that remain now, north-east of Wormsley Church. Talbot died on 7 September 1274 and was buried in the priory he had founded, as were many of his descendants.

Talbot, Gilbert (1276-1346), 1st Baron Talbot, born on 18 October 1276, was the eldest son of Sir Richard Talbot (qv, d.1306) and Sarah. His younger brother, Richard (qv, d.1328), was Lord of Richard's Castle and another brother, Thomas, became a priest. He married Anne, daughter of William Botteler of Wem He and his brother Richard joined the rebellious barons at the Battle of Boroughbridge on 16 March 1322 where Humphrey

(VII) de Bohun (qv) was killed and they were captured. They were pardoned and Gilbert was required to do Edward II (qv) service in France. However he joined with Roger (V) Mortimer (qv) and Isabella's forces which returned to overthrow Edward. He survived Mortimer's fall and continued in lucrative service to Edward III (qv) in the Welsh Marches and Herefordshire, investigating disorders and raising troops in the county. He was appointed Edward's Lord Chamberlain. He restored Penyard Castle at Weston-under-Penyard, long a Talbot possession. Under its vegetation-choked ruins is said to be a great treasure of gems and gold, guarded by a monstrous bird. Talbot is recorded granting lands to the family's foundation of Wormsley. He sat in Edward III's parliament of 1331 and died at Eccleswell Castle on 20 February 1346.

Talbot, Gilbert (1332-87), 3rd Baron Talbot, son of Richard the 2nd Baron (qv, d.1356), was born in Eccleswell Castle. In 1352 he married Petronella Butler (*c.*1335-*c.*68) and they lived in Goodrich Castle. He was a founder of Balliol College and died in Valladolid, Spain.

Talbot, Gilbert (*c.*1346-99), younger brother of Sir John (qv, d.1355), followed King Edward III to France aged about 13, caught his eye and was given a pension. He travelled to Italy in the train of Humphrey (IX) de Bohun, Earl of Hereford (qv), to arrange Lionel, Duke of Clarence's marriage to a Visconti princess. He was MP for Berkshire in 1386 and a JP. He married three times, on each occasion with a view to obtaining a lucrative dowry: Margaret, widow of Sir John Blaumonster of Wighill, Yorks; Joan, Lady Lisle (d.1392), widow of John Wynow; and Margaret (d.1434), widow of Constantine, Lord Clifton. He fought under John of Gaunt (qv) with his own small retinue in the French wars and was rewarded with manors in Berkshire, and knighted. He accompanied Richard II (qv) to Ireland in 1394. He died on 6 February 1399, leaving as his heir an infant son, Richard (d.1413).

Talbot, John (d.1355), knight of Richard's Castle, married Juliana (d.1361), daughter of Roger, Lord Grey of Ruthin. Sir John's eldest son John (d.1375) inherited the Herefordshire estates.

Talbot, John (*c.*1387-1453), Earl of Shrewsbury, second son of Richard (qv, d.1396), was born at Goodrich Castle. He came to be styled Lord of Archenfield, Lord Furnival, Earl of Shrewsbury and Waterford. His widowed mother, Ankaret, married Thomas Neville, Baron Furnival, brother of the Earl of Westmorland and John married his daughter Maud. This brought him great influence with the new regime and he was called to sit in Henry IV's (qv) Parliament of 1409. He was appointed Lieutenant of Ireland in 1414 and helped his younger brother Richard (qv, d.1449) to preferment there. Talbot was a quarrelsome man and his feud with John Abrahall (qv) and the Skidmores (qv Thomas Skidmore) caused anarchy in the Archenfield area. On his return from Ireland, where he was Lord Lieutenant, in 1421 he found that Abrahall and the Skidmores had occupied his Archenfield lands and were murdering his tenants. In 1423 the people of Wormelow petitioned parliament for protection from their private armies. Talbot eventually prevailed against his violent neigh-

bours. Talbot's sister Alice married Sir Thomas de la Barre junior (qv, d.1420), who was involved in the feuding; on her husband's death in 1420 she and Lord John were appointed custodians of her son John de la Barre's (qv) Herefordshire estates. Talbot distinguished himself in the French wars during two campaigns in the 1340s, known as Henry VI's best general, and was created Earl of Shrewsbury. This earldom is thought by some to have been informally bestowed by the unstable Henry VI, and to have been used by Lord John without heraldic right. He was captured and ransomed once, and later, after the defection of the Burgundians, he was killed with most of his army at the Battle of Castillon in Aquitaine on 17 July 1453, the final battle of the Hundred Years War that marked the collapse of English ambitions in France. One of the few to escape was his rival Sir John (II) Skidmore (qv, d.1475). Talbot's son John, 1st Viscount Lisle, fell beside his father at Castillon. Lord John's heart was buried at the doorway of St Alkmund's, Whitchurch in Shropshire. The earl's grandson, Thomas 2nd Viscount de Lisle (1443-70) was killed in a duel, and the Talbot line ceased in the county. Nearly two hundred years later, 'brave Talbot, the terror of the French' was the hero of Shakespeare's *Henry VI, Part One.*

Talbot, Richard de (1120-75), son of a Hugh Talbot, was created Lord of Eccleswell and Linton by Henry II (qv). He built Eccleswell Castle, of which ruins on a mound and a dovecote remain, and married Matilda, daughter of Stephen Bulmer (not related to the Herefordshire family). Their son Gilbert (*c.*1150-after 1205) was born at Linton.

Talbot, Richard (1180-1234), Lord of Eccleswall and Linton, was a descendant of Richard (qv, d.1175). He married Alina Bassett and their sons were Richard, Bishop of London and Gilbert (qv, d.1274). King John stayed at Eccleswell Castle in 1216.

Talbot, Richard (1250-1306), son of Gilbert (qv, d.1274) and Gwenllian, was Lord of Eccleswell and Richard's Castle, with lands in the Credenhill area. He was Sheriff of Gloucester. He married Sarah daughter of William de Beauchamp and sister of the Earl of Warwick.

Talbot, Richard (1305-56), 2nd Baron, son of Gilbert, 1st Baron (qv, d.1346), married Elizabeth de Comyn (1299-1372), daughter of 'Red' Comyn, a powerful Scottish nobleman, and niece of Aymer de Valence, last of the Valence Earls of Pembroke. Her inheritance included Goodrich Castle, although Talbot might have already seized it in the fall of the Despensers, who had meanwhile taken possession. He was a royal steward and sat in Edward III's Parliament of 1332. He founded Flanesford Priory for Augustinian canons in 1348. After Richard's death Elizabeth married Sir John Bromwich.

Talbot, Richard (*c.*1285-1328), son of Richard (qv, d.1306) and Sarah, married Joan daughter of Hugh de Mortimer (qv) of Richard's Castle and their son John (1319-55) was born there. Richard is buried at Wormsley Priory.

Talbot, Richard (1361-96), 4th Baron, son of Gilbert (qv, d.1387) and Petronella, married Ankaret (1361-1413), the daughter and heir of John, Lord Strange of Blakemere, Shropshire. They lived at Goodrich Castle. Their eldest son was Gilbert (d.1419), 5th Baron Talbot.

Talbot, Richard (1389-1449), archbishop of Dublin, was born at Goodrich Castle the third son of Richard 4th Baron Talbot (qv, d.1396). He was educated at Oxford where with Bishops Trefnant and Mascall (qqv) he attempted to stem the spread of Lollardy. He was ordained deacon at Hereford in 1407 and priest next year at Lambeth. Bishop Mascall of Hereford made him a prebendary and gave him the Bromyard living. From 1407-12 he was precentor at Hereford. He became Dean of Winchester in 1414 and, in 1418, Archbishop of Dublin aged 29. He treated this as a political appointment, acting as justice, and when his brother John (qv, d.1453) was Lord Lieutenant, the Archbishop acted as his deputy. The brothers had a long-running feud with the Earl of Ormond. Talbot died on

15 August 1449 and was buried at the altar of St Patrick's Cathedral.

Talbot, Thomas (fl.1780), clergyman and physician, founded Hereford General Infirmary on the bank of the Wye. It was built with voluntary subscriptions and opened in 1783 with 55 beds.

Talbot, William de (b.*c.*1020), or Thalebot, of Badlestane, Bedfordshire, married Bastia Flaitel (1025-99) from a pre-Conquest Norman family living at Linton by Ross. Her father was Gerald Flaitel.

Tarleton, Banastre (1765-1833), army officer and politician, was born on 21 August 1765 in Liverpool. He was educated at University College, Oxford and the Middle Temple. After his father died he gambled his inheritance away. His mother bought him a commission in the Dragoon Guards and he was posted to America. He fought through the whole of the War of Independence with courage and ruthlessness but eventually surrendered at Yorktown. At home he was fêted as a hero and his portrait was painted by Reynolds and Gainsborough. He was a friend of the Prince of Wales and had a notorious affair with Mrs Robinson, 'Perdita', following her affair with Lord Malden (qv George Capel Coningsby). He entered Parliament where he spoke in support of slavery and was given a baronetcy. He married Priscilla Bertie, natural (illegitimate) daughter of the Duke of Ancaster, and they lived in Leintwardine House (in Leintwardine High Street) which he enlarged. He died there on 23 January 1833, survived by his wife. He was buried in St Mary Magdalene, Leintwardine, where there is a grand monument to him by Peter Rouw.

Tatham, Charles Heathcote (1772-1842), architect, was born in Westminster on 8 February 1772 and educated in Louth, Lincolnshire. He was employed in Henry Holland's (qv) London office where Tatham met influential people. He studied the classical architecture of Italy and published a book of his drawings (1796). He was commissioned by Edward Foley (qv) to design an interior at Stoke Edith House, the park gates and a cottage in the grounds. At Foley's death

in 1803 he made his monument in St Mary's Church, Stoke Edith. Tatham was an influence on Sir John Soane who acquired his important collection of classical fragments; these are now shown in Soane's London museum. Tatham died on 10 April 1842.

Taylor, Isaac (1720-88) of Ross, was a surveyor of estates and counties, drawing up maps such as that of 1754 of Herefordshire at a scale of one inch to a mile. His map of Hereford City (1757) shows Blackfriars preaching cross, which still stands, a similar one by the cathedral which doesn't, and the bishop's chapel, which Henry Egerton (qv) demolished. The old Market Hall is shown in High Town beside the Cooken Row, the Tolsey and other now demolished buildings, one of which must be the Old House – all that now remains of this historic centre of Hereford Market. The city walls with their gates are complete: it wasn't until 1780 that they began to be demolished. In the borders he engraved vignettes of local places and figures including a portrait of himself in ragged dress drawing the map, signed 'Isaac Taylor of Ross'. In a rococo cartouche is a dedication to the Earl of Oxford, High Steward of Hereford, Bishop Beauclerk (qv) *et al.* An old copy of this map hangs in St Peter's Church, Hereford. In 1772 Taylor published a county map of Worcestershire and in 1777 one of Gloucestershire. He married Eleanor Newman and they had a son and grandson, both called Isaac. They lived in the large town house, 54-55 High Street, Ross, where he acted as local surveyor and land agent. He had antiquarian interests and bought the papers of James Hill (qv). Taylor died in June 1788 and was buried in St Mary's churchyard behind his house.

Taylor, John (1578-1653), the 'Water Poet', was born in Gloucester on 24 August 1578 and educated at St Mary de Crypt school. He was apprenticed as a Thames ferryman in London and went to sea in the Elizabethan Navy. He is noted for his robust poems and prose descriptions of the many tours he made round Britain and abroad, to Prague for instance. He was a self-

publicist whose trips involved some gimmick, such as his journey up the Thames in a paper boat and his walk to Scotland and back without money. His rueful description of the accidents that befell him gained him a wide readership. On his 'last voyage and adventure', July to September 1641, he travelled to Shropshire by boat, hauling his 'monumental vessel' between rivers where necessary, covering a total of 1,200 miles he calculated. Reaching Herefordshire he stayed at Ross for his 63rd birthday, then at Hoarwithy and Hereford, locals vying with each other to feast and accommodate him. In Hereford he had three offers of dinner: from Mayor Edmund Ashton, from some vicars choral and from a group of gentlemen in a tavern among whom he names Philip Traherne (qv, d.1645). He gave the slip to them all, however, making his apologies in the book. As a waterman he drew attention to the obstacles to river journeys, then the least arduous form of travel, and advocated clearing away weirs. His eventful and exhausting life ended sadly in the unsympathetic environment of the Commonwealth. He was persecuted and fined in London where he was known to be a supporter of the king; his house was confiscated and his life threatened, forcing him to flee on foot to the Court in Oxford. His later work is jumbled and fragmented, reflecting the madness of the times, he said, and his distress. In 1647 he ran an alehouse in Westminster rashly called The Mourning Crown which he changed, after threats, to The Poet's Head. It failed to pay, though, and in old age he returned to his travels, visiting King Charles in 1648 for instance, during his imprisonment in Carisbrooke Castle on the Isle of Wight, to offer encouragement and sympathy. The authorities were predictably hostile and in 1649 confiscated his subscription list, leaving him without sponsors. Impoverished and ill, he died in London on 5 December 1653 and was buried in St Martin's in the Fields.

Taylor, Silas (1624-78), antiquary and Parliamentarian officer, was born at Much Wenlock, the son of Silvanus (qv), and educated at Shrewsbury School and New Inn Hall, Oxford. He enlisted in Massey's (qv) regiment in the Parliamentary army. John Aubrey (qv) says he lost his wife and children in a fire in London in 1645 and buried them in Hereford Cathedral. He was Commissioner for Sequestrations in Herefordshire in the Commonwealth and with Birch (qv) was co-governor of Hereford, where he lived with his father. He exercised his power in Royalist Hereford with civility and restraint, keeping the respect of the citizens, which would serve him well later but caused friction with his masters. He benefited from Parliament's redistribution of church lands, buying the bishop's manor at Bosbury when that property was forcibly auctioned in 1649; Litley Court in the parish of Hampton Bishop; the disused 'almshall' of the hospital of St Ethelbert; and a part share in the bishop's palace at Hereford with Birch. Aubrey said 'he lay'd out much money in building and altering'. He arranged concerts in music-starved, Puritan-garrisoned Hereford and brought Matthew Locke (qv) to Hereford. Locke conducted at a concert where so many Royalist gentry congregated that the garrison feared a rising. In his pamphlet attacking the radical preacher Richard Delamaine (qv) Taylor recalls with disapproval one of his frenzied sermons which he, his father and John Tombes (qv) attended. He found remains of Bishop Æthelstan's (qv, d.1056) 11th-century cathedral to the south of the present cathedral, which recent archaeological excavations substantiate. He was distressed at the sad condition of the cathedral library, created 40 years before by Thomas Thornton (qv), and made use of it to research his history of Herefordshire, unpublished but used by John Duncumb (qv). Taylor's work, for which he had designed a frontispiece, was left in Edward Harley's (qv, d.1700) keeping at Brampton Bryan and later transferred with the Harleian collection to the British Museum. With Edward Harley and John Scudamore (qv, d.1671) he found himself at odds with Cromwell's regime in London. He survived the Restoration with diminished fortunes but his earlier kindnesses paid off and he was left with some of his offices. He and his father had houses in Hereford and Westminster where Pepys remembered he had a fine organ. He composed music for King Charles II (qv) and in the 1660s published a book on an ancient form of land tenure called gavelkind which he dedicated to Edward Harley. Charles II, ever tolerant of old enemies, employed Taylor as keeper of armaments at Dunkirk where Harley was Governor. Later Taylor was made Commissioner of Stores at Harwich. Pepys liked him and enjoyed a play of his called *The Serenade*. Taylor continued his researches but died in debt, his papers in disarray, at Harwich on 4 November 1678 where he was buried in the parish church.

Taylor, Silvanus (fl.1650), lived at Harley near Much Wenlock, Shropshire, and in London. Active for Parliament in the Civil Wars, he was lieutenant of the Tower 1649-50, a member of the High Court of Justice and a member of the commission that tried John Lilburne, the Leveller firebrand, in 1649. As a member of Parliament's ruling County Commission of Hereford and neighbouring shires through the 1650s he bought sequestrated lands of the Royalist gentry and published books on the benefits of enclosing the commons. He and his sons Silas (qv) and Silvanus (d.1672) were all musical.

Tempest, Henry (1753-1819), 4th Baronet of Tong, Yorkshire, is said to have duped Susanna Lambert (qv), heiress of Barton Court and Hope End in Colwall, into marriage for her property, which having been achieved she and her father were then cast out. Tempest was born on 13 January 1753 and married Susanna in 1791: there was no child of the marriage. In 1799 he was High Sheriff of Herefordshire and in 1809 he sold Hope End to Edward Barrett (qv) and lived in Surrey. At his death on 29 January 1819 the baronetcy became extinct.

Theed, William (1764-1817) the elder, monumental sculptor, from Staffordshire, studied painting at the RA schools and in Italy. He was a ceramic modeller for Wedgwood and a silversmith and was elected RA. At the end of his life he made a fine wall tablet for Harriet Clive (qv under Edward Bolton Clive) at St Peter's, Wormbridge. Christopher Hewetson's piece in Ross Church for Thomas Westfaling (qv, d.1814) has been attributed by some to Theed Senior. His son, also William, was also a noted sculptor.

Thelwall, John (1764-1834), poet and radical, after acquittal from a charge of treason and a period of imprisonment in the Tower of London, moved to Llyswen, Breconshire with his wife Susan and children for the three years 1797-1800 to try farming. He often travelled to nearby Hereford for company in the Crown and Sceptre alehouse where he was observed by a government spy. These were paranoid years and the clientèle was considered Jacobinical. He met John Britton (qv) in a Hereford bookshop in 1798 and told him he was preparing to be a great epic poet. Henry Crabb Robinson (qv) called on him and also heard optimistic plans. His years in Llyswen however were the wettest of the 18th century and he returned to urban life.

Theulf (d.1123), Bishop of Worcester 1115-23, a canon from Bayeux, was a chaplain of Henry I who made him bishop. William of Malmesbury (qv under William) called him the fat despoiler of his cathedral. He lived at Hampton (later Court) near Leominster where he died on 20 October 1123. He was buried in Worcester Cathedral.

Thomas, the saint and doubting apostle, is associated with charitable giving, his feast day, 21 December, being just before Christmas. Sir Henry Baker (qv), vicar of Monkland, held his annual dole on this day and many churches, as at Ledbury, still have boards that itemise St Thomas's Day charities. Herefordshire women went Thomasing or mumping and sacks of grain would be set up at farm doors where a measure would be dealt out to them.

Thomas of Bosbury (d.1231), Dean of Hereford 1216-31, oversaw the completion in 1225 of the cathedral's lady chapel, where work had been interrupted during the Pope's interdiction in the reign of King John. It housed an altar to Mary and a shrine of St Ethelbert (qv), the cathedral's patrons, with a crypt below for the veneration of Ethelbert's relics. These had been dispersed during the 1055 sack of the cathedral but fragments remained and one of St Ethelbert's teeth had recently been presented by Philip de Fauconberg, archdeacon of Huntingdon and a canon at Hereford. The crypt was lit by perpetual candles and hung with gold and silver offerings. Access was through a stair down through the door which can still be seen in the north wall of the lady chapel, with another leading up into the close. Dean Thomas commissioned the *Life of Ethelbert* from Gerald of Wales (qv). He had St Ethelbert's Almshouses built in Castle Street in 1225 with gardens running down to the castle moat, funded by a donation from Canon Elyas and a tithe of the proceeds from the fair of St Denis (qv). He confirmed the charter for the foundation of the Hospital of St Katherine in Ledbury in 1231 and died the same year.

Thomas of Cambridge (14th century), master mason, constructed the chapter house of Hereford Cathedral, completing the work of John of Evesham (qv under John). A contract of 1364 exists between Thomas and Dean Birmingham (qv) and the building, ten-sided like the one at Evesham Abbey, was completed in *c.*1370.

William Stukeley (qv) sketched it on his 1721 visit as a fan vault springing from a central column and the stone now on the site was held to be the central vault-springer. The vault had fallen by Stukeley's time, however, and it is now thought to have actually been an open-span lierne vault – the stone being a corner-springer. The chapter house was stripped of its lead during the Civil Wars for the repair of the castle gatehouse and for making shot. Bishop Bisse (qv) removed more bits and it was ruinous by Henry Egerton's (qv) time. It was demolished with difficulty, so strong did it still prove.

Thomas, Francis (1794-1857), born at Kington, became a clerk of the State Paper Office and rose to be the secretary of the Public Record Office, and published books about his work.

Thomas, Joshua (1719-97), Baptist minister, was born on 22 February 1719 in Carmarthenshire and moved to Hereford aged 20 to be apprenticed to his uncle Simon Thomas, a mercer. He walked to Leominster for the nearest Baptist services and was baptised in 1740. He married Elizabeth Jones (*c.*1725-1807) and they had five children. He was minister at Hay and at other Marches Baptist communities, and in 1754 moved to be the minister of the Leominster Baptists for 43 years. Thomas translated theological works into Welsh, wrote *A brief history of the Baptist church at Leominster* and completed his great history of the Baptists: *Hanes y Bedyddwyr* (1778), translated into English in 1782. He died on 25 August 1797 in his Etnam Street manse and was buried in the Baptists' burial ground. His brothers Timothy and Zacharias, and his eldest son Timothy were all Baptist ministers.

Thomas, Philip Edward (1878-1917), writer and poet, was born in London to Welsh parents on 3 March 1878, and educated at St Paul's School and Lincoln College, Oxford. He married Helen Noble and they started a family in a tiny cottage in Kent. For 15 years Thomas struggled to support them through reviews, studies of writers and books on his walking trips, tramping the country roads between Kent and Wales for weeks, producing a large body of work, still uncollected. Amongst it is his edition of John Dyer (qv) and an early review of Thomas Traherne (qv). He loved Herefordshire:

Make me content
With some sweetness ...
From ... Herefordshire,
And the villages there. (From *Words*)

In 1914 he stayed with the Frost family who had taken a cottage at Leddington near Dymock and was later joined by Helen and the children in a rented cottage nearby. They travelled from Kent to Ledbury Station where they hired a cart for the next few miles. It was at a stop on this line that Thomas wrote his notes for the poem that was to become *Adlestrop*. Frost helped Thomas discover that he was a poet. Thomas, Frost and other poets walked and talked in this corner of Gloucestershire, Herefordshire and Worcestershire, forming the brief Dymock poets colony and producing the short lived *New Numbers* (qv Abercrombie). At the end of the year the fellowship broke up; Thomas was to enlist and Frost returned to America. Edward Thomas's career as a poet was brief; he was killed at the Battle of Arras on 9 April 1917.

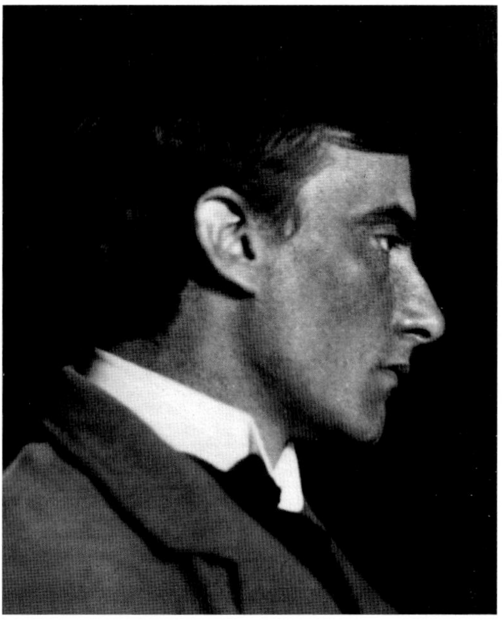

Thornhill, Hugh and **Robert** (16th century) bought the preceptory and lands at Harewood at the Dissolution of the monasteries. They sold it to the Browne (qv) family in 1547.

Thornton, Thomas (1541-1629), was born at Harrow, Middlesex and educated at Oxford University. He was a tutor at Christ Church, Oxford, where he was ordained and taught for 50 years. Amongst his students were Philip Sidney and William Camden (qqv). In 1570 he was a canon of Oxford, recommended by Sidney, upon whose early death he wrote Latin elegies. He was a canon of Worcester and in 1583 canon and precentor of Hereford; and for the last 30 years of his life he was Master of St Katherine's Hospital, Ledbury, lodging in the Master's House which, with its mediaeval hospital and chapel, still stands on Ledbury High Street. He was Vice Chancellor of Oxford University in 1583 and 1599. When Queen Elizabeth's (qv) commissioners visited Hereford Cathedral in 1583 they found the library in a terrible condition, mouldering in a leaky room above the west end of the cloisters with books and charters damp and in disarray. Dr Dee (qv) had also noted this on his visit in 1574. The commissioners required that the collection be protected from damage and theft and that a canon be appointed librarian. In 1590 it was moved into the lady chapel and there it stayed for the next 250 years. The first librarian was George Adams and another early one was John Best (qv) but Thornton was the organising spirit. He was familiar with Sir Thomas Bodley's work at Duke Humfrey's Library, Oxford, where bookcases held books chained upright, spines inward, instead of flat in chests as was customary. Thornton had a local carpenter build four similar standing cases and used Bodley's Birmingham ironmonger to supply chains, bars and locks – paid for by Thornton himself and completed in 1611. A few years later another four cases were bought by the Dean and Chapter and all 1,450 books were locked into the shelves, an arrangement that can still be seen, with ancient labels on the bookcase ends. The freed cloister room was used as the cathedral school room. The chained library, with the addition of books that Bishop Herbert Croft (qv) brought from the Jesuit College at Cwm, books from All Saints' chained library and from the vicars choral library which was originally separate, and the Mappa Mundi, can be seen in the new library building at the west end of the south cloister range. That this treasure should have survived and be so well housed now is due to Thornton and to the beneficence of Sir John Paul Getty junior who paid for the building when Dean and Chapter wanted to sell the collection. Amongst the treasures are the *Anglo-Saxon Gospel Book*; the important 1217 issue of Magna Carta; a 12th-century gospel book; a 14th-century Limoges enamel reliquary of St Thomas Becket; a copy of Voragine's *Golden Legend* printed by William Caxton in 1483; and Foxe's *Book of Martyrs*. The archive has an inventory of all Thornton's goods at the time of his death, including £50 worth of books. In his will he inveighs, as had Bishop Scory (qv) earlier, against the religious conservatism of his Herefordshire colleagues. He died in the Master's House in Ledbury on 15 April 1629 and was buried in Ledbury Church, where a wall monument shows him preaching.

Thurkil the White (fl.1020), a Danish thegn, follower of King Cnut, had been granted the manor of Fownhope. He is recorded in the 8th-century *Hereford Gospel Book* as present at a Shire Gemot or Court which sat at *Aegelnođes stane* or Aylton near Ledbury during Cnut's (qv) reign in about 1020. The court's dealings were minuted on a blank page in the Gospel Book. Bishop Æthelstan (qv) presided with Ranig (qv), Cnut's Danish Earl of Mercia and Bryning the Sheriff of Hereford responsible for the running of the court. All the thegns of the shire were present (*ealle đa đegnas on Herefordscire*), including Tofi the Proud, who represented the king, and Thurkil, who identifies himself as speaking for the defendant, his mother-in-law. She is being sued by her son Edwin, the son of Einion, for land at Wellington and Cradley. As Einion is a Welsh name, the lady is a Saxon princess and her kinswoman's husband Thurkil has a Danish name, one sees how nations mingled in Herefordshire at this time. The court sent three thegns: Leofwine of Frome, Ethelsige the Red and Winsige the seaman, to take a statement from the lady at Fawley, a few miles to the south. She was very angry with her son and convinced them that the land was hers to dispose of and she would leave everything to her kinswoman Leofflaed, Thurkil's wife, and nothing to Edwin. The court confirmed this and Thurkil rode to the cathedral to record the satisfactory result in the Gospel Book, now in Hereford Cathedral library.

Thynne: The family bought up all Weobley votes from 1754 and monopolised representation for the rest of the century. In 1789 they became Marquises of Bath.

Thynne, Henry Frederick (1735-1826), born in London, the second son of Thomas Thynne, 2nd Viscount Weymouth, changed his name to Henry, 1st Baron Carteret according to the conditions of his uncle Robert Cartteret's will, in which he was heir. He was MP for Weobley 1761-70. His relatives Viscount Thomas Thynne, and Lords George and John Thynne were subsequently variously elected, all supporting the administration, until 1832 when the Reform Act abolished the electoral rights of this ancient pocket borough and the 84 vote houses were pulled down. The 'vote houses' were uninhabited and often derelict properties which were the sole source of votes in this borough, all owned by the Thynnes.

Tilley, Luke one of five brothers, came to Ledbury in 1869 and established a printers, stationers and library in the High Street, and here he produced the Ledbury Free Press. The business thrived and he installed steam-powered printing machinery. His son John took over in 1915 and John's daughters followed him, running the press through most of the 20th century. There is still a printing company at the premises where the old linotype printing machinery can be seen.

Tirrel (or Torell): The family held the manor of Brinsop from the 12th to 15th centuries when it passed to the Danseys (qv Roger Dansey). Ralph Tirrel was a benefactor of Wormsley Priory in 1210 and another Ralph held two hides at Brinsop in 1340 in return for military service. The splendid hall of Brinsop Court manor house, built by the Tirrels at the start of the 14th century, survives intact.

Tombes, John (1602-76), clergyman and writer, born on 10 October 1602 in Bewdley, Worcestershire and educated at Magdalen Hall, Oxford, was a skilled linguist and graduated BD. In November 1630 he became vicar of Leominster Priory Church and married his first wife Elizabeth Scudder (1613-33), whose father was a Puritan preacher. They had a daughter, Elizabeth who died in 1658. After Elizabeth's death he married again in 1636 and had a son John. In 1640 he helped Lady Brilliana Harley (qv) to compile a list of lax practices amongst Herefordshire clergy for Parliament. He was a controversial minister but an exceptional preacher admired by John Scudamore (qv, d.1671). John Aubrey (qv) says Sir William Croft (qv, d.1645) had a house built at Leominster in order to hear his sermons. He offended people as diverse as George Fox and Thomas Traherne (qqv): he stood a table in the nave in place of an altar and refused to baptise infants, attracting the serious accusation that he was an Anabaptist. He believed the Cross was idolatrous and vestments papist. On the one hand he displeased the more extreme in the congregation with his comparative moderation, and they eventually separated themselves to meet in the house of John Pateshall (qv) in Bridge Street which became an early Baptist Chapel, and on the other hand his nonconformist thoughts offended the more conservative amongst his congregation who, in 1641, ejected him. He then preached in Bristol until the Royalist advance of 1643 drove him to London, but even here his rejection of paedobaptism caused offence. Cromwell was impressed with him however and made him minister of Bewdley where he founded a

Baptist Chapel, although he remained a Presbyterian, and indeed an Anglican, at heart. He held several celebrated disputes with that other moderate, Richard Baxter, who was preaching in the area. In 1646 he became vicar of Ross and in 1649 briefly Master of St Katherine's Hospital at Ledbury. In 1651 he was able to return to Leominster where a debate with Thomas Traherne (qv) is recorded. At the Restoration he conformed to the extent of taking the oath of supremacy to the Church of England, except that he would not baptise infants and finally even the tolerant Bishop Herbert Croft (qv) had him ejected. He married a third wife and settled in her parish of St Edmund's, Salisbury. Tombes was one of the great divines of the 17th century and a principled controversialist; his preaching and disputing were remarkable and his books celebrated. John Aubrey met him in Herefordshire and found him 'a very pious and zealous Christian'. He died at Salisbury on 22 May 1676 where he is buried in St Edmund's churchyard.

Tomkins, Benjamin (1714-79), son of Richard Tomkins (qv), inherited the cow Silver and her calf on the death of his father in 1723. She is often cited as the dam of the Hereford breed (qv). Tomkins was farming from 1738 at the Court House, Canon Pyon, joined from 1769 by his son Benjamin at nearby Black Hall and his nephew George at King's Pyon. In 1758 he moved his herd to Wellington Court and for the next 20 years he bred them for the characteristics he desired: a middle red colour with a white or bald face and deep, broad body, with stamina and the ability to put on weight quickly. They would breed prolifically and be long-lived. Tomkins also improved the Ryeland (qv) breed of sheep. There are Tomkins monuments in St Mary's Church, King's Pyon.

Tomkins, Richard (d.1723), a prosperous yeoman farmer of New House, King's Pyon was noted, with his son Benjamin (qv) and their friend William Galliers (qv), for his systematic breeding of the large, white-faced red cattle known as Herefords, valued by Tomkins as much for draught animals as for meat.

Tomkyns: of Garnstone and Monnington. In 1520 James Tomkyns married Eleanor, the daughter of William Synoghe (qv) from an old Weobley family, and with her and another wife he had 33 children. He acquired Monnington and Garnstone from descendants of the Audley family (qv). Tomkyns were MPs for Leominster and Weobley through the 17th century. They were connected by marriage to the Prices of Foxley. Their lands finally went to the Cornewall family (qv).

Tomkyns, James (1569-1636), son of Richard (qv), was educated at Gloucester Hall, Oxford and the Middle Temple. He built Monnington Court. He was mayor of Hereford in 1606-7. He was MP for Leominster and was responsible for the re-enfranchisement of Weobley in 1628. In Parliament he sat on the committee for the removal of obstructions on the Wye. He married Anne Boyle of Hereford and their sons William (d.1640) and Thomas (qv) were the first two MPs for Weobley. William's nephew James (d.1643) was in London when the Civil War broke out. He raised a troop for the king but was seized and hanged outside his door in Fetter Lane.

Tomkyns, Richard (16th century), son of James and Eleanor (qv Tomkyns family), was escheator for Herefordshire in 1585 and High Sheriff in 1591. He married Katherine, daughter of James Baskerville of Kyre Park, Worcs and their daughter Fortuna married Robert Perrot (qv) in 1611.

Tomkyns, Thomas (1605-74), younger son of James Tomkyns (qv), was MP for Weobley after his brother William's (qv under James Tomkyns) death. He was an active MP: Pepys who heard him speak called him a man 'of many mad motions'. Andrew Marvell praised him as well: as 'long as cider lasts in Hereford, /The girls shall always kiss thee, though grown old, /And in eternal healths thy name be troll'd.' He married Mary, a daughter of Sir Walter Pye (qv), and their daughter Anne married Roger Vaughan, (qv, d.1672). Secondly he married Lucy, daughter of Sir William Uvedale, a connection of the Price family of Foxley. Their son was Uvedale Tomkyns (qv). In about 1650, as a memorial to Charles I (qv), Thomas planted the mile-long avenue of pines, yews and chestnuts called Monnington Walk that Kilvert (qv) loved. As part of his daughter Anne's marriage settlement Garnstone Castle went to his son-in-law Roger Vaughan (qv, d.1672). In 1660 Tomkyns was elected to the Restoration Parliament as a Cavalier with Herbert Perrot (qv, d.1682). He was knighted in 1661. He was buried in Monnington Church.

Tomkyns, Uvedale (d.1692) lived at Monnington Court and rebuilt St Mary's Church Monnington-on-Wye in 1679 in the style of Charles II: the panelling, windows and font all remain with his arms above the porch. He married Mary (d.1728), daughter of Edward Capel of How Caple. They were buried in the chancel and his and Mary's initials are carved on the font cover and the communion table. They had no children and the estate went to Mary's brother John Capel and then to George Cornewall (qv, d.1819), whose Moccas estate was across the Wye.

Tompkins, Thomas (d.1629) drowned as a child in a pool at Llandinabo. His brass in St Dinabo's Church shows him in Stuart dress with a prominent cross round his neck, standing praying in the pool with a Latin inscription that contrasts the pure waters of his baptism with the muddy ones of his death.

Tomson, Giles (1553-1612), Bishop of Gloucester, the son of a London grocer, was educated at Merchant Taylors' School and University College, Oxford. He became a fellow of All Souls College, Oxford and graduated DD in 1602. He impressed Queen Elizabeth and was given the living of Pembridge in 1592 and later made a canon residentiary of Hereford by Bishop Herbert Westfaling (qv). The queen made him Dean of Windsor and her chaplain, and he continued as such under James I. He was appointed Bishop of Gloucester in 1611. He was a member of the Hampton Court Conference which James called to look at Puritan calls for reform, and was one of the scholars engaged in the revision of the Bible. He died on 14 June 1612.

Tonson, Jacob (1655-1736), printer, son of a barber-surgeon, was born in London. His mother had connections with the printing trade and Jacob became an apprentice. He learnt to spot best-sellers and signed up Dryden; he bought the manuscript of Milton's *Paradise Lost* cheap at the recently deceased poet's house and brought out a modern edition of Shakespeare. He established his authors as classics by publishing complete works with reliable texts in attractive, well-advertised editions. He founded the Kit-Kat Club as a meeting place for Whig society where every member had a standard sized portrait painted called a 'kit-kat'. In 1720 aged 65 he retired, leaving his nephew to manage the club and his other business ventures in London, and bought The Hazle with its vineyard at Ledbury from the Elton family (qv under Ambrose Elton, b.*c.*1604). He lived here for the last 16 years of his life with occasional visits to friends in London. Alexander Pope (qv) stayed with Tonson at The Hazle, once with his friend the Earl of Oxford (qv Robert Harley, d.1724) to whom he described Tonson as 'full of Matter, Secret History, Wit & Spirit'. Dryden described him:

With leering Looks, Bullfac'd, and Freckled fair,
With two left Legs, and Judas-colour'd Hair.
With Frowsy Pores, that taint the ambient Air.
(*Faction Displayed* 1705)

Tonson died at The Hazle on 18 March 1736 but was buried in London. His much-bullied nephew had predeceased him and Tonson's extensive fortune and properties went to his nephew's sons, who continued publishing the great literary figures of the day, such as Dr Johnson.

Tosny, Ralph de (*c.*1040-1102), or Toeni, was the son of Roger de Tosny and Godehildis of Conches in southern Normandy. He was a quarrelsome lord tolerated by Duke William for his fighting abilities and prominent at the Battle of Hastings. He married Isabel (d. after 1102), daughter of Simon de Montfort l'Amaury, who rode to battle with her husband and his knights. His sister Adelize married William fitz Osbern (qv), Earl of Hereford and their son was Roger de Breteuil (qv). Ralph had been granted estates in eastern England and when his nephew Roger, now 2nd Earl of Hereford, rebelled against the king in 1075 his Herefordshire lands including Clifford Castle were granted to Ralph. Ralph was not interested in his Herefordshire holdings and sublet them. He died on 24 March 1102 and was buried at Conches Abbey. His son Ralph's (b.1079) daughter Margaret de Tosny (1118-85) married Walter fitz Richard fitz Pons (qv Walter de Clifford), and their daughter was the famous Rosamund Clifford (qv).

Townsend, George Fyler (1814-1900), vicar of Leominster, was the son of George Townsend, originally from Kent and a prebend of Durham. He made the standard English translation of *Aesop's Fables*. In 1860 he published a revised edition of *The Arabian Nights* and in 1872 wrote *The Sea Kings of the Mediterranean*, a history of the Knights of Malta. In his *History of the Town and Borough of Leominster* (1860s) he discusses the origin of the name: *Llanllieni* 'the town in the rivers' and *Leofminstre* 'Leofric's (qv) minster'. He went on to be vicar of a parish in Westminster.

Trafford, Lionel James (1855-1900), soldier, was born in Gibraltar, the third of the four sons and two daughters of Charles Trafford of Michaelchurch Court, JP and DL. He was educated at Wellington College, Berks, and joined the army. As a captain in the Royal Sussex Regiment he fought in the Egyptian campaigns of the 1880s and was part of the failed attempt in 1885 to rescue General Gordon at Khartoum in the Sudan, by steamships sent up the Nile. He was mentioned in dispatches and decorated. Captain, later Major, Trafford kept a diary of this desperate venture with watercolour illustrations. After his discharge he received an inheritance from the death of an aunt and in 1893 bought Hill Court, south of Ross. After his premature death his distraught wife Ruth commissioned George Frederick Bodley (qv) to build the Paraclete Chapel near Hill Court at Hom Green, Walford as his memorial.

Traherne is a common name in Herefordshire with many spellings. They were especially common in Ledbury and Lugwardine, and in both places streets are named after them.

Traherne, John (1608-48), shoemaker and freeman of Hereford City, is recorded as being taken prisoner in a skirmish during one of the sieges of Hereford and having to be ransomed for £10. For more about his presence in Hereford during the siege, see the entry for Joyce Jefferies. He is probably the father of Thomas (qv) and Philip (qv, d.1723).

Traherne, Philip (1566-1645) was an innkeeper, twice mayor of Hereford, once in 1622 and again in 1643 after William Waller (qv) had withdrawn his occupying troops to Bristol. Traherne's second mayoralty followed the deaths of two previous incumbents, one William Price (qv) who had been roughly handled for letting in Waller. Traherne is mentioned by John Taylor (qv) in 1641 and noted as an organiser of the defences against the Scots. He married three times: Elizabeth, before 1604, with whom he had three daughters and two sons, one of whom was John qv, d.1648), who may have been Thomas and Philip Traherne's father. In 1612 he married Mary Torr alias Vincent at St Peter's, Hereford with whom he had James, Herbert and Thomas (d.1636). In 1638, in his 70s, he married Jane Lane. Philip Traherne is recorded in the donors' book for Hereford Cathedral library, as presenting a, now lost, copy of Shakespeare's First Folio for the use of the vicars choral. He died on 17 October 1645 aged 79. His gravestone in the south nave aisle of the cathedral was moved into the chapter house yard during Cottingham's (qv) renovations and is now illegible.

Traherne, Philip (1640-1723), also Traheron, the younger brother of Thomas (qv), married their friend Susanna Hopton's (qv) niece Susanna Blount (b.1649) in 1670 and in the same year was posted to Smyrna as chaplain to the Levant Company. He returned to Susanna in 1674 when his brother died, and was appointed rector of Hinton Martell near Wimborne, Dorset, where their five children were born. He had been one of his brother's pious circle, co-writing some of the manuscripts, and was Thomas's literary executor.

Traherne, Richard (fl.1685-1706) was the son of a John Traherne of Hereford. He matriculated at Christ Church on 3 March 1685 and was ordained. He was rector of Dinedor in 1692 and Little Birch in 1706.

Traherne, Thomas (1637-74), clergyman and devotional writer, was born in All Saints parish, Hereford, the older son of John Traherne (qv). The Trahernes were shoemakers said to have come from Ledbury. During his childhood Hereford was besieged three times and occupied twice with a garrison billeted on its citizens. His father was taken prisoner and King Charles was welcomed, having driven away the Scots: an extraordinary childhood. Traherne mentions the meanness of his surroundings and Aubrey (qv) says that as a child Thomas had a ghostly vision. Thomas was educated at the Cathedral School and Brasenose College, Oxford where he was sponsored by a group of Presbyterians appointed in the place of bishop, Dean and Chapter (qv William Lowe). He graduated in 1656 during the Protectorate and was presented to Credenhill rectory by Amabel, Dowager Countess of Kent (qv Henry Grey, d.1651), where he spent most of the rest of his life. He was quick to conform to the restored Church of England, travelling to Launton, Oxfordshire on 20 October 1660 to be ordained by Robert Skinner (qv Edward Skinner), Bishop of Oxford, the see of Hereford still being vacant. He contributed to the new chapel roof at Brasenose which can still be seen. Otherwise biographical material is scarce: he is mentioned in his churchwardens' accounts as being in residence at Credenhill up to the 1670s and is known to have acted as surrogate for the bishop in the consistory court. More can be deduced from his writings: in one of his *Poems of Felicitie* he writes about younger brother Philip's return from a stay at Lugwardine. In 1637 an Elizabeth Reed (qv under Reed family) married Thomas Traherne of Middle Court in Lugwardine and there were more of the name at nearby Wilcroft who may have looked after the boys. *Select Meditations* records his thoughts on his vocation in the rectory at Credenhill, his 'Hous of Paradice', before the Restoration. He refers to himself as garrulous, telling everyone he met about the love of God. He was part of a study-group which included the pious Lady Susanna Hopton (qv) and his brother and which met for prayer and talk of spiritual matters. Manuscripts exist which have clearly been circulated for they contain observations in other hands. His constant subject is God's *abundance* and *felicity* that are ours to enjoy. He ecstatically describes streets of Hereford jewelled and peopled with saints and angels and Herefordshire fields full of the ungathered wheat of heaven. His child's-eye vision of God's world looks forward to Blake and back to other writers of the *affirmative way* and to the Gospels themselves. In the second Century of the *Meditations* he writes 'He that delights not in love makes vain the universe', 'never was anything in this world loved too much' and 'you are as prone to Love as the sun is to shine'. At the end of his life Traherne was appointed chaplain to Sir Orlando Bridgeman, Charles II's principled Lord Keeper of the Seals, and died at his house in Middlesex on 10 October 1674, lamented by his friend Edward Harley (qv, d.1700): 'my worthy friend Thomas Traherne ... dead'. In a spoken will he had bequeathed his books and hat to brother Philip, but had already arranged for property he owned in Widemarsh Street, Hereford to be conveyed to the city as almshouses. He was buried in the chancel of Teddington Parish Church, Middlesex. The story of the rediscovery of his writings is extraordinary. *Roman Forgeries* was published in his lifetime and *Christian Ethicks* posthumously in 1675. Philip was his literary executor and his hand is found rewriting poems in a smoother manner. Otherwise his work was lost or shut away (as a 17th-century hand on one of the manuscripts complains). It is possible that the manuscripts spent the 18th century in the Skippe attics at Upper Hall, Ledbury as their reappearance follows a sale of papers from there, and George Skippe (qv) records buying *Christian Ethicks* on publication. In 1896 two manuscript books were bought for pence from barrows in Farringdon Road, London. They were recognised as Traherne's work by Bertram Dobell, who published the poetry (1903) and prose *Centuries of Meditations* (1906). In 1910 his notebooks and *Poems of Felicity* were found in the British Museum, in 1964 *Select Meditations* came to light and in 1967 a bound manuscript, later recognized as the *Commentaries of Heaven*, was pulled smouldering from a rubbish tip in Wigan. As recently as 1997 the manuscript of his long poem *The Ceremonial Law* was found uncatalogued in the Folger Library, Washington DC; and in the same year five more treatises were identified in the Lambeth Palace library. All these texts are now being published, revealing a major 17th-century Herefordshire mystic.

Trefnant, John (*c.*1350-1404), Bishop of Hereford 1389-1404, from Trefnant in north Wales, was educated at Oxford, graduating DD by 1376. He was a noted theologian, a lawyer with a large library of law books, and held offices in Church and Court. He was consecrated Bishop of Hereford in June 1389 by the Pope in Rome. He continued his diplomatic work for king and Pope but was known to have been much in his diocese by his recorded dealings with Lollards like Swinderby and Brut (qqv) in Herefordshire. Trefnant played a leading part in the abdication of Richard II (qv) in 1399, interviewing Richard in the Tower of London with Archbishop Courtenay and announcing the news of his abdication to parliament. Henry IV (qv) sent him to Rome to explain the matter to the Pope. It was in his time that the college of vicars choral was instituted: singing men in minor orders who were given accommodation on the south of Castle Street (their hall is a surprising survival). Trefnant rebuilt the south wall of the south transept in a late Perpendicular style with a daring amount of glass into which he incorporated his monument with its effigy.

Tregoz: The family have left their name in Eaton Tregoz parish on the Wye near Ross where Robert de Tregoz settled in the 12th century.

Tregoz, John de (1241-1300), Baron of Ewyas Harold, endowed the chapel of St John the Baptist at Eaton Tregoz in 1280; in 1325 his son William de Foy became priest there. His daughter Sybil married William Grandison, who succeeded to the estate.

Tregoz, Robert (I) de (1168-1215), a Sheriff of Wiltshire from Salisbury, married Sybil de Ewyas and was granted the barony of Ewyas Harold and lands at Eaton Tregoz, which preserves the name. At Ewyas Harold he strengthened the pre-Conquest castle (qqv Harold II, Alfred of Marlborough and William fitz Osbern). The striking motte remains.

Tregoz, Robert (II) de (d.1265), Baron of Ewyas Harold, where he was born, married Juliana, sister of Thomas Cantilupe (qv) and lived in Foy Castle, now vanished. A charter describes him holding 1,500 hides in the honour of Ewias with Sir Robert Whitney (qv, fl.1242). Tregoz was killed at the Battle of Evesham, fighting Prince Edward (qv Edward I) with Simon de Montfort (qv), and his lands and revenues were forfeit to the Crown. Juliana's head and that of her sainted brother can be seen carved as label stops in Foy Church.

Treherne, Richard was headmaster of Hereford Cathedral School from 1749 to 1762.

Trillek, John (*c.*1308-60), Bishop of Hereford 1344-60, was born in Hereford to a family from Tryleg, Monmouthshire. He and his brother Thomas were brought up in the household of their uncle, Bishop Adam Orleton of Hereford (qv). John went to Oxford, founding Trillock's Inn where clerks from Hereford could study, now part of New College, and studied at Paris University. His first benefice was Bromyard, and he accumulated others with royal offices. He was a canon at Hereford from 1327, and known to be resident, as he had a canon's house in the cathedral close, and was elected bishop while only 36, one of the last mediaeval bishops to be freely elected by a cathedral chapter. He was active in his diocese, moving between his episcopal manors, dealing with clerical discipline and matters arising from rural poverty. The diocese was devastated by the outbreak of the Black Death in the summer of 1348 and a third of the population of Herefordshire died. Trillek completed the shrine of the newly canonised Thomas Cantilupe (qv) in the north transept of his cathedral. Edward III (qv) and his Court were present in Hereford on 3 October to celebrate the new saint's feast day. His shrine was covered with gold and gems, a contrast with the death-filled streets of Hereford outside, but perhaps giving hope to the stricken diocese. The plague in fact abated in 1349. During Lent 1350 Bishop Trillek uncanonically but at the king's order, as part of national celebrations, instituted a period of thanksgiving for the end of the worst epidemic in European history. This was not the end of the plague as Dean William de Ferriby died in the outbreak of 1361. Reorganisation of the diocesan finances was also needed after the devastation brought by the plague and some of the bishop's palaces were sold, including Ledbury. Bishop Trillek's last years were unhappy; he had become physically and mentally frail and Dean Thomas Trillek oversaw diocesan affairs, an arrangement contested by the archdeacon of Shropshire, Henry Shipton, who held Trillek at Bishop's Castle. He died on 20 November 1360 and was buried in his cathedral. His brass can be seen on the north side of the choir showing him in episcopal robes with crozier. His crozier was buried with him but removed during 18th century work and is often on show in the chained library.

Trillek, Thomas (*c.*1312-72), Dean of Hereford 1353-61, younger brother of Bishop John Trillek, held a portion of Bromyard Church and was a canon of Hereford. In 1353 he was elected Dean of Hereford with a prebend in the collegiate church of Ledbury in 1355. He contracted with John de Evesham (qv under John) in 1359 to build a chapter house. He was Bishop Trillek's executor and in 1364 was appointed Bishop of Rochester. He died in late December 1372 and was buried in Rochester Cathedral. He was a learned man and part of his book collection survives in the Bodleian Library, Oxford.

Tudor, Owen (*c.*1400-61), Owain ap Meredudd ap Tudur, claimed descent from Cadwallader. He was present at Henry V's (qv) Court and after Henry's early death he caught the eye of his young widow Catherine de Valois, Shakespeare's 'fair Kate', mother of the infant king Henry VI, and without permission they contracted a morganatic marriage. Their two sons Edmund and Jasper were ennobled as uterine brothers of King Henry VI; the older, Edmund, fathered Henry VII (qv), while Jasper lived on through many vicissitudes to become a senior member of Henry's Court. Jasper Tudor was the leader of Henry's Lancastrian army defeated at Mortimers Cross by Edward of York (qv Edward IV). Owen Tudor was captured, amongst others such as Henry Scudamore (qv) and on 3 February 1461 was led out by Sir Roger Vaughan (qv, d.1471) to execution in Hereford Market Place. Owen is said to have reflected that 'the head that lies on this stock was wont to lie in Queen Catherine's lap'. Owen's head was displayed on Hereford Market Cross, where a mad woman washed it and lit candles around it. His remains were eventually buried in a chapel on the north side of the Greyfriars' Church outside the walls of Hereford, where his son erected a monument. With the suppression of the monasteries by his grandson Henry VIII, the church, chapel and monument were swept away. Queen Catherine, the daughter of mad king Charles VI of France, had died in 1437 aged 36, a victim of a congenital weakness that plagued the Valois family thought to have been porphyria. She was eventually buried with her first husband Henry V in Westminster Abbey. Her body was embalmed so well that it was later treated as an object of curiosity. On Shrove Tuesday 23 February 1669 Samuel Pepys picked up the corpse and, as a birthday present to himself, kissed her on the lips, as he confided to his diary.

Tully: A family of important breeders of Hereford white-faced cattle at Huntington in the early 18th century. Mr Tully's herd were of a greater size than those of Tomkins and Galliers (qqv). His three sons continued to develop the breed.

Turner, Joseph Mallord William (1775-1851), artist and innovative Royal Academician, painted several Herefordshire landscapes. His

Hereford Court sketchbook of the 1790s, now in the Tate Gallery, contains views of Wigmore Castle and Hampton Court. Other work in the Tate includes a sketch of the Blackfriars Cross before Scott's (qv) restoration. Turner's watercolour of the cathedral from the vicars choral cloister (1793) was presented to the Dean and Chapter by Frances Havergal (qv F.T. Havergal) and now hangs in the bishop's palace.

Turstin (*c.*1040- after 1086) or Thurstan, known as the Fleming or *de Lingen*, was the son of Rolf. He is shown carrying the papal banner beside Duke William in the Bayeux Tapestry to draw attention to William's legitimacy. He held the manor of Wigmore as tenant of William fitz Osbern (qv under William) and, after William's son had rebelled, as tenant of Ralph (I) de Mortimer (qv). He is recorded in the Domesday Book as the proprietor of Aylton. He married Agnes daughter of Alfred of Marlborough (qv). The Lingen and Whitney (qqv) families claim descent from him.

Twisleton-Wykeham-Fiennes, see under **Fiennes**

Tyler, John (1640-1724), Dean of Hereford (1692-1724) and Bishop of Llandaff, was born at Westhide on 16 August 1640, the son of John Tyler of Kington, and attended Lady Hawkins' School at Kington. He married Sarah, daughter of John Scudamore of Trecelly, Llangarron, then Dorothy, daughter of Sir William Cooke, of Highnam. He had no children but many relatives in Herefordshire, one being vicar of Shobdon. He graduated BA, MA and, in 1707, DD at Magdalen College, Oxford. He was vicar of Kentchurch, the patron being his Scudamore father-in-law, and a canon of Hereford in 1688. In the next year he became vicar of Brinsop and then of St Peter's, the civic church of Hereford. He was appointed chaplain to William and Mary and in 1693 became Dean of Hereford. When in 1706 he was consecrated Bishop of Llandaff he was allowed to continue as dean *in commendam*, a common practice at Hereford as Llandaff was poor and the living quarters dilapidated. He continued to live in Hereford deanery and Browne Willis (qv) accused him of neglecting the fabric of Llandaff Cathedral. Tyler died on 8 July 1724 and was buried in Hereford Cathedral where there is a memorial. He was interested in education and the availability of libraries and by his will established a poor school in Hereford.

Tysilio (d.640), a sainted bishop from whose name comes Sellack and Llancillo, was the son of Brochfael, King of Powys and his cult was centred in south Wales and Ergyng. He travelled to Brittany where he is known as St Suliac. His feast day is 8 November.

U V

Unett: a family centred on the Castle Frome area. In 1569 William Unett was granted a long lease for the payment of an annual rose on the moated manor house at Birchend, near Castle Frome. A descendant, who died before 1629, married Anne daughter of Ambrose Elton (qv, d.1659). An Alice Unett married Edmund Skippe of Upper Hall, Ledbury in 1609. The splendid table tomb in the chancel of St Michael's Church at Castle Frome shows the alabaster figures of a Unett man and his wife in the gorgeous costumes of the 1630s, children

kneeling round the base. In the next generation Richard and Elizabeth Unett lived at Mathon. Robert Unett of Birchend had a daughter Elizabeth who married Thomas Foley (qv) as his fourth wife in the 18th century. His Birchend manor house is now a humble farmhouse. The heroine of Edna Lyall's (qv) historical romance *In Spite of All* set in the Civil Wars is called Hilary Unett.

Vashon, James (1742-1827) son of Revd James Vashon (qv), was born at Eye. He enlisted in the Royal Navy at 13 under George Cornwall, a member of the neighbouring Cornwall family at Eye. He fought in the Mediterranean, through the American War of Independence and in the Napoleonic Wars, rising through 60 years' service to become Admiral of the White, and was knighted. Vashon Island, Washington, is named after him. He was twice married and had a son. In 1808 Sir James retired to Ludlow, where he was buried in St Laurence's Church.

Vashon, James Volant (b.1707), of Huguenot origins, was vicar of Eye, near Leominster and a lecturer at Ludlow. He married Mary Mayhew and they had a son, Sir James Vashon (qv, d.1827), and a daughter, Sarah, who married Humphrey Ballard of Ludlow. Sarah and Humphrey's son Volant Vashon Ballard CB (1774-1832) had an exemplary naval career, serving initially under his uncle Admiral James Vashon (qv) and rising to become Admiral of the Red.

Vaughan: The Welsh family Fychan were known to the bards and the subject of legends that link them with Caradoc (qv). The family was a source of law and culture in the Marches for centuries, as well as violent feuding. The legend of Black Vaughan was taken seriously in Kington for centuries. Their oldest house, Hergest Court, has been dated by tree-ring analysis to the early 13th century. They have connections with Bredwardine and Kinnersley Castles, the Courtfield and Moccas on the Wye. Their arms include three boys' heads with serpents round their necks. With the Vaughans there is a strong sense of the Marches as a separate region. They were interrelated with the other governing gentry of the Marches: the Herberts, Baskervilles, Devereux, Parrys etc., and with them often took the law into their own hands. A branch of the Vaughan family at Courtfield, Welsh Bicknor, maintained a recusancy through penal times; two of its members fought with Prince Charles Stuart at Culloden and followed him into exile, to be allowed back years later. The Vaughans produced celebrated officials for the Catholic Church following Catholic emancipation. Other Vaughans, including the twins Henry the Silurist and Thomas the alchemist, lived in Radnorshire, Montgomery and Merioneth.

Vaughan, Bernard John (1847-1922), born at Courtfield the sixth son of John Francis (qv) and Louisa, was a much travelled and sought-after Jesuit preacher.

Vaughan, Henry (b.*c*.1554), was the son of Watkyn (b.*c*.1520) and Joan (née Parry). He imparked Moccas and imported red deer from the Newcourt estate which his Parry mother had brought to the Vaughans. He married Eleanor Boyle and sent some of the famous deer from his new deer park to his brother-in-law the Earl of Cork for his Irish estate.

Vaughan, Herbert Alfred Henry Joseph Thomas (1832-1903), cardinal-archbishop of Westminster, the eldest son of John Francis (qv) and Louisa, was born on 15 April 1832. He studied at Stonyhurst, the Jesuit college, at Downside with the Benedictines and was ordained priest at Lucca in 1854. He was appointed Bishop of Salford aged 40, and in 1892 was made Archbishop of Westminster, becoming cardinal the following year. He founded St Bede's College, a Catholic school in Manchester in 1876. The building of Westminster Cathedral was his responsibility and after his death on 19 June 1903, the new cathedral was opened with his Requiem Mass.

Vaughan, John (1853-1925), youngest son of John Francis (qv) and Louisa, became auxiliary to the Bishop of Salford in 1909. After ordination he was appointed professor of mathematics at his brother Herbert's (qv) new school, St Bede's and was involved with missionary and pastoral work. He wrote several books of Catholic piety.

Vaughan, John Francis (1808-80), son of William Vaughan, was born at Courtfield, Welsh Bicknor. He was a magistrate and Deputy Lieutenant of both Hereford and Monmouth, and as such the senior Catholic in the shire. He married Louisa Eliza Rolls (1810-53) with whom he had 14 children and, after her death, his cousin Charlotte Weld (b.*c*.1821). Louisa was a pious convert and her five daughters became nuns and five of her sons priests. Charlotte's family were old Catholics; her uncle Thomas Weld was the first English cardinal since the Reformation. Vaughan died in Biarritz.

Vaughan or **Fychan, Roger** (d.1415), of Hergest Court and Bredwardine Castle, married Gwladys (d.1454) daughter of Sir Dafydd Gam of Brecon. They had three sons, Watkyn (qv, d.1456), Thomas (qv, d.1471) and Roger, (qv, d.1469), who were brought up with their Herbert half-brothers William, 1st Earl of Pembrokeshire (qv), and Richard. He was connected also with the Devereux and Baskerville (qqv) families. Roger and his father-in-law

Sir Dafydd were killed at Agincourt in defence of Henry V. The three sons were established at Bredwardine, Hergest and Tretower respectively. The alabaster effigy of a knight in the chancel of St Andrew's, Bredwardine could be Roger.

Vaughan, Roger (d.1471), the third and most prominent of the sons of Roger Fychan or Vaughan (qv, d.1415) and Gwladys, lived at Tretower (now conserved to represent a fortified manor house of Vaughan's time), which his half-brother William Herbert, 1st Earl of Pembroke, gave him. He fought for Edward, Earl of March (qv Edward IV) at Mortimers Cross and led Owen Tudor (qv) to his execution in Hereford after the battle. He was prominent in securing Wales for Edward, who knighted him and gave him offices in east Wales. He married Denise, daughter of Thomas ap Philip Vaughan of Talgarth, and their four daughters all married local gentry. With his second wife Margaret, Lady Powis (d.1480) he had an heir, Thomas (qv, d.1483), and a daughter who married Humphrey Kynaston, an outlaw of Shropshire. There were also several illegitimate children. After the Battle of Tewkesbury he pursued Jasper Tudor but Tudor turned the tables and caught and executed him at Chepstow in reprisal for the death of his father Owen Tudor (qv).

Vaughan, Roger (before 1558-1607) married Watkyn Vaughan's (qv, b.*c*.1520) wife's sister Elizabeth, who brought him her share of Parry and Scudamore lands. They lived in Kinnersley Castle, the old Norman home of the Vaughans, for many years. This he rebuilt in an Elizabethan style, and it still stands intact today, standing by St James's Church. His arms – a boy's head and serpent – appear on the splendid solar overmantel under a gorgeous plaster ceiling of Roger Vaughan's time. After his death Elizabeth sold the now brand-new castle to Francis Smalman (qv).

Vaughan, Roger (1584-1643) of Bredwardine was the son of Henry (b.*c*.1554) and Eleanor Boyle. He married Joan Husbands (b.1589) of Wormbridge. They had a son Henry (b.1609), of Moccas and Bredwardine, who married Frances Pye as her first husband (qv Water Pye). Henry and Frances had a son Roger Vaughan (qv, d.1672).

Vaughan, Roger (c.1636-72) was the son of Henry and Frances (qv Roger Vaughan d.1643), and married Anne (c.1640-74), daughter of Thomas Tomkyns (qv), his cousin. He was elected MP for Hereford 1662-72. He died at the naval battle of Solebay in the Third Anglo-Dutch War deeply in debt, leaving Herbert Westfaling (qv, d.1705), who had stood surety for him in some distress, and his half-brother Henry Cornewall (qv, d.1717), to tackle the debts.

Vaughan, Roger William (1834-83), Roman Catholic Archbishop, was born on 9 January 1834 at Courtfield, the second son of John Francis (qv) and Louisa. He was a frail child, educated at home in a pious atmosphere. He went to Downside in 1850 and took the Benedictine habit as Brother Bede. He studied at Rome and was ordained priest in 1859. He was professor of philosophy, then Prior of St Michael's Monastery, Belmont and published a biography of St Thomas Aquinas (1872). In 1873 he went to Sydney, Australia becoming archbishop in 1877. He reformed the Catholic education system and began Sydney Cathedral. Constant travel and public speaking told on his health and he retired home, dying on 18 August 1883. He was buried at Belmont but his body was later moved to the crypt of his cathedral in Sydney.

Vaughan, Rowland (1559-1628), second son of Watkyn Vaughan qv, b.*c*.1520), was born at Newcourt. He secured a place at Court through his aunt Blanche Parry (qv) and captained a company of men to resist the Armada. He fought in the Irish wars, returning ill to recuperate at his Bredwardine house. He is mentioned as *armiger* and as owning Whitehouse and Newcourt, both Parry properties. In 1585 he married his cousin Elizabeth (d.1611), daughter of Roger (qv, d.1607) and Elizabeth. He devised an innovative irrigation system to flood his valley lands along the River Dore at Turnastone downstream to his neighbour Sir James Scudamore's (qv, d.1619) property at Abbey Dore and increase their fertility. He employed John Abel (qv) to construct a 'trench-royall' with a sluice gate that would flood his fields at will. He published his findings in his *Most Approved and Long experienced Water Workes* (1610). Neighbours considered the idea eccentric but the lush results persuaded them to copy his methods. His son John and his descendants continued using the system for irrigation and transport, and remains of it can still be traced. Rowland had several other children, including a Jane who married a Parry. He was a litigious man and died in London during a law suit against a neighbour; he is buried in St Dunstan's in the West. A son of John's was Rowland Vaughan of Caer Gai, a notable Royalist and translator of Lewis Bayly's (qv) *Practise of Pietie* into Welsh.

Vaughan, Thomas (*c*.1400-69) of Hergest Court was Roger Fychan's (qv, d.1415) second son. He married Elen Gethin, 'the terrible', daughter of Cadwgan ap Dafydd, and they had three sons, Watkyn, Richard and Roger, and a daughter Elizabeth, who married Robert Whitney (qv, d.1494). Thomas and his two brothers with their Herbert kin fought for Edward IV (qv) at Edgecote where Thomas was killed. He is buried in Kington Church where there is a monument to him and Elen. He was known as 'Black Vaughan' probably because of his hair colouring, but later legend tells of his restless spirit terrorizing Kington in various forms such as a black hound or bull. The spirit is said to have been laid by 12 clergymen and confined under a stone in Hergest Pool. The tale may be a source of Conan Doyle's (qv) *Hound of the Baskervilles*. The bard Lewis Glyn Cothi (qv) sang the eulogy at his funeral. The *Red Book of Hergest* is an anthology of Lewis's poems, often praising the exploits of the Vaughans; the *White Book of Hergest* with its legends, eulogies and genealogies was tragically lost in a London bookbinder's fire.

Vaughan, Thomas (*c*.1410-83), courtier and son of Sir Roger (qv, d.1471) and Lady Margaret, was an esquire of the body to Henry VI and lived in a house called Garlick in London. He was appointed steward and receiver of the Beauchamp (Earl of Warwick) estates in Herefordshire and the Marches. By 1459 he was supporting the Yorkists and fled abroad after their defeat at Ludford Bridge. He returned the next year and married Eleanor, a Lancastrian widow, but fled after Warwick's defeat at St Albans in 1461. He was captured in the Channel by pirates with Henry's treasure and was ransomed by Edward Duke of York, now king (qv Edward IV). After 1471 he was a favoured royal servant, knighted in 1475 for his services to the young Prince Edward, and sat in Edward's Parliaments as knight of the shire for Cornwall. After Edward IV's death he was arrested by Richard Duke of Gloucester while he was accompanying Prince Edward to his coronation and summarily executed at Pontefract Castle. The Vaughans' Yorkist connections were pardoned by Henry VII (qv) but their influence waned in Tudor times. Thomas of Tretower was much eulogised by Welsh bards including Lewis Glyn Cothi. He was buried in Westminster Abbey, where his brass remains. In Shakespeare's *Richard III* Vaughan's ghost appears to warn Richard on the eve of the Battle of Bosworth.

Vaughan, Watkyn (d.1456), Roger's (qv, d.1415) eldest son, established himself at Bredwardine Castle, which guarded a crossing of the Wye. He married Elizabeth, daughter of Sir Henry Wogan. He was murdered at Bredwardine in 1456 and his Herbert and Devereux kin tried and summarily executed the suspects in Hereford. The heads of these families at that time were Sir Walter Devereux (qv, d.1459), recently bloodied from the Battle of St Albans, and the Earl of Pembroke (qv William Herbert), Watkyn's uterine brother. His eldest son Sir Thomas fought for the Yorkists at the Battle of Barnet in 1471 and killed Warwick the Kingmaker.

Vaughan, Watkyn (d.1504), grandson of Thomas (qv, d.1469) and Elen, married Elizabeth, daughter of Sir James Baskerville (qv, d.1494) and Catherine/Sybil née Devereux. Watkyn was given the lordships of Huntington and adjacent areas to oversee. He died on 6 January 1504.

Vaughan, Watkyn (b.*c*.1520) of Bredwardine Castle married Joan, daughter and co-heiress of Myles Parry (qv). Three of his sons were Henry, Walter and Rowland (qv, d.1628). He built a new property at Moccas in 1550, downstream from Bredwardine on the old Moccas Castle motte. After Watkyn's death his widow married one of the Cornewall family (qv) and Moccas passed into their hands.

Vaughan Williams, Ralph (1872-1958), composer, was born at Down Ampney, Gloucs where his father was vicar and went to Charterhouse School. He studied piano and violin at the Royal College of Music where Charles Hubert Parry (qv) of Highnam Court was professor of composition and later director; and at Trinity College, Cambridge. His interest in traditional folk music drew him to Herefordshire where he collected folk songs with his wife Ursula, noting the traditional songs of the villagers, hop pickers and gypsies. He met Ella Mary Leather (qv) in 1908 at the Three Choirs Festival in Hereford and they noted down folk songs in the villages. He visited her at Weobley the same year with an Edison phonograph to record the songs. Of this time he was to recall a girl singing an old ballad to two men at Ledbury, and a gypsy singing at Monkland in 1912. He returned each year until the First World War with Mrs Leather and Cecil Sharp (qv) to collect carols – one particularly notable from Yarkhill. He published the results

as *Twelve Traditional Carols from Herefordshire* (1912) and in the *Oxford Book of Carols* (1928). He continued to visit and in 1949 brought Gerald Finzi to Weobley after a Three Choirs Festival at Hereford. Vaughan Williams arranged the original music for John Stanhope Arkwright's (qv) *The Supreme Sacrifice,* although Revd Charles Harris's (qv) version has always been preferred. He died on 26 August 1958.

Vavasour, William (d.1659), Royalist army officer from Copmanthorpe, Yorkshire, saw military service in Europe. Returning in 1639 he was colonel of foot in the Second Bishops' War of 1640. On the outbreak of the Civil War he joined the king's forces and was captured at Edgehill in October 1642. He was held at Warwick Castle but made his way back to the Court at Oxford where the king appointed him commander-in-chief of his forces in Herefordshire and adjacent counties. He raised a regiment of foot and horse and, in 1643, was created a baronet. As Governor of Hereford he organised the siege of Brampton Bryan (qv Brilliana Harley). He besieged Col Massey (qv) in Gloucester but fell foul of the scheming that often troubled the king's armies. Although he was again appointed Governor of Hereford he became disheartened and resumed his military career abroad. He died at the siege of Copenhagen on 18 February 1659 in the service of Charles X of Sweden.

Venn, John (1802-90), vicar of St Peter's, Hereford (1833-70), was the son of Revd John Venn, rector of Clapham. The family was the philanthropic, evangelical centre of the Clapham Sect. His sister was Virginia Woolf's grandmother. His first parish was prosperous Pinner in Middlesex but, eager to help the poor, he transferred to needy St Peter's with St Owen's in Hereford. He married Frances Turton. Conditions were hard after the failure of the potato crop and poor harvests in the severe winters of 1838, '39 and '41. The new workhouse system was hated and many destitute people preferred to starve; one 85-year-old man hanged himself rather than live there. Venn initiated methods of self-help, founding a reading room and a literary institute with a library and arranging lectures on self-improvement. He founded the Hereford Friendly Society to encourage the provident and the Hereford Society for Aiding the Industrious (still a grant-making body) which brought significant social benefits to Hereford. Venn was secretary of this society throughout his life. It built a soup kitchen, a steam mill where the sale of cheap flour funded all Venn's other projects, and, to make use of the steam heat, a baths and wash house next door. The red-brick, industrial mill building still stands and the baths complex survives as a Masonic hall, the bath still in place beneath the floor. The road is still called Bath Street. The Portfield, between Commercial Street and Ledbury Road, was bought for allotments. Low interest loans were made and profits were divided amongst the workers and used to fund the Working Boys' Home (currently used by social services) and St Owen's primary school. Model cottages at low rents were built and still stand in Kyrle Street. The Society continues and owns the almshouses in Bath and Friar streets. Venn retired as vicar in 1870 and died 20 years later; his monument in the sadly neglected graveyard of St Peter's off Commercial Street has recently been renovated. The arch into the graveyard was built by Edward Lingen Barker (qv) in 1881 in memory of Venn's sister Emelia (1794-1881). Venn left extensive diaries and letters.

Verdin, Joseph (1838-1920) was born on 4 January 1838 into the salt manufacturing family Joseph Verdin & Sons of Northwich, Cheshire. He was JP, DL and an alderman for Cheshire and knighted in 1897. Sir Joseph presented schools to Northwich and Winsford and the Verdin Baths to Winsford. He retired to Garnstone Castle, near Weobley with his sister Mary in 1900. He was a JP in Herefordshire and in 1903 High Sheriff. He died at Garnstone on 28 December 1920.

Vere, Francis de (1561-1609), army officer and diplomat, was from Essex and a nephew of the Earl of Oxford. He served in the Low Countries under General Sir Thomas Baskerville (qv, d.1597) and himself commanded during successful campaigns, at one time with Ben Jonson and Gervase Markham (qv) in his

force. He was knighted on the field. He was MP for Leominster in 1593 under the patronage of the Earl of Essex. Aged about 40 Sir Francis married Elizabeth, the 16-year-old daughter of the lawyer Sir Julius Caesar. He has a flamboyant tomb in Westminster Abbey.

Vere, William de (*c.*1120-98), Bishop of Hereford 1186-99, the son of Aubrey, 3rd Earl of Oxford, Henry I's chamberlain, was brought up at Henry's Court. He made a pilgrimage to the Holy Land, accompanying his nephew Geoffrey de Mandeville who carried money from the king for the Templars and Hospitallers. The King of Jerusalem offered him employment but he was eager to return home. In 1186 he was made Bishop of Hereford. He widened the processional route in the cathedral and replaced the three eastern apsidal chapels with two square-ended eastern transepts with an antechapel between them onto which the lady chapel would be built. He also rebuilt Holy Trinity Church in Bosbury, adding aisles and the chancel. He had been a supporter of Thomas Becket (qv) and commissioned the Limoges casket to hold a relic of the saint, still regularly exhibited at the cathedral. During William's episcopate Hereford became a centre of scientific studies, attracting learned canons like Roger of Hereford, Gerald of Wales, Ralph and Walter Foliot, Walter Map, and Robert Grosseteste (qqv). He died on 24 December 1198 and is buried in the south choir aisle of the cathedral. His seal showing him in full vestments is in the archives.

Vergil, Polydore (1470-1555), celebrated humanist scholar from Urbino, came to England on papal business and stayed. He had various offices and prebends including that of Nunnington in the Herefordshire parish of Withington, secured perhaps through his friendship with Wolsey (qv), who was briefly Dean of Hereford. He is remembered for his *Anglica Historia*, reviled as Romish lies at the Reformation but appreciated later.

Vernon-Harcourt, Frances (d.1872) was the youngest daughter of Edward Harley, 5th Earl of Oxford and Earl Mortimer (qv, d.1849) and the Countess Jane (qv Jane Harley). Because of the irregularity of their parents' marriage she and her siblings were sometimes known as the Harleian miscellany. On 20 April 1835 she married Lt-Col Henry Venables Vernon-Harcourt, the son of the Archbishop of York. Hers are the sketches in Robinson's (qv) *Castles* and *Mansions and Manors of Herefordshire*. She died on 15 October 1872.

Victoria (1819-1901), queen and empress, rode into Ledbury aged 11 on a pony with her mother the duchess of Kent in 1830 after sight-seeing on the Malvern Hills. They went on to call on the Heywoods (qv Thomas Heywood) at Hope End. Victoria, while princess, was the patron of Ross and Archenfield schools, as the plaque on the old school in Wye Street, Ross tells us. There are many memorials to her long reign in the county, notably the west window at Hereford Cathedral.

Voyle, William, see under **William Lowe**

Voysey, Charles Francis Annesley (1857-1941), architect and designer, was born on 28 May 1857 in Hessle, Yorkshire where his father was vicar. He was not academically minded

and became an architect because qualifications were not needed. The Voyseys were descended from John Wesley (qv) to whom Charles bore a resemblance. He admired his father's free-thinking religious ideas and was troubled when he was expelled from the Church of England for heretical views. During 1874-9 he studied under J.P. Seddon (qv), who also had a strong influence on him, and he set up practice in London in 1881 designing wallpapers and textiles for which he became noted. He married Mary Evans in 1885 and they had two sons. He was famous for his private houses and, although counted as an Arts and Crafts architect, his social and aesthetic philosophy is his own. He was a great influence on the modernist architects of Europe. An important house is Perrycroft at Colwall (1893-4) with another, Bannut Tree House, nearby. His buildings were plain and rational although not cheap, with vernacular features like battered (with an angled face) and rendered walls. He designed all the details of his houses – hinges, shutters, even furniture and curtains – and was offended when clients wanted to change them. Typical motifs were the heart shape seen on ironwork or cut out of shutters, and birds. There is a carpet designed by him in the nursery at Berrington Hall. After his wife's death he lived alone in a small service flat in St James's, spending most of his time at his club. He died on 12 February 1941.

W Y

Wailes, William (1808-81), stained glass manufacturer, was born in Newcastle. He started experimenting with firing enamels as a grocer, and expanded his skill through studying in Germany. He was employed by A.W.N. Pugin (qv) and became one of the biggest 19th-century stained glass makers, noted for his bright, sharp colours. His work was shown at the Great Exhibition in 1851 and the same year he supplied the east window at St Mary Magdalen, Little Hereford, where he has signed his initials. In the 1860s he supplied a two-light window for the chancel of St John the Baptist, Upton Bishop and two windows for the north transept in Hereford Cathedral, in both cases as part of George Gilbert Scott's (qv) restoration. As one of his last jobs he made glass for the chancel of Holy Trinity, Bosbury, the east window commemorating Revd Edward Higgins (qv) of Bosbury House.

Walerand, Robert (d.1272), son of Sir William Walerand, the Sheriff of Wiltshire, and Isabella de Kilpeck, married Matilda (d.1307), eldest daughter of Ralph Russell of Dyrham. He was a supporter of Henry III (qv) and his chief counsellor throughout the Barons' Wars, fighting against Simon de Montfort (qv) at Lewes and Evesham. His chief seat was at Siston, Gloucs and he was Sheriff of Gloucester, but he owned great estates centred on Kilpeck. He and Matilda had no issue and his sister Alice's son Alan Plukenet (II) (qv) was his heir.

Waller, William (*c.*1598-1668), Parliamentarian officer from Kent, was educated at Magdalen and Hart Hall, Oxford. After his wealthy father's death he was knighted by James I and married Jane Reynell (d.1633). She and their son died and her monument in Bath Abbey also includes an alabaster statue of Sir William. His second wife was Anne, daughter of Thomas Finch, Earl of Winchelsea and they and their children lived in Winchester Castle from 1638. Waller felt preserved and chastened by providence and felt directed to enter Parliament to oppose the king, as MP for Andover. He raised a regiment of horse and by 1643 was Major-General of the West. He took Tewkesbury and with Colonel Massey (qv) marched his 3,000 strong army to Ross. He occupied Leominster and, leaving Birch (qv) in charge of a garrison there, marched on to Hereford. Arriving on 25 April 1643 he found feeble defences which Governor Sir Richard Cave (qv) had vainly been trying to encourage the citizens to strengthen. Massey fired into Hereford killing several citizens and Waller, making a feint, launched his main attack on Widemarsh Gate. Cave attempted a parley but surrendered the city when his garrison began to desert. Waller took Cave, Sir John Scudamore (qv, d.1671) and his son James (qv, d.1668), Fitzwilliam Coningsby (qv) the sheriff and Colonel Herbert Price prisoners. The surrender saved Hereford from being

sacked by Waller as Winchester had recently been; Waller's own home, Winchester Castle, had been ruined. But his occupation of Hereford was brief. The Herefordians were resentful and uncooperative and he was forced to withdraw to Gloucester, Royalist forces moving back in on 18 May. Hereford was Waller's turning point; there were no more successes and his great army gradually disappeared through lack of funds and reverses. As a Presbyterian he was distrusted by a radicalised Parliament in the hands of the independents and he was imprisoned and exiled. His wife Anne, a 'pretty, portable Armie' in herself, was a constant support. She accompanied him on campaigns, struggled through to him in prison and preached to the troops everywhere. On her death he married Lady Anne Harcourt (d.1661), widow of Sir Simon Harcourt, and they had three children. He left various writings examining his life including *Divine Meditations* where he searches for meaning in God's dealings with him. Anthony Wood, the Oxford biographer, says he was 'a brave little spark'. Waller died at Osterley House on 19 September 1668.

Walond, Richard (1760-1838), apiarist, was rector of Putley (1783-96) and Weston-under-Penyard from 1801, publishing his sermons in 1819. He married Anne Elizabeth Whishaw (d.1813) and they had a son, Richard (1778-1802) who was also ordained. Revd Walond was treasurer of Hereford Cathedral (1802-31). He was a keen apiarist and involved with the innovations of his friend Dr Bevan (qv).

Walpole, Horace (1717-97), 4th Earl of Orford, was born on 24 September 1717 in Arlington Street, Piccadilly; his father was Prime Minister Robert Walpole and Lord Nelson (qv) was a cousin. He was a much loved but sickly child of older parents. He was educated at Eton and King's College, Cambridge where he made friends with the poet Thomas Gray (qv), with whom he toured the Continent. He entered politics but it is as the purveyor of taste and malicious gossip and for his matchless letters that he is famous. He bought a house at Strawberry Hill on the River Thames at Twickenham which he decorated as 'gothick' and wrote gothic horror tales such as *The Castle of Otranto*. His friend Lord Richard Bateman (qv) asked for his help at Shobdon and he recommended the architect Henry Flitcroft (qv). The resulting Shobdon Court and Church were in the style known as Strawberry Hill Gothick. The Court has been

demolished but St John the Evangelist, the most beautiful building in Herefordshire of its date, is a major example of Walpole's influence and has recently been renovated. It must be due to Walpole that the Herefordshire School (qv) carvings from the old church were preserved in the Shobdon Arches on the hill. Two carved wooden Flemish panels owned by him can be seen in Yatton Church. Walpole died on 2 March 1797 and was buried in Houghton Church in the family tomb.

Walsham, John (d.1648) was the son of Sir John Walsham and Barbara Knill (qv under Knill family), the heiress of Knill Court. He married Elizabeth Ford, and their daughter and heir Elizabeth married Francis Garbett (qv).

Walsham, John (1830-1905), 2nd Baronet, was born at Cheltenham on 29 October 1830, the eldest of Sir John James Garbett Walsham's (qv) four sons. He was envoy to China from 1885 to 1892 and invested KCMG. He married Florence Campbell Scarlett (d.1915) in 1867 and they lived at Knill Court. He left two sons and a daughter.

Walsham, John Garbett (1771-1819) was born John Garbett, but later assumed his mother's name Walsham and lived at Knill Court. He was Deputy Lieutenant of Herefordshire and Radnorshire and colonel in the Radnorshire Militia. He married Anna Maria Hughes and their son was John James Garbett Walsham (qv).

Walsham, John James Garbett (1805-1874), 1st Baronet Walsham, was born on 6 June 1805. His father was John Garbett (qv, d.1857) and his mother Elizabeth, heiress of the Walsham family. Their home, Knill Court, a charming Tudor manor house, the site of the suicide of Sir Samuel Romilly (qv), stood in a beautiful wooded setting south of Presteigne. In 1826 John Walsham married Frances, second daughter of Matthew Bell. He was created 1st Baronet Walsham in 1831 as the closest descendant of Sir Thomas Morgan (qv, d.1716), and was Deputy Lieutenant. Sir John rebuilt Knill Court on a grander scale in 1867 and extended the gardens.

Walsham, John Scarlett (1869-1940), 3rd Baronet, son of John (qv, d.1905), sold the Knill estate with its now inconveniently large Knill Court. It became a school and burned down in 1943.

Walter, John (1584-1656), benefactor, was born in Hereford but educated in London where he became clerk of Draper's Hall. He married and had children. Thomas Fuller (qv) accorded him a place in his *Worthies* for his extensive charities. He founded almshouses, leaving property that he owned in Wye Bridge Street in Hereford to house poor widows and bequests both in London and Hereford. He died in London on 29 December 1656.

Walter of Lorraine (d.1079), Bishop of Hereford 1061-79, came to England in the 1050s as chaplain to Edith (qv), Edward the Confessor's queen. Walter was consecrated Bishop of Hereford in Rome by Pope Nicholas II in April 1061 and confirmed by the Conqueror. The see of Hereford had been managed by Bishop Ealdred of Worcester since the death of Bishop Leofgar (qv). Walter granted church land to the north of the Saxon town walls of Hereford, now the High Town area, to William fitz Osbern (qv) for his new market, doubling the area of the Saxon city. There had been a Saxon market at the east end of Castle Street. Walter was a learned man but was said by William of Malmesbury (qv) to have been killed by a servant girl whom he was pestering. There is no effigy of him in the cathedral and his burial place is not known. His successor was Robert de Losinga (qv), another Lotharingian.

Walter fitz Walter (1345-86), 4th Lord fitz Walter, held lands in Herefordshire. He fought in the Hundred Years War in France and his son, also Walter (1368-1406), fought against Glyn Dŵr.

Walwyn: A Norman name. Philip Walwyn owned Walwain Castle, Pembs. and held lands at Hay in the 1090s. Walwyns appeared in Herefordshire in the next century at Stoke Edith, at Longworth in Lugwardine and at Much Marcle, where they established themselves through marriage with the Audleys (qv), who were based at Mortimer's Castle at Much Marcle in the 14th century under their feudal lords the Mortimers (qv). King Harold had been Lord of Merkelan and after the Conquest it was granted to the de Lacys, worth £30 in the Domesday record, a large sum. The de Lacys forfeited the Lordship and it passed to de Balun, then Audley. The Walwyn name disappeared from Much Marcle and the charming old manor house, Hellens, passed in marriage to the MP and advocate of cider Charles Radcliffe Cooke (qv). The family survived longer in Lugwardine, Longworth Hall being rebuilt by James Walwyn (qv), and at Old Court, Colwall.

Walwyn, Edward (fl.1798) born Edward James, a distant relative of the family, inherited the Walwyn lands at Marcle and assumed the Walwyn name. He was friendly with the painter Joshua Cristall (qv) who painted his portrait (now in Hereford Museum, see below). Cristall and his wife brought up Walwyn's two daughters, one of whom, Mary Anne, married Robert Duffield Cooke. Their son Charles Walwyn Radcliffe Cooke (qv) became the proprietor of Hellens.

Walwyn, Fulke (b.1603), a relative of Sir Richard Walwyn (qv, d.1573), bought and restored Hellens, which had fallen into disrepair. He fought for the king in the Civil Wars, riding out through the gates at the back of Hellens, which were locked until his return. They have remained locked ever since. However, his son John (qv, d.1686) and Sir Henry Lingen, both wounded at the fight between Massey and Prince Rupert (qqv) at Ledbury in 1645, did return.

Walwyn, Humphrey (fl.1600), son of John Walwyn (qv, fl.1580s), was born in Colwall but lived in London, a member of the Worshipful Company of Grocers. He remembered Colwall in his will of 1614 and left money to fund a free grammar school in the village, now The Elms School. His name and manor is preserved in Colwall in the Old Court Nurseries, Walwyn Road.

Walwyn, James (1744-1800) of Longworth Hall, Lugwardine, was a captain in the army. He employed Anthony Keck (qv) to recast the house in Georgian fashion (1788). His daughter Lucy married Colonel John (II) Scudamore (qv) of Kentchurch. After Captain Walwyn's death Longworth passed to Archdeacon Lilly (qv) in 1805 and then to Walwyn's relative Robert Phillips (qv under Robert Biddulph Phillips). Walwyn's son Richard predeceased him; he was an antiquarian who collected important manuscripts of Herefordshire which went to Phillips and are now in Hereford Record Office.

Walwyn, John (1415-88), William (qv) and Joan's son, was born at Longford, Kingsland. He married Agnes (b.*c.*1420) daughter of John Milbourne of Burghill, and they had many sons and daughters.

Walwyn, John (fl.1580s), of Old Court, Colwall, is commemorated at St James's Church, Colwall on a wall plaque of 1587 which shows the family arms.

Walwyn, John (1622-86), of Hellens, was the son of Fulke Walwyn and Margaret Pye, who married *c*.1620 and had ten children. John married Mary Winnington in 1667. Their daughter Margaret and her husband John Noble, a mercer in the London of the 1690s, inherited the manor of Marcle.

Walwyn, Mehitabel (*c*.1678-1728) is said to have eloped, aged about 30, with John Pierce, the stable boy. After two years she returned to Hellens in disgrace and was confined by her unforgiving parents. She sadly scratched on her window pane 'It is a part of virtue to abstain from what we love if it will prove our bane' – lines from *The Faithfull Shepherd* in Richard Fanshawe's 1647 translation of Guarini's popular arcadian poem which formed the libretto of an opera seria by Handel (of 1712). The story is about the sacrifice of a young woman. Hetty died in this room, perhaps by her own hand. The room, and possibly Hetty's ghost, can be seen at Hellens, still with her bell pull hanging ominously.

Walwyn, Nicholas (1508-58), of Longworth Hall, was the son of Thomas Walwyn and Eleanor Vaughan. He married Eleanor, the daughter of John Lingen of Sutton, and they had ten children.

Walwyn, Nicholas (d.1685) of the Longworth branch died without male heirs and Longworth was sold to Bishop Herbert Croft (qv). When Croft died in 1691 it was bought back by a cousin of Nicholas, Dr James Walwyn, a wealthy sugar plantation owner.

Walwyn, Richard (b.*c*.1340), knight, son of Thomas (qv, b.*c*.1310), married Joan (*c*.1343-after 1393), daughter of Walter de Helyon (qv), the Audleys' franklin from whom Hellens is thought to have taken its name. Sir Richard was nine times called to Edward III's Parliaments and was High Sheriff 1336-42. He had sons Thomas II (qv) and William.

Walwyn, Richard (1387-1455), eldest son of Thomas (II) (qv) and Isabel of Hellens, married Clementia Write (*c*.1394-1456) in 1420. Their heirs form the Hellens branch of the family.

Walwyn, Richard (*c*.1502-73), knight, was the son of Thomas Walwyn (qv, d.1531) of Hellens. He married Dorothy, daughter of John Lacon. In January 1554 he was instructed by the government to raise a force and oppose Sir James Croft's (qv, d.1590) uprising. Croft had 12,000 Herefordshire men on the hill overlooking Pinsley Brook north of Eardisland in support of Wyatt's rebellion in protest at Queen Mary's (qv) marriage to the Spanish Philip I, but they flew when Sir Richard and the men of Leominster approached. Queen Mary, who had only recently secured the throne from the usurping Jane Grey (qv), knighted Walwyn and granted Leominster a charter. Walwyn's loyalty to the queen was unexpected as he had profited from the spoils of the Reformation, buying up the advowson and tithes of Clifford Priory at the Dissolution and Clifford Castle. Despite this Walwyn died bankrupt and Hellens was sold. He had sons Thomas and Richard (d.1578).

Walwyn, Richard (fl. mid 17th century), was a friend of Thomas Blount (qv) and read his historical notes.

Walwyn, Thomas (b.*c*.1310), son of Richard Walwyn of Bickerton, Much Marcle married Catherine of Hereford and had a son, Richard (qv, b.*c*.134).

Walwyn, Thomas (*c*.1470-1531) descended from Richard Walwyn, (qv, d.1455), of the Hellens branch, married Agnes (1460-1533), daughter and co-heir of Sir Simon Milbourne of Tillington. Their son was Richard Walwyn (qv, d.1573).

Walwyn, Thomas (I) (*c.*1370-1444), son of John Walwyn (*c.*1340-1416) of Stoke Edith, married Margaret; there were no children. He served in the household of Bishop John Trefnant (qv) and was present at the investigation of the Lollard Walter Brut (qv). He was an esquire of Richard II (qv) and elected to his Parliament of 1395. He and his nephew William Walwyn (qv, d.1452) were executors of Bishop Trefnant's will in 1404. He and his father John were also executors of Thomas (II) Walwyn's will.

Walwyn, Thomas (II) (*c.*1362-1415), born at Hellens, was the son of Sir Richard (qv, b.*c.*1340). He married Isabel Hathaway (*c.*1366-*c.*1430) of Ruardean and had sons Richard (qv, d.1455), William (qv) and Malcolm and two daughters, one of whom, Margaret (*c.*1398-1436), married William Croft (qv, d.1439). Walwyn was escheator for the county and was twice Sheriff of Hereford. In 1392 he is recorded as endowing a chantry in St Nicholas, Norton Canon with Kynard de la Bere (qv) and Thomas Oldcastle (qv). He is mentioned as a friend of Sir John Oldcastle (qv). He went to Ireland with Roger (VII) Mortimer (qv), his feudal overlord, on the king's business in 1394 and acted as his co-executor when Mortimer was killed. He was MP for Herefordshire in 1397 and 1404. He acquired Longworth Hall, Lugwardine, from William (V) Beauchamp (qv), whose service he had entered. He died at Hellens on 20 May 1415, leaving a chantry for himself and his family at Much Marcle Church. Dean Prophete (qv), who seems to have been a relative, was an overseer of his will. It would be nice to think the tomb chest in the Kyrle chapel of St Bartholomew's, Much Marcle of a couple in the height of the fashion of *c.*1400 shows Thomas and Isabel. He was a retainer of the Earls of March.

Walwyn, William, (*c.*1390-1452), younger son of Thomas (II) (qv) and Isabel, was born at Hellens. He married Joan, daughter of Sir Robert Whitney (qv, d.1402) and their heirs formed the Longworth branch of the Walwyns.

Ward, Harry Marshall (1854-1906), botanist, was born on 21 March 1854 in Victoria Street, Hereford, the eldest son of Francis Marshall Ward, professor of music, and his wife, Mary Hannah East. He studied natural sciences at Christ's College, Cambridge and travelled on the Continent and in Ceylon studying parasitism in plants. He married Selina Kingdon and they had a daughter and a son, Francis, who became a plant collector and explorer. He developed the important botanical institute at Cambridge and published many papers on disease and parasitism in plants. He identified 80 species of bacteria in the water of the Thames. He was a Fellow of the Linnaean Society and the Royal Society. Ward died at Torquay on 26 August 1906 and was buried in Cambridge.

Ward, John (1704-73), actor manager, was born in Ireland. He was the proprietor of a travelling company of players that toured the Midlands and Wales in the 18th century, regularly including Herefordshire. He was a Methodist and maintained strict discipline in the troupe. The Ward family home was in Leominster and they played regularly in the Forbury Chapel and at Kington Theatre. The young stage-struck Roger Kemble (qv) of Hereford joined them and married Ward's daughter Sally. They toured Herefordshire towns, Ledbury being a favourite where local gentry flocked to see them play at the Talbot and the George. When Ward retired in 1766 Kemble with Sally took over the troupe's management based at Leominster Theatre. Ward's granddaughter Sarah Kemble joined the company as did a player called William Siddons who married her, and as Sarah Siddons (qv) she became the most famous actor of her day. John Ward died on 30 October 1773 at his home in Leominster and he and his wife are buried in the Priory churchyard.

Ward, Thomas (1801-72), stationer and printer, was born in Melksham, Wilts. He moved to Ledbury and set up as a stationer, marrying Sarah Thackway (1811-1900) of Ledbury, who ran a similar business. He published his guide to the town, *Hints of Ledbury*, in 1831, and the family moved to London in 1838 with their son Thomas, working as printer-compositors. After Thomas's death Sarah returned home to Ledbury where she lived in St Katherine's Almshouses.

Warnecombe, Richard (before 1494-1547) of Ivington, was the son of John Warnecombe of Hereford. He was typical of the administrative officials who ran England and Wales at the time of the Reformation, serving city, county, bishopric and crown. In Hereford he was alderman, town clerk by 1518 and mayor in 1525 and 1540. He served as deputy steward and escheator in Herefordshire and was the civic servant of Bishops Booth and Foxe (qqv). Warnecombe, with John Scudamore (qv, d.1571), would have ensured the smooth transmission of the administration of the see of Hereford from pre- to post-Reformation policies. He was a JP and *custos rotulorum* (a keeper of records) and represented Hereford in Henry VIII's Parliaments in 1529, 1542 (when Catherine Howard was executed) and at four other times. He married Margaret, the daughter of Richard Philips of Hereford and widow of Richard Jones of Bullinghope, and they had three sons and six daughters. His Philips father-in-law was Mayor of Hereford six times between 1509 and 1532. Warnecombe bought the manor of Lugwardine from Sir John Brydges (qv, d.1557). He died on 17 November 1547 and was buried in Hereford Cathedral. The range of executors of his will – Dean Hugh Curwen, Richard Sparkford, archdeacon of Shropshire, the mayor Thomas Bromwich and John Scudamore – sums up the range of his business. His daughter Alice married first William Wigmore of Shobdon – their son Thomas (qv) was an MP – then Sir James Croft (qv, d.1590).

Warton, Robert (d.1557), alias Purefoy, Bishop of Hereford 1554-7, was educated at Gloucester College, Oxford. He was a Cluniac monk, prior of Bermondsey in 1525 and Bishop of St Asaph during the Dissolution. He witnessed Prince Edward's christening and the funeral of Jane Seymour. He was a commissioner for the peace in Herefordshire and the Marches. A Protestant under Edward, on the accession of Queen Mary he adapted to the restoration of Catholicism and was rewarded with the see of Hereford, replacing the Puritan Bishop John Harley (qv, d.1557) who had married during Edward VI's reign. Under Mary's instructions Warton set about depriving other married clergy. He died on 22 September 1557, and in his will he left his mitre, crozier and vestments to the cathedral and bequests to cathedral officers, his servants and the poor. His damaged effigy lies in the north-east transept of the cathedral and his richly embroidered orphrey is at St Michael's Church, Abergavenny.

Waterton, Hugh (*c*.1340-1409), royal official, was from Lincolnshire where his family were Lancastrian servants. Hugh served in France in 1373 under John of Gaunt (qv) and became his attorney. On his return he bought the manors of Credenhill and of Eaton Tregoz with its castle at Foy and deer park of 144 acres. He was Steward of Thomas de Mowbray (heir of the Duke of Norfolk) during his minority and married Ellen from the Mowbray family. He was an executor of Gaunt's will in 1397 and served his son Henry Bolingbroke, (qv Henry IV), as Privy Councillor and chamberlain. He was Constable of Bolingbroke's castles of Brecon and Hay, and accompanied him on pilgrimage to Jerusalem in 1393. He was knighted in 1396 and appointed JP in Herefordshire. When Bolingbroke took the throne as Henry IV, he was made Chamberlain of the Duchy of Lancaster. On the rebellion of Glyn Dŵr (qv) he became constable of the four important Marches castles of Monmouth, Grosmont, Whitecastle and Skenfrith, and was prominent in opposing Glyn Dŵr. He urged the king to send extra forces to the Marches and indeed a royal army was formed at Chester. While the king campaigned in Wales he was appointed keeper of Berkhamsted Castle where he was governor of Henry IV's younger children with the king's cousins Edmund (V) Mortimer (qv) – whose father had joined forces with Glyn Dŵr – and his younger brother Roger. Waterton joined the commission to negotiate Henry's son's marriage with Catherine of Valois. There were two surviving daughters from his Mowbray marriage, one of whom, Elizabeth, married John ap Harry (qv) of Poston, Vowchurch. Sir Hugh was buried in Foy Church; his altar tomb lies behind the pulpit.

Wathen, James (1751-1828), artist and writer, was born in Eign Street in All Saints parish, Hereford and was educated locally. His father, Thomas Wathen, was a leatherworker and his mother, Dorothy Taylor, a Bristol merchant's daughter. After his father's death James stayed on at home to look after his blind mother until her death aged 85 in 1801. He was 'Jemmy Sketch' in Hereford, a familiar sight sketching in the towns and countryside: a large number of his watercolour vignettes of vanished Herefordshire sites survive. By chance he was sketching Hereford Cathedral before the west front collapsed bringing with it half the cathedral nave, and in *A View of the West Tower and Front of Hereford Cathedral taken on the morning of 17 April 1786*, he shows deep cracks on the north-west tower. He drew a comparative illustration after the collapse and both were much published to his profit in the *Gentleman's Magazine* and elsewhere. His work is invaluable in showing how things were in the 1790s before the gates and huddled cottages were swept away. He was a strenuous walker and it is said he could outpace

a horse; he walked to and from London many times. When his mother died he travelled to India and the Far East, publishing on his return his illustrated *Journal of a Voyage to Madras and China* (1814). After the exile of Napoleon he brought out drawings and a description of St Helena. He boasted that he ate no meat and drank only tea. He died in Hereford aged 77 on 20 August 1828. Several of his sketches are held in Hereford City Library and most descriptions of the county include his views.

Watkins, Alfred (1855-1935), archaeologist and inventor, was born on 27 January 1855 at the Imperial Hotel in Widemarsh Street, Hereford, the sixth of Charles (qv) and Ann's eight surviving children. Alfred learnt little at his Hereford school at the Gate House, Widemarsh Street (later the Farmers Arms) and worked for his father in the brewery and mill, educating himself. A constant innovator, he claimed at the end of his life to have had psychic help with his inventions. He introduced electric light in the flour mill with a dynamo to power it in 1876, installed a rolling mill in the factory and, his own invention, a dough thermometer. With these he made his prizewinning Vagos loaf using a new wholemeal flour. He married Marion Mendam Cross (b.1859) on 2 April 1886 and

moved to Vineyard Croft, Hampton Park where they brought up their two children, Allen and Marion. He made his own pinhole camera and experimented with the whole process. He believed good photographs could be taken by ordinary people without expensive equipment and invented the Bee Meter which enabled prints to be easily developed at home. He set up Watkins Meter Co. in rooms in the mill making photographic equipment, followed by Watkins Time Tank, Watkins Time Thermometer and his plate-speed cards. H.G. Ponting, the photographer on Scott's Antarctic expedition, used Watkins' light meter for his celebrated photographs. Watkins published the popular *Photography: the Watkins Manual of Exposure and Development* (1900) and *Photography, its Principals and Applications* (1911) to explain the processes. He was a fellow of the Royal Photographic Society and president when their convention was held in Hereford in 1908. They awarded him the prestigious medal for scientific progress in photography. Watkins recognized the importance of bees in the rural economy and noted that feudal tenants of Archenfield were described in the Domesday record as paying their dues in honey. He was a founding member of the Herefordshire Bee-Keepers Association whose horse-drawn 'bee van' travelled round Herefordshire villages showing magic-lantern slide shows, using Watkins' slides of good practice in bee keeping. He was an advocate of currency reform – not the ultimately successful decimal system that was being advocated at the time, but an 'octaval' method which he saw as more easily divisible. His system involved the cent: the old halfpenny; the groat: 8 halfpence; the half-crown: 8 groats, and a pound: 8 half-crowns. He was a county magistrate and in 1914 elected county councillor for Tupsley. A keen archaeologist, he was an original thinker about the past. As a member of the Woolhope Naturalists' Field Club he published his survey of Herefordshire pigeon houses and his *Standing Crosses of Herefordshire* (1929) and for 30 years supplied most of the club's photographs. On 30 June 1921 at Blackwardine he noticed alignments of landscape features, mounds, stones, ponds and sacred places, which he called ley lines, an ancient network for the guidance of travellers. Later that year he addressed the Woolhope Club on his discovery, and published the book: *Early British Trackways* in 1922. Then followed *The Old Straight Track* and *The Ley Hunter's Manual*, both best-sellers. Watkins died on 7 April 1935 at his home, 5 Harley Court by the cathedral where a plaque commemorates him, and is buried in the cemetery on Westfaling Street. Much material, including his collection of photographs, photographic equipment and books, is held in Hereford City Museum.

Watkins, Charles (1821-88), son of farmers at Mitcheldean, came to Hereford as the landlord of the Three Crowns, Eign Street, Hereford, and married Ann Hill (d.1899), an Irish barmaid. They had ten children. He acquired the Imperial Inn (later Hotel) in Widemarsh Street and bought the Hereford Brewery on Bewell Street, renaming it the Imperial. He later established his Imperial Flour Mills off Friar's Street and the family grew prosperous. Suiting his new status, he built the large Holmer Park House with bricks from clay in the garden (*c.*1860); at Holmer can be seen material from Hereford's

Market Hall which Charles bought up when it was demolished. His businesses prospered and he bought the large Wistaston Court estate in Marden and rebuilt Wilcroft in Bartestree where he and Ann spent their last years. His son Alfred (qv) remembered services in Wistaston Chapel, but this was demolished in 1909.

Watkins, John (d.1594), Dean of Hereford 1574-93, was educated at All Souls College, Oxford and appointed rector of Ross-on-Wye. He became Dean of Hereford on the death of John Ellis (qv) and, like him, resisted Bishop Scory's (qv) visitation, and his attempt to rebuild the bishop's palace. Watkins complained about the bishop's nepotism: Lady Scory held three prebendal portions and his totally unsuitable son Sylvanus held one also. The dispute reached the Privy Council and Queen Elizabeth (qv) appointed a commission which reported in 1582. It dealt with the matter of unqualified office holders, placed the interpretation of statutes firmly with Dean and Chapter and raised the terrible state of the library, which was the responsibility of Dean and Chapter. As a result the books and manuscripts were moved to the security of the lady chapel and new provision for them was created there (qv Thornton). The secular use of this chapel – a worrying site of recent Catholic piety – was pleasing to bishop and chapter. Dean Watkins resigned in 1593 and, dying the next year, was buried in Ross churchyard.

Watkins, Morgan (fl.1653-72) was a Quaker preacher of Wigmore Grange and Eyton, where he had a farm. He was proficient in Welsh and Latin, and his name appears on a letter of support to Oliver Cromwell from Herefordshire dated 1653. He met George Fox (qv) when he toured the Marches in 1657, and travelled the country preaching, though he was much persecuted. He suffered in the plague-ridden prisons of the time including Newgate and Westminster Abbey Gatehouse, the horrors of which he describes in letters to Mary Pennington. He had returned to his Eyton farm by 1670 when cattle and equipment were distrained to pay a fine. He wrote various books including *The Perfect Life of the Son of God Vindicated* (1659).

Watkins, Morgan George (1836-1911), clergyman and antiquarian of Southwell, Nottinghamshire, was educated at Exeter College and ordained. He was rector of Barnoldby-le-Beck, Lincolnshire in 1861-85, diocesan inspector of schools 1872-84 and in 1885 vicar of Kentchurch. He wrote articles for the *Dictionary of National Biography* and continued John Duncumb's (qv) *Collections towards the History and Antiquities of the County of Hereford* following William Henry Cooke (qv), providing *The Hundred of Huntington* (1897) and *The Hundred of Radlow* (1902). He was president of the Woolhope Naturalists' Field Club in 1895.

Watson, John Boles (1748-1813), theatre manager, was born in Ireland and, stage-struck, met Roger Kemble's son, John Philip (qv under

Roger Kemble), who was similarly afflicted and together they tramped the land as strolling players. He built a theatre in Cheltenham that was patronised by George III and Queen Caroline, and from here his troupe toured the Midlands including Hereford where Roger Kemble had created his theatre in the dilapidated Half Moon on Broad Street. In 1783 Watson bought a plot next to the Half Moon and had local builder William Parker (qv) build a permanent theatre there, paying him from the takings. Watson's new theatre opened in 1785 and was a great success, entrance costing two shillings for the gallery, one shilling for the pit. The season was December to March but plays would also be put on during May Fair week, the Assizes, or during Races week as seemed profitable. When Kemble retired in 1793 Watson took over his players. His daughter Louisa married the tightrope walker John Richer (qv).

Watt, James (1769-1848), engineer, was the son of the engineer and inventor of the same name. He was born in Glasgow on 5 February 1769 then lived in Birmingham and Manchester. With Matthew Boulton he ran an engineering works at Soho, Birmingham which manufactured more efficient versions of the steam engines Watt's father pioneered. He had a country house near Kington and was friends with the Garbetts (qv Francis Garbett) of Knill. He was a shareholder of the Kington Tramway Company, which between 1811 and 1820 built a narrow-gauge horse tramway from Eardisley to Kington, crossing lands of the Harleys' Berrington estate. It was a mineral line carrying coal, quarried stone and iron, and was later extended alongside the River Arrow to the Burlingjobb limestone quarries where Watt owned lime kilns. The engineer was John Hodgkinson (qv). James Crummer (qv), Thomas Harley's (qv, d.1804) agent and friend of Watt, helped him buy farms on the Berrington estate which Harley was having to sell. The tramway linked the Hay Railway at Kington with the Brecknock and Abergavenny Canal at Hay. After 40 years' use it was bought by the Kington and Eardisley Railway: the track may still be followed. One of the original tram-

wagons was discovered in the quarry in the 1960s and has been conserved and is stored at Hereford Museum. Watt became a wealthy and highly respected citizen of Birmingham, living at Aston Hall. He died unmarried there on 2 June 1848. His grandson James Watt Gibbs Watt bought the Newport estate, Almeley from Emily Foley (qv) in 1863. He altered the Queen Anne house and employed William Nesfield (qv) to give an Italianate feel to the gardens.

Watts, George Frederic (1817-1904), artist, was born in Marylebone, London on 23 February 1817 the son of a piano salesman. His grandfather, George (b.1746) was a Hereford cabinet-maker who settled in London in the 1790s. Watts was a frail child with a precocious talent for drawing. He learnt to paint in a neighbour's studio in Dean Street, Soho and by copying the Elgin Marbles in the British Museum. The family was poor and several brothers died young. Watts supplemented family income by selling small oil portraits in the style of old masters. He entered the RA Schools and won a bursary for foreign travel. In Florence he was taken up by Lord Holland, who introduced him to influential friends in his circle. On his return to London he shared a studio in Mayfair and moved in bohemian circles, living with Sara and Thoby Prinsep. He fell in love with Sara's beautiful sister Virginia Pattle, and the eight Pattle sisters appear frequently in Watts' paintings, but in 1850 she married Charles Somers (qv Charles Somers Cocks), Viscount Eastnor, shortly to become

3rd Earl Somers. They remained friends and Watts was a frequent guest at Eastnor Castle, where there is a collection of his work. Watts was an advocate of mural painting in public spaces and decorated rooms in the new House of Lords and at the Somers' London house, 7 Carlton House Terrace. His influence is found in their daughter Lady Henry Somerset's (qv Isabella Caroline Somers Cocks) terracotta reliefs on a seat in Eastnor churchyard and around the drinking fountain on Eastnor village green. Aged nearly 50, Watts fell in love with 16-year-old actress Ellen Terry. Their marriage was a predictable disaster and he then adopted a young relation of the Prinseps, Blanche Clogstoun, later to marry Herbert Haldane Cocks (qv Arthur Herbert Cocks), and she appears in his paintings. In his 70s Watts married painter Mary Fraser Tytler (1849-1938), a Scottish admirer, and they settled in a house he had built at Compton near Guildford in Surrey with a gallery for his work. They discovered the work of brilliant young Hereford painter Brian Hatton (qv), having him to stay and introducing him to contacts. Watts' painting is dark and gravely symbolic in his final decades. He died, the most famous artist in Britain, on 1 July 1904 at his Kensington Studio, his ashes being brought to Compton, where his private gallery has been recently renovated and is open to the public.

Weatherly, Frederick Edward (1848-1929) was born on 4 October 1848 at Portishead near Bristol. The family had Herefordshire connections and he was educated at Hereford Cathedral School with a scholarship to Brasenose College, Oxford where he became a tutor. He married Anna Maria Hardwick (d.1920) and they had a son and two daughters. He studied law at the Inner Temple and became a

barrister. He wrote novels, children's stories and song lyrics like *Danny Boy* (1912), *The Roses of Picardy* (1916) and *The Green Hills of Somerset* which were popular in the 1920s, and an autobiography, *Piano and Gown*. Eric Coates set a series of his songs to music. He died at his home in Bath on 7 September 1929 and was buried in Bathwick Cemetery.

Weaver, Dorothy (1608-1692), born Benet, has a gravestone in the cathedral cloister:

> *She was a true loyalist, an eminent courageous instrument in the preservation of this*

City against the rebellious Scotts. And a great sufferer in the late rebellion against the late Charles the First. She departed this life the 6th day of April An Dm 1692 in the 84th year of her age.

The valour of her husband Captain Thomas Weaver is mentioned.

Weaver, Richard (1575-1642), son of Edmund and Margery Weaver of Yatton, a gentry family, was a member of the mercers' company in Hereford. His gravestone in the cathedral yard says he had been several times mayor and MP. It shows his arms with the motto *vivas post funera vivo* – 'Live now so that you may live hereafter' – a tag used by John Abel (qv).

Webb, John (1776-1869), clergyman and antiquary, the eldest son of William Webb (1738-91) of Castle Street, London. He was educated at St Paul's School and Wadham College, Oxford and married Sarah Harding (1776-1849). He was ordained in 1800 and became curate of Ravenstone, Leicestershire and then Ross. In 1812 he was rector of Tretire with Michaelchurch and paid for the rebuilding of St Mary's, Tretire in 1857 by T.H. Wyatt (qv). He was an historian, proficient in Norman French, and in 1819 was elected a fellow of the Society of Antiquaries. He wrote various papers, including one on the history of Gloucester Abbey and one on the preceptory of the Templars at Garway. He edited John Roe's *A Military Memoir of Colonel John Birch* for the Camden Society, and wrote the magisterial *Memorials of the Civil War ... as it Affected Herefordshire,* both completed and edited by his son, who brought them to print in 1873 and 1879 respectively. He was a poet, musician and antiquarian who discovered in Michaelchurch the Roman altar dedicated by Beccicus (qv), which he repaired and placed in St Michael's Church. Revd Webb died on 18 February 1869 at his son's rectory of Hardwick near Hay.

Webb, Thomas William (1806-85), astronomer and clergyman, son of John (qv), was born on 14 December at Ross rectory and educated at

home at Tretire where he acquired a love of natural history. He was educated at Magdalen Hall, Oxford, ordained deacon at Hereford Cathedral and became curate at St Denys (qv), Pencoyd near Ross and in 1843 married Henrietta Wyatt. In 1856 he became rector of the new parish of Hardwick near Hay and his father came to live with them. He made meticulous observations of nature – for instance, of spiders – and was an early photographer. He was a skilled astronomer, expert in optics, building a series of increasingly powerful telescopes in the rectory garden, up to a 9 inch reflector. Here he wrote *Celestial Objects for Common Telescopes* (1859) a guide for amateur astronomers still in use. He served on the British Association's moon committee and was active in the Selenographical Society. He was a member of a group of local astronomers including Revd Cooper-Key and George With (qqv), and a friend of Revd Kilvert (qv). He was a prebend of Hereford Cathedral. Webb died at Hardwick vicarage on 19 May 1885 and was buried at Mitchel Troy near Monmouth.

Wegg-Prosser, Francis Richard (1824-1911), MP and benefactor, was born on 19 June 1824 at Nuneham Courtney in Oxfordshire, son of Revd Francis Haggit and his wife Lucy. He was educated at Eton and Balliol where he was a noted mathematician and astronomer. He changed his name to Wegg-Prosser in 1849 by royal licence on inheriting the Belmont estate and fortune of Revd Dr Prosser (qv), his mother's uncle. He married Harriet Catherine (d.1893), daughter of the second Earl Somers (qv John Somers Cocks, d.1852) and they had two sons and two daughters. He was Conservative MP for Herefordshire from 1847 until 1852 when he converted to Roman Catholicism. He involved himself with charitable causes, building almshouses with their own chapel on the estate. There had been a Benedictine abbey at Belmont before the Dissolution and he dedicated his fortune to building another. Wegg-Prosser invited a Benedictine community to settle there and had Edward Welby Pugin (qv) build St Michael's Church (1854-57) and monastery, and remodel his house. From 1855 to 1920 it was the Roman Catholic Pro Cathedral for the diocese of Newport and Menevia. Its first bishop (qv Thomas Brown) is buried in the north transept. In 1920 St Michael's again became an abbey. Wegg-Prosser died at Belmont on 16 August 1911. There is a stained glass window commemorating him in All Saints, Clehonger designed by A.W.N. Pugin (qv) in 1850 and made by Hardman & Co. (qv).

Wellington, Alice and **Thomas** (fl.1600) were Roman Catholic villagers of Allensmore. They and other local people were excommunicated by Bishop Bennett (qv) for their 'firm recusancy', in his attempt to suppress what he saw as the rampant Catholicism of Herefordshire. When Alice died, Richard Heyns the vicar refused her burial in Allensmore churchyard, but at 5am on 21 May 1605 on Whitsun Tuesday Revd Heyns was woken by a crowd following a cross with staves and candles and chanting the proscribed Roman Catholic burial rite, bearing Alice's body to her grave. In the crowd Heyns recognized one James Cole, a weaver who acted as 'massing clerk' to Father Roger Cadwallador (qv), later martyred in Leominster. Heyns posted a servant to Bishop Bennett at Hereford who sent a constable to suppress the gathering. A fracas ensued and one of the funeral party, Leonard Marsh, was arrested. Word spread and at Belmont the constable's own party was ambushed and Marsh freed. News of the 'Whitsun riot' at Allensmore reached King James, who was incensed. He called out Sir Herbert Croft (qv, d.1629), of known Catholic sympathies, and he tactfully pacified the area. The Gunpowder Plot was uncovered only six months later.

Wentworth, Behning (fl.18th century) of Canon Bridge, Madley, married Anne daughter of William Bird (qv) and they lived in Hammersmith, London. Their daughter Frances (1786-1856) married William Atkins-Bowyer, a major in the forces of Halifax, Nova Scotia. Wentworth became secretary of Nova Scotia.

Weonard (7th century) was a popular saint in west Herefordshire and patron of the village of that name. In Celtic he was Gwainerth, a local woodcutter and follower of St Dubricius (qv) turned hermit. Thomas Blount (qv) reports seeing his stained glass image in St Weonards Church. It showed a long-bearded figure holding an axe, titled 'St Wenardus, heremyta', and there is modern glass of him still. He is said to be buried in a tump near the church in a golden coffin inscribed

Where this stood
Is another, twice as good.
But where that is, no man knows.

The bronze age mound is the home of pixies mentioned by Alfred Watkins (qv) in his *Old Straight Track*.

Wesley, John (1703-91), founder of Methodism, was born on 28 June 1703, the son of Samuel Wesley, rector of Epworth, Lincs. He was educated at Christ Church, Oxford where, dissatisfied with the formality of Anglican religion, he sought a more sincere piety. He was ordained an Anglican minister but his charismatic enthusiasm kept him from the normal church career. He visited America planning to convert the Indians but was himself deeply influenced by the Moravian brethren. On his return he toured Britain preaching with his

brother Charles. His journal records a visit to Leominster on 14 August 1746 where he preached to a boisterous crowd, from *Acts* 28.22: 'we desire to hear from you; with regard to this sect we know that everywhere it is spoken against'. Standing on a grave on the south side of the church he impressed the crowd but the churchwardens rang the bells and played the organ loudly, and Wesley moved to the Corn Market, collecting crowds as he went. He preached again at 5am in the morning and then at the stables in Harp Yard, Kington, now called the Old Gospel House. He left behind a group of followers, 'methodists' they began to be called because of the Wesley brothers' insistence on the need for discipline and method in their relations with God. A house church was set up in Bridge Street in Leominster; then land was bought in Etnam Street and a permanent Wesleyan Methodist church was built there with Sunday school attached. In 1749 John and Charles Wesley visited Ross and Hereford and in 1762 they stayed at the Swan and Falcon Inn in Hereford, later the City Arms. The Wesleys' piety inspired a religious renewal throughout Britain. Revd John Wesley died on 2 March 1791 at his house in London.

Wesley, Samuel Sebastian (1810-76), composer and organist, was born on 14 August 1810, the son of organist Samuel Wesley, in Hampstead, London. They were related to the Methodist Wesleys but distanced by the irregularity of their lives. Samuel senior was a brilliant musician handicapped by a bipolar condition, who offended his family by running off with an unsuitable woman whom he then refused to marry; he then absconded with their 16-year-old maid Mary Sutor, the mother of young Samuel and his six younger siblings. Samuel junior, also brilliantly precocious, was strong-minded and unreliable with inherited bipolar tendencies. Despite his impoverished background he was chosen as a boy to sing before George IV and at 16 was performing on the organ in churches and concert halls around London. Dean Merewether (qv) heard Wesley play and appointed him organist and choirmaster at Hereford Cathedral at £60pa. Here he found 'a mess of error', a broken organ, a desultory choir and dreary lodgings. However the organ was repaired and extensively improved for him and he was inspired by it to write his masterpiece *The Wilderness*, which was first performed on 10 November 1832 at the inauguration of the organ. In 1834 the Three Choirs Festival was at Hereford and Wesley

arranged a programme marked by his own secular tastes and with much work by his father and himself. He wrote memorable anthems at Hereford including *Blessed be the God and Father* (1835). Wesley was contemptuous of Dean and Chapter. He eloped with Merewether's sister, Mary Ann, and they married at Ewyas Harold Church in May 1835 and moved to Exeter where Wesley had secured the post of cathedral organist. Wesley's time at Hereford is commemorated by a stained glass window in the east nave wall high above the crossing. He continued to write good church music and got on as badly with his Exeter employers, soon moving on to Leeds where a new organ was provided, to Winchester, still writing excellent anthems and biting feeding hands, and to Gloucester, where he prepared the 1865 Three Choirs Festival. He published editions of his work that came to be highly thought of. Although unable to get on with colleagues or superiors he was loved by pupils. He was a keen fisherman. He died on 19 April 1876 of Bright's disease and was buried in Exeter.

Westall, Richard (1765-1836) was a painter and a friend of Thomas Lawrence; he painted historical subjects and portraits in a neo-classical style and illustrated books. A patron was Richard Payne Knight (qv), who thought him a leader in the picturesque style, and Westall often stayed at Downton Castle where there is still a good collection of his paintings. He was popular in his day, often compared with Rembrandt and Titian. At the end of his life he was Queen Victoria's (qv) drawing master.

Westfaling, Herbert (1532-1602), Bishop of Hereford 1586-1602, the child of German immigrants, was educated at Christ Church, Oxford where he became a prebend. He was chancellor of St Paul's and published the strongly Protestant *Treatise of Reformation in Religion* (1582). His long sermons were unpopular and even Queen Elizabeth's (qv) requests for brevity were ignored. At Hereford he found papist practices and, in 1593, had the presbytery whitewashed. He had no sense of humour – Francis Godwin (qv), his friend and successor never saw him laugh – but much integrity, and he was efficient and competent. He was at odds with Dean and Chapter, who stood on their ancient privileges and refused to allow his visitation. The venal Sylvanus Scory (qv under John Scory), son of the previous bishop, was particularly difficult to dislodge. He married Anne Barlow, daughter

of the Bishop of Chichester. He was fond of their four children, Herbert, Anne, Margaret and Elizabeth, and provided well for them, buying the manor of Mansell Gamage for his son. Elizabeth married Robert Walwyn of Newland in Worcestershire and became the mother of the Leveller William Walwyn. Westfaling died on 1 March 1602 and Samuel Baldwin (qv) made a monument, but this was broken up in the 1640s and now only his effigy remains in the cathedral, with the long beard and full lawn sleeves of the time. There is a Westfaling Street in Hereford. Herbert, the bishop's son, who predeceased his father, dying of the smallpox, married Frances Rudhall (qv) and has been found to be a scholar whose translation of Cicero is in the Bodleian Library.

Westfaling, Herbert (d.1638), of Mansell Gamage, was the grandson of Bishop Westfaling (qv). He married Elizabeth, daughter of John Frogmore of Claines, Herefordshire.

Westfaling, Herbert (1630-1705) was the son of Herbert Westfaling (qv, d.1638) of Mansell Gamage and his wife Elizabeth Frogmore and the great-grandson of the bishop (qv Herbert Westfaling, d.1602). He married Ann, daughter of Sir Thomas Edwards, and sat as MP for Hereford 1660-79. He was created a Knight of the Royal Oak at the Restoration and received the property of Rudhall Manor from his grandmother Lady Rudhall (qv John Rudhall, d.1636). He was Mayor of Hereford in 1683. His granddaughter Elizabeth married Dr Thomas Apperley (qv).

Westfaling, Herbert (1671-1743), of Rudhall Manor, was the son of Herbert Westfaling (qv, d.1705). He was educated at Magdalen Hall, Oxford, and married Anne, daughter and heir of Charles Chappell of Battersea. He represented Hereford in Parliament as a Whig 1717-27.

Westfaling, Herbert (1699-1773), son of Herbert Westfaling (qv, d.1743), was MP for Thetford 1754-61. He failed to represent Hereford, but was helped by Charles Fitzroy-Scudamore (qv under Frances Fitzroy-Scudamore, d.1750) to his previous seat of Thetford.

Westfaling, Thomas (d.1814), of Rudhall Manor. It was at Rudhall in 1798 that Dr Jenner (qv) read his paper on inoculation to Thomas Paytherus (qv), Westfaling and other colleagues. Westfaling was also a friend of Nelson (qv); they had met at the Hamiltons in Naples, and when Nelson was in Herefordshire in 1802 he stayed for a few days with Westfaling and his wife at Rudhall. He was entertained with a grand ball and fireworks, with cider passed round to the

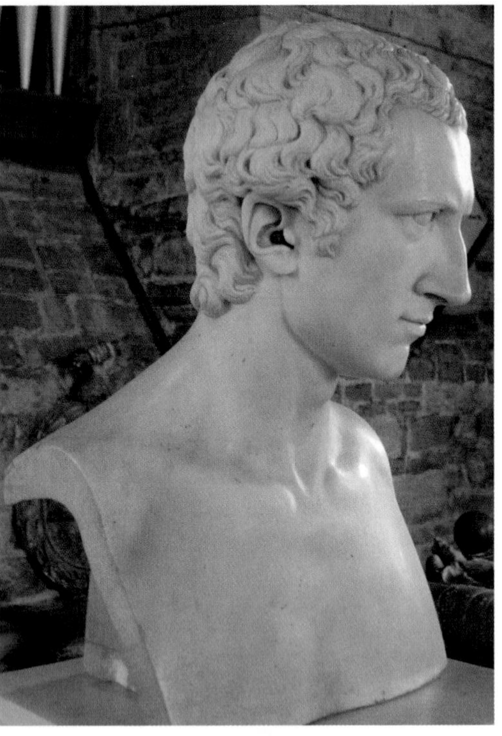

crowds of onlookers. Westfaling was buried in Ross Church, where there is a fine neo-classical bust of him above a relief of Charity with children, now thought to be the work of Christopher Hewetson (1739-99).

Westmacott, Richard (1775-1856), sculptor, was born on 15 July 1775, one of the 13 children of the London sculptor of the same name. He was apprenticed to his grand-

father, a monumental sculptor at the family firm producing church monuments and fireplaces. He studied in Rome under Canova and followed John Flaxman (qv) as professor of sculpture at the Royal Academy, carving monuments in the neo-classical style in his huge Westminster studio. There are fine works of his in Herefordshire: a typical monument is that in King's Caple Church of a mourning woman kneeling at an urn. In Ledbury Church there is a version of his famous wall plaque of a destitute family and another of a beautifully modelled woman kneeling by the plaque of Robert Myddelton Biddulph (qv, d.1814), while behind her his three children cry and comfort each other. He also worked at Moccas Church. He was a sociable man of energy and enthusiasm, and when Queen Victoria (qv) knighted him he took as his arms four bees. His son Richard took over his workshop when he retired and is represented in Herefordshire by a wall plaque at Weobley.

Weston, Henry (1850-1917), cidermaker, took the lease of Bounds Farm, Much Marcle in 1878 in the middle of an agricultural slump. He moved in with his new wife Emily Jane (1850-1933) and they had five daughters and four sons. They preceded the Hereford firm Bulmer (qv) by ten years. Conditions were right: they had cider and perry orchards, local people were eager for work and a railway line was being built through the area. His neighbour, MP Charles Radcliffe Cooke (qv) produced cider for which he was a tireless advocate in parliament and soon the bars of Westminster Palace stocked Weston's cider and perry and the business flourished. Steam power was introduced: the brand *Old Rosie* takes its name from one of their Aveling steam engines, currently being brought into working order again. Weston died on 21 June 1917 and was buried in St Bartholomew's churchyard, Much Marcle. Three of his sons Hubert, Stafford and Leonard took over the firm; Hubert was also famous for his herd of pedigree Herefordshire cattle. Henry's grandchildren continue to run this successful Herefordshire firm and Weston's shire horses are still seen, although now only pulling the carriage at weddings.

Wetherell, Nathan (1726-1806), Dean of Hereford 1771-1806, was from Durham. He was educated at Lincoln College and a Fellow of University College, Oxford where he was master from 1764 and vice chancellor. He married Richarda, daughter of Alexander Croke of Studley Priory and their son was the MP Sir Charles Wetherell. He lived in the master's lodge at his college and came to Hereford in the vacations, and when at Hereford he was commonly at odds with Bishop Beauclerk (qv). Signs of dilapidation at the cathedral were underestimated. Wetherell ordered a survey of the north-west tower where cracks had opened and masonry was falling. Thomas Symonds (qv, d.1791), a competent local surveyor, was appointed in 1771. He began filling in the space below the tower and set up braces, but deterioration continued and on Easter Monday 17 April 1786 the whole west end of the cathedral fell. Wetherell, the bishop and most of the chapter were away, despite the season, and hurried back. A wooden screen was put up so that services could be held and two years later James Wyatt (qv), a friend from Oxford, started rebuilding. Wetherell died on 29 December 1808 and was buried in his college at Oxford. His daughter Mary is memorialised in a stained glass window at Hereford Cathedral. Another daughter, Sarah (1777-1842) married Revd Thomas Lane Freer. Her children erected a neo-classical monument by Peter Hollins (qv) to her in St Lawrence, Bishopstone, the church of her son Revd Richard Lane Freer (qv).

Weyman, John (fl.1863-70) of Little Brampton, Shropshire was the owner of the celebrated racehorse The Colonel. Weyman's farm The Rock straddles the border with Shropshire at Richard's Castle, the paddocks where The Colonel was trained being in Herefordshire. His trainer was a farmworker called Roberts. The Colonel won the Radnorshire Stakes at Knighton and several steeplechases and hurdle races. In 1869 and 1870, ridden by George Stevens, he won the Grand National at Aintree, one of the few horses to win it more than once. The Colonel was then sold to a German stables for 2,000 guineas and is rumoured to have ended life as the Kaiser's charger.

Whall, Christopher Whitworth (1849-1924), stained glass designer, was born on 16 April 1849 in Thurning rectory, Huntingdon-

shire, where he learnt to love vernacular handicrafts. He studied art at the Royal Academy Schools, one teacher being Lord Leighton. He became interested in stained glass on the Continent. On his return he worked at Powell's glass works (qv Hardman) but, disapproving of the separation of art from labour, taught himself the full range of skills. He worked with Arts and Crafts artists like Lethaby and Seddon (qqv) and proved a good teacher himself. He married Florence Chaplain in 1884 and they had five children. His work in the lady chapel at Gloucester Cathedral (1898-1913) made him famous. Lethaby (qv) admired him and commissioned glass for All Saints, Brockhampton-by-Ross. He made the east window at St Mary, Sarnesfield (1922) and the memorial window to Charles Palairet (qv) in St Michael's, Ledbury. There are also examples of his work in the V&A.

Whall, Veronica (1887-1967), daughter of Christopher (qv), an artist in her own right, worked with her father at their studio at 1 Ravenscourt Park, Hammersmith. There is a window by her of St Martin in Ledbury Church. Her portrait of her father as St Christopher is in the singing gallery above the lady chapel at Gloucester.

Wharton, Nehemiah (fl.1641-49?), a Parliamentary trooper, was a sergeant in Denzil Holles's regiment. He had been apprenticed to a painter in London, and wrote him a series of letters describing conditions in Essex's (qv Robert Devereux, d.1646) army. He recorded how they took Hereford by stratagem in the Civil War in a letter of 7 October 1642: the march from Bromyard on terrible roads and in such cold weather that a soldier died, and the plundering of churches and gentry houses. Hereford shut its gates against them but the 'silly maior' was 'cozen'd' to open them and the city taken. The next day Wharton looked round Hereford, at the stout walls and gates, the market house, the stateliest in the land, and went into the cathedral, which he thought better than Worcester's. The people of Hereford were 'totally ignorant in the waies of God and much addicted to drunkenness and other vices, principally unto swearing, so that the children that have scarce learned to speake doe universally sweare stoutlye'. He noticed that Welsh was much spoken. The cathedral music astonished him and soldiers began to dance with each other in mockery. Wharton's regiment fought in the Battle of Edgehill later in the month and he may have been killed there.

Wheeler, Nicholas (1550-86), Roman Catholic priest, was born and grew up in Leominster where he was the star pupil of the grammar school. He was headmaster of a school at Monkton in Wiltshire noted for its Catholic sympathies, the proprietor of which was later executed for sheltering Catholic priests. He trained as a Jesuit priest at the English College at Douai, treasonable under a law of Elizabeth's, and then at Rheims. He returned to England on mission, ministering to sympathetic lawyers in the Inns of Court, helped by Fr Richard Davis (qv), a schoolfriend from Leominster. Davis remembered him as 'a man of fine complexion of body, affable and courteous'. He was soon arrested however and hanged, drawn and quartered at Tyburn on 21 January 1586. He and another Leominster-born priest Roger Cadwallador (qv) were beatified by Pope John Paul II in 1987.

White, Arnold Henry (1848-1925), journalist, was born on 1 February 1848 at Chapel House in All Saints parish, Hereford where his father, Edward White (1819-98), was a Congregationalist minister. The family moved to London and White, having failed to enter Parliament, became a journalist and political agitator. His crusade against corruption landed him in prison. He wrote *Efficiency and Empire* (1901) and a regular newspaper column under the pseudonym Vanoc where he expressed xenophobic views and found conspiracy in high places. In 1879 White married Helen Constance (1849-1918), only daughter of Lowell Price of Farnham Royal, Bucks and they had a son. He died at Farnham Common on 5 February 1925.

White, Matthew (d.1641), church musician and priest, was a vicar choral of Wells Cathedral and sang at the Chapel Royal before James I. He was awarded the degree of Mus.Doc. by Oxford University for his compositional abilities. In 1635 he was a vicar choral at Hereford and appointed succentor and vicar of St Nicholas, Hereford. He was dead by 16 October 1641 when a successor was appointed to the succentorship.

White, Thomas (1674-1748), architect and monumental sculptor of Worcester, was a pupil of Wren and built several churches in Worcester. He designed Worcester Guildhall and carved the statue of Queen Anne over the door. He made the fine wall monument to Captain Samuel Skinner (qv) in Ledbury Church *c.*1725. His portrait bust is surrounded by well-rendered naval equipment, smoke and spindrift. There is a monument in Bosbury Church to John Brydges (qv, d.1742) by White.

Whitefield, George (1714-70), Methodist preacher, was born in Gloucester at the Bell Inn, which his parents managed. Measles left him with a squint. He was educated at the Crypt School at St Mary de Crypt and Pembroke College, Oxford, where, a member of the Wesleys' Holy Club, he was converted to evangelical Christianity and ordained. He was both idolised and derided for his charismatic preaching. He spoke in Leominster on 30 April 1743 in Hereford and in Ross. His insistence on the need for new birth caused emotional outbursts. He worked closely with the Countess of Huntingdon (qv under Selina Hastings) and was frequently in America, where he died.

Whitney: A knightly family which takes its name from the village on the Wye opposite Clifford. They trace their descent from Eustace, son of Turstin (qv), who witnessed a charter here shortly after the Conquest. They served at the courts and in the wars of Richard II and Henry IV but disappeared into the female line in the 17th century.

Whitney, Eustace de (*c.*1256-*c.*1301), son of Sir Robert (qv, fl.1242), was granted free warren of his demesne lands in Pencombe, Little Cowarne, Whitney and Caldwell by Edward I (qv) at Leominster in 1284 (warren was land kept for hunting). The Whitney family granted land to St Peter's Abbey, Gloucester. He was summoned by Edward to fight the Scots in 1301 and died on the campaign. He married Mary de Mortimer, the daughter of Hugh Mortimer, a younger brother of Roger (III) de Mortimer (qv) and Agatha de Ferrers. Their children were Sir Eustace Whitney (qv, d.*c.*1352), Baldwin and Maud. Maud de Whitney married Giles de Briouze (qv under William (V) de Briouze) *c.*1280.

Whitney, Eustace de (1283-*c.*1352), son of Sir Eustace (qv, d.*c.*1301), was knighted in the Scottish war in 1301 after his father's death and in that year married Elizabeth de Fréville; Elizabeth had been born in Tarrington. Their heir was Robert (1318-80). Sir Eustace was MP for Hereford in 1313 and 1352. He was patron of Whitney Church of which his kinsman Thomas was rector.

Whitney, Eustace (*c.*1411-*c.*1468) was the son of Robert (qv, d.1441) and Joan, born at Clifford Castle. He married first Jennet the daughter of Sir Thomas Russell, and later Jane Clifford. He was MP for Herefordshire in 1468 and headed a commission sent to Wales by Henry VI in 1455. A daughter Eleanor (b.*c.*1426) married a James Scudamore (b.1419).

Whitney, John de (fl.1250), a brother of Sir Robert (fl.1242, qv), was killed in Hereford by a John of Oxford, and one of Edward I's first acts on becoming king in 1272 was to secure his widow Edith's possession of his property.

Whitney, Peryne (*c.*1373-1422), daughter of Sir Robert Whitney (qv, d.1402), married her neighbour Sir Thomas Clanvowe (qv) in 1392. She was one of the damsels of the chamber of Queen Anne (qv), wife of Richard II, and she and Sir Thomas were granted pensions by the queen. She was friendly with Henry IV's queen Mary, a de Bohun (qv) lady from Herefordshire. Peryne and her husband, a great poet, were buried at St Mary's, Yazor.

Whitney, Robert de (1210- after 1242), knight and Lord of Whitney, is described in a charter as holding 1,500 hides in the honour of Ewias with Robert (II) de Tregoz (qv, d.1265). He granted lands to Friar Walter, a hermit living on an island in the Wye. His brother Eustace was the 'parson of Pencombe' where Robert had land and was patron of the living.

Whitney, Robert (1348-1402) was the son of Sir Robert Whitney, (d.1380), and grandson of Sir Eustace de Whitney (qv, d.1352). His first wife was Janet Trussell and their daughter Joan married William Walwyn (qv, d.1452); and his second wife was Maud, daughter of Ralph Lord Cromwell, and they had a son Robert (qv, d.1441). Another child whose mother is uncertain was Thomas (qv, fl.1415). Sir Robert was a servant of Richard II (qv) engaged in diplomatic work abroad and MP for the shire in 1391. He was a Lollard sympathiser and sheltered the preacher William Swinderby (qv). He was Henry

IV's (qv) Knight-Marshal and died with many of his kin at the bloody Battle of Bryn Glas near Pilleth under Edmund (IV) Mortimer (qv) in 1402 when the men of Herefordshire were overwhelmed by Glyn Dŵr (qv). It is said that atrocities were committed on the field of battle.

Whitney, Robert (*c.*1379-1441), son of Robert (qv, d.1402) and Maud, was a servant of John of Gaunt (qv) and his son Henry Bolingbroke (qv Henry IV). His father and uncle were killed in the fighting against Glyn Dŵr (qv) and his houses sacked. In recompense Henry gave him the custody of Clifford Castle and the lordships of Clifford and Glasbury during the minority of Edmund (V) Mortimer (qv). He married Wintelan (or Wenllian), daughter of Sir Thomas Oldcastle (qv). Their daughter Ellen married John Skidmore (qv under his father, John (II) Skidmore). Sir Robert was Sheriff of Herefordshire in 1413, 1428, 1433 and 1437 and MP for Hereford in 1416 and 1422. He fought in Henry V's French wars and was captain of the garrison of Vire Castle. Like his father, he showed Lollard tendencies. He died on 12 March 1441 and was buried at Clifford.

Whitney, Robert (*c.*1436-94), son of Sir Eustace (qv, d.*c.*1468), married Constance Touchet and they had five sons, including Eustace, his heir, and five daughters, among them Joan, who married Sir Roger Vaughan. After Constance's death he married Elizabeth, also known as Alice or Alianor (d.*c.*1525), daughter of Thomas and Elen Vaughan (qv) of Hergest, occasioning an eulogy by the bard Lewis Glyn Cothi (qv). After her husband's death Elizabeth managed the large Whitney estates for 30 years, presiding in Pencombe manorial court. Robert was a Yorkist in the Wars of the Roses as were many in Herefordshire, fighting at Mortimers Cross in 1461.

Whitney, Robert (1491-1541), born at Whitney, married Margaret daughter of Robert Wye of Icomb, Gloucestershire where they took up their abode. He refused to attend the marriage of Henry VIII to Anne Boleyn but benefited from the dispersal of church lands at the Dissolution. A daughter Margaret married their neighbour Howell Penoyre (qv under Thomas ap Jenkin Penoyre) of the Moor.

Whitney, Robert (*c.*1525-67) was born at Icomb, the eldest son of Robert (qv, d.1541). He was a minor at his father's death and ward of Sir James Baskerville (qv, d.1572) of Eardisley. On being granted livery he married Sybil (d.*c.*1559) his guardian's daughter and they had three sons and two daughters: James and Eustace, who succeeded in turn to the estate; Robert; Blanche, who married Robert Greville; and Elizabeth, who married John Bryce. Sir Robert acknowledged another son, William, who he fathered on Catherine of Maesllwch, the daughter of a William Vaughan. Sir Robert was a commissioner for tax collection under Edward VI (qv) and in 1553 was knighted by Queen Mary. He was MP for the shire in 1559. While at Westminster his Hereford men were involved in a fracas for which Sir Robert was called before the Star Chamber and censured. After Sybil's death he married Mary, daughter of Sir James Berkeley, who claimed descent from Edward I. She was a widow of both Sir Thomas Perrot and Sir Thomas Jones and was said to have had a bastard son by Henry VIII (qv). Sir Robert died on 5 August 1567 and was buried at St Peter's, Whitney. Whitney estates were extensive through the shires of Hereford and Gloucester.

Whitney, Robert (1592-1653), born on 23 September 1592 at Whitney, was the eldest son of Eustace (d.1617) and Margaret. He married Anne (b.1589) daughter of Sir Thomas Lucy of Charlecote, Warks, celebrated as the magistrate from whose park Shakespeare was said to have poached deer and as the original of Justice Shallow (qv under Charles Lucy). They had many children, their daughter Lucy marrying William Smalman (qv) of Kinnersley. Whitney studied at Lincoln's Inn and was knighted by James I in 1617. In 1639 he was High Sheriff of Hereford and a commissioner for the collection of taxes. At the outbreak of the Civil War he sold lands to raise funds for the Royalist cause. He commanded a troop at the Battle of Worcester on 3 September 1651 when Cromwell crushed the second Civil War. He died soon after this and was buried at Whitney on 15 September 1653.

Whitney, Thomas (fl.1415), son of Sir Robert (qv, d.1402), was one of the Duke of Gloucester's lances at Agincourt in 1415. He was knighted and given a French estate by Henry V for his valour. His daughter Peryn married John Abrahall (qv).

Whitney, Thomas (1622-70) was the eldest son of Sir Robert (qv, d.1653) and Anne. In 1666 he married Elizabeth (1647-1761), daughter of Colonel William and Elizabeth Cope of Icomb, where the Whitney family had property. He was a founder knight of Charles II's new order of the Knights of the Royal Oak – a reward for the family's support in the Civil Wars. At his death the Whitney name ends and the Whitney-Clifford estates were divided amongst his four sisters – Anne Rodd, Lucy Booth, Elinor Wright, and Susan Williams. In 1676 Elizabeth married again, to Thomas Geers (qv, d.1700) of Canon Frome; she died in April 1676 and was buried at St James's Church, Canon Frome.

Whittington, Richard (*c.*1350-1423) was a merchant and mayor of London, now famous for his appearances with his cat in pantomimes. Pauntley Court, now in Gloucestershire but in the diocese of Hereford in the 14th century, is sometimes given as his birthplace but there are claims for Hope Sollers. William de Whyttington, Dick's grandfather, married Maud, daughter and heir of John de Sollers, and received Hope as Maud's dower, where they brought up their family. Their son, Sir William Whittington, was an outlaw at his death in 1360, leaving his son Dick penniless. The boy famously walked to London to an apprenticeship with a London merchant. Discouraged with his hard life in London and homesick for Herefordshire he set out to return but, resting on Highgate Hill, heard Bow Bells ring out 'Turn again Whittington thrice Lord Mayor of London'

and returned to his duties and celebrity. Asked to invest in one of his master's ships to Africa he offered his cat, all he had, and Puss proved so valuable as a mouser that his reward enabled him to set up as a merchant. He married his master's daughter Alice Fitzwarren, became rich and was Lord Mayor in 1397, 1406 and 1419. He subsidised Henry V's French wars, the rebuilding of Westminster Abbey nave and his own parish church of St Michael Paternoster Royal. He died in his house next door to this church.

Wigmore, Roger (d.1404), crown official, was the son of John Wigmore of Lucton. The family were retainers of the Mortimers (qv) and Wigmore was attorney for Roger (VII) Mortimer (qv) and also for Sir Walter Devereux (qv, d.1402). He was favoured by Richard II (qv) who loaded him with lucrative offices: he was his chamberlain and chief financial official, and MP for Herefordshire. He was able, however, to easily transfer his services to Henry IV (qv) on his usurpation.

Wigmore, Thomas (d.*c.*1601) was the son of William Wigmore of Shobdon and Alice, daughter of Richard Warnecombe (qv). His mother's second marriage was to Sir James Croft (qv, d.1590), whose influence helped Thomas become MP in Carmarthenshire and for Leominster. He was a JP, and Sheriff of Hereford in 1579-80. He feuded with Sir Thomas Coningsby (qv, d.1625) and was bound over to keep the peace. His son, Warncombe Wigmore, married Elizabeth, daughter of Jonathan Walwyn, in 1635. Another son, Thomas, distinguished himself in the Civil Wars on the King's side and was accounted one of the Nine Worthies of Herefordshire (see index).

Wigmore, William (*c.*1599-1665), Jesuit priest, was the son of Sir William Wigmore of Herefordshire and his wife, Anne, daughter of Sir John Throckmorton of Gloucestershire. His parents were Catholic although his father attempted some conformity with authorised religion. The family often used the surname Campion in honour of the martyred Jesuit Edmund Campion and many of William's relations were members of religious orders. William was educated at St Omer and became a Jesuit priest *c.*1632 and held offices in Jesuit colleges in France. He wrote *The Catholicke Doctrine of Transubstantiation* (1657) and died rector of a Jesuit house at Ghent on 28 September 1665.

Wilkes, John Bernard (1785-1869) was born and died in London. He was organist for Moravian communities at Merthyr, Llandaff and Leominster. While at Leominster he met Sir Henry Baker (qv), rector of Monkland, who loved organ music and had decent organs in his church and rectory. Wilkes found the music later called Monkland in the *Moravian Collection of Hymn Tunes* chiefly composed for private amusement by John Antes (*c.*1790). (Antes was a Moravian from America who came to England in 1781 and lived in Bristol.) Wilkes adapted this tune for Milton's hymn *Let us with a Gladsome Mind* and Baker included it in *Hymns Ancient and Modern* (1861).

Wilkinson, George (1814-90), builder and architect, was the son of William Wilkinson, carpenter of Witney, Oxon. Aged 20 he won the Poor Law Commissioners competition to build the Thame Union Workhouse, a model design which won him many orders, and in 1836 he built the workhouses in Bromyard, Ledbury, Leominster and Weobley for about £3,000 each. The Ledbury workhouse, in what is now Orchard Lane, housed some 150 inmates. In the mid 20th century a residential home was built in the grounds and Wilkinson's building was converted to private apartments. He moved to Ireland *c.*1840 where he built more workhouses and wrote a history of Irish architecture. He returned to England on retirement and died in Twickenham on 4 October 1890.

Willard, Frances Elizabeth (1839-98), suffragist, was born on 28 September 1839 in New York. Her work for the temperance movement brought her into contact with Lady Henry Somerset (qv Isabella Somers Cocks) at Eastnor Castle with whom she stayed for long periods. They travelled Britain together addressing meetings on reform. She died in New York on 17 February 1898. She left an autobiography, *Glimpses of Fifty Years* (1889).

Willason, John (16th century) of Sugwas married Alice the sister of Bishop John Skippe (qv) and they had a son Richard (qv). In 1542 he leased Upper Hall and estate in Ledbury cheaply from his episcopal father-in-law, and other church property in the county.

Willason, Richard (*c.*1538-1574), son of John (qv) and Alice, bought Ledbury chantry lands with John Harford (qv) of Bosbury and in 1541 leased the bishop's palace of Sugwas. Richard married Anne (d.1591), daughter of William (qv, d.1558) and Margery Elton of Ledbury. He because a wealthy landowner with much property in the Sugwas area. He died on 25 February 1574 and his wife commissioned a tomb from the Hereford sculptor John Gilden (qv, fl.1573) in Madley Church, which is still to be seen. Their daughter Anne married Alexander Denton (qv Anne Denton).

William (fl.1701), Hereford painter, was responsible for the second set of texts and wall paintings in Dore Abbey. William's signature remains as 'William ...er of H.....rd, painter, 1701'. William's work covered black letter text of 50 years before which can still just be seen.

Amongst elements of his work that survive is a skeleton leaning on a spade and Father Time who has a long forelock for grasping hold of, but is bald behind.

William III (1650-1702), Prince of Orange and King of Great Britain (II of Scotland), had married James II's daughter Mary. He was invited to supplant the Stuart dynasty when James converted to Catholicism and reign with Queen Mary, and landed in England in pursuit of this in 1688. In 1690 William and Mary granted a three-day fair to Hereford with a splendid seal, still attached, one of the finest in the country; and in 1697 William issued a Charter of Re-incorporation to the City of Hereford, as its status as an incorporated borough had been surrendered under Charles II. Hereford then governed itself under this 1697 charter until the Municipal Corporations Act of 1835. The charter also allowed an additional fair of two days to be held in February, making a total of four fairs in the year (February, Easter, June and October). This important charter was translated from the Latin and published by John Allen (qv) in 1820.

William fitz Norman (d.1071), a kinsman of the Conqueror, was rewarded after the Battle of Hastings with sequestered Saxon estates in Herefordshire. He was the direct feudal tenant of the king. He built castles, one at Kilpeck on the site of an ancient feature from Offa's (qv) time, from which to govern Archenfield. He was keeper of the Haye, the royal forest that ran south from Hereford, and Treville Forest around Kilpeck. His grandson was Hugh de Kilpeck (qv).

William fitz Osbern (*c.*1020-71), 1st Earl of Hereford, fought at Hastings with the Conqueror to whom he was related. His father Osbern had been killed defending the duke and he was William's most trusted friend. A strong, persuasive personality, he encouraged Duke William to invade England in 1066 when he was unenthusiastic. He was the Conqueror's right-hand man and with Bishop Odo governed England when the Conqueror returned to Normandy in 1067. William appointed him Earl of Hereford, granting him the Godwin estates (qv Godwin), and in 1069 he organised the pacification of the west midlands. Fitz Osbern started rebuilding Hereford, the city and castle, as his fortified base in the Marches after its sack in 1055 (qv Ælfgar). Ralph de Mantes' (qv under Ralph) stronghold was probably on high ground at the east side of Castle Green, but William erected a new wooden castle further west. He also began enlarging the Saxon *burh* of Hereford on the Widemarsh side by almost half as much again, providing for a market there, and using the old centre, the parish of St John the Baptist (qv) for a massive cathedral. The new market area, now called High Town, had roads that linked the new gates of Eign, Bye and St Owen's, a layout that survives today. It was given trading liberties and incentives such as fitz Osbern had accorded his towns in Normandy. He continued Harold's attacks against the Welsh of Brycheiniog and built a chain of castles along the border: Wigmore (which he gave to Turstin (qv), Clifford, Ewyas Harold (where a pre-Conquest castle stood), Monmouth and Chepstow. William fitz Osbern also had estates in Normandy to defend and was killed fighting in Flanders. Orderic Vitalis considered him the bravest of the Normans, witty, generous and loyal. He married Adelize, sister of Ralph de Tosny (qv), and their son was Roger de Breteuil (qv).

William of Ledbury (13th century) was elected Prior of the Benedictine House in Great Malvern and presented to Westminster Abbey who had jurisdiction over this house. In March 1280 the subprior wrote to Bishop Giffard of Worcester to inform him of the election. Giffard's visitation, however, resulted in William's deposition; he was accused of keeping some twenty mistresses and supporting them in luxury at the expense of his own community. This scandal has to be understood in the context of political antagonism between Bishop Giffard of Worcester and the Benedictine hierarchy. The case was attended by excommunications and counter excommunications but eventually Giffard was bought off by the Abbot of

Westminster and the king, and Prior William restored to office.

William of Leominster (late 13th century), author, a native of the town and a monk in its priory, was educated at Oxford. He wrote a commentary on the *Sentences* of Peter Lombard. Thomas Fuller (qv) calls him an illustrious writer.

William of Malmesbury (*c.*1090-*c.*1143) historian, was born in Wiltshire to a Norman father and English mother shortly after the Conquest. He entered the Benedictine monastery of Malmesbury and realised his aptitude for history. Prompted by William I's Queen Matilda, he wrote the *Gesta regum Anglorum* (1125) to update Bede's 8th-century history, setting English history in a continental context. This was followed by a history of the English bishops, and of the Popes. He travelled widely in difficult conditions researching primary material and describing abbeys and cathedrals and their histories. He visited Hereford and its cathedral searching out antiquities such as the *Anglo-Saxon Gospel Book*. He worshipped at St Ethelbert's (qv) shrine, restored since the destruction in the previous century, and wrote the saint's history, tracing his parentage. A classicist with a love of Cicero, Lucan and Virgil, he declined office at his abbey, preferring to remain a scholar and librarian. He was recording the current events of Stephen and Matilda's civil war when he died *c.*1143.

Williams, William (1788-1874), was born in Monnington and served with the 44th Regiment of Wellington's Army throughout the Napoleonic Wars. His memorial in St Mary's churchyard, Monnington says he was at the storming of Badajoz, and fought at Salamanca, Victoria, Hergenzoom and in the Battle of Waterloo. He died back in Herefordshire on 11 June 1874.

Williams-Ellis, Clough (1883-1978), architect, was born in Northamptonshire and educated at Trinity College, Cambridge, where he gave up science for architecture. With little training but much zest he set up an architectural practice in London, designing in a light, eclectic style which was increasingly appreciated. While he was at Llangoed Castle in Radnorshire in 1912, building in a freely interpreted Tudor style, he was commissioned by Peter Legh Clowes (qv under John Clowes) to rebuild the front of Burton Court, Eardisland and Quebec Cottage nearby. Williams-Ellis is remembered for the holiday village of Portmeirion (begun 1925); and for books on the horrors of modern architecture and what to do about it. He died aged 94 at his home Llanfrothen in north Wales on 8 April 1978.

Willis, Browne (1682-1760), antiquary, was born on 14 September 1682 at Blandford St Mary, Dorset the eldest son of Thomas Willis, and educated at Westminster School, Christ Church, Oxford and the Inner Temple. He lived at Whaddon Hall, Fenny Stratford, Bucks and at Burlton, Burghill which his father had bought from John Aubrey (qv). He married Katherine Elliot, whose dowry enabled him to devote himself to antiquarian interests. He was among the first to study church architecture as opposed to collecting biographical information from monuments. He viewed them with a conservator's eye and was critical of contemporary attitudes to church fabric, for instance of Bishop John Tyler's (qv) neglect of Llandaff. He rebuilt churches himself in what he felt was a 'correct' style. He corresponded with the great antiquarians of his age, amassing antiquarian documents now in the Bodleian and publishing much. The views of cathedrals he commissioned from John Harris and Walter Merricke record structures before the age of restoration and include Hereford Cathedral. He was noted for his eccentric dress and looked like 'a mumping beggar'. He died at Whaddon Hall on 5 February 1760.

Willis, Henry (1821-1901), organ builder, was born on 27 April 1821 in London, the eldest of the four sons of Henry Willis, a carpenter. His father, an amateur musician, apprenticed his son to the London organ builder John Gray of Gray and Davison and Henry learned to play on the organ of St Paul's. In his 20s he rebuilt the organs of Tewkesbury Abbey (1846) and Gloucester Cathedral (1847). In 1847 he married his organ pupil Esther Maria Chatterton and, after her death, her sister Rosetta. The organ he showed at the Great Exhibition of 1851 made him famous and was bought and installed in Winchester Cathedral. Others were ordered for St George's Hall, Liverpool and the Crystal Palace. English cathedrals clamoured for his organs and in 1879 Hereford bought one to replace the Renatus Harris (qv) organ that had stood on the pulpitum screen but had been dismantled during renovations. He also improved existing instruments, adding innovations such as mechanical blowing equipment. In 1893 Willis installed his new combination pistons at Hereford, and in the 1930s a complete rebuild was funded by the Hereford firm H.P. Bulmer (qv), whose woodpecker logo can be seen on the instrument. Willis heard of Revd John Baron's experiments at Upton Scudamore, Wiltshire with a small organ that fitted the chancel of a parish church, and built some 200 of these 'Scudamore' organs, often in suitably mediaeval forms. The family responsible for this village's name is a branch of the Herefordshire Scudamores. Willis was a small, obstinate, nervous man with a passion for yachting. He died on 11 February 1901 at his home in Kentish Town in London from pneumonia and was buried in Highgate Cemetery.

With, George Henry (b.1827) astronomer, born in London, was one of the first to train as a schoolmaster. In 1851 Richard Dawes (qv) offered him the mastership at the Blue Coat School, Hereford. He also taught science at Hereford Ladies' College and at the Cathedral School where he was a lay reader. He married Lavinia Baker (1824-90) at Alverstoke where they had a son; on moving to Hereford they had a further son and three daughters. With was an important astronomer able to construct the latest optical equipment and a colleague of Revd Cooper-Key and Revd Thomas Webb (qqv). He was a fellow of the Royal Astronomical Society and the Chemical Society and helped John Venn (qv) by experimenting with improved fertilizers for his Hereford Society for Aiding the Industrious. He was a friend of Michael Faraday and Thomas Huxley.

Wode, John del (fl.1419), servant of Colwall, is the subject of a charter of manumission by Bishop Edmund Lacy (qv), which states

... since from the beginning, nature created all men free of their condition and afterwards the ius gentium imposed upon some the yoke of servitude. We believe this to be truly an act of piety, to restore those who require this to their pristine freedom. For which consideration we have manumitted and have freed from every servile yoke ... John del Wode, son of William del Wode, our bondsman, a servant in our kitchen ... belonging to our lordship of Colwall.

Wolsey, Thomas (*c.*1471-1530), cardinal, the son of an Ipswich butcher, was educated at Magdalen College, Oxford when Richard Mayo (qv), later Bishop of Hereford, was the college's first president. Mayo granted Wolsey the prebend of Pratum Minus at Hereford Cathedral and made him dean in 1509. His one year tenure may have been in order to secure a pension, although cathedral documents show him raising money through an indulgence to pay for Bishop Booth's (qv) outer porch. Wolsey followed Mayo as almoner to Henry VIII and was a notorious amasser of benefices, rising with avidity and energy to become friend and counsellor of Henry VIII as Archbishop of York and cardinal. His sights were set on the papacy but he fell foul of the king's divorce. He was arrested for high treason, dying in disgrace on 29 November 1530 at Leicester Abbey on his way to the Tower. William Tyndale called him *Wolfsee* and characterised him as bewitching the king.

Wood, Elliott KCB (1844-1931), third son of Miles Astman Wood (qv, d.1898), joined the Royal Engineers and served in South Africa, Egypt and Sudan, where he was mentioned in dispatches and decorated. As Major-General in the Boer War he was responsible for the blockhouse system of defence. He was mentioned in dispatches, decorated and created KCB. He married Anne Beatrice, widow of Horace Dugmore and daughter of Lt-Col Robert Bourne (qv); they lived in Pembridge and later at Holmer Court. Sir Elliott was the first County

Commissioner for the Boy Scouts. In the First World War he joined the Hereford Volunteer Motor Corps. He wrote an autobiography, *Life and Adventures in Peace and War*.

Wood, John (1704-54), architect, was born in Bath in August 1704 the son of George Wood, a local builder. He laid out the circuses and crescents of Bath, grouping the houses to look like palaces. In 1728 William Brydges (qv under his father, William Brydges, d.1688) had him rebuild Tyberton Court, now destroyed, and St Mary's Church in brick in a classical style. The panelling in the apse is his work of 1728-31, as is the kneeling angel lectern. His son John continued his practice.

Wood, John Henry (1841-1914), entomologist and physician practising at Tarrington, was the son of Miles Astman Wood (qv, d.1898). In 1864 Dr Wood was appointed medical officer for the area by public subscription. He wrote many scientific papers on the *Microlepidoptera* and *Diptera*. He named two European butterflies, and the Mistletoe Moth, *Celypha Woodiana*, was discovered by him at Tarrington. His diary for 1891-94 can be seen in Hereford library.

Wood, Miles Astman (1807-98) was born in Newent and trained at Guy's Hospital and in Paris. He was a Member of the Royal College of Surgeons and *c.*1830 joined Dr Congreve Selwyn's established medical practice at Orchardleigh, New Street, Ledbury. He took over Dr Selwyn's practice and married Ann, daughter of Thomas Webb, banker of Ledbury and moved into Orchardleigh. He was a GP in Ledbury for some 60 years and was medical officer at the workhouse and at the cottage hospital. His two eldest sons John Henry (qv) and Miles (qv, d.1922) were also physicians. There is a monument to Dr and Mrs Wood in Ledbury Church and the present carillon was given in their memory.

Wood, Miles Astman (1842-1922), second son of Dr Miles Astman Wood (qv, d.1898), trained and qualified at King's College Hospital in London and ran Ledbury Dispensary with his father for many years, becoming medical officer at the workhouse and the cottage hospital after him. He lived at Orchardleigh with his sister Constance and was a local JP.

Wood, Thomas (fl.1787-1809), Hereford monumental mason, supplied the carved seal above the door of St Ethelbert's Almshouses (1804), and constructed, in a modified form, Nelson's Column (1806-09) on Castle Green designed by Hardwick (qv). There is a wall monument by him in Kinnersley Church to Elizabeth Allen (d.1787) and in Leominster Priory to Thomas Williams (d.1799).

Woodman, William (1654-*c.*1731) the elder, monumental mason, was responsible for the sumptuous Scudamore tombs in St Cuthbert's Church, Holme Lacy. He also made Bishop Monck's (qv) tomb – a large pyramid – in Westminster Abbey. Having completed his apprenticeship he was made free of the Mason's Company in London with a large workshop working in a conservative style. His son William continued to produce monuments into the 18th century in a more advanced manner.

Woodward, Thomas (1796-1872), organist, was originally from Worcester but his family moved to Herefordshire. He married Mary and they lived in Kington with their children. He and a son wrote hymns and school text books. By 1860 Mary had died and he and two daughters, Laura and Lucilla, moved to Ledbury, where he was organist at the church and secretary of a savings bank in Bank House by the church. Woodward, known locally as 'the professor', taught music from his house in South Parade. When he became elderly Laura took over as organist. He died on 23 June 1872, and he and Mary were buried at St Mary's Church Donnington, Ledbury parish church then being the subject of scandal (qv John Jackson).

Woodward, William (d.1691), a dissenting Presbyterian minister, was educated at Oxford during the Commonwealth and became a college tutor. At the Restoration he was a minister at Richard's Castle but was ejected for nonconformity. He was supported by Presbyterian Edward Harley (qv, d.1700) who valued him highly. After the 1687 Act of Toleration Woodward founded a congregation in Etnam Street, Leominster. After his death this group moved to Burgess Street as Independents, later becoming Sandemanians or Llewelyns (qv William Llewelyn).

Woodyer, Henry (1816-96), architect, born in Guildford, Surrey in August 1816, was educated at Eton and Merton College, Oxford. He studied in the architectural office of Butterfield and set up his own London practice. He was bohemian in manners and dress and enjoyed sailing his yacht, *Queen Mab*. He favoured the high church and a major work of his is Holy Innocents at Highnam, Gloucs. (1849-51). His restorations were original and distinctive. He rebuilt most of St Peter, Pudleston in the 1850s, supplying all the furnishings. In 1865 he rebuilt Colwall chancel in an Early English style. He married and in old age lived with his daughter at Padworth Croft, near Reading where he died of heart failure on 10 August 1896.

Wordsworth, William (1770-1850), poet, was born on 25 December 1770 in Cockermouth, Cumberland, the third of the five children of attorney John Wordsworth (1741-83) and his wife, Ann (1747-78). His intimate companionship with his sister, Dorothy (1771-1855), friendship with Coleridge (qv), marriage to Mary Hutchinson and association with the Lakes is well known. His wife Mary had relatives who lived in Herefordshire and the Marches and the families frequently visited one another. Wordsworth loved Herefordshire and the Wye:

How oft, in spirit, have I turned to thee,
O sylvan Wye! thou wanderer thro' the woods.
(from *Lines Composed … above Tintern*)

It was near Goodrich Church in 1792 with Dorothy and Coleridge that Wordsworth met the 8-year-old girl about whom he wrote *We are Seven*. An elderly servant of the Wordsworths died here and is buried in the churchyard. He was staying with friends in Ledbury when he heard the legend about Katherine Audley (qv):

When Human touch (as monkish books attest)
Nor was applied or could be, Ledbury bells
Broke forth in concert, flung adown the dells,
And upward high as Malvern's cloudy crest;
Sweet tones and caught by a noble Lady blest
to rapture.
And there, a saintly Anchoress, she dwelt.

Mary's brother Tom Hutchinson had taken Hindwell Farm four miles west of Kington, and his sister Sarah with her husband John Monkwell helped him work it. The Wordsworths often stayed there. The Hutchinsons later moved to Brinsop Court near Hereford, an easier journey for the Wordsworths by coach from Grasmere. Wordsworth first visited Brinsop in 1827 accompanied by his wife and Southey's (qv) eldest daughter. William, Mary and Dorothy are commemorated by a stained glass window by Comper (qv) in the chancel of St George's, Brinsop and their servant Jane Winder is buried in the churchyard. On a visit in 1835 with Mary he saw a Roman mosaic exposed at nearby Bishopstone, 'fresh and clear, as if its hues were of the passing year'. He wrote a poem about it, and about St Katherine, on returning to Brinsop. He also wrote an untitled sonnet to a Miss Loveday Walker, the daughter of the vicar of Bishopstone, whose pet dove was caught by a kite while she played the harp. William and Mary returned in 1837 with their daughter Dora. They visited friends at Leysters, staying with Revd Miller at Bockleton vicarage, who later cut 'W.W.' on a rock on the wooded hillside where Wordsworth used to admire the view. Leominster Morris Men dance annually at the stone. Wordsworth was interested in landscape design and on his next visit in 1841 he laid out the vicarage gardens at Brinsop and planted the cedar which still flourishes there. He admired Sir Uvedale Price (qv) and visited him at Foxley to discuss his ideas on landscape design. With Price he designed the winter gardens at Coleorton in Leicestershire for Sir George Beaumont. Wordsworth died on 23 April 1850 at Grasmere and Mary had his great autobiographical poem *The Prelude*, with its recollections of Herefordshire, published. In 1871 when Kilvert (qv), an admirer of Wordsworth, visited Brinsop he talked to the Wordsworths' Hutchinson niece who showed him a miniature of the poet. She remembered Wordsworth as a tall man and his sister as small and spare. She thought Dorothy, who deteriorated mentally in her later years, had overtaxed her health while young with the long walks they took. Dorothy would walk into Hereford from Brinsop for a thimble, she said.

Wren, Matthew (1585-1667), Bishop of Hereford in 1635, was born in London on 23 December 1585 and educated at Pembroke College, Cambridge, and was ordained. He was Master of Peterhouse in 1628. He married Elizabeth Cutler (d.1646) and they had 14 children. In 1634 he was Dean of Windsor and in 1635 appointed Bishop of Hereford. He tried to hold a visitation but as with his predecessor Bishop Lindsell (qv), Dean and Chapter refused to allow it. He moved on to Norwich and again to Ely in 1638. In his short time at Hereford he revised the cathedral's statutes in accordance with Laud's general overhaul of the church, doomed to imminent eclipse. He was a conservative churchman and urged that altars be restored to the east end of the church and protected by altar rails, and he instituted this at his cathedrals. Associated with Laud's Arminianism, he was an early target of Puritan reform and spent the Interregnum, 1642-60, in the Tower. He was released at the Restoration and restored to his see of Ely. He restored Pembroke College Chapel, vandalised by Puritans, in a classical style designed by his nephew Christopher Wren and on his death on 24 April 1667 was buried there.

MATTHEW WREN, D.D. LORD BISHOP OF ELY.
G. Vander Gucht Sculp.
Sapiens malis premi, sed non opprimi potest.

Wroth, Richard (15th century), a London parminter or parchment-maker, was a Herefordshire Lollard, a follower of Sir John Oldcastle (qv) whom he helped escape from the Tower of London.

Wroth, Robert was abbot of Dore Abbey 1347-62. He came from a Longtown family who had close links with the abbey, and were owners of Kentchurch before it passed to the Skidmores (qv). A William Wroth had been abbot 1274-81, and a Sir Robert Wroth contributed to the abbey building in 1286. A statue base in the abbey bears the inscription 'Robert Wroeth me fec[it]'.

Wulfgeat of Donnington left property in his will of *c.*1000AD to Leominster nunnery.

Wulviva see under **Godiva**

Wyatt, James (1746-1813), architect, was born on 3 August 1746 at Weeford in Staffordshire, the son of a farmer and general builder, all of whose sons were trained in different building skills. James, being artistic, was sent to study the architecture of Italy. He stayed with his brothers in London and attracted early notice with an Oxford Street building. Elected to the Royal Academy, he got fashionable commissions and became a prolific and widely travelled architect. He had a fixed rate for mileage and consultation fees, took on more work than he could manage and consequently sometimes failed to deliver, but customers record his zeal and charm. His charmed clients included George III and Oxford University, where he designed many college buildings, including the Radcliffe Observatory. He was highly eclectic, using neo-classical or gothic styles, and was equally capable of good interior design, furniture and fittings. He was one of the first to build with cast iron and prompted Smirke (qv) to use it at Eastnor Castle. John Butler (qv), the new Bishop of Hereford, was familiar with Wyatt's work from Oxford and recommended him to rebuild the western parts of the cathedral after the collapse of 1786. Wyatt began by patching up the nave damage

but after the death of three workmen when more of the roof collapsed he rebuilt the upper parts of the nave and removed the central spire: he was 'the Destroyer' to A.W.N. Pugin. His new west front was universally disliked, although John Matthews (qv) commissioned a mansion from him at Belmont in 1788 and he built Sufton Court for James Hereford (qv, d.1768). John Geers Cotterell (qv) commissioned him to build a new house at Garnons, Mansell Gamage but he never got round to it, although Repton (qv) painted it as a complete castle with battlements in his *Red Book*. Commissions ceased with the Napoleonic Wars however, and he had health problems as he aged; he neglected his practice and became increasingly muddled. By the time of his death he was penniless. He was killed in a carriage accident.

Wyatt, Thomas Henry (1807-80), architect, was born on 9 May 1807 in Roscommon, Ireland the eldest son of Matthew Wyatt (1773-1831), a barrister and his wife Anne. He was intended for a mercantile career but decided on architecture and was apprenticed to Philip Hardwick (qv). He married his cousin Arabella Wyatt (1807-75), took on a partner and, in 1860, his son Matthew. He could supply

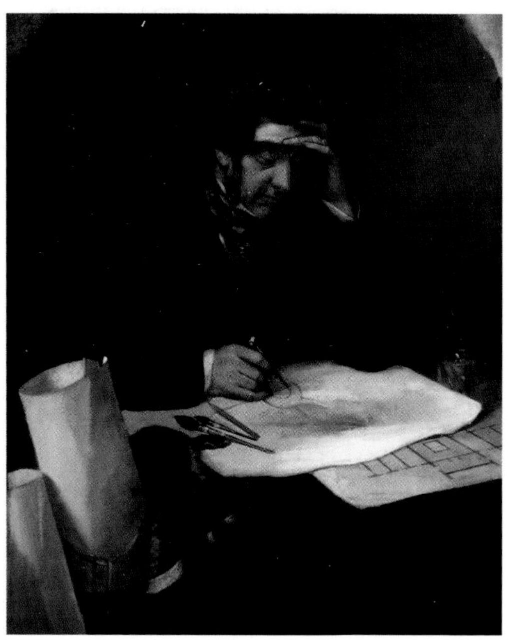

anything in any style and built or restored over 150 churches between 1830 and 1880. He built St Mary's, Tretire for Revd John Webb (qv) in 1855-56, replacing the Norman church, and his fittings are still in place. In 1873 he rebuilt Bredenbury Court in an Italianate style (now St Richard's School) and its two lodges and rebuilt St Andrew's Church, Bredenbury, all for William Henry Barneby (qv). He built the tower and a chapel at St Weonards (1874) and restored St Mary's, Humber (1878) where the pulpit is his. Wyatt died on 5 August 1880 in Great Russell Street, London.

Wyatville, Jeffry (1766-1840), architect, was born Wyatt, on 3 August 1766, into a dynasty of architects at Burton on Trent. He intended a naval career but was apprenticed in his uncle Samuel Wyatt's architectural office in 1785, transferring to James Wyatt (qv), who helped him attract patrons such as the Marquess of Bath, and was elected to the Royal Academy. He worked in Regency historical styles and was called in by Sir Richard Arkwright (qv) to make Hampton Court look more like a 15th-century castle. For iron-founder John Partridge he built Bishopswood House, Walford 1820-25, now demolished, like many of this period, although surrounding buildings survive – one now called Bishopswood House. Wyatt mediaevalised a comfortable early 18th-century wing and built cloisters in the courtyard. He worked at Chatsworth for the Duke of Devonshire, who called him 'a delightful man, good, simple like a child, eager, patient, easy to deal with', with an attractive Staffordshire and Cockney accent. The duke introduced Wyatt to George IV, who allowed him to change his name to the grander sounding Wyatville and knighted him. This began his association with Windsor which continued under William IV and Victoria. Sir Jeffry died on 18 February 1840 at his London home in Lower Brook Street and was buried in St George's Chapel, Windsor.

Wycherley, Richard (d.1502), was suffragan for the Bishop of Hereford from 1484 during Bishop Mylling's (qv) frequent absences, and Bishop of Worcester. He was master of St Katherine's Hospital, Ledbury, following John Vaughan in 1485 and found the master's house a convenient venue for the diocesan business of both sees as it was half way between the two cathedrals. Ordinations were carried out in Ledbury Church or the hospital chapel. Dendrochronological dating of timbers in the Master's House show part of it to have been built during Wycherley's tenure, and tiles of his period can be seen in the chapel.

Wycombe, William de was Bishop Robert de Béthune's (qv) chaplain and later Prior of Llanthony. The ill-disciplined monks and the enmity of Roger fitz Miles (qv) were too much for him and he retired to Canon Frome to write the saintly Bishop Robert's life with the aim, unrealised, of having him canonised.

Yapp, Arthur Keysall (1869-1936), President of the YMCA, was born at Orleton on 12 March 1869, oldest of the three children of Richard Keysall Yapp (1829-1873), and Jane Gammidge. The Yapps had farmed in the area for many years. His maternal grandfather, Timothy Gammidge, was a Congregational minister. On his father's death the family moved into

Leominster. He was educated at home and at Hereford County College. He joined the Young Men's Christian Association which he ran and developed over many years. He married Alice Higson and they had a son and a daughter. On the outbreak of the First World War he reorganised the YMCA into a world-wide facility for the forces, for which he was appointed KBE. He similarly placed the YMCA's facilities at the nation's service during the depression. He was buried in St George's, Orleton.

Yapp, Richard Henry (1871-1929), botanist, younger brother of Arthur Yapp (qv), was born in Orleton and educated in Leominster and the county school in Hereford. He graduated with first class honours at St John's College, Cambridge and was appointed botanist to the university expedition to the Malay States, on his return publishing papers on Malay plants. He was professor of botany at University College, Aberystwyth and President of the Ecological Society in 1921. From 1919 he was Mason professor of botany at Birmingham.

Yeomans, John (1803-42) of Moreton was a noted breeder of Hereford cattle, with his father Richard Yeomans (1767-1833) and grandfather John Yeomans (1736-98). They farmed at Howton Court, near Pontrilas. He married Anne Morgan (d.1894), who would later marry Thomas Duckham (qv), another noted Hereford cattle breeder. Yeomans shares credit for the development of this now widely spread breed with their Herefordshire neighbours Galliers, Tomkins and Tully (qqv).

Yorke, Philip James (1799-1874), chemist and army officer, was born at Ely on 13 October 1799, the eldest son of Revd Philip Yorke, prebendary of Ely (1770-1817) and Anna Maria (d.1835) daughter of Charles Cocks (qv), 1st Baron Somers. The next generation continued to intermarry with the Somers Cocks family and with the Biddulphs: Adelaide, daughter of John Michael Gordon Biddulph (qv), married Henry Yorke. Philip was educated at Harrow and reached the rank of lieutenant colonel in the Scots Fusilier Guards. In 1852 he was appointed colonel of the Herefordshire militia. He married Emily, daughter of Morgan Morgan Clifford (qv) of Perrystone Court. He was an amateur chemist and meteorologist and published papers with the Royal Institution. He made a lifelong study of the climate of Herefordshire, taking regular readings at his house near Ross. A weather station is still maintained in Ross. He died at his London house on 14 December 1874.

Young, Francis Brett (1884-1954), born in Halesowen, Worcs, trained as a physician and during the First World War served in East Africa. When his health broke down he was medically discharged and went to live on Capri with his wife where he started to write his west midlands novels. His first success, *The Dark Tower* (1915), deals with the Grosmont family in the fictional village of Trecastle, clearly in the Hereford-Radnor Marches. He moved to the Lake District where he produced a novel a year – *Portrait of Clare* (1927) is best remembered – until the Second World War. After the war he retired to South Africa where he died. His ashes were returned to Worcester.

Index of People

Page numbers in red denote main entries

A

C

D

E

F

G

H

I

J

K

L

N

P

Q

R

S

T

Y

Z

Bishops of Hereford

Red page numbers indicate bishops for whom there is a dictionary entry. Dates in brackets show the date/s of the bishopric.

Anglo-Saxon Bishops
Putta (676) 327
Tyrhtil (688)
Torhthere (710)
Walhstod (727), erected a gold and silver cross at the south of the cathedral.
Cuthbert (736) 121-2
Podda (741)
Ecca (*c*.747)
Ceadda (*c*.758)
Ealdbeorht (*c*.777)
Esne (*c*.781)
Ceolmond (*c*.787)
Utel (*c*.793)
Wulfheard (*c*.801)
Beonna (824)
Eadwulf (*c*.825)
Cuthwulf (fl.837-57), issued a charter which makes the first mention of a church at Hereford served by a group of clerks.
Mucel (*c*.857)
Deorlaf (*c*.857)
Cynemund (*c*.888)
Edgar (*c*.889)
Tidhelm (*c*.930)
Wulfhelm (*c*.937)
Ælfric (*c*.937)
Ethelwulf (*c*.951)
Æthelstan (1013) 5
Leofgar (1056) 250
Ealdred (1056)

Norman Conquest to the Reformation
Robert de Losinga (1061-79) 257-8
Gerard (1096-1100) 170
Reinhelm (1107-15) 333
Geoffrey de Clive (1115-9) 92
Richard de Capella (1121-7) 77
Robert de Béthune (1131-48) 39-40
Gilbert Foliot (1148-63) 161
Robert of Melun (1163-7) 272-3
Robert Foliot (1174-86) 162
William de Vere (1186-98) 404
Giles de Briouze/Braose (1200-15) 58
Hugh de Mapenore (1216-9) 262
Hugh Foliot (1219-34) 161-2
Ralph de Maidstone (1234-9) 261-2
Peter de Aquablanca (1240-68) 9-10
John de Breton (1269-75) 57
Thomas de Cantilupe (1275-82) 75-6
Richard Swinfield (1283-1317) 376
Adam Orleton (1317-27) 299
Thomas Charlton (1327-44) 85
John Trillek (1344-60) 395-6
Lewis Charlton (1360-9) 84-5
William Courtenay (1369-75) 111
John Gilbert (1375-89) 171
Thomas Trefnant (1389-1404) 394
Robert Mascall (1404-16) 267
Edmund Lacy (1417-20) 243
Thomas Polton (1420-1) 317
Thomas Spofford (1421-48) 368-9
Richard Beauchamp (1448-50) 32
Reginald Boulers (1450-3) 54
John Stanbury (1453-74) 370
Thomas Mylling (1474-92) 290-1
Edmund Audley (1492-1502) 15
Adriano Castellesi (1502-4)
Richard Mayo (1504-16) 271-2

Bishops during the Reformation
Charles Booth (1516-35) 52-3
Edward Foxe (1535-8) 164
John Skippe (1539-52) 361-2
John Harley (1553-4) 194-5
Robert Parfew (1554-7)

Post-Reformation bishops up to 1900
John Scory (1559-85) 345-6
Herbert Westfaling (1585-1602) 421-2
Robert Bennett (1603-17) 35-6
Francis Godwin (1617-33) 175
Augustine Lindsell (1634) 253
Matthew Wren (1634-5) 435-6
Theophilus Field (1635-6) 157
George Coke (1636-46) 97-8
Nicholas Monck (1660-1) 279
Herbert Croft (1662-91) 116
Gilbert Ironside (1691-1701) 224
Humphrey Humphreys (1701-12) 223
Philip Bisse (1713-21) 45-6
Benjamin Hoadly (1721-3) 212
Henry Egerton (1724-46) 147
James Beauclerk (1745-87) 33-4
John Harley (1787-8) 195
John Butler (1788-1802) 71
Folliott Cornewall (1802-8) 106
John Luxmoore (1808-15) 259-60
George Huntingford (1815-32) 223
Edward Grey (1832-7) 180
Thomas Musgrave (1837-47) 290-1
Renn Hampden (1848-68) 189
James Atlay (1868-94) 12-3
John Percival (1895-1917) 312

The Nine Worthies of Herefordshire

The Nine Worthies were Royalist leaders commemorated at the Restoration for their resistance to Parliament's invasion of the county in the 1640s:

Wallop Brabazon 56
Fitzwilliam Coningsby 101
Sir William Croft (d.1645) 119
Henry Lingen 254-5
John Prise of Wistaston 324
William Rudhall (d.1651) 342
John Scudamore (d.1671) 351-2
William Smalman 364
Thomas Wigmore of Shobdon 429

Index of Themes

Contents

Agriculture and Animals

Architects and Artisans

Artists, Actors and Musicians

Companies and Factories

Dramas, Deaths and Disasters

Folklore and Magic

Historical Events

Merchants and Manufacturers

Politics and Political Office

Pre-Normans and Normans

Public Service

Religions and Views

Rivers and Transport

Rogues, Roués and Eccentrics

Scholars and Experts

Societies and Institutions

Sports and Pastimes

Wars and Battles

The World and its Explorers

Writers and Publications

Index of Places

Index of Churches

Index of Castles and Houses

Picture Credits

Lascelles Abercrombie (p.2), *by Walter Stoneman*
Robert Adam (p.3), *by George Willison*
Thomas Allen (p.7), *by James Bretherton*
John Aubrey, *by an unknown artist*
Sir Richard Baggallay (p.17), *by Lock & Whitfield*
Elizabeth Barrett Browning (p.26), *by Field Talfourd*
Robert Bloomfield (p.47), *by Henry Bone*
Edward Blore (p.48), *by George Koberwein*
John Britton (p.60), *by John Wood*
Lancelot ('Capability') Brown (p.62), *by Nathaniel Dance (later Sir Nathaniel Holland, Bt)*
James Brydges, 1st Duke of Chandos (p.65), *by Herman van der Myn (or Mijn)*
Edward Coley Burne-Jones (p.71), *by George James Howard, 9th Earl of Carlisle*
William Camden (p.74), *by Marcus Gheeraerts the Younger*
Dora Carrington (p.79), *by Dora Carrington*
King Charles I (p.84), *by an unknown artist*
Ewan Christian (p.86), *by an unknown artist*
William Cobbett (p.93), *by George Cooke*
Lady Henry Somerset (Lady Isabella Caroline Somerset (née Somers-Cocks)) (p.95), *by Hayman Seleg Mendelssohn*
Samuel Taylor Coleridge (p.99), *by Peter Vandyke*
Sir (John) Ninian Comper (p.100), *by Beatrice Bright*
Sir George Cornewall Lewis, 2nd Baronet (p.108), *by George Richmond*
Charles Wolfran Cornwall (p.109), *by James Bretherton*
David Cox (p.111), *by Sir William Boxall*
David Cox Jr (p.112), *by Elliott & Fry*
Joshua Cristall (p.114), *by an unknown artist*
Oliver Cromwell (p.119), *by Samuel Cooper*
John Dee (p.127), *by Robert Cooper*
Daniel Defoe (p.128), *by Jeremiah Taverner*
Robert Devereux, 2nd Earl of Essex (p.131), *by Marcus Gheeraerts the Younger*
Robert Devereux, 3rd Earl of Essex (p.131), *by Renold or Reginold Elstrack (Elstracke)*
Charles Dickens (p.134), *by Samuel Laurence*
Arthur Conan Doyle (p.136), *by Henry L. Gates*
Michael Drayton (p.136), *by an unknown artist*
Sir William Dugdale (p.138), *by an unknown artist*
Sir Edward Elgar, Bt (p.149), *by Charles Frederick Grindrod*
Queen Elizabeth I (p.149), *by George Gower*
John Evelyn (p.154), *by Robert Walker*
Paul Foley (p.160), *by an unknown artist*
George Fox (p.164), *by R. Sawyer*
David Garrick (p.168), *by Robert Edge Pine*
Robert John Gibbings (p.171), *by Howard Coster*
Grinling Gibbons (p.171), *by Sir Godfrey Kneller, Bt*
Lady Jane Grey (p.181), *by an unknown artist*
Sir (Henry) Rider Haggard (p.186), *by George Charles Beresford*
Renn Dickson Hampden (p.189), *by William Henry Southwell*
Robert Harley, 1st Earl of Oxford (p.196), *by Sir Godfrey Kneller, Bt*
Selina Hastings, Countess of Huntingdon (p.199), *by an unknown artist*
Thomas Hearne (p.202), *by Henry Monro*
Henry Holland (p.215), *by George Garrard*
Gerard Manley Hopkins (p.216), *by Anne Eleanor Hopkins*
Charles Howard, 11th Duke of Norfolk (p.221), *by Thomas Gainsborough*
Henry James, 1st Baron James of Hereford (p.225), *by Carlo Pellegrini*
Richard Payne Knight (p.237), *by Sir Thomas Lawrence*
Thomas Andrew Knight (p.239), *by Richard James Lane*
Edward William Lane (p.245), *by Richard James Lane*
Stringer Lawrence (p.247), *by Thomas Gainsborough*
John Leland (p.249), *by Hans Holbein the Younger*
Johanna Maria ('Jenny') Lind (p.253), *by Eduard Magnus*
Charles Lucy (p.259), *by Rolfe's Portrait Studio*
John Masefield (p.268), *by Henry Lamb*
Henry Matthews, Viscount Llandaff (p.270), *by Sir (John) Benjamin Stone*
Sir Thomas Morgan, 1st Baronet (p.282), *by Elisabeth Bridgetta Gulston*
Axel Martin Frederik Munthe (p.289), *by Howard Coster*
Sir Roderick Impey Murchison, 1st Baronet (p.290), *by Stephen Pearce*
John Nash (p.292), *by Sir Edwin Henry Landseer*
Horatio Nelson (p.293), *by Sir William Beechey*
Florence Nightingale (p.296), by Sir George Scharf
Sir Frederick Arthur Gore Ouseley, 2nd Baronet (p.301), *by Lewis Carroll (Charles Lutwidge Dodgson)*
Sir (Charles) Hubert Hastings Parry, 1st Baronet, *by Elliott & Fry*
Richard Godfrey Parsons (p.305), *by Bassano Ltd*
Sir Joseph Paxton (p.307), *by Octavius Oakley*
John Percival (p.312), *by Henry Walter ('H. Walter') Barnett*
John Philips (p.313), *by an unknown artist*
Alexander Pope (p.318), *by Michael Dahl*
Sir Uvedale Price, 1st Baronet (p.321), *by an unknown artist*
Augustus Welby Northmore Pugin (p.326), *by an unknown artist*
Sir James Rankin, 1st Baronet (p.330), *by Bassano Ltd*
Humphry Repton (p.333), *by Samuel Shelley*
David Ricardo (p.335), *by Thomas Phillips*
George Bridges Rodney, 1st Baron Rodney (p.338), *by Sir Joshua Reynolds*
Sir Samuel Romilly (p.339), *by Samuel William Reynolds*
Prince Rupert (p.343), *by Gerrit van Honthorst*
Sir George Gilbert Scott (p.346), *by George Richmond*
Sarah Siddons (née Kemble) (p.356), *by John Downman*
Sir Philip Sidney (p.356), *by an unknown artist*
Ernest Simon (p.357), *by Lafayette Ltd*
Sir Robert Smirke (p.364), *by George Dance*
Robert Southey (p.367), *by Edward Nash*
John Speed (p.368), *by an unknown artist*
Philip Wilson Steer (p.371), *by George Charles Beresford*
George Edmund Street (p.373), *by Lock & Whitfield*
William Stukeley (p.374), *by Sir Godfrey Kneller, Bt*
Jonathan Swift (p.375), *by Charles Jervas*
Sir Banastre Tarleton, Baronet (p.383), *by Sir Joshua Reynolds*
John Taylor (p.384), *by R. Clamp*
Edward Thomas (p.387), *by Frederick Henry Evans*
Jacob Tonson (p.392), *by Sir Godfrey Kneller, Bt*
Ralph Vaughan Williams (p.402), *by Howard Coster*
Charles Francis Annesley Voysey (p.405), *by an unknown photographer*
Sir William Waller (p.407), *by an unknown artist*
Horace Walpole (p.407), *by John Giles Eccardt*
George Frederic Watts (p.417), *by Frederick Hollyer*
John Wesley (p.420), *by Nathaniel Hone*
Samuel Wesley (p.420), *by John Jackson*
Richard Westall (p.421), *by George Dance*
Sir Richard Westmacott (p.423), *by Charles Benazech*
William Wordsworth (p.434), *by Robert Hancock*
Matthew Wren (p.435), *by Gerard Vandergucht*
James Wyatt (p.436), *by Charles Turner*
Thomas Henry Wyatt (p.437), *by George Landseer*
Francis Brett Young (p.438), *by Helen Wilson*

© Logaston Press
James Atlay (p.13), Hereford Cathedral
John & Alice de la Barre (p.25), Clehonger Church
St Thomas à Becket and St Thomas Cantilupe stained glass (p.34), Credenhill Church
Robert Bennett (p.35), Hereford Cathedral
Robert & Margaret de la Bere (p.37) and John & Agnes de la Bere (p.38), Stretford Church
Robert de Béthune (p.39), Hereford Cathedral
Anthony Biddulph (p.41), Ledbury Church
Constance Biddulph (p.41), Ledbury Church
John Birch (p.44), Weobley Church
Charles Booth (p.53), Hereford Cathedral
Richard de Capella (p.77), Hereford Cathedral
George Coke (p.98), Hereford Cathedral
Richard & Eleanor Croft (p.118), Croft Church
Richard Dawes (p.126), Hereford Cathedral
Anne Denton (p.129), Hereford Cathedral
Walter Devereux, d.1402 (p.132), Weobley Church
St Dubricius (p.137), Hereford Cathedral
Edward II (p.144), Gloucester Cathedral
Edward of Woodstock (p.147), the Black Prince
Walter de Fresne (p.165), Moccas Church
St George stained glass (p.169), Brinsop Church
Godiva and Wulviva stained glass (p.174), Woolhope Church
Peter Grandison (p.178), Hereford Cathedral
John Harford, Bosbury Church
Richard Harford (p.191), Bosbury Church
Walter de Helyon (p.203), Much Marcle Church
King Henry II (p.204), V&A plaster court
King Henry III (p.205), V&A plaster court
John Hoskyns, d.1631 (p.220), Ledbury Church
John of Gaunt stained glass (p.229), Lancaster Priory Church
Sir John Kyrle, d.1650 (p.240), Much Marcle Church
William Langland stained glass (p.246), Little Malvern Priory
Augustine Lindsell (p.253), Hereford Cathedral
Robert de Losinga (p.258), Hereford Cathedral
Hugh de Mapenore (p.262), Hereford Cathedral
St Margaret (p.263), Byford Church
Richard Mayo (p.272), Hereford Cathedral
Robert de Melun (p.272), Hereford Cathedral
Sir John Milbourne (p.276), Burghill Church
Blanche Mortimer (p.178), Much Marcle Church
Daniel O'Rourke (p.300), Hereford Times foyer
Richard Pembridge (p.310), d.1345, Clehonger Church
Richard Pembridge, d.1375 (p.310), Hereford Cathedral
Francis Perrot (p.312), Monnington-on-Wye Church
Walter Pye (p.328), Much Dewchurch Church
Reinhelm (p.333), Hereford Cathedral
Rhys ap Gruffydd (p.335), St David's Cathedral
John and Mary Rudhall (p.341), St Mary the Virgin, Ross
William Rudhall, d.1530 (p.342), St Mary the Virgin, Ross
William Rudhall, d.1651 (p.342), St Mary the Virgin, Ross
James Scudamore, d.1668 (p.350), Holme Lacy Church
Samuel Skinner (p.360), Ledbury Church
Francis Smalman (p.364), Kinnersley Church
Thomas Spofford (p.369), St Mary the Virgin, Ross
John Stanbury (p.370), Hereford Cathedral
John Swinfield (p.376), Hereford Cathedral
Thomas Tompkins (p.391), Llandinabo Church
Unett tomb (p.398), Castle Frome Church
Roger Vaughan (p.399), Bredwardine Church
Thomas & Elen Vaughan (p.401), Kington Church
Thomas & Elizabeth Walwyn (p.411), Much Marcle Church
Herbert Westfaling (p.421), Hereford Cathedral
Thomas Westfaling (p.422), St Mary the Virgin, Ross

© Hereford City Museum and Art Gallery
Joyce Andrews (p.7), *by an anonymous artist*
John Scarlett Davis (p.126), *self portrait*
Brian Hatton (p.200), *self portrait*
Edward Hopton (p.217), *by an anonymous artist*
Joseph Hume (p.222), *by Thomas Ballard Snr*
John Kyrle, Man of Ross, d.1724 (p.241), *by Josef van Aken*
George Marshall (p.265), *by Brian Hatton*
Tom Spring (p.369), *by an anonymous artist*
Revd W.S. Symonds (p.378), *by an anonymous artist*
Edward Walwyn (p.409), *by Joshua Cristall*

© Hereford Cathedral Library
Herbert Croft (p.116)
Francis Tebbs Havergal (p.200)
John Napleton (p.292)
George Robertson Sinclair (p.358)

© Ridgebourne Archives
Richard Banks (p.21)
Richard William Banks (p.21)
William Hartland Banks (p.21)
Esther Crummer (p.120)

© John Leonard
Earl Thomas Coningsby, Hope-under-Dinmore Church (p.103)
Frances Coningsby, Hope-under-Dinmore Church (p.103)

© Torre Abbey Historic House & Gallery
Sir Samuel Meyrick (p.275), *by H.P. Briggs*

With thanks to Derek Foxton for the photograph of the portrait of John Venn (p.403) by Edmund Wood Gill which hangs in the offices of Hereford Society for Aiding the Industrious.